The **Rough Guide** to

The Dordogne and the Lot

written and researched by

Jan Dodd

With contributions from

Nana Luckham

ROUGH
GUIDES

NEW YORK • LONDON • DELHI

www.roughguides.com

Contents

Cave Art colour section following p.176

A Taste of Périgord colour section following p.304

◄◄ Château de Hautefort ◄ River Dordogne at Bergerac

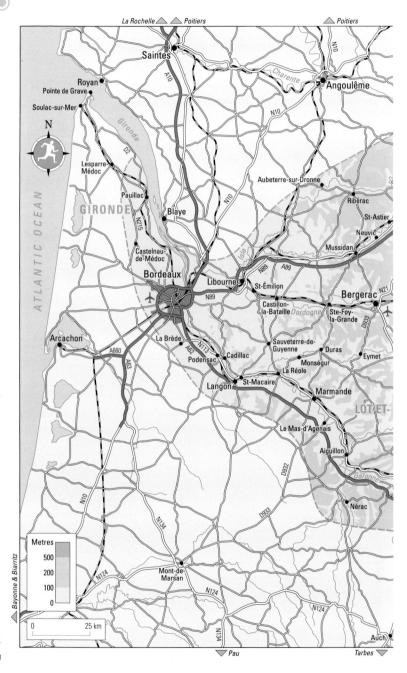

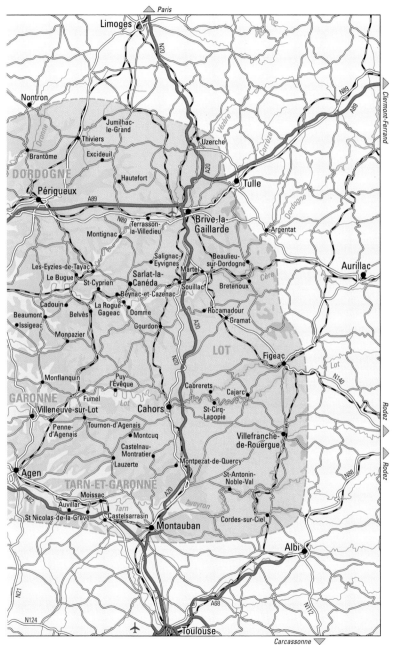

Paris

Clermont-Ferrand

Limoges

Nontron

Jumilhac-
le-Grand

Thiviers

Uzerche

Brantôme

Excideuil

DORDOGNE

Hautefort

Tulle

Périgueux

A89

Terrasson-
la-Villedieu

N89

Brive-la-
Gaillarde

Montignac

Argentat

Salignac-
Eyvignes

Beaulieu-
sur-Dordogne

Les-Eyzies-de-Tayac

Martel

Aurillac

Le Bugue

Sarlat-la-
Canéda

St-Cyprien

Souillac

Bretenoux

Beynac-et-Cazenac

Cadouin

La Roque-
Gageac

Rocamadour

Beaumont

Belvès

Domme

Gramat

Issigeac

Gourdon

LOT

Monpazier

Figeac

Lot

N140

Monflanquin

Puy
l'Évêque

Cabrerets

Cajarc

GARONNE

Fumel

Lot

Cahors

St-Cirq-
Lapopie

Rodez

Villeneuve-sur-Lot

Penne-
d'Agenais

Tournon-d'Agenais

Montcuq

Villefranche-
de-Rouergue

Castelnau-
Montratier

Rodez

Lauzerte

Montpezat-de-Quercy

Agen

TARN-ET-GARONNE

St-Antonin-
Noble-Val

N88

Moissac

Auvillar

St Nicolas-de-la-Grave

Castelsarrasin

Montauban

Cordes-sur-Ciel

Albi

Toulouse

Carcassonne

Introduction to

The Dordogne and the Lot

It was in the green, secluded valleys of the Dordogne and Lot region that prehistoric people penetrated deep into limestone caves to paint the world's earliest masterpieces of pot-bellied ponies, mammoths and muscular bison. Later occupants of the area expressed their faith in the Romanesque churches to be found on many a hilltop, and in the array of abbeys and towering cathedrals, while the legacy of a more bellicose era lies in the medieval fortresses perched on pinnacles of rock. A more intimate link with the past is recorded among the ancient farmhouses tucked into the landscape's folds.

In addition to this richly layered history, the Dordogne and Lot is endowed with a tremendous variety of scenery, from the dry limestone plateaux of the *causses*, sliced through with narrow gorges, to the wooded valleys of the Périgord Noir and the Bordeaux vineyards' serried ranks. Through these landscapes slide the great rivers that unify and define the region: the **Dordogne**, which flows 500km from the Massif Central west to the Atlantic coast and further south the **Lot**, writhing across country on its way to join the **Garonne**, which, along with its tributaries, the **Tarn** and **Aveyron**, marks this region's southern border.

It is a region best savoured at its own unhurried pace; there is always something to catch the eye, some forgotten corner to stumble upon, a market or a village *fête*. That isn't to say the region is undiscovered – indeed, some sights number amongst the most visited in France – but its heartland is still steeped in what the French call the *douceur de vivre*, the gentle way of life.

Where to go

The principal western gateway to the Dordogne and Lot region, and its only major city, is **Bordeaux**, whose sprawling suburbs belie a core of elegant eighteenth-century town houses, superb restaurants and a vibrant cultural life. After languishing for a period, Bordeaux is once again a city on the up, buoyed by the renown of its prime commodity, wine. The great **Bordeaux vineyards** lie mostly in the **Médoc**, though the prettiest scenery is that of the **Entre-Deux-Mers** with its wooded hills, closely followed by **St-Émilion**, which focuses around a small, captivating town – the home of Europe's largest underground church.

From near St-Émilion the Isle valley heads northeast to **Périgueux**, where an extraordinary Byzantine-style cathedral stands above a tangle of medieval lanes, and into a broad sweep of rolling pasture and woodland known as **Périgord Vert** (Green Périgord). This region's

Fact file

• The area covered by this guide amounts to some 30,000 square kilometres and has a population of under two million. Of these, around 750,000 live in Bordeaux, the region's main industrial centre, while elsewhere the economy is based primarily on agriculture and tourism.

• The most famous product is undoubtedly wine. It's the vineyards around Bordeaux that really put this region on the map – they extend over 1000 square kilometres and are divided into 57 different *appellations*. The average annual output is 700 million bottles produced by 6400 producers representing 12,600 individual châteaux.

• The Dordogne and Lot boasts two individual World Heritage Sites – the Vézère valley, with its prehistoric cave art, and the town and vineyards of St-Émilion – in addition to a dozen or so sights listed under the pilgrims' route to Santiago de Compostela in northern Spain. These include Bordeaux cathedral, Moissac's Romanesque abbey and the shrines of Rocamadour.

• Some of the world's finest examples of prehistoric art are to be found in the the limestone caves of the Vézère valley. The valley contains 25 decorated caves, of which only a handful are open to the public, and 147 other prehistoric sites. The most significant is Lascaux cave, where some 17,000 years ago our ancestors covered the walls with an extraordinary, vivid parade of beasts.

▲ Rocamadour

loveliest river is the Dronne and its most appealing town waterbound **Brantôme**, known for its rock-cut sanctuaries and plethora of restaurants. East of here is castle-country: **Château de Puyguilhem** stands out for its elegant Renaissance architecture, while the **Château de Hautefort** is one of the grandest castles in the Dordogne and Lot. Further east again, the rugby-playing town of **Brive-la-Gaillarde** hides not only an attractive old centre but also one of the region's best local history museums, and lies within easy striking distance of **Collonges-la-Rouge**, a village which merits a visit if only to marvel at its rich, red building stone.

South of Périgueux, in an area known as **Périgord Pourpre** (Purple Périgord) thanks to its wine production, vines cloak the slopes of the lower Dordogne valley around the pleasant riverside town of **Bergerac**. Of the local wines, most famous are the sweet whites of **Monbazillac**, whose glorious château dominates this stretch of valley. But the star of this area is the river itself, which loops through two immense meanders near **Trémolat** to create a classic Dordogne scene.

Trémolat marks the western border of **Périgord Noir** (Black Périgord), named for the preponderance of evergreen oaks with their dark, dense foliage. Here you'll find the greatest concentration of Périgord cottages with their steep, stone-covered roofs, and fortresses perched high above the river. Here, too, are the walnut orchards and flocks of ducks and geese, the source of so much of the produce featured in the region's markets. Of these the most vivid is **Sarlat**'s, held among the fine medieval and Renaissance houses built in honey-coloured stone. Close by, the beetling cliffs of the **Vézère valley** are riddled with limestone caves where prehistoric artists left their stunning legacy. **Les Eyzies**' archeological museum is a veritable treasure trove, though for sheer atmosphere you can't beat the **Grotte de Font-de-Gaume**, where the original paintings are on show. Returning to the Dordogne, the magnificent châteaux of **Beynac** and **Castelnaud**, eyeing each other across the river from their eyries, provide yet another archetypal image of the region.

Upstream from Sarlat, the abbey-church of **Souillac** offers remarkable Romanesque carvings, while the nearby pilgrimage town of **Rocamadour**, set halfway up a cliff-face, is equally compelling. Further east is the **Château de Castelnau**, a supreme example of medieval military architecture, and the Renaissance **Château de Montal**, with its exquisite ornamental detailing.

Shadowing the Dordogne to the south, the Lot flows through comparatively wild country where, even in high summer, it's possible to find quiet corners. The departmental capital, **Cahors**, is an appealingly unassuming town, home to France's best surviving fortified medieval bridge. Upstream, the perched village of **St-Cirq-Lapopie** provides the valley's most dramatic sight, while the nearby **Grotte de Pech-Merle** contains a dazzling display of prehistoric art. From here the pretty Célé valley cuts northeast to Figeac, which boasts a highly rewarding museum dedicated to the man who unravelled the mystery of hieroglyphics. West of Cahors, the atmospheric villages of **Monflanquin** and **Monpazier** represent outstanding examples of *bastides*, the "new towns" of the Middle Ages, built on a grid plan around arcaded squares.

The Garonne valley to the south is visually unexciting but hides an ace up its sleeve: the Romanesque carvings of the abbey-church at **Moissac** are among the finest of their kind. Further east, the narrow defiles of the **Gorges de l'Aveyron** are at their most dramatic around the attractive old town of **St-Antonin-Noble-Val** and **Najac**, where a semi-ruined fortress commands the valley. And it's worth continuing to **Villefranche-de-Rouergue**, a *bastide* town that springs into life on market days when stalls fill its superb central square – a scene that, in essence, has changed little for centuries.

When to go

Winters are wet and mild, with little snow or frost - on sunny days it's possible to sit outside even in December. **Spring** can be very variable: some years see glorious weather; in others it's cold and wet. Temperatures begin to pick

Joueurs de pétanque

9

▼ Moissac

up around May and can reach the 40s in mid-**summer**, though usually hover in the mid-20s. **Autumn** is similar to spring, though brings slightly more sunshine.

The most important factor in deciding when to visit is the **holiday seasons**. In July and August it seems the whole of northern France is heading south en masse, along with an invasion of north Europeans. By far the busiest period is mid-July through August, peaking in the first two weeks of August, when hotels and campsites are bursting at the seams and top-rank sights absolutely heaving. Conversely, from November to Easter many places close down completely. Overall, the **best time to visit** is September and early October, with May and June coming a close second.

	Jan	Feb	Mar	Apr	May	Jun	Jul	Aug	Sep	Oct	Nov	Dec
Agen												
Temp. max (°C)	9	11	14	16	20	24	27	26	24	19	13	9
Temp. min (°C)	2	3	4	6	9	13	15	14	12	9	5	2
Rainfall (mm)	64	63	58	60	79	60	50	58	48	59	58	61
Bordeaux												
Temp. max (°C)	9	11	14	16	20	23	26	26	24	19	13	10
Temp. min (°C)	2	3	4	6	10	12	14	14	12	9	5	3
Rainfall (mm)	100	84	78	75	79	58	48	57	76	85	88	100
Sarlat												
Temp. max (°C)	8	10	13	16	19	23	26	25	23	18	12	9
Temp. min (°C)	1	2	3	6	9	11	14	13	12	9	4	2
Rainfall (mm)	78	78	76	80	92	78	59	64	65	79	78	79

things not to miss

It's not possible to see everything that the Dordogne and Lot has to offer in one trip – and we don't suggest you try. What follows is a selective and subjective taste of the region's highlights: outstanding natural features, spectacular castles, history, culture and eye-catching architecture. They're arranged in five colour-coded categories to help you find the very best things to see, do and experience. All entries have a page reference to take you straight into the Guide, where you can find out more.

01 **Brantôme** Page **157** • Brantôme is renowned for its choice of waterside restaurants.

02 Cordes Page **374** • The picturesque medieval hill-town of Cordes-sur-Ciel, the pearl of the bastides, perches on a rocky pinnacle.

04 Vineyard visits Page **79** • Visit the cellars of Château Margaux and taste one of Bordeaux's leading wines.

03 Shopping in Sarlat Page **218** • One of the region's best markets is held in the beautiful town of Sarlat.

05 Truffles Page **171** • In winter, truffle sellers at local markets sell their famously expensive "black diamonds", renowned for their amazing aroma and said to be an aphrodisiac.

06 Bordeaux
Page **85** • The elegant eighteenth-century architecture of the Place de la Bourse is typical of the buzzing city of Bordeaux.

08 Bergerac
Page **188** • Once a bustling river-port, Bergerac is now a small but beguiling city.

10 Cadouin Abbey
Page **210** • The astonishing Cadouin Abbey was once a major pilgrimage site.

07 Bastide towns
Page **336** • Monpazier is one of the region's best-preserved bastide towns, built in the typical grid-style, with many buildings dating from the thirteenth-century.

09 The gardens of Manoir d'Eyrignac
Page **225** • Explore the ornate gardens of Manoir d'Eyrignac dating back to the eighteenth century.

11 Prehistoric caves
Page **227** • The caves and rock shelters around Les Eyzies contain stunning examples of prehistoric art.

12 **Sarlat** Page **221** • Lose yourself in Sarlat's old centre – an intriguing maze of narrow medieval lanes.

13 **Canoeing** Page **49** • Drifting along in a canoe is a good way to get some gentle sightseeing done.

14 **Château at Najac** Page **376** • The fairy-tale château of Najac set on top of a hill with an impressive view dominates the Aveyron.

15 **St-Antonin-Noble-Val** Page **371** • See St-Antonin-Noble-Val and the medieval houses from its glorious heyday sheltering under towering limestone cliffs.

16 **Summer festivals** Page **46** • Catch a colourful summer festival, held in every town and village.

17 **Local produce** Page **40** • Famous gastronomic treats from the region include foie gras and walnut oil, available from local markets.

18 **Ancient festivals** Page **130** • Twice a year the Jurade parades through St-Émilion.

19 **Limestone caves** Page **237** • Spectacular limestone caves pepper the Dordogne and Lot region.

20 **The Château de Hautefort** Page **172** •
Ornamental gardens and spectacular views surround the Château de Hautefort.

21 **Walnut oil** Page **224** • Walnut oil is still pressed according to the time-honoured method and can be bought straight from the mill.

22 **Pont Valentré** Page **302** • The Pont Valentré in Cahors is an outstanding example of a fortified medieval bridge.

Basics

Basics

Getting there

The quickest and most cost-effective way of reaching the Dordogne and Lot from most parts of the United Kingdom and Ireland is by air. From southeast England, however, the Channel Tunnel rail link to Paris via Lille, from where you can connect to the fast and efficient TGV services south to Bordeaux, provides a viable alternative. The Tunnel is the most flexible option if you want to take your car to France, though the cross-Channel ferries are often cheaper. It's also worth bearing in mind that if you live west of London, the ferry services to Roscoff, St-Malo, Cherbourg, Caen and Le Havre can save a lot of driving time. There are now direct flights from Montréal in Canada to Bordeaux, but from elsewhere in the US and Canada you'll be routed though Paris, Amsterdam or another European hub, with onward connections. There are also direct flights to Paris and other European hubs from Australia and New Zealand, though in general the cheapest air fares are via Asia. From South Africa, connections are usually made through Paris or Amsterdam.

Air fares increasingly depend on how far in advance you can book: the earlier the cheaper. But they will also depend on the **season**, with the highest prices around early June to the end of August, when the weather is best; fares drop during the "shoulder" seasons – roughly September to October and April to May – and you'll get the best prices during the low season, November to March (excluding Christmas and New Year when prices are hiked up and seats are at a premium). Note also that flying at weekends is generally more expensive; price ranges quoted below assume midweek travel. Note that all passengers departing France now pay a "solidarity tax" ranging from €1 for economy class to €10 for business class on flights within the EU and from €4 to €40 on all other flights. The tax, which is included in the ticket price, is designed to raise funds for medical aid to developing countries.

If France is only one stop on a longer journey, you might want to consider buying a **Round-the-World** (RTW) ticket. Some travel agents can sell you an "off-the-shelf" RTW ticket that will have you touching down in about half a dozen cities (Paris is on many itineraries); others will have to assemble one for you, which can be tailored to your needs but is apt to be more expensive. It's also worth noting that a **Rail pass** (see p.30) may be useful if you are visiting France as part of a longer European trip.

Booking online

Many airlines and discount travel websites offer you the opportunity to book your holiday **online**, cutting out the costs of agents and middlemen. Good deals can often be found through discount or auction sites, as well as through the airlines' own websites.

Online booking agents

ⓦ **www.cheapflights.co.uk** (UK & Ireland);
ⓦ **www.cheapflights.com** (US);
ⓦ **www.cheapflights.ca** (Canada);
ⓦ **www.cheapflights.com.au** (Australia & New Zealand);
ⓦ **www.cheapflights.co.za.** (South Africa).
All the above sites offer flight deals, destination information and links to other travel sites.
ⓦ **www.ebookers.com** Efficient, easy-to-use flight finder for UK departures, with competitive fares and car rental.
ⓦ **www.expedia.co.uk** (UK);
ⓦ **www.expedia.com** (US);
ⓦ **www.expedia.ca** (Canada);
ⓦ **www.expedia.com.au** (Australia). Discount airfares, all-airline search engine and daily deals.
ⓦ **www.flightcentre.co.uk** (UK);
ⓦ **www.flightcentre.us** (US);
ⓦ **www.flightcentre.ca** (Canada);

Fly less – stay longer! Travel and climate change

Climate change is a serious threat to the ecosystems that humans rely upon, and air travel is among the fastest-growing contributors to the problem. Rough Guides regard travel, overall, as a global benefit, and feel strongly that the advantages to developing economies are important, as is the opportunity of greater contact and awareness among peoples. But we all have a responsibility to limit our personal impact on global warming, and that means giving thought to how often we fly, and what we can do to redress the harm that our trips create.

Flying and climate change

Pretty much every form of motorized travel generates CO_2 – the main cause of human-induced climate change – but planes also generate climate-warming contrails and cirrus clouds and emit oxides of nitrogen, which create ozone (another greenhouse gas) at flight levels. Furthermore, flying simply allows us to travel much further than we otherwise would do. The figures are frightening: one person taking a return flight between Europe and California produces the equivalent impact of 2.5 tonnes of CO_2 – similar to the yearly output of the average UK car.

Fuel-cell and other less harmful types of plane may emerge eventually. But until then, there are really just two options for concerned travellers: to reduce the amount we travel by air (take fewer trips – stay for longer!), and to make the trips we do take "climate neutral" via a carbon offset scheme.

Carbon offset schemes

Offset schemes run by ⓦ www.climatecare.org, ⓦ www.carbonneutral.com and others allow you to make up for some or all of the greenhouse gases that you are responsible for releasing. To do this, they provide "carbon calculators" for working out the global-warming contribution of a specific flight (or even your entire existence), and then let you contribute an appropriate amount of money to fund offsetting measures. These include rainforest reforestation and initiatives to reduce future energy demand – often run in conjunction with sustainable development schemes.

Rough Guides, together with Lonely Planet and other concerned partners in the travel industry, are supporting a **carbon offset scheme** run by climatecare.org. Please take the time to view our website and see how you can help to make your trip climate neutral.

ⓦ**www.roughguides.com/climatechange**

ⓦ**www.flightcentre.com.au** (Australia);
ⓦ**www.flightcentre.co.nz** (New Zealand);
ⓦ**www.flightcentre.co.za** (South Africa).
Australian company offering good deals on flights and holidays from their branches around the world.
ⓦ**www.flyaow.com** Online air travel info and reservations.
ⓦ**www.lastminute.com** (UK);
ⓦ**www.lastminute.ie** (Republic of Ireland);
ⓦ**www.us.lastminute.com** (US);
ⓦ**www.au.lastminute.com** (Australia & New Zealand). Offers good last-minute holiday package and flight-only deals.
ⓦ**www.opodo.co.uk** Popular and reliable source of low UK air fares. Owned by, and run in conjunction with, nine major European airlines.
ⓦ**www.orbitz.com** (in US) Comprehensive Web

travel source, with the usual flight and hotel deals but also great follow-up customer service.
ⓦ**www.priceline.co.uk** (UK);
ⓦ**www.priceline.com** (US). Name-your-own-price website that has heavily discounted deals on standard fares. The tickets are non-refundable, non-transferable and non-changeable.
ⓦ**www.sta-travel.com** Worldwide specialists in independent travel, also student IDs, travel insurance, etc.
ⓦ**www.travel.kelkoo.co.uk** Useful **UK**-only price-comparison site, checking several sources of low-cost flights (and other goods and services) according to specific criteria.
ⓦ**www.travelshop.com.au** Australian website offering discounted flights, packages, car rental and insurance.

Ⓦ www.travelocity.co.uk (UK);
Ⓦ www.travelocity.com (US);
Ⓦ www.travelocity.ca (Canada);
Ⓦ www.travelzoo.co.uk (UK);
Ⓦ www.travelzoo.com (US);
Ⓦ www.travelzoo.ca (Canada). Great resource for news on the latest airline sales and car rental and hotel deals. Links take you direct to the seller's site.
Ⓦ www.zuji.com.au (Australia);
Ⓦ www.zuji.co.nz (New Zealand). Destination guides, hot Web fares and best deals for accommodation.

From the UK and Ireland

The choices available to people travelling to southwest France from the UK and Ireland are vast, ranging from coaches and cut-price airlines to tailor-made package tours. How you decide to go will depend on your budget, the time available and whether you want to take your own transport.

By plane

With the rapid increase in the number of no-frills services between the UK and Ireland to France, **flying** is becoming by far the most popular option, particularly if you are leaving from or heading to one of the regional airports. To find the best deals you should shop around, ideally at least a couple of months before you plan to leave, longer if it's peak season.

The cheapest fares are likely to be with one of the **low-cost airlines**, a number of which now operate direct flights to south-west France. New routes are opening all the time (and some closing), but at the time of writing **Ryanair** flies from Stansted to Bergerac, Biarritz (roughly 100km south of Bordeaux) and Rodez (60km southeast of Figeac), and from Dublin and Shannon to Biarritz; **easyjet** links Luton with Bordeaux

and Gatwick and Bristol with Toulouse; and **bmibaby** flies from Birmingham and Manchester to Bordeaux and from Manchester to Toulouse. Fares fluctuate, but at the time of writing, Ryanair is offering a one-way ticket from Stansted to Bergerac for around £16 including airport taxes and surcharges, while easyjet has one-way fares at £20 from Luton to Bordeaux. Tickets work on a quota system, so you'll need to book well ahead and travel off-peak to snap up such bargains. While they can be purchased by phone, tickets are slightly cheaper online.

It's always worth checking out the **traditional carriers**, such as British Airways, Air France, bmi (British Midland) and Aer Lingus. The cheapest tickets usually require you to stay over on a Saturday night and don't allow any amendments. Again, the further ahead you book, the better, but low-season return fares to Bordeaux start at around £60 from London, £120 from Edinburgh and €230 from Dublin.

Air France, or one of its partners, operates direct flights to Bordeaux from Dublin and via Paris Charles de Gaulle (Paris CDG) from London Heathrow, Aberdeen, Nottingham East Midlands, Edinburgh or Manchester (and various other regional airports), and then take an onward connection to Bordeaux or Toulouse. **British Airways** flies direct from Heathrow and Gatwick to Bordeaux and Gatwick to Toulouse; they also fly to Paris CDG from Heathrow, Birmingham, Bristol, Edinburgh, Glasgow and Manchester. From Northern Ireland, you'll be routed through London. **British European** (flybe) operates to Bergerac from Bristol, Birmingham, Exeter, Leeds Bradford and Southampton; to Bordeaux from Bristol, Norwich and Southampton; and to Toulouse from Bristol and

Travel advice

Australian Department of Foreign Affairs Ⓦ www.dfat.gov.au, Ⓦ www.smartraveller.gov.au
British Foreign & Commonwealth Office Ⓦ www.fco.gov.uk
Canadian Department of Foreign Affairs Ⓦ www.dfait-maeci.gc.ca
Irish Department of Foreign Affairs Ⓦ www.foreignaffairs.gov.ie
New Zealand Ministry of Foreign Affairs Ⓦ www.mft.govt.nz
US State Department Travel Advisories Ⓦ www.travel.state.gov

Travelling with pets

If you decide to take your dog (or cat) on holiday to France, the **Pet Travel Scheme (PETS)** enables you to avoid having to put it in quarantine when re-entering the UK as long as certain conditions are met. The animal must be micro-chipped with an ISO Standard chip, vaccinated against rabies, blood tested and have an official EU Pet Passport issued by a government-authorized vet. It must also be treated against ticks and tapeworm by a qualified vet within 48 hours of re-entering the UK. Details of the regulations are available at ⓦwww.defra.gov.uk/animalh/quarantine/index.htm or through the PETS Helpline (ⓣ0870/241 1710). Note also that you can only take your pet on certain routes – not on Eurostar, for example, nor some low-cost airlines – so check well in advance.

Birmingham. **Bmi** links Manchester with Bordeaux and Toulouse and Birmingham with Bordeaux. From Ireland, **Aer Lingus** has direct flights from Dublin to Bordeaux and Toulouse. It also flies from Dublin and Cork to Paris CDG.

A good place to look for **discount fares** is the classified travel section of papers such as the *Independent* and the *Daily Telegraph* (Saturday editions), the *Observer*, *Sunday Times* and *Independent on Sunday*, where agents advertise special deals. In London, check the back pages of the listings magazine *Time Out*, the *Evening Standard* or the free travel mag *TNT*. Independent travel specialists such as STA Travel do deals for students and anyone under 26, or can simply sell a scheduled ticket at a discount price.

Airlines

Aer Lingus UK ⓣ0870/876 5000, Republic of Ireland ⓣ0818/365 000, ⓦwww.aerlingus.com.
Air France UK ⓣ0870/142 4343, ⓦwww.airfrance.co.uk, Republic of Ireland ⓣ01/605 0383, ⓦwww.airfrance.com/ie.
bmi (British Midland) UK ⓣ0870/607 0555, Republic of Ireland ⓣ01/407 3036, ⓦwww.flybmi.com.
bmibaby UK ⓣ0871/224 0224, Republic of Ireland ⓣ1890/340 122 ⓦwww.bmibaby.com.
British Airways UK ⓣ0870/850 9850, Republic of Ireland ⓣ1890/626 747, ⓦwww.ba.com.
British European UK ⓣ0871/700 0535, Republic of Ireland ⓣ1890/925 532, ⓦwww.flybe.com.
easyjet UK ⓣ0905/821 0905, Republic of Ireland ⓣ1890/923 922, ⓦwww.easyjet.com.
Ryanair UK ⓣ0871/246 0000, Republic of Ireland ⓣ0818/303 030, ⓦwww.ryanair.com.

By train

Eurostar operates high-speed passenger trains daily from Waterloo International to the Continent via the **Channel Tunnel**; most but not all services stop at Ashford in Kent (50min from London). Services depart roughly every hour (from around 5.30am to 8pm) for Paris Gare du Nord (2hr 50min), a few of which stop at Lille (1hr 40min), where you can connect with TGV trains to Bordeaux and Toulouse.

Standard **fares** from London to Lille start at £55 for a non-refundable, non-exchangeable return. The next option is the changeable "semi-flexible" ticket (from £120), where you can change the dates but it is non-refundable and must include a Saturday night away. Both these deals have limited availability, so it pays to plan ahead; tickets go on sale 120 days before the date of travel. Otherwise, you're looking at £250 for a fully refundable ticket with no restrictions.

Tickets can be bought online or by phone from Eurostar (add £5 per booking), as well as from travel agents and mainline train stations. Note that Inter-Rail, Eurail and Eurodomino **rail passes** (see p.30) entitle you to discounts on Eurostar trains. For information about taking your **bike** on Eurostar, see p.34.

Train contacts

Eurostar UK ⓣ0870/518 6186, ⓦwww.eurostar.com.
International Rail UK ⓣ0870/084 1410, ⓦwww.international-rail.com.
Rail Europe UK ⓣ0870/837 1371, ⓦwww.raileurope.co.uk.
Trainseurope UK ⓣ0871/700 7722, ⓦwww.trainseurope.co.uk.

By ferry

Though slower than travelling by plane or via the Channel Tunnel, the ferries and catamarans plying the waters between Dover and Calais offer the cheapest means of travelling to France **from the UK** and are particularly convenient if you live in southeast England. Even if your starting point is west of London, it may still be worth heading to one of the south-coast ports and catching a ferry to Brittany or Normandy. If you're coming from the north of England or Scotland, you could consider the overnight crossings from Hull and Rosyth to Zeebrugge (Belgium) operated by P&O Ferries and Superfast Ferries respectively. Another option is taking a ferry from Portsmouth to Santander (with Brittany Ferries) or Bilbao (P&O Ferries) in northern Spain. Crossing times are long (20–34hr), but the route north into the Dordogne, by car or train, is a relatively short one – it's roughly 200km from Bilbao to Bordeaux. By comparison, it takes at least eight hours by motorway from Calais to Bordeaux, a journey of around 870km.

From Ireland, putting the car on the ferry from Cork or Rosslare (near Wexford) to Cherbourg or Roscoff in Brittany cuts out the drive across Britain to the Channel. The crossing takes around thirteen hours from Cork and eighteen hours from Rosslare. Again, you'll need to add another eight hours or so for the drive down to Bordeaux.

Ferry **prices** have been coming down in the face of fierce competition from the low-cost airlines and the new breed of high-speed ferries. One-way fares for a car and up to five passengers are now available for as little as £20 with Norfolkline on the Dover-Dunkerque route and £30 with SpeedFerries to Boulogne, while return fares on the Dover-Calais route start at around £50 return. From Ireland return fares for a car and two adults start at around €400 on the Cork to Roscoff route; one-way fares from Rosslare to Roscoff start at €99 for a car plus driver. Fares are slightly more expensive if booked by phone, and note that you'll need to plan well ahead to get these bargains. Most ferry companies also offer fares for foot passengers, typically around £20 return on cross-Channel routes; accompanying bicycles can usually be carried free in the low season,

though there may be a small charge during peak periods.

In general, the further ahead you book the cheaper the fare and it's well worth playing around with dates and times to find the best deals: midweek, nightime sailings are usually cheapest. An easy way to compare prices is via Ferry Savers (☎0870/192 1351, ⓦwww.ferrysavers.com) and EuroDrive (☎0870/442 9807, ⓦwww.eurodrive.co.uk), both of which offer cut-price fares; the latter caters only for people taking their cars across the Channel.

When calculating costs, it's worth remembering of course that you'll have to add in the price of petrol and the tolls on any motorways you take in France. The Michelin website (ⓦwww.viamichelin.fr) allows you to find the cost of tolls on any particular journey; it's also a handy route planner. For contact details of information services regarding roadworks and general traffic conditions, see p.31.

Ferry contacts

Brittany Ferries UK ☎0870/366 5333, ⓦwww.brittanyferries.co.uk; Republic of Ireland ☎021/427 7801, ⓦwww.brittanyferries.ie. Poole to Cherbourg; Portsmouth to Caen and St-Malo; Plymouth to Roscoff and Santander (March–Dec); and Cork to Roscoff (April–Oct).

Condor Ferries ☎0870/243 5140, ⓦwww.condorferries.co.uk. Poole (June–Sept) and Weymouth to St-Malo; Portsmouth to Cherbourg (Aug only).

Irish Ferries UK ☎0870/517 1717, Republic of Ireland ☎0818/300 400, ⓦwww.irishferries.com. Rosslare to Roscoff (May–Sept) and Cherbourg.

LD Lines UK ☎0870/428 4335, ⓦwww.ldlines.co.uk. Portsmouth to Le Havre.

Norfolkline UK ☎0870/870 1020, ⓦwww.norfolkline.com. Dover to Dunkerque.

P&O Ferries UK ☎0870/240 0565, ⓦwww.poferries.com. Dover to Calais; Portsmouth to Bilbao; Hull to Zeebrugge (Belgium).

Sea France ☎0870/443 1653, ⓦwww.seafrance.com. Dover to Calais.

SpeedFerries ☎0870/220 0570, ⓦwww.speedferries.com. Dover to Boulogne.

Superfast Ferries UK ☎0870/234 0870, ⓦwww.superfast.com. Rosyth (near Edinburgh) to Zeebrugge (Belgium).

Transmanche Ferries ☎0800/917 1201, ⓦwww.transmancheferries.com. Newhaven to Dieppe.

Via the Channel Tunnel

It's a long drive south to the Dordogne and Lot from the north coast of France (upwards of eight hours using the motorways as far as possible), but if you do want to take your car – and don't fancy a long sea journey and a short drive into the region from northern Spain (see p.23) – the simplest way is to load it on to one of the drive-on drive-off shuttle trains operated by **Eurotunnel** (℡0870/535 3535, ⓦwww .eurotunnel.com). The service runs continuously between Folkestone and Coquelles, near Calais, with up to three departures per hour at peak times (one every two hours from midnight to 6am) and takes 35min (slightly longer at night), though you must arrive at least 30min before departure. It is possible to turn up and buy your ticket at the check-in booths, but you'll pay the highest rate on the day and at busy times booking ahead is strongly recommended. Standard **fares** start at £49 one-way if you book far enough ahead and/or travel offpeak, rising to £161. Fully refundable and changeable FlexiPlus fares cost £199 return.

If you don't want to drive too far when you've reached France, you can take advantage of SNCF's **motorail**, which you can book through Rail Europe's Motorail department (℡0870/241 5415, ⓦwww.raileurope .co.uk), putting your car on the train in Calais for the journey south to Brive or Toulouse. The service is operational only between late-May and early September and this is a relatively expensive option: Calais–Brive, for example, costs from around £300 one way for a car and two adults travelling in the low season, rising to over £500 at peak times (July and August).

By bus

Eurolines (UK ℡0870/580 8080, Ireland ℡01/836 6111, ⓦwww.eurolines.com) runs regular bus-ferry services from London Victoria to Bordeaux, Brive, Souillac, Cahors, Montauban and Toulouse; off-season you may have to change at Lille. Adult return **fares** start at around £90 for Bordeaux if you book at least thirty days in advance, with a journey time of roughly sixteen hours. Regional return fares from

the rest of England and Wales are available, as are student, youth and seniors discounts. The **Eurolines pass** offers Europe-wide travel (including Toulouse) for fifteen or thirty days. Prices range from £135 for an adult fifteen-day pass in the low season (£115 for under-26s) to £299 for a peak-season thirty-day pass (£245 for under-26s).

Package tours and specialist operators

Any travel agent will be able to provide details of the many operators running **package tours** to the Dordogne and Lot (see below), which can be exceptional bargains. Some deals are straightforward travel-plus-hotel affairs, while others offer tandem touring, air-and-rail packages and stays in country cottages. If your trip is geared around specific interests – such as cycling or self-catering in the countryside – packages can work out to be much cheaper than the same arrangements made on arrival. Packages can also be a good idea if you are on a tight schedule – particularly for city breaks, as these deals often include free transfers to your hotel and guided tours or even theatre tickets as well as flights and accommodation, leaving you more time to enjoy your holiday. In addition to the **specialist tour operators** listed below, bear in mind that most of the ferry companies (see p.23) also offer their own travel and accommodation deals. You'll also find operators listed on the Holiday France website (ⓦwww.holidayfrance.org.uk), run by the Association of British Tour Operators to France.

Travel agents and tour operators

Alabaster & Clarke ℡01730/893 344, ⓦwww .winetours.co.uk. Treat yourself to a luxury tour of the Bordeaux vineyards with Britain's biggest wine-tour specialist.

Alan Roger ℡0870/405 4055, ⓦwww .alanrogers.com. Independent campsite specialist, with details of inspected sites as well as pitch-and-ferry and full holiday options.

Allez France ℡0845/330 2056, ⓦwww .allezfrance.com. Self-drive, fly-drive and rail-drive accommodation packages throughout the Dordogne and Lot.

Belle France ☎0870/405 4056; ⓦwww
.bellefrance.co.uk. Walking and cycling holidays in
the Dordogne and Lot.

Canvas Holidays ☎0870/192 1154, ⓦwww
.canvasholidays.co.uk. Offers tailor-made caravan
and camping holidays.

Cycling for Softies ☎0161/248 8282, ⓦwww
.cycling-for-softies.co.uk. An easy-going cycle
holiday operator. Although luggage transfer is not
included in the deals, this can be arranged for an
additional fee.

Equine Adventures ☎0845/130 6981, ⓦwww
.equineadventures.co.uk. Explore the Dordogne or
the Bordelais vineyards on horseback.

Eurocamp ☎0870/901 9410, ⓦwww.eurocamp
.co.uk. Self-drive, go-as-you-please holidays with tent
or mobile home.

France Afloat ☎0870/011 0538, ⓦwww
.franceafloat.com. French canal and river cruising
specialist, covering the Lot, Canal latéral à la Garonne
and the Canal du Midi.

French Affair ☎020/7381 8519, ⓦwww
.frenchaffair.com. Fly-drive and a wide range of self-
catering accommodation in the Dordogne and Lot.

Grape Escapes ☎0870/766 7617, ⓦwww
.grapeescapes.net. Tailor-made holidays exploring
the Bordeaux vineyards.

Headwater ☎01606/720 099, ⓦwww.headwater
.com. Upmarket activity holidays (walking, cycling and
canoeing) off the beaten track, including "gastronomic
cycling" tours in the Dordogne and independent
walking holidays in the Lot.

HF Holidays ☎020/8905 9556, ⓦwww
.hfholidays.co.uk. Walking and cycling specialist
offering guided and independent tours in this region.

Hoseasons ☎01502/502 588, ⓦwww.hoseasons
.co.uk. Boating holidays on the Lot and Baïse rivers.

Inntravel ☎01653/617 949, ⓦwww.inntravel
.co.uk. Broad range of activity holidays, including
riding, walking and cycling, as well as travel and
accommodation-only packages, from this well-
established specialist tour operator.

Joe Walsh Tours Republic of Ireland ☎01/676
0800, ⓦwww.joewalshtours.ie. Flight agent plus
escorted tours and pilgrimage tours including
Rocamadour.

Keycamp Holidays ☎0870/700 0740, ⓦwww
.keycamp.com. Caravan and camping holidays,
including transport to France.

Naturetrek ☎01962/733 051, ⓦwww.naturetrek
.co.uk. Professionally organized wildlife tours
including the Dordogne and Lot valleys.

North South Travel UK ☎ & ⓕ01245/608 291,
ⓦwww.northsouthtravel.co.uk. Friendly, competitive
travel agency, offering discounted fares worldwide –
profits are used to support projects in the developing

world, especially the promotion of sustainable tourism.

STA Travel UK ☎0870/1630 026, ⓦwww
.statravel.co.uk. Specialists in low-cost flights and
tours for students and under-26s, though other
customers are welcome.

Trailfinders UK ☎0845/0505 940, ⓦwww
.trailfinders.com. Well-informed and efficient agent
offering flights, tours and other services to
independent travellers.

VFB Holidays ☎01242/240 340, ⓦwww
.vfbholidays.co.uk. Independent and escorted
holidays in hotels or self-catering, with a good range
of cottages, farmhouses and villas to choose from.

Walking Safari Company ☎01572/821 330,
ⓦwww.walkeurope.com. Interesting selection of
walking, cooking and wine tours.

From the US and Canada

The only direct **flights** from the US or
Canada to the Dordogne and Lot region is
the weekly Montréal to Bordeaux service
offered by **Air Transat**. However, most major
airlines operate scheduled flights to Paris,
from where you can take a domestic flight
(check there's no inconvenient transfer
between Charles de Gaulle and Orly airports)
or transfer to the rail network. **Air France**
has the most frequent and convenient
service, but their fares tend to be on the
expensive side. Other airlines offering
services to Paris from a variety of US cities
include: **American Airlines** from New York,
Boston, Chicago, Dallas and Miami; **Continental** from New York and Houston; **Delta**
from Atlanta, Cincinnati and New York;
Northwest from Detroit; and **United** from
Chicago, Philadelphia and Washington DC.
Air Canada offers non-stop services to Paris
from Montréal and Toronto. Another option is
to take one of the other **European carriers**,
such as British Airways, Iberia or Lufthansa,
from the US or Canada to their home base
(London, Madrid and Frankfurt respectively),
then continue on to Paris or direct to
Bordeaux.

Thanks to such intense competition, trans-
atlantic **fares** to France are very reasonable.
A typical return fare for a midweek flight to
Paris costs from around US$550 from
Houston, US$700 from Los Angeles and
US$550 from New York. From Canada,
prices to Paris start from CAN$950 from
Montréal and Toronto or CAN$1100 from
Vancouver. Air Transat's return fares on the

non-stop Montréal–Bordeaux route start at around CAN$950.

If you're visiting Europe as part of a longer trip, you might want to consider buying a **Round-the-World (RTW)** ticket. The most comprehensive and flexible deals are offered by Sky Team, oneworld and Star Alliance. Prices are either mileage-based or calculated according to the number of continents you visit. They also depend on your itinerary, but RTW tickets including Paris start at around US$4000 from the US and CAN$4000 from Canada, excluding taxes and surcharges.

These international alliances and some local carriers also offer regional **air passes** covering travel around Europe. Details vary from one airline to another, but the basic rule is that the pass must be booked at the same time as the main ticket. With oneworld's Visit Europe pass, for example, you have to buy a minimum of two flights within Europe costing between US$85/ CAN$95 and US$345/CAN$380 depending on the distance, not including taxes and other surcharges.

Hundreds of **tour operators** specialize in travel to France, and many can put together very flexible deals, sometimes amounting to no more than a flight plus car or train pass and accommodation. If you're planning to travel in moderate or luxurious style, and especially if your trip is geared around special interests, these packages can work out to be cheaper than the same arrangements made on arrival.

More economical are the numerous **package tours**, such as walking or cycling trips, boat trips along canals and any number of theme tours based around history, art, wine and so on. Just a few of the possibilities are listed below, and any travel agent will be able to recommend others.

Airlines

Air Canada Canada ☎1-888/247-2262, ⓦwww .aircanada.ca.
Air France US ☎1-800/237-2747, ⓦwww .airfrance.com; Canada ☎1-800/667-2747, ⓦwww.airfrance.ca.
Air Transat Canada ☎1-866/847-1112, ⓦwww .airtransat.com.
American Airlines US ☎1-800/433-7300, ⓦwww.aa.com.

British Airways US and Canada ☎1-800- AIRWAYS, ⓦwww.ba.com.
Continental Airlines US domestic ☎1-800/523-3273, international ☎1-800/231-0856, ⓦwww .continental.com.
Delta US and Canada domestic ☎1-800/221-1212, international ☎1-800/241-4141, ⓦwww .delta.com.
Iberia US and Canada ☎1-800/772-4642, ⓦwww.iberia.com.
Lufthansa US ☎1-800/645-3880, Canada ☎1-800/563-5954, ⓦwww.lufthansa-usa.com.
Northwest US ☎1-800/225-2525, ⓦwww.nwa .com.
United Airlines US ☎1-800/864 8331, ⓦwww .united.com.
US Airways US domestic ☎1-800/428-4322, international ☎1-800/622-1015, ⓦwww.usair .com.

Courier Flights

Air Courier Association US ☎1-800/461-8556, ⓦwww.aircourier.org. Courier flight broker. Membership (US$40 for a year, plus $5 monthly fee) also entitles you to up to 85 percent of international published fares and guaranteed lowest prices.
International Association of Air Travel Couriers US ☎308/632-3273, ⓦwww.courier.org. Courier flight broker. One year's membership costs US$35 on the Internet or US$45 in the US and US$50 elsewhere.

Tour operators

Adventure Center ☎1-800/228-8747 or 510/654-1879, ⓦwww.adventurecenter.com. Hiking and "soft adventure" specialists. The eight-day "Dordogne and Discovery" includes a bit of canoeing, walking and cycling.
Backroads ☎1-800/462-2848 or 510/527-1555, ⓦwww.backroads.com. Luxury cycling and walking tours of the Bordeaux vineyards and the Dordogne and Vézère valleys.
Butterfield and Robinson ☎1-866/551-9090, ⓦwww.butterfield.com. Activity holidays with first-class accommodation. Holidays include week-long biking tours in the Dordogne valley, including family options.
Classic Journeys ☎1-800/200-3887 or 858/454-5004, ⓦwww.classicjourneys.com. Cultural walking tours along the Vézère and Dordogne valleys.
Cross-Culture ☎1-800/491-1148 or 413/256-6303, ⓦwww.crosscultureinc.com. Small-group tours to Bordeaux and its vineyards.
Cyclomundo ☎1-800/520-VELO, ⓦwww .cyclomundo.com. Defines itself as the "bike rider's

travel agency", specializing in custom-made "biking à la carte" trips. Also offers a few scheduled trips, including a culinary romp round Périgord and wine-tasting around Bordeaux.

Discover France ☎1-800/960-2221, ⓦwww .discoverfrance.com. Specialist in self-guided cycling and walking holidays in France, including the southwest.

Euro-Bike & Walking Tours ☎1-800/321-6060, ⓦwww.eurobike.com. Ten- and seven-day bike or walking tours of the Dordogne valley, overnighting in luxury hotels.

Infohub ⓦwww.infohub.com. Online operator offering a wide range of escorted and self-guided cultural, gastronomy and activity holidays.

STA Travel US ☎1-800/781-4040, ⓦwww .statravel.com. Specialists in low-cost flights and tours for students and under-26s, though other customers are welcome.

The International Kitchen ☎1-800/945-8606 or ☎312/726-4525, ⓦwww.theinternationalkitchen .com. Cooking vacations staying in a Bordeaux wine château or in the Dordogne or the Quercy. Also offer upscale vineyard tours.

Viator ⓦwww.viator.com. Online bookings for local tours and sightseeing trips including Aquitaine.

Wilderness Travel ☎1-800/368-2794, ⓦwww .wildernesstravel.com. Specialists in escorted hiking and cultural adventures, Wilderness Travel offers an eight-day jaunt around the castles and caves of the Dordogne.

From Australia, New Zealand and South Africa

There are scheduled flights to Paris **from Sydney**, Melbourne, Brisbane, Perth and Auckland, all of which involve at least one stop en route. Alternatively, you can fly via another European hub and get a connecting flight to Bordeaux from there. Flights via Asia or the Gulf States with a transfer or overnight stop in the airline's home port are generally the cheapest option. However, some airlines will route you through the US. **From South Africa**, both South African Airways and Air France operate daily non-stop flights from Johannesburg to Paris. With other airlines you'll be routed through another European hub such as London, Amsterdam, Madrid or Frankfurt, from where you can pick up a connecting flight to Bordeaux.

The cheapest return **fares** start at around Aus\$2000 from Sydney, Perth and Darwin and NZ\$2000 from Auckland. From South Africa, you're looking at anything upwards of R700 from Johannesburg and R1000 from Cape Town.

If you're planning to visit France as part of a longer trip, then **Round-the-World (RTW) tickets** offer greater flexibility and better value than a standard return flight. The most comprehensive and flexible deals are offered by the three big airline alliances: Sky Team, oneworld and Star Alliance. Prices are based either on the overall mileage or on the number of continents you visit and on your itinerary, but you should figure on at least Aus\$3100/NZ\$3600/R18,500 excluding taxes and surcharges.

If you intend to do a fair amount of travelling within Europe, it's worth considering one of the **air passes** offered by these international alliances and some local carriers. Details vary from one airline to another, but the basic rule is that the pass must be booked at the same time as the main ticket. With oneworld's "Visit Europe" pass, for example, you have to buy a minimum of two flights within Europe, costing between Aus\$115/NZ\$135/R645 and Aus\$485/NZ\$570/R2725 depending on the distance; taxes and other surcharges are extra.

Finally, if you wish to travel in style, and especially if your visit is going to be geared around special interests such as walking, cycling, art or wine, you may wish to consider one of the **package tours** offered by the operators overleaf. Though organized tours are inevitably more restrictive than independent travel, they may work out to be cheaper than making the same arrangements on arrival and can help you make the most of your time if you're on a tight schedule.

Airlines

Air France Australia ☎1300/390 190; New Zealand ☎09/302 0854; ⓦwww.airfrance.com.
Air New Zealand Australia ☎132 476, ⓦwww .airnz.com.au; New Zealand ☎0800/737 000, ⓦwww.airnz.co.nz.
British Airways Australia ☎1300/767 177; New Zealand ☎09/966 9777; South Africa ☎011/411 8600; ⓦwww.ba.com.
Cathay Pacific Australia ☎131 747; New Zealand ☎09/379 0861 or 0800/800 454; ⓦwww .cathaypacific.com.

Emirates Australia ☎1300/303 777; New Zealand ☎0508/364 728; ⓦwww.emirates.com.

Gulf Air Australia ☎1300/366 337; ⓦwww.gulfairco.com.

Iberia South Africa ☎011/783 1102; ⓦwww.iberia.com.

KLM Australia ☎1300/392 192; New Zealand ☎09/921 6040; ⓦwww.klm.com.

Korean Air Australia ☎02/9262 6000; New Zealand ☎09/914 2000; ⓦwww.koreanair.com.au.

Lufthansa Australia ☎1300/655 727; New Zealand ☎0800/945 220; ⓦwww.lufthansa.com.

Malaysia Airlines Australia ☎132 627; New Zealand ☎0800/777 747; ⓦwww.malaysiaairlines.com.

Qantas Australia ☎131 313; New Zealand ☎0800/808 767 ; ⓦwww.qantas.com.

Singapore Airlines Australia ☎131 011; New Zealand ☎0800/808 909; ⓦwww.singaporeair.com.

South African Airways South Africa ☎0861/359 722; ⓦwww.flysaa.com.

Thai Airways Australia ☎1300/651 960; New Zealand ☎09/377 0268; ⓦwww.thaiair.com.

Virgin Atlantic Australia ☎1300/727 340; ⓦwww.virgin-atlantic.com.

Travel and tour agents

Adventure World Australia ☎02/8913 0755, ⓦwww.adventureworld.com.au. Agent for Headwater, specialist in independent and guided walking and cycling holidays. Also accommodation passes and car rental.

Australians Studying Abroad (ASA) Australia ☎03/9822 6899, ⓦwww.asatravinfo.com.au.

All-inclusive 10-day lecture tour from Toulouse to Bordeaux exploring villages, châteaux and vineyards en route.

French Travel Connection ⓦwww.frenchtravel.com.au. Online agent offering everything to do with travel to and around France, including accommodation, canal boats, walking tours, train travel, cookery classes, car rental and more.

Passport Travel Australia ☎03/9867 3888, ⓦwww.travelcentre.com.au. Agent for Sherpa Expeditions escorted and self-guided walking and cycling holidays.

Peregrine Adventures Australia ☎1300/854 444, ⓦwww.peregrine.net.au. Small-group adventure specialist offering guided and independent walking and cycling holidays in the Dordogne.

STA Travel Australia ☎134 STA or 03/9207 5900, ⓦwww.statravel.com.au; New Zealand ☎0800/474 400, ⓦwww.statravel.co.nz; South Africa ☎0861/781 781 ⓦwww.statravel.co.za. Specialists in low-cost flights and tours for students and under-26s, though other customers are welcome.

Trailfinders Australia ☎1300/780 212, ⓦwww.trailfinders.com.au. International travel experts with advice and deals on flights and holiday packages.

Travel Notions Australia ☎02/9552 3355, ⓦwww.unitednotions.com.au/travelnotions. Representative of leisurely "Cycling for Softies" holidays (see p.25) offering graded bike rides through the Dordogne and the Lot.

Viator ⓦwww.viator.com. Online bookings for local tours and sightseeing trips including Aquitaine.

Getting around

France has the most extensive train network in Western Europe. The nationally owned French train company, the SNCF (Société Nationale des Chemins de Fer), runs fast, modern trains between all the main towns in the Dordogne and Lot, and even between some of the minor ones. In rural areas where branch lines have been closed, certain routes (such as Agen to Villeneuve-sur-Lot) are covered by buses operated by the SNCF or in partnership with independent lines. It's an integrated service, with buses timed to meet trains and the same ticket covering both.

The private **bus services** that supplement the SNCF services can be confusing and uncoordinated. A few areas, such as around Bordeaux and Brive, are reasonably well served. Throughout the rest of the region, though, services are often extremely sporadic and usually cater for schoolchildren or locals heading for the weekly markets, and so are not greatly useful to visitors. Where services do exist, approximate journey times and frequencies can be found in the "Travel Details" at the end of each chapter.

To really do the region justice, however, you'll need your own transport. Whether it be **car** or **bicycle**, it's important to note a number of French road rules and peculiarities. **Hitching** is also an option, but is not easy and is becoming less and less popular. For information about **walking**, **trekking** and **canoeing**, as well as other activities, see "Sports and outdoor pursuits", p.48.

Transport will inevitably be a large item of expenditure if you move around a lot. It's worth investigating the various train passes (see p.30) and many discounts available, although French trains are good value in any case. Two sample one-way fares are

Left luggage

As part of the "Vigipirate" anti-terrorist campaign, left-luggage facilities at train stations, bus stations and the like have been closed down. Apart from carrying your bags with you, the only option is to leave them at your hotel.

Bordeaux to Périgueux, €18, and Périgueux to Les-Eyzies €7. Buses are cheaper, though prices vary enormously from one operator to another; a one-way bus ticket from Périgueux to Sarlat, for example, costs €9, as opposed to around €13 by train. Bicycles generally cost between around €10 to €15 per day to rent.

By train

SNCF has pioneered one of the most efficient, comfortable and user-friendly railway systems in the world. Pride and joy of the French rail system is the high-speed **TGV** (*train à grande vitesse*; Ⓦwww.tgv.com), capable of up to 300kph. The region's principal stations served by the TGV are Bordeaux (3hr from Paris), Agen (4hr), and Montauban (4hr 30min) and its main rail corridors run north–south (Paris–Bordeaux, Limoges–Périgueux–Agen and Paris–Brive–Toulouse), with the important exception of the main line cutting southeast from Bordeaux via Agen and Montauban to Toulouse. Three cross-country lines strike out northeast and east from Bordeaux: to Limoges via Périgueux; Brive via Périgueux; and along the Dordogne valley to Bergerac and Sarlat. Another line serves the Médoc peninsula to the north of Bordeaux. The Lot valley is less well covered.

For **train information** and reservations, you can either phone (☎36.35; €0.34 per minute) or consult Ⓦwww.voyages-sncf.com. Regional **timetables** and leaflets covering particular lines are available free at stations. *Autocar* (often abbreviated to *car*) at the top of a column means it's an SNCF

Rail passes

Rail Europe (@ www.raileurope.fr) issue a number of rail passes for travel within France. Note that these passes must be purchased in your home country. The **France Railpass** allows between three and nine days of unlimited travel within a month, while the **Saverpass** offers the same for two or more people travelling together. Prices range from £117 (US$212) to £222 (US$491) per person for the regular pass travelling in second class and from £100 (US$190) to £187 (US$372) for the Saverpass; first-class passes and children, youth and senior passes are also available.

Passes are also available covering France in combination with other European countries. European residents can purchase the **Inter-rail Pass** which entitles you to unlimited travel within the specified period and geographical area. The passes come in over-26 and (cheaper) under-26 versions, and cover 29 European countries plus Morocco. For residents outside Europe there are various **Eurail** passes. See the relevant websites on below for further details and current prices.

bus service, on which rail tickets and passes are valid.

Tickets for all SNCF trains can be bought online with a credit card through @ www .sncf.com (allow at least nine days if booking from abroad), which has an English-language option, or by phone and at any train station (*gare SNCF*). At stations, it's easiest to use the counter service, though if there are language problems or long queues the touch-screen computerized system gives instructions in English and is a good way to check various fares and times. All tickets – but not passes (see box) or Internet tickets printed out at home – must be **validated** in the orange machines located at the entrance to the platforms; it is an offence not to follow the instruction *Compostez votre billet* (Validate your ticket).

Fares are cheaper if you travel off-peak (*période bleue* or blue period) rather then during peak hours (*période normale* or *période blanche*, normal or white period) – in general, peak period means Monday mornings and Friday and Sunday evenings. A leaflet (*le calendrier voyageurs*) showing the blue and white periods is available at train stations. In addition, on certain mainline routes a limited number of **discount tickets** known as tarifs Prem's (one-way fares from €20 on regional trains and €25 on TGVs) can be bought online between two months and two weeks in advance. Even cheaper Internet-only TGV fares (from €19 one-way) can be purchased

through @ www.idtgv.com on services from Paris to Bordeaux and Toulouse; tickets go on sale four months before departure and you'll have to be able to print out your ticket. A discount of between 15 and 35 percent on regular fares is also available to anyone who books a return journey covering at least 200km and including a Saturday night away (this fare is known as a Découverte Séjour). All these discount fares carry certain restrictions, so check when you book. **Seat reservations** are obligatory on all TGV trains and are included in the ticket price.

Aside from the regular lines, in summer there are two special tourist trains. The Autorail Espérance runs along the Dordogne valley between Sarlat and Bergerac (see p.224), while the Chemin de Fer Touristique de Haut Quercy operates on a disused line between Martel and St-Denis (see p.275). Neither of these routes are covered by normal rail passes.

Rail contacts

In the UK and Ireland

Rail Europe (SNCF) UK ☎ 08708/371 371, @ www.raileurope.co.uk; @ www.sncf.co.uk.

In North America

Europrail International Canada ☎ 1-888/667-9734, @ www.europrail.net.
Rail Europe US ☎ 1-877/257-2887; Canada ☎ 1-800/361-RAIL, @ www.raileurope.com.

In Australia and New Zealand

Rail Plus Australia ⓣ 03/9642 8644, New Zealand ⓣ 09/377 5415, ⓦ www.railplus.com.au.

In South Africa

World Travel ⓣ 011/628 2319, ⓦ www .world-travel.co.za.

By bus

The most convenient **bus services** are those operated as an extension of rail links by SNCF, which run between train stations and serve areas not accessible by rail. In addition to SNCF buses, private, municipal and departmental buses can be useful for local and some cross-country journeys, though be prepared for early starts and careful planning – the timetable is often constructed to suit market and school hours – if you want to see much outside the main towns. All buses are, generally speaking, cheaper and slower than trains.

There's a frustrating lack of coordinated departure information for buses around the Dordogne, where you'll have to rely on local tourist offices for help. However, the Conseils Généraux of the Gironde, Lot and Corrèze produce comprehensive **timetables** – or, in the case of the Gironde, a map and individual leaflets – detailing all the routes in the *département*; you can get copies by writing to the departmental tourist offices (see p.63), or in person from tourist offices in the main towns.

Larger towns usually have a *gare routière* (bus station), often next to the *gare SNCF*.

Mileage chart	
Bordeaux to Agen	140km
Bergerac	90km
Brive	215km
Cahors	200km
Montauban	220km
Périgueux	140km
Sarlat	160km
Périgueux to Agen	140km
Bergerac	50km
Brive	75km
Cahors	130km
Montauban	180km
Sarlat	65km

However, the private bus companies don't always work together and you'll frequently find them leaving from an array of different points (the local tourist office should be able to tell you where these are).

Driving

Driving in the Dordogne and Lot can be a real pleasure – and is often the only practical means of reaching the more remote sights. There are three **autoroutes** in the area: the A20 cuts south from Limoges to Toulouse via Cahors; the A62 runs along the Garonne from Bordeaux to Toulouse; and the A89 links Bordeaux with Périgueux and Brive. Motorway **tolls** are payable in cash or by credit card (get in the lane marked CB) at the frequent tollgates (*péages*). For an idea of the costs involved, the tolls for a car from Bordeaux to Périgueux add up to €8.20 and €12.60 from Bordeaux to Montauban, less for a motorbike. Outside the busiest periods and if you're in a hurry, it is well worth paying this to avoid the slow and congested, toll-free national roads (marked, for example, N21 or RN21 on signs and maps). The smaller *routes départementales* (marked with a D) are generally uncongested and make for a more scenic drive, though may occasionally be in relatively poor condition.

For up-to-the-minute **information** regarding traffic jams and roadworks on *autoroutes*, ring the 24-hour, multilingual service Autoroutel (ⓣ 08.92.70.70.01; 00.34 per min) or consult ⓦ www.asf.fr. Traffic information for other roads can be obtained from the Bison Futé recorded information service (ⓣ 08.26.02.20.22; €0.15/min, ⓦ www .bison-fute.equipement.gouv.fr); both services are in French only. The Michelin website (ⓦ www.viamichelin.fr) is also useful when planning your route.

There are times when it's wiser not to drive, most obviously in Bordeaux, where **parking** can be difficult and expensive; if you're renting a car here, it's best to do so at the airport. The region's other towns and cities are all of a manageable size – just follow signs for *centre ville* or the tourist office and you'll normally find a car park nearby. **Congestion** can be a problem throughout the region in July and August, most notably around major towns and tourist spots, including the most scenic stretches of the Dordogne, Lot and Aveyron valleys. The cost of **fuel** can also be a discouraging factor. At the time of writing, petrol prices were hovering around €1.40 a litre for unleaded (*sans plomb*), slightly more for four-star (*super*) and €1.20 a litre for diesel (*gazole* or *gasoil*); you'll find prices lowest at out-of-town hypermarkets. Note that in rural areas most petrol stations close at night, on Sundays and on bank holidays, and some may also close on Mondays. Some stations are equipped with 24-hr pumps, but these only work with French bank cards.

If you run into **mechanical difficulties** you'll find garages and service stations in the Yellow Pages of the phone book under "*Garages d'automobiles*"; for **breakdowns**, look under "*Dépannages*". If you have an accident or theft, you should contact the local police – and keep a copy of their report in order to file an insurance claim. Within Europe, most vehicle **insurance** policies cover taking your car to France; check with your insurer. However, you're advised to take out extra cover for motoring assistance in case your vehicle breaks down; contact your insurer or one of the motoring organizations listed below for a quote.

Rules of the road

US, Canadian, Australian, New Zealand and all EU **driving licences** are valid in France, though an International Driver's Licence makes life easier. The minimum driving age is 18 and you must hold a full (not a provisional) licence. Drivers are required to carry their licence with them when driving, and you should also have the insurance papers with you. If the vehicle is rented, its registration document (*carte grise*) must also be carried.

Since the French drive on the right, drivers of right-hand drive cars must adjust their **headlights** to dip to the right. This is most easily done by sticking on black glare deflectors, which can be bought at motor accessory shops and at the Channel ferry ports or the Eurostar terminal. It's more complicated if your car is fitted with High-Intensity Discharge (HID) or halogen-type lights; check with your dealer about how to adjust these well in advance. Motorcyclists must drive with their headlights on, and must also wear a **helmet**.

By law all non-French vehicles must display their **national identification letters** (GB, etc), either on the number plate or by means of a sticker. Even if your car has flashing **hazard-warning lights**, you're recommended to carry a red triangle in case the lights fail or you break down on a blind corner. You are also strongly advised to carry a spare set of bulbs, a fire extinguisher and a first-aid kit. **Seat belts** are compulsory front and back, and children under 10 years are not allowed to sit in the front of the car. It is illegal to use a hand-held **mobile phone** while driving.

The law of *priorité à droite* – **giving way** to traffic coming from your right, even when it is coming from a minor road – has largely been phased out. However, it still applies on a few roads in built-up areas and the occasional roundabout, so it pays to be vigilant at junctions, especially in rural areas where old habits die hard. A sign showing a yellow diamond on a white background gives you right of way, while the same sign with a diagonal black slash across it warns you that vehicles emerging from the right have priority. *Stop* signs mean you must stop completely; *Cédez le passage* means "Give way".

Unless otherwise indicated, **speed limits** are: 130kph (80mph) on *autoroutes*; 110kph (68mph) on dual carriageways; 90kph (55mph) on other roads; and 50kph (31mph) in towns. In wet weather, and for drivers with less than two years' experience, these limits are 110kph (68mph), 100kph (62mph) and 80kph (50mph) respectively, while the town limit remains constant. Fixed and mobile radar detectors are now widely used on French roads. The legal blood **alcohol limit** is 0.05 percent alcohol (0.5 grams per litre), and police frequently make random breath tests and saliva tests for drugs are becoming increasingly common. There are increasingly stiff **penalties** for driving violations, which can mean fines of up to €75,000, your licence confiscated on the spot and a prison sentence in the most serious cases.

Car rental

Car rental in France costs upwards of €75 for a day and €250 for a week, but is usually cheaper if arranged before you leave home or online. You'll find the big firms represented in Bordeaux and most major towns, with addresses detailed throughout the Guide. Local firms can be cheaper but most don't offer one-way rentals and you need to check the small print carefully. It is difficult to rent cars with automatic transmission in France. If you can't drive a manual, try to book an automatic well in advance, possibly before you leave home, and be prepared to pay a much higher price for it.

The **cost** of car rental includes the minimum car insurance required by law. Under the standard contract you are liable for an excess (*franchise*) for any damage to the vehicle. This starts at around €500 for the smallest car and can be covered by credit card. You should return the car with a full tank of fuel or face paying an exorbitant fuel charge.

To rent a car in France you must be over 21 and have driven for at least one year, some companies stipulate two. Most companies charge **drivers under 25** an extra insurance premium, typically €25 per day. OTU Voyage (☎01.55.82.32.32; ⓦwww.otu.fr), the student travel agency, can arrange car rental for young drivers at discounted rates.

Car rental agencies

Alamo US ☎1-800/462-5266, ⓦwww.alamo .com.
Argus Car Hire Republic of Ireland ☎01/499 9600, ⓦwww.arguscarhire.com.
Auto Europe US & Canada ☎1-888/223-5555, UK ☎0800/358 1229, Republic of Ireland ☎1800/943 075, South Africa ☎0800/911 532; ⓦwww .autoeurope.com.
Avis US & Canada ☎1-800/331-1212, UK ☎0870/606 0100, Republic of Ireland ☎021/428 1111, Australia ☎136-333 or 02/9353 9000, New Zealand ☎09/526 2847 or 0800/655 111, South Africa ☎011/923 3660; ⓦwww.avis.com.
Budget US ☎1-800/527-0700, Canada ☎1-800/268-8900, UK ☎08701/565656, Republic of Ireland ☎09/0662 7711, Australia ☎1300/362 848, New Zealand ☎0800/283-438; ⓦwww .budget.com.
Dollar US ☎1-800/800-3665, Canada ☎1-800/848-8268; ⓦwww.dollar.com.
Enterprise Rent-a-Car US & Canada ☎1-800/261-7331; ⓦwww.enterprise.com.

Europcar US & Canada ☎1-877/940 6900, UK ☎0870/607 5000, Republic of Ireland ☎01/614 2800, Australia ☎1740/504 000, South Africa ☎011/574 4457; ⓦwww.europcar.com.
Europe by Car US ☎1-800/223-1516, ⓦwww .europebycar.com.
Hertz US ☎1-800/654-3001, Canada ☎1-800/263-0678, UK ☎08708/448 844, Republic of Ireland ☎01/676-7476, Australia ☎03/9698-2555, New Zealand ☎0800/654 321, South Africa ☎021/935 4800; ⓦwww.hertz.com.
Holiday Autos US & Canada ☎866/392-9288, UK ☎0870/400 4461, Republic of Ireland ☎01/872 9366, Australia ☎1300/554 432, New Zealand ☎0800/144 040, South Africa ☎011/234 0597; ⓦwww.holidayautos.com.
National US & Canada ☎1-800/227-7368, UK ☎0870/400-4581, Republic of Ireland ☎021/432-0755, Australia ☎02/1432 0755, New Zealand ☎03/366-5574, South Africa ☎0800/011 323; ⓦwww.nationalcar.com.
SIXT US & Canada ☎1-888/749-8227, UK ☎0870/1567 567, Republic of Ireland ☎061/206 088, Australia ☎03/9824 2273, South Africa ☎0860/031 666; ⓦwww.e-sixt.com.
Suncars UK ☎0870/500 5566, Republic of Ireland ☎1850/201-416; ⓦwww.suncars.com.
Thrifty US & Canada ☎1-800/847-4389, UK ☎0808/234-7642, Republic of Ireland ☎1800/515-800, Australia ☎1300/367 227, New Zealand ☎03/359 2721, South Africa ☎0861/002 111; ⓦwww.thrifty.com.

Motoring organizations

In the UK and Ireland

AA UK ☎0800/085 2840, ⓦwww.theaa.com. Republic of Ireland ☎01/617 9999, ⓦwww .aaireland.ie.
RAC UK ☎0800/550 055, Republic of Ireland ☎1890/483 483; ⓦwww.rac.co.uk.

In the US and Canada

AAA US ☎1-800/AAA-HELP, ⓦwww.aaa.com.
CAA Canada ☎613/247-0117, ⓦwww.caa.ca.

In Australia and New Zealand

AAA Australia ☎02/6247 7311, ⓦwww.aaa.asn .au.
New Zealand AA ☎0800/500 213, ⓦwww.aa .co.nz.

In South Africa

AA South Africa ☎083/843 22, ⓦwww.aasa.co.za.

Scooter and motorbike rental

Scooters are relatively easy to find and, though they're not built for long-distance travel, are ideal for pottering around the local area. You also don't need a licence to drive them, just a passport or some form of ID. Places that rent out bicycles often also rent out scooters; you can expect to pay at least €40 a day for a 50cc machine, less for longer periods. For anything more powerful you'll need a full **motorbike** licence. Rental prices are around €60 a day for a 125cc bike. Expect to leave a hefty deposit by cash or credit card – over €1000 is not unusual – which you may lose in the event of damage or theft. Crash helmets are compulsory on all bikes, and the headlight must be switched on at all times.

Hitching

If you're intent on **hitching**, you'll have to rely almost exclusively on car drivers, as lorries very rarely give lifts. Even so, it won't be easy. Looking as clean and respectable as possible makes a very big difference, as conversations with French drivers soon make clear. Experience suggests that hitching the less-frequented D-roads is much quicker, while in rural areas a rucksack and hiking gear will help procure a lift from sympathetic drivers.

Autoroutes are a special case. Hitching on the *autoroute* itself is illegal, but you can make excellent time going from one service station to another. Alternatively, tollgates (*péages*) are the second best (and legal) option, but ordinary approach roads can be disastrous. Look out for the free *autoroute* maps showing all the service stations, tollgates, exits, etc.

For long-distance rides, and for a greater sense of security, you might consider using the **national hitching organization** Allostop (30 rue Pierre-Sémard, 75009 Paris; ☏01.53.20.42.42, ⊛www.allostop.net) or Covoiturage (⊛www.covoiturage.com), a car-sharing pool where passengers can also register for lifts.

By bicycle

Bicycles (*vélos*) have high status in France, where cyclists are given respect both on the roads and as customers at restaurants and hotels. In addition, local authorities are actively promoting cycling, not only with urban cycle lanes but also with comprehensive networks in rural areas (frequently using disused railways). The Aquitaine tourist authority (see p.63) produces a useful bilingual brochure, *L'Aquitaine à Vélo*, detailing a number of itineraries in the region, while that in Entre-Deux-Mers (see p.119) issues a range of leaflets entitled *Cyclotourisme en Entre-Deux-Mers*.

Hotels are nearly always obliging about looking after your bike, even to the point of allowing it into your room. Most towns have well-stocked retail and **repair shops**, where parts are normally cheaper than in Britain or the US. However, if you're using a foreign-made bike with nonstandard metric wheels, it's a good idea to carry spare tyres.

The **train** network runs various schemes for cyclists, all of them covered by the free leaflet *Guide Train + Vélo*, available from most stations. Trains marked with a bicycle in the timetable and a number of TGVs (listed in the above booklet) allow you to take a bike free either in the dedicated bike racks or in the luggage van; in the latter case it's essential to reserve a slot (costing €10) on TGVs and recommended on other services at least several days in advance during busy periods. Otherwise, you can take your dismantled bike, packed in a carrier measuring 120cm by 90cm, for free on TGVs and other trains with sufficiently large luggage racks. Another option is to send your bike parcelled up as registered baggage through Sernam (☏08.25.84.58.45, €0.15/min) for a fee of €39; delivery should take two days, bearing in mind that the service doesn't operate at weekends.

Eurostar allows you to take your bicycle as part of your baggage allowance provided it's dismantled and packed in a bag no more than 120cm by 90cm. However, Eurostar encourage people to register their bikes and send them unaccompanied with their registered baggage service, Esprit Europe (☏08705/850 850, ⊛www.espriteurope.co.uk) for £20 one way, with a guaranteed arrival time of 24 hours; you can register your bike, which does not need to be dismantled, from ten days before departure. **Ferries**

usually carry bikes free (though you may need to register it), as do some **airlines** such as British Airways, while others now charge – remember to check when making your booking.

Bikes – either mountain bikes (*vélos toutterrain* or VTT) or hybrid bikes (*vélos toutchemin* or VTC) – are often available to **rent** from campsites and hostels, as well as from specialist cycle shops and some tourist offices for around €15 per day. The bikes are often not insured, however, and you will be presented with the bill for its replacement if it's stolen or damaged; check your travel insurance policy for cover.

As for **maps**, a minimum requirement is the IGN 1:100,000 series (see p.58) – the smallest scale that carries contours. The UK's national cyclists' organisation, the CTC (☎0870/873 0061, ⊛www.ctc.org.uk), can suggest routes and supply advice for members (£33 a year, or £53 for a family of four and £12 for under 18s and students under 26 years). They run a particularly good insurance scheme. Companies offering specialist bike touring **holidays** are listed on pp.24, 26 & 28. For **guide books** aimed at cyclists, see p.401.

By boat

Boating makes a leisurely way to explore the Lot and Garonne valleys. From April to October the **River Lot** is navigable for house boats from St-Cirq-Lapopie downstream to Luzech (65km), and from Fumel down to its confluence with the Garonne (78km). For the rest of the year the current is too swift and the river too high to be safe. But the Lot is a capricious river at any time, so it pays to follow the guidelines provided by rental companies carefully.

The other option is to potter along the **Canal latéral** which tracks the Garonne eastwards from Castets-en-Dorthe, near Langon, to Toulouse (190km), where it joins the Canal du Midi. You can also combine the Canal latéral with the River Lot and the **River Baïse** south to Nérac.

The main specialist **operators** are detailed in the box below, while a number of the tour agents listed in "Getting There" (see pp.24, 26 & 28) also offer boating holidays. Boats are usually rented by the week, though shorter periods are also available outside the July and August peak. **Rates** range from €750 to €2500 per week for a four- to six-person boat, depending on the season and level of comfort. No licence is required, but you'll receive instruction before taking the controls. You should also be given a **carte de plaisance**, guaranteeing that the boat is insured and in good working order.

Boat rental companies in France

Babou Marine ☎05.65.30.08.99, ⊛www.baboulen-jean.fr
Crown Blue Line France ☎04.68.94.52.73, ⊛www.crownblueline.com
Locaboat Plaisance ☎03.86.91.72.72, ⊛www.locaboat.com
Nautic ☎04.67.94.78.93, ⊛www.nautic.fr
Nicols ☎02.41.56.46.56, ⊛www.nicols.com

Accommodation

At most times of the year you can turn up in any town in the Dordogne and Lot region and find a room or a place in a campsite. Booking a couple of nights in advance can be reassuring, however, as it saves you the effort of trudging round and ensures that you know what you'll be paying; many hoteliers, campsite managers and hostel managers speak at least a little English. In most towns, you'll be able to get a simple double for around €35, though expect to pay at least €50 for a reasonable level of comfort. We've detailed a selection of hotels throughout the Guide, and given a price range for each (see below); as a general rule the areas around train stations have the highest density of cheap hotels.

Problems may arise between mid-July and the end of August, when the French take their own vacations en masse. During this period, hotel and hostel accommodation can be hard to come by and you may find yourself falling back on local tourist offices for help. Some offer a **booking service**, though they can't guarantee rooms at a particular price, and all provide lists of hotels, hostels, campsites and bed-and-breakfast possibilities. With **campsites**, you can be more relaxed about finding an empty pitch somewhere for a tent, though it may be more difficult with a caravan or camper van.

Hotels

Most French hotels are **graded** from zero to five stars. The price more or less corresponds to the number of stars, though the system is a little haphazard, having more to do with ratios of bathrooms-per-guest and so forth than genuine quality, and some of the unclassified and single-star hotels can actually be very good. What you get for your money varies enormously between establishments.

For under €30, there won't be soundproofing and the showers (*douches*) and toilets (WC or *toilettes*) may well be communal (*dans le palier*). However, you should have your own bidet and washbasin (*lavabo*), often partitioned off from the rest of the room in an area referred to as a *cabinet de toilette*. The shared showers down the hall are usually free but sometimes you'll be charged a couple of euro per shower, in which case it might be worth upgrading to an en-suite room. Over €30 should get you a room with its own bath or shower though not necessarily toilet, and, though the decor may not be anything to write home about, comfortable furniture. For around €50 you should expect a proper, separate bathroom (*salle de bain*) and TV, while at over €85 you'll find something approaching luxury. Hotels with one star or above have a telephone in the rooms, though some phones can only receive calls. **Single rooms** – if the hotel has any – are only marginally cheaper than doubles, so sharing always slashes costs, especially since most hotels willingly provide rooms with **extra**

Accommodation price codes

All the hotels and *chambres d'hôtes* listed in this book have been price-coded according to the following scale. The prices quoted are for the **cheapest available double room in high season**, although remember that many of the cheap places will also have more expensive rooms with more facilities. In the case of a hostel, we give the price of a **dormitory bed**.

❶ Under €30	❷ €30–40	❸ €40–55	❹ €55–70
❺ €70–85	❻ €85–100	❼ €100–125	❽ €125–150
❾ Over €150			

beds for three or more people at good discounts.

Breakfast, which is not normally included, will add between €5 and €15 per person to a bill, sometimes more – though there is no obligation to take it. The standard breakfast consists of orange juice, a hot drink and croissant and/or bread and orange juice, though smarter places now run to yoghurt, fruit and cereals and may even offer a buffet. By way of comparison, a coffee and croissant in a café will set you back around €4–5. The cost of eating **dinner** in a hotel's restaurant can be a more important factor to bear in mind when picking a place to stay. It's actually illegal for hotels to insist you take half-board (*demi-pension*), though a few do, especially during the summer peak. This is not always such a bad thing, however, since you can sometimes get a real bargain.

Note that many family-run hotels close down for two or three weeks a year. In smaller towns and villages they may also close for one or two nights a week, usually Sunday or Monday. Details are given where relevant in the Guide, but dates change from year to year and some places will close for a few days in low season if they have no bookings. The best precaution is to phone ahead to be sure.

A very useful option, especially if you're driving and looking for somewhere late at night, are the modern **chain hotels** located at motorway exits and on the outskirts of major towns. They may be soulless, but you can count on a decent and reliable standard. Among the cheapest (from around €30 for a three-person room with communal toilets and showers) is the one-star Formule 1 chain (☎08.92.68.56.85, €0.34 per min; ⊛www .hotelformule1.com). Other budget chains include B&B (☎01.72.36.51.06, €0.34 per min; ⊛www.hotel-bb.com), the slightly more comfortable Première Classe (☎01.64.62.46.46; ⊛www.premiereclasse .fr) and Etap Hôtel (☎08.92.68.89.00, €0.34 per min; ⊛www.etaphotel.com). Slightly more upmarket are Ibis (☎08.92.68.66.86, €0.34 per min; ⊛www.ibishotel.com) and Campanile (☎01.64.62.46.46; ⊛www .campanile.fr), where en-suite rooms with cable TV and direct dial phones cost between €55 and €75. Top of the range chain hotels are the Novotel (☎08.25.01.20.11, €0.15 per min; ⊛www.novotel.com), Mercure (☎08.25.88.33.33, €0.15 per min, ⊛www .mercure.com) and Sofitel (☎08.25.01.20.11, €0.15 per min, ⊛www.sofitel.com), all of which tend to be in more attractive or at least more central locations. It's worth noting that these chains generally offer good online discounts.

Aside from the chains, there are a number of **hotel federations** in France. The biggest and most useful of these is **Logis de France** (83 av d'Italie, 75013 Paris; ☎01.45.84.83.84, ⊛www.logis-de-france.fr), an association of over 3000 hotels nationwide; standards are generally good, though can occasionally be a bit erratic. The organization produces a free annual guide, which you can obtain from your nearest French tourist office (see p.63), from Logis de France itself or from member hotels. Two other, more upmarket federations worth mentioning are Châteaux & Hôtels de France (84 av Victor-Cresson, 92441 Issy-les-Moulineaux; ☎01.72.72.92.02, ⊛www .chateauxhotels.com) and Relais du Silence (17 rue d'Ouessant, 75015 Paris; ☎01.44.49.90.00, ⊛www.silencehotel.com).

Bed-and-breakfast and self-catering

In country areas, in addition to hotels, you will come across *chambres d'hôtes*, **bed-and-breakfast accommodation** in someone's house, château or farm. Though the quality varies widely, on the whole standards have improved dramatically in recent years and the best can offer more character and greater value for money than an equivalently priced hotel. If you're lucky, the owners may also provide traditional home cooking and a great insight into French life. In general, prices range between €40 and €80 for two people including breakfast; payment is almost always expected in cash. Some offer meals on request (*tables d'hôtes*), usually evenings only, while others are attached to *fermes auberges*, farm-restaurants serving local produce (see p.41 for more). Again, we've detailed a number of *chambres d'hôtes* throughout the Guide and tourist offices will also be able to provide lists. Or contact Gîtes de France, (see overleaf).

If you're planning to stay a week or more in any one place it might be worth considering renting **self-catering accommodation**. This will generally consist of self-contained country cottages known as *gîtes* or *gîtes ruraux*. Many *gîtes* are in converted barns or farm outbuildings, though some can be quite grand.

You can get lists of both *gîtes* and *chambres d'hôtes* from **Gîtes de France** (59 rue St-Lazare, 75439 Paris; ☎01.49.70.75.75, ◍www.gites-de-france .fr), which every year publishes a number of national guides, such as *Nouveaux Gîtes Ruraux*, listing new addresses, *Chambres et Tables d'Hôtes* and *Chambres d'Hôtes de Charme* (€20–22), and more comprehensive regional or departmental guides which include photos (€5–20). All these guides are available online or from the Paris headquarters and departmental offices of Gîtes de France, as well as from local bookstores and tourist offices. Tourist offices will also have lists of places in their area which are not affiliated to Gîtes de France.

You'll also find self-catering accommodation, much of it foreign-owned, advertised on the Internet: ◍www.frenchconnections.co .uk, ◍www.cheznous.co.uk and ◍www .bvdirect.co.uk are well-established sites; or try one of the agents listed in the Travel Shop section of the Maison de la France website, ◍www.franceguide.com. In Britain, try looking at the classified ads in the Sunday newspapers, such as the *Observer* and *Sunday Times*. Another option is to contact one of the holiday firms that market accommodation/travel packages (see pp.24, 26 & 28 for a brief selection of these).

Departmental Offices of Gîtes de France

Aveyron 17 rue Aristide-Briand, BP 831, 120008 Rodez ☎05.65.75.55.55, ◐gites.de.france. aveyron@wanadoo.fr.

Corrèze Immeuble Consulaire, BP 30, 19001 Tulle ☎05.55.21.55.61, ◐gites.de.france@correze. chambagri.fr.

Dordogne 25 rue Wilson, BP 2063, 24002 Périgueux ☎05.53.35.50.24, ◐dordogne.perigord. tourisme@wanadoo.fr.

Gironde 21 cours de l'Intendance, 33000 Bordeaux ☎05.56.81.54.23, ◐gites33@wanadoo.fr.

Lot place François-Mitterrand, 46000 Cahors; ☎05.65.53.20.75, ◐gites.de.france.lot@wanadoo. fr.

Lot-et-Garonne 11 rue des Droits-de-l'Homme, 47000 Agen ☎05.53.47.80.87, ◐gites-de-france.47@wanadoo.fr.

Tarn-et-Garonne 7 bd Midi-Pyrénées, BP 534, 82000 Montauban ☎05.63.21.79.61, ◐gitesdefrance@cg82.fr.

Hostels, foyers and gîtes d'étape

There aren't that many **youth hostels** – *auberges de jeunesse* – in the Dordogne and Lot region, but at between around €12 and €16 per night for a dormitory bed, sometimes with breakfast thrown in, they are invaluable for single travellers on a budget; per-person prices of dorm beds are given throughout the Guide. Some hostels now offer rooms, occasionally en suite, for couples or families, but these don't necessarily work out to be cheaper than hotels – particularly if you've had to pay a taxi fare to reach them, for example. However, one or two, notably the hostel at Cadouin (see p.211), are beautifully sited, and allow you to cut costs by preparing your own food in their kitchens, or eating in their cheap canteens.

Those hostels that do exist in this region, all detailed in the Guide, are run either by the municipality or by the French **hostelling association**, the Fédération Unie des Auberges de Jeunesse (FUAJ); see opposite for contact details. To stay at FUAJ hostels you normally have to show a current HI (Hostelling International) **membership card**. It's usually cheaper and easier to join before you leave home, provided your national Youth Hostel association (see opposite) is a full member of HI. Alternatively, you can purchase an HI card in certain French hostels for €15.30 (€10.70 for those under 26), or buy individual "welcome stamps" at a rate of €2.90 per night; after six nights you are entitled to the HI card.

One or two larger towns, such as Ville-franche-de-Rouergue and Périgueux, provide hostel accommodation in Foyers de Jeunes Travailleurs, **residential hostels** for young workers and students, where you can usually get a private room for upwards of €12. On the whole they are more luxurious than youth hostels and normally have a good cafeteria or canteen.

In the countryside, another hostel-style alternative exists: **gîtes d'étape**. Aimed primarily at hikers and long-distance bikers, *gîtes d'étape* are often run by the local village or municipality and are less formal than hostels. They provide bunk beds and primitive kitchen and washing facilities from around €10, and are marked on the large-scale IGN walkers' maps and listed in the individual Topo guides (see p.402). More information can be found in the Gîtes de France booklet *Gîtes d'Étapes et de Séjours* (€10), and in *Gîtes d'Étape et Refuges*, published by Rando Éditions, available in French bookshops for €19.90 or online at ⑩www.gites-refuges.com.

Youth hostel associations

France

Fédération Unie des Auberges de Jeunesse (FUAJ), 27 rue Pajol, 75018 Paris ☎01.44.89.87.27, ⑩www.fuaj.org.

UK and Ireland

Youth Hostel Association (YHA) England & Wales ☎0870/770 8868, ⑩www.yha.org.uk. Annual membership £15.95; under-26s £9.95.
Scottish Youth Hostel Association ☎01786/891 400, ⑩www.syha.org.uk. Annual membership £8; under-18s £4.
Irish Youth Hostel Association ☎01/830 4555, ⑩www.anoige.ie. Annual membership €20; under-18s €10.
Hostelling International Northern Ireland ☎028/9032 4733, ⑩www.hini.org.uk. Adult membership £13; under-18s £6.

US and Canada

Hostelling International-American Youth Hostels ☎301/495-1240, ⑩www.hiayh.org. Annual membership US$28; under-18s free.
Hostelling International Canada ☎1-800/663 5777, ⑩www.hihostels.ca. Adult membership (up to 28 months) CAN$35; under-18s free.

Australia and New Zealand

Australia Youth Hostels Association ☎02/9565-1699, ⑩www.yha.com.au. Annual membership Aus$52; under-18s Aus$19.
Youth Hostelling Association New Zealand ☎0800/278 299 or 03/379 9970, ⑩www.yha .co.nz. Annual membership NZ$40; under-18s free.

Camping

Practically every village and town in France has at least one **campsite** to cater for the thousands of people who spend their holiday under canvas. Most sites open from around Easter to September or October. The vast majority are graded into four **categories**, from one to four stars, by the local authority. One- and two-star sites are very basic, with toilets and showers (not necessarily with hot water), but little else, and standards of cleanliness are not always brilliant. At the other extreme, four-star sites are far more spacious, have hot-water showers and electrical hook-ups. Most will also have a swimming pool – sometimes heated – washing machines, a shop and sports facilities, and will provide refreshments or meals in high season. At three-star sites you can expect a selection of these facilities and less spacious plots. A further designation, **Camping Qualité** (⑩www.campingqualite .com), has been introduced to indicate those campsites with particularly high standards of hygiene, service and privacy. For those who really like to get away from it all, **camping à la ferme** – on somebody's farm – is a good, simple option. Lists of sites are available at local tourist offices.

Though **charging systems** vary, most places charge per site and per person, usually including a car, while others apply a global figure. As a rough guide, a family of four with a tent and car should expect to pay from €10 per day at a one-star site, rising to €30 or more at a four-star. In peak season and if you plan to spend a week or more at one site, it's wise to book ahead, and note that many of the big sites now have caravans and chalet bungalows for rent.

If you're planning to do a lot of camping, it's worth getting hold of an **international camping carnet** (CCI), which gives discounts at member sites and serves as useful identification. Many campsites will take it instead of making you surrender your passport during your stay, and it covers you for third party insurance when camping. You can obtain the carnet from national motoring organizations (see p.33) or, in the UK, from the Camping and Caravanning Club (☎0845/130 7631, ⑩www .campingandcaravanningclub.co.uk).

The Fédération Française de Camping et de Caravaning (☎01.42.72.84.08, ⓦwww.ffcc.fr) publishes an annual guide (€16) covering 11,000 campsites, details of which can also be found online at the excellent Camping France website ⓦwww.campingfrance.com. If you'd rather have everything organized for you, a number of companies specialize in **camping holidays**, including Canvas Holidays, Keycamp and Eurocamp (all listed on p.25).

Lastly, a word of **caution**: never camp rough (*camping sauvage*, as the French call it) on anyone's land without first asking permission. If the dogs don't get you, the guns might – farmers have been known to shoot first and ask later. On the other hand, a politely phrased request for permission will as often as not get positive results. Camping on public land is not officially permitted, but is widely practised by the French, and if you are discreet you're not likely to have problems.

Food and drink

The cuisine of the Dordogne and Lot region is, at heart, country cooking (*cuisine de terroir*), plain and simple fare, revolving around duck and goose, garlic, a host of mushrooms, walnuts and whatever else the land has to offer. It's the sort of cuisine best sampled in little family-run places, where it's still possible to eat well for €15 or less. That said, every restaurant worth its salt offers a *menu du terroir*, featuring local specialities – indeed, it sometimes seems hard to find anything else, and in summer especially you'll be craving less hearty fare. Relief is at hand, however, in the more adventurous – and expensive – *gastronomique* restaurants found throughout the region, and most mid-priced establishments now offer at least a smattering of fish dishes. But real fish and seafood fanatics should head for Bordeaux – a city famed for the range and quality of its restaurants – and the towns and villages along the Gironde estuary. Be aware that the uniformity of menus at some middle-of-the-road restaurants can become tiring, and do be prepared for some disappointments, especially in prime tourist spots. See **A taste of Périgord** colour section for more on the region's speciality food and drink.

In the rarefied world of **haute cuisine**, where the top chefs are national celebrities, a battle has long been raging between traditionalists, determined to preserve the purity of French cuisine, and those who experiment with different flavours from around the world to create novel combinations. At this level, French food is still brilliant – in both camps – and the good news is that prices are continuing to come down. Many gourmet palaces offer weekday lunchtime menus where you can sample culinary genius for under €40.

Vegetarians can expect a lean time in the Dordogne and Lot region – the very concept is alien to most local chefs. There are very few specifically vegetarian restaurants, though crêperies, pizzerias and Chinese or North African restaurants can be good standbys. Otherwise the best you can hope for is an omelette, salad or plate of vegetables – often tinned – at an ordinary restaurant. Occasionally they'll be willing to replace a meat dish on the fixed-price menu (*menu fixe*); at other times you'll have to pick your way through the *carte*. Remember the phrase "*Je suis végétarien(ne); est-ce qu'il y a quelques plats sans viande?*" (I'm a vegetarian; are there any non-meat dishes?). **Vegans**, however, should probably forget about eating in restaurants and stick to self-catering. See the food glossary on p.410 for other useful vocabulary.

With the exception of Bordeaux and the larger towns, the Dordogne and Lot is also not well provided with restaurants serving **foreign cuisine**. The most common – and usually good value for money – are Vietnamese, Chinese or North African outlets.

Breakfast and snacks

A croissant or *pain au chocolat* (a chocolate-filled, light pastry) with hot chocolate or coffee in a café-bar is generally the most economical way to eat **breakfast**, costing around €4. If there are no croissants left, it's perfectly acceptable to go and buy your own snack at the local baker or patisserie. The standard hotel breakfast comprises bread and/or pastries, jam and a jug of coffee or tea, and orange juice if you're lucky, from around €5. More expensive hotels might offer a buffet comprising cereals, fruit, yogurt and the works.

At **lunchtime**, and sometimes in the evening, you'll find places offering a *plat du jour* (daily special) at between €8 and €12, or *formules*, a limited menu, typically offering a main dish and either a starter or dessert for a set price. *Croques-monsieur* or *croques-madame* (variations on the toasted-cheese sandwich) are on sale at cafés, brasseries and many street stands, along with *frites* (potato fries), *gauffres* (waffles), *glaces* (ice creams) and all kinds of fresh-filled baguettes (these very filling sandwiches usually cost between €3 and €5 to take away).

Crêpes, or pancakes with fillings, served up at ubiquitous crêperies, are popular lunchtime food. The savoury buckwheat variety (*galettes*) provide the main course; sweet, white-flour crêpes are dessert. They can be very tasty, but are generally poor value in comparison with a restaurant meal; you need at least three, normally at over €5 each (€3 for the sweet variety), to feel full. **Pizzerias**, usually *au feu de bois* (wood-fired), are also very common. They are somewhat better value than crêperies, but quality and quantity vary greatly.

For **picnics**, the local outdoor market or supermarket will provide you with almost everything you need. You'll often find a wonderful selection of cooked meat, prepared snacks, ready-made dishes and assorted salads at charcuteries (delicatessens), which you'll find in some villages, and in most supermarkets. You purchase by weight, or you can ask for *une tranche* (a slice), *une barquette* (a carton) or *une part* (a portion) as appropriate. Boulangeries (bakers) provide bread and sometimes double as patisseries, selling a mouthwatering array of cakes and pastries.

Meals

There's no difference between restaurants (or *auberges* or *relais* as they sometimes call themselves) and brasseries in terms of quality or price range. The distinction is that **brasseries**, which resemble cafés, serve quicker meals at most hours of the day, while **restaurants** tend to stick to the traditional meal times of noon to 2pm, and 7pm to 9pm or 9.30pm, sometimes later in larger towns and during the summer months. In touristy areas in high season, and for all the more upmarket places, it's wise to make reservations – easily done on the same day in most cases. In small towns it may be impossible to get anything other than a sandwich from a bar after 9.30pm or so; in Bordeaux, however, a few town-centre brasseries will serve until 11pm or midnight.

When hunting for places to eat, don't forget that **hotel restaurants** are open to non-residents, and can be very good value. Indeed, in many small towns and villages, you'll find these are the only restaurants, but in country areas keep an eye out for **fermes auberges**, farm restaurants where the majority of ingredients are produced on the farm itself. These are often the best places to sample really traditional local cuisine at very reasonable prices; a four-course meal for between €15 and €35 is the norm, including an apéritif and wine, but reservations are a must. Since restaurants change hands frequently and have their ups and downs, it's always worth asking locals for recommendations; this will usually elicit strong views and sound advice.

Prices, and what you get for them, must be posted outside. Normally there's a choice between one or more *menus fixes* – with a set number of courses and a limited choice – and choosing individually from the *carte* (menu). **Menus fixes**, often referred to simply as *menus*, are normally the cheapest option, typically around €12–15 at lunchtime (*le déjeuner*) for a three- or four-course menu, rising to €15–20 or more at dinner (*le dîner*). At the bottom end of the price range, menus revolve around standard dishes such as steak and chips (*steak frites*), chicken and chips (*poulet frites*) and various stews (such as *daubes*). But further up the scale they can represent much the best-value way of sampling regional specialities, sometimes running to five or more courses. Going **à la carte** offers greater choice and, in the better restaurants, unlimited access to the chef's inventiveness – though you'll pay for the privilege.

In the vast majority of restaurants a **service charge** of fifteen percent is included in prices listed on the menu – in which case it should say *service compris* (*s.c.*) or *prix net*. Very occasionally you'll see *service non compris* (*s.n.c.*) or *servis en sus*, which means that it's up to you whether you leave a tip or not. Wine (*vin*) or a drink (*boisson*) is sometimes included in the cost of a *menu fixe*. Otherwise, the cheapest option will be the house wine, usually served in a jug (*pichet*) or carafe; you'll be asked if you want *un quart* (0.25 litre), *un demi* (0.5 litre) or *une litre* (1 litre). As for choosing a bottle of wine, if you're worried about the cost, ask for *vin ordinaire* or the *vin de table*.

In the Guide the lowest price menu, or sometimes the range of menus, is given. Where average *à la carte* prices are given it assumes you'll have three courses, but excludes wine.

The French are extremely well disposed towards **children** in restaurants. Not only do they offer reduced-price children's menus (albeit often just salad, steak and chips and ice cream) but they also create an atmosphere – even in otherwise fairly snooty establishments – that positively welcomes kids; some even provide games and toys.

One final note is that you should always call the waiter or waitress *Monsieur* or *Madame* (*Mademoiselle* if a young woman), never *Garçon*.

Drinking

In France **drinking** is done at a leisurely pace whether it's a prelude to food (*apéritif*), or a sequel (*digestif*), and cafés are the standard places to do it. Every bar or café has to display its full price list, including service charges. You normally pay when you leave, and it's perfectly acceptable to sit for hours over just one cup of coffee, though a small tip will always be appreciated.

Wine

Though alcohol consumption at lunchtime is on the decline, **wine** (*vin*) is drunk at just about every meal or social occasion. Red is *rouge*, white *blanc* and rosé *rosé*. The house wine served in restaurants can be very good value in this wine-producing region, or opt for a bottle of AOC (*appellation d'origine contrôlée*) wine if you want a more sophisticated taste. You can buy a very decent bottle of wine for €6 in a shop or from the producer, while €10 and over will get you something worth savouring. By the time restaurants have added their considerable mark-up, wine can constitute an alarming proportion of the bill.

The basic **wine terms** are: *brut*, very dry; *sec*, dry; *demi-sec*, sweet; *doux*, very sweet; *mousseux*, sparkling; *méthode champenoise*, mature and sparkling. There are grape varieties as well, but the complexities of the subject take up volumes. A glass of wine is simply *un verre de rouge*, *rosé* or *blanc*. *Un pichet* (a pitcher) is normally a quarter-litre, but you may need to specify the size: a quatre litre (*un quart*), or a half (*un demi*). A glass of wine in a bar will typically cost around €3 to €6.

The best way of **buying wine** is directly from the producers (*vignerons*) at their vineyards or at Maisons or Syndicats du Vin (representing a group of wine-producers), or Coopératifs Vinicoles (producers' co-ops). At all of these you can usually sample the wines first. It's best to make clear at the start how much you want to buy (particularly if it's only one or two bottles) and you will not be popular if you drink several glasses and then fail to make a purchase. The most interesting option is to visit the vineyard itself, where the owner will often include a tour of the *chais* in

Wines of the region

The area around Bordeaux comprises one of the world's great wine-producing regions. The **Bordelais vineyards** stretch over 100km north–south and 130km east–west, divided among 57 different *appellations* and thousands of individual châteaux. The vast majority produce red wines, most famously those of the Médoc and St-Émilion, for example, but the area also produces quality white wines – the dry Graves and the velvety sweet Sauternes being the most notable. Don't overlook the lesser-known Bordeaux wines, such as Entre-Deux-Mers, where you can still find very drinkable wines at much lower prices.

The same goes for the vineyards further inland. Around **Bergerac**, the sweet, white Monbazillac is the star, though the aromatic whites of Montravel and the reds of Pécharmant are also worth looking out for. There are also some very palatable Côtes de Bergerac and Côtes de Castillon, the best of which resemble the neighbouring St-Émilion wines but for half the price. In a similar vein are the up-and-coming wines of **Duras** and **Buzet** to the south. Further east, the fine dark, almost peppery reds from **Cahors** provide one of the region's most distinctive tastes.

The quality of the local *vins de pays*, though very variable, can still be exceptional for the price, but for better quality vintages you need to concentrate on the **AOC (appellation d'origine contrôlée) wines**. But be aware that within each *appellation* there is enormous diversity generated by the different types of soil, the lie of the land, the type of grape grown, the ability of the wine to age, and – last but by no means least – the individual skills of the viticulturist.

Wine production is an extremely complex business and it's not difficult to feel intimidated by the seemingly innate expertise of all French people. Many individual wines and *appellations* are mentioned in the text, but trusting your own taste is the most important thing. Knowing the grape types that you particularly like (or dislike), whether you prefer wines fruity, dry, light or heavy, is all useful whether you are discussing your choice with a waiter, wine merchant or the producer themselves. The more interest you show, the more helpful advice you are likely to receive. And if you want to take it further, you can sign up for introductory wine-tasting courses in Bordeaux and St-Émilion.

For more information on the region's main wine-producing areas, see p.78 for Bordeaux, p.189 for Bergerac and p.296 for Cahors.

which the wine is produced and aged. The most economical method is to buy *en vrac*, which you can do at some wine shops (*caves*), filling an easily obtainable plastic five- or ten-litre container (generally sold on the premises) straight from the barrel. Supermarkets often have good bargains, too.

Beer

Light Belgian and German **beers**, plus various French brands from Alsace, account for most of the beer you'll find. Draught beer (*à la pression*) – very often Kronenbourg – is the cheapest drink you can have next to coffee and wine; *un pression* or *un demi* (0.33 litre) will cost around €3 to €4. For a wider choice of draught and bottled beer you need to go to special beer-drinking establishments such as the English- and Irish-style pubs found in larger towns and cities. A small bottle at one of these places can cost up to twice as much as a *demi* in an ordinary café-bar. Buying bottled or canned beer in supermarkets is, of course, much cheaper.

Spirits and liqueurs

Strong alcohol, including **spirits** (*eaux-de-vie*), such as cognac and armagnac, and **liqueurs** such as locally made walnut liqueurs (*vins de noix*), are always available. *Pastis* – the generic name for aniseed drinks such as Pernod or Ricard – is served diluted with water and ice (*glace* or *glaçons*). It's very refreshing and not expensive. Among less familiar names, try Poire William (pear brandy), or Marc (a spirit distilled from grape pulp). Measures are generous, but they don't come cheap: the same applies for imported spirits such as whisky (*Scotch*). Two drinks designed to stimulate the appetite – *un apéritif* – are Pineau (cognac and grape juice) and Kir (white wine with a dash of cassis – blackcurrant liqueur – or with champagne instead of wine for a Kir Royal). For a post-meal *digestif*, don't miss out on armagnac, oak-aged brandy from the south of the Garonne but available in bars and restaurants throughout the region. **Cocktails** are served at most late-night bars, discos and clubs, as well as at upmarket hotel bars; they usually cost at least €5.

Soft drinks

On the **soft drink** front, you can buy cartons of unsweetened fruit juice in supermarkets, although in cafés, the bottled (sweetened) nectars such as apricot (*jus d'abricot*) and blackcurrant (*cassis*) still hold sway. Fresh orange or lemon juice (*orange/citron pressé*) is a much more refreshing choice on a hot day – the juice is served in the bottom of a long ice-filled glass, with a jug of water and sugar to sweeten it to your taste. Other soft drinks to try are syrups (*sirops*) of mint, grenadine and other flavours mixed with water. The standard fizzy drinks of lemonade (*limonade*), Coke (*coca*) and so forth are all available. Bottles of **mineral water** (*eau minérale*) and spring water (*eau de source*) – either sparkling (*gazeuse*) or still (*plate*) – abound, from the big brand names to the most obscure spa product. But there's not much wrong with the tap water (*l'eau de robinet*) which will always be brought free to your table if you ask for it.

Coffee, tea and hot chocolate

Coffee is invariably espresso – small, black and very strong. *Un café* or *un express* is the regular; *un crème* is with milk; *un grand café* or *un grand crème* are large vesions. In the morning you could also ask for *un café au lait* – espresso in a large cup or bowl filled up with hot milk. *Un déca* is decaffeinated, now widely available. Ordinary **tea** (*thé*) – Lipton's nine times out of ten – is normally served black (*nature*) or with a slice of lemon (*au citron*); to have milk with it, ask for *un peu de lait frais* (some fresh milk). *Chocolat chaud* – **hot chocolate** – unlike tea, lives up to the high standards of French food and drink and can be had in any café. After meals, **herb teas** (*infusions* or *tisanes*), offered by most restaurants, can be soothing. The more common ones are *verveine* (verbena), *tilleul* (lime blossom), *menthe* (mint) and *camomille* (camomile).

The media

A limited range of English-language newspapers and news magazines are on sale in Bordeaux and in larger towns in the rest of the Dordogne and Lot region. Those which are printed locally, such as the *International Herald Tribune*, are available on the day of publication; others usually arrive the following day and are heavily marked up. You'll find a wider choice of mostly British papers in the main tourist centres and those areas with a strong expat population. French newspapers, radio and television will be of little interest unless you are fairly competent in French.

Newspapers and magazines

Of the **French daily papers**, *Le Monde* (@ www.lemonde.fr) is the most intellectual; it is widely respected, but somewhat austere, even though it now carries such frivolities as colour photos. *Libération* (@ www.liberation .com), founded by Jean-Paul Sartre in the 1960s, is moderately left-wing, pro-European, independent and more colloquial, with good, if slightly narrow, coverage. Rigorous left-wing criticism of the French government comes from *L'Humanité* (@ www.humanite.fr), the Communist Party paper, though it is struggling to survive. The other nationals are all firmly right-wing in their politics: *Le Figaro* (@ www.lefigaro.fr) is the most widely read. The top-selling tabloid, predictably more readable and a good source of news, is *Aujourd'hui*, while *L'Équipe* (@ www.lequipe.fr) is dedicated to sports coverage. The widest circulations are enjoyed by the **regional dailies**; in this area, *Sud Ouest* (@ www.sudouest.com) and *La Dépêche* (@ www.ladepeche.fr), based in Bordeaux and Toulouse respectively. For visitors, they are mainly of interest for their listings, and for their free supplements covering events in the area during July and August.

Weeklies of the *Newsweek/Time* model include the wide-ranging and socialist-inclined *Le Nouvel Observateur* (@ www .nouvelobs.com), its right-wing counterpart *L'Express* (@ www.lexpress.fr) and the centrist with bite, *Marianne* (@ www .marianne-en-ligne.fr). Comprising mainly translated articles, *Courrier International* (@ www.courrierinternational.com) offers an overview of what's being discussed in the media around the globe. The best investigative journalism is to be found in the weekly satirical paper *Le Canard Enchaîné*, while *Charlie Hebdo* is a sort of *Private Eye* or *Spy Magazine* equivalent. There's also *Paris-Match* (@ www.parismatch.com) for gossip about stars and royalty. **Monthlies** include the young and trendy *Nova* (@ www .novaplanet.com), which has good listings of cultural events.

Moral censorship of the press is rare. On the newsstands you'll find pornography of every shade alongside knitting patterns and DIY. You'll also find French **comics** (*bandes dessinées*), many of them aimed at the adult market, with wild and wonderful illustrations; whole bookshops, even museums, are devoted to them.

With so many Brits now living in the Dordogne, it's not surprising to find two **local English-language papers**. *The News* (@ www.french-news.com) and *The Connexion* (@ www.connexionfrance.com) cater primarily to the expat community but also run general background stories. Both are published monthly.

Radio

If you've got a **radio**, you can tune into English-language broadcasts. The websites of the BBC (@ www.bbc.co.uk/worldservice), Radio Canada (@ www.rcinet.ca) and Voice of America (@ www.voa.gov) list their world service frequencies around the globe. The French equivalent is Radio France International (RFI; @ www.rfi.fr), which broadcasts on 89 FM and 738 MW in French and various foreign languages including English. For news in French, there's the state-run France Inter (89.7 FM), Europe 1 (183 LW or various FM frequencies) or round-the-clock news on France Info (105.5 FM).

Television

French TV has six channels: three public (France 2, France 3 and Arté/France 5); one subscription (Canal Plus – with some unencrypted programmes); and two commercial open broadcasts (TF1 and M6). Of these, TF1 (www.tf1.fr) and France 2 (www.france2.fr) are the most popular channels, showing a broad mix of programmes. TV5 (www.tv5.org) is the French-language world service channel. In Bordeaux, local cover is provided by TV7. In addition there are any number of cable and satellite channels, which include CNN, BBC World, BBC Prime, Eurosport, MTV, Planète, which specializes in documentaries, Ciné

Classics and Jimmy (*Friends*, *Seinfield* and the like in English). The main French-run music channel is MCM.

Arté/France 5 (also known as La Cinquième; www.arte.tv) is a joint Franco-German cultural venture that transmits simultaneously in French and German: offerings include highbrow programmes, daily documentaries, art criticism, serious French and German movies and complete operas. Arté broadcasts from 7pm to 3am, while France 5 (www.france5.fr) uses the frequency to put out educational programmes the rest of the time. **Canal Plus** (www.canalplus.fr) is the main movie channel, with repeats of foreign films usually shown at least once in the original language. **France 3** (www.france3.fr) is strong on regional news and more heavyweight movies, including a fair number of undubbed foreign films. The main French **news** broadcasts are at 8pm on TF1 and France 2.

Festivals

It's hard to beat the experience of arriving in a small French village, expecting no more than a bed for the night, to discover the streets decked out with flags and streamers, a band playing in the square and the entire population out celebrating the feast of their patron saint. As well as Fête de St-Jean (around June 21, the summer solstice) and Bastille Day (July 14), both celebrated with fireworks and other events in every town and village throughout the region, there are any number of festivals – both traditional and of more recent origin – throughout the Dordogne and Lot.

In such dedicated **wine** country, there are inevitably festivals coinciding with the grape harvest, when each village stages its own celebrations. The biggest wine jamboree, however, is Bordeaux's Fête du Vin, which takes place in alternate years, while St-Émilion's Jurade hosts a more stately procession in spring to announce the judging of the new wines and in autumn to kick off the harvest.

The region's cathedrals, churches and châteaux make superb venues for festivals of **music** and **theatre**. All the major towns, and many of the smaller, put on at least one such festival a year, usually in summer, when you can often catch free performances in the streets. Anyone interested in contemporary theatre should make a beeline for Périgueux in early August, when international mime artists gather for Mimos, one of France's most exciting and innovative festivals.

Popular local culture is celebrated in the Félibrée, a festival established in 1903 to promote and safeguard the local *Occitan* (or *Oc*) language and culture. The **Félibrée** takes place on the first Sunday in July, when there is a procession, an *Occitan* Mass and – of course – a blow-out Périgordin meal. Nowadays the celebrations also continue for around ten days either side of the Félibrée itself in the form of folk concerts, crafts demonstrations, theatre and so forth. It's a peripatetic festival which takes place in a different town in the Dordogne *département* each year; contact the tourist office in Périgueux for the latest information.

More recent introductions are the **historical spectaculars** held at places such as Castillon-de-Bataille, where the final battle of the Hundred Years' War is re-enacted by hundreds of local thespians. Such events may be touristy, but the atmosphere – most are held at night – and general enthusiasm more than compensate.

For details of the region's most important and interesting festivals, see the boxes at the beginning of each chapter of the Guide.

Sports and outdoor activities

The Dordogne and Lot region offers a wide range of sports – both spectator and participatory. Although you can watch local teams play big-league sports such as football, you'll find that locally popular games such as rugby are more worthwhile seeking out. You also have the choice of a variety of outdoor activities, including hiking, cycling, trekking and water-borne diversions such as canoeing.

Spectator sports

Although Bordeaux boasts a major-league **football** team, which has regularly produced national players, the sport that raises the most passion in this region is **rugby**. Southwest France has a rich rugby heritage and local teams are renowned for their style and the spirit with which they play. At a local, everyday level, the rather less gripping game of **boules** is the sport of choice, played in every town and village.

Football and rugby

By far the most prominent **football** team in the region is Bordeaux's **FC Girondins** (ⓦ www.girondins.com), whose home ground is Stade Chaban-Delmas, in the city's southwestern suburbs. Top-rank players such as Zidane, Deschamps, Wiltord and Lizarazu – all members of France's winning 1998 World Cup squad – all played for Bordeaux at one time or another. Founded in 1881, the club dropped briefly out of the First Division in 1991, before staging a comeback to reach the final of the European UEFA Cup in 1996. They lost to Bayern-Munich and then continued through a frustrating run of near misses in national and European competitions, until in 1999 they came top of the French First Division (now known as League 1) and then brought home the League Cup three years later. The Girondins finished the 2005-6 season second behind Olympique Lyonnais in League 1.

Despite the influence of France's footballing prowess, **rugby** remains the most important and closely followed field game throughout this region. Virtually every town worth its salt boasts a team and if you go along to a match you'll soon get swept up in the camaraderie. If you're here in season (mid-September to mid-May), it's well worth going along; unless it's a final, tickets are easy to buy at the gate. The top teams to look out for are Agen, Brive and

Montauban, all of which play in the First
Divison (Top 14) and attract international
players, while Bordeaux, this time represented by Stade Bordelais, ranks in the
Second Division (Pro D2). The high point in
local rugby in recent years was when Brive
won the European Cup in 1997.

Boules

Once the preserve of elderly men in berets,
boules, and its variant *pétanque* (in which
contestants must keep both feet on the
ground when throwing), has been growing in
popularity in recent years and broadening of
appeal to include more young people and
women. There is even a world championship
and talk – not all of it in jest – of getting
boules recognised as an Olympic sport. The
game is similar to English bowls, but the
terrain is always rough (never grass) and the
area much smaller. Two equally numbered
teams (from one to three persons) find a
space of hard, gravelly ground and throw a
cochonnet (jack or, literally, piglet) six to ten
metres. From a fixed spot each player
proceeds in turns to launch a total of three
balls (two in a six-person match), aiming to
place their metal *boules* closest to the
cochonnet at the end of the exchange. A
point is gained for each ball that is closer
than the nearest ball of the opposing team.

The jack is then thrown again and play
continues until one side scores 13. Matches
invariably draw a crowd of onlookers, and
you will not be considered rude if you stop
to observe. The best times to watch are
during village *fêtes*, which invariably include
a tournament, drawing out the best players.
If you want to hone your *boules* skills, sets of
varying degrees of quality are available in
sports shops and supermarkets throughout
the region.

Outdoor pursuits

As with much of rural France, the Dordogne
and Lot region provides a fantastically wide
range of **outdoor activities**. One of the most
popular – and highly recommended – is
walking, taking advantage of the extensive
network of footpaths, including several long-
distance routes. **Cycling** is also a great way
to get about as long as you stick to the

quieter back roads, while the more leisurely
pursuit of **canoeing** has an extremely high
profile in this region in the summer months.
Details of these and other activities are
outlined throughout the Guide, and local and
departmental tourist offices (see p.63) will
also provide in-depth information about
activities in their area. Alternatively, contact
the appropriate national federation (see p.50)
who can put you in touch with their regional
or departmental offices.

Walking and cycling

Walking is without doubt the best way to
enjoy this region of France. Well-maintained
long-distance paths known as *sentiers de
grande randonnée*, or simply **GRs**, cut
across country, signed with red and white
waymarkers and punctuated with campsites
and *gîtes d'étapes* – walkers' hostels – at
convenient distances. Some of the main
routes in the region are the GR6, linking Ste-
Foy-la-Grande in the west to Figeac; the
GR36, which wanders southeast from
Périgueux via Les Eyzies and Cahors to the
Gorges de l'Aveyron; and the GR65, the
great pilgrimage route passing through
Figeac, Cahors and Moissac on the way to
Santiago de Compostela in Spain.

The entire GR65 and parts of the GR36
and GR6 are described in a **Topo-guide**
(available outside France in good travel
bookshops) which gives a detailed account
of the route, including maps, campsites,
refuges, sources of provisions, etc. In
France, the guides are available from
bookshops and some tourist offices, or
direct from the principal French walkers'
organization, the Fédération Française de la
Randonnée Pédestre (see p.50 for details).

In addition, many tourist offices produce
guides to their local footpaths; where there is
no tourist office, try asking at the *mairie*.
Particularly noteworthy are the guides
produced by Sarlat tourist office detailing
walks in the Périgord Noir, and the free
pamphlets describing various options in the
Gironde.

The region's minor roads and demarcated
cycling routes provide plenty of opportunities for cyclists; it's best to avoid main roads
if you want to enjoy yourself, particularly in
the high season. Again, many tourist offices

can provide details of cycle paths in their area. Among the long distance routes, there's the "Grand Traversée du Périgord" running 180km from Mareuil in the far northwest via Brantôme, Périgueux and Les Eyzies to Monpazier. In the Lot-et-Garonne, the "Véloroute" follows the River Lot 80km from Aiguillon northeast to Fumel and Bonaguil. And in the Gironde a disused railway has been converted into a cycle – and walking – route stretching from just outside Bordeaux to Sauveterre-de-Guyenne in the Entre-Deux-Mers and will eventually continue to La Réole and beyond. Even Bordeaux itself has an impressive network of cycle lanes. For more on cycling in France, see p.34.

For recommendations on walking and cycling **maps**, see p.59. **Guidebooks** to look out for are listed on p.400 and p.401.

Canoeing

Canoeing is hugely popular in the Dordogne and Lot region, and in the summer months every navigable river has outfits renting canoes and organizing excursions. Most popular are the Dordogne itself, particularly the stretch between La Roque-Gageac and Beynac, where you pass beneath some of the region's most dramatic castles, and the Vézère, where you can stop off at various points to visit the valley's prehistoric sights. Both are particularly busy, however, in summer. Other, quieter options include the River Lot, through the Aveyron gorges and the smaller Dronne, Dropt and Célé rivers. The Célé is a beautiful river and its upper reaches offer more exciting canoeing through wilder country.

You can **rent** two- to three-person canoes and single-seater kayaks on all these rivers, as detailed in the Guide; every tourist office also stocks lists of local operators. Although it's possible to rent by the hour, it's best to take at least a half-day and simply cruise downstream. The company you book through will provide transport as required. Prices vary according to what's on offer, but you can expect to pay €15–20 per person for a day's rental.

On the Dordogne and Lot rivers you can make **longer excursions** of up to two weeks, either accompanied or on your own,

sometimes in combination with cycling or walking. Various tour operators offer canoeing packages (see p.25, p.26 and p.28), or you can book direct with the local company. Two of the biggest along the Dordogne valley are Safaraid (⚏05.65.37.44.87, ⓦwww .canoe-kayak-dordogne.com) and Copeyre Canoë (⚏05.65.37.33.51, ⓦwww.copeyre .com), both of which maintain a number of bases between Argentat and Beynac. As an example, you can expect to pay around €100 to €150 per person for a seven-day outing – plenty of time to paddle the most interesting stretch from Beaulieu to Limeuil (220km) – and see a few sights on the way; rates include transport, tent and waterproof containers.

The length of the canoeing **season** depends on the weather and the water levels. Successive droughts have caused some rivers almost to dry up in recent summers. Better to come in spring or early summer to be on the safe side. Most operators function daily in July and August, on demand in May, June and September, and close between October and April when the rivers are too high for inexperienced canoeists. One or two, however, stay open throughout the year. All companies are obliged to equip you with lifejackets (*gilets*) and teach you basic safety procedures. You must be able to swim.

If canoeing is to be a major part of your holiday, it's well worth investing in Peter Knowles' *White Water: Massif Central* **guidebook** (see p.401).

Other activities

Horse riding is another excellent way of enjoying the countryside. Practically every town in the Dordogne and Lot, and many farms, have equestrian centres (*centres équestres*) where you can ride with a guide or unaccompanied – depending on your level of experience – on the marked riding trails that span the region. Local and departmental tourist offices can provide details, or you can contact the Comité Nationale du Tourisme Équestre (overleaf).

In the limestone regions of the Dordogne and Lot **rock climbing** (*escalade*) and **caving** (*spéléologie*) are popular activities. Several local canoe rental outfits, such as

Couleurs Périgord and Kalapaca offer beginners' courses and half-day or full-day outings. Again, further information is available from tourist offices or the appropriate national federation.

More placid activities include **golf, fishing** – local tourist offices will assist you in obtaining a licence – and **swimming**. There are many river beaches along the Dordogne and Lot rivers, usually well signposted, and on smaller rivers such as the Célé. An alternative is to head for one of the real or artificial lakes which pepper the region. Many have leisure centres (*bases de plein airs*) at which you can rent pedaloes, windsurfers and dinghies, as well as larger boats and jet-skis (on the bigger reservoirs). It's worth noting, however, that in high summer, when the water is at its lowest, pollution warnings have been issued on rivers and lakes in the region. Check with local tourist authorities for the current situation.

National sports federations

Canoeing Fédération Française de Canoë-Kayak, 87 quai de la Marne, 94344 Joinville-le-Pont ☎01.45.11.08.50, ⓦ www.ffck.org.
Caving Fédération Française de Spéléologie, 28 rue Delandine, 69003 Lyon ☎04.72.56.09.63, ⓦ www.ffspeleo.fr.
Cycling Fédération Française de Cyclotourisme, 12 rue Louis-Bertrand, 94207 Ivry-sur-Seine ☎01.56.20.88.88, ⓦ www.ffct.org.
Golf Fédération Française de Golf, 68 rue Anatole-France, 92300 Levallois-Perret ☎01.41.49.77.00, ⓦ www.ffg.org.
Riding Comité Nationale de Tourisme Équestre, 9 bd Macdonald, 75019 Paris ☎01.53.26.15.50, ⓦ www.ffe.com.
Rock climbing Fédération Française de la Montagne et de l'Escalade, 8–10 quai de la Marne, 75019 Paris ☎01.40.18.75.50, ⓦ www.ffme.fr.
Walking Fédération Française de Randonnée Pédestre, 14 rue Riquet, 75019 Paris ☎01.44.89.93.93, ⓦ www.ffrp.asso.fr.

Culture and etiquette

As a very broad generalization, French social conduct is a balance between Mediterranean exuberance and the more cool-headed, north European approach to life. Family ties are still strong, with much socializing taking place within the extended family, while many city migrants maintain close ties with their rural roots, often returning to the ancestral home for holidays.

The French tend to **dress** smartly; even casual-wear is often studiedly chic. That said, dress codes are reasonably flexible. Even in quite classy restaurants, for example, some men will wear jackets and ties and others a smart polo-neck or open-neck shirt; women could wear anything from a little black number and pearls to smart trousers. Scruffiness is generally regarded as a lack of respect both towards yourself and the people around you. You'll certainly get a better reception if you take a little care how you look.

In a similar vein, it helps to observe certain **social conventions**. When entering a shop,

post office or the like, even at a supermarket check-out, it's polite to greet everyone with at least a *Bonjour* (Hello), better still *Bonjour Monsieur/Madame/Mademoiselle*, and to leave with an *Au revoir* (Goodbye). When being introduced to someone it's customary to shake hands. When you know them better, greet them with a kiss on both cheeks. This holds even if it's a big group – you have to do the whole round. And when dealing with officialdom, it always pays to be polite.

Even basic attempts at speaking French are appreciated, especially outside Bordeaux and the main tourist centres, where you'll find fewer people who feel comfortable speaking English. If you're struggling, it's worth writing down what you want to say: many people can read and write English even if they find the spoken **language** hard going.

Another aspect of French culture is, of course, its famously liberal and open attitude as towards **sexual mores**. This extends to a general tolerance towards gays and lesbians (see p.56 for more). Perhaps surprisingly, however, **the Pill** (*la pillule*) is available only on prescription. Condoms, on the other hand, are widely available in supermarkets, pharmacies and street dispensers.

Shopping and markets

The quickest and most convenient places to shop are the hypermarkets and supermarkets you'll find in and around every major town. Even some villages have a "superette". But more interesting by far are the specialist food shops and, of course, the markets which are still held at least once a week in towns throughout the region.

Clothing and shoe sizes

Women's dresses and skirts

American	4	6	8	10	12	14	16	18
British	8	10	12	14	16	18	20	22
Continental	38	40	42	44	46	48	50	52

Women's blouses and sweaters

American	6	8	10	12	14	16	18
British	30	32	34	36	38	40	42
Continental	40	42	44	46	48	50	52

Women's shoes

American	5	6	7	8	9	10	11
British	3	4	5	6	7	8	9
Continental	36	37	38	39	40	41	42

Men's suits

American	34	36	38	40	42	44	46	48
British	34	36	38	40	42	44	46	48
Continental	44	46	48	50	52	54	56	58

Men's shirts

American	14	15	15.5	16	16.5	17	17.5	18
British	14	15	15.5	16	16.5	17	17.5	18
Continental	36	38	39	41	42	43	44	45

Men's shoes

American	7	7.5	8	8.5	9	10	10.5	11	11.5
British	6	7.0	7.5	8	8.5	9.5	10	10.5	11
Continental	39	40	41	42	43	44	44.5	45	46

Many of these **markets** have been held on the same day for centuries. One of the region's biggest and best is that at Sarlat, but the competition is fierce and it's worth including several market days in your itinerary. In winter time, you'll also find most towns in the Dordogne and Lot hold *marchés aux gras* when whole fattened livers of duck and goose are put up for sale alongside the other edible bits of the fowl. Often these events double up as truffle markets and are one of the few places in France where **bargaining** is acceptable. For a list of the region's most important and interesting markets, see the boxes at the beginning of each chapter of the Guide.

Not surprisingly, **souvenirs** from this region tend to revolve around food and wine. Small tins of pâté and the many varieties of chocolates, sweets and biscuits are relatively easy to carry. Unless you've got your own car, of course, bottles of wine and liqueurs, and jars of walnut oil and the vast array of preserved meat, soups and so forth present more of a problem.

Boutiques in Bordeaux and the other main towns are good for **clothes** and shoe shopping (see the conversion chart on the previous page for equivalent sizes) and also for perfumes and cosmetics.

Non-EU residents are entitled to **tax-free** prices on certain goods totalling over €175 (including tax) bought in the same shop on the same day. To reclaim the VAT (*TVA* in French) you will need an export sales certificate (*bordereau de vente à l'exportation*) from the shop. It consists of two sheets which must be signed by the retailer and yourself. Present the certificate and the goods at customs when leaving the EU, which must be done within three months of purchase. When you get home, send the pink sheet back to the retailer – it must be received within six months of the date of sale. The refund will normally be paid into your bank account.

Travelling with children

France is an excellent country in which to travel with kids. They are generally welcome everywhere and young children and babies in particular will be fussed over, though noisy children tend to be frowned upon. Note also that French mothers rarely breast-feed in public. As for things to do, there are many family-oriented theme parks in the Dordogne and Lot region and no end of leisure activities geared towards children.

In general, children under four years travel free on **public transport**, including SNCF trains and buses, while those aged between 4 and 12 pay half fare. **Museums** and other sights are usually free to children under 12 and half price for under-18s.

Hotels charge by the room, with a small supplement for an additional bed or cot, and family-run places will usually babysit or offer a listening service while you eat or go out. Some youth hostels are now starting to offer family rooms. Most **restaurants** provide children's menus. While they tend to be of the steak-and-chips followed by ice cream variety, a few places now offer more interesting – and healthy – fare. You'll have no difficulty finding disposable nappies/diapers (*couches à jeter*) and French supermarkets stock a vast range of baby foods, including a few organic options nowadays. Many **baby foods** have added sugar and salt, however, and French milk powders tend to be sweeter than elsewhere. A logo of a baby's bottle on bottled water indicates that it's suitable for making up formula.

Local tourist offices will have details of specific activities for children, which might include everything from farm visits, nature walks or treasure hunts in a maze (*labyrinthe*) to paintball and forest rope-ways for older children. All the bigger campsites put on extensive programmes in summer.

One thing to be aware of – not that you can do much about it – is the difficulty of negotiating a child's buggy over cobbled streets in the medieval town centres. And in parks the lawns are usually out of bounds, so sprawling horizontally with toddlers and napping babies is usually not an option; look out for signs saying *pelouse interdite*.

Travel essentials

Costs

Although prices have been rising steadily in recent years, the Dordogne and Lot is not an outrageously expensive place to visit, at least compared to other northern European countries, largely because of the relatively low cost of accommodation and eating out. When and where you go, however, will make a difference: in prime tourist spots hotel prices can go up by a third during July and August.

Average costs

For a reasonably comfortable existence, including a double room in a mid-range hotel, a light restaurant lunch and a proper restaurant dinner, plus moving around, café stops and museum visits, you need to allow around €100 a day per person. But by counting the pennies, staying at youth hostels or camping, and being strong-willed about extra cups of coffee and doses of culture, you could manage on €40–50 a day each, to include a cheap restaurant meal – less if you restrict yourselves to street snacks or market food.

Youth and student discounts

Once obtained, various official and quasi-official youth/student ID cards soon pay for themselves in savings. Full-time students are eligible for the **International Student ID Card** (ISIC; ⓦ www. isic.org or www.isiccard .com), which entitles the bearer to special air, rail and bus fares and discounts at museums, theatres and other attractions. It also gives you access to a free 24-hour helpline to call in the event of a medical or legal emergency. You have to be 26 or under to qualify for the **International Youth Travel Card**, while teachers are eligible for the **International Teacher Card**, offering similar discounts.

The cards all cost the same amount: £7 in the UK; €13 in the Republic of Ireland; US$22 in the US; Can$16 in Canada; Aus$18 in Australia; and NZ$20 in New Zealand. They are available through universities and student travel specialists such as STA Travel, USIT and Travel CUTS.

Taxes and tipping

The majority of goods and services in France are subject to **value added tax** (*taxe sur la valeur ajoutée* or *TVA* in French), usually at a rate of 19.6 percent, which is included in the price. Most local authorities also levy a **tourism tax** on hotel and *chambres d'hôte* accommodation, generally not more than €1 per person per night depending on the category; in some areas this tax only applies in peak season. While the tax is not included in room rates, it must be clearly indicated as a separate item.

Hotels and almost all restaurants include a **service charge** of fifteen percent in their prices (*service compris*). It's therefore not necessary to leave an additional cash **tip** at restaurants unless you feel you have received service out of the ordinary; if so, an extra two or three percent is plenty. It's customary to tip porters, tour guides and taxi drivers one or two euros, and to leave the small change at cafés.

Crime and personal safety

In the more rural parts of the Dordogne and Lot region crime is extremely rare. However, petty theft is a problem in Bordeaux and, to a lesser extent, in other major towns; you should also be careful in crowds, especially during festivals. In urban areas and at prime tourist spots cars with foreign number plates also face a high risk of break-ins. Vehicles are rarely stolen, but luggage makes a tempting target.

It obviously makes sense to take the normal **precautions**: don't flash wads of notes around; carry your bag or wallet securely; never leave cameras, mobile phones or other valuables lying around; and park your car overnight in a monitored parking, garage or, at the very least, on a busy and well lit street. It's wise to keep a separate record of cheque and credit card numbers, and the phone numbers for cancelling them (see p.59). Finally, make sure you have a good insurance policy (see p.57).

There are two main types of **police** in France – the Police Nationale and the Gendarmerie Nationale. The former deals with all crime, parking and traffic affairs within large and mid-sized towns, where you will find them in the Commissariat de Police. The Gendarmerie Nationale covers the rural areas.

If you need to **report a theft**, go to the local Gendarmerie or Commissariat de

Emergency numbers

Police ☏17
Medical emergencies/ambulance ☏15
Fire brigade/paramedics ☏18
Rape crisis (Viol Femmes Informations) ☏08.00.05.95.95
All emergency numbers are toll-free

Police (addresses of commissariats are given in the Guide for the major towns), where they will fill out a *constat de vol*. The first thing they'll ask for is your passport, and vehicle documents if relevant. Although the police are not always as cooperative as they might be, it is their duty to assist you if you've lost your passport or all your money.

If you have an **accident** while driving, you must fill in and sign a *constat d'accident* (declaration form) or, if another car is also involved, a *constat aimable* (jointly agreed declaration); these forms should be provided with the car's insurance documents. The police can impose on-the-spot fines for minor **driving offences** and take away your licence for anything more serious (see p.32 for more).

Pedestrians should take great care when crossing roads. Although the authorities are trying to improve matters, many French drivers pay no heed to pedestrian/zebra crossings. Never step out onto a crossing assuming drivers will stop. Also be wary at traffic lights: check cars are not still speeding towards you even when the green man is showing.

Drug use is just as prevalent in France as anywhere else in Europe – and just as risky. People caught smuggling or possessing drugs, even just a few grams of marijuana, are liable to find themselves in jail. Should you be **arrested** on any charge, you have the right to contact your consulate (addresses are given on p.64), though don't expect much sympathy.

The majority of **racism** in France is focused against the Arab community, although black and Asian visitors may also encounter an unwelcome degree of curiosity or suspicion from shopkeepers, hoteliers, bar and club owners and the like. It generally takes the form of hotels claiming to be booked up, though the police in Bordeaux and the larger towns such as Périgueux and Montauban may demand to see your papers or even to search you. Carrying your passport at all times is a good idea.

If you suffer a **racial assault**, contact the police, your consulate or one of the local anti-racism organizations (though they may not have English-speakers): SOS Racism

(29 rue Bergeret, 33000 Bordeaux; ☎05.56.31.94.62, ⓦwww.sos-racisme.org); and Mouvement contre le Racisme et pour l'Amitié entre les Peuples (MRAP; Périgueux ☎06.11.30.74.65 or Paris ☎01.53.38.99.99, ⓦwww.mrap.asso.fr).

Disabled travellers

The French authorities have been making a concerted effort to improve facilities for disabled travellers. Though haphazard parking habits and stepped village streets remain serious obstacles for anyone with mobility problems, ramps and other forms of access are gradually being added to hotels, museums and other public buildings. All but the oldest hotels are required to adapt at least one room to be wheelchair accessible, and a growing number of *chambres d'hôtes* are doing likewise. Accessible hotels, sights and other facilities are gradually being inspected and, if they fulfill certain criteria, issued with a "Tourisme & Handicap" certificate.

Most **train stations** now make provision for travellers with reduced mobility. Spaces for wheelchairs are available in first-class carriages of all **TGVs** for the price of the regular, second-class fare; note that these must be booked in advance. For other trains, a wheelchair symbol in the timetable indicates services offering special on-board facilities, though it's best to double-check when booking. SNCF publishes a free booklet, *Le Mémento du Voyageur Handicapé et à Mobilité Réduite*, which details facilities and services available on TGV and regional express trains. You can usually find it at main train stations, and the information is also on their website at ⓦwww.voyages-sncf.com/voyageurs_handicapes/.

Drivers of **taxis** are legally obliged to help passengers in and out of the vehicle and to carry guide dogs. Specially adapted taxis can be arranged in Bordeaux through Mobibus (☎05.56.16.61.66) as long as you give at least a week's notice. Elsewhere, such services are generally only available to local residents, but ask at the local tourist office or *mairie* for further information. All the big **car rental** agencies can provide automatic cars if you reserve sufficiently far in advance, while Hertz offers cars with hand controls on request – again, make sure you give them plenty of notice.

As for finding suitable **accommodation**, listings produced by Logis de France (see p.37) and Gîtes de France (see p.38) indicate places with specially adapted rooms. It's essential to doublecheck when booking that the facilities meet your needs.

French readers headed for the Lot should get a copy of the excellent **guidebook**, *Le Guide de Globe Roller; Voyages Accessible dans le Lot* (Éditions Divona), by local resident and wheelchair user, Jonathan Dupire. It details accessible accommodation, transport, attractions and other tourist facilities graded according to the level of mobility. It's available at certain local tourist offices or from the association Voyager Accessible, La Borde Rouge, 46150 La Bastide du Vert (☎06.13.72.86.20; €10 plus postage). *Handitourisme*, published annually by Petit Futé (ⓦwww.petitfute.com) covers similar ground but for the whole of France.

For general **information** about accessibility, special programmes and discounts contact one of the organizations listed below before you leave home.

Contacts for travellers with disabilities

In France

Access Tourisme Service 8 rue St-Loup, 45130 Charsonville ☎02.38.74.28.40, ⓦwww.access-tourisme.com. Organised and customized holidays for people with special needs including adapted vehicle rental, accessible hotels and even travel companions if required.

APF (Association des Paralysés de France) 17 bd Auguste-Blanqui, 75013 Paris ☎01.40.78.69.00, ⓦwww.apf.asso.fr. National association that can answer general enquiries and put you in touch with their departmental offices.

In the UK and Ireland

Access Travel 6 The Hillock, Astley, Lancashire M29 7GW ☎01942/888 844, ⓦwww.access-travel.co.uk. Tour operator that can arrange flights, transfer and accommodation. This is a small business, personally checking out places before recommendation.

Holiday Care The Hawkins Suite, Enham Place, Enham Alamein, Andover SP11 6JS ☎0845/124 9971, ⓦwww.holidaycare.org.uk. Provides free lists of accessible accommodation and tourist sights plus information on financial help for holidays.

Irish Wheelchair Association Blackheath Drive, Clontarf, Dublin 3 ☎01/818 6400, ⓦwww.iwa.ie. Useful information provided about travelling abroad with a wheelchair.

In the US and Canada

Accessible Journeys 35 West Sellers Ave, Ridley Park, PA 19078 ☎1-800/846-4537 or 610-521-6959. Well-established travel agent offering tailor-made and group tours for disabled travellers.

Directions Unlimited 720 North Bedford Road, Bedford Hills, NY 10507 ☎1-800/533-5343. Travel agency specializing in tours to Europe for people with disabilities.

Mobility International USA 132E Broadway, Suite 343, Eugene, OR 97401 ☎541/343-1284, ⓦwww.miusa.org. Provides information and referral services and international exchange programs.

Society for Accessible Travel and Hospitality (SATH) 347 5th Ave, Suite 610, New York, NY 10016 ☎212/447-7284, ⓦwww.sath.org. Non-profit educational organization that offers tailored travel tips to people with various disabilities.

Electricity

The **electricity** supply in France is almost always 220V, using plugs with two round pins. If you need a transformer, it's a good idea to buy one before leaving home, though you can find them in big department stores.

Gay and lesbian travellers

In general, France is more liberal on homosexuality than many other European countries. The legal age of consent is 16 and civil unions between same-sex couples were made legal in 1999. That said, same-sex marriages are still illegal in France and in 2004 Noël Mamère, the controversial mayor of Bègles, near Bordeaux, created quite a furor by conducting the country's first gay marriage. The courts annulled it the following year, but the couple propose to appeal to the European Court of Human Rights.

On a day-to-day level, the French mostly consider sexuality to be a private matter and homophobic assaults are extremely rare. In the Dordogne and Lot region there's a thriving gay and lesbian community in Bordeaux and smaller groups in Cahors and in other towns and cities. Nevertheless, **gays** tend to be discreet outside specific gay venues, parades and the prime gay areas of Bordeaux. **Lesbians** tend to be extremely discreet. You should expect to be received with tolerance, but not necessarily a warm welcome.

Two useful general **guidebooks**, though in French only, are *France Gay et Lesbien* published by Petit Futé (ⓦwww.petitifute.com) and *Le dykeGuide* (ⓦwww.dykeplanet.com), aimed primarily at lesbians. Both are published annually and are available at FNAC stores and major booksellers or direct from the publishers. The English-language *Spartacus International Gay Guide* (ⓦwww.spartacusworld.com) has an extensive section on France and contains some info for lesbians. *Têtu* (ⓦwww.tetu.com) is France's best-selling gay/lesbian magazine, with events listings and contact addresses; you can buy it in bookshops, newsagents or through their website, which is also an excellent source of information. Another useful source of information is the password-protected website ⓦwww.ooups.com, the French-language version of gay.com.

Contacts for gay and lesbian travelers

In the UK

Madison Travel ☎01273/202 532, ⓦwww.madisontravel.co.uk. Established travel agents specializing in packages to gay- and lesbian-friendly mainstream destinations.

ⓦwww.gaytravel.co.uk Online gay and lesbian travel agent, offering good deals on all types of holiday. Also lists gay- and lesbian-friendly accommodation.

In the US and Canada

Alyson Adventures ☎1-800/825-9766, ⓦwww.alysonadventures.com. Activity vacations for gay and lesbian travellers, including bike tours of southwest France.

Discover France ☎1-800/960-2221, ⓦwww.discoverfrance.com. Gay-friendly tour agent offering tailor-made cycling and walking holidays in southwest France.

gaytravel.com ☎1-800/GAY-TRAVEL or 1-800/429-8728, ⓦwww.gaytravel.com. The premier site for trip planning, bookings, and general information about international gay and lesbian travel.

International Gay & Lesbian Travel Association ☎1-800/448-8550 or 954/776-2626,

ⓦwww.iglta.org. Trade group that can provide a list of gay- and lesbian-owned or -friendly travel agents, accommodation and other travel businesses.

Health

Visitors to the Lot and Dordogne region have little to worry about as far as health is concerned. No vaccinations are required, there are no nasty diseases to be wary of and tap-water is safe to drink. The worst that's likely to happen is a case of sunburn or an upset stomach from eating too much rich food – or a hangover from all that wonderful wine. If you do need treatment, however, you should be in good hands: the French healthcare system is rated one of the best in the world.

Under the French health system, all services, including doctor's consultations, prescribed medicines, hospital stays and ambulance call-outs, incur a charge which you have to pay upfront. **EU citizens** are entitled to a refund (usually between 70 and 100 percent) of medical and dental expenses, providing the doctor is government registered (*un médecin conventionné*) and provided you have a European Health Insurance Card (EHIC; *Carte Européenne d'Assurance Maladie*) which has replaced the E111 form. Note that everyone in the family, including children, must have their own card, which are free. In the UK you can apply for them online through the Department of Health website (ⓦwww. dh.gov.uk), by phone (☎0845/606 2030) or by post – forms are available from post offices. Allow between one and three weeks depending on the method chosen. Even with the EHIC card, however, you might want to take out some additional insurance to cover the shortfall. A stay in hospital, for example, can still leave you with a hefty bill. All **non-EU visitors** should ensure they have adequate medical insurance cover.

For minor complaints go to a **pharmacie**, signalled by an illuminated green cross. You'll find at least one in every small town and even some villages. They keep normal shop hours (roughly 9am–noon & 3–6/7pm), though some stay open late and, in larger towns, at least one (known as the *pharmacie de garde*) is open 24 hours according to a rota; details are displayed in all pharmacy windows.

For anything more serious you can get the name of a **doctor** from a pharmacy, local police station, tourist office or your hotel. Alternatively, look under "Médecins" in the Yellow Pages (*Pages Jaunes*) phone directory. The consultation fee is in the region of €21 for a general practitioner and €25 for a specialist. You'll be given a statement of treatment (*Feuille de Soins*) for later insurance claims. Any prescriptions will be fulfilled by a pharmacy and must be paid for; little price stickers (*vignettes*) from each medicine will be stuck on the *Feuille de Soins*.

In serious **emergencies** you will always be admitted to the nearest general hospital (*centre hospitalier*). Phone numbers and addresses are given in the Guide for all the main cities. The national number for calling an ambulance is ☎15.

Insurance

Even though EU citizens are entitled to health care privileges in France, it's advisable to take out an insurance policy before travelling to cover against theft, loss and illness or injury. Before paying for a new policy, however, it's worth checking whether you are already covered: some all-risks home insurance policies may cover your possessions when overseas, and many private medical schemes include cover when abroad. In Canada, provincial health plans usually provide partial cover for medical mishaps overseas. Students will often find that their student health coverage extends during the vacations and for one term beyond the date of last enrolment.

After investigating these possibilities, you might want to contact a specialist travel insurance company, or consider the Rough Guides travel insurance deal outlined overleaf. A typical **travel insurance policy** usually provides cover for the loss of baggage, tickets and – up to a certain limit – cash or cheques, as well as cancellation or curtailment of your journey. Most exclude so-called dangerous sports unless an extra premium is paid: in the Dordogne and Lot this would include rock climbing and potholing. Many policies can be chopped and changed to exclude coverage you don't need – for example, sickness and accident benefits can often be excluded or included at will.

If you do take **medical coverage**, ascertain whether benefits will be paid as treatment proceeds or only after your return home, and if there is a 24-hour medical emergency number. When arranging **baggage cover**, make sure that the per-article limit will cover your most valuable possession. If you need to make a claim, you should keep receipts for medicines and medical treatment, and in the event you have anything stolen, you must obtain an official statement from the police (called *un constat de vol*).

Rough Guides has teamed up with Columbus Direct to offer you **travel insurance** that can be tailored to suit your needs. Products include a low-cost **backpacker** option for long stays; a **short break** option for city getaways; a typical **holiday package** option; and others. There are also annual **multi-trip** policies for those who travel regularly. Different sports and activities (trekking, skiing, etc) can usually be covered if required.

For eligibility and purchasing options, see our website (🌐www.roughguidesinsurance .com). Alternatively, UK residents should call ☎0870/033 9988; Australians should call ☎1300/669 999 and New Zealanders should call ☎0800/55 9911. All other nationalities should call ☎+44 870/890 2843.

Internet

An increasing number of hotels and *chambres d'hôtes* offer **Internet access** to guests, either in the rooms or at reception. Some also offer Wifi. You'll find a sprinkling of cyber cafés in Bordeaux and other main towns; rates vary from around €2 to €4 per hour. In the rural heartland of the Dordogne and Lot, however, such facilities are still few and far between.

Laundry

Laundries are still reasonably common in French towns – just ask in your hotel, or the tourist office, or look in the phone book under "*Laveries automatiques*" or "*Laveries en libre-service*". They are often unattended, so come armed with small change. Machines

are graded in different wash sizes, costing in the region of €4 to €5 for 7kg. Most hotels forbid doing any laundry in your room, though you should get away with just one or two small items.

Mail

The French mail service is fast, reliable and efficient. **Post offices**, known as La Poste and identified by bright yellow-and-blue signs, are generally open from around 9am to 5pm or 6pm Monday to Friday, and 9am to noon on Saturday. Those in smaller towns and villages usually also close from noon to 2pm.

You can receive mail using the **poste restante** system available at the central post office in every town. It should be addressed (preferably with the surname first and in capitals) "Poste Restante, Poste Centrale", followed by the name of the town and its postcode. You'll need your passport to collect your mail and will have to pay €0.53 per item. Mail is only kept for fifteen days.

For sending letters, remember that you can buy **stamps** (*timbres*) with less queueing from *tabacs* and newsagents. Standard letters (20g or less) and postcards within France and to European Union countries cost €0.53, €0.75 to South Africa and €0.90 to North America, Australia and New Zealand. Inside larger post offices is a row of yellow *guichets automatiques* – automatic ticket machines with instructions available in English with which you can weigh letters and packages and buy the appropriate stamps; sticky labels and tape are also dispensed. For further information on postal rates, among other things, log on to the post office website 🌐www.laposte.fr.

You can also change money at post offices, send faxes and do photocopying. To post your letter on the street, look for the bright yellow **postboxes**.

Maps

In addition to the **maps** in this guide and the various free town plans you'll be offered along the way, the one extra map you might want is a good, up-to-date road map of the region. The best are the regional maps produced by Michelin (1:300,000) and IGN (1:250,000; 🌐www.ign.fr). In both cases you'll need to buy three maps (Aquitaine,

Midi-Pyrénées and Auvergne-Limousin) to cover the entire area encompassed by the Guide. Alternatively, both companies issue large spiral-bound road atlases covering the whole of France at around the same scale.

If you're planning to walk or cycle, it's well worth investing in the more detailed IGN maps. The Carte de Randonnée (1:25,000) series is specifically designed for walkers, while the Carte de Promenade (1:100,000) is ideal for cyclists.

Money

France is one of the twelve European Union countries which have adopted a single currency, the **euro** (€). The euro is divided into 100 cents (also called *centimes*). There are seven notes – in denominations of 5, 10, 20, 50, 100, 200 and 500 euros – and eight different coins: 1, 2, 5, 10 and 50 cents, and 1 and 2 euros. Euro coins feature a common EU motif on one face, but different country-specific motifs on the other. No matter what the motif, all euro coins and notes can be used in any of the twelve member states: Austria, Belgium, Finland, France, Germany, Greece, Ireland, Italy, Luxembourg, Portugal, Spain and the Netherlands.

At the time of writing, the **exchange rate** is hovering around €1.50 to the pound, €0.80 to the US dollar, €0.70 to the Canadian dollar, €0.60 to the Australian dollar, €0.50 to the New Zealand dollar and €0.10 to the South African rand. For the most up-to-date exchange rates for these and other currencies, consult ⓦ www.oanda.com/convert/classic.

Credit and debit cards

By far the best way to access money in France is to use your **credit** or **debit card** to withdraw cash from an **ATM** (known as *un distributeur de billets* or *un point argent*); most machines give instructions in several European languages. You'll need a four-digit personal identification number (PIN) to use your cards in France. Note that there is often a transaction fee, so it's more efficient to take out a sizeable sum each time rather than making lots of small withdrawals.

Credit and debit cards are also widely accepted in shops, hotels and restaurants,

Lost or stolen cards

To cancel **lost** or **stolen cards,** call the following 24-hour numbers: American Express ☏01.47.77.72.00; Diners' Club ☏08.10.31.41.59; MasterCard ☏01.45.67.84.84; Visa ☏08.00.90.11.79.

though some smaller establishments don't accept cards, or only for sums above a certain threshold. Visa – called Carte Bleue in France – is almost universally recognized, followed by MasterCard (also known as EuroCard). American Express ranks a bit lower. Be aware that whereas some foreign cards still work by means of a magnetic strip, French cards are equipped with a chip and require the user to input their PIN when making a purchase. If you're asked to tap in your PIN or told your card has been rejected, it's worth explaining that yours is *une carte à piste* and not *une carte à puce*.

Traveller's cheques

Traveller's cheques are obviously safer than cash and also provide a useful backup to credit cards. The problem is that they're becoming increasingly difficult to cash. In Bordeaux you can change them at the exchange bureaux in the airport and in the city centre (see p.80). Elsewhere, post offices in larger towns usually accept most popular brands such as American Express, Visa, Thomas Cook and Citicorp in major currencies; remember to take some form of ID. You may be charged a small commission depending on the brand.

The usual fee for buying cheques is one or two percent, though this may be waived if you buy the cheques through a bank where you have an account. It pays to get a selection of denominations. Make sure to keep the purchase agreement and a record of the cheque serial numbers safe and separate from the cheques themselves. In the event that cheques are lost or stolen, the issuing company will expect you to report the loss immediately to the relevant office; most companies claim to replace lost or stolen cheques within 24 hours.

Wiring money

Having **money wired** from home using either MoneyGram International (⊛ www.moneygram .com) or Western Union (⊛ www.westernunion .com) is never cheap, but it is much simpler and more convenient now it's possible to wire money over the Internet or by phone using a Visa or MasterCard credit or debit card. Details are available on the company websites.

It's also possible to have money wired directly from a bank in your home country to a bank in France, although this is somewhat less reliable because it involves two separate institutions and usually takes a minimum of two days.

Banks and exchange

Core **banking hours** are Monday to Friday 9am to noon and 2 to 4.30pm. Some branches close on Monday, while others stay open at midday and may also open on Saturday morning. All are closed on Sunday and public holidays (see box).

Banks no longer offer **currency exchange**. The only places where you can still change currency are at the *bureaux de change* in Bordeaux airport and in the city centre (see p.98). Very occasionally local tourist offices also offer exchange facilities (detailed in the Guide).

Opening hours and public holidays

Basic **hours of business** are 9am to noon and 2pm to 6pm. Many shops and other businesses in Bordeaux stay open throughout the day, as do most tourist offices and museums throughout the region in July and August. Otherwise, almost everything closes for a couple of hours at midday, sometimes longer. Small food shops often don't reopen till halfway through the afternoon, closing around 7.30pm or 8pm, just before the evening meal. Supermarkets also tend to stay open to at least 7pm.

The standard **closing day** is Sunday, though some food shops, particularly bakeries (*boulangeries*), and newsagents are open in the morning. Some shops and businesses, particularly in the rural areas, also close on a Monday.

Public holidays

January 1 New Year's Day
Easter Monday
Ascension Day (forty days after Easter)
Pentecost or Whitsun (seventh Sunday after Easter)
May 1 Labour Day
May 8 Victory in Europe (VE) Day 1945
July 14 Bastille Day
August 15 Assumption of the Virgin Mary
November 1 All Saints' Day
November 11 Armistice Day 1918
December 25 Christmas Day

Museums tend to open around 9 or 10am, close for lunch from noon until 2pm or 3pm, and then run through to 5pm or 6pm. In summer some stay open all day and close later. Museum closing days are usually Monday or Tuesday, sometimes both. Many state-owned museums have one day of the week when they're free or half price. Reductions are generally available for those over 60 and under 18 (for which you'll need your passport as proof of age) and for students under 26 (see below), while many are free for children under 12, and almost always for kids under 4.

Churches are generally open from around 8am to dusk, but may close at lunchtime and are reserved for worshippers during services (times of which will usually be posted on the door). Country churches are increasingly kept locked; there may be a note on the door saying where to get the key, usually from the priest's house (*le presbytère*) or someone else living nearby, or from the *mairie*.

France celebrates eleven **public holidays** (*jours fériés*), when banks and most shops and businesses (though not necessarily restaurants), and some museums, are closed.

Smoking

In February 2007 the France government introduced a ban of smoking in most public places, including stations, museums, shops and government offices and plan to extend it to bars, hotels, restaurants and clubs by January 2008. Anyone found smoking will be fined 75 euros though how strictly the ban will be enforced remains to be seen.

Studying

It's relatively easy to be a **student** in the Dordogne and Lot region, specifically Bordeaux, which boasts one of France's major universities. Foreigners pay no more than French nationals to enroll for a course, and the only problem then is to support yourself, though you'll be eligible for subsidized accommodation, meals and all the student reductions. In general, French **universities** are fairly informal, but there are strict entry requirements, including an exam in French, for undergraduate degrees, but not for postgraduate courses. For full details and prospectuses, contact the Cultural Service of any French embassy or consulate (see p.64). Embassies and consulates can also provide details of **language courses** at French universities and colleges, which are often combined with lectures on French "civilization" and usually very costly. You'll find ads for lesser language courses advertised all over the place.

It's also worth noting that if you're a full-time **non-EU student** in France, you can get a temporary work permit enabling you to work during vacations, including the summer after you qualify, so long as your visa is still valid.

Further useful resources are the government-run Agence EduFrance (ⓦwww.edufrance.fr), set up to promote French higher education abroad, and ⓦwww.studyabroad.com, with listings and links to study and work abroad programmes. Alternatively, contact the organizations listed below.

Study abroad programmes

AFS Intercultural Programs UK ☎0113/242 6136, US ☎1-800/AFS-INFO, Canada ☎1-800/361-7248 or 514/288-3282, Australia ☎1300/131736 or ☎02/9215-0077, NZ ☎0800/600 300 or 04/494 6020, South Africa ☎11/447 2673, international enquiries ☎01-212/807-8686, ⓦwww.afs.org. Global

UN-recognized organization running summer programmes to foster international understanding.
Australians Studying Abroad ☎03/9509 1955, ⓦwww.asatravinfo.com.au. Study tours focusing on art and culture.
Erasmus EU-run student exchange programme enabling students at participating universities in Britain and Ireland to study in one of 31 European countries. Grants available for three months to a full academic year. Anyone interested should contact their university's international relations office, or check the Erasmus website ⓦhttp://ec.europa.eu/education/programmes/socrates/erasmus/erasmus_en.html.

Telephones

French **telephone numbers** have ten digits. Numbers beginning with ☎080 are free-dial numbers; those beginning ☎081 and ☎086 are charged as a local call; anything else beginning ☎08 is premium-rated. Numbers starting ☎06 are mobile numbers and therefore also expensive to call.

You can make domestic and international **phone calls** from any telephone box (*une cabine*) and can also receive calls – look for the number in the top right-hand corner of the information panel. The vast majority of phones require a **phone card** (*une télécarte*), which come in 50 and and 120 units (€7.40 and €14.75 respectively) and are available from post offices, *tabacs* and newsagents amongst other places. You can also use **credit cards** in many call boxes.

France Télécom's (ⓦwww.francetelecom .fr) **rates** and charging structures are not only horribly complicated but change frequently – fortunately in the downward direction on the whole. At the time of writing, calls within France from public phones are charged at around €0.20 per minute when calling a fixed phone and €0.35 to mobiles. International calls cost around €0.40 per minute to the UK, €0.55 to the US and Canada, and €1.60 to Australia, New Zealand and South Africa. Off-peak rates (roughly 20 percent cheaper) apply to international calls made on weekdays between 7pm and 8am and all day Saturday and Sunday and public holidays. Note that when using a hotel phone, they usually add a significant mark-up to the above rates.

One of the most convenient ways of **phoning abroad** from France is via a telephone charge card from your phone company back home, though check first whether France is covered. Using a PIN number, you can make calls from most hotel, public and private phones that will be charged to your home phone account or to a credit card. Since most major charge cards are free to obtain, it's certainly worth getting one at least for emergencies, but bear in mind that rates aren't necessarily cheaper than calling from a public phone.

Another option is one of the **pre-paid phone cards** (cartes téléphoniques) on sale at tabacs and newsagents which you can use from a public or private telephone. At the time of writing, Symacom (⬆www.symacom .fr) was giving the best rates and quality of service with its "Continental" cards priced at €15 and €7.50. The €15 card, for example, gives you over two hours to the UK, US, Canada and Australia from a phone box and between 30 and 50 hours from a private phone; you pay a small connection charge on top.

To avoid payment altogether, you can, of course, make a reverse charge or **collect call** – known in French as téléphoner en PCV – by contacting the international operator (see below).

Mobile phones

If you want to use your **mobile/cell phone** in France, contact your phone provider before leaving home to check whether it will work locally, and what the call charges are – they tend to be pretty exorbitant, and remember that you're likely to be charged extra for incoming calls. If you want to retrieve messages while you're away, you'll have to ask your provider for a new access code, as your home one is unlikely to work abroad.

French mobile phones operate on the European GSM standard, so many **US cellphones** won't work in France unless they are "tri-band". The quickest and cheapest option is probably to change your phone and/or service provider. Alternatively, you could rent a phone through companies such as Cellhire (⬆www.cellhire.com), though it's debatable how much you'd actually save given the additional costs such as insurance and delivery charges. You

would also have to let people know your new, local number.

If you're going to be in France more than just a couple of weeks and making a lot of local calls, it may be worth buying a French **SIM card** and a prepaid phone card. For this you'd have to make sure your phone is "unlocked", in other words it will work with other providers. Again, you'll get a local number. Expect to pay upwards of €15 for a starter kit including a SIM card and around €5 worth of calls credited to your account. You can buy the kits in France at one of the high street shops run by the three main French operators, the largest of which are Orange and SFR, followed by Bouygues Télécom. It's also possible to buy a French SIM card through various Internet telecoms companies before leaving home.

The **network coverage** in France is pretty good, and getting better all the time. However, you may still find gaps in the depths of the countryside – just head for the top of a hill or a town and you should pick up a signal again.

Calling home from France

Note that the initial zero is omitted from the area code when dialling the UK, Ireland, Australia and New Zealand from abroad.
UK international access code + 44 + city code.
Republic of Ireland international access code + 353 + city code.
US and Canada international access code + 1 + area code.
Australia international access code + 61 + city code.
New Zealand international access code + 64 + city code.
South Africa international access code + 27 + city code.

Useful telephone numbers

Directory enquiries ☏118 712 or ☏118 218.
International operator ☏08.36.59.31.23.
Speaking clock ☏36.99.

Time

France lies in the **Central European Time Zone** (GMT+1). This means it is one hour ahead of the UK, six hours ahead of Eastern Standard Time, and nine hours ahead of Pacific Standard Time. Between April and

October France is eight hours behind eastern Australia and ten hours behind New Zealand; from November to March it is ten hours behind southeastern Australia and twelve hours behind New Zealand. Daylight Saving Time (GMT+2) in France lasts from the last Sunday of March to the last Sunday of October.

Toilets

The standard of cleanliness in public **toilets** (*les toilettes*, or *vay say* – WC) is often poor. Those in train stations and department stores, where you commonly pay a nominal sum, are usually OK, as are the Tardis-like public toilets found on the streets. These have automatic doors that open when you insert the requisite coins, and are cleaned automatically once you exit; children under 10 aren't allowed in on their own. You'll still find the occasional squat toilet and unenclosed urinals, especially in bars and cafés.

Tourist information

The French Government Tourist Office (Maison de la France, ⊛www.franceguide .com) increasingly refers you to their website for information, though they still produce a number of useful brochures, alongside stock items such as the Logis de France book (see "Accommodation", p.37). For information specific to the Dordogne and Lot region, including lists of hotels and campsites, festivals, activities and so on, you could try contacting the regional or departmental tourist offices (see below) before you leave home. And, of course, there's also the vast, if not always reliable, reservoir of information available on the Internet.

Tourist offices

In the Dordogne and Lot region you'll find a tourist office – usually an **Office du Tourisme** (OT) but sometimes a **Syndicat d'Initiative** (SI) – in practically every town and many villages (addresses, contact details and opening hours are detailed in the Guide). For the practical purposes of visitors, there is little difference between them; sometimes they share premises and call themselves an OTSI. In small villages where there is no OT

or SI, the *mairie* (town hall) will offer a similar service.

All these offices can provide specific local information, including listings of hotels and restaurants, leisure activities, bike rental, bus times, markets, laundries and countless other things; many can also book accommodation for you. If asked, most offices will provide a town plan (for which you may be charged a nominal sum), and will have maps and local walking guides on sale. In Bordeaux and the larger towns you can usually also pick up free events guides or at least a list of summer festivals, while those in the wine regions will additionally provide information on local vineyards, and in peak season may also conduct vineyard tours.

French government tourist offices abroad

Australia Level 13, 25 Bligh St, Sydney, NSW 2000 ☎02/9231 5244, ⊛au.franceguide.com.
Canada 1981 Avenue McGill College, Suite 490, Montréal, QUE H3A 2W9 ☎514/288 2026, ⊛ca .uk.franceguide.com.
Ireland ☎1560/235 235, ⊛ie.franceguide.com. Info by phone and Internet only.
New Zealand Contact the office in Australia.
South Africa PO Box 41022, 2024 Craighall ☎11/880 8062, ⊛www.za.franceguide.com.
UK 178 Piccadilly, London W1J 9AL ☎09068/244 123, 60p per min, ⊛uk.franceguide.com.
US ☎514/288 1904, ⊛us.franceguide.com; 9454 Wilshire Blvd, Suite 715, Los Angeles, CA 90212; 205 North Michigan Ave, Suite 3770, Chicago, IL 60601; 444 Madison Ave, New York, NY 10022.

Regional and departmental tourist offices

Aquitaine Comité Régional du Tourisme d'Aquitaine, Cité Mondiale, 23 Parvis des Chartrons, 33074 Bordeaux ☎05.56.01.70.00, ⊛www .tourisme-aquitaine.info.
Aveyron Comité Départemental du Tourisme de l'Aveyron, 17 rue Aristide-Briand, BP 831, 12008 Rodez ☎05.65.75.55.75, ⊛www.tourisme-aveyron .com.
Corrèze Comité Départemental du Tourisme de la Corrèze, 45 quai Aristide-Briand, 19000 Tulle ☎05.55.29.98.78, ⊛www.vacances-en-correze.net.
Dordogne Comité Départemental du Tourisme de la Dordogne, BP 2063, 25 rue Wilson, 24002 Périgueux ☎05.53.35.50.24, ⊛www .dordogne-perigord-tourisme.fr.

Gironde Comité Départemental du Tourisme de la Gironde, 21 cours de l'Intendance, 33000 Bordeaux ☏ 05.56.52.61.40, ⓦ www.tourisme-gironde.cg33 .fr.

Lot Comité Départemental du Tourisme du Lot, 107 quai Cavaignac, 46000 Cahors ☏ 05.65.35.07.09, ⓦ www.tourisme-lot.com.

Lot-et-Garonne Comité Départemental du Tourisme du Lot-et-Garonne, 71 rue Péchabout, 47000 Agen ☏ 05.53.66.14.14, ⓦ www.lot-et-garonne.fr.

Midi-Pyrénées Comité Régional du Tourisme Midi-Pyrénées, 54 bd de l'Embouchure, BP 2166, 31022 Toulouse ☏ 05.61.13.55.55, ⓦ www .tourisme-midi-pyrenees.com.

Tarn-et-Garonne Comité Départemental du Tourisme du Tarn-et-Garonne, 7 bd Midi-Pyrénées, BP 534, 82005 Montauban ☏ 05.63.21.79.09, ⓔ cdt82@wanadoo.fr.

Visas and entry requirements

Citizens of European Union (EU) countries can travel freely in France, while those from Australia, Canada, New Zealand and the United States, among other countries, do not need a visa for a stay of up to ninety days. However, the situation can change and it's advisable to check with your nearest French embassy or consulate before departure.

All non-EU citizens who plan to remain longer than ninety days should apply for a **long-stay visa**, for which you will have to show proof of – among other things – a regular income or sufficient funds to support yourself and medical insurance. For further information about visa regulations consult the Ministry of Foreign Affairs website: ⓦ www.diplomatie.gouv.fr.

French embassies and consulates

Australia Embassy: 6 Perth Avenue, Yarralumla, ACT 2600 ☏ 02/6216 0100, ⓦ www.ambafrance-au.org. Consulate: St Martins Tower, 31 Market St, Sydney, NSW 2000 ☏ 02/9261 5779, ⓦ www .consulfrance-sydney.org.

Britain Embassy: 58 Knightsbridge, London SW1X 7JT ☏ 020/7073 1000, ⓦ www.ambafrance-uk.org. Consulates: 21 Cromwell Road, London SW7 2EN ☏ 020/7073 1200, ⓦ www.consulfrance-londres .org; 11 Randolph Crescent, Edinburgh EH3 7TT ☏ 0131/225 3377, ⓦ www.consulfrance-edimbourg.org.

Canada Embassy: 42 Promenade Sussex, Ottawa, ONT KIM 2C9 ☏ 613/789 1795, ⓦ www .ambafrance-ca.org. Consulates: 777 Main St, Suite 800, Moncton, NB E1C 1E9 ☏ 506/857 4191, ⓦ www.consulfrance-moncton.org; 1 place Ville-Marie, Bureau 2601, Montréal, QC H3B 4S3 ☏ 514/878 4385, ⓦ www.consulfrance-montreal .org; 25 rue St-Louis, Québec, QC G1R 3Y8 ☏ 418/694 2294, ⓦ www.consulfrance-quebec .org; 3 Bloor St East, Suite 2200, Toronto, ONT M4W 1A8 ☏ 416/925 8041, ⓦ www.consulfrance-toronto.org; 1130 West Pender St, Suite 1100, Vancouver, BC V6E 4A4 ☏ 604/681 4345, ⓦ www .consulfrance-vancouver.org.

Ireland 36 Ailesbury Rd, Ballsbridge, Dublin 4 ☏ 01/277 5000, ⓦ www.ambafrance-ie.org.

New Zealand 13F, 34–42 Manners St, PO Box 11-343, Wellington ☏ 04/384 2555, ⓦ www .ambafrance-nz.org.

South Africa Embassy: 250 Melk St, Corner Middel St, Nieuw Muckleneuk, Pretoria, 0181 ☏ 12/425 1600, ⓦ www.ambafrance-rsa.org. Consulates: 3F Standard Bank Bldg. 191 Jan Smuts Av, P.O. Box 1027, Parklands 2121, Johannesburg ☏ 11/778 5600, ⓦ www.consulfrance-jhb.org; 2 Dean Street Gardens, P.O. Box 1702, 8001 Cape Town, ☏ 21/423 1575, ⓦ www.consulfrance-lecap.org.

US Embassy: 4101 Reservoir Rd NW, Washington DC 20007 ☏ 202/944-6195, ⓦ www.ambafrance-us.org. Consulates: Prominence in Buckhead, Suite 1840, 3475 Piedmont Rd NE, Atlanta, GA 30305 ☏ 404/495-1660, ⓦ www.consulfrance-atlanta.org; Park Square Building, Suite 750, 31 St James Ave, Boston, MA 02116 ☏ 617/834-4400, ⓦ www .consulfrance-boston.org; 205 North Michigan Ave, Michigan Plaza, Suite 3700, Chicago, IL 60601 ☏ 312/327-5200, ⓦ www.consulfrance-chicago .org; 777 Post Oak Blvd, Suite 600, Houston, TX 77056 ☏ 713/572-2799, ⓦ www.consulfrance-houston.org; 10990 Wilshire Bd, Suite 300, Los Angeles, CA 90024 ☏ 310/235-3200, ⓦ www .consulfrance-losangeles.org; Espirito Santo Plaza, 1395 Brickell Av, Suite 1050, Miami, FL 33131 ☏ 305/403-4150, ⓦ www.consulfrance-miami.org; 1340 Poydras St, Suite 1710, New Orleans, LA 70112 ☏ 504/523-5772, ⓦ www.consulfrance-nouvelleorleans.org; 934 Fifth Ave, New York, NY 10021 ☏ 212/606-3600, ⓦ www.consulfrance-newyork.org; 540 Bush St, San Francisco, CA 94108 ☏ 415/397-4330, ⓦ www.consulfrance-sanfrancisco.org.

Weather information

To check on the **weather** outlook, check the Météo France website ⓦ www.meteo.fr or call their recorded information service on ☎08.92.68.02 plus the number of the *département*: Aveyron 12; Corrèze 19; Dordogne 24; Gironde 33; Lot 46; Lot-et-Garonne 47; Tarn-et-Garonne 82 (call charge €0.34 per min).

Working

Specialists aside, most non-EU citizens who manage to survive for long periods of time in France do it on luck, brazenness and willingness to live in pretty basic conditions. In Bordeaux and the larger towns, bar and club work, teaching English, translating, working as an au pair or busking, are some of the ways people scrape by; in the countryside, the options come down to seasonal fruit- or grape-picking, teaching English or DIY oddjobbing. Remember that, while unemployment in France has been dropping, it is still relatively high. The current rate in Bordeaux stands at around ten percent, dropping to between eight and nine percent in the rest of the region, in line with the national average of just under nine percent.

EU citizens are free to work in France on the same basis as a French citizen. This means you no longer have to apply for a residence or work permit except in very rare cases – contact your nearest French consulate for further information.

Non-EU citizens, however, will need a work permit (*autorisation de travail*) and a residence permit; again contact your nearest French consulate or, if already in France, your local *mairie* or *préfecture* to check what rules apply in your particular situation.

France has a **minimum wage** (the SMIC – *Salaire Minimum Interprofessional de Croissance*), indexed to the cost of living; standing at €8.27 per hour at the time of writing. Employers, however, are likely to pay lower wages to temporary foreign workers who don't have easy legal resources, and make them work longer hours. By law, however, all EU citizens at least are entitled to exactly the same pay, conditions and trade union rights as French nationals.

If you're looking for something secure, it's important to **plan well in advance**. A good starting point is one of the books on working abroad such as *Work Your Way Around the World* by Susan Griffith, *Live and Work in France* by Victoria Pybus and *Summer Jobs Abroad* by David Woodworth and Victoria Pybus, all published by Vacation Work (9 Park End St, Oxford OX1 1HJ; ☎01865/241 978, ⦿www.vacationwork.co.uk). You might also want to search the French version of the online recruitment resource Monster (⦿www .monster.fr) and also Jobs d'Eté (⦿www .jobs-ete.com), which focuses on summer jobs for students.

In France, check out the "Offres d'Emploi" (Job Offers) in the national and regional papers, and try the youth information agency CIDJ (Centre d'Information et de Documentation Jeunesse; ⦿www.cidj.asso.fr), 101 quai Branly, 75015 Paris, or the Centre Régional d'Information Jeunesse Aquitaine in Bordeaux (see p.81), which has information about temporary jobs in the region. The national employment agency, ANPE (Agence Nationale pour l'Emploi; ⦿www.anpe.fr), with offices all over France, advertises temporary jobs in all fields and, in theory, offers a whole range of services to job-seekers from within the European Union, but it is not renowned for its helpfulness to foreigners. Non-EU citizens will have to show a work permit to apply for any of their jobs.

Teaching English

Finding a job **teaching English** is also best done in advance. Late summer is usually the best time. You don't need fluent French to get a post, but a degree and a TEFL (Teaching English as a Foreign Language) or similar qualification are normally required. The annual *EL Gazette Guide to English Language Teaching Around the World* gives a thorough breakdown of TEFL courses available and provides all sorts of practical information, including lists of schools. The guide is produced by EL Gazette Ltd, Unit 3, Constantine Court, 6 Fairclough St, London E1 1PW (☎020/7481 6700, ⦿www .elgazette.com), who also publish the monthly *EL Gazette* which is filled with job advertisements. Other useful resources are *Teaching English Abroad*, published by Vacation Work (see p.65) and the TEFL website ⦿www.tefl.com, with its database of English-teaching vacancies, amongst all sorts of other information. The British Council also has information on placements for

English-language assistants in France at ⓦ www.britishcouncil.org/learning-ie-teaching-exchange.htm. If you apply for jobs from home, most schools will fix up the necessary papers for you.

It's just feasible to find a job when you're in France, but you may have to accept semi-official status and no job security; look under "Enseignement: Langues" in the local Yellow Pages for addresses of schools, or ask in the local Chambre de Commerce et d'Industrie (Chamber of Commerce). Offering private lessons (via university noticeboards or classified ads, for example), you'll have lots of competition, but it's always worth a try.

Au pair work

Au pair work is usually arranged through an agency, such as L'Acceuil Familial des Jeunes Etrangers (AFJE; 23 rue du Cherche-Midi, 75006 Paris; ☎01.42.22.50.34, ⓦwww.afje-paris.org), which specializes in arranging combined au pair and language study placements in partnership with Alliance Française. You'll find other agencies listed in Vacation Work's *The Au Pair and Nanny's Guide to Working Abroad*, by Susan Griffith and Sharon Legg, and on the International Au Pair Association (IAPA) website (ⓦwww .iapa.org).

Terms and conditions are never very generous, but should include board and lodging and pocket money and some form of travel pass if appropriate. Prospective employers are required by law to provide a written job description, so there is protection on both sides. Even so, it's wise to have an escape route (such as a ticket home) in case you find the conditions intolerable and your employers insufferable.

Other work opportunities

The American/Irish/British **bars and restaurants** in the main towns sometimes have vacancies. You'll need to speak French, look smart and be prepared to work very long hours.

Temporary jobs in the **travel industry** revolve around courier work – supervising and working on bus tours or summer campsites. Again, you'll need good French (and another European language will help) and should preferably write to tour operators in early spring. Getting work as a courier on a campsite is slightly easier. It usually involves putting up tents at the beginning of the season, taking them down again at the end, and general maintenance and trouble-shooting work in the months between; Canvas Holidays (see box, p.25) is often worth approaching.

An offbeat possibility, if you want to discover rural life, is being a **working guest** on an organic farm. The period can be anything from a week to a couple of months and the work may involve cheese making, market gardening, beekeeping, wine producing and building. For details of the scheme and a list of addresses in the Dordogne and Lot region, contact World-Wide Opportunities on Organic Farms (WWOOF; ⓦwww.wwoof.org/home .asp), with branches in Britain, the US, Canada, Australia and New Zealand, among other places.

Guide

Guide

Bordeaux and its vineyards

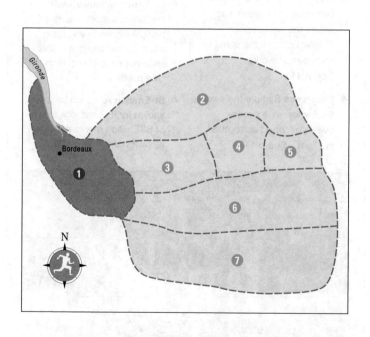

CHAPTER 1 # Highlights

✳ **Bordeaux** Lively, stylish city whose wealth of elegant eighteenth-century architecture takes some beating. See p.73

✳ **Medoc vineyards** Explore the vineyards that produce some of the world's most famous wines. See p.99

✳ **Château de la Brède** This picturesque château was where the philosopher Montesquieu wrote some of his greatest works. See p.111

✳ **Sauternes** Sample the sweet Sauternes wine evocatively described as "bottled sunlight". See p.113

✳ **Château de Roquetaillade** One of the region's most impressive and well-preserved fortresses features fairy-tale interiors. See p.117

✳ **Entre-deux-Mers** Its rolling hills dotted with Romanesque churches, this is without doubt the prettiest of Bordeaux's wine regions. See p.118

✳ **La Sauve-Majeure** Twelfth-century sculptors illustrated biblical stories in engaging detail on the capitals of this semi-ruined abbey church. See p.119

✳ **St-Émilion** Although best known for its wine, the town of St-Émilion merits a visit in its own right. See p.130

△ Château Piction-Longueville

Bordeaux and its vineyards

F rance's second largest Atlantic port, **Bordeaux**, is at heart a trading city, built on revenues from wine exports and from the expansion of colonial trade in the eighteenth century. The legacy of this wealth is a city centre dignified by grand avenues, civic monuments and graceful rows of town houses. For many, the architecture alone provides sufficient attraction but Bordeaux also boasts several rewarding museums, any number of superb restaurants and a thriving cultural and nightlife scene. It is also the area's principal administrative centre – capital of both the Aquitaine *région* and the Gironde *département* – and, with its European air services and good train connections, a major gateway to the Dordogne and Lot region.

Before setting off into the Dordogne heartland, however, there are the Bordeaux **vineyards** – one of the world's foremost wine-producing regions – to explore. Neatly tended rows of vines stretch down the Médoc peninsula in the north and then south and east of Bordeaux along the Garonne and Dordogne valleys for more than fifty kilometres. The northern peninsula is the place to start. The countryside may not be the most enticing – the **Médoc** vineyards are flat and monotonous – but the châteaux – Margaux, Palmer, Mouton-Rothschild and Lafite – are world-famous, and there are also any number of lesser-known producers to visit. Some have established wine-related museums as an added attraction. Médoc wines are mostly reds, while to the southeast of Bordeaux the **Graves** is known for its dry white wines and the **Sauternes** for sweet, golden-coloured whites, some of which, such as those of Château d'Yquem, are amongst the most highly sought-after wines in the world. There are, however, a couple of non-wine-related diversions in the region as well: the moated fourteenth-century **Château de la Brède**, home of the philosopher Montesquieu, and in the very south of the region the **Château de Roquetaillade**. Although dating from the same period, the latter is of particular interest for its exuberant late-nineteenth-century makeover by architect Viollet-le-Duc.

Heading north across the Garonne from the Sauternes, the **Entre-Deux-Mers** may not be the most prestigious of Bordeaux's wine regions but it is by far and away the prettiest. The vineyards here are interspersed with pasture, orchards and woodland across rolling hills topped with sun-soaked villages. Many of these settlements, such as the well-preserved **Sauveterre-de-Guyenne** and

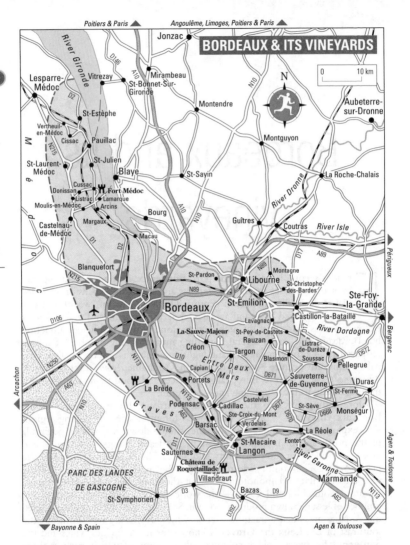

Monségur, are *bastides*, medieval new-towns built on a strict grid-pattern around a central market square (see box on p.336). The Entre-Deux-Mers is also home to a number of once-wealthy abbeys in various states of ruin. The best is the twelfth-century **La Sauve-Majeure**, in the west of the region, where fragments of wall shelter the most beautiful array of carved capitals.

Religion and wine come together again in **St-Émilion**, north of the Entre-Deux-Mers, where they combine to produce the region's most enchanting wine-town. It sits on a south-facing slope overlooking the Dordogne valley, a huddle of grey-white houses, towers and spires encircled by vines; in 1999 both town and vineyards were inscribed on UNESCO's World Heritage list. St-Émilion largely owes its existence – and certainly its name – to an eighth-century hermit whose cave, and the vast subterranean church next door, now provide the town's most compelling sights. Not forgetting, of course, the surrounding wine châteaux. This combination of historical monuments, fine wine and attractive countryside makes St-Émilion a perfect place to spend at least a couple of days.

The Bordeaux region is relatively well covered by **public transport**. There are train services along the Garonne and Dordogne valleys, though the latter is rather sporadic, and a branch line north through the Médoc. Rather more comprehensive are the buses, though here, too, services are being cut back all the time. Some routes duplicate the trains, while others cut across country to places such as Sauveterre-de-Guyenne, Monségur and La Sauve. If you intend to use the buses a lot, pick up a Trans-Gironde route-map and the relevant timetables from the tbc information booth in Bordeaux (see p.81). That said, to make the most of the region, and particularly when it comes to visiting the vineyards, you will need your own transport. Renting a car is the obvious solution, but **cycling** is also an option. Outside Bordeaux, the back roads are pleasant to cycle on and the departmental authorities have established a number of dedicated cycle paths, of which the most useful is that from Bordeaux to Sauveterre in the Entre-Deux-Mers.

Bordeaux

Big and obviously wealthy, with a population of around three quarters of a million, **BORDEAUX** is very much an Atlantic city, characterized by a monumental, Parisian-style grandeur and sophistication, as opposed to the Mediterranean warmth of its local rival, Toulouse. The French novelist Stendhal called it "the most beautiful town in France". That's perhaps overstating it a bit, but Bordeaux has undergone a transformation in recent years and it's possible once again to see what he meant. Many of the magnificent eighteenth-century buildings have been cleaned of their grime – the place de la Bourse in particular looks absolutely stunning – and the riverfront is, after years of debate, finally being reclaimed for pedestrians.

Especially attractive is the relatively compact and unusually homogeneous eighteenth-century centre, paid for by the expansion of colonial trade in the eighteenth century. The **architecture** grabs your attention, notably the marvellous ironwork and sculptural embellishments found on the more bourgeois residences. Here and there remnants of an older city survive, including a few fragments of what the Romans called Burdigala and some fine churches, of which **Cathédrale St-André**, inscribed on UNESCO's World Heritage List, is by far the most outstanding. There's also a clutch of engaging **museums** detailing the history of the city and its region. All this, in addition to some fabulous restaurants and plenty of reasonably priced hotels, makes Bordeaux well worth a couple of days' stopover.

Some history

Bordeaux was founded by the Bituriges Vivisci, a local Gaulish tribe, some time around the third century BC. In 56 BC it was absorbed peacefully into the Roman Empire as the capital of the Aquitania administrative region. Successive Germanic invasions in the third century AD prompted the construction of stout defensive walls, following the route of present-day cours de l'Intendance, rue des Remparts and cours d'Alsace-Lorraine, but the city nevertheless fell to the Visigoths in 409. After peace was finally re-established in the tenth century,

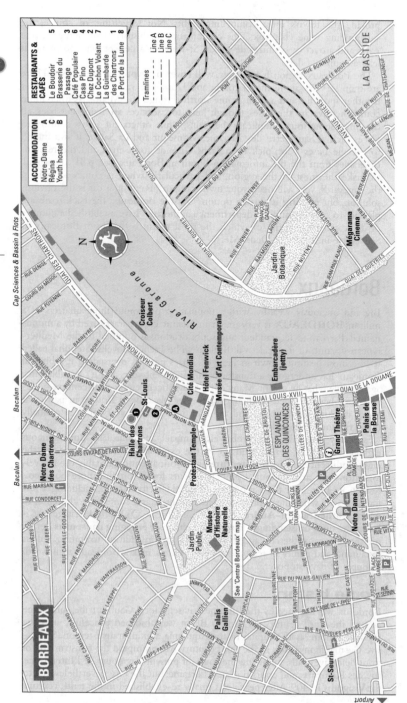

Go with the gurus

the Baldès family, even makes New Black Wine, using a variant of the 19th-century heating process to achieve the colour.

"My other favourites include Château du Cèdre, Domaine de Maison Neuve, Domaine la Bérangeraie and the tiny, English-owned Domaine du Garinet, where Mike and Sue Spring make three different cahors, together with a rosé and two white *vins de pays*. It's a relaxed region, and often you can just drop in, but it's worth ringing in advance."

Make it happen Brittany Ferries (0870 907 6103, www.brittany-ferries.co.uk) and P&O Ferries (0871 664 5645, www.poferries.com) run cross-Channel car ferries. For vineyard details, visit www.vindecahors.fr; for a list of local tourist offices, which stock a wine route brochure, the Circuit du Vignoble de Cahors, go to www.tourisme-lot.com. Le Vert (00 33-5 65 365136, www.hotellevert.com), at Mauroux, is a lovely inn, with doubles from £65. Walks France (05 65 31 83 39, www.walksfrance.com) has eight-day wine-themed walking holidays in the region; for details, e-mail james@walksfrance.com.

JOHN TORODE ON FOOD
Thailand

The Aussie chef runs Smiths of Smithfield, in London, and co-hosts MasterChef on BBC2.

ut also we

unhesitatingly
aried is Venice
hat you go on
ears in which
(2009 is the
Biennale time
is a conceptual
cars and roads.
nals.

of course, is

JEFF BANKS ON SHOPPING
New York

A long-time presente of The Clothes Show the designer runs the Jeff Banks fashion label, with lines in menswear and interiors.

"The last time I was in Bloomingdale's, Beyoncé whirl surrounded by 7(

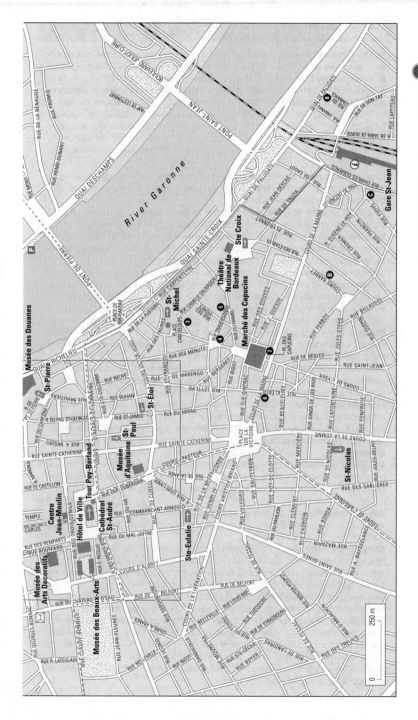

Festivals, events and markets

As you might imagine, the majority of **festivals** and **events** in the Bordeaux region revolve around wine. Nearly all the different *appellations* have at least one *portes ouvertes*, usually at a weekend, when you can visit participating châteaux without an appointment and sample some of their wares for free; the two most important of these events are listed below. Then in autumn, most villages celebrate the end of the grape harvest with a *fête des vendanges* in mid- to late-October. This normally takes the form of a big meal (to which members of the public are welcome, though you'll have to reserve in advance) and some form of entertainment, followed by dancing. Contact the tourist office of the relevant town for further information.

First weekend in April Médoc: Les Portes Ouvertes dans les Châteaux. Some eighty châteaux and wine cooperatives representing the Médoc's eight *appellations* offer free tastings over two weekends.

Late April or early May St-Émilion: Portes Ouvertes dans les Châteaux. Around eighty châteaux open their *chais* and offer free tastings over a long weekend.

Early May Pauillac: La Fête de l'Agneau. A weekend dedicated to Pauillac lamb, raised on the surrounding salty meadows. Events include herding the sheep to the summer pastures, sheepdog trials and a special Mass.

Late June or early July Bordeaux: Fête du Vin ⓦwww.bordeaux-fete-le-vin.com. In even-numbered years the city celebrates its wine heritage with a massive jamboree on the esplanade de Quniconces lasting four days. In addition to sampling the wines, there are introductory tasting lessons, concerts, street performers and a wine auction, amongst other events. The festival culminates in a spectacular fireworks display over the river. In odd-numbered years there's a more modest Fête du Fleuve with nautical parades, regattas, concerts and, of course, wine and food stalls along the quays (ⓦwww.bordeaux-fete-le-fleuve.com).

Third Sun in June St-Émilion: Fête de Printemps. Members of the Jurade (see p.133) dust off their finery for a procession through the town. They then announce the evaluation of the new vintage from the top of the Tour du Roi.

First weekend in July Monségur: 24 Heures du Swing ⓣ05.56.61.89.40, ⓦwww .swing-monsegur.com. The centre of Monségur is closed to traffic for its jazz festival featuring French and international artists. Concerts take place in the cafés, on the streets and under the market hall, many of them free, but tickets are required for the big-name events.

Mid-July Fort Médoc: Jazz Fort Médoc ⓣ05.56.94.43.43. Weekend jazz festival hosting big-name international acts in the semi-ruined fort where the audience sits on hay-bales. There are local wines on sale and a firework display on the last night.

July & August Pauillac: Soirées guinguette sur les quais. More tastings of Médoc wines, plus concerts, markets and open-air restaurants along the banks of the Garonne on three Saturday evenings.

Early September Pauillac: Marathon des Châteaux du Médoc ⓦwww .marathondumedoc.com. Some 9,000 runners descend on the Médoc, many in fancy dress, to be serenaded by musicians as they run through the vineyards. Followed by a party on the quay and more festivities the following day.

First weekend in September Langon: Foire du Vin et du Fromage. Over 150 wine and cheese producers from throughout France as well as displays of traditional crafts.

Third Sun in September St-Émilion: Ban des Vendanges. Following their spring outing (see above), the Jurade once again parade through the town. This time they also induct new members of the Jurade and attend Mass in the Collegiate church before announcing the start of the harvest from the Tour du Roi.

Dec Bordeaux: Grand Marché de Noël. From early December stalls selling Christmas goodies set up along the allées de Tourny.

Bordeaux came into the hands of the counts of Poitou, later titled the **dukes of Aquitaine**, who ruled a vast area stretching from the Loire to the Pyrenees. In 1152 the then Duchess Eleanor of Aquitaine (see box on p.387) married Count Henry of Anjou, and when he was crowned King Henry II of England two years later, Bordeaux began three centuries under **English rule**. Though the local lords – an unruly lot – initially balked at the takeover, they were soon won over when they found themselves at the heart of a very profitable business exporting wine to England.

Bordeaux boomed as a result. A succession of new walls had to be built in the thirteenth and fourteenth centuries to encompass the expanding city – some of the stones were brought as ballast in ships returning home from the wine run. But the good times came to a grumbling halt as France and England battled it out during the Hundred Years' War. When the conflict ended in 1453 at Castillon-la-Bataille, not far east of Bordeaux, the city reluctantly surrendered to **French rule** under Charles VII. Their new overlords even felt it necessary to beef up their military presence by building a couple of smaller forts and the vast Château Trompette; this fortress was eventually destroyed in 1818 to make way for today's esplanade des Quinconces. Nevertheless, local rebellions against high taxes and trade restrictions, amongst other things, continued into the late seventeenth century.

Things began to take off again in the early 1700s as Bordeaux entered its second and most significant **golden age**, this time based on a rapid opening up of trade – including slaves – with Africa and the Caribbean. One of only thirteen ports permitted to trade with the Antilles, as the French West Indies were known, by the end of the century Bordeaux's crescent-shaped "port de la lune" had become the most important in France. Its ships carried manufactured goods, flour, salted beef and wine on the outward journey, returning home with cane sugar, cotton, coffee and cacao; for a long time sugar-refining was one of the city's major industries. This new-found prosperity led to another building boom. The Royal Intendants, most notably Claude Boucher (1720–43) and his successor the **marquis de Tourny** (1743–57;), began knocking down the city's medieval walls, replacing them with the grand boulevards and triumphal arches you see today. The wealthy merchants quickly developed a taste for luxury, erecting fine mansions furnished with exotic woods. Strangely enough, despite all this construction, there was no attempt to bridge the Garonne – this wasn't achieved until Napoleon stopped here on his way to Spain in 1808 and ordered the construction of the elegant Pont de Pierre.

Even today, central Bordeaux boasts only two bridges, and the **modern city** remains concentrated on the river's left (west) bank, though this is changing fast under an ambitious urban renewal scheme initiated by the dynamic mayor, the ex-prime minister Alain Juppé. During his first two terms of office from 1995 to December 2004, when he was barred from public office for fourteen months in the wake of a scandal about party financing in Paris dating back to the 1980s, Juppé succeeded in reinvigorating the once staid city. Under his mandate new public spaces were created and some of the more important landmarks given a much-needed spring-clean – the city's long-neglected riverfront in particular has benefited, now the scene for the hugely successful Fête du Vin and Fête du Fleuve (see box opposite) and is just spectacular at night. Other major works include a state-of-the-art tram system linking central Bordeaux with its suburbs, together with a park-and-ride scheme to reduce city-centre congestion, plus a network of gardens, footpaths and cycle paths along the Garonne. For the most part the changes have been welcomed by the Bordelais, who re-elected Juppé as mayor in

Along with Burgundy and Champagne, the **wines of Bordeaux** form the "Holy Trinity" of French viticulture. Despite producing as many whites as reds, it is the latter – known as claret to the British – that have graced the tables of the discerning for centuries. The countryside that produces them encircles the city, enjoying near-perfect climatic conditions and soils, ranging from limestone to sand and pebbles. The region now produces around 5.5 million hectolitres, equal to some 700 million bottles, of AOC (*Appellation d'Origine Contrôlée*) wines, of which just under a third are exported. The vast majority of this is red wine.

It was the **Romans** who introduced vines to the region during the first century AD. In the early thirteenth century, after a long period of decline the **English**, accompanied by local Benedictine monks, began planting new vineyards around Bordeaux, precipitating a golden era for producers and merchants. Wine bound for England went tax-free and the volume exported in 1307 – around 700,000 hectolitres in total for the whole region – was not reached again until the 1950s. The next great boost came in the mid-seventeenth century when the **Dutch** started draining the marshy land north of Bordeaux, giving rise to the Médoc vineyards. They also invented the technique of burning sulphur inside barrels to disinfect and preserve the wood which, coincidentally, also helped to preserve the wine. Since it no longer deteriorated after six months or so – to the benefit of vineyards further from Bordeaux – the merits of ageing were soon discovered, first in the cask and then, during the eighteenth century, in the bottle. By this time all the great Bordelais vineyards had been planted, ushering in a period of prosperity which lasted until **phylloxera** (see "Contexts" on p.398) hit in the late nineteenth century. On the whole, the Bordeaux vineyards weathered the crisis reasonably well and the top names continue to dominate the world's quality wine market despite increasing competition from New World wines.

In the lower echelons, however, things are not so rosy. Europe's **"wine lake"** is now estimated at over 1.5 million hectolitres, a combination of overproduction, falling consumption and increasing competition; in France, some would also add charges of complacency and arrogance as local wine producers sat on their laurels and failed to adapt to new methods and new markets. As part of a package of temporary measures (all backed up with buckets of EU aid), for the first time in the history of the Bordelais AOC wines, in 2005 some of the harvest was distilled into industrial alcohol. Producers are also being asked to scale back their production and, in the longer term, the Conseil Interprofessionnel du Vin de Bordeaux (CIVB) has recommended at least 10,000 ha be taken out of production by 2009; so far a mere 1800 ha have been grubbed up. Much effort is also going into improved marketing, especially abroad, and developing "wine tourism" – the latest buzzword among the Bordelais. Amongst a variety of initiatives, you'll find more châteaux now open their doors to the public; some offer wine-tasting or cooking classes, others upscale accommodation or wine-related museums.

The **classification** of Bordeaux wines is an extremely complex affair. At the lowest level, the AOC label is a guarantee of both origin and quality found throughout France. In the Bordeaux region there are 57 *appellations*, starting with the general Bordeaux and Bordeaux Supérieur, which can come from anywhere in the Gironde *département*. Within this broad category, districts producing better wines, such as Graves and Haut-Médoc, are entitled to use their more specific *appellation*. Finally, come the villages and communes known for the very finest wines – Margaux, Pauillac and Sauternes, to name but three.

In addition, some individual vineyards around Bordeaux were classified in 1855. What were then considered the region's best wines were graded into five **grands crus**, or "great growths", based largely on the prices the wines had fetched over the previous century. Of the reds, only the Médoc wines and a single wine from the Graves (Haut-Brion) were deemed worthy of consideration and of these, just four were voted Premiers Grands Crus Classés: Margaux, Lafite, Latour and Haut-Brion. Of the sweet Sauternes wines, which were classified at the same time, Château d'Yquem alone merited the title Premier Cru Supérieur. With the exception of Château Mouton-Rothschild, which moved up a class to become the Médoc's fifth Premier Cru in 1973, there have been no official changes since, so divisions between the Grands Crus should not be taken too seriously. Since then, additional categories, such as Crus Bourgeois and Crus Artisans, have been devised, both of which include some excellent wines. Rather unjustly, St-Émilion wines were not classified until 1954.

Nearly all Bordeaux wines are blended; in other words they contain at least two, usually three, **grape varieties**. To a large extent the type of grapes grown depends on local soil conditions. There is enormous skill in deciding the exact proportions required – which varies from year to year and is almost always done after vinification – to bring out the best in the wines. Bordeaux reds comprise a blend of Cabernet Sauvignon, the oldest of the Bordeaux grapes, Cabernet Franc, Merlot and, in smaller proportions – if at all – Malbec and Petit-Verdot. The whites, on the other hand, can contain only Sémillon, Sauvignon and Muscadelle grapes.

For more on Bordeaux's most important individual wine regions see the following: **Médoc** p.100; **Graves** p.110; **Sauternes** p.114; **St-Émilion** p.131. Details of introductory **wine-tasting courses** can be found on p.99, p.106 and p.134 for Bordeaux, Pauillac and St-Émilion respectively.

Vineyard visits

Touring the vineyards around Bordeaux and sampling a few local wines is a pleasure not to be missed. Many of the larger producers now offer properly organized **visits** – often in English if you ring ahead – of their vinification plant and ageing cellars (*chais*), but rarely inside the château itself. They increasingly charge a fee, usually in the region of €5 to €7, though this generally includes **tastings**. In a few cases you have to make an **appointment** several days, or even weeks, in advance, sometimes in writing. Other producers are happy for you just to roll up within specified hours. But even so it is advisable to phone ahead, especially outside the main summer season, to ensure someone will be there. And note that the majority of producers don't accept visitors during **harvest time** (generally late Sept–early Oct).

Where the **smaller vineyards** are concerned, the visits are a lot more ad hoc. Some charge, but may waive the fee if you make a purchase, while others offer them free. Nevertheless, it's worth bearing in mind that these are commercial operations and that, while there's no compulsion to buy, the purchase of just one or two bottles will be much appreciated – and seems fair recompense for the time spent showing you round.

In the Guide we recommend vineyards open to visitors in each of Bordeaux's wine regions. There are, of course, hundreds more. The local **Maison du Vin** will be able to provide you with detailed lists and will often offer advice or help make appointments. For those without their own transport, getting to most of these vineyards is hard work. In which case, the simplest thing is to take one of the **guided tours** offered by tourist offices in each of the wine districts – see the Guide for details. Bordeaux tourist office, for example, runs excellent bilingual tours covering a different region each afternoon (1 April–15 Nov daily; 16 Nov–31 March Wed & Sat; €28). Tastings are generous and expert tuition on how to go about it is part of the deal.

2006. It remains to be seen what further plans he has for the city but, for the moment a least, there's a definite buzz in the Bordeaux air.

❶ Arrival and information

Bordeaux's **airport** (ⓦwww.bordeaux.aeroport.fr) lies 12km west of the city centre. Its facilities include **information desks** (daily 5.30am–11pm), a Travelex **bureau de change** (Mon–Fri & Sun 6am–9pm, Sat 6am–8pm) and several 24-hour ATMs; all the major **car rental** companies are also represented (see "Listings", p.98). From the airport the Jet'bus shuttles into town (every 45min; €6.80), taking around thirty to 45 minutes, with stops at the train station and then by request on the allées d'Orléons near the tourist office and on place Gambetta, before looping back to the airport. Alternatively, a taxi will cost €30–35.

The **gare SNCF**, with its own small tourist office (May–Oct Mon–Sat 9am–noon & 1–6pm, Sun 10am–noon & 1–3pm; Nov–April Mon–Fri 9.30am–12.30pm & 2–6pm; ☏05.56.91.64.70) is at the heart of a somewhat insalubrious area, nearly 3km south of the centre. Tram line C, which stops on the esplanade des Quinconces near the tourist office, will save you the hike.

There's no central **gare routière** in Bordeaux. For the moment most regional bus services drop you at various points around the esplanade des Quinconces. However, there are plans to relocate them into the suburbs, near appropriate tram stations. If you're leaving Bordeaux by bus, ask at the tourist office or the TBC tram offices (see "City Transport", opposite) for the latest situation. Eurolines buses stop outside the train station.

If you're driving, the easiest option is to use one of the city-centre underground **car parks**, such as beneath the allées de Tourny and place des Grands-Hommes (€2.20/€1.50 respectively for the first hour; €17.80/€16 for 24 hr). Cheaper alternatives, are to leave your car on the east bank of the Garonne near the Pont de Pierre, if you can find a space, and hop on a tram into the centre or to use the park-and-ride scheme (€2.60) available at some suburban tram stations; the closest to the centre are at Stalingrad and Galin on line A. Bear in mind that much of central Bordeaux – the oblong of streets between place Gambetta, the cathedral and the river – is closed to non-local traffic. In addition, the area between the Jardin Public and the river is closed entirely to traffic on the first Sunday of each month from 10am to 7pm.

Information and tours

Bordeaux's main **tourist office**, 12 cours du 30-juillet (May, June, Sept & Oct Mon–Sat 9am–7pm, Sun 9.30am–6.30pm; July & Aug Mon–Sat 9am–7.30pm, Sun 9.30am–6.30pm; Nov–April Mon–Sat 9am–6.30pm, Sun 9.45am–4.30pm; ☏05.56.00.66.00, ⓦwww.bordeaux-tourisme.com), can book accommodation free of charge and stocks a number of useful **maps** and information leaflets; ask for their *Plan-Guide du Patrimoine* (Heritage Tour Map; €1) and the free magazine *Bordeaux Tourisme*, which details special exhibitions and other events. Look out, too, for *Spirit* (ⓦwww.spiritonline.fr), another freebie featuring a mix of articles and listings, partly in English, which you'll find here and in hotels and restaurants around Bordeaux. The tourist office also organizes various **guided tours**, both around Bordeaux centre on foot and by tram and into the surrounding wine regions. The most popular of these wine tours is a half-day visit to one of the "Great Bordeaux Vineyards" (1 April–15 Nov daily; 16 Nov–31 March Wed & Sat; €28) – highly recommended, particularly if you're short of time. For those who'd rather do it themselves, staff here can also provide detailed information on the wine regions, including suggestions for château visits and *dégustations* (see p.79 for more on visiting the vineyards). For information on **boat tours** of the harbour and trips further afield, see p.79.

For **student information** CIJA (Centre d'Information Jeunesse Aquitaine, 5 rue Duffour-Dubergier (℡05.56.56.00.56, ⓦwww.info-jeune.net), has vast amounts of information and useful noticeboards. CROUS, 18 rue du Hamel (℡05.56.33.92.00, ⓦwww.crous-bordeaux.fr), caters for university students and those in higher education.

City transport

Central Bordeaux is eminently walkable, but for longer journeys the best option is the efficient new **tram system** (daily 5am–1am; ⓦwww.infotbc .com). It consists of three lines: line A runs east–west via the Pont de Pierre and the Hôtel de Ville (the *mairie*), beside the cathedral; line B cuts southwest from the northern quays through the city centre, with stops at Quinconces, place Gambetta, the Hôtel de Ville and place de la Victoire; and line C heads north from the train station along the quays to Quinconces and the Jardin Publique. Transfers between the lines are possible at the Quinconces, Hôtel de Ville and Porte de Bourgogne (at the west end of the Pont de Pierre) stops. Trams run roughly every ten to twenty minutes depending on the line and the time of day; if you can, try to avoid the morning and evening rush hours (roughly Mon–Fri 7–9am & 5–7pm), particularly on line A. **Tickets** are available from machines at each stop (only coins accepted), from nearby *tabacs* listed on the machines or from one of the three tbc trams at the train station, at 9 place Gambetta and on esplanade des Quinconces near the tourist office. A single-ride ticket costs €1.30, but it's cheaper to buy a "Tickarte", a carnet of five (€5) or ten (€10) tickets. Alternatively, If you're going to be moving about a lot, it pays to buy a Tickarte Bordeaux Découverte, giving unlimited travel for one, two or three consecutive days (€4.10, €7.10 and €9.20 respectively). Tickets are valid for unlimited travel up to one hour on trams and city buses (see below); you must punch the ticket every time you get aboard.

All tickets and passes are valid on the extensive **city bus** network, although in this case you can also buy single-ride tickets from the conductor. The most useful services are likely to be line #16 between the train station and Gambetta, stopping on cours de la Marne near the youth hostel, and Le Bus du Soir, a **nightbus** comprising eleven routes that operate from around 9.30pm until roughly 1am. Route #S7 runs from the train station, handy for the clubland area along quai de Paludate, to place de la Victoire and place Gambetta, while #S1 serves the northern quays.

Cycling is an increasingly popular and pleasant way to get around Bordeaux. There are numerous cycle lanes and paths, including a riverside route (also designed for walking, jogging and other activities) from Pont de Pierre north along the quays to the Chartrons district and then turning inland to Bordeaux's leisure lake, Le Lac. **Bike rental** is available from Pierre Qui Roule at 32 place Gambetta (℡05.57.85.80.87, ⓔinfo@pierrequiroule.fr; Mon 2–7pm, Tues–Sat 10am–7pm), which also rents out in-line **skates**, and Macadam Sport at 27 quai des Chartrons (℡05.56.51.75.51; ⓔmacadamsport@wanadoo.fr; Mon–Sat 10am–1pm & 2–7pm). Count on around €8–10 for a half day and €10–15 for a day for a bike and slightly less for skates.

There are also 24-hour **taxi** stands at the train station, on rue Esprit-des-Lois near the tourist office and at the top of cours Clémenceau near place Gambetta. Alternatively, call Taxi Télé (℡05.56.96.00.34).

Accommodation

The area around the train station – particularly rue Charles-Domercq and cours de la Marne – has any number of one- and two-star **hotels**, though this isn't the most appealing or convenient area to stay. Better to head for the city centre, where you'll find a good choice, from the basic to the luxurious. Rooms are generally not difficult to come by, with the notable exception of the week of the Fête du Vin (even-numbered years) and Fête du Fleuve (odd-numbered years) in June, when Bordeaux is packed to the gunnels. All the hotels listed below are marked on the map on p.84, except where indicated below.

Acanthe 12–14 rue St-Rémi ☎05.56.81.66.58, @www.acanthe-hotel-bordeaux.com. Spick-and-span hotel with unfussy but comfortable en-suite rooms in a great location just behind place de la Bourse. Great value for the city centre, so book ahead. (See map on p.86) ❸

Ariane 5 rue de Lurbe ☎05.56.52.27.72, ℗05.56.48.07.17. Welcoming and attractive little hotel with well-kept rooms offering good-value accommodation just outside the Golden Triangle. Private garage available (€8). ❸

Bayonne Etche-Ona 4 rue Martignac and 11 rue Mautrec ☎05.56.48.00.88, @www.bordeaux-hotel.com. The *Bayonne* and *Etche-Ona* are in fact two separate buildings with not a lot to choose between them. Rooms are small at the cheaper end and comfortable rather than oozing character, but the location, mod cons such as broadband Wi-fi access in all rooms and attentive service make this one of the top options in the city centre. (See map on p.86) ❼

Bristol 4 rue Bouffard ☎05.56.81.85.01, @www.hotel-bordeaux.com. A relaxed two-star hotel just south of place Gambetta offering a range of functional rooms, all en suite with TV and phones, in the main building as well as very basic budget accommodation in its annexes close by (a popular alternative to the youth hostel); ask to see several rooms as they vary considerably. *Bristol* ❷–❸; annexes ❶

Une Chambre en Ville 35 rue Bouffard ☎05.56.81.34.53, @www.bandb-bx.com. This stylish *chambre d'hôtes* in the old city makes a good option if you're looking for somewhere with character. The rooms, blending modern with traditional touches, are unusually spacious and all en suite. ❺

La Maison du Lierre 57 rue Huguerie ☎05.56.51.92.71, @www.maisondulierre.com. Stylish hotel with the atmosphere of a *chambre d'hôtes* near place de Tourny. It has just twelve rooms – not huge but attractively decorated, with wooden floorboards and cheerful fabrics – and a lovely little courtyard garden. Private garage available (€10). ❺

Notre-Dame 36–38 rue Notre-Dame ☎05.56.52.88.24, @www.hotelnotredame.free.fr. Quiet, refined establishment offering good value for money in an area of old streets just north of esplanade des Quinconces. Air conditioning and generous bathrooms come as standard, though the decor is unexciting. The cheapest rooms are on the small side for two people. (See map on p.74) ❸

De La Presse 6–8 rue Porte-Dijeaux ☎05.56.48.53.88, @www.hoteldelapresse.com. This family-run hotel in the pedestrianized heart of Bordeaux represents good value for the level of service; rates are at the bottom of this price range. Its rooms are plain but bright and well proportioned, with big beds and three-star comforts as minibar and air conditioning. Closed one week at Christmas. (See map on p.86) ❺

Des Quatre Soeurs 6 cours du 30-Juillet ☎05.57.81.19.20, @4soeurs.free.fr. Popular, efficient and friendly hotel in an ideal spot next to the tourist office. The narrow foyer is all nineteenth-century pannelling, while the rooms are decked out in cream and blue, with hand-painted furniture and gleaming bathrooms. Cheaper rooms are a touch boxy for the price. ❺

Régina 34 rue Charles-Domercq ☎05.56.91.66.07, ℗05.56.91.32.88. The best value for money near the train station, the *Régina* is open 24 hours, offering simple, neat rooms of a good size. The cheapest have a shower but no toilet and, while all rooms are equipped with phones, only some have TVs. Ask for a quieter room at the back. Closed 15–30 Dec. (See map on p.74) ❷

La Tour Intendance 14 & 16 rue de la Vieille-Tour ☎05.56.44.56.56, @www.hotel-tour-intendance.com. This pleasant hotel tucked into a quiet corner off place Gambetta boasts a cheerful little lobby and somewhat expensive en-suite rooms – disappointingly plain in the main building but more stylish, if decidedly cramped, in the nearby annexe. You can also use their garage for €10 per night. Closed Christmas and New Year. ❻

Youth Hostel 22 cours Barbey ℡05.56.33.00.70, ⓦwww.auberge-jeunesse-bordeaux.com. Situated off cours de la Marne, this modern hostel is a 10min walk – or a short bus ride (line #16) – northeast of the train station. It's in a bit of a seedy area, but they've tightened up on security. All rooms (for two, four or six people) are equipped with showers (toilets are in the corridor), and there's a kitchen, plus Internet access. Annual membership card (€1.50) required. €19.90 per night per person, including breakfast. (See map on pp.74–75, p.84 & p.86) ❷

The City

Bordeaux is spread out along the west bank of the Garonne River, with the eighteenth-century old town lying between the place de la Comédie to the north, cours d'Albret to the west and cours Victor-Hugo to the south. Cutting north–south through this district, the old Roman road, the die-straight **rue Ste-Catherine**, forms the city's spine and its principal shopping street. To the east of this you'll find the imposing buildings of the riverfront and **quartier St-Pierre**, its narrow streets lined with grand mansions from Bordeaux's glory days, while westwards the triple spires of the cathedral provide a focal point for the city's museum district. There are a couple of sights further south of rue Ste-Catherine, namely the churches of St-Michel and Sainte Croix, before heading north again across the vast, open square of the esplanade des Quinconces to the **quartier des Chartrons**, where Bordeaux's wine merchants once lived and worked. West of centre, there are some very scant remains of the city's Roman past to be found beyond the welcome greenery of the Jardin Public and one last church, St-Seurin, which is worth a detour for its delicate alabaster carvings and collection of sarcophagi. Finally, the **east bank** of the Garonne merits a quick jaunt, if only for the views back across the river and a stroll along the quays to see a very contemporary botanical garden.

The Grand Théâtre and the Golden Triangle

The social hub of eighteenth-century Bordeaux was place de la Comédie and the impeccably classical **Grand Théâtre**, built on the site of a Roman temple, at the northern end of rue Ste-Catherine. Completed in 1780 by the architect Victor Louis, this lofty building is decorated with an immense colonnaded portico topped by statues of the nine Muses and three Graces. Inside, a monumental stone staircase – the inspiration for Paris's Opéra Garnier and using natural light to great effect – leads to the theatre itself, now restored to its original blue, grey and gold colour scheme. Its walls are covered in sumptuous *trompe l'oeil* and the dome in allegorical scenes, lit by a massive crystal chandelier. The best way to see it is to attend one of the operas, concerts or

Bordeaux's architecture

As you explore the old city centre, now a conservation area, look out for the splendid detailing of the **eighteenth-century architecture**. In addition to intricate wrought-iron balconies, balustrades, locks and door-knockers, these aristocratic facades are enlivened by sculpted animals and human faces – many are thought to be portraits of the original owners – above the doors and windows. Though such *mascarons* had been used to decorate buildings for some time, the practice reached its peak in eighteenth-century Bordeaux. Not surprisingly, bunches of grapes and the figure of Bacchus, god of wine, also feature strongly, as does Neptune, the sea god. The local, porous building-stone tends to blacken easily, but recent restoration projects have returned many of these frontages to their original gleaming white – to glorious effect.

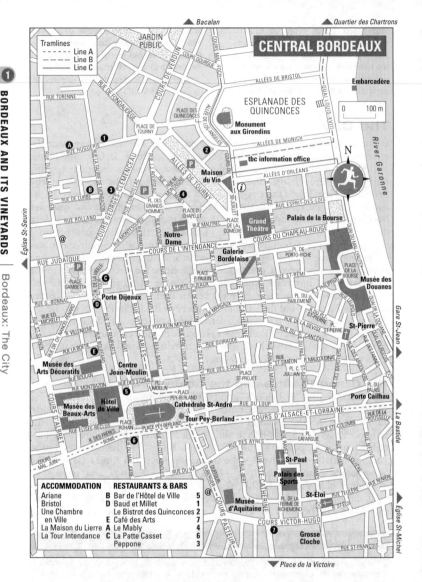

CENTRAL BORDEAUX

ACCOMMODATION		RESTAURANTS & BARS	
Ariane	**B**	Bar de l'Hôtel de Ville	**5**
Bristol	**D**	Baud et Millet	**1**
Une Chambre		Le Bistrot des Quinconces	**2**
en Ville	**E**	Café des Arts	**7**
La Maison du Lierre	**A**	Le Mably	**4**
La Tour Intendance	**C**	La Patte Casset	**6**
		Peppone	**3**

ballets staged throughout the year (see p.96) – alternatively, sign up at the tourist office (see p.80) for one of their informative **guided tours** (1hr; €5.50), though note that these are fairly infrequent in winter.

Smart streets radiate outwards from place de la Comédie – among them ritzy cours de l'Intendance, where **Goya** spent the last years of his life (1824–28) at no. 57 – west to café-lined place Gambetta. Once a majestic space laid out in the early eighteenth century to replace a malodorous rubbish dump, the *place* is now little more than a busy roundabout. Marooned in its midst, a valiant attempt at an English garden marks where the guillotine lopped off three hundred heads

△ Bordeaux Grand Théâtre

at the time of the Revolution, while its southeastern corner is occupied by the Neoclassical Porte Dijeaux, one of several triumphal arches erected in the mid-1700s. From here **cours Georges-Clemenceau** leads northeast to place de Tourny, which commemorates the eighteenth-century administrator Marquis Louis Aubert de Tourny, a prime mover in the city's rejuvenation, who supervised much of the rebuilding. The sandy, tree-lined allées de Tourny then cuts back to the place de la Comédie, enclosing an area of chic boutiques and attractive residential streets known as the **Golden Triangle**. Its focus is the lovely, circular **place des Grands-Hommes**, its centre now filled with a striking ironwork market hall completed in 1900, though it feels far more recent with its clean lines and expanse of glass (see "Shopping and markets", p.98).

The triangle is also home to Bordeaux's only Baroque church, the late-seventeenth-century **Notre-Dame** (Mon 2.30–5.30pm, Tues–Sat 8.30am–noon & 2.30–5.30pm, Sun 10am–noon & 2.30–5.30pm). The gently curved facade of this former Dominican chapel comprises a pleasing arrangement of columns, friezes, scrolls and pinnacles centred on a bas-relief of the Virgin Mary presenting a rosary to St Dominic. Inside, light plays off the smooth planes of curved and arched stone, providing a perfect backdrop for elements of typically extravagant Baroque decoration: magnificent gilded ironwork, vigorous statuary adorning the altar and *trompe l'oeil* frescoes in the side chapels, where you'll also find an interesting collection of religious paintings.

Place de la Bourse and the Quartier St-Pierre

East of place de la Comédie, cours du Chapeau-Rouge (the Red Hat), named after a venerable *auberge* once located here, leads to the banks of the Garonne and the imposing **place de la Bourse**. This superb, U-shaped classical ensemble is centred on the Grand Pavilion, in fact a relatively small building topped with a pinnacled grey-slate lantern; to either side stretch the Palais de la Bourse, the former stock exchange, to the north and the Hôtel des Douanes, the old

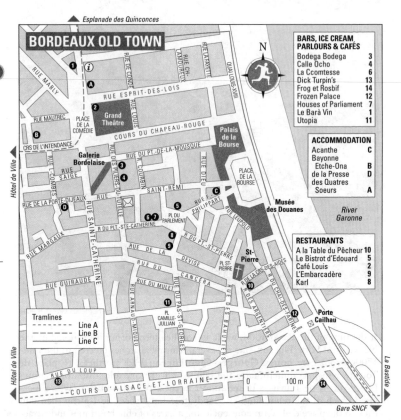

BORDEAUX OLD TOWN

BARS, ICE CREAM PARLOURS & CAFÉS

Bodega Bodega	3
Calle Ocho	4
La Ccomtesse	6
Dick Turpin's	13
Frog et Rosbif	14
Frozen Palace	12
Houses of Parliament	7
Le Barà Vin	1
Utopia	11

ACCOMMODATION

Acanthe	C
Bayonne	
Etche-Ona	B
de la Presse	D
des Quatres	
Soeurs	A

RESTAURANTS

A la Table du Pêcheur	10
Le Bistrot d'Edouard	5
Café Louis	2
L'Embarcadère	9
Karl	8

Tramlines
- - - - - Line A
- - - - - Line B
――――― Line C

0   100 m

Gare SNCF ▼

River Garonne

La Bastide ▶

◀ *Hôtel de Ville*

customs house, balancing it to the south. When the square was first laid out in the early eighteenth century, it was known as the place Royale in honour of Louis XV, and its focal point was an equestrian statue of the king. Come the Revolution, however, the statue was melted down for cannon and wasn't replaced until the 1860s when the present Three Graces fountain was installed. The impressive bulk of the Hôtel des Douanes contains the **Musée des Douanes** (Tues–Sun 10am–6pm; €3), detailing the history of the French customs service. Apart from one or two good late-nineteenth-century representations of Bordeaux's quays thronged with ships, the most engaging displays relate to the efforts of customs officials – wickedly caricatured in contemporary cartoons – to prevent smuggling and displays of the booty they've seized over the years.

Inland from place de la Bourse, **quartier St-Pierre** encompasses the area from cours du Chapeau-Rouge to cours d'Alsace-Lorraine in the south and west to rue Ste-Catherine. This is the heart of Bordeaux's old town, an area of narrow streets lined with typical Bordelais mansions (see box on p.83). Its residents were a mixed bunch, from merchants and members of parliament – the old parliament house once stood on place du Palais to the south – to artisans whose trades are recorded in the street names: rue des Bahutiers (chest-makers); rue des Argentiers (gold and silversmiths); and rue du Cancéra (coopers, in the local dialect). To see the best of the quarter, take rue Fernand-Philippart from behind place de la Bourse to lovely, paved **place du Parlement**. Though the surrounding buildings span more than two centuries, from 1760 on, this square remains one of Intendant Tourny's most successful creations; not rigidly uniform, and small enough to be intimate, but without the architecture losing its sense of nobility. In summer it is filled with tables spilling out of the surrounding cafés and restaurants. A short walk to the southeast, **place St-Pierre** is even smaller and less formal. It is dominated by the attractive fourteenth- and fifteenth-century church of St-Pierre, with its delicate arched windows and a symmetry offset by the adjacent belfry, though there's little to see inside.

Further south, down rue des Argentiers, the ornate, almost fairy-tale **Porte Cailhau** – topped by an array of exaggerated pinnacles – takes its name from the stones (*cailloux*, or *cailhaux* in dialect) used as ships' ballast that were unloaded on the neighbouring quay. It is one of Bordeaux's only two remaining medieval city gates, erected in the late fifteenth century in honour of an early victory by Charles VIII in the Italian Wars (1494–1559). A statue of the monarch, holding an orb and sceptre, decorates the gate's eastern facade.

Cathédrale St-André and the Hôtel de Ville

Bordeaux's old town west of rue Ste-Catherine is dominated by the **Cathédrale St-André** (Mon 2–7pm, Tues–Fri 7.30am–6pm, Sat 9–7pm, Sun 9am–6pm), whose most eye-catching feature is the great upward sweep of the twin steeples over the north transept, an effect heightened by the adjacent but separate bell tower. Of the earlier eleventh-century church, in which Eleanor of Aquitaine married Louis VII in 1137, only the west wall remains. In the thirteenth and fourteenth centuries the building was almost completely remodelled, with a much higher nave and the addition of a finely carved **Royal Door**, depicting the Last Judgement, in the north wall; according to local legend, the door was closed permanently after Louis XIII and Anne of Austria, daughter of the king of Spain, passed through it on their wedding day in 1615. The tympanum above the adjacent door – the main entrance – features the Last Supper and Christ's Ascension.

The cathedral's interior holds no great interest, apart from the **choir** which provides one of the few complete examples of the florid late-Gothic style known as *Rayonnant*. Some of the **carvings** are also worth closer inspection: in the ambulatory around the choir look out for an expressive statue of the Virgin with St Anne as a child, and a small and very gaunt St Martial, the legendary founder of the church, fashioned out of alabaster in the fifteenth century; the capitals on the far side of the Sacrament Chapel, behind the altar, tell the story of the birth of Christ and the flight into Egypt in superb detail; finally, flanking the cathedral's west door, under the organ loft, are two powerful Renaissance-era bas-reliefs of the descent into hell and the Resurrection.

In 1440 Archbishop Pey-Berland, who also founded Bordeaux University, laid the corner stone of the cathedral bell tower, built on a separate site as was the custom at the time. It's worth climbing the fifty-metre-high **Tour Pey-Berland** (June–Sept daily 10am–6pm; Oct–May Tues–Sun 10am–12.30pm & 2–5.30pm; €5) – topped by a gilded statue of Notre-Dame d'Aquitaine – for fine views over the cathedral and the city's red-tiled roofs to the river beyond.

West of the cathedral the **Hôtel de Ville** (45min guided tour; Wed 2.30pm; €2.50), formerly Archbishop Rohan's palace, was completed in 1784, marking the arrival of Neoclassical architecture in Bordeaux. The downstairs reception rooms are decorated with beautifully crafted carved wooden panelling and *trompe l'oeil*, while the grand stone staircase is a masterpiece of stonemasonry. Since 1837 the city council has met here in suitably sombre surroundings laden with Republican motifs reminding them of their civic duties.

The museum district

The cream of Bordeaux's museums lie scattered in the streets around the cathedral. Directly behind the Hôtel de Ville, with its entrance on cours d'Albret, the **Musée des Beaux-Arts** (daily except Tues 11am–6pm; free) offers a small but worthy selection of European painting from the fifteenth to the early twentieth century, as well as temporary exhibitions (€5). Only a fraction of the three-thousand-strong collection is on view at any time, featuring works by Reynolds, Titian, Rubens, Delacroix, Matisse and Marquet (a native of the city) amongst many others. Delacroix's *La Grèce sur les ruines de Missolonghi* is probably the most famous work, but look out, too, for the superb play of light in Henri Gervex's *Rolla* in the museum's north wing.

Far more engaging, however, is the **Musée des Arts Décoratifs** (daily except Tues 2–6pm; free), two blocks further north in rue Bouffard. It occupies the handsome Hôtel de Lalande, built in the 1770s as the home of a local wine merchant and member of parliament; today it is in remarkably good repair, with its high-ceilinged rooms, parquet floors and plasterwork mostly intact. Some of the wall coverings, such as the attractive grey-wash paper in the Salon des Panoramiques, the first room on the left as you enter, have been relocated from other Bordelais houses, as has the extensive collection of period furniture, miniatures, portraits, clocks and glassware. The most remarkable items are the beautiful displays of mainly French porcelain and faïence, including some Oriental-inspired designs. There's also an attractive *salon de thé*-cum-restaurant in the museum's courtyard (closed Sun).

Continuing clockwise around the cathedral brings you to the **Centre Jean-Moulin** (Tues–Sun 2–6pm; free), a moderately interesting museum dedicated to the Resistance, on place Jean-Moulin. Among all the documentation – unfortunately not translated – on the ground floor look out for a pint-size, collapsible motorbike that was dropped by parachute from British planes towards the end of the war and a replica of a cockle canoe (see box). The second floor hosts a room dedicated to the concentration camps and a gallery for temporary exhibitions, while upstairs again is a mock-up of Jean Moulin's office in Nice, where he worked undercover as an art dealer while coordinating the Resistance movement. Arrested in 1943, he was tortured and died on the way to Germany.

The Cockleshell Heroes

On the night of December 7, 1942, in the midst of World War II, a British naval submarine dropped ten Royal Marine commandos in their two-man "cockle" canoes at the mouth of the Gironde estuary. Their mission, code-named **Operation Frankton**, was to paddle 120km up the Garonne to Bordeaux and block the harbour by scuttling as many ships as possible; with the British navy blockading the Channel ports, Bordeaux was a vital German supply route. The mission got off to a bad start: one canoe was swept away and another overturned when it hit the tide race at the mouth of the estuary; a third sank soon after. The six crew either drowned or were captured and shot. Undeterred, the remaining four commandos continued upriver, paddling under cover of darkness and lying up during the day. They finally reached Bordeaux harbour on the night of December 11 and attached their limpet mines, seriously damaging at least five ships and blocking the harbour for several months. They then set off to walk 160km northwards to link up with the French Resistance. Two were betrayed along the way and executed, leaving just two of the original team to make it back to London via Spain and Gibraltar in April 1943. Major "Blondie" Hasler, the leader of the mission, died in 1987 and Marine Billy Sparks in 2002, the last of the "Cockleshell heros".

There's also an engaging, grainy film of Moulin doing Charlie Chaplin impressions in the snow, and numerous caricatures and sketches he produced under the pseudonym Romanin.

A short walk or tram-ride south past the Tour Pey-Berland, down rue Duffour-Dubergier, the excellent **Musée d'Aquitaine** (Tues–Sun 11am–6pm; free) is perhaps the best of the city's museums, despite frustratingly poor labelling in any language – it's well worth forking out for the English-language audio-guide (€2.20). The museum charts the history of Bordeaux and its region from prehistoric times to the present day, with a section devoted to artefacts brought back from around the world by local merchants, missionaries and colonial administrators. Best, though, are the ground-floor rooms covering the prehistoric and Gallo-Roman eras and containing a number of important finds; look out for the 20,000-year-old bas-relief of Venus carrying a crescent-shaped horn (known as the "Vénus à la Corne") with her pendulous breasts and stout hips, which was found at Marquay near Les Eyzies (see p.229). Moving into the Gallo-Roman rooms, the startling change in scale and level of sophistication of the exhibits amply illustrates the explosion of art that occurred at this time. There are some superb mosaic floors, goldware and statues: a magnificent Hercules in bronze from the second century AD and an almost perfect white marble Diana from the fourth or fifth centuries. But the piece that stands out most amongst all the gods and goddesses is the poignant funerary statue of a young girl erected by her father. She stands clutching her cat to her chest while a cockerel pecks at its tail. The medieval collection, upstairs, reveals some glorious religious sculpture, including the tomb of Curton, a thirteenth century knight, and an impressive rose window. Later, look out for the elaborate funeral monument of the Renaissance essayist Michel de Montaigne (see p.202), who served as mayor of Bordeaux from 1581 to 1585.

A couple of minutes' walk east of the museum along cours Victor-Hugo, a heavy Gothic tower, the fifteenth-century **Grosse Cloche**, straddles rue St-James. A remnant of the city walls, the gate also doubled as a bell tower for the medieval city hall. Until 1945 the start of the grape harvest and all other major events in the city were marked by peals of the big, single bell hanging between the gate's sturdy towers.

The southern districts

Bordeaux's **southern districts** were developed outside the medieval walls after the twelfth century as an artisans' quarter of coopers, carpenters and ships' chandlers, and as home to the sailors and stevedores who worked the boats and unloaded their cargoes at the nearby quays. Though there are signs of gradual gentrification, for the moment this is still very much a working-class area, with the only sights being a huge, atmospheric flea market and a couple of historic churches. If you have time to spare, however, it's worth taking a quick wander round the backstreets just to see what you stumble across.

The main **flea market** takes place on Sunday mornings (see "Listings" on p.98 for more) when it fills the wide square in front of the Gothic **Église St-Michel**, which you reach from cours Victor-Hugo by heading south down rue des Faures. Started in the mid-fourteenth century and not completed for another two hundred years, the church is one of Bordeaux's most famous landmarks thanks to its soaring **bell tower** (June–Sept daily 2–7pm; €2.50) – at 114m, it is the second tallest in France afer Strasbourg. The original fifteenth-century spire was destroyed in a storm in 1760 and not restored until Paul Abadie (1812–84), the architect of Paris's Sacré-Coeur, got to work on it in 1861. You can now climb La Flèche, as it is known, for more sweeping views and also descend into the crypt, which until 1990 housed around 60 mummi-fied corpses; photos of the decidedly goulish crowd line the walls.

The tower of St-Michel stands apart from the body of the church (Mon–Sat 9am–6pm, Sun 9–11.15am), where the main point of interest inside is the stained glass windows. These striking examples of postwar religious art were commissioned in the 1960s to replace those destroyed by World WarII bomb damage. Four craftsmen designed the windows, including Gérard Lardeur, whose St Michael weighing the souls presides over the south door, and Pierre Gaudin, who chose the massacre of the innocents for his theme in the second chapel on the left as you enter via the west door. In the first chapel on the right, don't miss the charming statue of St Ursula sheltering some of her fellow virgin-martyrs – alongside a few bishops, one of whom recently lost his head to a thief or vandal – under her outspread cloak.

Rue Camille-Sauvageau leads further south to the district's older and more attractive, honey-coloured **Église Sainte-Croix** (Thurs 9.30am–noon, July & Aug also Sat 3.30–6.30pm). This Benedictine abbey-church is said to have been founded by Clovis, the first Merovingian king (481–511) and a Christian convert, in 510 AD. It was heavily restored in the twelfth and thirteenth centu-ries, by which time it had become one of the region's most important religious foundations. In fact, old engravings show that the church was even better-look-ing before the ubiquitous Paul Abadie added the north tower and remodelled its Romanesque facade in the 1860s. Nevertheless, the irregular assembly of arches and columns provide a pleasing frame for the deep-set west door with its rhythmic carvings. By contrast the interior boasts very little decoration save a few carved capitals and faded murals. As you enter, note the sarcophagus in the first chapel on the left which holds the body of the abbot, (later St Mommolin) who was buried here in 643 AD. Further on, to the left of the altar, there's also an unusual bald-headed representation of Christ on the Cross. It's believed that the fifteenth-century, lime-wood statue might originally have sported a wig for extra realism, as some Spanish figures do.

North through the quartier des Chartrons

Back in the centre of town, cours du 30-Juillet leads north from place de la Comédie into the bare, gravelly – and frankly unattractive – expanse of the **esplanade des Quinconces**. Said to be Europe's largest municipal square, it was laid out in the early nineteenth century on the site of the Château Trompette (see p.107). At its eastern end stand two tall columns, erected in 1829 and topped by allegorical statues of Commerce and Navigation; at the opposite end is the **Monument aux Girondins**, a glorious late-nineteenth-century fantasy of statues and fountains built in honour of the influential local deputies to the 1789 Revolutionary Assembly, later purged by Robespierre as moderates and counter-revolutionaries (see p.391). During the last war, the occupying Germans made plans to melt the bronze statues down, only to be foiled by the local Resistance, who got there first and, under cover of darkness, dismantled them piece by piece and hid them in a barn in the Médoc for the duration of the war. It was only in 1983 that the monument was reassembled. It is, again, highly allegorical: at the top of the column Liberty breaks free from her chains; beneath her, facing the river, the French cockerel stands over three empty pedestals representing the Girondin deputies; on the opposite, west side, a trio of voluptuous nudes symbolize Bordeaux flanked by the rivers Garonne and Dordogne. The best statues by far, though, are the rescued bronze compositions in the fountains, particularly the powerful, semi-mythical horses with their webbed and clawed feet.

The district north of the esplanade is known as the **quartier des Chartrons** after the Carthusian monks who settled here in the fourteenth century and began draining the marshy land. They were followed in the next century by Dutch and other European wine merchants who avoided taxes by loading their boats outside the city walls. As business prospered in the seventeenth and eighteenth centuries, they built themselves offices, as well as comfortable houses complete with stone-lined cellars, for ageing the wine. Though most of the merchants, or *négociants*, have moved on, the Chartrons district still has a gentrified feel and its quiet streets make it a pleasant area to wander.

Starting on the quayside, the first sight you come to is the Neoclassical **Hôtel Fenwick** overlooking shady cours Xavier-Arnozan. Built in 1795 to house America's first French consulate, it is a grand affair, topped with two viewing towers, presumably to enable the consul to keep an eye on happenings in the port. The maritime theme is echoed by a pair of ships' prows emerging either side of the main door. Across cours Xavier-Arnozan, with its entrance on rue Ferrère, the **Musée d'Art Contemporain** (Tues–Sun 11am–6pm; free; temporary exhibitions €4) occupies a converted early-nineteenth-century warehouse for colonial imports. The vast, arcaded hall provides a magnificent setting for the mostly post-1960 works by artists such as Daniel Buren, Richard Long, Sol LeWitt and Christian Boltanski. Few pieces from the permanent collection are on display at any one time, the main space being filled by temporary exhibitions, so it's hit-and-miss as to what will be on offer. There's a suitably arty – and highly rated – café-restaurant on the roof (Tues–Sun 11.30am–6pm).

Rue Notre-Dame, which runs north from cours Xavier-Arnozan, has become a centre for **antique shops**. At its southern end, the bulk and austerity of the Protestant Temple, or chapel, built in the 1830s along pure Classical lines, comes as something of a shock after the fussy, bourgeois facades around it, while further along, a left turn beside the church of St-Louis brings you into an attractive, café-lined square, in the middle of which stands the graceful **Halle des Chartrons**, a market hall built in 1869, now used to stage a variety of temporary exhibitions.

Returning to the riverside, you may still find the navy destroyer **Croiseur Colbert** dominating the quai des Chartrons. The rusting vessel, which has become an increasingly unwelcome feature of Bordeaux's waterfront, is scheduled to go in 2007. From here it's a pleasant stroll north along the quays, past former warehouses now converted into shops, cafes and restaurants. At the far end, **Cap Sciences** (Tues–Fri 2–6pm, Sat & Sun 1–7pm; €5.50; ⓦwww .cap-sciences.net) is a showcase for the region's scientific, technical and industrial community, with lots of interactive exhibitions (in French) aimed predominantly at school children.

The last sight in the area is the **Base Sous-Marine** (Tues–Sun: April–June & Sept 2–7pm; Oct–March 2–6pm; closed July & Aug; free; ☏05.56.11.11.50), an old German submarine base overlooking the yacht harbour on boulevard Alfred-Daney in the Bacalan district to the north of the quartier des Chartrons. The brooding grey structure, with concrete walls and roof up to 9m thick, now houses a contemporary art gallery with changing exhibitions – phone ahead to make sure it's open. Alternatively, you get a good view from the south side of the harbour, accessible from rue Lucien-Faure.

The Jardin Public south to St-Seurin

West of the Chartrons district, across cours de Verdun, the formal **Jardin Public** (daily 7am to sunset; free) represents one of the city's rare open green spaces. It began life in the mid-1700s as a tree-filled park, another of Intendant

Tourny's improvements, but later had to be redesigned after serving as a parade ground in the Revolution. This second, smaller garden follows English styling in its landscaped lake and lawns – for a change, you're allowed to walk and sit on the grass. It also contains a botanical garden and the **Muséum d'Histoire Naturelle** (closed for renovation until 2011).

Behind the garden to the southwest stretches a quiet, provincial quarter of two-storey stone houses. Concealed among the narrow streets, next to rue du Dr-Albert-Barraud, a large chunk of brick and stone masonry, rather grandly titled the **Palais Gallien**, is all that remains of Roman Burdigala's arena, whose terraces could hold an estimated 15,000 spectators.

Further south again, **Église St-Seurin** (Tues–Fri 8.30–11.30am & 2–6.30pm, Sat 8.30–11.30am & 2.30–5.30pm), on place des Martyrs-de-la-Résistance, was built on the site of a Gallo-Roman burial ground. Though the church's exterior reflects numerous remodellings since it was founded in the sixth century, it is of interest more for its fourth-century crypt (Sat 2.30–5.30pm; free) and collection of intricate alabaster carvings. The soft white stone was imported from England in the fourteenth and fifteenth centuries. The first group you come to, just before the altar opposite the equally ornate Gothic bishop's throne, comprises fourteen bas-relief panels portraying the lives of St Seurin, a fifth-century bishop, and St Martial, a third-century evangelist from Limoges, in superb detail. The life of the Virgin Mary is the subject of the second group in the chapel to the left of the choir; unfortunately, these twelve panels were replaced in the wrong order after a nineteenth-century clean-up.

The sarcophagus of St Seurin rests under the altar table, but there are more sarcophagi to be seen in the **burial site** (June–Sept daily 2–7pm; €2.50) accessed from outside the church's south door. Various ancient burial methods can be seen from a simple covering of tiles to terracotta jars for children and sarcophagi from the Roman and Merovingian eras. Many have been left much as they were discovered, all jumbled on top of one another, though the best have been removed either to the crypt or the Musée d'Aquitaine (see p.89).

Across the Pont de Pierre

The **Bastide district**, on the east bank of the Garonne, is the scene for various urban renewal projects tied in with the new tram system. To get there take tram line A or walk over the long, low **Pont de Pierre**, which adds a touch of Mediterranean warmth to the city. This was the Bordeaux's first bridge, constructed after Napoleon struggled to ferry his troops across en route to the Spanish campaigns; its seventeen arches are said to commemorate each of his victories.

Immediately over the bridge, head north along the riverbank where Bordelais come at weekends to picnic in the shady gardens. The views from here, looking across to the place de la Bourse, are without doubt the finest in Bordeaux, particularly at night when the buildings along the quays are floodlit.

If you want something to aim for, continue north for about five minutes and you'll come to the **Jardin Botanique** (June–Aug 8am–8pm; Sept–May 8am–6pm; free). Inaugurated in 2003, this is the first stage of a new botanical garden project which will eventually hold a museum, greenhouses and a herbarium. It comprises eleven different ecosystems, including an aquatic area and the sand dunes and pine forests of the Atlantic coast, as well as beds devoted to various staple crops such as millet, oats and rice. Following the latest trends in garden design, it is almost Zen in its pure lines and division of space. A little more time is needed for the trees to soften some of the harder edges, but it's interesting to see nevertheless.

Eating and drinking

Bordeaux is packed with a bewildering choice of **restaurants**, many of them top-notch, and because of its position close to the Atlantic coast fresh seafood features prominently on many a menu. Being a student city, there's also no shortage of **cafés** and **bars** to explore. You can pick up picnic fare at the **supermarket** in the basement of the Grands-Hommes building, and at the many **gourmet food shops** around: on rue Montesquieu, just off the square, Jean d'Alos runs the city's best fromagerie, with dozens of farm-produced cheeses. In the Grands-Hommes building itself is Baillardran, a confectioner specializing in the succulent little *canelé* cakes which were once made by the Bordeaux nuns – surprising, since they are laced with rum. In a similar vein, Cadiot-Badie, at 26 allées de Tourny, is worth popping into as much for the

△ Bordeaux street life

old-world decor as its scrumptious handmade chocolates, while little cubes of praline and wine-soaked raisons dipped in chocolate and cinnamon known as *pavés de Bordeaux* (Bordeaux cobblestones) are available at Darricau, 7 place Gambetta. For more specialist food and wine shops, see p.98.

Restaurants

The best single area to trawl for **restaurants** is around place du Parlement and place St-Pierre, where you'll find something to please all tastes and budgets. Few places stand out and some may find it too touristy, but the fierce competition keeps the prices down. There are numerous sandwich bars and fast-food outlets at the south end of rue Ste-Catherine and spilling into studenty place de la Victoire. After a night on the town, join the workers at the Marché des Capucins for a hearty **breakfast** at one of several all-night café-bars such as *Le Cochon Volant*. In summer, *guinguettes* – open-air **riverside stalls** selling shrimps, king prawns and other seafood – set up along the quai des Chartrons and on Sunday morning locals come here to feast on oysters and white wine after browsing the market. For locations of the following eating places see the maps on pp.74–75, p.84 and p.86.

A La Table du Pêcheur 16 rue de la Cour-des-Aides. Just off place St-Pierre, this is one of the quieter and better places to eat in the old centre. It's recommended for its excellent fresh fish, much of it grilled over the open fire, not to mention the friendly service and very reasonable prices: there's a lunchtime *formule* (two courses including a glass of wine) for €11 and a menu at €18. Closed Sun & Mon.

Baud et Millet 19 rue Huguerie ☎05.56.79.05.77. The ultimate cheese-and-wine feast, with dishes

such as a flaky-pastry starter filled with goat's cheese and an anchovy-and-olive *tapenade* to aubergine stuffed with Gorgonzola and vegetables and braised Camembert with apples flambéed in calvados, consumed around a few tables at the back of a wine shop – choose your own bottle from the shelves. Choose between a cheese buffet with salad (€19.50) or a three-course menu at €24. Closed Sun.

Le Bistrot d'Édouard 16 place du Parlement. Undeniably touristy these days, but recommended for its moderate prices and position on this lovely square, with outdoor seating in summer. There are good-value, three-course menus (€12.90-23.90) offering a choice of regional dishes as well as salads and other standard brasserie fare. Open daily.

Le Bistro des Quinconces 4 place des Quinconces ℗05.56.52.84.56. Typical, old-fashioned brasserie which doubles as a café and bar. In fine weather locals vie for the outdoor tables. The eclectic *carte* includes dishes such as salmon or beef tartare and fish *parillada* (a selection of grilled fish). The weekday lunch menu is at €19; expect to pay €30–35 for dinner. Daily 8am–1am.

Le Boudoir 7 rue Traversanne ℗05.56.94.20.45. Faded sofas, bric-a-brac, books and games give this little "café cantine" in the midst of the St-Michel quarter a decidedly bohemian air. Local artists and artisans come here for the inventive home cooking, along the lines of spinach and goat's cheese in flaky pastry or spicy roast duck and lots of fresh vegetables, from a menu which changes daily. A three-course lunch costs €13, dinner €20. July & Aug dinner only Tues–Fri; Sept–June open for lunch daily and for dinner Wed–Sat.

Brasserie du Passage 14–15 place Canteloupe ℗05.56.91.20.30. After strolling round the St-Michel flea market, head for this fun bar-brasserie with tables on the square or in an antique hall, formerly a banana-ripening warehouse. It serves simple but tasty fare such as eggs with foie gras and entrecote in Bordelaise sauce, and some of the cheapest beers in town. There's a lunch menu at €12, rising to €17 in the evening. Reservations recommended for lunch at weekends. Closed Wed.

Café des Arts 138 cours Victor-Hugo. A Bordeaux institution and one of the city's few old-style cafés, its ambience dates from 1930s faded relics. It offers typical brasserie fare, with a good-value lunchtime *formule* at €10.50 and a *plat du jour* at €8.50, and has the advantage of serving till late. Daily 8am–2am.

Café Louis place de la Comédie. If you want to dine in sumptuous surroundings – all *trompe l'oeil*, gilded mirrors and chandeliers – without breaking the bank, try this café-restaurant in the Grand Théâtre. The short, uncomplicated menu includes salads, seafood and grills, or there are daily specials. Interesting selection of wines, too. The lunchtime *formule* is priced at €16.50; in the evening count on €30–40 *à la carte*. Closed Sun eve & Mon.

Casa Pino 40 rue Traversanne. The atmosphere is more workers' cantine than haute-cuisine at Bordeaux's best-known Portuguese restaurant, which attacts a mixed crowd of artisans,

market-goers, tourists and business people with its hearty portions. The €11 menu, served at lunch and weekday evenings (Fri & Sat €20), including wine and coffee is excellent value. Otherwise, expect to pay €20 from the *carte*. Closed Sun & July.

Chez Dupont 45 rue de Notre-Dame ℗05.56.81.49.59. Bustling, old-fashioned brasserie-restaurant in the Chartrons district with wooden floors and retro styling. Their market menus include toothsome dishes such as langoustine with ginger and artichoke carpaccio with foie gras, followed perhaps by grapefruit gratin with gingerbread ice cream. Prices are very reasonable, with a *plat du jour* for €7.50, and full menus from €14.50. Reservations are recommended in the evening – and there's a surprise in store in the toilet! Tues–Sat.

Le Cochon Volant 22 place des Capucins ℗05.57.59.10.00. Traditional home cooking in copious quantities in a cheerful, red-and-white-tiled room – formerly a butcher's shop – in a corner of the Capucins marketplace. The restaurant attracts an eclectic crowd, from businessmen and bureaucrats to local artisans and is a popular breakfast spot among clubbers. Reservations recommended for dinner. *Plat du jour* at €7.50, lunch menu at €11 and in the evening count on €20–25 upwards *à la carte*. Open for lunch and dinner Tues & Wed and for breakfast, lunch & dinner Thurs–Sun. Closed Mon.

L'Embarcadère 3 rue du Pas-St-Georges ℗05.56.52.23.29. Smart, popular Parisian-style brasserie specializing in fresh seafood. At lunchtime there's a *formule* of a salad and *plat du jour* for €10.90. Evening menus start at €19.80 for three courses, and they also do dramatic seafood platters (€18–45). Closed Sun & Mon.

La Guimbarde des Chartrons 10 place du Marché-des-Chartrons. Regulars and tourists rub elbows at this friendly little café-restaurant on the Chartrons market square. Dishes are marked on the slate boards: €8 for a main dish and €12 for three courses including wine or coffee. It's all fresh and well cooked. Closed Sat & Sun.

Karl 6 place du Parlement. From coffee and croissant with freshly squeezed orange to vast cooked platters, this is *the* place to come for breakfast (8.30am–3pm). It has a good range of cakes, pastries and ice creams to eat in or take away, and serves light meals all day. Daily 8.30am–8pm.

Le Mably 12 rue Mably ℗05.56.44.30.10. Informal, friendly and unsurprisingly popular restaurant offering good value and a warm atmosphere among its mirrors, candles and sepia shots. There's a lunchtime *formule* at €17 while evening menus start at €22 for three courses. The food is plentiful and of excellent quality, using lots of fish and local produce, with dishes such as rabbit and hazelnut terrine followed by roast seabass with lemon thyme. Closed Sun & Mon.

La Patte Casset 12 rue Maréchal-Joffre ℡05.56.44.11.58. It's worth going out of your way to sample this attractive restaurant with its tiny, olive-tree-filled courtyard opposite Bordeaux's law courts – it's best to reserve for lunch on weekdays (buffet at €7.50 or two courses for €12.50). In the evenings, the slate-board menu features dishes such as fresh gazpacho, spicy tuna and raspberry *millefeuille*. Three courses will set

you back €35–40. Closed Sat eve & Sun.
Peppone 31 cours Georges-Clémenceau. One of central Bordeaux's better Italian restaurants, popular for its tasty, thin-crust pizzas (€12). Closed Sun.
Le Port de La Lune 58–59 quai de Paludate ℡05.56.49.15.55. Big, noisy brasserie with a great atmosphere out on the southern quays next to the *Comptoir du Jazz* (see p.97); the photos, the sound system and their motto – "jazz-abuse is good for your health" – give you some idea of the priority here. The food is reasonable and varied, with a three-course menu including coffee and wine at €22. Daily noon–1am.

Cafés, ice cream parlours and bars

Surprisingly, Bordeaux lacks any truly grand, people-watching **cafés**. Though *Café Regent* on place Gambetta is the place to be seen, there are prettier spots to be found in the old city – try place Camille-Jullian, for example, or place du Parlement. There's no shortage of **bars**, including a growing band of English and Irish **pubs**. Student action mostly focuses around place de la Victoire, where places offer cheap drinks, DJ nights, live sport and theme evenings; all are packed on Thursday nights. Bordeaux's well-established **gay** scene is concentrated near the Hôtel de Ville.

Le Bar à Vin Maison du Vin, 3 cours du 30-Juillet. Not much in the way of ambience, but the wine bar of the CIVB (see p.99) offers the best value in Bordeaux (€2–5 per glass) and expert advice from the trained sommeliers who serve as bar staff. Cheese or ham platters cost €3–4.50. Daily 11am–10pm.
Bar de l'Hôtel de Ville (BHV) 4 rue de l'Hôtel-de-Ville. Friendly little gay and lesbian café-bar which stages a variety of free events every other Sunday between May and September as well as impromptu theme nights in summer. Daily 6pm–2am.
Bodega Bodega 4 rue des Piliers-de-Tutelle. Large wine bar with a Spanish ambience, also serving sangria and beer, and pretty authentic tapas (from €4 per dish, or a selection of seven for €23.50) to soak it all up. Occasional live music on Thursday evenings. Mon–Sat noon–3pm & 7pm–2am.
Café Populaire 1 rue Kléber. Bordeaux's clubbers gather at *Café Pop* for a drink or a meal – the food is good value and plentiful – or a warm-up bop before heading down to the quai de Palu-date (see overleaf). Things really get going after midnight, when the volume goes up a notch or three and everyone hits the dance floor. Tues–Sat 8pm–2am.
Calle Ocho 24 rue des Piliers-de-Tutelle. Bordeaux's best-known and liveliest salsa bar is bursting at the seams on Friday and Saturday

nights. They serve real Cuban rum and *mojitos*, and the music is loud. Mon–Sat 5.30pm–2am.
La Comtesse 25 rue du Parlement-St-Pierre. More like an antique shop than a bar, this tiny place is decked out with old paintings, chandeliers, distressed woodwork and faded sofas set off against bare, stone walls. The music is equally eclectic, with a preference for techno, jazz and fusion. Daily 6pm–2am.
Dick Turpin's 72 rue du Loup. Opposite a wiste-ria-filled courtyard, this is a pretty good rendition of an English town pub, with a relaxed, friendly atmosphere and a mixed clientele. Happy hour 5–8.30pm. Mon–Sat 3pm–2am, Sun 5.30pm–midnight.
Frog et Rosbif 23 rue Ausone. Big, Brit-ish-style pub-restaurant and microbrewery – house beers include Bord'Ale (best bitter) and Darkitaine (stout) – housed in a former women's prison. There's all the usual fare: pub grub (burg-ers, fish and chips, curries and crumble, with main dishes around €10), darts, quiz nights, theme nights and live sports screenings, as well as a happy hour (5.30–8.30pm) and cheap drinks on Thursdays (student night). July & Aug Mon–Fri 7pm–2am, Sat & Sun 5.30pm–2am. Sept–June Mon–Fri 5.30pm–2am, Sat & Sun noon–2am.
Frozen Palace 28 rue du Chai-des-Farines. Fabulous homemade ices and sorbets (one scoop for €2, three for €4) in inspired flavours

that might include organic lavender or raspberry and vervaine. Tues–Sun: April, May & Sept 3–7pm; July & Aug 3–10pm depending on the weather.
Houses of Parliament 11 rue Parlement-Ste-Catherine. A central location and delights such as John Smith's and Newcastle Brown on tap plus the usual standards – happy hour (5–8pm), quiz nights, student nights, ladies' nights, live sport, pool and so forth – ensure a good crowd at this London-style pub. Mon–Fri 5pm–2am, Sat & Sun 2pm–2am.

🏃 **Utopia** 5 place Camille-Jullian. Even if you're not going to see a film, the *Utopia's* café-restaurant makes an atmospheric place for a drink or light meal (salads and open sandwiches from €5.50 up) – or you can sit out on the square in fine weather. Daily 11.30am–10.30pm.

Entertainment and nightlife

Bordeaux's cultural life runs the gamut from classical theatre to avant-garde performance art and big-name rock concerts. A vibrant late-night scene focuses among the clubs and discos lining the southern quays, though some of the scene has now shifted to the northern docks. To find out what's happening in and around Bordeaux, ask at the tourist office or get hold of one of the free **listings** guides: *Spirit* (with an English section) and *Bordeaux Plus*. To buy **tickets** for city and regional events, contact the venue direct or head for the Box Office (℡05.56.48.26.26, ⓦwww.boxoffice.fr) in the nineteenth-century Galerie Bordelaise arcade wedged between rue Ste-Catherine and rue des Piliers-de-Tutelle. Both FNAC, 50 rue St-Catherine (℡08.92.68.36.22, €0.34 per min, ⓦwww.fnacspectacles.com), and Virgin Megastore (℡08.92.39.28.00, €0.34 per min, ⓦwww.virginmega.fr) on place Gambetta also have ticket outlets.

Theatre and classical music

The city's most prestigious **theatrical events** take place in the sumptuous Grand Théâtre, which hosts a huge varied programme of opera, ballet, contemporary dance and classical music. So much so, in fact, that performances often spill over into the Théâtre National de Bordeaux on square Jean-Vauthier near Eglise Sainte Croix, and the unlovely Palais des Sport on place de la Ferme-de-Richemont, near cours Victor-Hugo; tickets and information are available from the Grand Théâtre (℡05.56.00.85.95, ⓦwww .opera-bordeaux.com) or from the ticket outlets mentioned above. Théâtre Fémina, 20 rue de Grassi (℡05 56 52 45 19, ⓦwww.theatrefemina.fr), is another lovely old theatre putting on operetta, song recitals and comedy, often featuring big French names. Occasional **classical concerts** also take place in Bordeaux's churches, notably the cathedral, but also Notre-Dame, Sainte-Croix and St-Seurin, which are well worth looking out for. More informal **café-théâtre** and modern performance arts get a strong showing in venues throughout the city. A couple of the more accessible include La Comédie Gallien, 20 rue Rolland (℡05.56.44.04.00, ⓦwww .comediegallien.com) and Théâtre Onyx, 11–13 rue Fernand-Philippart (℡05.56.44.26.12, ⓦwww.theatreonyx.net).

Cinema

When it comes to **cinema**, the best venue, where you're also most likely to find *Version Originale* (VO) films is the Utopia on place Camille-Jullian (℡05.56.52.00.03, ⓦwww.cinemas-utopia.org/bordeaux), housed in a converted church complete with frescoes and Gothic arches, not to mention five screens and a popular café-restaurant (see above). It's also worth seeing what's on at the repertory Cinéma Jean Vigo, 6 rue Franklin (℡05.56.44.35.17,

@www.jeanvigo.com), near place des Grands-Hommes. UGC Ciné Cité, 13–15 rue Georges-Bonnac (☎08.92.70.00.00, €0.34 per min), off place Gambetta, serves up more standard, Hollywood fare, some of it in VO, while films at the vast, new seventeen-screen Mégarama (☎08.92.69.33.17, €0.34 per min, @www.megarama.fr), across the Pont de Pierre in the old Gare d'Orléans, are mostly subtitled.

Live music

Jazz and blues fans are well catered for in Bordeaux and there's no shortage of more **contemporary music** either at venues scattered round the city. Ticket prices generally start at around €5, while opening hours and days vary – it's a good idea to phone ahead to be on the safe side.

Le Blueberry 61 rue Camille-Sauvageau ☎05.56.94.16.87. Jazz and blues concerts take place most evenings at this little club in the St-Michel district. Daily 7pm–2am. Closed Aug.
Cercle des Arts Traditionnels (Le CAT) 24 rue de la Faïencerie ☎05.56.39.14.74. A good venue for world music out in the northern, industrial Bacalan district.
Chez Alriq quais de Queyris ☎05.56.86.58.49. This *guinguette* (open-air eatery) offers a lovely riverside setting and concerts most evenings – outdoors in summer – focusing on blues, jazz and world music. Find it over on the east side of the river at the north end of quais des Queyries. Tues–Sat 3pm–2am, Sun 12.30–7pm.
Comptoir du Jazz 58 quai de Paludate ☎05.56.49.15.55, @www.leportdelune.com.

Jazz and blues fans should head for this cosy club attached to the *Port de la Lune* restaurant (see p.95) on the southern quays. Entry is generally free but you are expected to buy at least a drink. Daily 7pm–2am.
Le 4 Sans 40 rue Armagnac ☎05.56.49.40.05, @www.le4sans.com. This huge club-cum-disco behind the station pulls the crowds with its big-name DJ nights and gigs ranging from jazz to rock to salsa. Fri & Sat 11pm–4.30am.
Rock School Barbey 18 cours Barbey ☎05.56.33.66.00 @www.rockschool-barbey. com. Rock is alive and kicking at Bordeaux's very own rock music school and concert hall – not much in the way of decor but brilliant acoustics. Concerts take place several times a week, starting at 9pm.

Dance clubs

The majority of Bordeaux's **dance clubs** are spread out along southerly quai de Paludate. Recently, however, a couple of river barges in the northern docks have been converted into unusual dance clubs, though drink prices tend to be slightly higher up there. Since venues are constantly changing – places often come and go within six months – it's best to ask around for the latest hot spots. Wherever you opt for, things don't really get going until midnight and continue till 4am. Entry is usually free.

Dame de Shanghai Bassin à Flot No. 1, quai Armand-Lalande ☎05.57.10.20.50, @www .damedeshanghai.com. The bigger of two wooden barges moored in Bordeaux's northern docks, this one with Chinese-themed decor and a playlist strong on electro. The crowd is slightly older and wealthier than you'll find on the quai de Paludate. Wed–Sun 11pm–4am.
Deck Club Bassin à Flot No. 2, rue Lucien-Faure ☎05.56.43.02.54. Smaller and more select than the neighbouring *Dame de Shanghai*, the *Deck Club* is best in summer when you can get outside for a breath of air.

Palais de la Grosse 49 quai de Paludate ☎05.56.49.36.93. Welcoming venue with a rela-tively varied playlist and popular with the gay and lesbian crowd. Mon–Sat 11pm–4am.
Shadow Lounge 5 rue Cabanac ☎05.56.49.36.93, @www.leshadowlounge.com. One of Bordeaux's more established venues. The music is pretty eclectic, as is the decor: choose between the white Winter Garden or the distinctly baroque Shadow Lounge itself, all classy chandeliers and velvet drapes. It's also very selective, so you'll need to dress up. Thurs–Sat 11pm–4am.

Listings

Airlines Air France ☎08.20.82.08.20; Aer Lingus ☎01.70.20.00.72; Air Transat ☎08.25.12.02.48; Bmi Baby ☎08.90.71.01.81; British Airways ☎08.25.82.54.00; easyjet ☎08.99.70.00.41; Lufthansa ☎08.26.10.33.34.

Airport Bordeaux-Mérignac ☎05.56.34.50.50, ⓦ www.bordeaux.aeroport.fr.

Banks and exchange The main banks along cours de l'Intendance and allées de Tourny offer 24hr ATMs. For changing money, there's a bureau de change at the airport and American Express in the city centre at 11 cours de l'Intendance (Mon–Fri 9.30am–5.30pm). Both handle the major foreign currencies and brands of traveller's cheques.

Boat trips The *Aliénor* (☎05.56.51.27.90, ⓦ www.bordeaux-resto.com) offers a varied programme, from dinner cruises and theme nights to a full day's jaunt with a stop at Bourg or Blaye, heading downstream, or Cadillac (cruise only €20; with *plat du jour* €30; full menu €45); you can take your own picnic. Boats leave from the Embarcadère des Quinconces on quai Louis-XVIII. In July and August the same company also run 90-minute harbour cruises on the *Aliénor II* (Mon–Fri 3pm & 4.30pm; €10), while the *Ville de Bordeaux* (☎05.56.52.88.88) offers a similar guided historical tour of the riverfront (Mon & Thurs 3pm; €10).

Books and newspapers The best place for English-language papers is the Relay Livres newsagent in the basement of the gare SNCF, under the main ticket desks. Otherwise, try Presse Gambetta on place Gambetta. France's largest independent bookstore, Mollat, 15 rue Vital-Carles (ⓦ www.mollat.com), has a good selection of local guides and maps, and stocks the city's widest range of English-language titles. Also worth a look is Bradley's Bookshop, 8 cours d'Albret (ⓦ www.bradleys-bookshop.com).

Bus departures Most regional bus services currently leave from various points around the esplanade des Quinconces, though there are plans to move them out of the centre to departure points near an appropriate tram station. For information on the latest situation contact CITRAM Aquitaine (☎05.56.43.68.43; ⓦ www.citram.com) or drop in at the "tbc" information office on the esplanade des Quinconces (see p.81), which also stocks bus timetables. Buy your tickets on the bus. Eurolines buses leave from outside their office opposite the train station at 32 rue Charles-Domercq (☎05.56.92.50.42, ⓦ www.eurolines.fr).

Car rental All the main car rental firms have offices in or around the train station and at the airport (numbers given in that order): Avis ☎08.20.61.16.74, ☎08.20.61.16.73 ⓦ www.avis.fr; Budget ☎05.56.91.41.70, ☎05.56.47.84.22 ⓦ www.budget.fr; Europcar ☎08.25.00.42.46, ☎05.56.34.05.79 ⓦ www.europcar.fr; Hertz ☎05.57.59.05.95, ☎08.25.00.24.00 ⓦ www.hertz.fr; National/Citer ☎05.56.92.19.62, ☎05.56.34.20.68 ⓦ www.national.fr and Sixt ☎05.56.92.08.35, ☎05.56.34.08.15 ⓦ www.sixt.fr.

Consulates Great Britain, 353 bd du Président-Wilson ☎05.57.22.21.10, ⓦ www.amb-grandebretagne.fr; USA, 10 place de la Bourse ☎05.56.48.63.80, ⓦ www.amb-usa.fr. The nearest Canadian consulate is in Toulouse: ☎05.61.52.19.06, ⓔ consulat.Canada.toulouse@wanadoo.fr. In Paris there are embassies for Australia ☎01.40.59.33.00, ⓦ www.france.embassy.gov.au; Ireland ☎01.44.17.67.00, ⓔ paris@dfa.ie; New Zealand ☎01.45.01.43.43, ⓦ www.nzembassy.com/france; South Africa ☎01.53.59.23.23, ⓦ www.afriquesud.net.

Hospital Centre Hospitalier Pellegrin, place Amélie-Raba-Léon (☎05.56.79.56.79), to the west of central Bordeaux, on tram line A.

Internet access Cyberstation, 23 cours Pasteur (Mon–Sat 9.30am–2am, Sun 2pm–2am); I-phone, 24 rue Palais-Gallien (daily 10am–midnight).

Police Commissariat Central, 23 rue François-de-Sourdis (☎05.57.85.77.77), west of centre on tram line A.

Post office The central post office is located at 52 rue Georges-Bonnac, 33000 Bordeaux. You'll find useful sub-post offices at 27 allées de Tourny and beside the junction of rue des Pilliers-de-Tutelle and rue St-Rémi.

Shopping and markets The main fresh-food **market** is the vast marché des Capucins (Tues–Sun 6am–1pm), while on Sunday mornings there's a lively food market towards the south end of the quais des Chartrons (7am–2pm). The square in front of St-Michel is the venue for flea markets (Tues–Fri and, the biggest, Sun morning) with more general fare on offer on Mondays and Saturdays (7am–4pm). Bordeaux's principal **shopping** streets are rue Ste-Catherine and rue Porte-Dijeaux. You'll find lipsmacking luxury food shops in and around place des Grands-Hommes, while antiques sellers gather at the south end of rue Notre-Dame in the Chartrons district. The main **wine shops** are all concentrated near the tourist office. La Vinothèque, right next door at 8 cours du 30-Juillet, stocks a broad range, mostly from the Bordeaux region. L'Intendant, 2 allées de Tourny (ⓦ www.chateauprimeur.com), specializes in Premiers

Grands Crus Classés (see p.79) and holds over 15,000 bottles in a specially designed circular tower with the oldest vintages at the top, while Badie, 62 allées de Tourny, also offers a good range of wine and local liqueurs. Maison des Millésimes at 37 rue Esprit-des Lois (ⓦwww.jackswines .com) sells more than six hundred Bordeaux wines and offers the opportunity to taste certain bottles. Bordeaux Magnum, as its name suggests, specializes in magnums (holding 1.5 litres) of Bordeaux wines and on Thursday evenings (5–8pm) holds free tasting hosted by a local producer; find it at 3 Rue Gobineau, behind the Maison du Vin.

Wine-tasting courses In summer (May–Oct) the Conseil Interprofessionnel du Vin de Bordeaux (CIVB) at La Maison du Vin, 3 cours du 30-Juillet (ⓣ05.56.00.22.88, ⓦecole.vins-bordeaux.fr), opposite the tourist office, holds introductory two-hour wine-tasting courses in English (Mon–Sat; €20). Reservations and further information available from the tourist office. For more serious study, their Wine School offers longer courses in various languages; the three-day "wine weekend", for example, costs €640 per person (including board and lodging) and the beginner's intensive three-day course €375.

The Médoc

The landscape of the **Médoc**, a long, thin slice of land northwest of Bordeaux wedged between the forests bordering the Atlantic coast and the Gironde estuary, is in itself rather monotonous. Its gravel plains occupying the west bank of the brown, island-spotted river rarely swell into anything resembling a hill, but these soils sustain Bordeaux's best vineyards, producing some of the world's finest **wines**. Until Dutch civil engineers were employed to drain the Médoc in the early seventeenth century, the area was largely marshland, good only for sheep, corn or wheat, and most transport was by water. A century later the sand and pebble ridges had been planted with vines and the area never looked back.

The D2 **wine route**, forking off the N215 just north of Bordeaux, passes through a string of small, prosperous towns sitting in an island of vines. While none is particularly interesting in itself, each is surrounded by an incredible concentration of top-name châteaux, many of which are open to visitors by appointment. First stop for most people is **Margaux**, home to the great Château Margaux and within easy reach of Château Palmer and many other Grands Crus Classés. From here it's a hop northwards across remnants of marsh and lesser vineyards before reaching **St-Julien** and the biggest of the wine towns, **Pauillac**. Again the châteaux come thick and fast on the waves of higher ground, led by the Rothschilds' estates and Château Latour, until the wine route reaches its end at **St-Estèphe**.

As you travel through the area, particularly around Margaux and Arcins, you'll see signs saying *non au contournement* or simply *non*, protesting against a proposed motorway and bridge across the Gironde. This is part of a plan for an

Estuary Pass

If you intend visiting a number of sights in the Médoc, it's worth getting a **Pass'Estuaire**, a free pass which entitles two people to discount prices on 38 sites around the Gironde estuary. The pass, which is available free at participating sites including Château Maucaillou (p.103) and Château Lannessan (p.103), Fort Médoc (p.103) and the museum at Pauillac (p.107).

The wines of the Médoc

The Médoc wine area is divided into two regional *appellations*: Haut-Médoc, from Bordeaux to St-Estèphe, and Médoc (sometimes known as Bas-Médoc), the area at the northern tip of the peninsula, which in general produces lower-quality red wines. Confusingly, when people talk about Médoc wines in general, they are usually referring to the far more important Haut-Médoc. This is where you'll find the "big six" communes with their individual labels – Margaux, St-Julien, Pauillac, St-Estèphe, Moulis and Listrac – and all the region's classified vineyards.

The Médoc as a whole produces almost exclusively **red wines**, from the grape varieties of Cabernet Sauvignon, Merlot, Cabernet Franc and, to a lesser degree, Malbec, Petit Verdot and Carmenère. Tannin-rich Cabernet Sauvignon is the quintessential Médoc grape. It gives body, bouquet, colour and maturing potential to the wine, while Merlot makes it rounder and softer. In general these are more delicate, distinctive wines showing greater finesse than the heartier St-Émilion (see p.131), particularly when properly aged, but there is a certain amount of variation. In **Margaux**, for example, where the soils are more sandy, wines contain a larger proportion of Merlot. Consequently these are the most supple and feminine of the Médoc wines and can be drunk younger, though they also age extremely well. Further north a higher clay content makes for darker, fuller-bodied wines around **St-Julien**, though they still mature relatively quickly, while the very gravelly soils of **Pauillac** favour Cabernet Sauvignon – hence a high concentration of top-rank vineyards producing very individual wines which benefit from ageing. The region's most fruity, full-bodied wines, often compared to St-Émilion, come from **St-Estèphe**, on the northern border of Haut-Médoc.

The majority of Médoc vineyards date from the late seventeenth and early eighteenth centuries. In 1855 the most prestigious wines were ranked into five **Crus Classés** ("Classified Growths") by a committee of Bordeaux brokers in order that only the best should be represented at the Great Exhibition in Paris. Much has changed since then and it is now generally acknowledged that, while the Premiers Crus ("First Growths") remain valid, the lower four rankings need a complete overhaul. There has been some tinkering over the last few years, including relegating a number of the poorer wines from the bottom of the table. The best noses in the business also spent more than eighteen months before refining the classification of the so-called **Crus Bourgeois**, some of which are considered superior to a number of Crus Classés and equal in price, in 2003. The ranking was sub-divided into Crus Bourgeois Exceptionnel, with just nine wines making the grade, 87 Crus Bourgeois Supérieur and 151 plain Crus Bourgeois, while 243 wines previously carrying the Cru Bourgeois label were delisted (many have appealed). Even so, purists still sniff that it's merely a marketing ploy and not a guarantee of true quality. Further down the scale again come the lowly but rapidly improving **Crus Artisans**. Indeed, with prices rising ever higher, it's among this last group that you'll probably find the best value for money in the Médoc. As a very general rule of thumb, expect to pay from €15 for a Cru Bourgeois, slightly less for Crus Artisans, while classified wines start at around €20 a bottle and can cost at least ten times that amount for the most sought-after names and vintages.

outer ring-road to the west of Bordeaux linking the A10 to the A63. The most northerly of the proposed routes cuts through the Médoc at Arcins and has, not surprisingly, raised a lot of opposition in the area. A public enquiry is due to take place in late- 2008 or early 2009.

Considering the number of visitors it attracts, the Médoc is surprisingly short of affordable or attractive places to stay, perhaps because many people come on a day-trip from Bordeaux. It's worth taking a little more time, however, and spending at least one night in the region. While it's easier to explore with your own car (see p.98 for Bordeaux rental outlets), there are regular **bus services** from Bordeaux via Margaux and St-Julien to Pauillac, and also a country **train** line which roughly tracks the D2 as far as Pauillac and then continues on to Lesparre, Soulac-sur-Mer and the Pointe-de-Grave.

To get to and from the east side of the Gironde, there's a handy car **ferry** between Lamarque and Blaye (see p.104). From mid-June to mid-September foot passengers and cyclists are served by a former river barge which makes the crossing from Vitrezay to Pauillac several times a week depending on the tides (€5; ℡05.46.49.89.89). Note that it's not possible to join this boat from Pauillac to Vitrezay.

Margaux and around

The small village of **MARGAUX**, some 20km north of Bordeaux on the D2, basks in the reflected glory of the surrounding châteaux, and not without reason. Château Margaux itself, arguably the prettiest in the Bordeaux region, sits right on the doorstep, while the renowned Château Palmer is within striking distance. With its helpful Maison du Vin, a couple of restaurants and even two hotels, the village makes a natural place to start exploring the Médoc.

Unless you've already picked up information in Bordeaux (see p.99), first stop should be the **Maison du Vin** (Jan–March Tues–Fri 10am–noon & 2–6pm; April & May 10am–1pm & 2–7pm; June–Sept Mon–Sat 10am–7pm, Sun 11am–4pm; Oct–Dec Mon–Sat 10am–noon & 2–6pm; ℡05.57.88.70.82, ℮syndicat .margaux@wanadoo.fr), on the main road through the village. They don't offer tastings, but sell a selection of local wines at châteaux prices and can advise on vineyard visits. It's necessary to book at least two weeks in advance (longer in summer) to visit the impeccable *chais* of **Château Margaux** (℡05.57.88.83.83, ⓦwww.chateau-margaux.com; by appointment only Mon–Fri 10am–noon & 2–4pm; closed Aug and during harvest; free), beyond the church on the east side of the village. Even without an appointment, however, it's worth approaching as far as the gates just to see its elegant Neoclassical facade, the work of Bordelais architect Louis Combes. The château's wine, a classified Premier Cru and world-famous in the 1940s and 1950s, went through a rough patch in the two succeeding decades but has improved markedly since the estate was bought by a Greek family in the 1980s, and is now back as one of Bordeaux's premier wines.

Just south on the D2, with its owners' French, English and Dutch flags clearly visible across the vines, **Château Palmer** (℡05.57.88.72.72, ⓦwww .chateau-palmer.com; by appointment only April–Oct Mon–Fri 10am–noon & 2–6.30pm; Nov–March Mon–Fri 9am–12.30pm & 2–5.30pm; free) is contrastingly welcoming to visitors. It is also Neoclassical in style, but this time with a strong hint of the Loire in its steep, grey-tiled roof and corner turrets. The very English name derives from a General Charles Palmer, from Bath, who bought the estate in 1814 only to mismanage it completely and go bankrupt. The wines were nevertheless classified in 1855 and now rank among Margaux's best. Another relatively easy place to visit is **Château Lascombes** (℡05.57.88.97.43, ⓦwww.chateau-lascombes.com; by appointment only daily 9.30–11.30am & 2–4.30pm; free), also a Cru Classé, on the northern outskirts of the village; it's of interest for its high-tech, computerized vinification methods.

In the village of **LABARDE**, 4km southeast of Margaux on the D209, **Château Siran** (℡05.57.88.34.04, ⓦwww.chateau-siran.com; daily 10.15am–6pm; free, tasting €5) occupies a pale ruby-coloured *chartreuse*. They produce a range of wines from a Haut-Médoc and a Bordeaux-Supérieur up to an excllent Cru Bourgeois Exceptionnel, recognised in the 2003 classification. As an added attraction, since 1980 they have followed the example of Mouton-Rothschild (see p.106), commissioning topical labels from well-known artists – most notably Joan Miró on a theme of the Football World Cup in 1982 – for their top wine under the Château Siran name.

Just to prove the area isn't exclusively about wine, Margaux village is also home to an artisan **chocolate maker**, Mademoiselle de Margaux (ⓦwww .mademoiselledemargaux.fr; April–Sept Mon–Sat 10am–1pm & 2–6.30pm; Oct–March Mon–Fri same hours), across the road from the Maison du Vin. Here, too, they offer tastings of their produce, such as *sarments du Médoc*, shaped appropriately like vine clippings, and the luscious *guinette*, a bitter cherry soaked in armagnac and dipped in dark chocolate.

Practicalities

Buses on the Bordeaux–Pauillac route stop in the centre of Margaux village, while the **gare SNCF** lies less than a kilometre to the southwest. The Maison du Vin (see p.101), which also doubles as a **tourist office**, can provide information about **accommodation** in the area, but the choice is rather limited. Within Margaux itself, on the main road coming in from the south, there's the moderately expensive but very comfortable *Le Pavillon de Margaux* (☎05.57.88.77.54, ⓔle-pavillon-margaux@wanadoo.fr; ➒), with a restaurant (lunch *formule* at €15, menus from €28). Your other option is the *Relais de Margaux* (☎05.57.88.38.30, ⓦwww .relais-margaux.fr; ➒) in its own grounds 2km east of the village. This complex comprises a modern luxury hotel with a couple of restaurants (main restaurant from €45; brasserie lunch menu at €19) plus golf course and spa facilities.

Besides the hotels, you can **eat** at Margaux's *Auberge de Savoie* (☎05.57.88.31.76; closed Sun eve & Jan), next to the Maison du Vin, with a lovely interior courtyard and good traditional food and menus at €26–42. Better still, head 4km south to the village of Labarde, to join the vineyard workers in the welcoming ⅍ *Auberge des Grands Vins* (weekday lunch menu €12, otherwise from €17; closed Sun, Mon & Tues eve), a country inn specializing in meats, fish and even cheese grilled on the open fire. Or, in spring and summer (April–Oct), there's nothing to beat the two *guinguettes* – casual, open-air restaurants – beside the river at **MACAU** port, 6km south of Margaux, where they serve platters of prawns, winkles, crabs and other delicacies straight from the Gironde (dishes €5–15).

North towards St-Julien

Northwest of Margaux lie the two less-well-known Haut-Médoc *appellations*, **Moulis** and **Listrac**. At just six hundred hectares, Moulis has the smallest area under vines, while Listrac boasts the highest elevation at a grand 43m above sea level. The **wines** are full-bodied and, while there are no classified châteaux in the district, there are some notable Crus Bourgeois and Crus Artisans. To draw the tourists, a couple of châteaux have set up their own museums, which merit a quick visit, and on the coast there's also a ruined fort to provide some relief from the wine trail. If you're looking for a base in the Médoc, this area is worth considering since there are some more affordable accommodation options over to the west, particularly around Castelnau-de-Médoc.

To sample some of the wine that **MOULIS-EN-MÉDOC** has to offer, head north on the D2 from Margaux for about 8km before turning left on the D5 to **Château Maucaillou** (℡05.56.58.02.58, ⓦwww.chateau-maucaillou.com; daily: May–Sept 10am–5pm; Oct–April 10–11am & 2–4pm; €7 including tasting, *chai* and tasting or museum only €4.60). The château, constructed in 1875 in a fanciful mix of architectural styles, produces an elegant, fruity Cru Bourgeois Supérieur as well as Haut-Médoc and Bordeaux AOC wines. The guided tour introduces you to the mysteries of modern wine production by visiting the vinification room and the *chai*, while you also see how things used to be in the unusually informative museum. Exhibits – mostly labelled in English – take you from planting via pruning and harvest to bottling, covering corks and cooperage on the way.

LAMARQUE village, just east of the D2, has the distinction of being home to an eleventh-century castle with turrets, ramparts and stone mullion windows. **Château de Lamarque** (℡05.56.58.90.03, ⓦwww.chateaudelamarque.com; Mon–Fri 9am–noon & 1–5pm; free), signed down a long alley in the middle of the village, is also a wine domaine, producing a Cru Bourgeois Supérieur and a rosé wine, unusual in this area. Unfortunately the guided tour doesn't take you inside the castle, but the vinification plant still has the traditional wooden vats, though they're only for show – inside each wooden casing is a modern vat.

Pick up some picnic provisions in the village before heading for the next stop, signed east off the D2 a little further north. On the banks of the Gironde, **Fort Médoc** (daily: April–Sept daily 9am–12.30pm & 1–7pm; Oct–March 10am–12.30pm & 1–5.30pm; €2.20) was designed by the prolific military architect Vauban to defend the estuary, and thus Bordeaux, against British attack in the late seventeenth century. It formed the western end of a chain of three forts slung across the river, the others being Blaye and the island Fort Paté, but Fort Médoc soon began subsiding in the marshy ground and was abandoned. Though little remains of the buildings, Vauban's signature is still apparent in the moats, grassy ramparts and in the star-shaped ground-plan, and in summer the ruins have a leafy charm, marred only by a view of the nuclear power station across the river just north of Blaye. A very slow restoration project is under way, in aid of which there's an annual **jazz festival** in mid-July (see box on p.76 for details).

Like Château Maucaillou above, **Château Lanessan** (℡05.56.58.94.80 ⓦwww .lanessan.com; daily 9.30am–noon & 2–5.30pm; €5.50) distinguishes itself with a small museum, in this case showcasing horse-drawn carriages, in addition to its two highly rated but reasonably priced Haut-Médoc Crus Bourgeois Supérieurs. It's signed west off the D2 down a dirt track about 5km north of Lamarque, not long after **CUSSAC** village; note that it's the second château you come to at the end of the track. As with so many Médoc châteaux, Lanessan was rebuilt in the late nineteenth century, in this case by someone with a taste for neo-Tudor gables, mullions and tall skinny chimneys, and also with a passion for horses. The stable block, where the museum is housed, was the last word in luxury: wood-lined stalls, marble water-troughs, even a tap for running water installed long before the château boasted such amenities. Not surprisingly, the carriages some of these pampered beasts pulled are also in immaculate condition. There are only ten in all, dating from 1884 to 1903, but the guide will explain what they were used for and point out their special features, such as their particular braking, lighting or suspension systems. Appropriately, Lanessan is also now home to the Bordeaux International Carriage Driving School and, if you phone a day or so in advance, you can tour the domaine by carriage (90min; €80 for up to five people).

Practicalities

Lamarque and Cussac are both stops on the Bordeaux-Pauillac **bus** route while **trains** stop at the less convenient Listrac-Moulis **gare SNCF**, midway between Moulis and Lamarque. Those with their own transport can cross the Gironde here on the Lamarque–Blaye **ferry** (30min; ☎05.57.42.04.49); there are at least four sailings per day in winter rising to ten during the summer peak.

As for **accommodation** in the area, one of the wings of *Château Maucaillou* (see previous page) has been converted into a rather grand *chambre d'hôte* (☎05.56.58.01.23; ⑤). The other options are around the workaday town of **CASTELNAU-DE-MÉDOC**, on the main N125 Bordeaux–Pointe de Grave road 4km southwest of Moulis. *Domaine de Carrat* (☎ & ☎05.56.58.24.80; ③; closed Christmas school hols) is a friendly *chambre d'hôte* 500m southwest of Castelnau on the N125 and down a long drive. Its three spacious rooms, all en suite, occupy an old stable block among the pine trees; no meals, but kitchen facilities are available. Or, for something much grander, book well ahead to stay in one of four large *chambre d'hôtes* decorated with family heirlooms in 🛏 *Château du Foulon* (☎05.56.58.20.18, ⊛www.au-chateau.com/Foulon.htm; ⑤; closed Christmas & New Year), a lovely nineteenth-century château surrounded by fifty hectares of park on the southern edge of Castelnau.

Five kilometres further north along the N125, **LISTRAC** is home to a small modern hotel, the *Auberge des Vignerons* (☎05.56.58.08.68, ☎05.56.58.08.99; ③; closed two weeks in Feb) on the main road with simple rooms and a decent restaurant (closed Sat lunch, Sun eve & Mon; lunch menus from €16, eves from €24). A more attractive alternative is the *chambr d'hôte* at *Château Cap Léon Veyrin* (☎05.56.58.07.28, ⊛capleonveyrin@aol.com; ③), a working vineyard 3km east of Listrac, on the edge of **DONISSAN** village.

When it comes to **eating**, by far the best restaurant in the area is the 🛏 *Lion d'Or* (☎05.56.58.96.79; closed Sun & Mon, also July & two weeks at Christmas) in **ARCINS** on the D2 a couple of kilometres south of Lamarque. Not only is the cooking excellent – from homemade pheasant terrine to local lamb or rabbit stew – and good value with a menu at €13.30 (Sat eve *à la carte* only, from around €30), but you can even take your own wine – local reds only. If they're full or closed, head to **LAMARQUE** and the very agreeable *L'Escale* (July & Aug daily; Sept–June closed Tues), down by the port; in season look out for elvers or young eels (*pibales*), shad (*alose*), lamprey (*lamproie*) and other local delicacies on their well-priced regional menus (€16–26).

St-Julien to Pauillac

After crossing lower, marshy land given over to poplars and pasture, the D2 wine route crests a slight rise before being met by the vines of **St-Julien**. Here you're back among the big-name estates – including Talbot, Branaire and Léoville-Barton, the latter graced by a beautiful eighteenth-century *chartreuse* still owned by the Irish Barton family. Here on the undulating higher ground the estuary is more in evidence and **Château Beychevelle** (☎05.56.73.20.70, ⊛www.beychevelle.com; May–Sept Mon–Sat 10am–noon & 1.30–5pm; Oct–April Mon–Fri same hours; free; visit with tasting by appointment only; €8) in particular takes full advantage of this, with its long prospect down sloping lawns to the river over a kilometre away. Its name recalls that the duc d'Epernon, Grand Admiral of France, lived here in the seventeenth century; as ships passed by the command was issued to *baisse-voile* ("strike sail") in salute. The château itself is a classic,

△ Château Pichon-Longueville

long, low, white-stone Médoc mansion surrounded by immaculate lawns and iron railings.

Two kilometres further on you pass through **ST-JULIEN** village, where the **restaurant** *Le St-Julien* (☎05.56.59.63.87; €35 *à la carte*; closed Sun) – not to be confused with the *Relais St-Julien* in the same village – is known for its excellent local dishes. Otherwise, there's no reason to linger here. Better instead to press on northwards to the neighbouring **Pauillac** district and the most important of the Bordeaux vineyards: no fewer than three of the five Premiers Crus come from these stony soils. Vineyards here occupy larger single tracts of land than elsewhere in the Médoc, and consequently neighbouring wines can differ markedly: a good vintage Lafite is perfumed and refined, whereas a Mouton-Rothschild is strong and dark and requires lengthy ageing to reach its best.

Though not among the top three, **Château Pichon-Longueville** (☎05.56.73.17.17, ⓦwww.pichonlongueville.com; by appointment only daily 9–12.30am & 2–5pm; free), one of the first châteaux you come to from the south, is not only a striking building but its state-of-the-art facilities provide one of the area's most interesting visits. Since acquiring the estate in 1987, the French insurance group AXA has invested enormous sums in restoring the château and in completely rebuilding the vinification plant and *chais* which are now partially underground. Their design allows year-round visits and enables you to see everything from where the grapes are sorted to the bottling plant and a store room containing one million precious bottles.

In the nineteenth century, Baron Joseph de Pichon-Longueville decided to divide his domaine equally between his two sons and three daughters. In the end, only two of the children inherited: Raoul took over the boys' share, including the main château, while Virginie inherited the larger portion of land overlooking the river. Nowadays, **Château Pichon-Longueville Comtesse de Lalande** (☎05.56.59.19.40, ⓦwww.pichon-lalande.com; by appointment only May–Aug Mon–Sat 9–11.30am & 2–4.30pm; Sept–April Mon–Fri 9–11.30am & 2–4pm; free), immediately over the road from its sibling, is once again owned by a woman, May Eliane de Lencquesaing. Apart from its Grands

Giant of the skies

Components of the **Airbus A380**, the world's largest aeroplane capable of carrying some 550 passengers, are made in factories in Germany, Spain, Britain and France. They are then assembled in Toulouse, 250 kilometres west of Bordeaux. Smaller pieces, such as the cockpit, are moved in a special cargo plane, but the wings and body sections are too big. Instead they have to go on an extraordinary – and costly – journey by boat, barge and road through southwest France. Specially adapted cargo boats bring the pieces up the Gironde as far as Pauillac, where they're offloaded onto a huge tailor-made barge. The barge chugs upstream to Bordeaux, where it has to get under the low-slung Pont de Pierre. This delicate operation involves partially submerging the barge and waiting for low tide when it can squeeze under the bridge with just centimetres to spare. It's then plain sailing down to Langon. Here the pieces are put on lorries 50m long, 8m wide and with no less than 96 tyres – yes, also built specially – for the last leg of the journey on a specially modified road. It takes the convoys three nights to cover the 240km from Langon to Toulouse travelling at an average speed of 25kph. It's all very impressive, and worth seeing if you're in the area when a cargo is passing through; ask at the tourist offices in Pauillac, Bordeaux and Langon. It does make you wonder, however, if it wouldn't just have been so much simpler to build the assembly plant in Bordeaux.

Crus wines, there are lovely views from the terrace and an extensive collection of glassware, from Roman times to contemporary artworks by Chihuly and others, on display in the former orangerie.

A visit to **Château Mouton-Rothschild** (☎05.56.73.21.29, Ⓦwww.bpdr .com; by appointment only Mon–Thurs 9.15–12.30am & 2–5.30pm, Fri 9.15am–12.30pm & 2–4.30pm; €5, or €13 with one tasting), 2km northwest of Pauillac, on the other hand, is more about the mystique of the place. Though it is now one of the area's three Premiers Crus – the others being Lafite-Rothschild and Latour, with its distinctive round tower – Mouton-Rothschild was ranked only as a Second Growth until the classification was revised in 1973. That this happened was largely thanks to the efforts of Baron Philippe de Rothschild (1902–88), a great publicist and innovator who built up the estate after 1922 and the first producer to bottle all his wines at the château to ensure quality. The *mouton*, by the way, does not refer to a sheep, but is believed to derive from the little hill (*monton* in local dialect) on which the best vines grow; the two rams on the family crest made their appearance later, as a visual pun.

The château itself (not open to the public) is pretty but surprisingly unassuming. The old underground *chais*, however, are suitably atmospheric, the tunnel walls thick with a purple-black deposit accumulated over decades of condensing wine vapour. Two of the tunnels contain the family's private cellar of some 90,000 bottles of the world's top wines and there is also a priceless archive of every vintage produced on the estate over more than a century. Since 1955 international artists – Braque, Henry Moore and Warhol amongst others – have been invited to design the labels for each vintage, while even greater art treasures are in store, from Mesopotamian wine jugs to French tapestries, in the next-door museum of "wine in art" created by the baron in 1926, where the tour ends.

As these great estates developed in the eighteenth century, so **PAUILLAC** grew into a bustling port, then faded somewhat after the arrival of steamships, which sailed on up to Bordeaux, before undergoing a revival in recent years. It is now easily the largest town in the Médoc but, while its little fishing harbour and riverfront are pretty enough, they can't counteract the looming presence of the nuclear power plant across the Gironde, while immediately east is the dock where components of the Airbus A380 planes are offloaded onto barges (see box opposite). Nevertheless, it serves as a reasonable base, with transport services, banks, a post office and a few accommodation options in the area. It is also home to an endearing museum, **Le Petit Musée d'Automates** (July & Aug Mon–Sat 10.30am–7pm, Sun 2.30–7pm; May, June, Sept Tues–Sat 10am–12.30pm & 2.30–7pm; July & Aug Tues–Sat 10am–1pm & 2–7pm, Sun 2–7pm; Oct–April Thurs–Sat 10am–12.30pm & 2.30–7pm; €3); turn up rue Aristide-Briand from the quay near the jetty and it's a few doors along on the right. Behind the Aladdin's cave of a shop the owners have created several anthropomorphic scenes of animals' lives, of which the highlight is a chaotic classroom. Great for kids.

Practicalities

Pauillac is the terminus for **buses** from Bordeaux; they stop on the riverfront near the *mairie* and at the **gare SNCF** on the northern edge of town, about five minutes' walk from the centre. The big and helpful **Maison du Tourisme et du Vin** (July & Aug Mon–Sat 9.30am–7pm, Sun 10am–1pm & 2–6pm; Sept–June Mon–Sat 9.30am–12.30pm & 2–6pm, Sun 10.30am–12.30pm & 3–6pm; ℡05.56.59.03.08, ⓦwww.pauillac-medoc.com) lies south along the waterfront. They can help book accommodation (€3) and make appointments to visit the surrounding châteaux (€3.90 per château). They also run their own vineyard tours (€8; no children under 8 years old) as well as various other activities, including river cruises (mid-July to late Aug five departures each Sunday; €10), and sell a broad range of Médoc wines at châteaux prices.

Wine also features strongly at **festivals** in Pauillac, one of the most active towns in the Médoc. Events include the Fête de l'Agneau in May (see box on p.76 for details), summer night markets and organized walks – even a marathon through the vines. Walking and biking are good ways to explore this area. The tourist office can provide route maps and **bike rental** is available through Sport Nature, 6 rue du Maréchal-Joffre (℡05.57.75.22.60), heading north from the town centre.

Pauillac even offers **Internet** access at its Espace Multimédia, 20 route de la Rivière (Mon 2–6.15pm, Tues–Fri 10am–12.30pm & 2–6.15pm), a short walk south of the tourist office.

The best place to **stay** in central Pauillac is the attractive *chambre d'hôte* 🏠 *La Rivière* with pretty rooms and a garden at the quieter, north end of the quays (℡05.56.59.19.62, ⓦwww.chambres-dhotes-pauillac.com; ❹). The other alternative is the rather overpriced *Hôtel de France et d'Angleterre* (℡05.56.59.01.20, ⓦwww.hoteldefrance-angleterre.com; ❹; closed mid-Dec to early Jan) facing the little harbour; rooms vary, so ask to see several. In the area around Pauillac, there's another excellent *chambre d'hôte* about 8km northwest near the village of **CISSAC**: *Château Gugès* (℡05.56.59.58.04, ⓦwww.chateau-guges.com; ❹), in a large nineteenth-century house attached to a vineyard on the road to Gunes; with just two rooms, you'll need to book well ahead. If money is no object, treat yourself to a night at the plush *Château Cordeillan-Bages* (℡05.56.59.24.24, ⓦwww .cordeillanbages.com; closed Dec to mid–Feb; ❾; menus €60–110, restaurant closed Mon & lunchtime Tues & Sat), a seventeenth-century manor house with 25 immaculate rooms on Pauillac's southern outskirts. The hotel doubles as a very upmarket school where you can take courses in appreciation of local wines and gastronomy (℡05.56.73.19.33). At the other end of the scale, there's a spruce,

welcoming riverfront **campsite** *Les Gabarreys* (℡05.56.59.10.03, ⓔcamping
.les.gabarreys@wanadoo.fr; closed Nov–Easter) a kilometre south of the tourist
office on route de la Rivière.

Most **restaurants** in Pauillac are conveniently located on the riverfront across
the road from the harbour. Best of the bunch is *Le St-Martin* (weekday lunch
menus from €11.90, eves & weekends from €16.50; closed Mon & Christmas
hols), offering Gironde sturgeon with ginger and saffron butter and snails with
Roquefort among other local specialities, plus some vegetarian dishes. Next
along, *La Salamandre* (weekday lunch menus from €12, or from €23 eves &
weekends) is a popular café, bar, tobacconist and restaurant all rolled into one.
It covers all bases foodwise, too, from generous pizzas and salads to fusion
food, though you're best off sticking to the simpler dishes. For something a
little more classy, *Le Pauillac* offers lots of seafood and well-prepared regional
cuisine (℡05.56.59.19.20; lunch menus from €17, eves & weekends from €21).
Another good option is the *Café Lavinal* (℡05.57.75.00.09; Sept–June closed
Sun) in the village of **BAGES**, a couple of kilometres southwest of Pauillac.
This café-brasserie belongs to the same group as the *Château Cordeillan-Bages*
hotel (see previous page), so the cooking is pretty top-notch but at more affordable prices; a *plat du jour* (weekday lunches only) will set you back €10 and a
full *à la carte* meal in the region of €40. Across the square, *Au Baba d'Andréa*
(Tues–Sat) is a traditional style **bakery** where you can buy wonderful breads,
pastries and – of course – *rhum baba* baked in an open oven.

St-Estèphe

North of Pauillac, the wine commune of **St-Estèphe** is Médoc's largest
appellation, consisting predominantly of Crus Bourgeois vineyards and producers belonging to the local *cave coopérative*, **Marquis de St-Estèphe**, on the
D2 (Jan–March Mon–Fri 8.30am–12.15pm & 2–6pm; April–Dec Mon–Fri
8.30am–12.15pm & 2–6pm, Sat 10am–noon & 2–5pm). One of the *appellation's* five Crus Classés is produced at the the unmistakable **Château Cos
d'Estournel** (℡05.56.73.15.50, ⓦwww.estournel.com; by appointment only
Mon–Fri 9am–12.30pm & 2–5.30pm; free), also on the D2 about 4km north of
Pauillac. There's no château as such but its *chais* are housed in an over-the-top
nineteenth-century French version of a pagoda, clearly visible from the road,

Aquitaine caviar

While most people associate **sturgeon** and **caviar** (the eggs of sturgeon) with Russia
and Iran, in the early twentieth century local fishermen produced up to five tonnes of
caviar a year from European sturgeon caught in the Gironde estuary. By the 1970s
the haul had dwindled to nothing thanks to overfishing and habitat loss through
dredging and building barrages and, in 1982, the Euoprean sturgeon was declared a
protected species. It is Europe's biggest freshwater fish, adult males growing up to
1.5m long and 15 kilos in weight. The Gironde is the only waterway in Europe where
the species can still be found, swimming upstream each year from April to June to
breed in the Dordogne and Garonne rivers. As with wild salmon and the lamprey (see
box on p.130), the fry then migrate downstream to the estuary and eventually to the
open sea. A program introduced in 1982 to rescue the species has seen only limited
success and the fish remains critically endangered. The caviar and sturgeon meat
you'll find in local restaurants comes from locally farmed Russian sturgeon.

complete with a door which supposedly once adorned the sultan of Zanzibar's palace. The exotic touches are the work of Louis-Gaspard d'Estornel, who founded the vineyard in 1811. He made such a success exporting his wines to India that he earned the nickname the Maharajah of St-Estèphe. When one of his consignments arrived in India the sale fell through, so he shipped it back again. He discovered the wine had improved markedly during the long sea voyage, presumably due to the constant temperature and rocking motion. So began a bizarre but highly profitable practice where wines were shipped to India and back and then sold at a premium, marked "Retour des Indes".

The village of **ST-ESTÈPHE** itself is a sleepy affair dominated by its land-mark, the eighteenth-century *church of St-Étienne*, every inch of its interior painted, gilded and sculpted; the choir is particularly beautiful. The small, active *Maison du Vin* (June & Sept Mon–Fri 10am–5.30pm, Sat 1.30–5.30pm; July & Aug Mon–Sat 10am–7pm; Oct–May Mon–Fri 10am–12.30pm & 1.30–5pm; ℡05.56.59.30.59, ✉mv-se@wanadoo.fr), is hidden in the church square.

St-Estèphe marks the end of the wine-route. Beyond here you enter a more hilly, but also more marshy area which wasn't reclaimed until the nineteenth century. Local vineyards produce high-quality table wines mostly under the Médoc *appellation*, which often need laying down for several years. It's worth making a brief excursion to visit the pretty, rose-coloured **Château Loudenne** (℡05.56.73.17.80, ⓦwww.lafragette.com; Apri–Oct daily 9.30–11am & 2.30–5.30pm; Nov–March by appointment only Mon–Fri, same hours; €5), some eight kilometres north of St-Estèphe. Loudenne produces a very drinkable Cru Bourgeois Supérieur under the Médoc AOC as well as white and rosé Bordeaux wines. The museum is very well laid out, following a year in the life of the vineyard, and includes some rare pieces, such as an astonishingly large Spanish terracotta fermenting jar. Afterwards, take the time to wander round the gardens and down to the river.

Instead of retracing your steps, lovers of Romanesque architecture should loop back inland via the village of **VERTHEUIL-EN-MÉDOC** to visit the eleventh-century **Église St-Pierre**. Inside the abbey church, located on the central square, you'll find some fine carved capitals, echoed by the carved wooden choir stalls of a later date.

Practicalities

The nearest **train** station is at Pauillac. For an elegant place to **stay**, head south two kilometres to the village of **LEYSSAC**, where *Château Pomys* (℡05.56.59.73.44, ⓦwww.chateaupomys.com; ⑤) offers ten comfortable rooms and an elegant restaurant (menus €18 & €35; closed Mon) in a mansion set in its own park; it's also a working vineyard producing a Cru Bourgeois St-Estèphe. There are also several welcoming *chambres d'hôtes* in the area, including *Le Clos de Puyzac*, 3km west in **PEZ** village (℡05.56.59.35.28, ✉stephmetzger@wanadoo.fr; ③) and, in **VERTHEUIL**, the very comfortable ⚘ *Château le Souley* (℡05.56.41.98.76, ⓦwww.lesouley.com; ④) which also offers *table d'hôte* on request.

As for places to **eat**, your best bet is *Le Peyrat* (May–Sept closed Sun eve; Oct–April closed Sat eve & Sun), on the banks of the Gironde one kilometre east of St-Estèphe. Unfortunately, the views are again dominated by the nuclear power station opposite, but it's the food you've come for: honest country cooking, such as eels in parsley and *magret* laced in local honey, or scallops with cèpes in season. The four-course weekday lunch menu will set you back just €11; evening and weekend menus start at €16.

Graves

The **Graves** region, encompassing a crescent of vineyards hugging the left bank of the Garonne southeast of Bordeaux, is the oldest of the city's wine-producing areas, originally planted during Roman times. Though now largely eclipsed by the Médoc, red Graves wines once provided the bulk of Bordeaux's wine exports, notably from the Pessac-Léognan *appellation* on the city's southern outskirts, where Château Haut-Brion still maintains a toehold amongst the suburban sprawl. The Graves heartland contains a series of wine towns which were once bustling river ports and are now linked by the main Bordeaux–Toulouse train line and busy N113. This isn't an area in which you'll want to

Graves wines

The name **Graves** derives from *grabas*, the local term for the bed of sand and river pebbles, over three metres thick in places, deposited over the centuries by the Garonne. Though hostile to most other crops, these harsh, gravelly soils provide the perfect conditions for vines – not only are they well drained but the stones' reflected heat also ensures good, all-round ripening. The region contains three main *appellations*: **Graves** and **Pessac-Léognan**, both producing red and dry white wines, and the medium-sweet **Graves Supérieures**. Within this area the Sauternes enclave merits its own *appellation* (see p.114).

Until the eighteenth century Graves was Bordeaux's foremost wine-producing region. The red wines in particular were much in demand, with as much as sixteen million litres being exported annually to London by the late twelfth century, a figure that was not equalled until the 1960s. Graves' golden age, however, was between the fifteenth and eighteenth centuries when many of today's great vineyards developed. Most notable among these was **Château Haut-Brion** where modern techniques introduced by the Pontac family revolutionized the production process. The Pontacs were also the first to market their wine under its château name, an event recorded by the London diarist Samuel Pepys in 1663: "Drank a sort of French wine, called Ho Bryan, that hath a good and most particular taste that I ever met with."

As the Médoc's star rose in the eighteenth century, so Graves' began to wane. Outbreaks of oïdium and then the deadly **phylloxera** in the late 1800s led many growers to turn their land over to pine trees, the only other crop able to tolerate such stony soils, and by 1935 the area under vines had decreased from 50 square kilometres to a mere 15 square kilometres. In the postwar period, however, Graves wines have enjoyed a **renaissance** and previously neglected vineyards are once again producing quality wines. In recognition of this fact a **classification** system was introduced in the 1950s establishing sixteen Crus Classés, all of which fall within the Pessac-Léognan area. (Previously, only Château Haut-Brion was deemed worthy, being granted Premier Cru Classé status when Bordeaux wines were classified in 1855.)

Red wines comprise around seventy percent of Graves output. In general they have more body than the Médoc reds and age well over five to ten years to yield a fine, aromatic wine. Their distinctive flavour results from the balance of Cabernet Sauvignon, Merlot and Cabernet Franc grape varieties. Dry white Graves – a blend of Sémillon, Sauvignon and Muscadelle grapes – have evolved considerably over recent years to rank among the region's finest. The best, now often aged in oak barrels, peak at three to four years of age. Though Graves Crus Classés fetch up to €50 a bottle, the majority of Graves wines sell for well under €15.

linger, but it's worth ducking off the main roads to visit fourteenth-century **Château de la Brède**, home to the philosopher Montesquieu, and at least some of the Graves' myriad wine producers. A good starting point is **Portets**, one of the more appealing riverside towns with a clutch of châteaux noted for their gardens or architecture as well as their wines. For other ideas, call in at **Podensac**'s well-run information centre, the Maison des Graves, which showcases a broad selection of local producers.

The region is poorly served by **public transport**. Local trains track the River Garonne, stopping at Portets, Podensac and Barsac, while the only useful bus services are those from Bordeaux to La Brède.

La Brède

One of the first villages you come to on leaving Bordeaux is surprisingly free of vines. Instead, sleepy **LA BRÈDE** is famous as the home of the philosopher Baron de La Brède et de Montesquieu who was born in nearby **Château de la Brède** in 1689.

The little **Château de la Brède** (45min guided tour: April–June Sat, Sun & public hols 2–6pm; July–Sept Mon & Wed–Sun 2–6pm; Oct–11 Nov Sat, Sun & public hols 2–5.30pm; €6.50; park only €2.50), now owned by a private foundation, is located just west of the village. It is encircled by a picturesque moat and a vast park, created by Montesquieu, which help soften the building's somewhat austere edges.

Though he spent his winters in Paris hobnobbing with fellow philosophers, Montesquieu revelled in the peace and quiet of his country retreat. This is where he wrote some of his best-known essays, among them the highly influential political treatise *L'Esprit des Lois* ("*The Spirit of Laws*"), and where he amassed a fabulous library of five thousand books, which was so weighty that the ceiling of the entrance hall below had to be strengthened with six stout, oak pillars. Sadly, they are no longer required. In 1926 Montesquieu's cash-strapped descendants were forced to sell 1500 volumes, followed in 1939 by his manuscripts; the remaining books were donated to Bordeaux library for safekeeping in 1995.

Other of Montesquieu's possessions have survived, including several sturdy travelling trunks and furniture he brought back from his travels. His writing table occupies pride of place in the wood-panelled bedroom downstairs which he used towards the end of his life. Here, too, is a rare likeness – a profile in bas-relief sculpted just before he died in 1755. In his old age, his sight failing but his mind as sharp as ever, Montesquieu obliged his secretary to sleep in a small, adjoining bedroom, ready to take notes whenever inspiration struck. Records show that few secretaries sustained the onslaught for long.

There's a well-organised **tourist information** office (Mon–Sat: 15 June– 15 Sept 10am–1pm & 2–6pm; 16 Sept–14 June 9am–noon & 2–6pm; ℡05.56.78.47.72, ⓦwww.otmontesquieu.com) on the main road going through the village, which offers wine tours (15 June–15 Sept daily; €10 per person) amongst other activities.

If you're in La Brède around lunchtime, book a table at the little **restaurant** *La Table du Cercle de l'Avenir Brédois* (℡05.56.20.27.30; Mon–Thurs lunch only, Fri lunch & dinner; closed Aug), in the village centre just behind the *mairie*. It is run by an association created in 1904 to promote the local wines and serves traditional cuisine. A *plat du jour* costs €10 and the *menu du jour* €15 at lunchtime, rising to €25 on Friday evenings.

Portets to Podensac

PORTETS, set slightly off the N113 east of La Brède, is one of the Graves' more promising riverside towns with its neat church square and a quiet picnic spot down by the *halte nautique*. The main reason for coming here is to visit the delightful **Château de Mongenan** (mid-Feb to June, Nov & Dec Sat, Sun & public hols 2–6pm; July & Aug daily 10am–7pm; Sept & Oct daily 2–6pm; closed Jan to mid-Feb; €6) on Portets' western outskirts. This pretty little château contains a museum of eighteenth-century life commemorating one of its former owners, Antoine de Valdec de Lessart, who served as foreign minister under Louis XVI before being executed during the Revolution. Rare original documents, period costumes, faïence and fabrics fill every corner. There's a room devoted to de Lessart's herbarium as well as a *lieu à l'anglaise* – an indoor toilet complete with grape-draped cover, all the rage in the late 1700s – and a somewhat spooky mock-up of a Masonic lodge.

In 1741 de Lessart's predecessor, Baron de Gasq, created a beautiful, walled botanical garden inspired by Jean-Jacques Rousseau. It still exists today in front of the house, heavy with the perfume of old-fashioned roses, herbs, aromatic and medicinal plants alongside almost-forgotten varieties of vegetables. The family also continues traditional methods of wine production and you can end the visit by sampling their oak-aged red and white Graves. Tastings are also available in nearby **Château de Portets** (℡05.56.67.12.30; Mon–Fri by appointment only; free), a much grander building a few hundred metres away overlooking the river, which also once belonged to the de Gasq family. You can't see inside, but the lovely formal garden is worth a visit – and the wines are good.

For information about other local vineyards, head south another 8km to **PODENSAC** where you'll find the helpful **Maison des Graves** (May–Oct Mon–Fri 9.30am–6.30pm, Sat, Sun & public hols 10.30am–6.30pm; Nov–April Mon–Fri 9am–6pm; ℡05.56.27.09.25, ⓦwww.vins-graves.com) on the town's western edge. Their cellars represent over three hundred wines from 150 properties in the Graves and Pessac-Léognan regions; prices are only a few cents

---

Riding the wave

If you're exploring the lower stretches of the lower Garonne and Dordogne rivers in spring or autumn, don't be surprised to see dozens of surfers, kayakers and jet-skiers surfing *up* the river on a **tidal bore** – a series of about a dozen waves up to two metres high which race upstream for 150km at between 15 and 30kph. These waves form when exceptionally high tides funnelled up a narrow and gently sloping estuary push up and over the water flowing downstream. Though hardly the most thrilling ride in the world, surfing the *mascaret*, as it is known locally, first became popular in the late 1970s on the Garonne between Cambes and Cadillac. Then the action moved north to the Dordogne River, focusing around St-Pardon, just downstream from Libourne. It's now become something of a tradition, helped by the fact that this is the last tidal bore still running in France; the rest have fallen victim to flood-protection schemes and other forms of river management.

Apart from St-Pardon, the best spots to witness the *mascaret* are the Gironde estuary near Margaux and the Garonne between Portets and Podensac. The biggest waves are likely to occur at the time of the spring and autumn equinox (around 21 March 21 and Sept 23) – autumn is generally better because the level of the river is lower and the effect is therefore more pronounced. Spectators need to get in position shortly after low tide, and make sure to stand on a bridge or somewhere well above the water to avoid getting swamped, if not washed away.

above châteaux rates. To help narrow the choice, it's possible to sample a couple of wines for free. Though staff can't arrange châteaux visits for you, they provide a list of those that accept visitors together with a useful map of the region (*Carte oe notouristique Graves & Sauternes*).

One of the larger vineyards in the area and one of the easier to visit is **Château de Chantegrive** (℡05.56.27.17.38, ⓦwww.chantegrive.com; Mon–Sat 9am–12.30pm & 1.30–5pm; free) on the southwest edge of Podensac. It's of interest mainly for its ultra-modern vinification techniques and superb red-wine *chais* of over six hundred oak barrels. They produce a range of well-rated Graves red wines in addition to a prestigious, oak-aged dry white and a sweet wine under the Cérons *appellation*.

Sauternes, Barsac and Langon

The little River Ciron forms the eastern boundary of a region famous for a sweet white wine justly described as "bottled sunlight". Compared with the Graves, the **Sauternes** hills are slightly higher, the landscape more rolling and every inch of space is covered with neat rows of vines presided over by noble châteaux. The foremost of these, **Château d'Yquem**, requires a bit of organizing to visit, but plenty of others are more than happy to offer tastings and tours of their *chais*. **Château de Malle** also provides a rare opportunity to peek inside a lived-in château and stroll around its elegant Italianate garden. The region boasts a number of recommended restaurants, both in Sauternes village itself and across the Ciron in **Barsac**, which has its own sweet white *appellation*. The main service town here is **Langon**, just outside the Sauternes region to the east, which also provides a convenient jumping-off point for the extravagantly decorated **Château Roquetaillade**, one of several local "Clémentine" fortresses built by relatives of Pope Clément V.

You can reach both Barsac and Langon via **public transport**, either by local trains on the Bordeaux–Agen line or by regional bus services operating out of Bordeaux (see p.98). If you want to explore slightly further inland, though, particularly around Sauternes, you really need your own transport.

Sauternes village

SAUTERNES itself is a trim but sedate village dominated by a pretty church at one end, and the *mairie* and **Maison du Sauternes** (Mon–Fri 9am–7pm, Sat & Sun 10am–7pm; ℡05.56.76.69.83, ⓦwww.maisondusauternes.com) at the other. The *maison* is a treasure trove of golden bottles with white-and-gold labels sold at château prices. Cheapest is their own, blended *Duc de Sauternes* at just over €11 a bottle; free tastings available.

Sauternes wines

The distinctive golden wine of **Sauternes** is certainly sweet, but also round, full-bodied and spicy, with a long aftertaste. It's not necessarily a dessert wine, either: the balance of sugar and acidity marries well with Roquefort and other strong cheeses, delicately flavoured fish and foie gras. Sauternes should be drunk chilled but not icy, somewhere around 8–10°C.

The main grape variety is Sémillon, blended with Sauvignon and usually a tiny amount of Muscadelle for its musky aroma. Gravelly terraces with a limestone sub-soil help create the smooth, subtle Sauternes taste, but mostly it's due to a peculiar microclimate of morning autumn mists and hot, sunny afternoons which causes the *Botrytis cinerea* fungus, or **"noble rot"**, to flourish on the grapes. By penetrating the skin, the mould allows water to evaporate, thus concentrating the sugars and pectins and intensifying the flavours.

Harvest time is a nerve-racking period for Sauternes producers. The climate has to be just right for *Botrytis* to work its magic: too much rain and the grapes soak up water again like a sponge; leave it too late and there's a risk of frost damage. As a result, harvests are both unpredictable and time-consuming. Each grape is individually picked only when it's reached the exact point of shrivelled, rotting maturity, a process which can take up to two months with pickers passing over the same vine again and again. Many grapes are rejected, giving an average yield of perhaps only one glass per vine – as opposed to one to three bottles elsewhere in the region. Though they can be drunk young and fruity, Sauternes develop their full body only at around ten years and are not truly at their best until at least twenty, even thirty years old. Not surprisingly, this is a luxury drink, with bottles of Château d'Yquem, in particular, fetching hundreds, sometimes thousands, of euros. In 2006, a 1787 Château d'Yquem became the most expensive bottle of wine in the world when it was sold at auction to an American for around €80,000.

Sauternes wines first came to the fore in the seventeenth century, when they were much prized in Holland. Such was their importance, in fact, that the wines were included in the **classification** at the Paris exhibition in 1855, when Château d'Yquem was awarded Premier Cru Supérieur. At the same time 21 other producers – now 26 as a result of land subdivision – were designated Crus Classés.

You can pick up information about visiting Sauternes châteaux, among other things, at the helpful **tourist office** (May–Oct Mon 2.30–6.30pm, Tues–Sat 10am–1pm & 2.30–6.30pm; ☎05.56.76.69.13, ⓦwww.sauternais-graves-langon.com) halfway down the hill towards the church. They also offer various excursions, including half-day vineyard tours by minibus (€10 per person) and two days' grape-picking (Sept–Oct; €114 per person), and **bike rental** should you wish to cycle around the vineyards.

The only **accommodation** in the village is the small, simple and friendly hotel *Les Ormeaux* (☎05.56.76.61.19, Ⓔsauternes.lesormeaux@wanadoo.fr; ❷; closed Christmas & New Year hols) near the *mairie*, with shower cubicles in the rooms but a shared toilet. It also doubles as a café-bar – offering sandwiches and snacks – and a newsagent. At the other end of the spectrum, the ⚹ *Relais du Château d'Arche* (☎05.56.76.67.67, ⓦwww.chateaudarche-sauternes.com; ❽), about one kilometre north of the village, is a wine château offering elegant rooms in a lovely seventeenth-century chartreuse. Signed just across the road from the *Relais* is an attractive *chambre d'hôte Le Caplane* (☎05.56.76.61.17, Ⓔlecaplane@wanadoo.fr; ❹), with two pleasant rooms and a swimming pool. Alternatively, try the more modest *Domaine du Ciron* (☎05.56.76.60.17, Ⓕ05.56.76.61.74; ❸; meals on request €20), about a kilometre southeast of Sauternes.

There are a couple of good **eating** opportunities in the village itself. The *Auberge Les Vignes* (☎05.56.76.60.06; closed Sun eve, Mon & Jan) is a cosy little restaurant beside the church, with regional specialities such as *grillades aux Sarments* (meats grilled over vine clippings), a great wine list and a well-priced €12 menu on weekdays (other menus at €18 and €25). Otherwise, there's the more refined *Le Saprien* (☎05.56.76.60.87; closed Mon & for dinner Sun & Wed; also closed Christmas & Feb school hols; menus from €25), opposite the tourist office, with the added bonus of a shady summer terrace. They also serve *grillades aux Sarments* and modern variations of local dishes such as calves' sweetbreads in a curry and Sauternes sauce and *lamproie au Sauternes* – the latter definitely an acquired taste.

The châteaux

The Sauternes *appellation* covers some 240 producers tending over twenty square kilometres of vines. The landscape is peppered with handsome châteaux, the majority of which offer tastings. Below are a few recommendations.

Right on the southern edge of Sauternes village, **Château Filhot** (☎05.56.76.61.09, ⓦwww.filhot.com; Mon–Fri 9am–noon & 2–6pm, Sat & Sun by appointment; free) was one of the Crus Classés designated in 1855. The elegant Neoclassical edifice looks out over its balustrades and terraces to an English-style park dotted with grazing sheep. Its vineyard, which belongs to a branch of the same Lur-Saluces family who owned Château d'Yquem, is one of the largest in Sauternes with an annual production of around 100,000 bottles.

Heading north, another Cru Classé vineyard is to be found at the **Château La Tour Blanche** (☎05.57.98.02.73, ⓦwww .tour-blanche.com; Mon–Fri 9am–noon & 2–5pm, Sat & Sun by appointment; free), near Bommes village. This domaine is now a wine school and the visits are particularly good for those wanting to delve into the more technical aspects of wine making. Alternatively, head for the family-run **Château Clos Haut-Peyraguey** (ⓦwww .closhautpeyraguey.com; daily 9am–noon & 2–6pm; free), on the road north from Sauternes to Preignac, where you're guaranteed a warm welcome and a tour round the *chai*. Unfortunately, the same can't be said for **Château d'Yquem** further east along the same ridge of hills. Though you can walk

△ Château d'Yquem

around the park (Mon–Sat), to visit this world-famous château, the region's sole Premier Cru Supérieur, you have to apply in writing at least one month in advance (℡05.57.98.07.07, ⓦwww.chateau-yquem.fr; visits Mon–Fri 2pm & 3.30pm; free); those in the wine business get priority. There's no sign at the entrance, but it's easy enough to spot, a honey-coloured sixteenth-century manor house with pepper-pot towers looking down over Château Lafon. The wines of Château d'Yquem were already highly valued in the sixteenth century but really came to prominence in the mid-1800s when the Lur-Saluces family perfected the technique of selecting the overripe grapes. In 1999, the domaine was taken over by the Louis Vuitton Moët Hennessy group after a bitter row among the inheritors, ending over four hundred years of Lur-Saluces history.

Continuing northwards, the next hill belongs to **Château de Suduiraut** (℡05.56.63.61.90, ⓦwww.suduiraut.com; Mon–Fri 9am–noon & 2–5.30pm by appointment only; free) surrounded by a walled park and looking down over the Garonne valley. The long, low château is now used for seminars, but you'll be shown round the *chai* and get a peek at the formal seventeenth-century gardens designed by Le Nôtre, before tasting their Premier Cru Classé and AOC Sauternes wines.

Château de Malle (℡05.56.62.36.86, ⓦwww.chateau-de-malle.fr; April–Oct daily 2–5.30pm; also 10am–noon, by appointment only; €7), in the lowlands just beyond the motorway, straddles the Graves and Sauternes *appellations*. Alongside a Cru Classé, it produces not only a cheaper AOC Sauternes but also Graves reds and dry whites. This is one of the few local châteaux you can actually see inside, albeit only four rooms, heavy with wood panelling and period furniture under the watchful gaze of ancestral portraits. More engaging is the manicured Italian park complete with fountains, statues, terraces and an open-air theatre which is particularly interesting. The château was built in the early seventeenth century by Jacques de Malle, a member of the Bordeaux parliament, before passing into the ubiquitous Lur-Saluces family by marriage.

Barsac

BARSAC, immediately west of the River Ciron, is a potentially attractive village ruined by the main road cutting through its centre. Although they fall within the Sauternes region, Barsac's sweet white **wines** are permitted their own *appellation*. In general they are lighter and fruitier than the neighbouring Sauternes, but it's a very subtle difference and the grape varieties, harvesting and production process (see box on p.114) are pretty much identical. To find out more about the area, call in at the **Maison du Vin** (daily 10am–12.30pm & 2.30–6.30pm; ℡05.56.27.15.44, ⓦwww.maisondebarsac.fr) which doubles as a tourist office and showcase for Barsac wines; find it on the main road, opposite the church.

On a back lane a couple of kilometres west of Barsac, **Château de Myrat** (℡05.56.27.09.06; year-round by appointment only; free) is a medium-sized vineyard which has been revitalized in recent years. You only get a glimpse of the château, hiding among trees behind wrought-iron gates, but the old-fashioned *chais* contain some nice antique presses and huge wooden collecting vats. The end product is a velvety-smooth Cru Classé.

Though there are no decent hotels in the area, there's a very nice place to **eat**, *Le Cap* (℡05.56.63.27.38; closed Sun eve, Mon & three weeks in Oct; menus from €19), further east along the Garonne banks just before **PREIGNAC**. It's in a delightful position, with views across the river to Sainte-Croix-du-Mont (see p.122) and a pretty, wisteria-covered terrace.

Langon

With its transport connections and hotels, **LANGON**, 8km east of Sauternes village, provides a convenient base for exploring the Sauternes region, as well as for heading further north into Graves, the southern reaches of Entre-Deux-Mers just across the Garonne (see p.118), or south to the **Château de Roquetaillade** (see below). Two hundred years ago the town was an important river-port, linked to Bordeaux by passenger-steamer in 1818. And now the river has come back into its own, with barges transporting the giant components of the Airbus A380 passenger plane from Bordeaux to Langon, from where they continue their journey by road (see box on p.106). That apart, Langon has nothing particular in the way of sights beyond **St-Gervais church**, whose Chartres-like steeple dominates the old town centre. There's a very active cultural centre here, though: **Les Carmes**, 8 place des Carmes (℡05.56.63.14.45, ⓦwww.centrecultureldescarmes.fr), which puts on a varied programme of theatre, dance, music and circus arts throughout the year.

The heart of Langon is place du Général-de-Gaulle. From here cours du Général-Leclerc leads west to the **train station**. You can pick up regional **buses** on cours du Général-Leclerc or at the station. The **tourist office** is located just off the central square at 11 allées Jean-Jaurès (July & Aug Mon 2–6pm, Tues–Sat 9.30am–12.30pm & 2–6pm; Sept–June Mon 2–6pm, Tues–Sat 10am–noon & 2–6pm; ℡05.56.63.68.00, ⓦwww.sauternais-graves-langon.com). They organize various excursions, including a half-day mini-bus tour of the Graves and Sauternes vineyards (€10 per person) and can help arrange châteaux visits if you'd rather do it independently. They also offer **bike rental** and have detailed maps of the cycle tracks and footpaths crisscrossing the area.

By far the most appealing of Langon's **hotels** is the central, three-star *Claude Darroze*, 95 cours du Général-Leclerc (℡05.56.63.00.48, ⓦwww.darroze.com; closed two weeks in Jan & three in Oct; ❹). Its clutch of simple but very comfortable rooms play second fiddle to one of the region's top restaurants, offering imaginative cuisine in elegant surroundings or, in summer, on a quiet shady terrace (menus €39–74). If they're full, the best alternative is the *Horus*, 2 rue des Bruyères (℡05.56.62.36.37, ⓦwww.hotel-restaurant-horus-langon.com; closed three weeks at Christmas; ❸), located on a rather busy roundabout near the *autoroute* toll booths about 500m from the centre. Though characterless, the rooms are perfectly adequate, all with bathroom, TV and phone, and there's a decent in-house restaurant (menus from €13).

Apart from the hotel **restaurants** mentioned above, the *Cercle des Amis Réunis* (Tues–Sun, lunch only), opposite the tourist office on allées Jean-Jaurès, is a bustling brasserie serving a standard range of salads, main courses and menus (from €12.50) at lunchtime.

Château de Roquetaillade

The **Château de Roquetaillade** (Easter–June, Sept & Oct daily 2.30–6pm; July & Aug daily 10.30am–7pm; Nov–Easter Sun, public hols & school hols 2.30–5pm; €7, or €8.50 including farm museum; ⓦchateauroquetaillade.free.fr) sits in a large park about 7km south of Langon. With its solid central keep, crenellations and massive walls, it bears a strong resemblance to an English fortress – not so surprising given that it dates from the early 1300s when Aquitaine belonged to the English Crown and new ideas of military architecture were being introduced. The castle was built by Cardinal Gaillard de la Mothe, nephew of Pope Clément V, and has been in the same family ever since, which partly explains why it is so well preserved. Another reason is the spunky character of former owner Marie Henriette de Lansac, who reputedly saved Roquetaillade from destruction in the Revolution. When the labourers arrived to demolish the castle she is said to have doubled their pay, asking them in return not to touch anything except the "good wine of Roquetaillade".

Even so, the castle you see today is not entirely genuine – the interiors in particular underwent extensive renovations in the late nineteenth century under the creative hands of **Viollet-le-Duc**, a restorer much in vogue at the time, but who has since been widely criticized for his fairy-tale conception of medieval architecture. At Roquetaillade, one of his colleagues went to work on the twelfth-century chapel with a colourful hotchpotch of Oriental, North African and European motifs. Viollet-le-Duc saved his own energies for the main castle where he added an extra gateway, decorative windows and machicolations around the parapet to create what he considered a medieval look.

Contemporary engravings show that, in fact, Viollet-le-Duc didn't tamper too much with the original facade, but **interiors** are another matter. The work was commissioned in 1886 by the then owner, Mauvesin, who wanted nothing but the best and could afford it thanks to his highly profitable Médoc vineyards. Viollet-le-Duc set about the task with gusto. He filled the entrance hall with a monumental white-stone staircase, painted every inch of wall – including two charming tricolour-winged angels in the Pink Room which presage the arrival of Art Nouveau – and even designed a complete dining-room suite. So long did all this take, however, that Mauvesin ran out of money in the mid-1870s when the architect was only halfway through the Great Hall. A small engraving shows what he had in mind, but it's still an impressive room, dominated by a suitably exuberant Renaissance chimneypiece remarkably similar in style to those at Cadillac (see p.120). As you leave the castle's inner courtyard, look back at the carvings over the door: the two middle faces depict Mauvesin and his wife; that on the left, with the smile, is said to be Viollet-le-Duc.

Entre-Deux-Mers

The landscape of **Entre-Deux-Mers** (literally "between two seas") – so called because it is sandwiched between the tidal waters of the Dordogne and Garonne – is the prettiest of the Bordeaux wine regions. It's an area of gentle hills and scattered medieval villages, many of them *bastides* (see box on p.336) founded by the English during the Hundred Years' War, the most typical examples of which are **Sauveterre-de-Guyenne** and **Monségur**. Earlier builders and craftsmen left a legacy of Romanesque churches decorated with splendid carvings, which reached their apogee in the ruined abbeys of **La Sauve-Majeure**, **Blasimon** and **St-Ferme**. Moving on a few centuries, the artist Toulouse-Lautrec spent much of his life at Château Malromé near **Verdelais**, while François Mauriac wrote some of his greatest novels at Malagar, just outside **St-Macaire**. Further along the Garonne, **La Réole** boasts the oldest town hall in France. In **Rauzan**, in the far north of Entre-Deux-Mers, you can ring the changes with a visit to an underground river system.

Entre-Deux-Mers produces a wide variety of **wines**, but is best known for the dry whites which are regarded as good but inferior to the super-dry Graves (see p.110). The vineyards of Cadillac, Loupiac and Sainte-Croix-du-Mont, three *appellations* overlooking the Garonne, also produce a sweet white wine comparable with many Sauternes, but at lower prices. Several Maisons du Vin scattered throughout the area provide tastings and advice on vineyard visits, as well as the opportunity to buy. For more general **information** about the region, contact the Office du Tourisme de l'Entre-Deux-Mers, 4 rue Issartier, Monségur (☎05.56.61.82.73, ⓦwww.entredeuxmers.com).

While most of the sights of Entre-Deux-Mers are widely scattered, a surprising number are still just about accessible by **public transport**. Trains on the Bordeaux–Agen line stop at Langon (see p.117) and La Réole. These two towns are also the start of several useful if sporadic bus routes, notably to Cadillac, Monségur, St-Ferme and Sauveterre-de-Guyenne. From Sauveterre buses also head west to La Sauve-Majeure, en route to Bordeaux, and northwards via Blasimon and Rauzan to Libourne, where they connect with trains on the Bordeaux–Paris mainline. For the more active, a disused railway line has been transformed into a dedicated surfaced cycle track from Latresne train station, on the outskirts of Bordeaux, to Sauveterre. Another eight circular routes have also been marked out; local tourist offices stock maps and brochures.

La Sauve-Majeure

The one place you should really try to see is the ruined Benedictine abbey in the centre of Entre-Deux-Mers, about 23km east of Bordeaux, at **LA SAUVE-MAJEURE** (June–Sept daily 10am–6pm; Oct–May Tues–Sun 10.30am–1pm & 2–5.30pm; €5; ⓦwww.monum.fr). Set in a tranquil valley of small vineyards and cornfields, it was once all forest here, the abbey's name being a corruption of the Latin *silva major* ("big wood"). It was founded in 1079 by a hermit later known as St Gérard and became an important stop for pilgrims en route to Spain's Santiago de Compostela. Thanks to royal and papal backing, at its height La Sauve boasted over seventy dependent priories stretching from England to Spain, but then fell into slow decay. Only the apse and stumps of wall topped by a defiant octagonal bell tower (worth the climb) still remain.

Despite such neglect, a series of outstanding **sculpted capitals** – big, bold and several unusually low on the walls – has survived from the twelfth century. The finest are those around the transepts and choir, some illustrating stories from the Old and New Testaments, others showing fabulous beasts and vegetal motifs. In the little chapels either side of the apse, look out for Adam clutching his throat as Eve hands him the apple, and Daniel upside down in the lions' den. But the most remarkable scene occurs on a capital on the southern wall, near the entrance to the tower, where the story of John the Baptist is depicted in astonishing detail. On one side Salome dances as Herod twirls his moustache in appreciation; on the other you see John's head being removed from the prison.

There's a small museum at the abbey entrance, containing keystones from the fallen roof and fragments of painted wall, and the nearby grange now houses the **Maison du Vin** (June–Sept daily 10.30am–6pm; Oct–May Mon–Fri 10.30am–noon & 2–5pm; ℡05.57.34.32.12, ⓦwww.vins-entre-deux-mers .com) showcasing the dry white wines of the Entre-Deux-Mers.

If you have the time, stroll over to the parish church of **St-Pierre**, visible on the neighbouring hill, where St Gérard is buried (ask at the *mairie* if the church is locked). Though built around the same time as the abbey, the church has survived intact, including its thirteenth-century frescoes (all bar one retouched in the nineteenth century) showing St James and pilgrims on their way to Compostela.

La Sauve is on the **bus** route from Bordeaux to Sauveterre-de-Guyenne (see p.126). There's nowhere to stay in the village, but you can **eat** well at the ⚹ *Restaurant de l'Abbaye*, just below the ruins (closed Sun eve & Mon), which offers an interesting selection of country classics and modern dishes (menus from €11).

Cadillac

Twenty kilometres south of La Sauve-Majeure, on the banks of the Garonne, **CADILLAC** is as famous for its name as for the dour Renaissance **château** dominating the town. According to local legend, Antoine Laumet, the founder of Detroit, Michigan – home city of General Motors – originally came from Cadillac. Sadly, this is just too good to be true. He was born in St-Nicolas-de-la-Grave (see p.126), and on emigrating to Canada simply took the name of Lamothe de Cadillac, even though he had no connections with the town. It's a recorded fact, however, that Cadillac was founded by the English in 1280, from when a surprisingly long stretch of original wall still exists, punctuated by two gates: Porte de l'Horloge to the south and westerly Porte de la Mer. Though it lacks any particular charm, Cadillac's range of accommodation and eating options make it a useful base.

In the late sixteenth century the newly named duc d'Épernon, a favourite of Henri III, was given permission to reconstruct a medieval castle at the confluence of the rivers Œuille and Garonne. His **Château de Cadillac**, on the north side of town (June–Sept daily 10am–1.15pm & 2–6pm; Oct–May Tues–Sun 10am–12.30pm & 2–5.30pm; €5), took nearly thirty years to build and was so luxurious – with sixty bedrooms, twenty fireplaces, tapestries and richly painted woodwork – that it was said to rival the king's own palaces. No doubt it yielded rich pickings to the revolutionaries who sacked the place in the 1790s, after which its echoing halls were turned into a notoriously harsh **women's prison**, the Maison Centrale de Force et de Correction. It's this last usage which seems most fitting as you cross the wide, bare courtyard, and which also provides the most interesting exhibits inside. Very little remains of the original decoration, though some of the Italianate painted ceilings and the magnificent Renaissance **fireplaces** with their over-exuberant plasterwork have now been restored on the ground floor. Look out, too, for the unusual collection of Aubusson tapestries in the Queen's apartments. They depict six illustrious women, including Artemesia, Lucretia and Cleopatra, the latter dressed in incongruous seventeenth-century ruffles as she tempts her lover, Antony, with a pearl.

Upstairs is contrastingly sober, and houses displays about the history of the château and its occupants, including photos and documents relating to the prison, the majority of whose inmates were guilty of infanticide – often committed in the place of abortion. Conditions were extremely strict: absolute silence, a bread-and-water diet and no privacy. The great halls were converted into overcrowded dormitories and even the fireplaces were pressed into service as makeshift latrines.

While building his château, the duc d'Épernon was also planning a grand mausoleum for himself in the nearby **church of St-Blaise**. Though his funeral monument was largely destroyed during the Revolution, the celebrated bronze statue of *Renommée* – a winged trumpeter – somehow survived (the original is in the Louvre). The church's ornate altarpiece dates from the same period. It features two statues of the duke and duchess's patron saints, Ste Marguerite and St John, to either side of a crucifixion scene.

Cadillac's sweet white wines – the result of a microclimate similar to that in Sauternes (see box on p.114) – are featured in a smart showroom, **La Closière** (May–Sept Mon-Fri 10am–12.30pm & 1.30–5.30pm; Oct– April Mon–Fri 9.30am–12.30pm & 1.30–5pm; ☎05.57.98.19.20, ⓦwww .premierescotesdebordeaux.com), signed just out of town on the D10 to Langon. It also stocks other regional wines, notably under the Premières Côtes de Bordeaux *appellations*, in addition to offering free tastings and advice on vineyard tours.

Practicalities

Cadillac's nearest **gare SNCF** lies across the Garonne at Cerons, from where a taxi will cost around €10, while **buses** between Bordeaux and Langon stop outside the ramparts on place de Lattre-de-Tassigny. The **tourist office** (April–June Tues–Sun 9.30am–12.30pm & 2–6pm; July–Sept daily 9.30am– 12.30pm & 2–7pm; Oct–March Tues–Sat 9.30am–12.30pm & 2–6pm, Sun 9.30am–12.30pm; ☎05.56.62.12.92 ⓦwww.entredeuxmers.com) is conveniently located in front of the château on place de la Libération; Internet access available.

The only decent **hotel** in Cadillac is the modern *Château de la Tour* (☎05.56.76.92.00, ⓦwww.hotel-restaurant-chateaudelatour.com; ❸), with a garden, swimming pool, Wi-fi Internet access and a good restaurant (menus €15–55; March–Nov daily; Dec–Feb closed Sun eve), beside the D10 just north of town. There are, however, several excellent **chambres d'hôtes** in the area. Pick of the bunch, ⚹ *Château de Grand Branet* (☎05.56.72.17.30, ⓦchateaugrandbranet.free.fr; ❹; closed Jan), a wine château 11km north near **CAPIAN** village, offers splendid accommodation in big, en-suite rooms, with *table d'hôte* on request. Other options include *Château Le Vert* (☎05.56.23.91.49, Ⓔchateaulevert@wanadoo.fr; ❸), 7km northwest on the D11 to Targon, and the more modest *Château du Broustaret* (☎05.56.62.96.97, ⓦwww.broustaret .net; closed Nov–Easter; ❸), signed off the D11 roughly 5km from Cadillac. Just outside Cadillac a small, two-star **campsite** (☎05.56.62.72.98; closed mid-Sept to mid-June) sits on the banks of the Garonne, or there's a more welcoming and attractive *camping à la ferme* at the *Domaine de Chicoye* (☎05.56.62.01.79; closed mid-Sept to Easter), near Loupiac on the road to Sainte-Croix-du-Mont (see p.122).

When it comes to **eating**, there's a clutch of cafés and brasseries around central place de la République, also the venue for a Saturday-morning market. The town's top restaurant, *L'Entrée Jardin*, is beside the bridge at 27 av du Pont (☎05.56.76.96.96; closed Sun eve, Mon and one week mid-Aug; weekday lunch menus from €11, Sun & eves €19–34), where imaginative dishes such as roast pigeon with vanilla and mullet with mango chutney are served. *Le Palais*

Gourmand, 7 rue Porte-de-la-Mer (Tues–Sun), just inside the city walls, is a friendly little place serving decent salads and a choice of local dishes; menus from €11.50.

Upstream to Verdelais

Either side of Cadillac the Entre-Deux-Mers plateau edges closer to the Garonne. There are good **viewpoints** all along the escarpment, but one of the finest is from the village of **SAINTE-CROIX-DU-MONT** about 6km to the southwest. Aim for the terrace running in front of the church and the medieval Château de Tastes, now the *mairie*, perched on the cliff edge. The **cliff** itself is also of interest. Its top layer, ranging in thickness from three to eight metres and extending back under the village, is composed of fossilized oyster shells deposited some 25 million years ago. The bed has been hollowed out in various places into shallow caves, one of which used to form an unusual showroom for the local wine growers' association. At the time of writing, however, the **Maison des Vins** (April to mid-Oct Mon, Tues, Thurs & Fri 2.30–6.30pm, Sat, Sun & public hols 10.30am–12.30pm & 2.30–7.30pm) had been relocated to beside the church, possibly only temporarily. The views aren't quite so good, but you can still raise a glass of their sweet white wine (€2 per glass, or €2.50 for a *dégustation* of 4 wines), which merits its own *appellation*, to the rival Sauternes vineyards on the far side of the Garonne.

A few kilometres east of here, **VERDELAIS** offers more views and an ornate Baroque **church**, every inch covered with votive plaques dedicated to a miracle-performing statue of the Virgin and Child. Verdelais' first recorded miracle took place in 1185 and pilgrims have been flocking here ever since. Many of them left gifts of paintings, silver hearts and bejewelled cloaks for the statue in thanks, and a fraction of the collection is on display at the nearby **Musée d'Art Religieux** (⌀05.56.62.02.04; July & Aug daily 3–6.30pm; Sept–June phone for opening times; €3). The most interesting exhibits are the paintings portraying young children returned to health, and various storm-tossed ships – you'll also find lovely scale-model boats donated by shipwrecked sailors.

Verdelais' main claim to fame these days, however, is the **tomb of Toulouse-Lautrec** (see box opposite) which lies across the road in the church cemetery; go straight ahead from the entrance gate to find it last on the left. From here you can walk on up past the Stations of the Cross, represented here by sculpted tableaux, for views south to Langon and west to Sainte-Croix.

Henri Toulouse-Lautrec spent his summers a couple of kilometres northeast of Verdelais in the enchanting **Château Malromé** (⌀05.56.76.44.92, ⓦwww .malrome.com). His mother, the Countess Adèle de Toulouse-Lautrec, bought the château in 1883 and had it renovated in neo-medieval style according to the then-fashionable ideas of Viollet-le-Duc (see p.118). She also rescued its neglected vineyard, which now produces eminently palatable red and white wines and a "clairet", a light red wine drunk chilled in summer. Sadly, the house is no longer open to the public, though there are plans to turn it into a hotel, but visitors coming for a *dégustation* (Mon–Fri 10am–6pm by appointment; free) or to eat at the wine-bar restaurant *L'Ombrière* (Fri lunch & dinner; menus €20 and €25, tapas €7; reservations required) are welcome to walk around the grounds.

Toulouse-Lautrec

Known for his provocative portraits of Parisian low-life, **Henri Toulouse-Lautrec** was born in Albi, northeast of Toulouse, in 1864. His father, Count Alphonse de Toulouse-Lautrec, was a highly eccentric man with a passion for hunting, illicit affairs and bizarre outfits, who married his first cousin. This genetic mismatch is blamed for Henri's stunted growth and delicate constitution, exacerbated by two childhood accidents which left him permanently crippled. Nevertheless, encouraged by an uncle and two family friends who spotted his artistic talent, Henri went to study in Paris under Bonnat and Cormon before setting up his own studio in **Montmartre** in 1884.

Henri was in his element there. He produced hundreds of paintings and sketches portraying the unglamorous reality of life in the cabarets, theatres, bars and brothels of *fin-de-siècle* Paris. Among his most famous works are those associated with the **Moulin Rouge**, which Henri began to frequent in 1890, recording events offstage as well as the great music-hall artists of the day: Yvette Guilbert, Jane Avril and May Belfort, among others. The portraits are often grotesque, with a strong element of caricature, but his affection for his subjects shines through. This is particularly true of his works in the *maisons closes*, when the prostitutes – if not their clients – are treated with great sympathy and sensitivity.

The bohemian life and excess of alcohol gradually took its toll. In 1900 Henri returned to southwest France to set up a studio in Bordeaux where the café and theatre world provided ample subject matter. But the following year, as his health began to deteriorate, he was taken back to Château Malromé, where he died on September 9, aged 37 years. Though originally buried in the nearby cemetery of St-André-du-Bois, in 1908 Henri's body was moved to **Verdelais**, where his mother eventually joined him.

Thanks to the uncompromising nature of much of his work, Toulouse-Lautrec met with very little critical success during his lifetime. His portraits were far too shocking for mainstream contemporary tastes and even in the 1920s both the Louvre and Toulouse city refused the family's gift of six hundred paintings, posters and sketches. The magnificent collection went instead to Albi. Since then Toulouse-Lautrec has been recognized as one of the founders of modern advertising, while his dynamic, almost calligraphic lines and bold swathes of colour have won worldwide acclaim.

St-Macaire and around

Just across the Garonne from Langon (see p.117), and some 12km southeast of Cadillac, **ST-MACAIRE** provides a more attractive alternative base, though it's a bit dead out of season. The town was founded in the first century AD by an itinerant Greek monk called Makarios. Later it grew wealthy on the wine trade, so that by the mid-fourteenth century the population had reached six thousand, only to decline from the early 1600s onwards as the river shifted and the port silted up. These days St-Macaire musters a mere 1600 souls but still retains several of its original gates and battlements as well as a beautiful medieval church.

St-Macaire's glory days are also still evident in the number of dignified edifices, the homes of wealthy merchants, many of which are now being done up. Some of the most handsome lie just inside **Porte Benauge**, the main north gate, and around the old market square, **place Mercadiou**, to the east. The **church of St Sauveur**, on the other hand, occupies an abandoned river cliff on the south side of town. Nothing remains of the original Benedictine priory beyond a fragment of cloister-wall, but the fourteenth-century murals inside the church are what everybody comes to see. They were somewhat crudely restored – and embellished – in 1825, but even so present a fine spectacle. While the scenes behind the altar are based on St John the Evangelist's Revelation, his miracles and martyrdom in a vat of boiling oil are depicted over the transept.

Admirers of the Nobel-prize-winning novelist **François Mauriac** (1885–1970) should pay a visit to his bolt-hole and source of inspiration, **Malagar** (June–Sept daily 10am–12.30pm & 2–6pm; Oct–May Wed–Fri 2–5pm, Sat, Sun & public hols 10am–12.30pm & 2–5pm; €5.50; ℡05.57.98.17.17, ⓦwww .malagar.asso.fr), on the hills about 3km north of St-Macaire. The little château has been preserved largely as he left it, including the desk where he wrote one of his most famous novels, *Nœud de Vipères* (*Vipers' Tangle*), published in 1932. In the adjacent François Mauriac Centre you can see many original documents, alongside photos and videos of the great man. The centre also puts on a varied programme of cultural events throughout the year.

Practicalities

At least one **train** a day stops at the **gare SNCF**, less than half a kilometre north of town, or there are more frequent services to Langon (see p.117), from where **buses** headed for Bordeaux will drop you outside Porte Benauge. St-Macaire's efficient **tourist office** (April & May Tues–Sun 10am–1pm & 3–7pm; June–Sept daily 10am–1pm & 3–7pm; Oct–March Wed–Fri 2–5pm, Sat & Sun 10am–noon & 2–5pm; ℡05.56.63.32.14 ⓦwww.entredeuxmers.com) occupies a handsome, sixteenth-century merchant's house just inside the gate. The office doubles as a showroom promoting regional produce, which here means honey and wine. Staff can help arrange visits to the *chais* and in July and August local wine-makers offer tastings in the tourist office.

The nicest **hotel** in town is *Les Feuilles d'Acanthe* (℡05.56.62.33.75, ⓦwww .feuilles-dacanthe.com; ❹) occupying another beautifully restored building opposite the tourist office. The decor is stylish and modern, featuring exposed stone walls and terracotta tiles, in addition to gleaming en-suite bathrooms. It even boasts a jacuzzi-solarium, while their *Le Pampaillet* restaurant serves traditional and regional dishes – menus start at €19. A cheaper alternative – and good for families – is *Les Tilleuls* (℡05.56.62.28.38, ⓦwww.tilleul-medieval .com; ❸), just outside Porte Benauge, where studio rooms come with kitchens. Or you can eat in their cheerful restaurant, *Le Mediéval* (daily for lunch & for dinner Fri & Sat; menus from €14.50), which is popular for its hot-stone grills and attractive summer terrace, not to mention very reasonable prices.

St-Macaire's best **restaurant**, however, is *L'Abricotier* (℡05.56.76.83.63; Tues–Sun; closed Tues eve & mid-Nov to mid-Dec; menus from €20) west of town on the busy N113. It may not look much from the outside but this is one of the region's top addresses. It's best in summer when tables spread out into the pretty, walled garden, but the food remains excellent all year, featuring shad, lamprey and other local fish as well as game in season. They also have three very comfortable rooms, again with kitchenettes (❸); advance booking is essential.

La Réole and around

LA RÉOLE, 20km east of St-Macaire along the same escarpment, hides some good medieval architecture among its narrow, hilly streets, but somehow feels cramped and dowdy as opposed to quaintly aged. That said, France's oldest town hall and the well-preserved Benedictine abbey – with expansive views over the Garonne and the surrounding countryside – reward a stroll through the town, while a quirky museum nearby is also worth a visit. Good transport connections and a choice of restaurants make La Réole a possible overnight stop, but you'll have to go out of town to find any particularly inspiring accommodation.

In medieval times La Réole was the region's second largest town after Bordeaux. To ensure their loyalty, Richard the Lionheart granted its townspeople a certain degree of self-government and ordered the building of a town hall. Even today, La Réole is fiercely proud of what is France's oldest surviving Hôtel de Ville, overlooking place Georges-Chaigne on the north side of the old town. Not that there's much to see. The big, open hall downstairs has a few carved capitals, while proclamations were presumably made from the modest balcony on the north side; the first-floor meeting hall is open occasionally for exhibitions.

From here, walk south down rue Peysseguin, one of La Réole's most atmospheric streets with one or two handsome town houses and a smattering of half-timbered facades, and turn right along semi-pedestrianized rue Armand-Caduc to find the **church of St-Pierre**. Here, too, is the entrance to the former cloister of the **Benedictine abbey**, founded in the tenth century by the bishop of Bazas; the name La Réole derives from Regula, meaning Benedictine Rule. The abbey was rebuilt in the early 1700s but by the time it was complete revolution was in the air and in 1791 the buildings were taken over by the local administration, which is still in residence. The building's main attributes are – at its east end – a grand stone staircase with an elegant iron banister lit by a graceful, elliptical lantern, and some good wrought ironwork by local master-craftsman Blaise Charlut, who was also responsible for the screens in Bordeaux Cathedral (see p.87). You can admire the best of his craftsmanship in the gates of the southern door from where a pretty double staircase leads down onto a wide terrace overlooking the Garonne. On a clear winter's day it's even possible to see the Pyrenees from here.

Just the other side of the Garonne and the Canal des Deux-Mers, the village of **FONTET** is home to the delightfully wacky **Musée d'Artisanat Monuments en Allumettes** (Feb–Sept daily 2–6pm; Oct–Nov Sun & public hols 2–6pm; closed Dec & Jan; €4) dedicated to scale models made of matchsticks. So far the enthusiastic owner has used over 670,000 – he buys them without sulphur direct from the manufacturers – to create his architectural models of Notre-Dame and the abbey of La Réole, among others. His current masterwork is a magnificent rendition of the Château de Versailles, complete with lights and fountains, which has so far consumed 230,000 matches and taken eight years to build; he reckons it will take another four years to complete. Needless to say, sparking up is strictly forbidden. Afterwards, walk along the canal to find a pleasant picnic spot beside the *halte nautique*.

Also worth a visit on your way north to Sauveterre (see overleaf) is the **Château de Lavison** (℡05.56.71.48.82; May–15 Sept daily 2.30–6pm; 15 Sept–April by appointment only; free), north of St-Sève on the D129. This thirteenth-century fortress once belonged to Edward 1 of England and, later, was used by the Black Prince as a hunting lodge. In the fifteenth and sixteenth centuries, the castle was enlarged and made into a more comfortable residence, which it remains to this day, furnished with some splendid family heirlooms. The guided tour ends with a visit to the *chais* to sample the domaine's very palatable AOC wines.

While you're in the vicinity, head west to Bagas, where in the early fifteenth century the monks of La Réole built a lovely **fortified mill** on the River Dropt.

Practicalities

La Réole's **gare SNCF** is located a little way east of town, from where it's a steep ten-minute walk to the centre. If you're travelling by **bus** you'll have to come via Sauveterre-de-Guyenne (see below); buses stop on central place de la Libération while some also take in the train station. The **tourist office**, on place Richard-Coeur-de-Lion (June–Sept Mon 2.30–6.30pm, Tues–Sat 9.30am–12.30pm & 2.30–6.30pm, Sun 9.30am–12.30pm; Oct–May Mon 3–6pm, Tues–Sat 9.30am–12.30pm & 3–6pm; ☎05.56.61.13.55, ✉lareole@entredeuxmers.com, occupies one of the half-timbered buildings beside the former Hôtel de Ville. In addition to the usual lists and leaflets, they also stock an English-language brochure (€2) outlining a walking tour of the main sights, and sell local wines.

While there's no hotel **accommodation** to speak of in or around La Réole, there's a good choice of **chambres d'hôtes** nearby. Three kilometres north on the D21 to St-Sève you'll find the stylish and very popular ⚘ *Domaine de la Charmaie* (☎05.56.61.10.72, ⓦmonsite.wanadoo.fr/domainedelacharmaie; ❹), and the cheaper and more rustic *Au Canton* (☎05.56.61.04.88, ✉monique-bauge@aol.com; ❹). Slightly further north, just off the main D670 to Sauvet-erre, *La Camiranaise* (☎05.56.71.11.26, ⓦwww.lacamiranaise.free.fr; ❹), is another good option. All three provide meals on request. Finally, La Réole's well-run, two-star **campsite**, *Le Rouergue* (☎05.56.61.13.55; closed Nov–May), lies just across the old suspension bridge, with great views back to the abbey.

La Réole's top **restaurant** is the light and airy *Les Fontaines* on rue de Verdun (☎05.56.61.15.25; closed Sun eve & Mon; also two weeks each in Feb & Nov), with a terrace looking across to the old Hôtel de Ville. The food consists of classic French cuisine, albeit with a modern touch, and there's a wide choice of menus from €16.50–47. There's a Provençal touch to the menu at *La Régula*, just off rue Armand-Caduc at 31 rue André-Benac (closed Sun eve & Wed; lunch menus from €12.50, eves from €16.50), though they also serve regional specialities. That said, the best place to sample no-nonsense local dishes is at the *Auberge Réolaise* (☎05.56.61.01.33; closed Thurs eve & Fri; also closed two weeks in Nov; menus €10–25), on the N113 just east of town. Don't be put off by the location or the grungy decor – the food's good, as long as you stick to local dishes, such as lamprey, shad or a hearty rabbit stew. In summer, head to Fontet, where *Les Fontines* (☎05.56.61.10.20; Tues–Sun; closed Oct–March) has an attractive garden down by the canal. It's popular with families and on week-days offers an excellent value lunch menu for €11 (€16 dinner & weekends), including hors d'œuvre and dessert buffets; you'll need to book at weekends. Don't expect any fireworks at these prices, but their daily specials are usually worth trying.

La Réole's main **market** takes place on Saturday mornings on the esplanade des Quais along the Garonne – a good place to stock up on picnic provisions. On Sunday mornings rather fewer stalls set up on place de la Libération.

Sauveterre-de-Guyenne and around

The majority of *bastides* in Entre-Deux-Mers were founded by the English. Of these, perhaps one of the most typical is **Sauveterre-de-Guyenne**, 14km north of La Réole, which was established under Edward I in 1281. The surrounding coun-tryside is peppered with Romanesque churches, some with lovely carved portals, such as at **Castelviel** and **Blasimon**. With its large, arcaded central square, gate towers and gridiron street plan, **Sauveterre-de-Guyenne** is a particularly good example of a *bastide* (see box on p.336). The ramparts themselves were demolished in 1814, replaced by what is now a ring-road, but they must have been a bit battered – Sauveterre changed hands ten times during the Hundred Years' War before finally falling to the French in 1451. The town boasts no real sights of its own, but is big enough to merit cafés, restaurants and other services grouped round place de la République, the venue for a lively Tuesday-morning **market**.

Sauveterre has bus connections to Libourne and La Réole; **buses** stop on place de la République and/or the ring road. You can find out more about these services and get other local information at the **tourist office** (15 June–15 Sept daily 9.30am–12.30pm & 2.30–6.30pm; 16 Sept–14 June Mon–Fri 9am–noon & 2–6pm, Sat 9am–noon & 3–6pm; ℡05.56.71.53.45, ⓦwww.entredeuxmers .com) in the southwest corner of the central square. It also offers bike rental and has maps of the region's marked cycling routes. The building is also home to the **Maison des Vins** (same hours) which sells local wines at producers' price.

As there's nowhere particularly attractive to **stay** in Sauveterre, it's better instead to head for one of the nearby *chambres d'hôtes*. The English-owned *Le Moulin de Saquet* (℡05.56.71.66.45, ⓦwww.le-moulin-de-saquet.com; ④) is in a lovely peaceful location near the village of **DAUBÈZE** about 5km west of Sauveterre. There's a clutch of places to **eat**, however, in Sauveterre, of which the best is *Les Arcades* (weekday lunch menus from €11, eves & weekends from €17) on the northwest corner of place de la République. This café-restaurant-bar attracts a mix of locals and tourist traffic with its simple but well-cooked dishes and good-value menus.

Around Sauveterre-de-Guyenne

Seven kilometres southwest of Sauveterre, through a rolling landscape of vines and windmills, lies the tiny, flowery village of **CASTELVIEL**, worth a visit for the carved south portal of its twelfth-century church. Though they're a bit worn in places, it's still possible to make out a wealth of detail on the portal's five tiers. The outer arch depicts scenes from rural life; on the second the Vices confront the Virtues; the third, which resembles a tug-of-war, represents the faithful united by their common bond. Monsters, biblical characters and layers of interlocking vegetation overspill from the remaining tiers to two small, flanking arches.

The same distance east of Sauveterre on the D230, the main claim to fame of **CASTELMORON-D'ALBRET** is as the smallest commune in France. The village comprises just 3.5 hectares and owns none of the surrounding agricultural land. With its wash-house, former seneschal's house and tiled market hall, and, of course, the inevitable potter, it's a picturesque spot almost verging on the twee.

Seven kilometres north of Sauveterre, **BLASIMON**, founded by the English in 1322, was one of the very last *bastides* constructed in the region. The town occupies a rocky promontory looking north over the Gamage valley and a ruined **abbey** (Sat & Sun 9am–6pm) established by Benedictine monks in the seventh century; if you want to visit on a weekday, phone the guardian M Mercadier (℡05.56.71.54.25) the day before and he'll unlock it for you. The cloister and abbey buildings, which were obviously fortified at some time, were abandoned in the thirteenth century, but the church itself has survived. Again, it's the twelfth century Romanesque carvings round the west door that are most absorbing. The elongated, sinuous figures of the Vices and Virtues are so incredibly delicate it's hard to believe their age. In other places the soft stone has weathered badly, though not so much that you can't identify the angels adoring the Lamb of God on the inner tier, hunting scenes on the outer edge, and at least get the gist of the exuberant motifs around. The interior is contrastingly unadorned save for the captivating faces on the capitals to either side of the entrance door. **Tourist information** is available at the Domaine Départemental de Blasimon (June–Sept Mon–Fri 9am–12.30pm & 4–7.30pm, Sat & Sun 9–11am & 5.30–7.30pm; closed Oct–May; ☏05.56.71.59.62, ⓦwww .entredeuxmers.com) rather inconveniently located 3km northwest on the Rauzan road. The complex comprises a park with a swimming lake (supervised in July & Aug), snack bar, tennis courts, playground and a **campsite**, the three-star *Camping du Lac* (same contact details; closed Oct–May).

RAUZAN, six kilometres northwest of Blasimon, is dominated by its semi-ruined **castle** (July & Aug daily 10am–noon & 2–6pm; Sept–June Tues–Sun 10am–noon & 2–5pm; €3; ⓦwww.rauzan.fr), founded by English forces in the run up to the Hundred Years' War. Although it's now slowly being restored, there's not a great deal to see inside – but the views from the keep are impressive. In 1845 an underground river was discovered running beneath Rauzan and has since been made good use of by the townspeople for everything from lovers' trysts to shelter for Resistance fighters during World War II. Now known as the **Grotte Célestine** (☏05.57.84.08.69, ⓦwww.rauzan.fr; by appointment: July & Aug daily 10am–noon & 2–6pm; Sept–June Tues–Sun 10am–noon & 2–5pm; €6.50) it now provides an enjoyable excursion, particularly for children, as you splosh along the river bed equipped with helmet and waders to admire the limestone concretions and learn about their formation. Note that there's a minimum height restriction of 1.2m (4ft) tall to enter.

Both Blasimon and Rauzan lie on the **bus** route between Sauveterre and Libourne, although there's only one service a day (Mon–Fri) in each direction. Rauzan boasts an excellent, shady **campsite** with a pool, ⚑ *Camping du Vieux Château* (☏05.57.84.15.38, ⓦwww.vieux-chateau.com; closed Nov–March), in the valley beneath the castle ramparts. The nearest hotel **accommodation**, however, is the very grand *Isabeau de Naujan* (☏05.57.55.14.30, ⓦwww .domaine-de-naujan.com; ❻; closed Jan & Feb), a handsome fourteenth-century château a couple of kilometres west of Rauzan in the village of **ST-VINCENT-DE-PERTIGNAS**. While the rooms have been rather too heavily modernised, they're very comfortable and it's in a lovely location. There's a restaurant (menus €20 & €38; reservations requested) and swimming pool and you can taste the domaine's AOC wines.

If you're looking for somewhere simple to **eat** in the area, a good choice would be the *Auberge Gasconne* (☏05.57.40.52.08; closed Sun eve & Mon, also last two weeks in Aug) in **ST-PEY-DE-CASTETS**, 6km northwest of Rauzan. It's a typical village inn, with an excellent €11 weekday lunch menu and other menus from €16 to €28.50. They're open for dinner on Friday and Saturday, but other evenings are by appointment.

Monségur

On the eastern fringes of the Entre-Deux-Mers region, some 20km northeast of La Réole, **Monségur** makes a good base for exploring the fertile Dropt valley and neighbouring Duras (see p.130). It's also within striking distance of the **abbey of St-Ferme**, home to more exquisite carvings.

Like Sauveterre-de-Guyenne, **MONSÉGUR** is another good example of a *bastide*, in this case occupying a hill top site. It was founded a couple of decades earlier, in 1265, also by the English, and though its **market square** is much more confined, there are one or two attractive houses in the narrow streets. Where the ramparts once stood a grassy two-kilometre walkway now takes you almost three quarters of the way round the town; the north side affords bucolic views over the Dropt valley. That just about exhausts Monségur's sights, but it makes up for it with some reasonable options for eating out or even an overnight stay, and if you happen to visit on the first weekend in July you'll also hit its biggest annual bash, the 24 Heures du Swing **jazz festival**, which takes place throughout the town (see p.76).

Monségur is served by **buses** from La Réole and Sauveterre. The **tourist office** is located east of the central square at 33 rue des Victimes (June–Sept Tues, Wed, Fri 9am–noon & 2–6pm, Thurs 10am–noon & 2–6pm, Sat & Sun 9am–noon; Oct–May Tues & Fri 9am–noon & 2–5pm; ☏05.56.61.89.40, ⓦwww.entredeuxmers.com). There's a great traditional **market** on Friday mornings under the nineteenth-century *halle* and a *foire au gras* (foie-gras market) on the second Sunday in December and in February, while May brings a riot of colour with its *foire aux fleurs*.

As far as **accommodation** is concerned, your best bet is ♯ *Sous le Cep d'Antan* (☏05.56.61.60.28, ⓦwww.souslecep-dantan.com; ❹), an attractive and welcoming *chambre d'hôte* on the market square which also has a good restaurant. Campers are served by the small, two-star **campsite,** *L'Étoiles du Drot* (☏05.56.61.67.54; closed Oct–March), just below the village on the La Réole road.

For **eating**, the rustic *Les Tilleuls* (lunch only; closed Sat & Sun), on place des Tilleuls to the west of the main market square, offers a hearty, no-nonsense *menu du jour* at just €11 including wine, or a *plat du jour* at €7.50. Alternatively, *Les Colonnes* (menus €10–19.50) is a spick-and-span pizzeria on the market square which also serves decent salads and regional dishes and hosts jazz concerts on Tuesday evenings. For something more stylish, you'll find beautifully presented and flavourful dishes at ♯ *Sous le Cep d'Antan* (☏05.56.61.60.28; menus €18.50–35; closed Tues), also on the market square, with a delightful interior courtyard shaded by a four-hundred-year-old vine, while *Les Charmilles,* just outside Monségur on the road to St-Ferme (☏05.56.61.19.96; closed Sun eve, Mon & Tues, also three weeks in Oct & Jan–March), boasts a wonderful riverside location and inventive dishes such as crab tartare (menus at €23 & €29 in the main restaurant; weekday lunches at €12.50 on the terrace). Slightly further afield, *La Ferme Gauvray* (☏05.56.71.83.96; Wed–Sun lunch, by appointment only; menus €15–33.50), 8km west of Monségur in the village of Rimons, is a popular ferme-auberge serving all manner of duck-based delicacies.

St-Ferme and around

The last stop in Entre-Deux-Mers is **ST-FERME**, 11km north of Monségur. The village clusters round the solid, grey **abbey** – founded by Benedictine monks sometime before the eleventh century – from which it takes its name. The fortifications added to the abbey buildings during the Hundred Years' War came in handy again during the Wars of Religion when Protestant forces attacked on at least two occasions. Happily, the **church** (daily 8am–7pm) withstood the onslaught. There's no grand portal, but instead the twelfth-century craftsmen went to work on the **capitals** in the three bays around the altar. Best of the lot is the first pillar on the far wall of the north bay, depicting Daniel being saved from lions with two angels above, while on the opposite wall of

1

Bloodsucking delicacy

The **lamprey** (*lamproie*) is one of those gastronomic delicacies not everyone has the stomach for. This primitive eel-like fish never developed jaws but is equipped instead with a powerful tooth-lined sucker for a mouth. With this it attaches itself to passing prey – generally larger fish – and proceeds to suck their blood. That doesn't really justify slitting it open alive to drain the blood, but that's what happens to hundreds of lampreys caught each spring in the Garonne and Dordogne rivers when, like salmon, they swim upstream to breed. Local chefs then slice them up and cook them for several hours with leeks in red wine, mixing in the blood just before serving. Garlic croutons add texture.

In 1990, Ste-Terre, a former fishing village on the Dordogne near St-Émilion, declared itself the world's lamprey capital and instigated a lamprey festival (late April), when members of the lamprey brotherhood parade in their finery and drink a toast to the unfortunate fish before everyone tucks into tureens of lamproie à la Bordelaise. If you're curious to see what they look like, head to the **Jardin de la Lamproie** (Tues–Sat 10am–12.30pm & 2–6.30pm, Sun 2–6.30pm; free) in Lavagnac, on the river just west of Ste-Terre. There's a tank of them in the exhibition hall and a video presentation and you can also buy ready-prepared jars of lamprey, should you be so inclined. Lamprey appears on restaurant menus throughout the region at around €20.

the same bay, David aims his sling at Goliath. Other recognizable scenes feature Adam, Eve and the serpent, behind the altar, and Daniel again with two lions on the last pillar on the right of the southernmost bay.

The rest of the abbey, which was rebuilt during the Renaissance, houses the local *mairie* and can be visited only on a **guided tour** (June–Sept Tues–Sat 2.30–6pm; Oct–May Tues–Fri 2.30–5pm; €3.50). Not that there's not a great deal of interest inside. Apart from the monks' scriptorium and an eighteenth-century fresco representing Justice, the highlight is a lively stained-glass window by local English artist Jennifer Weller, illustrating abbey life in the Middle Ages.

A couple of kilometres east of St-Ferme on the D127 to Duras, the welcoming **chambre d'hôte** *Manoir de James* (T05.56.61.69.75, Wwww.manoir-de-james.com; closed mid-Dec to mid-Jan, July & Aug; ❹) occupies a quiet spot among fields. The rooms are a touch expensive, but big and airy, with sizeable bathrooms, plus there's a swimming pool and the English-speaking owners can help arrange visits to local wine producers.

The countryside north of St-Ferme is attractive, too. Take the D16 towards St-Foy-la-Grande, then turn left just before Pellegrue on the D126 to find a succession of castles between **AURIOLLES** and **LISTRAC-DE-DURÈZE**. Cutting back southwest, signs indicating "Butte de Launay" lead you to a grassy hillock outside **SOUSSAC** with 360-degree views.

St-Émilion

Roughly 40km east of Bordeaux, or directly north of Sauveterre along the D670, is the oldest wine town in France. It lies at the heart of one of the world's most densely cultivated wine regions, located on the north bank of the

The wines of St-Emilion

Louis XIV described **St-Émilion wines** as the "nectar of the gods". The best – notably the wines of Château Ausone and Château Cheval-Blanc – certainly rate on a par with the top Médocs (see p.100). They are the heartiest of the Bordeaux reds, though within the region there is considerable variety due to its complex geology and the fact that many producers are still small, family-run businesses – the average vineyard is a mere 70,000 square metres.

St-Émilion wines were not included in the 1855 **classification** (see p.78), partly for local political reasons (the Bordeaux-based merchants who selected the wines tended to look down on St-Émilion), but won great acclaim in the Paris Exhibition of 1867 and again in 1889, when sixty producers collectively won the Grand Prix. It wasn't until 1954, however, that the wines were fully classified. They were subdivided into two *appellations* – St-Émilion and St-Émilion Grand Cru – and then the latter category organized in three tiers, Grands Crus, Grands Crus Classés and Premiers Grands Crus Classés, of which the top is further subdivided into "A" and "B" wines. The system is unique in that all the wines are tasted and the Grands Crus reviewed each year, while the two top tiers are reclassified every ten years. Following the last major overhaul in 2006, 46 wines are at present entitled to the Grands Crus Classés label and fifteen to Premiers Grands Crus Classés; Ausone and Cheval-Blanc are the only top-ranked "A" wines.

The two St-Émilion *appellations* cover the eight villages of the medieval jurisdiction, the Jurade (see p.133), with a total of 5400 square kilometres under vines and an average annual production of around 250,000 hectolitres (well over three million bottles). More than half of this is exported. In addition, wines produced in the four "satellite" communes to the north – St-Georges, Montagne, Puisseguin and Lussac – are entitled to the St-Émilion name, but preceded by that of the commune: Montagne St-Émilion, for example.

The region's **soils** range from sand-gravel on the Dordogne valley floor to the limestone plateau around the town, in places capped with layers of clay, and the coarse gravel plains of the north and east. Merlot is the predominant **grape variety**, followed by Cabernet Franc (here called Cabernet Bouchet) and with smaller quantities of Cabernet Sauvignon and, occasionally, Malbec. The end result is a smooth, round wine which ages well, though some are ready to drink after only five years. But even a brief tasting session will reveal the tremendous variety among these wines which, combined with the relatively small output from some vineyards, adds to the prestige, and price, of the best ones. A bottle of Château Ausone, for example, will set you back at least €200, but among the Grands Crus you should be able to find some very fine wines, good enough for laying down, for between €15 and €20 a bottle.

For more information on these wines, call in at St-Émilion's **Maison du Vin** (see p.134). For general tips on visiting vineyards see p.79.

River Dordogne shortly before it flows into the Gironde. The **vineyards** alone justify a visit, but there's a lot more to St-Émilion than first meets the eye. The town has hardly grown in size beyond its original twelfth-century ramparts, an appealing collection of old grey houses nestled in a south-facing amphitheatre of low hills, with the green froth of the summer's vines crawling over its walls. Underneath its pretty, cobbled streets, the hillside has been hollowed out to create Europe's largest **underground church** and is riddled with catacombs and quarries that provide ideal conditions for storing the precious wine. Some of St-Émilion's most famous **wine châteaux**, notably Ausone and Belair, sit right on its doorstep, while the limestone plateau to the north is peppered with countless châteaux, country houses and Romanesque churches hemmed in by the rows of pampered vines.

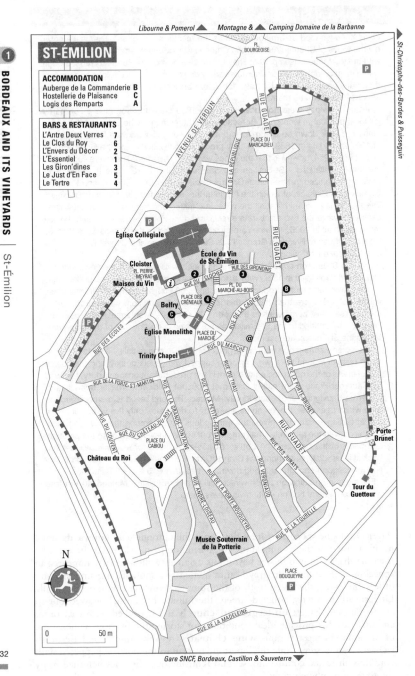

St-Christophe-des-Bardes & Puisseguin ▶

ST-ÉMILION

ACCOMMODATION
Auberge de la Commanderie	**B**
Hostellerie de Plaisance	**C**
Logis des Remparts	**A**

BARS & RESTAURANTS
L'Antre Deux Verres	7
Le Clos du Roy	6
L'Envers du Dècor	2
L'Essentiel	1
Les Giron'dines	3
Le Just d'En Face	5
Le Tertre	4

PL. BOURGEOISE

PL. BOURGEOISE

RUE GUADET

AVENUE DE VERDUN

RUE DE LA RÉPUBLIQUE

PLACE DES MARCADIEU

Église Collégiale

École du Vin de St-Émilion

Cloister
PL. PIERRE-MEYRAT

Maison du Vin

RUE DES GIRONDINS

RUE DU CLOCHER

PL. DU MARCHÉ-AU-BOIS

Belfry

PLACE DES CRÉNEAUX

Église Monolithe
PLACE DU MARCHÉ

RUE DE LA CADÈNE

Trinity Chapel

RUE DU MARCHÉ

RUE DES ÉCOLES

RUE DE LA PORTE-ST-MARTIN

RUE DE LA GRANDE-FONTAINE

RUE DU THAU

RUE DE LA PORTE-BRUNET

RUE DU COUVENT

RUE DU CHÂTEAU-DU-ROY

PLACE DU CABIOU

Château du Roi

RUE DE LA PETITE-FONTAINE

RUE ANDRÉ-LOISEAU

RUE DE LA PORTE-BOUQUEYRE

RUE GUADET

RUE DES JURATS

RUE VERGNIAUD

RUE DE LA TOURELLE

Porte Brunet

Tour du Guetteur

Musée Souterrain de la Potterie

PLACE BOUQUEYRE

N

0   50 m

RUE DE LA MADELEINE

While the Romans had introduced vines to the area before the third century, the history of St-Émilion really starts some five hundred years later when the **monk Émilion** (or Émilian), arrived here from Brittany and decided to stay. Making his hermitage in an enlarged natural cave he soon gathered a sizeable following, drawn as much by tales of miracle cures as by his piety. After Émilion's death in 767, the religious community continued to grow until the town boasted a population of around 10,000 (as opposed to under 3000 today) when it passed into the hands of the English Crown in 1152 as part of the duchy of Aquitaine. Richard the Lionheart considered the town sufficiently important to grant it the status of a self-governing commune, later ratified in a charter dated 1199 by his successor and brother King John. Thus was born the **Jurade**, an assembly presiding over local justice, taxes, defence, and, of course, the town's economic lifeblood, wine. Indeed, so sought-after was St-Émilion wine that when King Edward II of England reconfirmed the Jurade in 1312, following a brief period when the town was under French rule, he did so in exchange for "fifty barrels of clear, pure and good wine, to be delivered by Easter". Despite such strong English affiliations, St-Émilion retained its privileges after the Hundred Years' War and right up until the Revolution. The Jurade resurfaced again in 1948, but is limited strictly to promoting and maintaining the quality of the wine.

The worldwide fame of St-Émilion was sealed when it was added to UNESCO's World Heritage list in 1999 and now over a million visitors descend on the town each year, the majority during the summer months of July and August. To avoid the worst of the crowds it's best to come in the early morning or late afternoon, and better still to stay overnight here, though accommodation tends to be expensive. St-Émilion is also a feasible day-trip from Bordeaux, either by yourself, or with one of the vineyard tours organized by the Bordeaux tourist office (see p.79).

Arrival and information

St-Émilion's **gare SNCF** lies down in the valley 2km to the south. Since only four trains a day stop there at best, you could also alight at more frequently served Libourne, 7km further west on the Bordeaux–Paris line, and call a taxi from there (℡06.77.75.36.64 or 05.57.25.17.59; around €15 during the day and €20 after 7pm). The alternative is an only slightly less sporadic **bus** service (Mon–Sat three daily; operated by Marchessau, ℡05.57.40.60.79) from Libourne train station, which drops you on place Bourgeoise, the roundabout at the north end of rue Gaudet, St-Émilion's main street. CITRAM (℡05.56.43.68.43, ⓦwww.citram.com) also lays on two return services a day from Bordeaux, with a change at Libourne, in July and August and on weekends in September. If you're driving, note that the town centre is closed to traffic during the day but that there's free **parking** behind the gendarmerie just north of place Bourgeoise.

The super-efficient **tourist office**, on place des Créneaux beside the belfry (daily: April–June, Sept & Oct 9.30am–12.30pm & 1.45–6.30pm; July & Aug 9.30am–8pm; Nov–March 9.30am–12.30pm & 1.45–6pm; ℡05.57.55.28.28, ⓦwww.saint-emilion-tourisme.com), produces a useful guide outlining the main activities and attractions, including details of around ninety local vineyards where visitors are welcome. This is also where you need to sign up for tours of the Église Monolithe (see p.136). From May to September you can join one of their bilingual vineyard **tours** (Mon–Sat; €9.60), and they also rent out **bikes** for those who would rather be independent. For

Internet access, head down the main street to the *Saint Émilion Web Bar*, 37 rue Guadet (Fri & Sat 11am–midnight, Sun–Thurs 11am–10pm), which also offers Wi-fi access, not to mention wines by the glass and finger food for those that want to surf in style.

The town's **Maison du Vin**, which represents about a third of local producers, is round the corner from the tourist office on place Pierre-Meyrat (daily: Aug 10am–7pm; Sept–July 9.30am–12.30pm & 2–6.30pm; ℡ 05.57.55.50.55, ⓦ www.vins-saint-emilion.com). They sell a large selection of wines at châteaux prices and in season also offer bilingual introductory **wine-tasting courses** (mid-July to mid-Sept; €17; 1hr). Alternatively, the nearby **École du Vin de Saint-Émilion**, 4 rue du Clocher (℡ 05.57.24.61.01, ⓦ www.vignobleschateaux .fr), puts on courses year round (April–Oct Mon–Sat 11am; Nov–March by appointment only; €20; 1hr 30min) in addition to selling wines – not just from this region – and related accoutrements.

As you would expect, the most important of St-Émilion's annual **events** revolve around wine. In June members of the Jurade dust off their finery for the Fête de Printemps, and again in September to announce the harvest (see box on p.131 for more). Over a long weekend in late April or early May (Sat–Mon) some eighty châteaux throw their doors open to the public, while throughout the year keep an eye out for concerts held in the châteaux – accompanied by a tasting of course.

Accommodation

St-Émilion offers a number of good but expensive **hotels**, while for those on a stricter budget there are some very reasonably priced **chambres d'hôtes** and a **campsite** in the surrounding area. Note that most hotels close in December and January, while in summer (notably July and August) and during the two main festivals (see above), everywhere gets booked up weeks in advance, with some places hiking their prices by as much as a third. The tourist office won't make reservations for you, but they will be able to advise on where rooms might still be available.

In St-Émilion

Auberge de la Commanderie 2 rue de la Porte-Brunet ℡ 05.57.24.70.19, ⓦ www .aubergedelacommanderie.com. Small but comfortable rooms with sparkling bathrooms, though the bold colour scheme and minimalist decor, with old postcard shots of St-Émilion superimposed on the walls, won't be to everyone's taste. Despite its address, the hotel is located about halfway along rue Gaudet. Closed mid-Dec to mid-Feb. ④

Hostellerie de Plaisance place du Clocher ℡ 05.57.55.07.55, ⓦ www.hostellerie-plaisance .com. This is St-Émilion's top hotel, with a prime location next to the belfry and stunning views from its terraced garden. There are only seventeen rooms and three suites, some verging on the Baroque, split between the main building and two annexes. It has all the four-star comforts you'd expect – and prices to match. The restaurant offers equally high-class cuisine and a lengthy wine list (menus €33–85). Closed Jan. ⑨

Logis des Remparts 18 rue Gaudet (℡ 05.57.24.70.43, ⓔ logis-des-remparts@wanadoo .fr). Though its rooms don't have a great deal of character, this clean, tidy three-star at the lower end of this price bracket makes a good alternative if the *Auberge de la Commanderie* is full. The plus points are its terrace and pool, not to mention a breakfast that's a cut above the norm. Closed mid-Dec to mid-Jan. ⑥

Around St-Émilion

Bonsaï Relais rte de Castillon ℡ 05.57.25.25.07, ⓦ www.bonsai-hotels.fr. A few kilometres west of St-Émilion on the main D670, this modern chain hotel is the cheapest around. The rooms are predictably boxy but comfortable enough, all with en-suite facilities and satellite TV, and there's a pool, garden and restaurant (menus €14–29). ③

Camping Domaine de la Barbanne rte de Montagne ☎05.57.24.75.80, ⓦwww .camping-saint-emilion.com. Excellent three-star campsite 3km north of St-Émilion signed off the D122 Montagne road. In the midst of vines and next to a large lake, with two swimming pools (one heated), canoes and tennis courts amongst other facilities. Closed mid-Sept to March. ❶

Château Meylet La Gomerie, rte de Libourne ☎05.57.24.68.85, ⓦchateau .meylet.free.fr. An exceptionally welcoming and well-kept *chambre d'hôte* among the vines less than 2km outside St-Émilion on the D243 to Libourne. The rooms are all light and airy with good modern bathrooms. No meals, but there's a kitchenette. Bikes available. ❸

Château Millaud Montlabert rte de Pomerol ☎05.57.24.71.85, ⓕ05.57.24.62.78. A more rustic but nevertheless homely and well-equipped *chambre d'hôte* in a typical Girondin farmhouse 4km northwest of St-Émilion on the D245 to Pomerol. Again, there's a kitchenette but no meals, and you can sample the owners' Grand Cru wines. ❸

Château de Roques Puisseguin ☎05.57.74.55.69, ⓦwww.chateau-de-roques .com. Another vineyard location for this hotel in a rambling château about 10km northeast of St-Émilion on the D17. The ten rooms are unfussy but elegant and all en suite. Ancient grain stores beneath the château now serve as the *chais*, which you can visit. There's also a restaurant (menu €20–32) and billiard room and bikes are available. Closed Christmas & New Year hols. ❸

Le Relais de Franc Mayne La Gomerie, rte de Libourne ☎05.57.24.62.61, ⓦwww.chateau-francmayne.com. Set well back from the busy D243 to Libourne just outside St-Émilion, this newly opened château hotel offers very grand accommodation, complete with plasma TV screens, and decked out in rich purples or reds and with imaginative bathrooms. There's also a billiard room, salon and private garden and tours of the *chais* available on request (see p.139). At the bottom end of this price category. ❾

The Town

St-Émilion is built on a steep south-facing hill (flat shoes strongly recommended), with its belfry providing a convenient landmark in the town centre above the rock-hewn church with its entrance on place du Marché. From beside the belfry rue du Clocher and its extension, rue des Girondins, run east to meet St-Émilion's main street, **rue Gaudet**, which links place Bouqueyre in the south with northerly place Bourgeoise on the plateau.

A good place to get your bearings is beside the belfry on **place des Créneaux**, from the terrace of which you get a marvellous view over the huddled roofs. Better still, if you have the energy, climb the **tower** itself (same hours as the tourist office; €1) for a panorama that sweeps beyond the town walls over the vines' serried ranks. The other point to starting your explorations here is that you can sign up for a tour of the underground church (see below) at the tourist office on place des Créneaux.

While you're waiting for the tour to begin, take a look in the peaceful fourteenth-century **cloister** accessed via the tourist office (same hours; free). Though it belongs to the Collégiate church (daily 9.30am–12.30pm & 2–7pm; free), the connecting door is sealed up; instead, to reach the church turn right outside the tourist office and keep going to enter via its north door. Inside, look out for the twelfth-century frescoes of St Catherine's martyrdom on the south wall of the nave, and next to it a lovely slender Virgin squeezed onto the protruding wall, but the main draw is the statue of **St Valéry** on the transept's southeast wall, near the chapel of the martyrs. Carved and painted in the sixteenth century, he bears a staff, sack, gourd, scythe and a natty pair of pointy slippers – the work is not particularly outstanding, but the man is: St Valéry is none other than the patron saint of St-Émilion wine growers and was, according to local tradition, the brother of Jesus.

The rock on which this upper part of St-Émilion is built is a veritable honeycomb. It's estimated that 120,000 square metres have been excavated from under

△ St Emilion

the town alone, including the vast subterranean **Église Monolithe** (guided tours daily from 10am according to demand; 45min; €6 from the tourist office). The tour starts in a dark hole beside the place du Marché, supposedly the **cave** where St Émilion lived a hermit's life in the eighth century. A rough-hewn ledge served as his bed and a carved seat as his chair, where women trying to conceive reputedly still come to sit in the hope of getting pregnant. Back outside, directly above the "cave" is the simple thirteenth-century **Trinity Chapel**, built in honour of St Émilion and converted into a cooperage during the Revolution; fragments of frescoes are still visible, including the benediction of a kneeling figure which some say is Émilion. On the other side of the yard, a passage tunnels beneath the belfry to the **catacombs**, where three chambers dug out of the soft limestone were used as a cemetery and then later, through lack of space, as an ossuary from the eighth to the eleventh century. In the innermost chamber – discovered by a neighbour enlarging his cellar 55 years ago – an eleventh-century tombstone bears the inscription "Aulius is buried between saints Valéry, Émilion and Avic"; St Émilion's remains were later moved to the Collegiate church and then disappeared during the Wars of Religion.

The **church** itself is an incredible place. Simple and huge, the entire structure – barrel-vaulting, great square piers and all – was hacked out of the rock by Benedictine monks between the ninth and twelfth centuries. It is nearly forty metres long, twenty wide and eleven metres at its maximum height. The central pillars were fitted with massive, metal braces after cracks were discovered in the bell tower above. The whole interior was painted at one time, but only faint traces have survived the damp and the Revolution, when saltpetre was collected from the walls to make gunpowder. But you can still see various bas-relief carvings around the altar: a pair of four-winged angels, two zodiacal signs and a strange and badly damaged scene of a man with a spear standing between a horned monster and an angel musician.

In the lower part of town, a couple of minutes' walk from place des Créneaux down rue de la Grande-Fontaine, a warren of underground galleries makes an unusual home for the ever-expanding **Musée Souterrain de la Poterie**, 21 rue André-Loiseau (daily 10am–7pm; €4); ask to borrow their excellent English-language guide. This private collection covering two thousand years of pottery and ironwork from southwest France is a treasure trove of all sorts of interesting and unusual pieces, from earthenware fire-dogs sporting human faces to glazed roof finials (*épi de faîtage*) in the form of birds or humans, including a smartly turned-out gentleman in a top hat. Also on display are works by well-known contemporary potters such as local artist Michel Jouhanneau and Consuelo de Mont Marin.

Some of the rock dug from the museum's galleries undoubtedly went into building the massive square keep of the **Château du Roi** (daily: April–June, Sept & Oct 9.30am–12.30pm & 1.45–6.30pm; July & Aug 9.30am–8pm; Nov–March 9.30am–12.30pm & 1.45–6pm; €1) presiding over St-Émilion from the west, and constructed in the thirteenth century as a forceful reminder of the king's power in this otherwise independent town. Nowadays it comes into its own in June and September when the members of the Jurade, in their red and white robes, proclaim from its summit the judging of the new wines and the start of the grape harvest.

Eating and drinking

On a sunny spring or autumn day, when it's not too busy, there's nothing better than to sit at one of the **cafés** on place du Marché beneath the sky-piercing belfry. There are a number of inevitably touristy **restaurants** on the square, but you'll do better in the quieter streets around, or head out to one of the surrounding villages. For picnic fodder, there's a Sunday-morning **market** on place Bouqueyre at the south end of rue Gaudet, and a small supermarket right at the north end of town beyond the roundabout. You'll find a boulangerie and patisserie on rue Gaudet. While you're in St-Émilion you should try the local **macaroons** (*macarons*) – for three generations the Blanchez family (situated at 9 rue Gaudet near the post office) has been baking these tiny melt-in-the-mouth biscuits to the original recipe devised by Ursuline sisters in 1620.

L'Antre Deux Verres place du Cabiou. Enjoy a glass of St-Émilion – including some interesting and less well-known names – in the rock-hewn *cave* or on the terrace of this relaxed wine bar off the beaten track near the Château du Roi. For food, there's a choice of *tartines* (open sandwiches) and cheese or charcuterie platters, salads and the like, or full menus at €14.50 and €25. A glass of wine starts at €3–4, or €7 for a St- Émilion Grand Cru. Closed Jan & Feb.

Le Clos du Roy 12 rue de la Petite-Fontaine (☎05.57.74.41.55). Reservations are recommended at St-Émilion's most appealing restaurant, where the subtle, inventive cuisine includes a large number of fish and seafood dishes, such as wild turbot or skate with aubergines and tomato *confit*. It need not break the bank, either, with a two-course weekday lunch *formule* at €20 and menus from €28 to €46. Closed Tues & Wed; also three weeks from mid-Feb, two weeks late-Aug/early Sept & one week in Nov.

L'Envers du Décor rue du Clocher. Very popular bar-bistro just along from the tourist office, with a good range of local wines by the glass (from €5) and serving slightly refined takes on brasserie fare. Salads and starters cost upwards of €7 and main dishes €10–18, while full menus come in at €15 and €25. Closed two weeks at Christmas & New Year.

L'Essentiel 6 rue Gaudet. For those with money to burn, this relentlessly modern wine bar offers a unique opportunity to taste Grands Crus Classées wines by the glass (around €30 for one of the top names). Cheese platters cost €10. Daily 10am–9pm.

Les Giron'dines rue des Girondins. *Les Giron'dines'* back terrace makes a nice spot for a light, leisurely lunch of delicious home-made tarts and salads (€10–18), or there's a full menu at €16 (€26 on public hols). Closed Sun eve & Mon, and for dinner mid-Oct to April.

Le Just d'En Face rue de la Porte-Brunet. Tapas, hot pies, crêpes and other simple meals in a garden setting on the far side of rue Gaudet. Prices start at around €7, with grills at €16. Closed Wed.

Le Tertre rue du Tertre-de-la-Tente ℡05.57.74.46.33. For a splurge, try this romantic little restaurant on the cobbled street leading down to the market square. You're in for

well-prepared classic cuisine plus a few surprises, such as a hot foie gras and Sauternes soup served with poached oysters. Weekday lunch menus start at €18, and €25 at dinner and on weekends. Closed mid-Nov to mid-Feb, also Wed & Thurs mid-Feb to April.

Around St-Émilion

Auberge du Village St-Christophe-des-Bardes. Locals come to this village inn for a traditional workers' lunch (three courses including wine for €12), though you can just opt for a *plat du jour* (€7) or eat from the *carte* (€23 for three courses). Open daily for lunch and for dinner Fri–Sun. Closed during school hols in Nov & Dec/Jan.

Les Marronniers Montagne ℡05.57.74.60.42. Another popular option, this time in bright and breezy surroundings on the east edge of Montignac village. Various *formules* and menus are on offer; a three-course

lunch will set you back €13 (Mon–Fri) and dinner €20. There's also an extensive *carte* ranging from salads and *moules-frites* to excellent steaks. Good choice of local wines, too. Closed Sun eve & Mon.

Le Vieux Presbytère Montagne (℡05.57.74.65.33). Smart but still affordable restaurant tucked behind Montagne church which serves classic dishes alongside more imaginative fare. The *menu du marché* (€20 for three courses including a glass of wine) represents excellent value. Closed Sun eve & Mon.

A tour of the vineyards

The **vineyards** of St-Émilion are the first ever classified by UNESCO as being – in combination with the town – of sufficient cultural, historical and scenic importance to merit inclusion on the World Heritage list. Every spare inch of ground is covered with vines. Their trellised rows march from the valley floor up over the lip of the plateau, accentuating its gentle undulations, and nestle round the pale-grey limestone walls of the myriad **châteaux**. On the whole these are more modest buildings than you'll find in the Médoc or Sauternes wine regions, though St-Émilion does have its share of handsome seventeenth- and eighteenth-century piles. Most are still family homes, and therefore not open to the public, the one exception being a weekend in late April/early May when about eighty châteaux accept visitors under the *portes ouvertes* initiative organized by St-Émilion tourist office; some also host the occasional concert. But the real reason to visit is the wine, and from that point of view owners are more than happy to receive visitors – provided you phone ahead. Below is a representative selection of the region's tremendous variety where English-language tours are usually available on request.

Illustrious Ausone

One of St-Émilion's most prestigious vineyards, Château Ausone claims a long and distinguished past. Its name recalls **Decimus Magnus Ausonius**, a renowned Gallo-Roman poet whose domains here produced highly prized wines as early as the fourth century. "My wine," Ausonius wrote, "is as celebrated in Rome as the town of Burdigala (Bordeaux) itself." Ausonius was born in Burdigala in 309. The son of an eminent doctor, he practised law for a while before becoming a respected teacher and tutor to the emperor's son, Gratian. After Gratian became emperor in 367, Ausone's star rose even further and in 379 he was appointed consul of Gaul. Four years later, however, Gratian was murdered. Ausone retired to his estates to pen his verses and tend his vines. He died around 394, at the ripe old age of 85.

To start your vineyard tour there's no need to do more than stroll round St-Émilion's western ramparts to find **Château Belair** (☎05.57.24.70.94, ⓦwww.chateaubelair.com; by appointment Mon–Sat; free) on the hillside just outside the town. They produce one of the region's top wines, a Premier Grand Cru Classé since 1954, using various traditional techniques which are explained during the tour. Belair is also of interest for its underground vinification plant and ageing cellars, the latter spread over three kilometres of tunnels on three levels. The tunnels are the remnants of old stone quarries and, after quarrying was banned in 1872, were first used for cultivating mushrooms, before the owners of Belair and other châteaux along this hillside realized that their constant temperature (around 12–16°C) and high humidity were ideal for ageing and storing wine.

A kilometre or so northwest of St-Émilion on the Libourne road, **Château Franc-Mayne** (☎05.57.24.62.61; ⓦwww.chateau-francmayne.com; daily by appointment; €6 including tasting) provides another interesting excursion through a warren of tunnels, seeing how the blocks of stone were cut and how the vine roots seek out the tiniest crevaces. The visit ends in the rock-hewn tasting room sampling the château's Grand Cru. Neighbouring **Château Franc-Pourret** (☎05.57.51.07.55, ⓦwww.ouzoulias-vins.com; by appointment Mon–Fri; free if you buy) is a more modest, family-run vineyard and has the distinction of being one of only a handful producing organic wines – including a Grand Cru – in St-Émilion.

Three kilometres east along the same scarp on the D243, just beyond the village of **ST-CHRISTOPHE-DES-BARDES**, **Château Laroque** (☎05.57.24.77.28, ⓦwww.chateau-laroque.com; by appointment Mon–Fri; tastings €3) is one of the area's largest and oldest vineyards. You approach through elaborate wrought-iron gates, then down a long alley of cedars towards the seventeenth-century château overlooking immaculate lawns and Italianate statues in one direction and the River Dordogne to the south. The round tower standing slightly apart is all that remains of the original feudal château while the *chais* occupy the outbuildings across the courtyard. Château Laroque attained Grand Cru Classé status in 1996 following two decades of investment and technical innovation.

In the same commune but just north of St-Christophe on the D130 Parsac road, **Château Toinet-Fombrauge** (☎05.57.24.77.70; daily 10am–noon & 2–7pm; free if you buy) is a good example of a small, family-run vineyard. Not that their wines are anything to sneeze at – in addition to the standard St-Émilion they produce a very reasonable Grand Cru at just over €11 a bottle.

The next stop on this vineyard tour takes you a kilometre or so northwest of St-Émilion to visit **Château Laniote** (☎05.57.24.70.80; daily 8am–noon & 1.30–6pm; free) signed off the D243 Libourne road. This is another Grand Cru Classé, but produced on a much smaller scale than at Château Laroque, and of interest for those wishing to go into the technical intricacies of wine-making in more detail. In addition to the actual visit, a short video presentation allows you to see the whole process from start to finish. They also offer an introductory wine-tasting course (by appointment, €20).

To learn about the history of wine and viticulture in the region, continue three kilometres further north to the hilltop village of **MONTAGNE** with its pretty Romanesque church and **Ecomusée du Libournais** (April–11 Nov Mon–Fri 10am–noon & 2–6pm; closed 11 Nov–March; €5.50), which also doubles as a **tourist office** (☎05.57.74.50.35, ⓔtourisme.lussac@wanadoo.fr; April–Oct daily 9.30am–12.30pm & 2–7pm). The eco-museum combines replica artisans' workshops with displays concerning the life of the vine and the process of vinification, though none of the documents is translated. Afterwards you can follow a four-kilometre nature trail through the vines – ask at the museum for the map and explanatory leaflet. Or head north again on the Lussac road to visit the **Moulins de Calon**, a group of five windmills on a suitably windswept hilltop 1.3km from Montagne, one of which has been restored to working order. The owner, at nearby **Château Calon**, offers guided visits (℡05.57.51.64.88; Mon–Fri 9am–noon & 2–6pm; free), if you'd like to look inside. You can also visit their *chais* (by appointment) and sample wines produced under the St-Georges St-Émilion and Montagne St-Émilion *appellations*.

Travel details

Trains

Bordeaux to: Agen (at least 1 hourly; 1hr–1hr 50min); Angoulême (at least 1 hourly; 1hr–1hr 35min); Barsac (1–6 daily; 35min); Bergerac (2–5 daily; 1hr 10min–1hr 50min); Brive (1–2 daily; 2hr 15min); Langon (6–16 daily; 20–45min); Lesparre (3–7daily; 1hr 10min–1hr 40min); Libourne (at least 1 hourly; 25min); Margaux (4–7 daily; 35min–1hr 5min); Moulis-Listrac (4–8 daily; 45min–1hr 10min); Paris (at least 1 hourly; 3hr–3hr 30min); Pauillac (4–7 daily; 55min–1hr 25 min); Périgueux (6–10 daily; 1hr 10min–1hr 50min); Podensac (1–10 daily; 20–35min); Portets (1–10 daily; 20–25min); La Réole (6–10 daily; 30–55min); St-Émilion (4–10 daily; 30min–1hr); St-Macaire (1–3 daily; 25–45min); Sarlat (4–6 daily; 2hr 40min–3hr 30min); Toulouse (at least 1 hourly; 2hr–2hr 40min).

Buses

Bordeaux to: La Brède (Mon–Fri 8 daily; 1hr); Cadillac (2–11 daily; 1hr); Castelnau-de-Médoc (3–6 daily; 50min); Langon (2–11 daily; 1hr 30min); Libourne (4–11 daily; 50min–1hr); Listrac (3–6 daily; 55min); Margaux (2–8 daily; 45min); Pauillac (2–8 daily; 1hr 15min); St-Julien (2–8 daily; 1hr); St-Macaire (Mon–Fri 4 daily; 1hr 20min); La Sauve-Majeure (Mon–Sat 2–4 daily; 40min); Sauveterre-de-Guyenne (Mon–Fri 1 daily; 1hr 20min); Verdelais (2–5 daily; 1hr 15min).

Langon to: Bordeaux (1–15 daily; 1hr30–1hr 45min); Cadillac (1–9 daily; 30–40min).
Lesparre to: Bordeaux (3–6 daily; 1hr 30min); Castelnau-de-Médoc (3–6 daily; 40min); Listrac (3–6 daily; 35min).
La Réole to: Monségur (Mon–Sat 1–3 daily; 10–15min); St-Ferme (Mon–Fri 1–2 daily; 20min). Sauveterre-de-Guyenne (Mon–Sat 1–4 daily; 15min–1hr).
St-Émilion to: Libourne (July–Sept 2–5 daily; Oct–June Mon–Sat 3 daily; 7min).
Sauveterre-de-Guyenne to: Blasimon (Mon–Fri 3 daily; 10min); Bordeaux (Mon–Fri 1 daily; 1hr 45min); Libourne (Mon–Fri 3 daily; 1hr); Monségur (Mon–Fri 1–2 daily; 35min–1hr); Rauzan (Mon–Fri 3 daily; 20min); La Réole (2–8 daily; 1hr 20min); St-Ferme (Mon–Fri 1–2 daily; 30min–1hr); La Sauve-Majeure (Mon–Fri 1 daily; 45min).

Ferries

Lamarque to: Blaye (4–10 daily; 30min).

Planes

Bordeaux to: Lille (1–6 daily; 1hr 20min); Lyon (2–7 daily; 1hr 10min); Marseille (3–5 daily; 1hr 5min); Nantes (1–7 daily; 45min); Nice (1–2 daily; 1hr 15min); Paris CDG (5 daily; 1hr 20min); Paris Orly (1–4 hourly; 1hr 10min); Strasbourg (2–10 daily; 1hr 25min).

2

Périgueux and the north

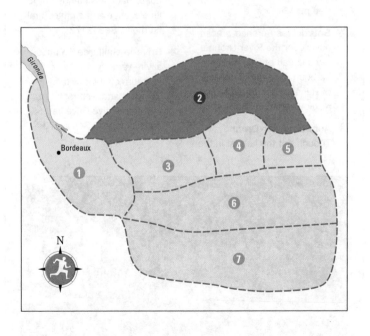

CHAPTER 2 # Highlights

✳ **Périgueux** From prehistoric and Gallo-Roman remains via Renaissance-era mansions to the cathedral's Byzantine extravagance, Périgueux has something for everyone. See p.145

✳ **Brantôme** Stroll the willow-fringed waterways of this beguiling town, then settle down to some serious eating. See p.157

✳ **Bourdeilles** Perched precariously over the River Dronne, the château of Bourdeilles harbours a splendid collection of Renaissance furniture and religious statuary. See p.160

✳ **Aubeterre-sur-Dronne** Though not the largest in the region, Aubeterre's subterranean church is both mysterious and awe-inspiring. See p.163

✳ **Château de Puyguilhem** A perfect example of early French Renaissance architecture. See p.166

✳ **Château de Hautefort** Built to rival the châteaux of the Loire, Hautefort stands out for its elegance and architectural harmony. See p.172

✳ **Brive-la-Gaillarde** An unusually rewarding local history museum coupled with a compact and well-restored city centre give Brive its special appeal. See p.173

△ Brantôme

Périgueux and the north

The north of the Dordogne *département* is its least known and most rural corner, a land with few people and large tracts of pasture and woodland, its intimate green valleys lending it the name of the **Périgord Vert**. It extends north and east to the departmental border and is bounded to the south by the **Périgord Blanc**. This latter region of limestone plateaux and wide, gentle valleys cuts a broad swathe across the heart of the Dordogne, following the course of the River Isle. On its way the river flows through just one major city, **Périgueux**, capital of both Périgord Blanc and the whole *département*. It is easy to spend a day or two exploring the old city centre with its pineapple-capped cathedral, Roman remains and archeological museum – a first taste of the wealth of prehistoric art to come – but it's in the countryside around that the region's best attractions lie.

One of the loveliest stretches is the **Dronne valley**, which shadows the Isle to the north. At **Brantôme** the Dronne's still, water-lilied surface mirrors the limes and weeping willows along its banks, before flowing on past the twin fortresses of **Bourdeilles** to **Ribérac**, a market town much-loved by the British, and **Aubeterre** on the Charente border. As at Brantôme, the river-carved cliffs at Aubeterre were hollowed out into primitive churches by twelfth-century monks. Others built dozens of little Romanesque churches on the sunny hills around, while south of the Dronne their successors helped tame the marshy, insalubrious plateau of the **Double**. In doing so they created the pine and chestnut forests which blanket the area today.

Upstream from Brantôme, two tributaries of the Dronne lead northeast to the tiny village of **St-Jean-de-Côle** and the **Château de Puyguilhem**, a marvellous Renaissance pile whose towers, gun-ports and machicolations were intended for decorative purposes rather than to be used in anger. Further northeast again there's no mistaking the warlike nature of **Jumilhac** castle's granite hulk, though its roof towers add a nicely fanciful touch. As a break from the châteaux trail, connoisseurs of foie gras should head south to the little museum in **Thiviers**, while truffle-lovers might like to press on to **Sorges**, where there's a marked path through truffle country and another small museum to explain it all. These two towns are close to the southeast border of the Périgord Vert, where the scenery becomes softer and more open again towards the lovely Auvézère valley. Here, in a spectacular

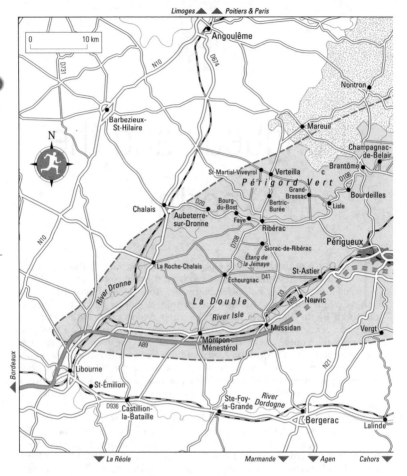

spot high over the river, the **Château de Hautefort** marks a return to the Périgord Blanc.

East of Hautefort, across the border in the Corrèze *département*, **Brive-la-Gaillarde** lies on an important crossroads and provides an alternative to Périgueux as a gateway to the region. For such a large city, Brive has a surprisingly compact and enjoyable old centre, where the historical museum is well worth visiting. The countryside around also holds a few surprises, from the national stud at **Arnac-Pompadour** to the appropriately named **Collonges-la-Rouge**, a village built of a rich, red sandstone.

Both Périgueux and Brive are major **transport** hubs. In addition to domestic airports, with frequent flights to Paris, they both have reasonable train connections to other towns in the region. Local bus services, however, are very sporadic.

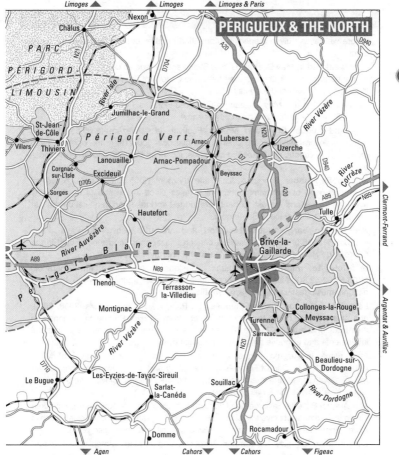

Périgueux

PÉRIGUEUX, capital of the Dordogne, is a small, busy market town for a province made rich by tourism and specialized farming. Its name derives from the Petrocorii, the local Gaulish tribe, but it was the Romans who transformed it into an important settlement. Whilst a few **Roman remains** survive, among them a recently excavated villa and an impressive sacred tower, it is the city's **medieval and Renaissance core** that gives Périgueux its particular appeal. Pretty, stone-flagged squares and a maze of narrow alleys harbour richly ornamented merchants' houses, while above it all rises the startlingly white spire of **St-Front Cathedral**, flanked by its cluster of pinnacled, Byzantine domes. A nineteenth-century reconstruction, the cathedral looks best at night – particularly from across the river – when floodlights soften the sharper edges and accentuate its exotic silhouette. The city is also home to the **Vesunna Gallo-Roman Museum** and the **Musée d'Art et d'Archéologie du Périgord** with their important archeological collections.

Where we haven't given a specific information number, contact the relevant tourist office.

First weekend in May Beatrice Burée: Snail Festival. Locals celebrate the snails by preparing and cooking them in their thousands; they are then consumed throughout the village by locals and tourists alike.

Second weekend in May St-Jean-de-Côle: Les Floralies. Flower stalls fill the village centre for a large and highly rated flower show.

July and August Brive and around: Festival de la Vézère (℡ 05.55.23.25.09, ℮ festival.vezere@wanadoo.fr). Operas and classical concerts in the open air (with picnics) or in various châteaux and churches, including Uzerche and Arnac-Pompadour.

July to September Périgueux: La Truffe d'Argent (℡ 05.53.02.82.21). A festival of French song open to amateurs, which takes place in the streets on Thursday evenings in July and August. Entrants are judged and take part in a final on the last night, which takes place in September.

Mid-July to early August Hautefort and around: Festival du Pays d'Ans (℡ 05.53.51.13.63). A mix of classical concerts, jazz, opera and theatre held in the Château de Hautefort and other châteaux and churches hereabouts.

Mid-July to mid-August Ribérac: Musiques et Paroles en Ribéracois (℡ 05.53.92.52.30). Aimed at fostering young talent from around the world, this international music festival takes place over five days.

Late July Brântome: Festival Européen du Pain. Held in even years (2008, 2010, etc), this two-day bread-fest attracts bakers from all over Europe to demonstrate their traditional artisans' loaves. There's also a Mass, displays of antique agricultural implements and a mobile bread-oven amongst other things.

First week in August Périgueux: Mimos, the International Festival of Mime (℡ 05.53.53.18.71). One of France's most exciting and innovative contemporary art festivals, with street artists and more formal ticketed events. Clowns, acrobats and workshops provide fun for all the family.

Mid-August Brive-la-Gaillarde: Les Orchestrades. Over ten days, some seven hundred young instrumentalists give free classical concerts in the streets of Brive culminating in a grand open-air concert when they all play a specially commissioned piece.

Late-August to early September Périgueux and around: Sinfonia en Périgord (℡ 05.53.04.78.49). A ten-day celebration of Baroque and Renaissance music, in Périgueux's St-Étienne church and in the nearby abbeys of Chancelade and Brantôme.

First weekend in November Brive: La Foire du Livre. A book fair held in Brive's market hall, which attracts some three hundred authors and artists presenting their new works, and around ten thousand book-lovers keen to snap up signed editions.

Early November Périgueux: Salon International du Livre Gourmand. **Biennial** (2008, 2010, etc) book fair dedicated to wine and gastronomy. Events take place over four days in the theatre (1 allée d'Aquitaine), and include book exhibitions, cooking demonstrations and opportunities to sample the results.

Markets

The most important **weekly markets** in this region are: Brântome (Fri); Brive (Tues & Sat); Excideuil (Thurs); Périgueux (Wed & Sat); Ribérac (Fri); and Thiviers (Sat). In winter many local towns hold **foie gras**, **truffle** and **walnut markets**, generally on the same day as their weekly market.

Some history

Périgueux began life some time after the fourth century BC as a fortified settlement inhabited by the **Petrocorii** ("Four Tribes"), whose craftsmen were noted for their ironwork. After 51 BC, however, the area came under Roman rule and a thriving town known as **Vesunna** (Vésone in French) began to develop, complete with amphitheatre, temples and luxurious villas. By the first century AD its population had reached an estimated 20,000, but the glory was shortlived. Vesunna, like many other towns, had neglected its defences under the *pax romana* and was caught unprepared by a succession of **barbarian invasions** in the third century. When Germanic tribes swept through the area in 275 AD, the population used stone from the surrounding civic monuments to construct defensive walls which helped the town survive, but in a much reduced state. As it faded it became known as La Cité des Pétrocores, then simply **La Cité**.

In the meantime, **St Front** arrived on the scene some time in the fourth century to convert the local population to Christianity. After giving La Cité a new breath of life by founding what eventually became St-Étienne Cathedral, St Front was later buried on a neighbouring hilltop, or *puy*, where his tomb became a pilgrimage centre. By the thirteenth century it had spawned a small but prosperous town of merchants and artisans known as **Le Puy-St-Front**, which began to rival La Cité, now the seat of the counts of Périgord. Though the two communities were joined by an act of union in 1240, they continued to glare at each other over their encircling walls – indeed, at the start of the **Hundred Years' War** La Cité sided with the English and Le Puy with France. For a while following the Treaty of Brétigny in 1360, Périgueux, as it was now known, fell under English rule, but the loyal burghers of Le Puy soon rallied to Charles V, and by 1369 Périgueux had been liberated by Bertrand du Guesclin, who then chased the English back towards the coast. Even so, by the early fifteenth century the city was in ruins, its population decimated by war, plague and famine and its buildings crumbling through neglect.

With peace, however, came renewed prosperity and a building boom that left Périgueux its wonderful legacy of **Renaissance** architecture, though much was lost or damaged during the **Wars of Religion**: despite being predominantly Catholic, Périgueux was held by the Protestants for six years after 1575, during which time they vandalized many religious buildings, amongst them St-Étienne. This proved to be the final blow for La Cité, which fell into slow decline, culminating in the transfer of cathedral status to St-Front in 1669.

Up to this time La Cité and Le Puy-St-Front remained firmly inside their respective walls, separated by open space, but in the eighteenth century Périgueux began to expand into today's **modern city**. In the process the medieval walls gave way to wide boulevards, while in the nineteenth century the canal and railway brought further development to what was by then the capital of Périgord. The old city centre was left largely untouched, so that in 1979 some twenty hectares were designated a preservation district. Nevertheless, Périgueux is still the *département*'s most industrialized town: its biggest current claim to fame – a result of 1970s decentralization policies – is the printing works where all French postage stamps, are produced.

Arrival and information

Périgueux boasts a small domestic **airport** at Bassillac, 7km east of the city, with daily flights to and from Paris. There are no facilities – though rented cars can be picked up here if booked in advance – and no convenient bus links, but a taxi into town will take less than twenty minutes (around €15). On the

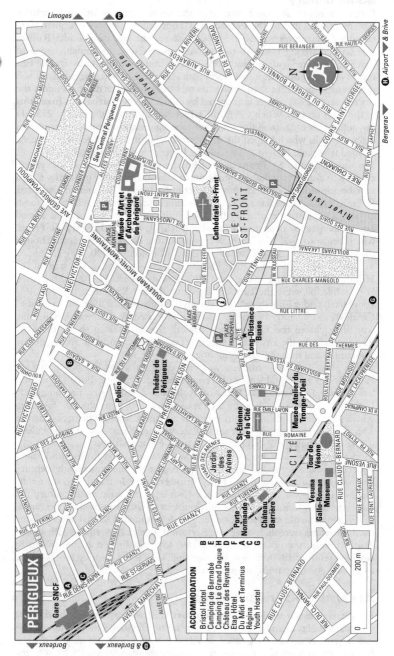

PÉRIGUEUX

ACCOMMODATION
Bristol Hotel   B
Camping de Barnabé   E
Camping Le Grand Dague   H
Château des Reynats   D
Etap Hôtel   F
Du Midi et Terminus   A
Regina   C
Youth Hostel   G

opposite side of the city, the **gare SNCF** lies roughly ten minutes' walk from the centre, along rue des Mobiles-de-Coulmiers and rue du Président-Wilson, or you can take bus #1 (direction Boulazac) to place Bugeaud or St-Front (€1.50). If you're **driving** you can park for free along the river below St-Front Cathedral, or there's plenty of pay-parking along allées Tourny, to the north of the centre, in place Montaigne to the east and underneath place Francheville. **Long-distance buses** pull in behind Place Francheville on rue de La Cité (see p.156 for more details). The *place* is also where you'll find the **tourist office** (Oct–May Mon–Sat 9am–1pm & 2–6pm; June–Sept Mon-Sat 9am-6pm, Sun 10am–1pm & 2–6pm; ☎05.53.53.10.63, ⊛www.ville-perigueux.fr). Here you can pick up free city **maps**, including one in English with recommended walking routes, and book up for their excellent **city tours** covering medieval and Renaissance Périgueux or the Gallo-Roman city (mid-June to mid-Sept Mon–Sat 10.30am, 2.30pm & 4pm, Sun 3pm; rest of the year Mon–Sat 2.30pm only; €5). The medieval tour is particularly recommended as it takes you into some of the city's hidden corners. Though the tours are predominantly in French, some guides also speak English; ask in advance.

Accommodation

Surprisingly, central Périgueux doesn't offer a particularly good range of **hotels**. There are only a couple of reasonable options in the old city itself, while the other alternatives are located within walking distance of the centre, with the best value for money to be found near the train station. For anything smarter you'll have to head further out. There is, however, a conveniently located **youth hostel** and a choice of **campsites**.

Apart from *Ibis*, which is marked on the central Périgueux map (p.157), all the accommodation listed is marked on the main Périgueux map (p.148).

Hotels

Bristol Hotel 37 rue A. Gadaud ☎05.53.08.75.90, ⊛www.bristolfrance.com This place looks pretty bland from the outside, but inside it's perfectly comfortable with airy, cool rooms, free Internet access and friendly, knowledgeable owners. ❸–❹

Château des Reynats av des Reynats ☎05.53.03.53.59, ⊛www.chateau-hotel-perigord .com. In the village of Chancelade, roughly 5km northwest of central Périgueux; the plush rooms (some in a newer annexe) and excellent restaurant in this little nineteenth-century château make it one of the city's top hotels. Restaurant closed for lunch on Sat, Sun & Mon; in winter also for dinner Sun & Mon (menus from €30). Closed Jan. ❻

Etap Hôtel 33 rue du Président-Wilson ☎05.53.05.53.82, ⊛www.etaphotel.com. One of the new breed of Etap Hôtels, for once located in the city centre rather than on the outskirts. Otherwise the formula is the same (a large double bed with single bunk above, an en-suite shower and toilet, and satellite TV), though the rooms are more spacious than usual. ❷

Ibis 8 bd Georges-Saumande ☎05.53.53.64.58, ⊛www.ibishotel.com. Comfortable but unexciting two-star hotel in an unsympathetic building right on the riverfront below St-Front Cathedral. All rooms are en suite. ❸

Du Midi et Terminus 18 rue Denis-Papin ☎05.53.53.41.06, ℻05.53.08.19.32. Simple, spruce hotel opposite the station. The cheapest rooms (with a washbasin but no shower or toilet) are rather small for two people, but there's a recommended restaurant offering good-value regional cuisine (menus from €12.50; Nov–May closed Sat & Sun eve). ❷

Régina 14 rue Denis-Papin ☎05.53.08.40.44, ℮comfort.perigueux@wanadoo.fr. Pleasant two-star hotel opposite the station offering cheerful rooms with high ceilings and windows to match (double-glazed on the front). All rooms are en suite and have satellite TV. ❸

Hostel and campsites

Camping de Barnabé Barnabé-Plage ☎05.53.53.41.45, ⊛www.barnabe-perigord.com. Charming two-star campsite fifteen minutes' walk northeast of the city along the Isle. It has a lovely riverside location, with an overspill site on the other bank, linked by boat. Bar with snack meals available in summer (April–Oct). Open all year.

Camping Le Grand Dague Atur ☎05.53.04.21.01, ⊛www.legranddague.fr. Lost in the hills 7km southeast of Périgueux, this spacious and immaculate Dutch-owned four-star site is worth seeking out if you've got your own transport. Easter–Sept.

Youth Hostel (Foyer de Jeunes Travailleurs) rue des Thermes-Prolongés ☎05.53.06.81.40, ⊜contact@fjt24.fr. With only sixteen bunk beds (four to a very small room), reservations at this

HI-affiliated hostel, five minutes' walk from the city centre along bd Lakanal, are essential from July to September. Each room has its own shower and washbasin, though no toilet, and rates include sheets and a buffet breakfast. Lunch and dinner are available, there's a large TV lounge and at weekends you can use the kitchen facilities. No curfew; €12.80 per person. For stays of four nights or longer there are single rooms available at €15.

The City

Périgueux's compact **historic centre** – much of it pedestrianized – sits on the west bank of the River Isle, occupying a rough square formed by the river, the tree-shaded cours Tourny to the north, boulevard Michel-Montaigne to the west and cours Fénelon to the south. Though the hilltop **Cathédrale St-Front** provides a natural magnet, the surrounding streets hide some particularly fine Renaissance architecture as well as the **Musée d'Art et d'Archéologie du Périgord**, with its collection of Paleolithic tools, and a remnant of **medieval wall**. The main commercial hub is concentrated around rue Taillefer, running from the cathedral west to place Bugeaud, and along pedestrianized rue Limogeanne to the north. At the southwest corner of the old town lies the wide, place Francheville, from where rue de la Cité leads westwards towards Périgueux's other principal area of interest, **La Cité**, centred around a rather mutilated church. This is where you'll find the smart new Gallo-Roman Museum, **Vesunna**, featuring the foundations of a Roman villa, and an engaging **Musée Atelier du Trompe-L'oeil**. Everything is within easy walking distance, making it possible to explore the city comfortably in a day.

From the Tour Mataguerre to place de la Clautre

There's still a slight medieval air to **Le Puy-St-Front**, the district tumbling downhill from the cathedral west to place Francheville and to cours Fénelon in the south. Its confined and cobbled alleys harbour Périgueux's oldest build-ings – the former homes of wealthy merchants – as well as the last remaining fragment of the medieval fortifications; Le Puy was originally surrounded by 28 defensive towers, of which only stout, circular **Tour Mataguerre**, protect-ing the southwest corner, remains. The tower, beside the tourist office, makes a good place from which to start exploring the city. According to legend, it was named after an English captain imprisoned here during the Hundred Years' War, but the present structure dates from the late fifteenth century, when it was rebuilt using leper labourers. It's only accessible on guided tours organized by the tourist office (see p.149); there's little to see inside – just the prison and a simple guardroom above – but views from the roof are good.

From beside Tour Mataguerre, rue de la Bride runs into rue des Farges, where, at no. 6, you'll find Périgueux's most venerable building, **Maison des Dames de la Foi**, dating from the late twelfth century. The name, "House of the Ladies of Faith", refers to a convent established in the seventeenth century for young Protestant women wishing to convert to Catholicism. Two hundred years earlier, during the Hundred Years' War, it's said that du Guesclin stayed here while preparing to liberate nearby Chancelade Abbey from the English. Although the house is slowly being restored, it's in pretty

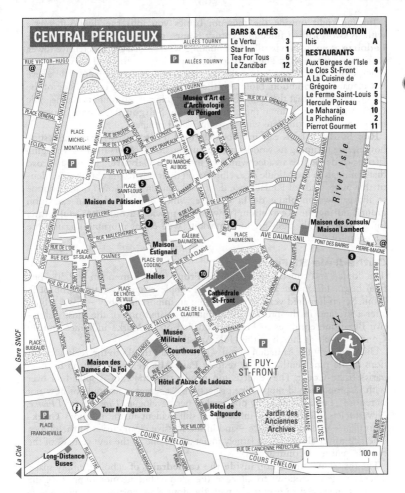

CENTRAL PÉRIGUEUX

BARS & CAFÉS
Le Vertu 3
Star Inn 1
Tea For Tous 6
Le Zanzibar 12

ACCOMMODATION
Ibis A

RESTAURANTS
Aux Berges de l'Isle 9
Le Clos St-Front 4
A La Cuisine de
  Grégoire 7
Le Ferme Saint-Louis 5
Hercule Poireau 8
Le Maharaja 10
La Picholine 2
Pierrot Gourmet 11

bad shape – in fact, you'd be forgiven for walking straight past, as the only evidence of its more illustrious history is the blocked-in window arches on the second floor.

At the top of rue des Farges, the **Musée Militaire** (Jan–March Wed & Sat 2–6pm; April–Dec Mon–Sat 2–6pm; €4) contains a vast and rather chaotic array of military memorabilia, one of the foremost such collections in France. Covering everything from the Franco-Prussian War to the Gulf War and today's UN peacekeeping missions, the exhibits are of rather specialized interest, but there are some noteworthy pieces. Look out for the fine collection of Oriental uniforms – the Zouaves' natty red trousers and embroidered jackets are particularly striking – and poignant sketches of trench life in World War I. But perhaps the most unusual displays, on the third floor, relate to the French colonial wars in Indochina (today's Vietnam, Laos and Cambodia), among them a couple of tattered Viet Minh flags.

Turning right outside the museum brings you into rue de l'Aubergerie with its two fortified fifteenth-century houses, of which **Hôtel d'Abzac de Ladouze** at no. 16, a typically dour building with an octagonal defensive tower, is the more interesting. The massive, blind arch low on the wall is evidence of much older foundations, while the incongruous ornamental balustrade above is a Renaissance addition. Note also the cockleshell carving on the side of the tower, indicating that the house once received pilgrims en route to Santiago de Compostela. Further down the street, **Hôtel de Saltgourde**, at no. 6, sports an impressive tower complete with a machicolated parapet.

Rue St-Roch leads east from below Hôtel d'Abzac past several interesting houses, one retaining its wood-timbered upper storey, others their overhanging latrines or decorative arcaded windows, to **rue du Calvaire**. This was the road that criminals in the Middle Ages climbed on their way to the courthouse, identifiable by its studded Renaissance door. The condemned would then continue to the gallows on **place de la Clautre**, which also served as an execution ground during the Revolution. Nowadays it provides a more peaceful setting for a twice-weekly fresh-produce **market** (Wed & Sat mornings) against the backdrop of the cathedral.

Cathédrale St-Front

The domed and coned **Cathédrale St-Front** (daily 8am–noon & 2.30–7pm; free) began life in the sixth century as a simple chapel over the tomb of St Front. Seven hundred years later – by then an important abbey – it was rebuilt after a fire and in the process the architects created one of the most distinctive Byzantine churches in France, modelled on St Mark's in Venice and on Constantinople's Church of the Holy Apostles.

Unfortunately, the cathedral of today is no beauty, thanks to the zealous attentions of the nineteenth-century restorer **Paul Abadie**, who went on to build Paris's Sacré-Coeur. The result is too regular, and the roof is spiked all over with ill-proportioned nipple-like projections; "a supreme example of how not to restore", Freda White tartly observed in her travelogue, *Three Rivers of France*. Nevertheless, the Byzantine influence is still evident in the interior's Greek-cross plan – unusual in France – and in the massive clean curves of the domes. The bell tower also survived largely intact and is one of the few vestiges of the twelfth-century reconstruction.

The overriding impression **inside the cathedral** is of echoing, empty space. There are few windows to alleviate the gloom, but it's not oppressive: the architects managed to play tricks with the domes' supporting columns, whose hollow centres belie the weight of stone above. The extravagant copper and glass chandelier over the central altar is another Abadie touch, designed for the wedding of Napoléon III in Paris's Notre-Dame, but the main attraction is a handsome Baroque **altarpiece** in the far eastern bay. Carved in oak and walnut, it depicts the Assumption of the Virgin Mary, with a humorous little detail in the illustrative scenes from her life of a puppy tugging the sheets off the infant Jesus's bed. Nearby, a particularly muscle-bound Hercules supports an equally ornate pulpit.

North of the cathedral

North of the cathedral crowd the renovated buildings of the **Renaissance** city. Though we suggest a few highlights to aim for below, the best approach is simply to wander, taking any enticing alley that strikes your fancy. If you head generally north, you'll emerge on cours Tourny near Périgueux's wide-ranging municipal museum.

The longest and finest street in this part of town is narrow **rue Limogeanne**, leading north from place de la Clautre via rue Salinière. Among the proliferating souvenir shops stand elegant mansions, now turned into swish boutiques and delicatessens, its most notable facade belongs to **Maison Estignard** at no. 5, whose elaborate architecture – mullions, dormer windows and ornamental columns – is typical of the Renaissance. It's also worth popping into the more sober courtyard of no. 3 to see a salamander carved above the inner door; this was the insignia of Francis I (1515–47), who brought Italian Renaissance style to France. Opposite, impasse Limogeanne leads into a series of courtyards and passageways known as **galerie Daumesnil** after the famous general born at 7 rue de la Clarté in 1776 (see box on p.154). The area, contain-

△ Périgueux

ing a mix of architectural styles, comprises one of Périgueux's most successful restoration projects.

Though nearby place du Coderc and place de l'Hôtel-de-Ville are both strong contenders, **Place St-Louis**, to the west of rue Limogeanne, is probably the prettiest of Périgueux's squares. In its southeast corner stands the handsome, turreted **Maison du Pâtissier** – built by a man who made his fortune from *pâté en croûte* (pâté in a pastry crust) – with a lovely Renaissance door bearing a warning on its lintel: "Remember death awaits us all. Let he who takes pleasure in speaking ill of those who are no longer with us, know that this house is forbidden to him. The supreme glory is to offend the wicked." There are more fine houses over to the east of rue Limogeanne on rue de la Constitution; from here the lanes begin to drop steeply to the river, where you'll find the fifteenth-century **Maison des Consuls** beside the bridge. It's a grand house with a semi-fortified third-floor gallery, while **Maison Lambert** next door – added in the sixteenth century – is almost lost behind a double gallery edged with sturdy balustrades. Sadly, both have seen better days.

The last sight in this area is the **Musée d'Art et d'Archéologie du Périgord** (April–Sept Mon & Wed–Fri 10.30am–5.30pm, Sat & Sun 1–6pm; Oct–March Mon & Wed–Fri 10am–5pm, Sat & Sun 1–6pm; €4, free Oct to May Mon–Fri noon–2pm; ⓦmusee-perigord.museum.com), housed in a grand, nineteenth-century building at the top of rue St-Front, overlooking the broad, tree-lined allées Tourny. The museum is best known for its extensive and important prehistoric collection and some beautiful Gallo-Roman mosaics. Exhibits include a 70,000-year-old human skeleton, the oldest yet found in France and a delicate engraving of a bison's head. However, these and many of the more fragile items on display are copies, and the museum's old-fashioned layout makes it hard to appreciate what's on offer.

Daumesnil: the peg-leg general

A devoted follower of Napoleon Bonaparte, **Baron Pierre Daumesnil** (1777–1832) was fiery, impetuous, loyal, patriotic and, above all, brave. He first distinguished himself during the Italian campaign (1796–97) when he rescued the drowning Napoleon from a river during the Battle of Arcole. Then at Acre in 1799 Daumesnil threw himself in front of his hero when a bomb landed at Napoleon's feet. It failed to explode, but Daumesnil, by now a major, was less lucky at the **Battle of Wagram** in Poland in 1809, when his left leg was so badly mutilated that it had to be amputated. Three years later he was promoted to general and made **governor of the Château de Vincennes** – the country's largest arsenal – which he twice refused to hand over to the allied European armies fighting Napoleon. The second time, in 1815, he declared: "I will give up Vincennes when you give me back my leg". Nevertheless, Daumesnil was forced to retire a few months later following Napoleon's defeat at Waterloo, and he eventually died of cholera in 1832, though his wooden leg was preserved and is now on display in Paris's Musée de l'Armée. In Périgueux you'll find a statue of him towards the south end of boulevard Michel-Montaigne, proudly pointing at his peg-leg.

La Cité

Remnants of the Roman town of Vesunna, now known as **La Cité**, lie southwest along rue de la Cité from place Francheville. Named after a local divinity, Vesunna was an important and prosperous town: by the first century AD it extended over some seventy hectares, complete with a forum, basilica, thermal baths and a seven-kilometre-long aqueduct. Today the most visible vestiges – a ruined amphitheatre, the remains of a temple complex and an excavated villa – lie scattered around the hulk of Périgueux's first cathedral, St-Étienne-de-la-Cité.

Approaching from the east, **St-Étienne**'s domes dominate La Cité. It was founded by St Front in the fourth century, then rebuilt in its present form, with a Romanesque nave comprising big square bays, some six hundred years later. The original building comprised four bays but two were destroyed, along with the bell tower, by Huguenots in 1577, leaving the church's west facade roughly truncated. The first bay you enter is the older of the two, dating from the eleventh century: the dome is more massive, the windows smaller and fewer and the stone less regular. The second bay was added a century later, then restored as an exact copy in the 1600s. Apart from being lighter and higher, its main feature is the line of decorative columns along the walls which stand out in the otherwise unornamented church.

The pretty **Jardin des Arènes** (daily: April–Sept 7.30am–9pm; Oct–March 7.30am–6.30pm; free), a circular garden northwest of St-Étienne, conceals a few remnants – comprising an entrance arch and traces of the foundations – of an enormous **amphitheatre** capable of holding twenty thousand people or more. Built in the first century AD, it was dismantled two hundred years later to construct defensive walls (see p.147), of which you can see a fragment, the **Porte Normande**, along nearby rue Turenne. In the panic, the walls were cobbled together with whatever came to hand: a column, some capitals, a carved lintel, all pilfered from neighbouring monuments.

Heading southeast from here, past the empty carcass of twelfth-century Château Barrière and across the train lines, you reach Périgueux's most imposing Roman monument, the **Tour de Vésone**, in another public garden (same times as des Arènes; free). This high, circular tower was once the sanctuary of a temple dedicated to Vesunna's eponymous guardian goddess. The gaping breach on the north side is said to have been created when St Front exorcized the pagan gods; more prosaically, the bricks and stones probably went into local building works.

Just behind the tower on rue Claude Bernard is the swish new **Vesunna** (July & Aug daily 10am–7pm; Sept–Dec & Feb-April Tues–Sun 10am–12.30pm & 2–5.30pm; April-June Tues-Sun 10am-12.30pm & 2-6pm; T05.53.53.00.92, Wwww.semitour.com; €5.50), a Gallo-Roman museum housed in a striking modern glass building, and built around the well-preserved remains of a grand Roman villa, which were discovered by chance in 1959.

The villa was no humble abode. It was complete with at least sixty rooms, an under-floor central heating hypocaust, thermal baths and colonnaded walkways around the central garden with its cooling pond and fountain. Around the walls you can see the remains of first-century murals of river and marine life, the colours still amazingly vibrant, and here and there, graffiti of hunting scenes, gladiatorial combat and even an ostrich – no doubt the work of some bored Roman teenager.

With time to spare, it's worth dropping by the **Musée Atelier du Trompe-L'oeil**, 5 rue Émile-Combes (Tues–Sat 10.30am–12.30pm & 2.30–6.30pm, Sun 3–6pm; €5; Wwww.museedutrompeloeil.com), as you head back into central Périgueux. This small, privately owned museum, which traces the history of *trompe-l'oeil* from prehistoric cave-paintings to the present day, doubles as a showroom and workshop for one of France's leading practitioners; there are even examples of her handiwork in the toilets. She also runs occasional courses of between two to five days for beginners upwards.

Eating, drinking and entertainment

There are several good places to **eat and drink** in Périgueux, particularly in the old city. In addition to those recommended below, all of which are marked on the central Périgueux map (p.151), there are several **cafés** along boulevard Michel-Montaigne. On place Francheville you'll find the multiscreen **CAP Cinema** (T08.36.68.04.45), and the Nouveau Théâtre de Périgueux (NTP) at 1 allée d'Aquitaine (T05.53.53.18.71) puts on a varied programme of **theatre**, dance, concerts and variety shows.

Restaurants

Aux Berges de l'Isle 2 rue Pierre-Magne T05.53.09.51.50. Pretty little restaurant at the east end of Pont des Barris (entrance through the *Hôtel des Barris*), offering unrivalled views of the cathedral and traditional cuisine at reasonable prices. Specialities include lamprey, soufflé of foie gras and Limousin beef. There's a wide choice of menus, starting at €13 for two courses. Closed Sun eve & Mon.

Le Clos St-Front 5 rue de la Vertu T05.53.46.78.58. This elegant restaurant has a well-earned reputation for its inventive and well-priced menus, starting at €21. The dishes are beautifully presented, not huge but extremely satisfying and include delights such as sautéed calamari with cardamom and chocolate pudding with szechuan pepper. Food is served in the dark pink dining room or in summer you can dine in the shady courtyard, which provides a haven of peace right in the city centre. Closed Sun eve & Mon Oct-May.

A la Cuisine de Grégoire 12 rue de la Sagesse T05.53.46.69.75. Small menu of fresh local produce served in a cosy little dining room, including grills, duck, fish and fresh vegetables from the local markets. The choice is limited but the dishes are well executed and the welcome warm.

La Ferme Saint-Louis 2 pl St-Louis T05.53.53.82.77. Either book ahead or get there early if you want to eat on the terrace of this excellent restaurant on one of Périgueux's prettiest squares. It serves a limited but well-priced menu, with a starter and main course at €24 (lunchtime only), or €27 for three courses. The food is all freshly prepared, portions are good and the service impeccable. Closed Sun & Mon.

Hercule Poireau 2 rue de la Nation ☎05.53.08.90.76. One of Périgueux's best-known restaurants, in a stone-vaulted room with cheerful red-check fabrics, offering top-quality local cuisine at surprisingly affordable prices. This is rich fare: house speciality is the luxurious *rossini de canard* (duck with a slice of foie gras in a truffle sauce). Menus from €19 to €42. Closed Wed.

Le Maharaja 3 rue Denfert Rochereau ☎05.53.53.88.82. One of the few Indian & Pakistani restaurants in the region serves up tasty vindaloos, and jalfrezis with menus from €11 at lunchtime and €29 in the evenings. Closed Sun & Wed lunch.

La Picholine 6 rue du Puy-Limogeanne ☎05.53.53.86.91. Don't be put off by the location, in a rather grungy corner tucked off place St-Louis – the food is tasty and very reasonably priced. The southern, Mediterranean flavours also make a welcome change: roast vegetables, *aïoli* and lashings of olive oil, accompanied by Provençal wines. Lunchtime menus start at €11, evenings at €14. Closed Sun. July & Aug open daily.

🏃 Pierrot Gourmet 6 rue L'Hôtel de Ville ☎05.53.35.32. Principally a gourmet deli and rotisserie, there are also a few tables for diners and table service from 10am-5pm daily. The food is fresh and top quality and includes a range of wonderful yet simple dishes such as mushroom paté, pears poached in red wine and pastas.

Bars and cafés

Star Inn 17 rue des Drapeaux. Snug Anglo-Irish pub behind the Musée d'Art at d'Archéologie du Périgord, patronized by a mixed crowd of local expats and Anglophiles. Happy hour Mon–Thurs 8–9pm, book exchange, board games and – of course – darts and quiz nights. Mon–Sat 8pm–1am.

🏃 Tea For Tous 28 rue Equillerie. Tea shop featuring over fifty types of teas from all over the world, from English breakfast to Moroccan mint. Also serves delicious cakes and desserts such as pear and chocolate crumble and cherry *clafoutis*. Tea with scones or cake costs €5.80.

La Vertu 11 rue de la Vertu. Appealingly eccentric bar where, in summer, you can lounge in wooden deck chairs outside in the quiet square . As well as a good choice of wines and beer, *La Vertu* serves cocktails, tapas and ice creams. Opening times are erratic.

Le Zanzibar 2 rue Condé. Bar with a tropical feel, a long list of exotic cocktails and imported island beers as well as a good selection of tapas. Salsa every Wednesday. Tues–Sat 6.30pm–1am.

Listings

Airlines Airliner (☎08.20.82.08.20, ⊛www .airfrance.com) operates daily flights to Paris Orly.

Airport Bassillac ☎05.53.02.79.71.

Bike rental Cycles Cum's, across the river at 41 bis cours St-Georges, ☎05.53.53.31.56; Cycles Évasion Peugeot, near the train station at 46 rond point Chanzy, ☎05.53.05.21.80.

Boat trips From mid-June to mid-September boats depart from beneath the cathedral for a fifty-minute excursion along the Isle (€6.50; ☎05.53.24.58.80).

Books and newspapers Maison de la Presse, 11 place Bugeaud, stocks the widest selection of English-language newspapers and magazines and has a decent selection of local guidebooks. Otherwise, try Librairie Marbot at 21–23 bd Montaigne, which also stocks a few English-language novels.

Bus departures Long-distance buses leave from the bus stop on rue de la Cité, behind place Francheville. Most routes are operated by CFTA, which has an information office on site (☎05.53.08.43.13). Tickets are available on board.

Car rental Near the train station, try: Ada-Autoloc 24, 4 bis rue Henri-Barbusse ☎05.53.05.40.28; Avis, gare SNCF ☎05.53.53.39.02; Europcar, 7 rue Denis-Papin ☎05.53.08.15.72; Sixt, 12 rue Denis-Papin ☎05.53.35.94.76. Hertz, 20 cours Montaigne ☎05.53.53.88.88, is in the city centre. You can also arrange to pick up cars at the airport.

Hospital Central Hospitalier, 80 av Georges-Pompidou (☎05.53.07.70.00), to the north of centre off bd Michel-Montaigne.

Internet access Net Runner, 11 rue Victor-Hugo (Mon–Wed & Fri 10am–midnight, Tues & Thurs noon-midnight; Sat & Sun 2pm-midnight); Intergames, rue Pierre-Magne (Mon-Sat 10am-7pm).

Markets Périgueux's largest markets take place on Wednesday and Saturday mornings principally in place de la Clautre, place du Coderc (both fresh foods) and place Francheville (Wed only; clothes and household goods). There's also a small, daily fresh-food market in place du Coderc's covered hall (8am–1pm). In winter (mid-Nov to mid-March), stalls selling foie gras and truffles set up in place St-Louis for the annual *marchés de gras* (Wed & Sat am).

Police Commissariat de Police, rue du 4-Septembre ☎05.53.06.44.44.

Post Office The central post office is at rue du 4-Septembre, 24000 Périgueux.

Shopping The best place to look for regional produce is along rue Taillefer, where Pierre Champion (no. 21) sells local wines and truffles as well as duck and goose in all its guises; browse also among the tempting specialist shops on rue Limogeanne. Apart from the markets listed above, you can buy picnic food in the Monoprix supermarket on place Francheville.

Taxis Call Allo Taxi Périgueux on ☎ 05.53.09.09.09. Alternatively, there's a taxi stand outside the train station and another on place Bugeaud.

Brantôme, the lower Dronne valley and the Double

Thirty kilometres north of Périgueux, the town of **Brantôme** is often described as the "Venice of Périgord". While that's rather overdoing it, the river walks and waterside restaurants are what draw most people here, with the added attraction of a Benedictine abbey's troglodyte vestiges. By contrast, the country along the **River Dronne** remains largely undisturbed. It is tranquil, very beautiful and restoring, best savoured at a gentle pace, perhaps by bike or even by canoe along the river. **Bourdeilles**, the first sizeable town downstream from Brantôme, was the seat of one of Périgord's four baronies (see p.386), as its great tower testifies, while the Renaissance château next door contains a marvellous collection of furniture. From the foot of the castle, the Dronne meanders through water meadows to one of the Dordogne's most famous market towns, **Ribérac**. Though Ribérac itself holds little else of interest, it makes an agreeable base from which to visit a crop of Romanesque churches scattered in the countryside around. **Aubeterre-sur-Dronne**, with another, better-preserved troglodyte church and a splendid position, represents the final stop along the river. From here, if time allows, plunge south into the empty, enclosed world of the **Double** forest. Among isolated pockets of habitation, the spire of a Cistercian abbey provides a rare landmark and a focus for exploring the area's farms and myriad lakes, before dropping south again to a little-visited Renaissance château at **Neuvic**.

While there is no public transport along the Dronne valley or into the Double, there are **buses** from both Périgueux and Angoulême to Brantôme and Ribérac. From Angoulême, on the Paris–Bordeaux train line, there is also a bus service to Aubeterre.

Brantôme

When local monks dug a mill-stream across a tight meander of the River Dronne about a thousand years ago, they created the island on which **BRANTÔME** now stands. It's a pretty setting, with gardens and parks surrounding much of the town, the mill beside an ancient dog-leg bridge and a Romanesque belfry silhouetted against the wooded scarp behind. The **abbey** and the **caves** at the base of this hill constitute Brantôme's principal sight, while the range of accommodation in the area makes the town worth considering as an alternative base to Périgueux.

The Town

Aerial views show Brantôme's **old centre** packed onto an almost circular island, seemingly tethered to the surrounding bank by its bridges. A modern bypass takes the worst of the traffic, but in summer it's still a bottleneck along the main road, rue Gambetta, which cuts north across the island to place de Gaulle on the far bank of the Dronne.

The town owes its existence to some rock-shelters – where the first hermits set up home around the fifth century – and a spring now hidden behind the church and convent buildings of the former **Benedictine abbey** standing on the river's far north bank. The first church was built under the cliffs here sometime before 817 – according to local tradition, it was Charlemagne (742–814) who founded the abbey with the endowment of St Sicaire's relic, one of the infants massacred by Herod. It had a rocky start, but by its twelfth-century heyday the abbey supported 24 parishes and had spawned a thriving town. Nevertheless, things started going downhill again with the Hundred Years' War and, after being rebuilt on several occasions, the abbey was finally abandoned after the Revolution. The present buildings, which date from the seventeenth century but were heavily restored two hundred years later, house the **Hôtel de Ville**, whose staring, serried windows still hint at ascetic institutional life. Not that self-denial was a virtue associated with this monastery's most notorious abbot, Pierre de Bourdeilles, the sixteenth-century author of *Les Dames Galantes* and other scurrilous tales of life at the royal court.

The abbey **church** recalls some of this history. The death of St Sicaire is the subject of a stained-glass window behind the altar, while bas-reliefs to either side depict the Massacre of the Innocents and Charlemagne offering Sicaire's relic to the church. After a quick look in the neighbouring chapterhouse, with its palm-frond vaulting, next stop is the **caves** (July & Aug daily 10am–7pm; April–June & Sept Mon & Wed–Sun 10am–noon & 2–6pm; Feb, March & Oct–Dec Mon & Wed–Sun 10am–noon & 2–5pm; €6), accessed through this northeast corner of the Hôtel de Ville. Despite being used as a quarry over the years, there's still considerable evidence of the monks' earlier troglodytic existence. The most interesting of the caves contains a large, rather crude **sculpture** of the Last Judgement, believed to date from the fifteenth century, in the aftermath of the Hundred Years' War. On a plinth decorated with geometric symbols and eight faces, each in different headgear, two angel trumpeters flank the skeletal image of Death, while the figure of God, faintly etched and massive, looms out of the rock above. The cave's right-hand wall bears a much finer Crucifixion scene in front of a very European-looking Jerusalem.

A later, more worldly generation of monks built themselves an Italianate walled garden, now a public **park**, to the south of the abbey and across the old stone bridge from the water mill. It's a pleasant picnic spot, and a walk along the balustraded **riverbanks** is a must. In summer you can also take a 45-minute **boat trip** around the island from beside the old bridge (Easter–early Oct; €6.50).

The more modern bridge directly in front of the abbey leads into rue Puy-Joli, Brantôme's main shopping street, where you'll find the engaging **Musée de Rêve et Miniatures** at no. 8 (opening hours available by telephone on ☏05.53.35.29.00; €6.50). Though not to everyone's taste, the six doll's houses and displays of furniture through the ages, including real silver and glassware all shrunk to one-twelfth normal size, show stunning craftsmanship – some pieces of furniture even have working locks and keys. These days, the museum mostly serves as a function room hired out for conferences and events.

Practicalities

Buses on the Périgueux–Angoulême route, timed to connect with TGV trains in Angoulême, stop on the Champs de Foire, at the south end of rue Gambetta. The **tourist office** is located in the Hôtel de Ville (July & Aug daily 10am–7pm; April–June & Sept Mon & Wed–Sun 10am–noon & 2–6pm; Feb, March & Oct–Dec Mon & Wed–Sun 10am–noon & 2–5pm; ☏05.53.05.80.52, www.ville-brantome.fr). For more than 450 years the streets of central Brantôme have been filled with a Friday-morning **market**, its stalls augmented in winter (Dec–Feb) with truffles, foie gras and local walnuts. Between May and September, you can rent **canoes** and **bikes** (only a handful, so reservations are recommended) from Brantôme Canoë, just out of the centre on the road east to Thiviers (☏05.53.05.77.24, Ⓦwww.brantome-canoe.com).

Accommodation

Brantôme has a good range of **accommodation** options, either in the town itself or close by. Those with a tent should head for the well-run **municipal campsite,** just east of Brantôme on the D78 Thiviers road (☏05.53.05.75.24; May–Sept).

Hôtel Chabrol 57 rue Gambetta ☏05.53.05.70.15, Ⓦwww.lesfrerescharbonnel.com. Comfortable, pretty rooms decked out in wood and florals overlooking the river, excellent service and a well-rated restaurant (see *Les Frères Charbonnel* below) make this one of Brantôme's most popular hotels. Closed mid-Nov to mid-Dec & Feb. ❸

Château de la Borie-Saulnier Champagnac-de-Belair ☏05.53.54.22.99, Ⓦperso.orange .fr/chateaudelaboriesaulnier. Set in extensive grounds, and with a pool, this imposing château offers five rooms full of period furniture and family knick-knacks. It's signposted off the D82 4km northeast of Brantôme. Evening meals on request. Closed mid-Oct to mid-April. ❹

Maison Fleurie 54 rue Gambetta ☏05.53.35.17.04, Ⓦwww.maisonfleurie.net.

Stylish, centrally located English-owned *chambre d'hôte* with a pool and a quiet courtyard garden. Closed two weeks in Feb. ❹

Moulin de l'Abbaye 1 rue de Bourdeilles ☏05.53.05.80.22, Ⓦwww.moulinabbaye.com. If you're feeling self-indulgent, treat yourself to a night of luxury in this beautiful old mill to the west of the abbey. Restaurant menus from €45 (closed for lunch Mon–Fri). Hotel & restaurant closed Nov–April. ❾

Hôtel Versaveau 8 place de Charles-de-Gaulle ☏05.53.05.71.42. This friendly hotel is the cheapest option in Brantôme, with just eight simple rooms above a decent restaurant (menus from €10). Closed three weeks in Nov & Sat Sept–May. ❶

Eating and drinking

The **café-bars** on place du Marché, across the river from the abbey church, are a popular spot for a drink. Alternatively, to the east of rue Gambetta the *Auberge du Hussard*, 6 rue Georges-Saumande (3pm–midnight), offers a quirky setting as you sup your drink: ices, coffees, teas and a good range of beers, including local artisanal brews, are served in an antique shop. As for eating, Brantôme has an unusual number of top-quality **restaurants** for such a small town; there's also one particularly good option a short drive away, while the hotels listed above are also decent places for a meal.

Restaurants

Au Fil de l'Eau 21 quai Bertin ☏05.53.05.73.65. Under the same management as the *Moulin de l'Abbaye* hotel, and specializing in well-prepared and not too expensive fish dishes. At its best in fine weather, when tables are set out on the riverbank to the west of the centre. Menus from €22. Closed mid-Sep to Easter, and Wed & Thurs all year except July & Aug.

🏃 **Les Frères Charbonnel** *Hôtel Chabrol*, 57 rue Gambetta ☏05.53.05.70.15. This hotel restaurant is in the gourmet class, but is still good value with menus from €27. Specialities of the

house include lemon sole with truffles (Oct–June closed Sun eve & Mon, also closed mid-Nov to mid-Dec, & Feb).

🏃 **Les Jardins de Brantôme** 33–37 rue Pierre-de-Mareuil ☏05.53.05.88.16. Though it doesn't look much from the outside, the food here is consistently good and there's a delightful garden behind for summer dining. It's at the far end of rue Pierre-de-Mareuil, a small street running north from place de Gaulle. Menus range from €11 to €23. Closed Wed & Thurs.

Moulin du Roc Champagnac-de-Belair ☏05.53.02.86.00, Ⓦwww.moulinduroc.com. For a real splurge in an idyllic waterside setting, head 6km east of Brantôme to find this very gracious hotel-restaurant beside the bridge as you come into Champagnac-de-Belair from the west. Apart from Sundays, lunch costs just €32 including a cocktail, two glasses of wine and coffee; Sunday and evening menus start at €45. Closed Jan & early Feb; also closed Wed lunchtime from Nov–May.

Bourdeilles

BOURDEILLES, 16km down the Dronne from Brantôme by the beautiful D106 back road, is relatively hard to reach – perhaps the most appealing way is by canoe (see p.159 for rental from Brantôme). It's a sleepy backwater, an ancient village clustering round its **château** (Feb, March & mid-Nov to Dec Mon, Wed, Thurs & Sun 10am–12.30pm & 2–5.30pm; April–June & Sept to mid-Nov daily except Tues 10am–12.30pm & 2–6pm; July & Aug daily 10am–7pm; €5.50; ⓦ www.semitour.com) on a rocky spur above the river. The château consists of two buildings: one a thirteenth-century fortress, the other a subdued Renaissance residence begun by the lady of the house, Jacquette de Montbrun, wife of André de Bourdeilles, as a piece of unsuccessful favour-currying with Catherine de Medici – unsuccessful because, though she passed through the area, Catherine never came to stay and so the château remained unfinished. The Renaissance château is now home to an exceptional collection of **furniture** and **religious statuary**. Among the more notable pieces are some splendid Spanish dowry chests; the gilded bedroom suite of a former Yugoslav king; and a sixteenth-century Rhenish entombment whose life-sized statues embody the very image of the serious, self-satisfied medieval burgher. The *salon doré*, the room Catherine de Medici was supposed to sleep in, has also been preserved. Its elaborate furnishings and floor-to-ceiling decoration seem almost guaranteed to give a restless night. To clear your head, climb the octagonal **keep** and look down on the town's clustered roofs, the weir and the boat-shaped mill parting the

△ Bourdeilles, River Dronne

current, and along the Dronne to the cornfields and the manors hidden among the trees.

There's a small **tourist office** just downhill from the château entrance (April–Sept daily 3–6pm; ℡05.53.03.42.96, Ⓦwww.bourdeilles.com). For a simple, old-fashioned **hotel**, *Les Tilleuls* (℡ & Ⓕ05.53.03.76.40; ❸; closed Nov–Feb; menus from €10), right across the street, makes a reasonable place to stay, or try the more comfortable *Hôtel du Donjon* opposite (℡05.53.04.82.81, Ⓦwww .hotel-ledonjon.com; ❸; closed Jan–Easter) which serves delicious regional cuisine in its leafy garden restaurant (menus from €20). More upmarket again is the very stylish *Hostellerie les Griffons* (℡05.53.45.45.35, Ⓦwww.griffons.fr; ❻; closed mid-Oct to Easter) in a sixteenth-century house beside the hump-back bridge, with top-notch regional cuisine (menus from €25).

If you're heading along the Dronne to Ribérac, (see below) you could stop for lunch at the *Moulin du Pont* (menus from €12; closed mid-Nov to Feb), a **restaurant** 8km downstream near the village of **LISLE**. Get here early to sit on the terrace with the weir on one side and the restaurant's trout ponds on the other. You could even arrive by river; **canoe** rental is available in Bourdeilles from Canoës Bourdeilles Loisirs (℡05.53.04.56.94; mid-June to mid-Sept) at the *Hôtel du Donjon*.

Ribérac and around

Surrounded by an intimate, hilly countryside of woods, hay meadows and drowsy hilltop villages, **RIBÉRAC**, 30km downstream from Bourdeilles, is a pleasant if unremarkable town whose greatest claim to fame is its Friday **market**, bringing in producers and wholesalers from all around. There's nothing really in the way of sights, but the country around is dotted with numerous **Romanesque churches** that provide a focus for leisurely wandering – before setting off, you might want to collect information on these from Ribérac's tourist office (see p.162). Nowadays many are kept locked, but the route described below takes in a representative sample of those that are more likely to be open. Their most distinctive features are a line of domes over the nave and the lack of decoration, just the occasional carved portal or capitals. Many have also been heavily fortified.

A couple of hundred metres from the centre on the hill to the east of town, Ribérac's own **Collégiale Notre-Dame** (mid-June to mid-Sept daily 2–7pm; rest of the year open for exhibitions only; free), now an exhibition and concert hall, makes a good place to start exploring. It's a pleasing building, with its squat tower and semicircular apse designed on a grander scale than its country cousins, but the west end and interior have been extensively altered; if it's open, it's worth popping in to see the recently restored seventeenth- and eighteenth-century frescoes. The **church of St-Pierre** in the village of **FAYE**, 1km west of Ribérac on the D20, on the other hand, has great charm even though it's no architectural beauty. Its diminutive single nave seems barely able to carry the fortress of a tower above. There's more reason to stop at **BOURG-DU-BOST**, 6km further downstream, where the **Notre-Dame** (daily 9am–7pm) harbours some very faded twelfth-century murals: the four Evangelists inside the dome, and the twelve Apostles around the choir.

From here the route cuts north and climbs to an undulating plateau with good views back over the Dronne's river meadows, then meanders through a string of villages. The first one to aim for is **ST-MARTIAL-VIVEYROL**, roughly 15km due north of Ribérac. Its church (daily 9am–6pm) more resembles a castle keep; the windows are reduced to narrow slits, there's just a single, simple door at ground level and the belfry doubles as a watchtower with, behind it, a guardroom along the length of the nave big enough to hold the whole village. Looping southeast around Ribérac, the **church of St-Pierre-et-St-Paul** (daily 9am–7pm) in **GRAND-BRASSAC** is unusual in that sculptures were added over its north door. They show Christ in majesty flanked by St Peter and St Paul above a frieze of the Adoration with traces of earlier paintwork.

The last of the Romanesque churches, **St-Pierre-ès-Liens** (daily 9am–7pm), is also one of the most prettily sited. It lies in wooded country 6km south of Ribérac and is best approached from the west with the roofs of **SIORAC-DE-RIBÉRAC** clustered behind. From the hastily erected rubble walls it's easy to see where, in the fourteenth century, the nave was raised a couple of metres and a guard tower added at the west end. Again, there are almost no windows and the walls are up to three metres thick – which explains why the nave is so surprisingly narrow.

Practicalities

Ribérac lies on the south bank of the Dronne. Its main street starts in the south as rue Jean-Moulin, runs through the central **place Nationale** and then continues northwards as rue du 26-Mars-1944. From place Nationale, rue Gambetta heads east to **place de Gaulle** and the vast market square beyond. **Buses** for Périgueux and Angoulême stop on the other side of this square near the Palais de Justice, which is where you'll also find Ribérac's **tourist office** (July & Aug Mon–Fri 9am–7pm, Sat 10am–1pm & 2–7pm, Sun 10am–1pm; Sept–June Mon–Sat 9am–noon & 2–5pm; ☎05.53.90.03.10, ⊛www.riberac .fr). The office doubles as a ticket office for SNCF, and in July and August they organize tours of the Romanesque churches, guided walks and farm visits. You can rent **bikes** at Cycles Cum's, 35 rue du 26-Mars-1944 (☎05.53.90.33.23), and at the campsite (see below), beside the entrance to which Canoës Ribérac (☎05.53.90.54.42, ⊛www.canoriberac.free.fr; mid-June to mid-Sept) rents out **canoes** and can arrange two-day trips along the Dronne.

Accommodation, eating and drinking

There are two good **hotels** in Ribérac. The cheaper is the *Hôtel du Commerce* at 8 rue Gambetta (☎05.53.91.28.59; ❷; closed Sun eve & Mon), with simple but cheerful rooms and a decent restaurant (menus from €12). More attractive and excellent value is the *Hôtel de France*, on the north side of place de Gaulle at 3 rue Marc-Dufraisse (☎05.53.90.00.61, ⊛www.hoteldefranceriberac.com; ❸; closed Mon, mid-Nov to mid-Dec & last three weeks in Jan), with a terrace garden and a restaurant of some originality and local renown (menus at €15 and €23; closed Mon & lunchtime on Tues & Sat). There's also a two-star municipal **campsite** just across the Dronne on the Angoulême road (☎05.53.90.50.08, ⊜ot.riberac@perigord.tm.fr; June to mid-Sept).

For **accommodation around Ribérac**, you could try the *chambre d'hôte* accommodation, 4km southeast of Ribérac at *La Petite Clavelie* (☎05.53.91.25.21, ⊛www.lapetiteclavelie.free.fr; ❷), where you'll be given a hearty welcome and delicious home cooking (meals on request; €15).

Ribérac's two hotels are both good places to **eat**. Locals tend to patronise *Le Vieux Frêne* (closed Wed eve & Mon, also in Oct), immediately across the Dronne and beside the bridge. It's a simple, rustic place where you can still get a four-course weekday lunch for €11 including hors-d'oeuvre buffet and a carafe of wine; other menus start at €18. For a **drink**, you can't beat the old-style *Café des Colonnes* on place de Gaulle.

Aubeterre-sur-Dronne

Touristy but very beautiful, with its ancient galleried and turreted houses, **AUBE-TERRE-SUR-DRONNE** hangs on a steep hillside above the river, some 30km west of Ribérac. Its principal curiosity is the cavernous subterranean **church of St-Jean** (daily: mid-June to mid-Oct 9.30am–noon & 2–7pm; mid-Oct to mid-June 9.30am–12.30pm & 2–6pm; €3.50), in the lower town northeast of Aubeterre's lime-shaded central square, **place Trarieux**. Carved out of the soft rock by twelfth-century Benedictine monks, it took at least a century to excavate the twenty-metre-high chamber and gallery above. It's from up here that you get the best views over the capacious baptismal font, designed for total immersion, and the two-tiered, hexagonal structure, possibly a reliquary, cut from a single piece of rock – its precise arches seem strangely out of place against the rough walls. The side-chapels are riddled with rock-hewn tombs, while a now blocked-off tunnel connects the gallery with the château on the bluff overhead.

On the opposite, southwestern hillside, the upper town consists of a single street of houses culminating in the **church of St-Jacques**, where only the beautiful, sculpted west facade remains of the original twelfth-century church. The great tiered and decorated arch around the main door is lovely, but don't overlook the frieze of zodiacal signs on the smaller arch to the left: Taurus, Aries and Pisces are easy enough to recognize, then come Capricorn, Aquarius and Sagittarius. The other half of the frieze is missing.

Aubeterre's **tourist office** (April–June & Sept Mon–Sat 10am–noon & 2–6pm; July & Aug Mon 2–7pm, Tues–Sun 10am–7pm; Oct–March Mon–Sat 2–6pm; ☎05.45.98.57.18, ⓦwww.aubeterresurdrone.free.fr) faces onto the town's main car park to the northwest of place Trarieux. There are two reasonable **hotels** to choose from: the Dutch-owned *Hôtel de France*, a simple place on the central square (☎05.45.98.50.43, ⓦwww.hoteldefrance-aubeterre .com; ❷), and the *Hostellerie du Périgord* (☎05.45.98.50.46, ⓦwww.hostellerie-perigord.com; ❸), down by the bridge on the Ribérac road. The latter offers bright en-suite rooms, a small pool and a recommended **restaurant** (menus €15.50–36; closed Sun eve & Mon). There's also a three-star municipal **campsite** (☎05.45.98.60.17; mid-June to mid-Sept) just across the bridge, with a small beach nearby and the possibility of **canoe** rental (☎05.45.98.51.72) in summer. On weekdays there is a daily **bus** to Angoulême, which departs from near the Gendarmerie on the main road to the south of the bridge, while Chalais, which is on the Angoulême–Bordeaux train line, is only 12km away; call ☎05.45.98.28.11 if you need a **taxi**.

The Double and beyond

South of the Dronne valley the landscape and atmosphere change dramatically as you enter the region known as the **Double**. This high, undulating plateau is strewn with lakes and brooding **forests** of oak, chestnut and pine, interspersed with pockets of vines and scattered farmhouses. The larger lakes, such as the **étang de la Jemaye**, have been developed for tourism and in summer the Double is a popular destination for walkers, cyclists and nature-lovers; the best place to pick up information is Ribérac tourist office (see opposite). Until the late nineteenth century, however, the Double was largely uninhabited thanks to its poor soils and malarial marshes. Then Napoléon III decreed that it should be drained and planted with maritime pines in similar fashion to the great Landes forest further south.

This work was partly carried out by Trappist monks who arrived from Port-Salut in 1868. They settled near the only village of any size, **ÉCHOURGNAC**, plum in the middle of the plateau nearly 20km southwest of Ribérac, where they founded the **Abbaye de Notre-Dame de Bonne-Espérance**. Since 1923 the walled abbey has sheltered a small community of Cistercian sisters – these days numbering about thirty, some under a vow of silence – who not only continued in the monks' spiritual footsteps but also in their role as local cheese-makers. But the enterprising and energetic sisters didn't stop there. In their well-stocked **shop** opposite the church entrance (summer Mon–Sat 10am–noon & 3–5.45pm, Sun 10–10.45am, 2.30–4.45pm & 5.30–7pm; winter Mon–Sat 10am–noon & 2.30–5.15pm, Sun 10–10.45am & 2.30–4.45pm; phone for confirmation ℡05.53.80.82.50) you'll find the original Le Trappe Échourgnac, a firm, orange-crusted cheese with a smoky flavour, and a new version laced with walnut liqueur, as well as jams, pâté, jellied sweets and handicrafts from missions around the world.

Five kilometres east of the abbey, on the D41 from Échourgnac, the **Ferme du Parcot** (May, June & Sept Sun 2–5.30pm; July & Aug daily same times; €4) has been preserved as a more typical example of local architecture. With walls of mud and straw on latticed timber frames, protected by a limestone plaster, these farm buildings are quite unlike the sturdy stone houses found elsewhere in the Dordogne. They date from 1841 and, from the grandeur of the barn, it seems the farmer was relatively affluent. In true rural style, however, the house itself, which was inhabited up to 1990, consists of just two very spartan rooms containing a few bits and pieces of furniture and old implements. The farm also marks the start of a gentle **nature trail** (2.5km; accessible all year) through the fields and forest to a fishing lake. To fortify yourself before setting off on the trail, you can **eat** at the *Auberge de la Double* (℡05.53.80.06.65; closed eve and Dec) in Échourgnac, a little village inn which serves weekday lunches at €11 and at €23 on Sundays.

If you're heading back to Périgueux from here, it's worth dropping down to the Isle valley, which marks the edge of the Double to the south and east, to visit an imposing Renaissance château with a botanical garden on the outskirts of **NEUVIC**, roughly 15km east of Échourgnac. As you head east across the valley floor, a great bank of red-tiled roofs pinpoints the largely sixteenth-century **Château de Neuvic** (daily tours: July & Aug 3pm & 5pm; €5.50 including garden; ⓦwww.chateau-parc-neuvic.com), which now makes an unusually grand school for deprived children. Since the interiors have been extensively modified, there's not a lot to see beyond some badly damaged frescoes and an elegant eighteenth-century salon furbished with pastoral scenes. But it's the scale of the building, and particularly its handsome western facade, that grabs the attention. The best vantage point is from the **botanical garden** to the west of the château (daily: April–June, Sept & Oct 10am–noon & 1.30–6.30pm; July & Aug 10am–7pm; €3.80), though you'll find your attention diverted by a wonderful collection of sculptures created by the pupils.

Cross back over the Isle and head upstream on the D3 for another 10km to find good eating options in the attractive town of **ST-ASTIER**. The smartest is *La Palombière* (℡05.53.04.40.61; menus from €12 to €41; closed Sun eve, Mon all day & Tues eve, also late Aug to mid-Sept and two weeks in Feb), with its pretty terrace beside the towering abbey church. *Le Calzone* opposite the tourist information office serves excellent pizzas and large salads from €6, while the *Auberge du Chapeau Rouge* (℡05.53.04.97.32; menus from €10; closed Mon & Sat & evenings except in July & Aug, and two weeks in late Aug & in Dec–Jan) is one of those glorious, no-nonsense locals' places where you can have a *plat du jour* for €7. To find it walk west from the church through place Gambetta and fork right in front of the post office along rue Montaigne.

While there is no **public transport** in the Double, both St-Astier and Neuvic are on the Périgueux to Bordeaux train line from where there are several services a day; they are also on the bus route (school term-time only) to Mussidan, though services are few and far between.

St-Jean-de-Côle to Hautefort

This sweep across the northern reaches of the Dordogne *département* starts among the lush river valleys of the Périgord Vert, where the enchanting village of **St-Jean-de-Côle** sits on a tributary of the River Dronne. The country around – gentle, rolling and green – is home to the Renaissance **Château de Puyguilhem**, set against oak woods, and the **Grotte de Villars**, a cave system which provides a modest taster of those along the Vézère valley to the south. From Villars the route cuts east and south through the towns of **Thiviers** and **Sorges**, respectively centres of foie gras and truffle production, as described in their small museums. North of Thiviers, the **Château de Jumilhac** merits a detour for its sheer scale and severity, softened by a bristling roof line, if nothing else. A very different castle awaits to the east of Sorges, among the higher, grander landscapes of the Périgord Blanc, where, beyond the attractive town of **Excideuil** with its own impressive castle, the **Château de Hautefort** presents a magnificent sight on its commanding spur, endowed with an elegance quite unlike the normal rough-stone fortresses of the Dordogne.

Those relying on public transport can reach Thiviers by **train** from Périgueux, and there are limited **bus** services from Périgueux and Thiviers to Excideuil. It is even possible to reach Hautefort by bus, but the timings are such that you'll have to stay two nights in the village.

St-Jean-de-Côle and around

Twenty kilometres northeast of Brantôme, **ST-JEAN-DE-CÔLE** ranks as one of the loveliest villages in the Périgord Vert. An ancient church and château constitute its major sights and, with a hotel and a couple of restaurants, it makes a good lunchtime or overnight stop. From here the splendid **Château de Puyguilhem** lies within easy striking distance, and on the return journey you could loop north via the **Grotte de Villars**, notable for its formations rather than the smattering of prehistoric artwork.

Tiny and very picturesque without being twee, St-Jean's unusually open, sandy square is dominated by the charmingly ill-proportioned late-eleventh-century **church of St-Jean-Baptiste**. The view as you approach is harmonious enough – layers of tiled roofs from the low, square market-hall to the steeply pitched belfry – but on entering the single, lofty bay it becomes apparent that the nave was never completed, due to a lack of funds. Beside the church stands the rugged-looking **Château de la Marthonie** (not open to the public) which dates from the twelfth century, but has since acquired various additions in a pleasingly organic fashion. Apart from a huddle of houses round the square, the rest of the village consists of a line of pastel-plastered cottages stretching west to a hump-backed bridge over the River Côle and the inevitable water mill. The whole ensemble makes a perfect backdrop for the Floralies **flower festival**, held on the second weekend in May.

St-Jean's **tourist office** (mid-June to Sept Mon–Fri 9.30am–1pm & 2–7pm, Sat & Sun 2–7pm; Oct to mid-June Mon, Tues, Thurs & Fri 9.30am–12.30pm & 2.30–5.30pm, Sat & Sun 2.30–5.30pm; ℡05.53.62.14.15,

) is on the square, as is the attractive **restaurant** *La Perla*, serving well-prepared sandwiches, salads and light lunches (menus from €17.50; closed Mon & Tues, & Nov–March). Though it doesn't have the same views, you'll also eat well at the village **hotel**, the wisteria-covered *Hôtel le St-Jean* (Ⓣ05.53.52.23.20, Ⓔlesaintjean@ville-saint-jean-de-cole.fr; ❷; menus from €14.50, closed Sun eve & Mon) on the main road near the entrance to the square. It's a real old-fashioned country place, nothing fancy but welcoming and well maintained.

Around St-Jean-de-Côle

About 10km west of St-Jean, just outside the village of **VILLARS**, the **Château de Puyguilhem** (Feb, March & mid-Nov to Dec Tues–Thurs & Sun 10am–12.30pm & 2–5.30pm; April–June & Sept to mid-Nov daily 10am–12.30pm & 2–6pm; July & Aug daily 10am–7pm; €5.50; Ⓦwww.semitour.com) is a perfect example of early French Renaissance architecture. It was erected at the beginning of the sixteenth century by the La Marthonie family of St-Jean-de-Côle on the site of an earlier and more military fortress. The lake that once filled the foreground has long gone, but the château still makes an enchanting prospect, with its steep roofs, stone balustrades, mullion windows, carved chimney stacks and an assortment of round and octagonal towers reminiscent of contemporaneous Loire châteaux.

Though the **interior** suffered more from neglect and pillaging, it too has been beautifully restored and contains some noteworthy pieces of furniture and Aubusson tapestries. Its most remarkable features, however, are two magnificent fireplaces: the first, in the guardroom, depicts three Greek soldiers, while upstairs in the banqueting hall the theme is continued with six of the twelve Labours of Hercules. Both are heavily restored, but no less remarkable for that. The sculptors also went to work on the entrance hall and main staircase, leaving a wealth of oak, vine and acanthus leaves, thistles, fleur-de-lis and a few salamanders for good measure. Right at the top, it was the turn of the master carpenters, whose superb hull-shaped roof timbers have lasted five hundred years.

The ruined Cistercian **abbey of Boschaud**, 3km away in the next valley south, merits a quick visit while you're in the area. Standing in the middle of a field, it's reached by a lane not much bigger than a farm track. Though the pure, stark lines of the twelfth-century architecture hold a certain appeal, the abbey's real charm rests in the fact that it is – for once – unfenced, unpampered and free.

In 1953 speleologists discovered an extensive cave system in the hills 3km north of Villars, part of which has been opened to the public. While the **Grotte de Villars** (daily: April–June & Sept 10am–noon & 2–7.30pm; July & Aug 10am–7.30pm; Oct 2–6.30pm; €6.90; Ⓦwww.grotte-villars.com) boasts a few prehistoric paintings – notably of horses and a still unexplained scene of a man and bison – the main reason for coming here is the variety of **stalagmites** and, in particular, **stalactites**. Some are almost pure white and as fine as needles, others ochre yellow, and there are also cascades, semicircular basins and hanging curtains of semi-translucent calcium carbonate. The final cave you come to contains the **paintings**, dating from 17,000 years ago, the same age as those at Lascaux (see p.243). And look out, too, for the claw marks further back from the entrance, where generations of tiny bear cubs have left their imprints.

Thiviers and Jumilhac

Not far east of St-Jean-de-Côle, and linked by a pleasant cycle ride along a disused train line, the small market town of **THIVIERS** sits on the main road

Foie gras

It is generally agreed that it was the Egyptians who first discovered the delights of eating the **enlarged livers** of migratory geese and ducks gorging themselves in the Nile delta, and that it was the Romans who popularized the practice of force-feeding domesticated birds, generally with figs. Indeed, the first-century cook Apicius wrote a number of recipes for what we now call foie gras, literally "fat liver". For many the name is off-putting enough, let alone the idea of force-feeding the birds, while for others a slice of the succulent, pale rose-coloured liver is a pleasure not to be missed.

Foie gras is produced throughout southwest France and also in Alsace, Brittany and the Vendée. However, the yellowish-hued livers from the Périgord, where the birds are traditionally fed on local yellow – as opposed to white – maize, and where producers jealously guard their methods of preparation, are particularly sought after. Périgord farmers now favour hybrid Mulard or Barbary **ducks** over the more traditional **geese** for a variety of reasons: they fatten more quickly, are easier to raise and force-feed, and the liver is easier to cook with. The softer goose livers, on the other hand, have a more delicate flavour and smoother texture. They are also larger – 600g to 700g for an average goose liver (*foie gras d'oie*) as opposed to 500g for duck (*de canard*).

So how do the livers get so big? The young birds are raised outside to the age of four months, after which they are kept in the dark and fed over one kilo per day of partly cooked maize for between two and three weeks. During this time the livers can quadruple in size. This **gavage**, or force-feeding, was traditionally carried out using a funnel to introduce the grain into the bird's throat and then stroking it down the neck by hand. Modern techniques follow the same principle but use a mechanized feeder. It's not nearly as terrible as it sounds and most small producers are very careful not to harm their birds, if for no other reason than a stressed bird will produce a rancid liver.

All round, it's best to **buy** foie gras from small family concerns, either direct from the farm – local tourist offices can advise – or at the region's many *marchés aux gras* that take place from November to March. If you're buying fresh liver, choose one which is not too big, is uniform in colour and firm but gives slightly to the touch; the market price averages around €30–40 per kilo for foie gras of duck and €50–60 for goose. The alternative is the ready-prepared preserved version, of which there is a bewildering variety. The majority is de-veined, seasoned (wherein the secret recipes) and then sterilized by cooking briefly (*mi-cuit*) before being vacuum-packed or sealed in jars, either of which is preferable to the canned varieties; the tin taints the flavour. When choosing, check that it is locally produced and then look for the label *foie gras entier*, in other words consisting of one or more whole lobes, or simply *foie gras* which is composed of smaller pieces but is still top-quality liver. Next step down is a *bloc de foie gras* made up of reconstituted liver (sometimes *avec morceaux*, visible pieces of lobe) pressed together. Below that come all sorts of *mousses*, *parfaits*, pâtés and so forth, each of which has to contain a specified minimum percentage of foie gras and to indicate this on the label.

One of the best ways to eat foie gras is cold, with a slice of plain country bread and a glass of Sauternes (see p.114) or other sweet white wine; use a fine, sharp knife dipped in hot water to cut it into thin slices. *Foie gras poêlée*, in which escalopes of foie are heated gently with apples, strawberries or other seasonal fruits, is also sublime.

and rail links between Périgueux, 40km to the south, and Limoges. The N21 bypasses the town these days, leaving its old centre – comprising a clutch of pretty, old houses round the church and along pedestrianized rue de la Tour – relatively peaceful. The one exception is during the Saturday **market**, when the streets present a lesson in local agriculture: walnuts, apples, Limousin beef, pork, duck and goose and all manner of associated foodstuffs. From mid-November to mid-March the *foies* come out in force at the *marché au gras*, some of them destined to go into the local speciality, *L'autre fois de Thiviers*, consisting of duck or goose liver robed in pâté (see the box on p.167 for more on foie gras). Thiviers' accommodation options make it a good base should you wish to make a detour to visit the **Château de Jumilhac** to the north.

Up until the 1920s Thiviers was an important centre for porcelain, a few pieces of which are displayed in a small **museum** (€1.50) accessed via the tourist office (see below). But the pretty blue-and-white porcelain plays second fiddle to the museum's prime concern – the history and production of foie gras. Thiviers' only other claim to fame is that **Jean-Paul Sartre** spent some of his early childhood and subsequent school holidays here with his grandparents. In this case, though, there is merely an inconspicuous plaque – above an estate agent at the top end of rue Jean-Jaurès near the church – since Sartre recorded his memories of the place in less than complimentary terms.

The **gare SNCF**, with services to Bordeaux, Périgueux and Limoges, is located just a few minutes walk north of Thiviers' centre. In school term-time a **bus** departs for Excideuil from the station at 7.40am (Mon–Fri; 30min). The helpful **tourist office**, on central place Foch (July & Aug Mon–Fri 10am–1pm & 2–6pm; Sat 9am–1pm & 3–6pm; Sun 10am–1pm; rest of the year Mon–Sat 10am–1pm & 2–6pm; ℡05.53.55.12.50), can provide information on farm visits and walks in the local area, as well as lists of *chambres d'hôtes* and other **accommodation** options. One of the nicest places to stay is the attractive and well-priced *Hôtel de France et de Russie*, 51 rue du Général-Lamy (℡05.53.55.17.80, Ⓦwww.thiviers-hotel.com; ❸; closed Feb & Nov), on the road north from the tourist office. At the other end of the scale, there's a well-run, three-star **campsite**, *Le Repaire* (℡ & Ⓕ05.53.52.69.75; May–Sept), beside an artificial lake on the eastern outskirts of Thiviers. In addition to the hotel **restaurants** mentioned above, the sunny little *Crêpatou* (Mon–Thurs lunch only; Fri–Sun lunch & dinner) behind the tourist office is worth a look, offering crêpes and salads for around €8, as is *L'air du Temps* on the corner of rue A. Rousseille, on the way into town from the *gare SNCF*, whose menu features panfried venison with juniper and pigeon *gallotine* with dates; menus from €17.50. Finally, you can even log onto the **Internet** at *Le Thiber.lien*, 30 rue du Général-Lamy (Mon 2.30–6.45pm; Tues–Sat 10.30am–12.15pm & 2.30–6.45pm; Sun 3pm–6pm).

Château de Jumilhac

In its upper reaches the Isle valley narrows down between steep, wooded banks to become a mini-ravine. One of its rocky bluffs, some 20km northeast of Thiviers, is home to the vast **Château de Jumilhac** (45min guided tour: June–Sept daily 10am–7pm; March–May & Oct–Nov Sat, Sun & school holidays 2–6.30pm; Nov–Feb Sun 2–5pm; €6, €7.50 including gardens; reservations ℡05.53.52.42.97). While elements of the original thirteenth-century château remain – such as the stone-paved ground-floor rooms and the family chapel – the present structure largely owes its existence to an ironmaster, Antoine Chapelle, later count of Jumilhac, who made his fortune manufacturing arms for the future Henry IV during the Wars of Religion.

The body of the château is suitably uncompromising: the hard, grey stone allowed for little decorative detail, and what windows there are mostly consist of narrow slits. But the roof is another matter, adorned with no fewer than eight different **towers**, from great grey-slate wedges to pinnacled turrets and a jaunty

△ Château de Jumilhac

pepper pot, topped off with delicate lead statues depicting the angels of justice or more mundane pigeon-shaped weather-vanes.

Inside, however, austerity reigns once again. This is particularly so in the cramped, ground-floor rooms, which date back to the thirteenth century, but also extends to the medieval rooms above, of which the much-vaunted **spinner's room** provides the focus of the tour. Not so much for its architecture – it's a small vaulted chamber decorated with naive frescoes of animals and flowers – but for the story attached. The spinner in question was Louise de Hautefort, wife of the then count of Jumilhac, who was imprisoned here for thirty years (1618–48) for her alleged infidelity. Not one to mope, Louise took to painting the walls and spinning to occupy her time. Or so it seemed. The shepherd who regularly called under her window, and from whom she bought her wool, was of course her lover in disguise, and the spindles were used to carry secret messages between them. According to one legend, the story ended in the lover being killed in a duel, while another has him retiring to a monastery. To give you some idea what all the fuss was about, there's a portrait of Louise, supposedly painted at the time of her release but still beautiful, defiantly holding her spindle aloft.

The two wings enclosing the courtyard were added later in the seventeenth century and are gradually being restored by the château's present owners, descendants of Antoine Chapelle, who bought it back from the state in 1927. So far the most interesting room on view is the west wing's grand **reception room**, with its oak panelling and elaborate chimneypiece carved by Limousin craftsmen. They are also re-laying the formal gardens, though these need a few more years to mature.

For more than two centuries Jumilhac has been closely associated with **gold**. The nearby mines closed in 2001, but you can learn more about the history of gold here and further afield in the **Galerie de l'Or** (mid-June to mid-Sept daily 10.30am–12.30pm & 2–6.30pm; €3.50), a succinct but well-presented museum overlooking the grassy square in front of the château. Visit in summer and you can even try your luck **panning for gold** in the Isle River (July & Aug, call ℡05.53.55.33.88 for hours; €4); it's not uncommon to find tiny specks, but don't expect to make your fortune.

Practicalities

Jumilhac's **tourist office** (Jan–March & Dec Wed–Sat 2–6pm; April, May, Oct & Nov Tues 2–6pm, Wed–Sat 10am–12.30pm & 2–6pm; June & Sept Wed 2–6.30pm, Thurs–Sun 10am–12.30pm & 2–6.30pm; July & Aug daily 10am–1pm & 2.30–7pm; ℡05.53.52.55.43, ⓦwww.pays-jumilhac.fr), located just down from the Galerie de l'Or, is a mine of information on local activities and accommodation.

One of the most attractive **places to stay** is *Les Vignes de Chalusset* (℡05.53.52.38.25; ❸; meals on request €14), a pretty and very welcoming **chambre d'hôte**, 5km east of Jumilhac, signed off the St-Yrieix road, with a pool and extensive grounds. Another good option is the three-star *La Chatonnière* **campsite** (℡05.53.52.57.36, ⓦwww.chatonniere.com; June to mid-Sept), beside the river just over a kilometre from Jumilhac on the same road. If you're in Jumilhac around lunchtime, try the *Lou Bouëïradour* **restaurant** (Sept–June closed Wed eve), named after an implement used for blanching chestnuts, across the square from the tourist office. Their good-value regional menus start at €11.

Sorges

A small town on the Périgueux road about 15km south of Thiviers, **SORGES** is worth visiting simply for its informative **Musée de la Truffe** (Feb to mid-June & Oct to Jan Tues–Sun 10am–noon & 2–5pm; mid-June to Sept daily 9.30am–12.30pm & 2.30–6.30pm; €5), located just off the main road to the south of the old centre. The dry limestone plateau around Sorges is particularly prolific for **truffles** – in the early 1900s the commune averaged 6000kg per year, and the largest black truffle discovered so far, a monster weighing well over a kilo, was found near Excideuil (see below) in only 1999. By way of comparison, most truffle-hounds would be happy with a mere couple of hundred grams. You'll unearth all manner of similar facts and figures in the museum, the brainchild of an enterprising local mayor – a former *trufficulteur* – from how the fungus forms to how to create your own truffle-oak orchard, all helpfully translated into English. The tips on choosing a good truffle and what to do with it afterwards will come in handy if you happen to be in Sorges for the annual **truffle market** (the Sunday nearest January 20), or if you're tempted by one of the preserved specimens on sale in the museum. You can also pick up details of a three-kilometre nature trail that gives an idea of how and where truffles grow (see also the box opposite).

The museum doubles as Sorges' **tourist office** (same hours; ℡05.53.05.90.11), and the town also boasts a very comfortable, reasonably priced **hotel**, called what else but *Auberge de la Truffe* (℡05.53.05.02.05, ⓦwww.auberge-de-la-truffe.com; ❸). Though it's on the main road, the rooms are all double-glazed and most face onto the garden and pool behind, or there's a quieter annexe (*Hôtel de la Mairie*) by the church. Even if you're not staying, try their excellent **restaurant** – naturally, truffles feature strongly (menus from €16; closed Mon lunchtime all year & Sun eve Oct–March).

Excideuil

The old route between Périgueux and Limoges used to run up the Isle and Loue rivers to **EXCIDEUIL**, 15km east of Sorges, where two huge medieval

The black diamonds of Périgord

The **black truffle** of Périgord, *tuber melanosporum*, is one of those expensive delicacies that many people find overrated. This is mainly because it's usually served in such minute quantities or is combined with such strong flavours that its own subtle, earthy taste and aroma are completely overwhelmed. Really to appreciate the truffle, it should be eaten in a salad, omelette or simple pastry crust, or, as the writer Colette advised, "eat it on its own, fragrant and coarse-skinned, eat it like the vegetable that it is, hot, and served in generous quantities".

Part of the truffle's mystique inevitably stems from its supposed **aphrodisiac** virtues. Perhaps the most famous proponent was Napoleon I, who attributed the conception of his son to having eaten a basket of Périgord truffles. Madame de Pompadour (see p.179) was also particularly partial to them. It was thanks to truffles, she said, that she retained Louis XV's favours for so many years.

The truffle is a **fungus** that grows entirely underground, and a fussy one at that. It prefers shallow, free-draining limestone soils rich in organic matter, a sunny position and marked seasonal differences, and requires the presence of certain species of oak, or occasionally lime or hazelnut, around the roots of which it grows. It's greedy, too, absorbing so much of the nutrients and water available that the vegetation overhead often dies. This tell-tale ring of denuded earth is just one of the clues truffle-hunters are on the lookout for. Others include small, yellow truffle-flies hovering just above the soil, and the distinct smell – which is where the pig, or generally these days the more amenable dog – comes in.

Even now the **life cycle** of the Périgord truffle – the most prized out of more than forty different varieties – is not completely understood, and attempts to cultivate them artificially have so far proved elusive. What is clear is that the spores are released in the spring and mature truffles are ready for harvest between December and early March. When ripe, the skin of a Périgord truffle is a deep purple-brown or black, while the lighter-coloured flesh is flecked with fine white veins. It should be firm to the touch and give off a pleasantly earthy aroma; an overripe truffle stinks.

The principal truffle **markets** take place at Périgueux, Sarlat and Brantôme, and at Lalbenque near Cahors in the Quercy. Prices these days average at €800–1000 per kilo. In the past, however, truffles were so common that they were considered a pest by vine growers. Ironically, the fungus proved a life-saver for many local farmers when phylloxera (see p.393) hit in the late nineteenth century, ushering in the truffle's "golden age". Since the 1950s the harvest has declined dramatically for a number of reasons – deforestation and rural depopulation amongst others – although there are signs of a revival with up to 90 hectares of truffle trees being planted each year in the Dordogne since 2000.

keeps still dominate the little market town. The **castle** was one of the region's most heavily fortified and for a while the viscounts of Limoges held court here. Following the Hundred Years' War, however, the fortress lay in ruins until relatively recently, when restoration was carried out. Now privately owned, you can enter only the precinct, but it's an impressive sight, particularly if you approach from the west. From the castle, rue des Cendres leads north into the tight knot of streets concentrated around place Bugeaud and the much-restored church, with its Gothic portal. This square and the nearby *halle* are the venue for a lively farmers' **market** on Thursday mornings, augmented in winter (Dec to early March) by an important *foire aux gras*.

Excideuil can be reached by **bus** from Périgueux (see p.145) and Thiviers (see p.166). There's a bus stop beneath the castle on place du Château, where you'll also find the **tourist office** booth (Jan & Feb Mon 3–5pm, Tues & Thurs

10am–noon & 3–5pm, Sat 10am–noon; March, April & Sept–Dec Mon 3–5pm, Tues–Fri 10am–12.30pm & 3–5pm, Sat 10am–12.30pm; May–Aug Mon 2.30–5.30pm, Tues–Fri 9.30am–12.30pm & 2.30–6.30pm, Sat 9.30am–12.30pm; ℡05.53.62.95.56, Ⓦwww.excideuil.fr) and a recently renovated **hotel**, the *Hostellerie du Fin Chapon* (℡05.53.62.42.38, Ⓕ05.53.52.39.60; ❷–❸), with good comfortable modern rooms with perks such as high speed Internet access and a **restaurant** serving simple but plentiful regional dishes. There's also a basic but prettily sited municipal **campsite** (℡05.53.62.43.72, Ⓔexcideuil@wanadoo.fr; July & Aug) by the river on the east side of town.

Hautefort

Southeast of Excideuil you cross the pretty Auvézère valley, the route of the GR646 footpath, and enter the limestone plateaux of the Périgord Blanc. The views are magnificent, and nowhere more so than around **HAUTEFORT** and its eponymous **château**, standing on a south-facing promontory some 20km from Excideuil and 40km northeast of Périgueux.

The **Château de Hautefort** (guided tours daily: Feb–March & Oct–Nov daily 2–6pm; April–June daily 10am–noon & 2–6pm; July & Aug daily 9.30am–7pm; closed Dec & Jan; €8; Ⓦwww.chateau-hautefort.com) is a stunning sight from whichever direction you approach, a magnificent example of good living on a grand scale, endowed with an elegance that's out of step with the usual rough stone fortresses of Périgord. Indeed, when the then marquis de Hautefort rebuilt it in the mid-seventeenth century, his ambition was to create a château worthy of the Loire.

The original fortress, which was built some time around 1000, in the twelfth century belonged jointly to the famous troubadour **Bertran de Born** (see p.386) and his brother Constantin, until Bertran persuaded his overlord, Henry II of England, to grant him sole ownership in 1185. The following year Constantin took his revenge and left the place in ruins – at which point Bertran went off to become a monk. The château's recent history has been no less troubled. After decades of neglect, in 1929 Hautefort was bought and meticulously restored by Baron Henri de Bastard and his wife. Then in August 1968, just three years after the work was completed, a **fire** gutted everything except the chapel in the southeast tower. A year later the indomitable baroness – her husband having died before the fire – set about the whole task again, and master craftsmen were called in to re-create everything from the staircases to the ornate chimneypieces. There's no disguising the fact that it's all brand new, but the quality of work is superb.

The approach lies across a wide esplanade, flanked by immaculate topiary gardens, and over a drawbridge to enter a stylish Renaissance **courtyard** opening to the south. The two wings end in a pair of round towers, whose great bulk is offset by grey-slate domes topped with matching pepper-pot lanterns; the southwestern tower, nearest the entrance, is the only part of the medieval château still standing. While the main building is equally symmetrical, the overall impression is one of rhythm and harmony rather than severity.

About the only furnishings saved from the fire were four sixteenth-century tapestries, now on display inside, but the real highlight is the **great hall**. This monumental room, 280 metres square, provides the perfect setting for two huge chimneypieces. Exact copies of the originals and carved from local walnut, each took five thousand hours' work.

After you've finished in the château and its thirty-hectare park, it's also worth wandering through the village to visit the **Musée de la Médecine** (June–Sept daily 10am–7pm; April–May & Oct Mon–Fri 2-6pm; €5; ⓦ www.muse-medi-cine-hautefort.fr) in the midst of an open square. It occupies part of a hospice for the poor founded in 1669 by the same marquis who rebuilt the castle, as its architecture – particularly the domed central chapel – suggests. One of the ground-floor rooms presents an early-nineteenth-century ward under the ministration of the Sisters of Charity. As if this wasn't sobering enough, things get worse upstairs among the displays of medical implements through the ages, culminating in examples of dental surgeries up to 1970 – they even have that awful smell.

The museum entrance lies through the **tourist office** (June–Sept daily 10am–7pm; Oct to mid-Dec & mid-Jan to May Mon–Fri 10am–noon & 2–6pm; ⓣ 05.53.50.40.27, ⓦ www.ot-hautefort.com), located in the hospice's north wing, where you can pick up details of places to visit along the Auvézère valley. For an overnight stay in Hautefort, there's a very pleasant **hotel** right under the castle walls, the *Auberge du Parc* (ⓣ 05.53.50.88.98, ⓕ 05.53.51.61.72; ❷; closed mid-Dec to mid-March) has five comfortable rooms and a good local **restaurant** serving Limousin beef and foie gras (menus from €15; closed Sun eve & Wed), and a lakeside campsite, *Le Moulin des Loisirs* (ⓣ 05.53.50.17.17, ⓦ www.moulin-des-loisirs.fr; Easter–Sept), less than 2km to the south. It is possible to reach Hautefort by public transport, but you'll have to stay two nights: a **bus** leaves Périgueux at 5.25pm (Mon–Fri), with the return service departing from Hautefort at 7.30am.

Brive-la-Gaillarde and around

A major road and rail junction, **Brive-la-Gaillarde** is the nearest thing to an industrial centre for miles around. Though it has no commanding sights, Brive does offer a few distractions, foremost of which is the Musée Labenche, focusing on local history, as well as a core of carefully restored old streets. It also makes an agreeable base for exploring the beautiful towns and villages around, and it's not that far to Lascaux and the upper reaches of the River Dordogne.

North of Brive, among the green fields and apple orchards of the southern Limousin, the hilltop town of **Uzerche** presents a grand array of turrets and towers caught in a loop of the River Vézère, while nearby **Arnac-Pompadour** is a must for anyone remotely interested in horses. Its château, from where Madame de Pompadour got her name, provides a stately back-drop to a national stud farm and a splendid racecourse. Heading south, first stop is the village of **Turenne**. Two sky-scraping towers and a number of noblemen's houses are all that remain of this once-powerful town, which enjoyed almost complete independence up to the eighteenth century. Nearby **Collonges-la-Rouge** also prospered under Turenne rule, but it is the unexpected shock of the red sandstone as much as the time-worn buildings that gives the village its special appeal.

All these places can be reached by public **transport**. Uzerche and Arnac-Pompadour lie on two different train lines between Brive and Limoges, while Brive is also the departure point for buses to Turenne and Collonges.

Brive-la-Gaillarde

The largely pedestrianized old centre of **BRIVE-LA-GAILLARDE** comes as a pleasant surprise after its sprawling suburbs. It is enclosed within a circular boulevard shaded by plane trees, from where all roads lead inwards

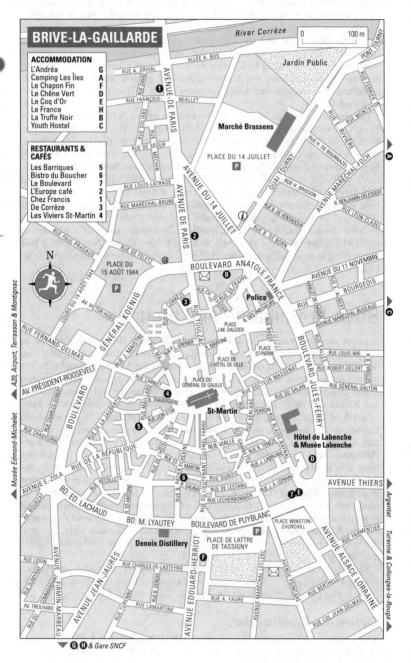

BRIVE-LA-GAILLARDE

River Corrèze

0   100 m

ACCOMMODATION

L'Andréa	G
Camping Les Îles	A
Le Chapon Fin	F
Le Chêne Vert	D
Le Coq d'Or	E
Le France	H
La Truffe Noir	B
Youth Hostel	C

RESTAURANTS & CAFÉS

Les Barriques	5
Bistro du Boucher	6
Le Boulevard	7
L'Europe café	2
Chez Francis	1
De Corrèze	3
Les Viviers St-Martin	4

Jardin Public

Marché Brassens

PLACE DU 14 JUILLET

BOULEVARD ANATOLE FRANCE

Police

PLACE 15 AOÛT 1944

St-Martin

Hôtel de Labenche & Musée Labenche

AVENUE THIERS

Denoix Distillery

PLACE DE LATTRE DE TASSIGNY

◀ **G H** & Gare SNCF

◀ Musée Edmond-Michelet   ◀ A20, Airport, Terrasson & Montignac

Turenne & Collonges-la-Rouge ▶

Argentat ▶

to the much-restored **church of St-Martin**. Brive's other main sight, the wide-ranging **Musée Labenche**, lies on the ring road to the southeast, while across the other side of town the local Resistance museum, the **Musée Edmond Michelet**, is of more specialist interest.

It's thought that Brive earned its nickname *la Gaillarde* during the Hundred Years' War when, for much of the time, it was a lone French stronghold surrounded by English. Opinions are divided, but the name "la Galliarde" (meaning strong, sprightly or bawdy) refers either to its fortifications or – the generally preferred option – the spirited, valiant nature of its people. The ramparts disappeared after the Revolution to make way for today's gardens and ring road, but the "Brivistes" themselves haven't changed, as they will happily tell you, citing their prowess on the rugby field as the prime example: Brive won the European Cup in 1997, were also runner-up the following year, and in 2000 made it to the finals of the French Cup.

Arrival and information

Brive is large enough to have its own **airport**, 4km to the west, from where there are regular flights to and from Paris. You can pick up an STUB city bus (line #1/3 Z. I. Brive Ouest–Malemort) from the main road running south of the airport, which then stops at various places on the boulevard ringing the old town. However, it's a bit of a hike from the airport terminal to the bus stop (a good 500m) and a taxi to central hotels costs just €3–4 (the bus fare is €1). A new airport for Brive-Souillac is set to open in 2007, and will be served with flights from the UK; for further information see ⒲www .aeroport-brive-souillac.com.

The **gare SNCF**, on the Paris–Toulouse and Bordeaux–Lyon main lines, is located on the south side of Brive, some ten minutes' walk along avenue Jean-Jaurès from the centre. The regional **bus** service is unusually comprehensive. Buses depart from various spots round town, including the gare SNCF and place du 14-Juillet to the north of the old centre, which is also where you'll find the **tourist office** (July & Aug Mon–Sat 9am–7pm, Sun 10am–1pm; Sept–June Mon–Sat 9am–noon & 2–6pm; ⓉO5.55.24.08.80, ⒲www.brive-tourisme .com). It occupies an old pumping station and water tower built in the form of a lighthouse, so you can't miss it. Staff have a fair amount of information in English, and look out too for the free *Limousin* guide produced annually by *The News* English-language paper.

Accommodation

There are several good cheap **hotels** around Brive station, and a choice of smarter establishments on the ring road. The municipal **campsite**, *Les Îles* (Ⓣ&Ⓕ05.55.24.34.74), is situated across the river nearly half a kilometre east from the old centre.

L'Andréa 39 av Jean-Jaurès ⓉO5.55.74.11.84, ⒲www.landrea.com. On the road down from the train station, this little hotel opts for an old-fashioned decor in its seventeen en-suite rooms. The owners run the cheerful and good-value Italian bistro downstairs (main dishes €6–10; closed Sun eve). ❷

Le Chapon Fin 1 place de Lattre-de-Tassigny ⓉO5.55.74.23.40, ⒲www.chaponfin-brive.com. This American-French-owned hotel occupies an attractive bourgeois house on the ring road. The rooms are comfortable enough and all en suite, but they play second fiddle to the restaurant serving regional specialities (menus from €15). ❹

Le Chêne Vert 24 bd Jules-Ferry ⓉO5.55.24.10.07, ⒲www.lechenevert.com. Mid-sized hotel next to the Musée Labenche with spacious (although somewhat old-fashioned) rooms with large windows allowing in plenty of light. Some rooms have small balconies. ❸

Le Coq d'Or 18 bd Jules-Ferry ⓉO5.55.17.12.92, ⒲www.hotel-coqdor.com. Recently renovated and under new ownership, this hotel has comfy, if rather small rooms decked out in pretty florals as well as a decent restaurant serving hearty local fare. ❸

Le France 60 av de la Gare ☎ 05.55.74.08.13, ⓦ www.lefrance.com. Budget hotel opposite the station offering a choice of functional rooms (either en suite or with shared toilet and shower) above a canteen-style restaurant (menus from €8). ❶

🏃 La Truffe Noir 22 bd Anatole-France ☎ 05.55.92.45.00, ⓦ www.la-truffe-noire .com. Despite being extensively restored, Brive's top hotel is still full of warm wood panelling and

cosy inglenooks. The rooms are equally tasteful, though rather small at the cheaper end, and there's an excellent restaurant – the house specialities of course feature truffles (menus from €24). ❻

Youth Hostel 56 av Maréchal-Bugeaud ☎ 05.55.24.34.00, ⓔ brive@fuaj.org. 78-bed HI hostel 25 minutes' walk across town from the train station. Facilities are excellent: most rooms have either two or three beds and share commu-nal washrooms, meals are available in season (April–Sept), as are snacks all year, and guests can use the kitchen. They also offer Internet access. No curfew. Closed mid-Dec to mid-Jan. €11.50 per person including sheets.

The Town

Brive's compact centre has been beautifully restored in recent years. As a focus for wandering the old streets, head first to the **church of St-Martin**, plum in the middle. Originally Romanesque in style, now only the transept, apse and a few comically carved capitals survive from that era. St Martin, a Spanish aristo-crat, arrived in pagan Brive in 407 AD on the feast of Saturnus, smashed various idols, and was promptly stoned to death by the outraged onlookers; some say his unmarked tomb is among those in the crypt. The only other point of interest is a large, twelfth-century baptismal font near the west door decorated with the symbols of the four Evangelists.

Numerous streets fan out from the surrounding square, **place du Général-de-Gaulle**, with a number of turreted and towered houses, some dating back to the thirteenth century. The most impressive is the sixteenth-century **Hôtel de Labenche**, southeast of the church on boulevard Jules-Ferry, now hous-ing a better-than-usual local history museum **Musée Labenche** (Mon & Wed–Sun: April–Oct 10am–6.30pm; Nov–March 10am–6pm; €4.50). As you enter, note the busts of the Labenche family leaning forward over each window. The museum's huge collection ranges from archeological finds, including some delightful Gallo-Roman bronzes complete with moulds, to nineteenth-century rural craft industries and a beautiful display of accordions made in Brive by the Dedenis factory prior to 1939. But the highlight is a rare collection of **Mortlake tapestries**. The Mortlake workshop, under the supervision of Dutch weavers, was founded by James I of England in 1620. Though they were only in business until the end of that century, they produced a number of impor-tant works which were highly prized at the time. The most interesting of the seven presented here are the three fox-hunting scenes – the colours are still exceptionally vibrant. In the centrepiece a lord and lady dance while another group play *quilles*, a local version of skittles, as dusk falls over the dregs of the hunt dinner.

The tone changes considerably at Brive's other museum, the **Musée Edmond Michelet** at 4 rue Champanatier (Mon–Sat 10am–noon & 2–6pm; free), portraying the Resistance and deportations during World War II through photo-graphs, posters and objects of the time, though little is explained in English. To get there take the main rue de la République west from St-Martin church as far as the ring road, from where the museum is signed straight ahead along avenue Émile-Zola. It occupies the former home of Edmond Michelet, one of Brive's leading *résistants*, who was arrested here in 1943 and deported to Dachau, but survived to become a minister in de Gaulle's postwar government.

Cave art

Thousands of years ago early inhabitants of the Dordogne and Lot region created some of the most expressive and moving prehistoric paintings, engravings and reliefs to be seen anywhere in the world. While these stunning works of art lie scattered throughout the area, hidden deep within limestone caves and on cliff walls, by far the greatest concentration is in the Vézère valley in the heart of the Dordogne.

▲ Lascaux

The first artists

The earliest signs of human habitation – in the form of flint tools – in the region date from around 450,000 years ago. However, things don't really start to get interesting until the appearance of **Cro-Magnon** people who swept across Europe a mere 40,000 or so years ago. Cro-Magnon are named after a rock-shelter near Les Eyzies where the first skeletons were discovered, but they are more broadly known as *Homo sapiens sapiens* – in other words, us.

The Cro-Magnon were **nomadic** people, tracking herds of reindeer across what was then steppe, only occasionally settling in riverside rock-shelters under the overhanging cliffs. Gradually they developed increasingly sophisticated **tools** using bone, ivory and antlers as well as stone, and then used fire to mould and strengthen them. They later crafted **ornaments** such as necklaces and also started to decorate their tools and stone blocks with crude engravings. By around 20,000 years ago the Cro-Magnon had honed their artistic skills sufficiently to depict supremely realistic animals on the walls of their rock-shelters, by means of **engraving** and **sculpting** with flints or **painting** with dyes made from charcoal, manganese dioxide and red ochre.

Top five caves to visit

☞ **Lascaux II** Superb replica of the summit of Cro-Magnon art. See p.243.

☞ **Grotte de Font-de-Gaume** Beautifully preserved paintings and engravings in a narrow tunnel. See p.232.

▼ Grotte de Rouffignac

☞ **Abri du Cap Blanc** Sculpted frieze of virtually life-size horses and bison. See p.233.

☞ **Grotte de Pech-Merle** "The chapel of mammoths" stands out among more than five hundred drawings. See p.312.

☞ **Grotte de Rouffignac** Hop on an electric train to view drawings of mammoths and woolly rhino in a kilometre-long cave. See p.235.

▲ Lascaux II

Into the caves

At the start of the **Magdalenian** era (named after another archeological site in the Vézère valley) about 17,000 years ago, there was a real explosion in the quantity and the level of sophistication of prehistoric art. It was prompted by the widespread use of the tallow lamp, fuelled with reindeer fat, which allowed artists to penetrate deep within the **limestone caves**. Here they covered the walls of passages and cavern ceilings with sometimes hundreds of drawings, paintings and engravings. In some places artists used the natural contours of the rock to produce supremely realistic, almost 3-D representations of horses, bison and other animals. Elsewhere, shading and other surprisingly advanced techniques were used to provide volume, perspective and a sense of movement. There are even drawings almost like caricatures, in which mammoths are portrayed with just a couple of lines.

▲ Grotte de Font-de-Gaume

Magic or ritual?

While the vast majority of Magdalenian art features wildlife, the occasional **human figures** also appear, as do various **abstract signs** – dots, rectangles and parallel lines being the most common – whose meanings are the subject of endless debate: some scholars believe they were forms of communication, or perhaps ritualistic symbols. There is also much speculation as to why prehistoric man produced these art works at all. Were they some form of ritual practice or magic to evoke a successful hunt? And why in such inaccessible spots? It seems likely that the caves were sanctuaries and, if not actually places of worship, they at least had spiritual significance. We will never know for certain, of course, but in many respects that only adds to the wonder and magic of these caves.

Visiting the prehistoric caves

To really appreciate the full power of these early artists you have to visit at least some of the region's "**decorated caves**". There are 25 in the Vézère valley alone, and more are being discovered all the time, though only a limited number are open to the public.

Visitor numbers to most caves are severely restricted either for conservation reasons or, in the case of Lascaux II, simply because the site can only hold up to 40 people at a time. At all of them you have to join a guided tour and at the most popular caves you need to buy tickets in advance, sometimes a week ahead or even longer during peak periods. Since it takes a bit of effort to visit these caves, unless you're a real prehistoric art buff, it's better to limit yourself to just two or three sites rather than risk losing that sense of magic.

▼ Lascaux sign

Returning to the centre, turn right along the ring road to find the **Denoix distillery**, founded in 1839, at 9 boulevard Maréchal-Lyautey (Tues–Sat 9am–noon & 2.30–7pm; free; Ⓦ www.denoix.com). The liqueurs produced here are centred around walnuts, notably a very mellow tipple called Suprême Denoix, but they have also resurrected a local mustard. Made with grape must and spices, Moutarde Violette de Brive was first devised in the fourteenth century for Pope Clément VI, a native of Corrèze. Not surprisingly for this area, it goes very well with duck.

Eating and drinking

In summer small **restaurants** and **bars** open in the gardens along the southern stretch of the ring road. Otherwise, avenue de Paris, leading north to the river, has a fair choice of places to eat as well as one of Brive's nicest cafés, the old-fashioned *L'Europe*, at no. 21.

Les Barriques 5 rue Maillard. Lunchtime sees this modern bar-brasserie packed with office workers. It offers a limited range of dishes ranging from around €7 to €10, or you can make your own salad from the self-service hors-d'oeuvre buffet. Not the sort of place where you'll be able to linger over your meal.

Bistrot du Boucher 8 rue Galinat. This stylish bistro tempts customers with a bewildering array of *formules*, menus and daily specials. A main dish will set you back €12, while the three-course menu is priced at €24 including wine or mineral water. It also serves until relatively late, around 11pm. July & Aug closed Sun.

Le Boulevard 8 bd Jules-Ferry. Though it doesn't look much from the outside, this is one of the nicest options along the southern boulevard. Beyond the chestnut-shaded terrace lurks a cosy dining room where locals come for delicacies such as a *feuilleté* of snails or veal with local mustard, followed perhaps by a walnut and hazelnut soufflé. Menus €11–22. Closed Sun eve & Mon.

🏃 **Chez Francis** 61 av de Paris ☎ 05.55.74.41.72. You'll need to book ahead for this friendly, cluttered restaurant down towards the river. The imaginative seasonal menus

feature the best of local ingredients, but prices are surprisingly affordable. At lunch you can have a *plat du jour* for just €9.50, while the fixed menus are priced at €14 and €21. A favourite haunt of writers, actors and artists during Brive's various festivals (see box on p.186), the walls, ceilings and lampshades are covered with messages of appreciation. Closed Sun & Mon, also ten days in Feb & two weeks in Aug.

De Corrèze 3 rue de Corrèze. Another popular, locals' place, this time to the north of St-Martin, with the choice of tiled floors and a handful of wooden tables under cheerful, sunflower cloths downstairs or a smarter stone-walled room above. The food is equally traditional and comes in hearty portions, with three-course menus starting at €8.50. Closed Sun.

Les Viviers St-Martin 4 rue Traversière. It's worth seeking out this little restaurant in a backstreet just west of St-Martin church for its wide-ranging *carte* including salads, pasta and plenty of local delicacies; it's especially well known for fish (menus €10–26). Another attraction is the possibility of eating outside, and this is one of the few places open on a Sunday. Closed two weeks in both March & Oct.

Listings

Airlines Airliner (☎ 08.20.82.08.20, Ⓦ www .airfrance.com) operates flights to Paris Orly every day except Saturday.
Airport Brive-Laroche ☎ 05.55.86.88.36. A new airport Brive-Souillac is due to open in 2007; for further information see Ⓦ www.aeroport-brive-souillac.com.
Bus departures Timetables for all the buses around the *département* are available from the tourist office (see p.175). Eurolines buses en route from Toulouse to London depart from outside the post office on place Winston-Churchill.

Car rental Near the train station, try: Avis, 56 av Jean-Jaurès ☎ 05.55.24.51.00; Europcar, 52 av Jean-Jaurès ☎ 05.55.74.14.41; Hertz, 54 av Jean-Jaurès ☎ 05.55.24.26.75; Sixt, 59 av Jean-Jaurès ☎ 05.55.23.56.28. All offer airport pick-ups.
Hospital Centre Hospitalier, bd Docteur-Verlhac ☎ 05.55.92.60.00.
Internet access You can log on at Ax'tion, 33 bd Général-Koenig (Tues–Sat 9am–7pm; Mon 1–7pm).
Markets The modern, open hall behind the tourist office is the venue for a famous market twice a week (Tues & Sat mornings) and three important *foires*

grasses for foie gras, truffles and other local produce held between December and February. During the first weekend in November each year the fruit and veg gives way to a book fair, La Foire du Livre, which attracts a number of well-known authors and artists.

Police Commissariat de Police, 4 bd Anatole-France ☎ 05.55.17.46.00.
Post office The central post office is at place Winston-Churchill, 19100 Brive-la-Gaillarde.
Taxis Call ☎ 05.55.24.24.24.

Around Brive

The country around Brive offers a variety of rewarding day-trips. To the north, **Uzerche** retains evidence of a more noble – and less peaceful – past in its mansions and fortified church perched above the river. Further west comes **Arnac-Pompadour**, home to one of France's best-known stud farms set in the grounds of a striking fifteenth-century château. The viscounts of **Turenne**, to the south of Brive, once ruled over vast tracts of Limousin and Périgord. Now only vestiges of their castle remain, though the aristocratic houses clustered in its lee have fared better, as has the viscounts' administrative centre, **Collonges-la-Rouge**, whose red sandstone lends it a warm, rosy appeal which survives the onslaught of visitors.

Uzerche

Thirty-five kilometres north of Brive, or a half-hour train ride along the course of the bubbling River Vézère, **UZERCHE** is impressively located above a loop in the river's course. It's worth a passing visit as the town has several fine old buildings dating from the sixteenth and seventeenth centuries when it was the capital of the Bas-Limousin, as this region was, and is, known. Despite the cramped site, on a long narrow knuckle of rock oriented north–south, the wealthier citizens managed to erect surprisingly substantial mansions. They also had a passion for towers, which can be best appreciated from across the river when their full height becomes apparent.

All traffic is funnelled along the main road running beside the river on the east side of Uzerche. From here steep steps lead up to the town's highest tower, that of the fortified **abbey church of St-Pierre**. Consecrated in 1097, the church combines Romanesque barrel vaults and carved capitals with a beautifully light and airy Limoges-style ambulatory and radiating chapels. South from the church, the place des Vignerons is a pretty spot with views out across the river, while to the north rue Pierre-Chalaud and rue de la Justice slope gently down past a number of fine Renaissance houses. One of the more ornate is the **Maison Eyssartier**, west of the abbey church at the bottom of the steeply sloping place de la Libération. It was originally owned by several generations of apothecaries – hence the pestle-and-mortar crest on the facade.

Uzerche's **gare SNCF** lies 2km north of the old town along the main road, while **buses** from Brive will drop you beside the river. The **tourist office** (mid-June to mid-Sept daily 10am–12.30pm & 2.30–7pm; during school holidays Mon–Fri 10am–noon & 2.30–5pm, Sat 10am–noon; rest of the year Mon–Fri 10am–noon; ☎ 05.55.73.15.71, Ⓦ www.pays-uzerche.com) is next door to the Maison Eyssartier; it's worth dropping in for their annotated walking route (in French only). If you need a place to **stay**, try the *Hôtel Ambroise* (☎ 05.55.73.28.60, Ⓦ www.logis-de-france.fr; ❷; closed Sun eve & Mon, & Nov; restaurant menus from €13), or there's a three-star municipal **campsite** (☎ 05.55.73.12.75, Ⓕ 05.55.98.44.55; May–Sept) 2km south along the river, from where you can rent **canoes** and **bikes** at the Base de la Minoterie (☎ 05.55.73.02.84, Ⓦ assoc.wanadoo.fr/vezere.passion).

Arnac-Pompadour and around

Roughly 20km west of Uzerche, and also accessible by train from Brive, **ARNAC-POMPADOUR** is dominated by its grey, turreted château over-looking one of the most picturesque racecourses in France. The town is probably most famous for its association with **Madame de Pompadour**, mistress of Louis XV, but it is also home to the country's second most important stud farm (*haras*), where Anglo-Arabs – the all-round horse used for racing, jumping, cross-country and dressage events – were first bred. As a result it's a very horsey place, although if you're in the area in mid-July, you might witness the annual donkey festival - **La Jounrnée Nationale de l'Âne** - a one-day fête that takes place on 14 July every year in honour of all things donkey related.

The present château largely dates from the fifteenth century. When the Pompadour line died out in 1745, it was ceded to Louis XV who promptly bestowed the title on his mistress. Though she never bothered to visit, the **Marquise de Pompadour** started breeding horses on her estate before being forced to sell for financial reasons in 1760; she nevertheless kept the title. On regaining possession of the castle the following year, Louis founded the Royal Stud, which became a **National Stud** in 1872. In between, the horses were sold off during the Revolution, but Napoleon I soon re-established the stud to keep his cavalry supplied. He sent four Arab stallions, booty from his Egyptian campaign, which were crossed with English thoroughbred mares to produce the first **Anglo-Arabs**.

The **château** itself was gutted by fire in 1834 and now houses the stud's headquarters. You can visit its terraces on a half-hour **guided tour** (daily: April–Sept 10–11.30am & 2–5.30pm; early Feb to March 2–5.30pm; Oct to early Feb 2–4.30pm; €1.60 - check with the tourist office for further info, see below), but the **dépôt des étalons**, where the stallions are kept, is more interesting (1hr guided tours daily: July–Sept 10–11am & 2–5.30pm; Oct–June 2.30–4.30pm; €4). It lies across the chestnut-shaded esplanade from the château. During the spring breeding season (March–June) there are fewer stallions in the *dépôt*, but this is the best time to visit the mares (*juments*) at the **Jumenterie de la Rivière** (45min guided tours daily: mid-Feb to March 2–4.15pm; April–June 2–5pm; July–Sept 3–5pm; €3.50), 4km southeast near the village of Beyssac. In late spring (May–June) the fields around are full of mares and foals, the best being kept for breeding, the rest sold worldwide as two-year-olds. At any time of year, however, you will see horses being exercised round the magnificent track in front of the château. In addition, from May to October there are frequent **race meetings**, as well as dressage and driving events, shows and open days; the tourist office (see below) can provide a calendar of events.

For those less enamoured of horses, the Romanesque **abbey church** of Arnac (part of the Pompadour domaines), 2km to the northwest, is of interest for its carved capitals. Though exceptionally high, enlarged photos beside each pillar help identify the striking images, including Daniel in the lions' den.

Arnac-Pompadour lies on a minor **train** line between Brive and Limoges. It can also be reached from Brive by **buses**, which stop by the château before terminating at the **gare SNCF**, 500m southeast on the D7 to Vigeois. The **tourist office** (daily: April–Sept 10am–noon & 2–6.30pm; Oct–March 2–6pm; ☏05.55.98.55.47, ✉office.tourisme.pompadour@wanadoo.fr), in the gate-house of the *dépôt des étalons*, sells tickets for the château, *dépôt* and Jumenterie, though at the last of these you can also buy tickets on the spot. There's even a reasonable place to **stay**: the *Hôtel du Parc* (☏05.55.73.30.54, ⓦwww .logis-de-france.fr; ❸; closed late-Dec to late Jan), behind the château. In addition to cheerful rooms and a small pool, the hotel boasts a good regional

restaurant (menus €10.50–49). The other option in the area is the modern *Auberge de la Mandrie* (T05.55.73.37.14, Wwww.logis-de-france.fr; ❸; closed Jan & Sun eve Nov–March), 4km west on the D7, with chalet rooms around a pool, and more refined cuisine (menus from €12.50).

Turenne

TURENNE, just 16km south of Brive, is the first of two very picturesque villages in the vicinity. In this case slate-roofed, mellow stone houses crowd under the protective towers of a once-mighty fortress. At their peak during the fifteenth century, the viscounts of Turenne ruled over a vast feudal domain containing some 1200 villages. Virtually autonomous, it was one of the most powerful estates in France. The viscounts retained the right to raise taxes and mint their own coins, amongst other privileges, up until 1738 when Louis XV bought the viscountcy in the aftermath of the Fronde rebellion (see p.391).

Although Louis also ordered that the castle be demolished, two towers still sprout from the summit; to reach them, take the lane running northeast from the main road and keep climbing. One of the towers is occupied by the present owners of the château, but the round **Tour de César** can be visited (April–June, Sept & Oct daily 10am–noon & 2–6pm; July & Aug daily 10am–5pm; Nov–March Sun 2–5pm; €3) and is worth climbing for vertiginous views away over the ridges and valleys to the mountains of Cantal. On the way up to the castle you pass a number of elegant Renaissance houses and the all-important salt store, as well as a **church** hurriedly thrown up in 1662 during the Counter-Reformation to bring the local populace back to Catholicism; take a peek inside at the gilded altar and unusual mosaic ceiling.

Buses from Brive stop on the main road near the **tourist office** booth (May & Sept Tues–Sun 11am–6pm; July & Aug Tues–Sun 10am–6pm; T05.55.85.94.38, Wwww.brive-tourisme.com), where you can rent **bikes** and pick up walking **maps** of the village (€1). The maps are also available at the nearby souvenir shop, from beside which the lane leads up to the castle. Follow it and you'll come to the old village square and a lovely small **hotel**, *La Maison des Chanoines* (T05.55.85.93.43, Wwww.maison-des-chanoines.com; ❻; closed Nov–Easter). The rooms are decorated with the same flair and imagination that's apparent in their **restaurant**, where you'll eat extremely well for around €30 (closed lunchtime Tues–Sat; reservations essential). Across the square, you can't miss the jolly facade of *La Vicomté* (lunch only; closed Nov–Feb), which offers views up to the château from its terrace and main dishes at around €10 or a traditional regional menu for €19. Another delightful option, as either a place to stay or eat, is to be found in the village of **Sarrazac**, in the depths of the country seven kilometres southeast of Turenne. The recently renovated ⚘ *La Bonne Famille* (T05.65.37.70.38, Wwww.labonnefamille.fr; ❸) is exactly what its name suggests: a traditional country inn run by an exceptionally welcoming family. The rooms, in an annexe, are nothing fancy but perfectly comfortable while the food is top-quality home cooking, all freshly prepared and served in hearty portions (lunch menus from €10, eve & weekends from €15; reservations recommended). Even the setting, beside the Romanesque village church, is just as it should be.

Collonges-la-Rouge

There's a great view back to Turenne as you head southeast on the D20 before cutting eastwards on pretty back lanes through meadows and walnut orchards to reach **COLLONGES-LA-ROUGE** some 10km later; alternatively, you can walk between the two on the GR446 footpath. The village is the epitome of bucolic charm, with its rust-red – even verging on mauve – sandstone houses, pepper-pot towers and pink-candled chestnut trees, although you need to time your visit carefully, as it is very much on the tourist route. Though small-scale, there is a grandeur about the place. This is where the nobles who governed Turenne on behalf of the viscounts built their mini-châteaux, each boasting at least one tower – there's a wonderful view of the bristling roofs as you approach from the west.

On the main square the twelfth-century **church** is unusual in having two naves, of which the shorter, north nave – the one used today – was a later addition. They came in handy during the sixteenth century when Turenne supported the Huguenot cause; here at least, Protestants and Catholics conducted their services peacefully side by side. Outside, the covered **market hall** still retains its old-fashioned baker's oven. On your way back up the main street, look out for the **Maison de la Sirène**, diagonally opposite the tourist office, which is named after the little mermaid sculpted above the entrance. Though battered, she's still charming as she preens herself, comb in one hand and mirror in the other. The building houses a rather unexciting municipal **museum** (July–Sept daily 10.30am–12.30pm & 3–6.30pm; €2).

Practicalities

Buses from Turenne and Brive pass Collonges on their way to the terminus at Meyssac (see overleaf). They stop on the main road at the northern entrance to the village. Follow this street south into the village and you'll come to the *mairie* and **tourist office** (daily: July & Aug 10am–7pm; Sept–June 10am–noon & 2–6pm; ☎05.55.25.47.57). A little further down, there's an attractive but slightly overpriced **hotel**, the *Relais de St-Jacques de Compostelle* (☎05.55.25.41.02, ⓔrelais-st-jacques@yahoo.fr; ❷–❹; closed mid-Nov to mid-March), with lovely views from the bedrooms and a decent restaurant (menus €15–40), and **chambre d'hôte** accommodation to the south of the village at the *Domaine de la Raze* (☎05.55.25.48.16, ⓦchambrelaraze.free.fr; ❸). If you want somewhere quieter, head east 2km to **MEYSSAC**, a smaller town built in the same red sandstone, to the very pleasant *Relais du Quercy* (☎05.55.25.40.31, ⓦwww .logis-de-france.fr; ❸; closed three weeks in Nov), with a pool and pretty restaurant (menus start at €12). Alternatively, there's a three-star **campsite**, *Moulin de la Valanne* (☎05.55.25.41.59; May–Sept), halfway between Collonges and Meyssac.

Collonges has a number of crêperies and snack bars in summer. Outside the season the choice of **restaurants** is more restricted, although both the hotel (see above) and *Le Prieuré* (menus from €17.50; closed Wed & Thurs except in July & Aug), beside the church, are safe bets. *Le Cantou*, on the main street, serves more modest regional dishes as well as brasserie-type fare for €8 to €10 (July & Aug open daily for lunch & dinner; Sept–June closed evenings & all day Mon; also closed last week of June & mid-Dec to mid-Jan).

Travel details

Trains

Brive-la-Gaillarde to: Arnac-Pompadour (3–4 daily; 40min); Bordeaux (1–2 daily; 2hr 30min); Cahors (5–8 daily; 1hr 10min); Paris Austerlitz (4–6 daily; 3hr–4hr); Périgueux (3–5 daily; 1hr); Souillac (5–8 daily; 25min); Toulouse (6–9 daily; 2hr–2hr 30min); Uzerche (4–8 daily; 20–30min).

Périgueux to: Bordeaux (8–14 daily; 1hr–1hr 30min); Brive (4–6 daily; 1hr); Neuvic (3–5 daily;

20–30min); St-Astier (6–11 daily; 10–15min); Terrasson (4–6 daily; 45min–1hr); Thiviers (7–11 daily; 20–50min).

Buses

Aubeterre-sur-Dronne to: Angoulême (Mon–Sat 1–2 daily; 1hr–2hr).

Brantôme to: Angoulême (3 weekly; 1hr); Périgueux (Mon–Fri & Sun 1–3 daily; 40min).

Brive to: Argentat (Mon–Sat 2 daily; 1hr 15min–1hr 30min); Arnac-Pompadour (Mon–Sat 1 daily; 2hr); Beaulieu-sur-Dordogne (school term Mon–Sat 1–3 daily, school holidays Tues, Thurs & Sat 1–2 daily, July & Aug Mon, Tues & Thurs–Sat 1–2 daily; 1hr–1hr 30min); Collonges-la-Rouge (Mon–Sat 1–4 daily; 25min–1hr); Meyssac (Mon–Sat 1–4 daily; 30min–1hr 5min); Turenne (Mon–Sat 1–3 daily; 20–40min); Uzerche (Mon–Sat 2 daily; 1hr–1hr 30min).

Périgueux to: Angoulême (1–3 daily; 1hr 45min); Bergerac (Mon–Fri 5 daily; school holidays 3 daily; 1hr); Bourdeilles (school term Mon–Fri 1 daily; 45min); Brantôme (Mon–Fri & Sun 1–3 daily; 40min); Le Bugue (school term Mon–Fri 1 daily; 1hr); Excideuil (school term Mon–Fri 5 daily, school holidays Mon–Fri 3 daily; 1hr); Hautefort (Mon–Fri 1 daily; 40min); Montignac (school term Mon–Fri 2–3 daily, school holidays Wed 1–3 daily; 1hr); Neuvic (school term Mon–Fri 1–3 daily; 40min); Ribérac (Mon–Fri 4 daily; school holidays 3 daily; 1hr); Sarlat (school term Mon–Fri 2–3 daily, school holidays Wed 1–3 daily; 1hr 30min); St-Astier (school term Mon–Fri 1–3 daily; 30min); Thiviers (school term Wed 1 daily; 40min); Villars (school term Fri 1 daily; 1hr).

Ribérac to: Angoulême (Mon & Fri 1 daily; 1hr); Périgueux (Mon–Fri 4 daily; school holidays 3 daily; 1hr).

Turenne to: Brive (school term Mon–Fri 1–2 daily; 20min); Collonges-la-Rouge (school term Mon–Sat 1 daily; 15min); Meyssac (school term Mon–Sat 1 daily; 20min).

Planes

Brive-la-Gaillarde to: Paris Orly (1–2 daily; 1hr 20min).

Périgueux to: Paris Orly (1–3 daily; 1hr 20min).

Bergerac and around

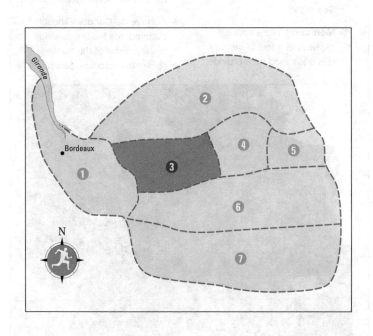

CHAPTER 3 **Highlights**

✳ **Bergerac** Surrounded by vineyards, this sleepy provincial town of cobbled squares and half-timbered facades makes for an atmospheric day's wander. See p.188

✳ **Church of St-Eutrope, Allemans-du-Dropt** Fifteenth-century frescoes depict the Last Judgement in spine-tingling detail. See p.198

✳ **Montcaret** The elaborate mosaics in a fourth-century villa unearthed here provide ample evidence of luxury living Roman-style. See p.202

✳ **Château de Montaigne** See where philosopher Michel de Montaigne wrote some of his most influential essays. See p.202

✳ **Cingle de Trémolat** A classic Dordogne meander, best viewed from the limestone cliffs to the north. See p.206

✳ **Abbaye de Cadouin** Though battered, the life-like carvings in the cloister of this austere abbey still resonate. See p.210

△ Pigeonnier at Allemans-du-Drop

Bergerac and around

n its lower reaches the Dordogne slides wide and slow through a landscape of vine-planted hills. This is the heart of the **Périgord Pourpre**, a major wine-growing area that blends seamlessly into the Bordelais vineyards to the west. For centuries the region's most important market town, port and commercial centre has been **Bergerac**, the second largest city in the Dordogne *département*, but still a pleasantly provincial place with a clutch of worthwhile sights amongst its twisting lanes. As to the wine region itself, its foremost sight is the Renaissance **Château de Monbazillac**, clearly visible on the ridge to the south and surrounded by its prestigious vineyards, originally planted by monks in the Middle Ages, which produce a very palatable sweet white wine. The high country further south of Bergerac, where the gentle River Dropt marks the border of the Dordogne and Lot-et-Garonne *départements*, wasn't always such a bucolic scene, as a glance at the remaining fortifications of **Issigeac** and particularly **Eymet** – the ramparts built in the run-up to the Hundred Years' War – goes to show. The prevailing sense of unease following more than a century of war, plague and famine is caught in the fifteenth-century frescoes of the Last Judgement in the little church of **Allemans-du-Dropt**, while further downstream at **Duras** another semi-ruined château dominates the valley.

To the west of Bergerac the Dordogne valley becomes wider, busier and less attractive. Nevertheless, there are one or two appealing sights, notably the Gallo-Roman remains at **Montcaret** and the nearby **Château de Montaigne**, where the eponymous philosopher wrote his original, wide-ranging *Essais*, before the river slips between St-Émilion's trellised vines (see p.130). North of here, the **Forêt du Landais** stretches north across the top of the Périgord Pourpre. It's a pretty region of wooded hills, meandering streams and sparse habitation, good for wandering, though without any particularly compelling sights.

Upstream of Bergerac, the pure waters of the River Couze, a tributary of the Dordogne, have spawned a paper-making industry at **Couze-et-St-Front**, where traditional, handmade paper is still produced to this day. Further east the Dordogne has carved two gigantic meanders at **Trémolat** and **Limeuil**; the views from the northern river-cliffs provide a classic Dordogne scene. Here also the Périgord Pourpre gradually gives way to wooded hills on the western edge of the Périgord Noir. The change is perhaps most obvious in the landscapes south of the river, where the *bastide* town of **Beaumont** and the nearby abbey of **St-Avit-Sénieur** stand isolated on the edge of a high, open plateau. Just a few kilometres to the east, however, **Cadouin**'s abbey church sits in a hidden valley deep among the chestnut forests.

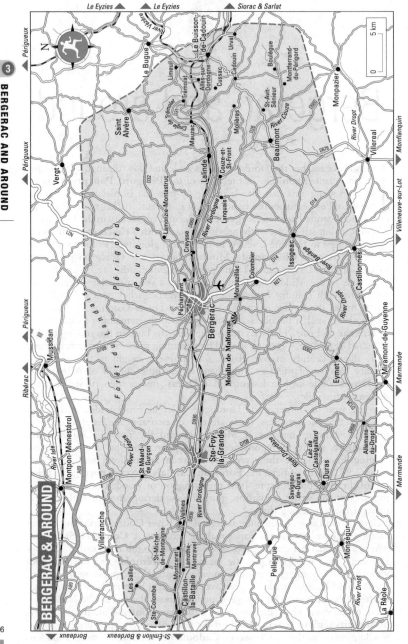

Overall, exploring this region by **public transport** is not easy. Although the Sarlat–Bordeaux train line runs along the Dordogne valley and through Bergerac, services to smaller intermediary stations are infrequent. Heading inland, away from the river, there are a couple of useful bus routes, but again services are few and far between.

Festivals, events and markets

Where we haven't given a specific information number, contact the relevant tourist office.

July and August Bergerac: Les Mercredis du Jazz (☏05.53.57.71.51). Free concerts by French jazz artists on Wednesday evenings in the Clôitre des Récollets.

Mid-July Bergerac: La Table de Cyrano (☏05.53.74.66.66). The old town is transformed into a gigantic outdoor restaurant for this magnificent food festival held over four days around July 14. Everyone eats at large, convivial tables, sampling local dishes and wines, and there are free concerts every night.

Third weekend in July Duras: Fête de la Madeleine. A combination of agricultural fair, town fête with music and feasting, and market stalls, culminating in a fireworks display on the Monday night.

Third Sunday in July Issigeac: Foire aux Paniers. Unique and hugely successful basket-weavers' fair held on the place du Château. Some sixty artisans from all regions of France demonstrate their different techniques and styles, including the local spiral-shaped baskets. Entry fee €2.

Last weekend in July Duras: Le Parvis (☏05.53.83.49.16). A highly rated local theatre troupe puts on three night-time spectacles over a weekend in the château courtyard. Tickets available from the château.

Late July to mid-August Bergerac and around: Été Musical en Bergerac (☏05.53.74.30.94). Performances of classical music, jazz and ballet in Bergerac, the Château de Biron, Monpazier, St-Avit and Cadouin.

Mid-July to mid-August Castillon-la-Bataille: La Bataille de Castillon (☏05.57.40.14.53, ⓦwww.batailledecastillon.com). Local citizenry stage a spectacular floodlit re-enactment of the battle that ended the Hundred Years' War. Some five hundred actors and fifty cavaliers take part, giving roughly a dozen performances over a month; €18 per performance.

August Dropt valley: Itinérance Médiévale en Vallée du Dropt (☏05.53.27.11.46). Medieval costume parades, jousting, fireworks, theatre and banquets are just some of the events taking place in towns and villages along the Dropt valley (including Duras, Eymet, Cadouin and Sauveterre) during this two-week festival.

Mid-August Bergerac: Les Tables de Roxane (☏05.53.74.66.66). A repeat of La Table de Cyrano (see above) but held around August 15 in odd-numbered years – on the place de la République.

Second Weekend in August Duras: Fête du Vin. Two-day wine-fest held beside the château with free tastings (you have to buy a glass at the entrance for €2). In the evening, hot-air balloons offer free rides from the foot of the château.

Late September to early October Bergerac: Fêtes des Vendanges (☏05.53.63.57.55, ⓦwww.vins-bergerac.fr). Various festivities take place in Bergerac – starting with a procession of *gabares* – and its surrounding wine villages over one week to celebrate the end of the grape harvest.

Markets

The main **markets** in this region are at Bergerac (Wed & Sat); Eymet (Thurs); Issigeac (Sun); Lalinde (Thurs); Ste-Foy-la-Grande (Sat).

Bergerac and around

Lying mostly on the Dordogne's north bank overlooking its wide flood plain, **BERGERAC** is a rather sleepy place for much of the year, but bursts into life for the summer tourist season, when cafés and restaurants spill out into the cobbled squares and alleyways. It suffered particularly badly during the Wars of Religion, but in recent years the old streets fanning out from the former port have been carefully restored to bring out the best in the rows of half-timbered cottages and more bourgeois, stone-built residences. Among several interesting and attractive reminders of the past, the main sights are a surprisingly rewarding **museum** devoted to tobacco and a former **monastery**, which in summer opens as an information centre on the local wines. Around Bergerac, the vineyards of **Monbazillac** and **Pécharment** provide rewarding excursions, the former easily combined with more extensive forays south, while there's another interesting museum, this time dedicated to river life, in the village of **Creysse** to the east.

Some history

The largest town in the Dordogne valley, Bergerac owes its existence and prosperity to the **river**. By the twelfth century it was already an important bridging point and port, controlling the trade between its Périgord hinterland and Bordeaux, particularly the burgeoning **wine trade**. Things began to take off after Henry III of England sought to keep the townspeople sweet by giving them certain privileges in 1254: they were exempted from local taxes, given the right of assembly and allowed to export their wines to Bordeaux unhindered. Local burghers took advantage of the new dispensations to ship their own wines first, while the less privileged were forced to sell later, at disadvantageous prices, and were also charged a tax of five *sous* per barrel. Bergerac's wine aristocracy were thus able to corner the lucrative foreign market until the seventeenth century, when the technique of ageing wines was discovered.

The town's heyday came in the decades preceding the Wars of Religion (1561–98) when Bergerac was among the foremost centres of **Protestantism** in southwest France. One of many truces between the warring factions was even signed here in 1577, but in 1620 the Catholic Louis XIII seized the town and ordered that the ramparts and fortress be demolished. Worse was to come when Catholic priests arrived to bring Bergerac back into the fold. They met with mixed success – the majority of the Protestant population fled, principally to Holland, where they soon established a long and mutually profitable business importing Bergerac wines.

Since then wine has continued to be the staple of the local economy. Up until the railway arrived in the 1870s, the bulk of it was transported by river, leading to a thriving **boat-building** industry all along the Dordogne. Though most have long disappeared, a few sturdy *gabares* are still being built to cater to the tourist trade.

Arrival and information

There are daily flights from numerous regional airports in the UK and also from Paris to Bergerac's **airport**, 4km southeast of the city on the Agen road; from here it's a ten to fifteen minute taxi ride to the centre (around €15). The **gare SNCF**, on the other hand, is located at the north end of cours Alsace-Lorraine, ten minutes' walk from the old town. Most **bus** services also terminate at the

The wines of Bergerac

The **Bergerac wine region** extends along the north bank of the Dordogne from Lamothe-Montravel in the west to Lalinde in the east, and south as far as Eymet and Issigeac. It comprises no fewer than thirteen different *appellations*, of which over half the total output (nearly 600,000 hectolitres, or 80 million bottles, in 2001) is red wine, although the region's most famous wine is the sweet white Monbazillac.

There is evidence of wine production around Bergerac since Roman times, but the vineyards really began to develop in the thirteenth century to supply the English market. Demand from Holland, for sweet white wines in particular, led to a second spurt in the sixteenth century and then again after the Wars of Religion, when Protestant émigré merchants virtually monopolized the market in Monbazillac wines. By the nineteenth century vines covered 100,000 hectares around Bergerac, only to be decimated by phylloxera in the 1870s; the area under AOC wines today covers a mere 12,000 hectares.

Pre-eminent among the Bergerac wines is **Monbazillac**. This pale golden, sweet white wine is blended from Semillon, Sauvignon and Muscadelle vines grown on the chalky clay soils of the valley's north-facing slopes. As with Sauternes, a key element is the cold, autumn-morning mists which lead to the development of *Botrytis cinerea*, or "noble rot", on the grapes (see p.114). The result is an intensely perfumed, concentrated wine best consumed chilled with foie gras, desserts or as an apéritif. Though they can't compare to the finesse of Sauternes, even a top-quality Monbazillac is eminently affordable at around €15 a bottle.

Pécharment, the best of the local reds, is often compared unfavourably to Bordeaux wines (see p.79), though some now rival a number of less prestigious St-Émilions. Pécharment wines are produced from Cabernet Sauvignon, Cabernet Franc and small quantities of Malbec or Merlot grapes, grown on the most favourable pockets of sand and gravel soils found to the north and east of Bergerac. They are thus far more complex and full-bodied than other Bergerac reds, and some will age well up to seven years.

You can sample the range of local AOC wines at Bergerac's Maison des Vins (see p.192). Alternatively, many producers offer **tastings and visits** to their *chais* – for a full list see the brochure *Route des Vins de Bergerac* available at the Maison du Vin or Bergerac tourist office. For general tips on visiting the vineyards, see the box on p.79.

station, though some stop on either place du Foirail or place de la République (see "Listings", p.194 for details). Driving in, you'll find free **parking** in the cobbled area beside the old port and on place du Foirail, a short walk east of the town centre.

Bergerac's main **tourist office** is at 97 rue Neuve-d'Argenson (July & Aug Mon–Sat 9.30am–7.30pm; Sept–June Mon–Sat 9.30am–1pm & 2–7pm; ☎05.53.57.03.11, ⓦwww.bergerac-tourisme.com). In summer they also open an annexe in the Clôitre des Récollets (July & Aug Mon–Sun 10.30am–1pm & 2.30–7pm; same number as above), and organize **guided tours** of the old town several times a week (July & Aug; 1hr 30min; €4).

Accommodation

Bergerac offers a choice of mid-level and budget **hotels** scattered around the town centre, in addition to one upmarket option on the northeastern outskirts. There's also a small, simple **campsite**, *La Pelouse* (☎ & ⒻF05.53.57.06.67; open all year), in a pleasant spot on the south bank of the river.

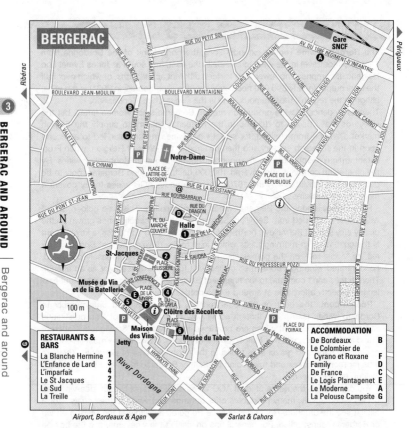

Airport, Bordeaux & Agen ▼   ▼ Sarlat & Cahors

De Bordeaux 38 place Gambetta ℡ 05.53.57.12.83, Ⓦ www.hotel-bordeaux-bergerac.com. With its gastronomic restaurant, swimming pool and small but pleasant garden lurking behind a rather austere 1930s facade, this is central Bergerac's top hotel. Most rooms have been renovated and upgraded with modern, ochre-coloured furnishings, there's a good buffet breakfast (€8) and the restaurant serves menus from €20. ④

🏃 **Le Colombier de Cyrano et Roxane** 17 place de la Myrpe ℡ 05.53.57.96.70. This lovely little *chambre d'hote* in a flagstone sixteenth-century cottage on place de la Myrpe is adorned with blue shutters, flower boxes and a tiny blue wooden door. The three doubles are full of old world charm with wooden beams, fireplaces; one room has its own leafy terrace. Price includes a hearty breakfast. ③

Family 3 rue du Dragon ℡ 05.53.57.80.90, Ⓕ 05.53.57.08.00. Family-run budget hotel with just eight en-suite rooms tucked in a corner of the central place du Marché-Couvert – booking is advisable at any time of year. Though on the small side, the rooms are clean and comfortable, equipped with TV and phone, shower units and good, firm beds. The restaurant, *Le Jardin d'Epicure*, also offers hearty, family cooking: *plats du jours* for €7.30 and menus from €17. ②

De France 18 place Gambetta ℡ 05.53.57.11.61, Ⓦ www.hoteldefrance-bergerac.com. A slightly cheaper option than the nearby *Bordeaux*, with a swimming pool squeezed into the back yard. The concrete-box exterior is a bit off-putting, but this recently renovated hotel has spanking new communal areas and comfortable rooms, although the bathrooms are on the small side. ③

Le Logis Plantagenet 5 rue du Grand Moulin ℡ 05.53.57.15.99, Ⓦ www.lelogisplantagenet.com. This restored fourteenth-century house has three roomy and rather plush doubles – all beams, wood

floors, rugs and country style furnishings – as well as a cosy residents' lounge and a courtyard garden. ❺
Le Moderne av du 108e Régiment-d'Infantrie ☏05.53.57.19.62, ⓕ05.53.61.80.50. Simple, cheerful rooms at a good price right opposite the station. Phone and TV are standard, though cheaper rooms share spruce communal toilets and showers, and those on the front are a little noisy. There's a decent bar-brasserie downstairs, with menus from €10. Closed Fri, also ten days in both Oct & Feb. ❶–❷

The Town

Although Bergerac sits astride the Dordogne, nearly everything of interest is located on the north bank. The best place to start is beside the old port where, in season, replica *gabares* pick up passengers for leisurely **river trips** (1hr; €6.50) along the Dordogne to a nature reserve home to herons, cormorants and kingfishers, amongst other wildlife; commentary is bilingual. Departures are at least four times daily from March to October, and up to once an hour in July and August (10am–8pm). For more information, call ☏05.53.24.58.80.

A short hop east of the port lies the entertaining **Musée du Tabac**, in the narrow lanes of the **vieille ville** which spreads gently uphill. A calm and pleasant area to wander, with drinking fountains on the street corners and numerous late-medieval houses, its main artery is the Grand'Rue, which runs north from the central church of St-Jacques to join rue de la Résistance, the old town's northern perimeter; these two form Bergerac's principal shopping streets. Just beyond their junction, across the wide place de Lattre-de-Tassigny, stands another useful landmark, the **Notre-Dame church**.

The Musée du Tabac

Rue de l'Ancien-Pont leads northwards from portside rue Hippolyte-Taine to the splendid seventeenth-century Maison Peyrarède, which houses the informative **Musée du Tabac** (March 15–Nov 15 Tues–Fri 10am–noon & 2–6pm, Sat 10am–noon & 2–5pm, Sun 2.30–6.30pm; Nov 16–March 14 Tues–Fri 10am–noon & 2–6pm, Sat 10am–noon; €3.50), detailing the history of tobacco (which used to be a major crop in the Bergerac region; Europe's major tobacco research centre is also based here), though rather glossing over its more dire medical effects. Nevertheless, this is a stunning collection of pipes, snuffboxes, cigar holders, tobacco jars, graters and various tools of the trade.

The museum occupies three floors, starting with the first discovery of tobacco in pre-Columbian America and its introduction to Europe in the mid-seventeenth century. Somewhat conveniently, the displays go only as far as the early twentieth century, before the question of health risks came to the fore. Though the plant takes its botanical name, Nicotiana, from the Frenchman Jean Nicot, who sent some leaves from Portugal to Catherine de Medici in 1561 to help cure her migraines, his compatriot André Thevet had already planted several seeds in his Angoulême garden five years earlier. With Catherine de Medici's endorsement, however, the "divine weed" took off. So popular did it become, among both men and women, that tobacco smoking soon had to be banned from churches as the smoke overpowered the incense. It was also widely consumed for medicinal reasons as a powder and in drinks, oils, pills and unguents. Such usage continued into the early nineteenth century, when tobacco came to be viewed with greater alarm, but mainly for moral rather than health reasons: tobacco consumption was blamed for laziness, brutality, criminality, madness and sexual perversion.

Tobacco's tale is told in great detail, accompanied by some marvellous illustrations and superb examples of the connoisseur's accoutrements. There are wooden graters etched with religious scenes, snuffboxes engraved with the busts of Napoleon and Marie Antoinette, blushing young beauties adorning porcelain pipe-bowls and hunting scenes fashioned out of meerschaum. Among many rare and beautiful pieces, the museum's prize possessions are an incredibly ornate Viennese meerschaum-and-amber cigar holder depicting a Sicilian wedding, and an intriguing machine, invented in the 1860s, for carving fourteen brier pipes at once. Look out, too, for the clay pipe in the ominous form of a skull with glittering glass eyes.

The rest of the old town

North of the museum, you cross the attractive place du Feu, one of many such well-restored squares in central Bergerac, to enter the **Cloître des Récollets**. This simple, galleried cloister dates from the seventeenth century when, in the aftermath of the Wars of Religion, Louis XIII dispatched five monks of the Franciscan Récollets order to bring Protestant Bergerac back to the faith. They were not warmly welcomed – it took a visit by Louis himself, in 1621, to assure their authority – but by the end of the decade the Récollets had succeeded in founding a new chapel and monastery. Not that they had the last word. After the Revolution, Bergerac's remaining Protestant congregation bought the chapel and re-established a temple on the site, which is still used for regular Sunday-morning worship.

The monks' vaulted grain and wine cellars, on the cloister's south side, are used nowadays for meetings of the Consulat de la Vinée, which decides those wines meriting the AOC label, while in summer the **Maison des Vins** occupies the monks' former reception rooms above (Feb–May & Sept–Dec Tues & Sat 10.30am–12.30pm & 2–6pm; June–Aug daily 10am–7pm; free; ⊤05.53.63.57.55, ⓔcivrb.poletouristique@vins-bergerac.fr). In addition to free tastings, they offer weekly wine-tasting lessons (mid-June to mid-Sept; €8; reservations required) and produce the very detailed *Route des Vins de Bergerac* as a guide to visiting the vineyards around the town.

On its north side the Cloître des Récollets opens onto one of Bergerac's most picturesque squares, the cobbled **place de la Myrpe** (also spelt Mirpe), lined with stone and half-timbered labourers' cottages. All very pretty now, but until not so long ago this frequently flooded area, within spitting distance of the

---

Cyrano de Bergerac

In 1897, the poet and playwright Edmond Rostand penned his most successful play, **Cyrano de Bergerac**. It tells the story of a guardsman and poet, renowned for his bravery and intellect, who falls in love with his cousin Roxane, but feels unable to declare his feelings because of his unattractive looks – in particular his large, protruding nose. Instead, he writes letters to her on behalf of one of his cadets, the handsome but dim-witted Christian, who has also fallen for her charms. First attracted by Christian's looks, Roxane falls in love with the soul revealed in the letters – not discovering until it is too late that it is in fact Cyrano's soul. Rostand's play has since been the subject of numerous adaptations, perhaps most famously the 1990 French film version staring Gérard Depardieu.

The lead character was inspired by a seventeenth-century soldier, playwright and free-thinking philosopher called Savinien de Cyrano, who was born in Paris and only decided to embellish his name while serving in a Gascon company. It seems Cyrano was well able to match the Gascon reputation for swaggering boastfulness and impetuosity. Not only was he a famous duellist, but many of his works were so outspoken that they had to be withheld from publication until after his death.

port, would have lived up to its name, meaning malodorous – which perhaps explains the presence of a statue, erected in 1977, honouring Edmond Rostand's fictional hero **Cyrano de Bergerac** in typically haughty pose, and with his formidable nose very much in evidence).

At the opposite end of place de la Myrpe, on the corner with rue des Conférences, the small **Musée du Vin et de la Batellerie** (Tues–Fri 10am–noon & 2–5.30pm, Sat 10am–noon; mid-March to mid-Nov also open Sun 2–6pm; €1.50) contains displays on viticulture, barrel-making and the town's once bustling river trade. This latter section is the most interesting, with models of the *gabares* alongside engravings showing men hauling them along the river – a practice banned in 1837 for humanitarian reasons – and early photos of Bergerac port. On the hillside above, up rue St-Jacques, stands the patchwork **church of St-Jacques** (Mon–Sat 8.30am–5pm). The church, a stop on the route to Santiago de Compostela, has had a chequered past. Founded in the twelfth century, it was partly destroyed in the Hundred Years' War, then rebuilt around 1537 only to be ruined three decades later in the Wars of Religion, when the stone was pillaged to erect ramparts against the Catholic armies and to build the square defensive tower which now forms the belfry. Reconstruction on a modest scale began in 1639 but, thanks to a donation by Louis XIV, the architects were able to enlarge their ambitions. Today's church is fairly modest, but has a certain grandeur in its narrow, high nave lit by stained-glass windows.

Rue St-James runs east from the church across the top end of pedestrianized **place Pélissière**, in the heart of the old town. An elegant town house, decorated with traditional musical instruments and cockleshells, faces down the square at no. 26, while further along are some rustic *colombage* facades. From here pretty **rue des Fontaines** continues uphill past prosperous, fourteenth-and sixteenth-century houses – no. 29 on the corner with rue Gaudra is particularly noteworthy with its large, arched windows and carved capitals – to the **market square**. The covered *halle* is the focus of a vast market on Wednesday and Saturday mornings, with more stalls on the square outside the **church of Notre-Dame** (Mon–Sat 8.30am–5pm), north of rue de la Résistance. While there, it's worth strolling into the nineteenth-century Gothic church to see two large oil paintings in the east chapel: *The Adoration of the Shepherds*, attributed to a pupil of Leonardo de Vinci, and *The Adoration of the Magi* from the Venetian School.

Eating and drinking

When it comes to **places to eat**, the streets of old Bergerac present the most promising hunting ground. Here you'll find cosy restaurants serving top-notch Périgord cuisine alongside more modest brasseries and an excellent Moroccan specialist. Don't forget, also, the hotel-restaurants mentioned above on p.190. The vine-shaded terrace of *La Treille*, overlooking the old port, at 12 quai Salvette, is a popular spot for a **drink**, while the best place to look for a **café** is on place Pélissière, with a few more workman-like places around the market hall and on place Gambetta to the west of Notre-Dame.

La Blanche Hermine place du Marché-Couvert ☏05.53.57.63.42. Cheerful crêperie offering an imaginative range of buckwheat crêpes as well as copious salads, grills and a more extensive evening menu – including such novelties as galette filled

with duck confit and minced peaches. Most dishes are under €8. Closed Sun and Mon & for two weeks at the end of August.

 **L'Enfance de Lard** place Pélissière ☏05.53.57.52.88. With just six tables,

reservations are recommended at this intimate, first-floor restaurant run by a delightful French-English team. From a small but innovative menu, try pan-fried foie gras – served in summer with a compote of cherries and chocolate – followed by meat grilled over a wood fire in front of you, and home-made desserts. There's a three-course menu at €30 including coffee, with a vegetarian option, and in winter they also stage dinner concerts once a month (€42 including wine). Open for dinner only; closed Tues & two weeks in Sept.

L'Imparfait 8 rue des Fontaines ℡05.53.57.47.92. Another highly-rated restaurant with an attractive high-ceilinged, stone dining room and a spacious summer terrace (reservations recommended for dinner in season). Fish features strongly, from salt-baked herbed sea bass to langoustine cooked with prawns, foie gras, fresh truffles and a sauce laced with Madeira and brandy. Menus – which change daily – start at €19 at lunchtime and €39 for dinner. Closed Dec–Feb.

Le St Jacques 30 rue St-Jâmes ℡05.53.23.38.08. This place has a charming shaded garden at the back complete with outdoor fireplace and stone walls strewn with lanterns and candles. It features a small menu of fresh regional cooking with a twist, including stuffed loin of pork with ginger and thyme and trout with an aniseed and balsamic sauce. Closed Mon. Menus from €22.50

Le Sud 19 rue de l'Ancien-Pont. Feast on *couscous Royale*, exotic salads and, if you still have room, home-made desserts or eye-boggling ice creams at this good-value, welcoming Moroccan restaurant. The decor is equally seductive with mosaic-tiled walls, carved wooden screens and flickering table lanterns. A three-course meal will set you back only €15–20, while in summer they also offer a light lunch menu (€11.50–13) on the terrace. There's a good choice of North African wines alongside one or two well-priced Bergeracs. Closed Mon.

Listings

Airlines Airliner ℡08.20.82.08.20, 🖳www .airfrance.com; British European ℡0044/13922 68500 (in UK), 🖳www.flybe.com; Ryanair ℡08.92.55.56.66, 🖳www.ryanair.com.
Airport Roumanière ℡05.53.22.25.25, 🖳www .Bergerac-aeroport.fr.
Bike rental For bike, scooter and motorbike rental, with airport pickups available, try Apolo Cycles, 31 bd Victor-Hugo ℡05.53.61.08.16, 🖳www.apolo-cycles .com. Otherwise, there's Périgord Cycles, 11 place Gambetta ℡05.53.57.07.19, offering bikes only.
Books and newspapers The best place to try for English-language papers is the Maison de la Presse, 33 rue de la Résistance, opposite the post office.
Bus departures Most buses around the region depart from outside the gare SNCF, with the exception of those for Lalinde (Les Cars Boullet; ℡05.53.61.00.46) which leave from place du Foirail, a five-minute walk east of the old town. The other routes out of Bergerac are: Villeneuve-sur-Lot (Les Cars Loiseau; ℡05.53.40.23.30), Périgueux (CFTA; ℡05.53.08.43.13) and Marmande via Issigeac and Eymet (Les Cars Bleus; ℡05.53.23.81.92).
Car rental Near the train station, try: Avis, 26 cours Alsace-Lorraine ℡05.53.57.69.83; Budget, 32 Avenue du 108e Régiment-d'Infantrie ℡05.53.74.20.20; Europcar, 3 av du 108e Régi-ment-d'Infantrie ℡05.53.58.97.97; Sixt, 14 av du 108e Régiment-d'Infantrie ℡05.53.74.20.00; Ucar, 31 bd Victor-Hugo ℡05.53.61.08.16,

🖳www.ucar-location.com. All offer airport pick-ups on demand.
Hospital Central Hospitalier Samuel Pozzi, 9 bd du Professeur Albert-Calmette, the eastern extension of rue du Professeur-Pozzi ℡05.53.63.88.88.
Internet access Available at Forum Espace Culture, 5–9 rue de la Résistance (Mon 2–7pm, Tues–Sat 10am–7pm).
Markets There's a fresh-food market from Monday to Saturday in the central *halle*, on place Gambetta and in front of Notre-Dame church, while Berger-ac's main market takes place on Wednesday and Saturday mornings in the *halle*. Place de la Myrpe is the venue for a flea market on the first Sunday of the month.
Police Commissariat de Police, 37 bd Chanzy ℡05.53.57.61.02.
Post Office The main post office is at 36 rue de la Résistance, 24000 Bergerac.
Taxis There's a taxi stand outside the station. Otherwise, call ℡05.53.23.32.32.
Tourist train In July and August a tourist train, the Autorail Espérance, runs along the Dordogne valley from Bergerac to Sarlat, via Lalinde and Le Buisson; en route they serve various local products, including paté, goat's cheese and a glass of wine. The train leaves Bergerac around midday (Mon–Sat), and takes an hour and a half to reach Sarlat; you then return on a regular SNCF service. Tickets cost €13 return (there are no one-way fares) and reservations are required: phone ℡05.53.59.55.39 to make a booking.

Around Bergerac

The area **around Bergerac** provides a couple of enjoyable excursions geared primarily around wine. On the hills to the south, **Monbazillac** is most famous for its sweet white wines, though the village also offers an imposing château housing a local history museum. East along the Dordogne there's an engaging museum of river life at **Creysse**, to the north of which the vineyards of **Pécharment** produce wines a cut above the surrounding Côtes de Bergerac and Bergerac *appellations*.

Monbazillac and around

Six kilometres south of Bergerac, **MONBAZILLAC** is the name not only of a village but also, more famously, of a château and a sweet white wine similar to those of the Sauternes (see p.114 for more on Monbazillac wines). Visible from across the valley floor, the handsome sixteenth-century **Château de Monbazillac** (April daily 10am–noon & 2–6pm; May & Oct daily 10am–12.30pm & 2–5pm; June–Sept daily 10am–7pm; Nov, Dec, Feb & March Tues–Sun 10am–noon & 2–5pm; €5.80; Ⓦ www.chateau-monbazillac.com) looks down over the gentle slopes of its long-favoured vineyards. An eye-catching blend of Renaissance residence and mock-medieval fortress, its corners reinforced by four sturdy towers, the château was a Protestant stronghold during the Wars of Religion. Surprisingly, it has survived virtually intact and now contains a moderately interesting **museum**. Best are the wine-related displays in the cellar, including antique bottles specially labelled for the Dutch market (see p.189), and the ground-floor grand salon with its richly decorated ceiling and a parquet floor of oak, pine and cherry wood. Upstairs again, two local personalities are remembered in the Baroque furniture of the equally exuberant Bergerac-born actor Jean Mounet-Sully (1841–1916), and a good collection of caricatures by SEM (aka Georges Goursat), born in Périgueux in 1863; SEM's most famous drawing of an animated scene in Paris's *Maxim's* restaurant still adorns the restaurant's menus.

The Château de Monbazillac now belongs to the local wine producers' co-operative, the **Cave de Monbazillac**, which produces the velvety sweet white wine. You can taste – and buy – the wines at the château or at the main **showroom** (Mon–Sat: Jan & Feb 10am–12.30pm & 2–6pm; March–June 10am–12.30pm & 1.30–7pm; July & Aug 9am–7pm; Sept–Dec 10am–12.30pm & 1.30–7pm; ☏05.53.61.52.52) located 2km west on the D933 Bergerac–Marmande road. Three kilometres further west again, you'll find a well-rated **restaurant**, the *Tour des Vents* (☏05.53.58.30.10; closed Mon & for dinner Sun & Wed, also closed Jan), beside the Moulin de Malfourat, a ruined windmill perched on the highest point for miles around. Though it's not an attractive building, the views from the restaurant's picture windows and terrace are superb – and the food is excellent value; menus start at €23.50.

After whetting your appetite at the Monbazillac, it's worth investigating some of the area's private **vineyards**. There are two good options to the east of Monbazillac near the village of **COLOMBIER**. The first you come to on the D14E, after about 4km, is the sixteenth-century **Château de la Jaubertie** (☏05.53.58.32.11, ✉jaubertie@wanadoo.fr; July & Aug Mon–Sat 10.30am–5.30pm; Sept–June Mon–Fri 10.30am–5.30pm; free), which was supposedly built by Henry IV for his mistress, Gabrielle d'Estrée, and later belonged to a doctor of Marie Antoinette. Now owned by the English Ryman family, the estate produces a variety of very reasonable wines under the Bergerac *appellation*; read Jeremy Joseph's *A Vineyard in Dordogne* (see "Books", p.400) to learn more about the Ryman's transformation of La Jaubertie. In Colombier itself, the **Domaine de l'Ancienne Cure** has won any number of awards for its high-quality Monbazillac, Bergerac and Pécharment wines – their Cuvée Abbaye and the highly concentrated L'Extase are particularly recommended. You can visit the *chais* by appointment (☎05.53.58.27.90, ⊛www.pays-de-bergerac .com/vins/domaine-ancienne-cure), but tastings are available at any time at their shop just below the village on the main N21 Bergerac–Agen road (April–Oct Mon–Sat 9am–7pm; Nov–March Mon–Sat 9am–6pm).

Creysse and Pécharment

Eight kilometres east of Bergerac, the village of **CREYSSE** lies strung out along the busy D660 Sarlat road. The only reason to stop here is the **Musée-Aquarium de la Rivière Dordogne** (daily: April, May & Oct 10am–12.30pm & 2–6pm; June–Sept 10am–noon & 2–7pm; €5.40) located under the riverside terrace in the village centre. The museum covers the history of **fishing** along the Dordogne, with examples of the different boats, nets and traps employed, but of greater interest is the surprising variety of river life. Display **tanks** contain examples of indigenous species such as salmon, trout, eel and bream, as well as zander, black bass and catfish, all of which were introduced in the nineteenth century. Also on show are a number of species found only in the Dordogne River: shad (*alose*) and sea lamprey (*lamproie*; see box on p.130) – both popular local dishes – which migrate upstream to breed, in addition to the increasingly rare river lamprey and a local type of sturgeon.

If you leave the river valley at Creysse, heading north, you're soon back among vine-covered hills. Some of this region's best red wines are produced around the village of **PÉCHARMENT**, 6km northeast of Bergerac. The family-run **Domaine du Haut-Pécharment** (☎05.53.57.29.50; daily 9am–noon & 2–7pm) is a good place to aim for. It stands in the thick of the vines with views across to Monbazillac, and produces a typically full-bodied, aromatic wine which ages well. The domaine is signed north off the D32 between Bergerac and Ste-Alvère. Opposite the turning, at the end of a long alley, the much grander **Château de Tiregand** (☎05.53.23.21.08; April–Oct Mon–Sat 9.30am–noon & 2–6pm; Nov–March Mon–Fri 9.30am–noon & 2–5.30pm) also offers tastings and, if you phone ahead, visits to its extensive park and seventeenth-century *chais*.

South of Bergerac

South of Bergerac, you gradually leave the vines behind as you cross an area of high, rolling country. First stop is **Issigeac**, with its picturesque medieval centre situated on a tributary of the Dropt. From there you can follow quieter back roads southwest along the **Dropt valley** to **Eymet**, a *bastide* of passing interest, and on to **Allemans-du-Dropt**, where the focus of interest is a remarkable series of frescoes in its otherwise unassuming church. Last but not least comes **Duras**, the town from which the twentieth-century novelist Margaret Duras took her pen-name after spending part of her childhood in the region. Duras's semi-ruined but still forbidding castle holds a commanding position on Périgord's southwestern border; if you continue down the Dropt from here you'll soon reach Monségur in the Entre-Deux-Mers region (see p.118), or, you can head north to Ste-Foy-la-Grande back in the Dordogne valley (see p.201).

As far as public transport is concerned, there is just one **bus** service from Bergerac to Marmande via Issigeac, Eymet and Allemans. Even using this, however, it will take careful planning and at least one overnight stop in Eymet, since there are only one or two buses a day in each direction, not always at convenient times.

Issigeac

An almost perfectly circular huddle of houses in the midst of pastureland and orchards 8km southeast of Colombier along the D14, **ISSIGEAC** owes its prosperity to the bishops of Sarlat who established a residence here in 1317. Only fragments of the

△ St-Eutrope, Allemans-du-Dropt

outer walls remain, and in recent years the village has been considerably tarted up, but otherwise its core of half-timbered medieval buildings is largely unspoiled and the narrow streets mercifully traffic-free.

The seventeenth-century **bishop's palace**, now containing various administrative offices, and the **Maison des Dîmes**, the former tax office, with its immense roof, command the village's north entrance. Behind the palace, and not much larger, the Gothic **church of St-Félicien** contains little of interest beyond some polychrome statues. Better instead to wander the old streets, starting with the **Grand'Rue**, leading south to Issigeac's most famous building known as the **Maison des Têtes** for its roughly carved, almost grotesque crowned and grimacing heads. It stands on the corner with rue Cardénal, at the east end of which a house with a half-timbered upper storey on a narrow stone pedestal – allowing carts to pass on either side – resembles nothing so much as a toadstool. From here, take rue Sauveterre circling southwest past more medieval houses and then cross over the southern end of the Grand'Rue to find the rue de l'Ancienne-Poste, which meanders generally back northwards to the Maison des Dîmes.

Issigeac receives sufficient visitors to have its own **tourist office**, located in a vaulted cellar beneath the bishop's palace (July & Aug Tues–Sat 10am–7pm, Sun 9.30am–1pm & 3–6pm; Sept to mid-Nov Tues–Sat 10am–12.30pm & 2.30–6.30pm, Sun 9.30am–1pm & 2–6pm; rest of the year call ☏05.53.58.79.62 for hours; ⓦwww.issigeac.fr). The busiest time is on Sunday mornings when the village fills with **market** stalls. If you are here on a Sunday, make sure you book ahead at ✝ *Chez Alain* (☏05.53.58.77.88; ⓦwww.chez-alain.com; Oct–June closed Sun eve, Mon & Tues lunch, also closed three weeks in Oct & Feb), a classy **restaurant** just across the ring road from the bishop's palace. They serve an excellent buffet lunch (€18), and other menus from €23 and specialities include langoustine tempura with spicy yogurt. **Buses** from Bergerac stop on place du Foirail on the southwest side of Issigeac.

Eymet

In contrast to Issigeac's meandering medieval streets, **EYMET**, 15km to the southwest, is laid out on a typical *bastide* chequerboard plan around a well-preserved arcaded central square, **place Gambetta**. Founded in 1270 by Alphonse de Poitiers (see p.388), Eymet changed hands on several occasions – not always by force – during the Hundred Years' War and later joined Bergerac as a bastion of Protestantism. Indeed, locals are still proud of the fact that in 1588 Henry of Navarre, the then leader of the Protestant armies and future King Henry IV, wrote a letter from Eymet to his mistress, Diane d'Andouins. With its corner tower and trefoil windows, the house in which he supposedly set pen to paper is the grandest on place Gambetta; it is naturally called the **Maison d'Amour**.

Apart from the square, with its Thursday-morning **market**, and the remnants of a château, there's not much else to see in Eymet. The town does, however, make a possible overnight stop for those relying on the limited bus services hereabouts. **Buses** stop on the main D933 which skirts Eymet to the east. There's a **tourist office** under the place Gambetta's arcades (May–Sept Mon–Sat 10am–12.30pm & 2–6.30pm; Oct–June Mon–Sat 2–5.30pm; ℡05.53.23.74.95, ⓦwww.eymet-en-perigord.com), and just off the D933 to the south, a comfortable **hotel**, *Les Vieilles Pierres* (℡05.53.23.75.99, ⓦwww .hotel-restaurant-vieilles-pierres.com; ❸; closed two weeks in Nov & in Feb; menus €10–35, closed Sat midday & Sun eve), with a pool and garden. Alternatively, there's a well-run two-star **campsite** between the château and the river (℡05.53.23.80.28; May–Sept).

The nicest place to **eat** is the *Maison d'Amour*, a crêperie and *salon du thé* on place Gambetta (closed two weeks in Oct & in Feb; also closed Mon–Wed in winter; ℡05.53.22.34.64), which is popular for its weekday breakfast *formules* (from €5), and well-stuffed *galettes* and salad platters. In July and August they also rent out **canoes** and **bikes** for some gentle exploration of the Dropt valley. For a **drink** head to *Le Pub*, also on place Gambetta, a lively little place with a good terrace, British beers and a decent menu of light lunches.

Allemans-du-Dropt

A good place to head – by whatever means of transport – is downstream 10km from Eymet to the tiny village of **ALLEMANS-DU-DROPT**, not much more than a homely little central square and the **church of St-Eutrope** (Mon–Sat 9am–6pm, Sun 9–10am & 11.30–6pm; free). The church's top-heavy lantern tower and grand west door – both nineteenth-century additions to the much-altered tenth-century building – are rather misleading; inside, the walls are covered with recently restored fifteenth-century **frescoes** depicting the Crucifixion and Last Judgement. A number of scenes have been lost or damaged over the years, but on the whole the paintings, which were only rediscovered in 1935, are unusually complete. They read from left to right as you enter, starting with the Last Supper and ending with a particularly graphic view of Hell. Despite the best efforts of St Michael, clad in medieval armour, a mere two souls seem bound for heaven while the damned are being carried off by the basket-load, or skewered on a spit, to be thrust into a boiling cauldron.

Once you've had enough of that, take a stroll to Allemans' western outskirts to see a splendid **pigeonnier** standing in a farmyard beside the D211 Pont de Duras road. Such pigeon-houses, which only noblemen had the right to build, are fairly common throughout southwest France, but this elegant hexagonal brick and oak-framed structure, raised up on seven pillars, each capped to prevent rats climbing up, is a particularly fine example.

Though Allemans is easy enough to find your way around, it's still worth picking up an English-language walking guide from the **tourist office** (mid-June to mid-Sept Mon–Sat 10am–12.15pm & 3–6.15pm; mid-Sept to mid-June Wed 9am–noon & 2–5pm, Fri 9am–noon; ☎05.53.20.25.59) beside the church; outside these hours ask at the little crafts shop opposite. **Buses** stop on place de la Mairie, southwest of the church, which is where you'll also find an old-fashioned country **hotel**, *L'Étape Gasconne* (☎05.53.20.23.55, Ⓦwww.letapegasconne-hotel.com; ❸). It's a quiet spot with a pool and a decent **restaurant** (closed lunchtime Sat; and for dinner Oct–April Fri & Sun) serving traditional fare; menus start at €11. There's also a low-key municipal **campsite** (☎05.53.20.23.37, Ⓕ05.53.20.68.95; May–Oct) beside the river, north across the old stone bridge from the village. In July and August you can also rent **canoes** here (☎06.89.60.68.31).

Duras

From Allemans, the Dropt winds its way northwest for 10km to where the castle-town of **DURAS** lords it over the valley from its rocky outcrop. The château towers were truncated during the Revolution, but they still afford fine views beyond the Dropt to the country around, an enchanting region of rolling hills topped with windmills, of pasture, orchards, woods and, particularly to the north, of vines. It was the wine trade which ushered in Duras's eighteenth-century golden era and which has, since 1937, played a part in its economic revival through the Côtes de Duras *appellation*, one of the first created.

The chequered history of Duras is evident in the mix-and-match architecture of the **Château des Ducs de Duras** which dominates the town (March–May & Oct daily 10am–noon & 2–6pm; June & Sept 10am–12.30pm & 2–7pm; July & Aug daily 10am–7pm; Nov–Feb Sat & Sun 10am–noon & 2–6pm; €4.50; Ⓦwww.chateau-de-duras.com). The château was founded in 1137, but then rebuilt after 1308 by Bertrand de Goth, nephew of Pope Clément V; it is said he used money confiscated from the Templars. Rebuilt again after the Hundred Years' War, it was then extensively remodelled during the more peaceful and prosperous late sixteenth and seventeenth centuries. The finishing touches were added in 1741, just in time to be thoroughly ransacked during the Revolution, after which the château was left to crumble until the commune bought it in 1969. They are still in the midst of a massive restoration project, but a fair number of rooms are open to the public, containing displays on archeology, rural crafts and agriculture amongst others. On your way round, look out for wells cut straight through the bedrock and freshwater tanks in case of siege, and a monstrous kitchen fireplace big enough to roast a whole ox. The dukes obviously liked to build on a grand scale – across a wide, open courtyard the entrance hall is impressive enough, and the ceremonial hall above is heated by no fewer than eleven chimneys.

Also worth a look is the **Musée Vivant du Parchemin** (daily: April–June & Sept 3–6pm; July & Aug 11am–1pm & 3–7pm; rest of the year by appointment only; €6; ☎05.53.20.75.55; Ⓦwww.museeduparchemin.com), a couple of minutes' walk northeast following the ramparts along boulevard

Jean-Brisseau. Established by two artisans, the museum-workshop provides a fascinating introduction to medieval parchment and the art of illumination. After a video presentation (English version available on request) and a short guided tour explaining, among other things, how parchment is made from hides and the different coloured inks from minerals, plant dies, oak galls and the like, you get to try your hand at a little fancy lettering with a goose-quill pen.

Practicalities

The nearby **tourist office**, at 14 boulevard Jean-Brisseau (July & Aug Mon–Sat 10am–7pm, Sun 3–5pm; Sept–June Mon–Fri 9am–12.30pm & 1.30–6pm; ☎05.53.83.63.06, ⓦwww.paysdeduras.com), has plentiful English-language information on the Duras region and also sells local wine, with free tastings in July and August, and can give advice on vineyard visits.

Also on boulevard Jean-Brisseau, near the museum and tourist office, the *Hostellerie des Ducs* (☎05.53.83.74.58, ⓦwww.hostellerieducs-duras.com; ❹) makes a very comfortable place to **stay**. In addition to a pool and flower-filled terrace, there's also an excellent **restaurant** serving upmarket regional cuisine, with menus from €15 (July–Sept closed for lunch Sat & Mon; Oct–June closed Sat lunch, Sun eve & Mon). Duras also has a wide choice of **campsites**, starting with a basic municipal site right under the château's north wall (☎05.53.83.70.18, ⓕ05.53.83.65.20; July & Aug only). Continue on this road, the D203 to Savignac, another 600m and you'll come to *Le Cabri*, a well-equipped *camping à la ferme* (☎05.53.83.81.03, ⓦwww.lecabri.eu.com; June–Sept). Finally, there's a three-star site beside the Castelgaillard leisure lake (☎ & ⓕ05.53.94.78.74; May–Sept), signed off the main D708 8km northeast of Duras, offering a variety of **activities** in season; if you're not camping, there's a small entry fee during the main holiday season.

West to Castillon-la-Bataille

Downstream from Bergerac, the steep north slopes of the Dordogne valley are once again clothed in vines all the way along to the more illustrious vineyards of St-Émilion (see p.130). The valley here is flat and uninteresting, dominated by a major road and rail line, but there are a few diversions en route. First is **Ste-Foy-la-Grande**, a pleasant enough town whose strict grid plan and arcaded central square reveal its origin as a *bastide*, though its prime interest lies in its transport links, hotels and other facilities. More immediately engrossing are the Gallo-Roman remains further west at **Montcaret**. The partially excavated villa with its well-preserved mosaics is one of the region's best. From Montcaret you can strike up into the hills to pay homage to the influential Renaissance thinker and confirmed sceptic, Michel de Montaigne, who wrote most of his famous *Essais* at the **Château de Montaigne**. Last stop is **Castillon-la-Bataille**, a busy market town famous for the nearby battleground where the Hundred Years' War came to a spectacularly bloody end. Its other attraction is a number of good-value red wines produced on the very border with St-Émilion.

Public transport along this stretch of the Dordogne is limited to **trains** on the Sarlat–Bordeaux line. With just a couple of trains per day between some of these towns, it requires careful planning and a fair bit of walking to reach the area's more interesting sites.

Ste-Foy-la-Grande

Heading west from Bergerac along the River Dordogne, the first place you come to of any size is the *bastide* town of **STE-FOY-LA-GRANDE**, whose die-straight streets retain a sprinkling of half-timbered houses. One of the finest, a grandiose sixteenth-century residence, is now occupied by the tourist office (see below) on the main street, **rue de la République**, running parallel to the river. Follow this road west and you reach the central place Gambetta, partially filled by the more modern *mairie* but still one of the town's most appealing corners. Also worth a wander is the riverside esplanade a short walk to the north, from where you can cross the river via the pont Michel-Montaigne to visit Ste-Foy's modest museum, the **Maison du Fleuve** (June–Sept Tues–Sun 2–5.30pm; €2.50), covering river life – its boats, fish and fishing – and its role in local history; if you've already seen the museum at Creysse (see p.196), however, you won't need to bother. But it's definitely worth timing your visit to Ste-Foy to catch the Saturday-morning **market**, one of the region's biggest and most important, when the whole town centre is closed to traffic.

Practicalities

Though Ste-Foy boasts few sights, it is worth considering as a base, particularly if you are travelling on to Montcaret (see overleaf) by public transport. The **gare SNCF** lies five minutes' walk south of town; from the station, turn left along avenue de la Gare then walk north along avenue Paul-Broca and then rue Victor-Hugo, Ste-Foy's major shopping street. Where Victor-Hugo crosses rue de la République, turn right to find the **tourist office** at no. 102 (June & Sept Mon–Sat 9.30am–12.30pm & 2.30–6.30pm; July & Aug Mon–Sat 9.30am–6.30pm Sun 10am–1pm; mid-Sept to mid-June Mon–Sat 9.30am–12.30pm & 2.30–5.30pm; ☎05.57.46.03.00, ⓦwww.paysfoyen.com).

For **accommodation** in central Ste-Foy, you can't do better than the *Grand Hôtel*, with its magnolia-shaded back terrace and airy, old-fashioned rooms, a little further to the left of the tourist office at 117 rue de la République (☎05.57.46.00.08, ⓦwww.logis-de-france.fr; ❸; closed two weeks in both Nov & Feb; menus from €18, closed Sat lunch & Wed). With your own transport, however, there's also the option of the *Escapade* (☎05.53.24.22.79, ⓦwww .escapade-dordogne.com; ❸; closed Nov–Jan, Oct–Easter closed Sun & Fri). Despite being only just south of the main D936, less than 4km west of Ste-Foy, this hotel has more of a country feel than one would expect. There are twelve unfussy rooms in a converted tobacco-drying barn as well as a pool, sauna, squash courts and gym in which to work off the chef's generous Périgord cooking (menus from €18.95; eve and Sun lunch only, reservations recommended). Another good-value **restaurant**, well known for its seafood, where you'll need to book a table, is *Au Fil de l'Eau* (☎05.53.24.72.60; closed Mon, Sun eve Sep–June & for 3 weeks in November), back in Ste-Foy at 3 rue de la Rouquette on the north side of Pont Michel-Montaigne; menus range from €14 (lunchtime Tues–Sat) to €53.

Anyone with a tent should head about 500m east along the river's south bank on avenue Georges-Clémenceau – the extension of rue de la République – to the three-star municipal **campsite** (☎05.57.46.13.84, ⓕ05.57.46.53.77; late April to mid-Oct). In season you can rent **canoes** from the *base nautique* (☎05.53.24.86.12; June–Sept) on the north side of the river opposite the campsite. Alternatively, **bike rental** is available from the Centre VTT, 62 boulevard Larégère (☎05.57.46.39.23).

Downstream to St-Michel-de-Montaigne

Travelling west on the D936 from Ste-Foy, garden-lovers might like to make a brief detour after about ten kilometres up into the hills north of the river to visit the **Jardins de Sardy** (April–Oct daily 10am–6pm; €5). Though not huge, the gardens – a combination of English and Italian style – occupy a pretty, sheltered spot overlooking the Dordogne. The centrepiece is an informal pond-garden set against the wisteria-covered farmhouse, where it's tempting to linger on the terrace over a cold drink or a light lunch (salad platters €8–12; July & Aug only, reservations required ☎05.53.27.51.45), surrounded by the heady scents of aromatic plants.

Three kilometres further along the main road, another right turn brings you to the village of **MONTCARET** and the remains of a fourth-century **Gallo-Roman villa** (daily: April–June & Sept 9.30am–12.30pm & 2–6pm; July & Aug 9.30am–1pm & 2–6.30pm; Oct–March 10am–12.30pm & 2–4.30pm; €4.60) with superb mosaics and an adjoining museum displaying some of the many objects found on the site. Only about one-tenth of the villa has been fully excavated, but it's more than enough to demonstrate the occupants' affluent lifestyle, from underfloor heating and a variety of hot and cold baths to a grand reception room measuring 350 square metres. The floors, baths and covered walkways were laid with elaborate mosaics, of which large areas have survived relatively intact, notably in the cold bath decorated with shellfish, dolphins and octopuses, and the more abstract pattern of shields and fish scales in the "dining room". This latter is the villa's best-preserved room and has been incorporated into the museum building; note, however, that from mid-November to mid-April those mosaics outdoors are covered to protect them from frosts and are therefore not on view.

Back lanes lead another three kilometres northwest to the sleepy village of **ST-MICHEL-DE-MONTAIGNE**, where Michel Eyquem, Lord of Montaigne (1533–92), wrote many of his chatty, digressive and influential essays on the nature of life and humankind. Even if you haven't read any of his works, it's worth making the pilgrimage to the **Château de Montaigne** (Feb–April, Nov & Dec Wed–Sun 10am–noon & 2–5.30pm; May–June, Sept & Oct Wed–Sun 10am–noon & 2–6.30pm; July & Aug daily 10am–6.30pm; closed Jan; €5.50; ⓦwww.chateau-montaigne.com), just beyond the village to the north, to learn more about this engaging, if somewhat quirky and complex, character.

The third son of a Catholic father and a mother from a wealthy Spanish-Portuguese Jewish family, Montaigne had an unusual education which involved everyone, including the servants, speaking to him in Latin, and being woken by a musician to ensure "his brain not be damaged". It certainly seems to have caused no harm, since Montaigne went on to become a councillor and later mayor of Bordeaux and was highly respected for his tolerance, wisdom and diplomacy. There is evidence that he also possessed a mischievous sense of humour – throughout the bitter Religious Wars, the Catholic Montaigne apparently took pleasure in ringing his chapel bell as loudly and as often as possible to annoy his Protestant neighbours. On the other hand, it must also be said that Montaigne, who held the Protestant leader Henry of Navarre in great esteem, played an important role in resolving the conflict, though he didn't live to see peace restored in 1598.

Though he attended Mass regularly before his death, and received the last sacrament, Montaigne's writings are renowned for their scepticism; in a typical outburst he declares, "Man is insane. He wouldn't know how to create a maggot, and he creates Gods by the dozen." His philosophical standpoint was essentially an argument for introspection – "if man does not know himself, then what can he know?" While it is criticized as being inconclusive, his legacy is rather his great originality of thought and his essays' wide-ranging questioning of generally accepted truths. His chapel occupies the ground floor of a four-teenth-century **tower** where Montaigne closeted himself away after 1571 to work on his three volumes of essays. Unfortunately his priceless library of more than a thousand books, all carefully annotated, were dispersed immediately after his death, but some trace of the philosopher can still be found in the Greek and Latin maxims he inscribed on the beams – note where he replaced some with later favourites. Indeed, it is something of a miracle that the tower exists at all, since the rest of the château was completely destroyed by fire in 1885; the subsequent reconstruction is not open to the public, though you are welcome to wander the extensive park.

Both Montcaret and Lamothe-Montravel, the nearest station to St-Michel-de-Montaigne, are served by infrequent **trains** from Bergerac via Ste-Foy to Castillon and St-Émilion, leaving you with an eight-kilometre walk and a long wait for the evening train. A better option would be to rent bikes in Ste-Foy (see p.201) and then follow the quieter side roads running parallel to the D936.

Castillon-la-Bataille

As you travel the final five kilometres west from Lamothe-Montravel to **CASTILLON-LA-BATAILLE** you'd be forgiven for not noticing as you cross the Lidoire valley. In 1453 this is where the French routed the English in the last major **battle** of the Hundred Years' War (see box below). There's nothing to mark the site, save an uninspiring monument to the English General Talbot on the spot where he supposedly died close to the River Dordogne, two kilometres east of Castillon, but every summer the local citizenry stage a spectacular floodlit re-enactment with some five hundred actors and fifty cavaliers (mid-July to mid-Aug; ☏05.57.40.14.53; ⓦwww.batailledecastillon.com).

The Battle of Castillon

What is now known as the **Hundred Years' War** had been rumbling back and forth through southwest France from 1337, but in the 1440s the French, led by the great military commander Bertrand du Guesclin, began to push the English armies back. In reply, the English despatched the equally renowned **Sir John Talbot**, Earl of Shrews-bury, with orders to regain the lost territory. He took Bordeaux in 1452 and had swept through to Castillon by July 1453.

Here a large French force was waiting for him camped beyond the town, but when the Castillon garrison withdrew without much of a fight, Talbot believed it would be an easy battle. Instead he was walking straight into a trap. The French had gathered three hundred pieces of artillery – a relatively new development – and ranged them in the hills either side of the valley. On **July 17**, after Talbot had heard Mass, a mes-senger reported mistakenly that the French were breaking camp and retreating when all they were doing was moving the baggage to the rear. Talbot hastily rallied his men and led them in pursuit straight into the mouth of the valley and a murderous cross-fire. Talbot and four thousand of his men were killed – if not immediately, then by the pursuing archers or simply drowning as they attempted to flee across the Dordogne. As news of the carnage spread, other English-held towns quickly capitulated, until more than a century of warfare finally came to an end.

The town makes the most of its history, and has one or two pretty corners, notably along the river and its one remaining medieval gate, but the only real reason to stop here is the helpful **Maison du Vin** facing the church across the central place de Gaulle (℡05.57.40.00.88, ⓦwww.cotes-de-castillon.com). They stock a representative sample of wines and can advise on vineyards in the area, where every day in season (May–Sept) a different wine producer opens his *chais* to visitors for free without having to make an appointment; Castillon's tourist office can provide further details. You're getting close to St-Émilion here and, while the Côtes de Castillon are no match for the big St-Émilion wines, since the early 1990s some have been making their mark – particularly when you consider that even the best cost only around €15 a bottle. Two names to look out for, both of which offer tastings by appointment, are **Château Cap de Faugères** (℡05.57.40.34.99, ⓦwww.chateau-faugeres.com), a couple of kilometres northwest from Castillon outside the village of Ste-Colombe, and **Vieux Château Champ de Mars** (℡05.57.40.63.49), some 7km north along the D123 and then right towards Les-Salles-de-Castillon.

Practicalities

Castillon's **gare SNCF** is located on the northeast side of town about five minutes' walk along rue Gambetta, while its **tourist office** is on place Marcel-Paul (Mon–Sat 9.30am–noon & 2–6pm; ℡05.57.40.27.58, ⓕ05.57.40.49.76); to find it, take rue Victor-Hugo heading west from the north end of place de Gaulle. There's really nothing much in the way of **hotels**, just the very basic *Bonne Auberge* at 12 rue du 8-Mai (℡05.57.40.11.56, ⓕ05.57.40.12.92; ❷–❸), at the south end of rue Gambetta. Better instead to head to one of the **chambres d'hôtes** around, such as the friendly *Chambre d'hôte Robin* (℡ & ⓕ05.57.40.20.55; ❸), in a small vineyard two kilometres north of Castillon on the D119 to Belvès; the tourist office can provide lists of others in the area. There's also a small two-star municipal **campsite**, *La Pelouse* (℡05.57.40.04.22; mid-May to early Sept), along the river to the east of Castillon.

When it comes to **eating**, head straight for the *Gourmandine* at 4 rue Waldeck-Rousseau (℡05.57.40.24.48; closed Sun eve & Wed, also one week both in late Aug and Nov), one block west of the tourist office, for their traditional dishes washed down with local wines (menus from €15). The other good option is the pizzeria-grill *Le Mounan*, just outside Castillon on the Bergerac road (menus from €10; closed Mon).

East to Le Buisson

The Dordogne River begins to get more interesting upstream from Bergerac, thanks largely to the two great meanders it makes near **Trémolat** and **Limeuil** before the hills begin to close in. The castles, abbeys and villages south of the river are also worth exploring, giving the option of two routes: along the Dordogne itself, or looping inland up the heavily wooded Couze valley to the village of **Cadouin**, with its austere abbey church and elaborately carved cloister.

Transport along the Dordogne valley is provided by **trains** on the Bergerac–Sarlat line. These call at most of the towns and even some villages, though note that in certain cases the services are fairly infrequent. The inland route is more problematic: there are **buses** from Bergerac along the river's north bank to Lalinde, and then a connection on to Cadouin by reservation only (Les Cars Boullet ℡05.53.61.00.46).

Along the Dordogne

Following the Dordogne east from Bergerac, the first sight of any interest is the half-completed **Château de Lanquais**, as much for the story behind its architecture as for its somewhat dilapidated interiors. The working paper mills at **Couze-et-St-Front** also merit a quick stop, while **Lalinde** provides hotels, transport and other tourist facilities, before you meet the first of the Dordogne's great loops, the **Cingle de Trémolat**. At the top of the second meander, the feudal village of **Limeuil** marks where the River Vézère flows into the Dordogne and where you pass into the Périgord Noir, while the final destination, **Le Buisson-de-Cadouin**, sits on an important rail junction on the Bergerac–Sarlat and Agen–Périgueux lines.

Lanquais and Couze-et-St-Front

The **Château de Lanquais** (April & Oct Mon & Wed–Sun 2.30–6pm; May, June & Sept Mon & Wed–Sun 10.30am–noon & 2.30–6.30pm; July & Aug daily 10am–7pm; €7), 15km east of Bergerac on the south side of the river, is described in tourist literature as "Périgord's unfinished Louvre". The story goes that in the mid-sixteenth century, when Bergerac and much of the surrounding country was under Protestant sway, Lanquais was owned by a Catholic, Isabeau de Limeuil, cousin to Catherine de Medici. In a brave – or foolhardy – move, Isabeau commissioned the architects of the Louvre in Catholic Paris to add a wing in similar style to her castle. Before the work could be completed, however, the Protestant armies besieged the château in 1577 and left the facade pitted by cannonballs.

They didn't destroy it, however, and you can still discern the change in styles where the Renaissance wing, with its dormer windows and ornamentation, was grafted on to the medieval fortress. It's an imposing rather than an attractive building and some of the interiors are in need of restoration, but there are one or two rooms worth a peep. As in many Périgord châteaux, it's the fireplaces that steal the show, notably that occupying one whole wall of the "blue salon" with its two enigmatic bulls'-skull carvings.

The present owners of the château have set aside two immense rooms with period furniture and en-suite bathrooms as **chambres d'hôtes** (℡05.53.61.24.24, ⓔculturesite@wanadoo.fr; ❼; closed Dec–March). Alternatively, there's cheaper but still very pretty *chambre d'hôte* accommodation half a kilometre south of the château at the welcoming *Domaine de la Marmette* (℡05.53.24.99.13; ❸). Evening meals are offered on request (€22 including wine), or there's a typical country **restaurant** in **LANQUAIS** village, just north of the château: the *Auberge des Marronniers* (℡05.53.24.93.78; closed Wed, and two weeks in both Feb–March & Oct) with good-value menus from €14.50.

Two kilometres from Lanquais you drop down to the Dordogne again at what was once an important paper-making centre, **COUZE-ET-ST-FRONT**. Of thirteen mills along the banks of the River Couze, only two still churn out handmade paper in time-honoured fashion. In the first, the fifteenth-century **Moulin de la Rouzique**, under a cliff in the town's northwest corner (daily: April–June, Sept & Oct 2–6.30pm; July & Aug 10am–7pm; €4.50), you can see paper being made and examine a collection of antique watermark paper in the drying rooms upstairs. At the equally venerable **Moulin de Larroque**, on the main road through the town centre, they make traditional cotton- and linen-rag paper (Mon–Fri 9am–noon & 2–5pm; free); there's also an array of paper products on sale (Mon–Fri 9am–noon & 2–6pm, Sat 10am–noon & 3–5pm).

Departing from Couze-et-St-Front, you have the choice either to continue east along the river to Lalinde or delve inland along the Couze valley to Beaumont (see p.209).

Lalinde

The only town of any size along this stretch of the Dordogne, **LALINDE** guards an important river-crossing 3km upstream from Couze and 23km from Bergerac. In 1267 Henry III of England chose the little settlement on the river's north bank to become the first English *bastide*. The central market square, grid plan and fragments of wall remain, but Lalinde's most attractive aspects are its riverside position and a large canal basin immediately to the north. The canal was built in the nineteenth century to bypass a dangerous set of rapids, made more hazardous in legendary times by the presence of a dragon, La Coloubre, which lurked in a cave on the opposite bank. According to legend, St Front (see p.147) got rid of the monster in the fourth century by burning it on an enormous bonfire on the hill above its lair – grateful citizens later erected the tiny clifftop **Chapelle de St-Front** in his honour.

Nowadays Lalinde is a bustling market town (Thursday is market day) and prosperous commercial centre. Its **gare SNCF** lies three minutes' walk across the canal, while **buses** stop on the central place de la Halle. The **tourist office** (July & Aug Mon–Sat 10am–7pm, Sun 10am–12.30pm; Sept–June Mon–Fri 9am–12.30pm & 2–5pm; ☎05.53.61.08.55, ⓦwww.lalinde-perigord.fr.st) is on the riverbank near the old bridge. You can rent **bikes** from the Centre VTT de Lalinde, Maison de l'Écluse (☎05.53.24.12.31), beside the canal bridge.

The town also has two good **hotel-restaurants**. Smarter of the two is *Le Château*, 1 rue de la Tour (☎05.53.61.01.82, ⓦwww.logis-de-france.fr; ❸–❹; Nov–March closed Sun, also mid-Nov to mid-Feb, and third week in Sept), overlooking the river to the west of the tourist office, and where the larger, more expensive rooms offer better value for their balconies and river views. The restaurant lives up to its reputation with dishes such as snails stuffed with foie gras and walnut butter, and spit-roast meats (menus at €25 and €40; July & Aug Mon & Tues closed lunchtime; rest of year closed Mon & lunchtime Tues). You'll also eat extremely well at the *Hôtel du Périgord*, 1 place du 14-Juillet (☎05.53.61.19.86, ⓦwww.logis-de-france.fr; ❸; Sept–June closed Sun eve & Mon, also two weeks in Dec & one in March), on the main boulevard de la Résistance to the north of central Lalinde. Despite its unpromising exterior, the rooms are well equipped and enlivened by the owner's bold abstract canvases – an artistic flair he also brings to his award-winning cooking, such as pigeon stuffed with foie gras, or soup with truffles *en croûte* (menus €15–45). Campers should head east along the river 1500 metres to the *Moulin de la Guillou*, a well-equipped two-star **campsite** (☎05.53.61.02.91; Easter–Sept).

Trémolat to Limeuil

Some 8km upstream from Lalinde the Dordogne snakes its way through two huge meanders, of which the first you come to, the **Cingle de Trémolat**, is the tighter and therefore more impressive. In July and August you can take an hour-long *gabare*-trip upstream from Mauzac, on the *cingle*'s west side, to Trémolat and back (2 daily; 1hr; €5.30; ☎05.56.48.60.59; ⓦwww.gabare.fr), but perhaps the best views are from the limestone cliffs to the north – follow signs to the Panorama de Trémolat, or on upwards to the Belvedere de Rocamadour – from where the whole meander is visible. Over to the east, a heavily fortified church tower pinpoints the picturesque village of **TRÉMOLAT**, where the *Bistrot d'en Face* makes a good pit stop (menus from €12). The **restaurant** belongs to the nearby *Vieux Logis* (℡05.53.22.80.06, ⓦwww.vieux-logis.com; ⑨), a beautiful luxury **hotel** in a former priory with a large pool, formal gardens – with a lovely terrace for summer dining (menus from €30) – and all sorts of cosy nooks and crannies. The restaurant also runs short cookery classes in the summer under the guidance of its top chef. Last but not least, there's an excellent three-star **campsite** (℡05.53.35.50.10, ⓕ05.53.06.30.94; May–Sept) beside the river less than a kilometre northwest of Trémolat on the road to the viewpoint. The **gare SNCF** is located just over a kilometre to the south of the village.

The D31 east from Trémolat takes you over the ridge for a bird's-eye view of the second meander. The road then drops down to the honey-stoned village of **LIMEUIL**, on the confluence of the Vézère and Dordogne rivers and an attractive sight, straggling down the hillside from the church. At the bottom is a grassy area beside the first of two bridges perpendicular to each other where, in summer, there are outdoor cafés and people canoeing and swimming in the river. Limeuil reached its first peak in the Middle Ages, thanks to its strategic location, and then another in the nineteenth century when local craftsmen built boats for the booming river trade.

The village has changed little since then, as you'll soon discover if you wander under the old gate and up narrow, central rue du Port on the way to the hilltop **park** (May Sat & Sun 10am–6pm; June & Oct also open Mon–Fri 2–6pm, Sat & Sun 10am–6pm; July–Sept daily 10am–7pm; Sept 10am–6pm; €3) where the château once stood. Afterwards, it's worth heading 1km northeast on the Le Bugue road to the **Chapelle St-Martin** (daily 9am–7pm; free); if it's locked, you can get the key from the house opposite. A Latin inscription inside this dumpy little Romanesque chapel records that it was dedicated to St Thomas à Becket, the archbishop of Canterbury murdered by Henry II's courtiers in 1170 after the king famously asked who would rid him of "this turbulent priest". The inscription goes on to relate that the chapel was founded in 1194 by Henry's son and successor, Richard the Lionheart, together with Philippe II (Philippe Auguste) of France on their return from the Third Crusade, "to beseech the pardon of God". There are also the remnants of fifteenth-century frescoes in the choir: to the right a Crucifixion scene and the Descent from the Cross; to the left the Flight from Egypt. Note also the *pisé* floor – giving the appearance of pebbles, but actually made of long, narrow stones placed upright – and the roof of stone slates, *lauzes*, over the choir. You'll meet these architectural features again and again as you penetrate deeper into the Périgord Noir.

The nearest **gare SNCF** to Limeuil is at Alles-sur-Dordogne, a couple of kilometres to the southeast, but there are more frequent services to Le Buisson (see overleaf) and Le Bugue (see p.236), 5km north on the Agen–Périgueux line. There's a small **tourist office** at the bottom of rue du Port (April & May Tues–Sat 3–6pm; June & Sept Tues–Fri 11am–1pm & 3.30–6pm, Sat & Sun 4–6pm; July & Aug Mon & Sat 3.30–6.30pm, Tues–Fri & Sun 10am–1pm & 4–6.30pm; Oct–March Tues 10am–noon & 3–6pm; ℡05.53.63.38.90, ⓦwww.limeuil-perigord.com) and, at the top of the same road, you'll find the appropriately named **hotel**, *Le Bon Acceuil* (℡05.53.63.30.97, ⓦau-bon-accueil-limeuil.com; ❷; closed Mon & mid-Nov to Easter). Rooms are spotlessly clean but basic – the cheapest come with either an en-suite toilet or a shower – but this is more than made up for by the vine-covered terrace, views along the valley and good, homely cooking (menus from €14). If you're looking for a **campsite**, try the three-star *Port de Limeuil* just across the river (℡05.53.63.29.76, ⓦwww.leportdelimeuil.com; April–Sept). You can rent **canoes** and **bikes** from Canoës Rivières Loisirs (℡05.53.63.38.73, ⓦwww.canoes-rivieres-loisirs.com), and there's also an excellent **riding centre**, La Haute Yerle, in Alles-sur-Dordogne (℡05.53.63.35.85, ⓦwww.rando-equestre-hauteyerle.com), which offers treks from half a day up to a week's circuit of the Périgord Noir.

Le Buisson-de-Cadouin

LE BUISSON-DE-CADOUIN, 5km south of Limeuil, is the last stop on this stretch of river. The town has nothing in the way of sights, but 2km southeast, the **Grottes des Maxange** (daily: Feb, Nov & Dec 2–5pm; March & Oct 9.30am–noon & 2–5.30pm; April–June & Sept 10am–6pm; July & Aug 9am–7pm; €6.50) hide unusually extensive displays of *excentriques*. These delicate limestone formations, some looping round on themselves, others suddenly veering off in a different direction, are believed to occur where water evaporates from extremely fine fissures in the rock. Here and there the walls glitter with star-like formations known as *aragonites*. The caves, which were discovered in 2000 in a working quarry, are also some of the more accessible in the region, with no stairs or narrow passages to negotiate.

Le Buisson is a junction on the Bordeaux–Sarlat and Agen–Périgueux train lines, and its **gare SNCF**, to the north of the town centre, is also the closest station to Cadouin (see p.210); for a **taxi** call Taxi Morante on ℡05.53.22.06.51. There's a well-run **tourist office** on place du Général-de-Gaulle (April & May Mon 2.30–5.30pm, Wed & Fri 10am–1pm & 3–6.30pm, Sat 10am–1pm; June & Sept also Tues & Thurs 10am–1pm; July & Aug Mon–Fri 10am–1pm & 3–6.30pm, Sat 10am–1pm; Oct–March Fri 10am–noon & 3–6pm; ℡05.53.22.06.09, ⓦwww.dordogne-vezere.com), a couple of minutes' walk south from the station and an **Internet** café on rue de la République, *Imprim'vite24* (Tues–Sat 9am–12pm & 2–7pm).

Less than two kilometres east on the road to Siorac, is a rather lovely **hotel**. ⚐ The *Manoir de Bellerive* (℡05.53.22.16.16, ⓦwww.bellerivehotel.com; ➐; closed Jan & Feb), an elegant little nineteenth-century château in an English-style park on the banks of the Dordogne, offers far more than you'd expect for the price. The rooms have been completely modernized, with gleaming en-suite bathrooms, and decorated with great flair: period furniture in the château

---

Cussac Cave

In September 2000, great excitement broke out among art historians and archeologists when a speleologist nosing around Cussac, near Buisson-de-Cadouin, stumbled on a previously unknown decorated cave containing more than one hundred **prehistoric engravings**. So important is Marc Delluc's discovery that it's been dubbed the "Lascaux of engraving", in reference to the famous Vézère-valley cavern (see p.243).

Cussac cave is particularly significant because of the number and size of the engravings. The biggest is a four-metre-long bison, while some scenes comprise as many as forty figures. They are also unusually well preserved, the outlines etched deep into the clay by artists sometime between 25,000 and 30,000 years ago. **Horses, bison, mammoths, rhinoceros** and **deer** all feature strongly, but there are also very rare representations of **birds**, as well as **female silhouettes, fertility symbols** and a strange long-snouted animal that has yet to be identified.

Because of the vulnerability of these caves (see p.243), it is unlikely that Cussac will ever be opened to the public. The local authorities, however, are keen to capitalize on the tourist potential. There's talk of creating a replica as at Lascaux, but in the meantime you can get a glimpse of what all the fuss is about at ⓦwww.culture.fr/culture/arcnat/cussac/en.

itself and more modern touches in the *orangerie* annexe. Their **restaurant**, *Les Délices d'Hortense*, won its first Michelin star in 2000 for delicacies such as macaroni of langoustines and spinach, or herbed roast pigeon (menus €35–85; open evenings only; closed Jan–March). There's also a tennis court, pool and a perfect breakfast spot on the terrace overlooking the Dordogne.

Inland via Beaumont and Cadouin

Where the River Couze joins the Dordogne at the paper-making town of Couze-et-St-Front (see p.205), this inland route strikes southeast to follow the quiet, green tributary valley. It was once a far more important routeway, as the *bastide* town of Beaumont, snug behind stout walls, clearly demonstrates. The colossal Gothic church here has survived in surprisingly good shape, better than the neighbouring abbey church of St-Avit-Sénieur, one of the biggest in the region, which was never completed due to a succession of fires, wars and lack of funds. Further upstream, the little chapel above the village of Montferrand-du-Périgord has also seen more prosperous times, but in this case its frescoes are still there – battered but largely visible. Another abbey church at Cadouin, further to the northeast, suffered a rather different fate when its holy relic, supposedly the shroud that covered Christ's head in the tomb, was found to be too recent by a thousand years and the pilgrims stopped coming. Nevertheless, its late-Gothic cloister is worth a look and the town's location, in a bowl of chestnut-forested hills, makes it the sort of place that's difficult to leave.

The Couze valley

The **Couze valley** has provided an important thoroughfare since Gallo-Roman times, and part of Edward's I's motivation for founding **BEAUMONT** in 1272, on a dominant spur 10km upstream, was to guard the route. As in many such *bastides*, the church, **St-Front**, was built for military as well as religious reasons – a final outpost of defence in times of attack – hence the bulky tower at each of the four corners and the well inside. Its only decorative touch comprises a frieze over the west door depicting the four animals symbolizing the Evangelists in the midst of mermaids, monsters and a man pulling a cheeky face. Nearby, the central square retains some of its arcades, and off to the west you'll find Porte de Luzier, one of the original sixteen town gates, but otherwise there's little to detain you. Beaumont does, however, boast a **tourist office** on the central square (June–Sept Mon–Sat 10am–1pm & 2–7pm, Sun 10am–1pm; Oct–June Mon–Fri 10am–noon & 2–5pm; ☎05.53.22.39.12, ⓦwww.pays-des-bastides.com), where you can pick up details of local *chambres d'hôtes*, walks and so forth.

On the other side of the valley, roughly 4km by road, the semi-ruined abbey of **ST-AVIT-SÉNIEUR** stares across at Beaumont from another rocky knoll. It grew up around the burial place of a fifth-century hermit, Avitus, who was born at Lanquais and later served in the Visigoth army until taken prisoner in 507 by the Frankish king Clovis, a recent convert to Christianity. At some point during his fourteen years' captivity in Paris, Avitus followed suit, and was then instructed in a vision to return to Périgord, where he lived as a hermit until his death in 570. Tales of his miracles soon attracted pilgrims and the simple chapel grew into a monastery, then the present **church** (daily 10am–noon & 2–6pm; free) was founded in the early twelfth century; an inscription records that the saint's bones were brought here in 1117. Like Beaumont's St-Front, it's another huge building, over fifty metres long and twenty wide, heavily fortified and plain save for the remnants of fifteenth-century geometric patterns painted on the walls and ceiling. In this case, however, the ravages of war and time have left deeper scars.

The D26 continues southeast up the narrowing valley for another 8km to the seemingly forgotten village of **MONTFERRAND-DU-PÉRIGORD**, where a clutch of typical Périgord houses shelters beneath the semi-ruined château. A single street leads up past a sixteenth-century market hall – bigger than some of the surrounding houses – to where a path takes off west through the woods. Roughly a kilometre later it comes out near the hilltop **church of St-Christophe**, standing on its own in a cemetery. It used to be the parish church but has gradually been diminished over the years to little more than a stocky bell tower – it's surprising to find that the twelfth- and fifteenth-century frescoes have survived. The moon's face smiles down as you enter, while to either side are scenes of the Last Supper and a monstrous mouth gobbling up souls. The oldest painting is that on the north wall of the choir, portraying St Leonard releasing prisoners. According to legend, Leonard was the godson of Clovis and refused a bishopric to become a hermit; his connection with prisoners dates from after his death when a crusader prince, released by his Arabic captors in 1103, went to pay homage at St Leonard's grave.

For **accommodation** or somewhere to **eat** in the area, you couldn't do better than the little creeper-covered country hotel back down on the main road. Owned by a young, friendly English–French couple, the *Lou Peyrol* (☎05.53.63.24.45, ⓦwww.hotel-loupeyrol.dordogne.com; ❷; closed Oct–Easter) has five rustic rooms, all but one en suite, and a restaurant with well-priced menus (five courses for €26; April–June & Sept closed Wed lunchtime).

Cadouin

At the same time that Augustinian monks were busy building their church in honour of St Avit (see p.209), the Cistercians founded a typically austere **abbey** in what is now the village of **CADOUIN**, 8km to the northeast up the D25. Their efforts were given a boost when, in 1117, Crusaders returning from the Holy Land gave them a piece of cloth believed to have been part of Christ's shroud. For eight hundred years it drew flocks of pilgrims – including Eleanor of Aquitaine, Richard the Lionheart and King Louis IX – until in 1935 the two bands of embroidery at either end were shown to contain an Arabic text from the early eleventh century. The cloth is now on display in the flamboyant Gothic **cloister**, accessed via a separate entrance to the north of the church door (April–June & Sept daily 9.30am–6.30pm; July & Aug daily 9am–7pm; Oct to mid-Nov daily 10am–12.30pm & 2–6pm; mid-Nov to Dec & Feb–March Tues–Sun 10am–12.30pm & 2–5.30pm; €8; ⓦwww.semitour .com) where it plays second fiddle to the finely sculpted but badly damaged capitals: look out for two merchants squabbling over a goose and the parable of Lazarus. There are some more good carvings on the cloister's north wall, either side of the abbot's seat, showing Jesus carrying the cross while two soldiers dice for his tunic, and a procession of monks alongside a prostrate Mary Magdalene – the remains of a Crucifixion scene.

Adjacent to the cloister stands the contrastingly austere Romanesque **church**, with its stark, monumental west wall and unusual double-tier belfry roofed with chestnut shingles. Inside, the triple nave is equally spartan and so high that the pillars appear to bulge outwards. You can still see the chains above the altar where the shroud was suspended in its casket, but the main point of interest is the stained-glass windows, installed around a century ago, retelling the story of the shroud's journey from Jerusalem.

△ Cadouin Abbey

If you've had enough of all these churches, the **Musée du Vélocipède** (daily 10am–12pm & 2–6pm; €5), just up the hill from the church, provides an engaging diversion. This unique collection of vintage bikes covers 150 years of cycling history, from the aptly named boneshaker of 1817 up to more user-friendly models produced towards the end of World War II. The owners have tracked down bicycles ridden by Victor Hugo and Jules Verne, a rare American penny-farthing and a bike from the first Tour de France in 1903, amongst many other weird and wonderful contraptions.

You can reach Cadouin by **bus** from Bergerac via Lalinde (see p.206), but the most convenient way to get here by public transport is to take the **train** to Le Buisson (see p.208) and then a taxi for the final 6km (count on around €8) otherwise it's about an hour-long hike up the steep hill. The village has its own summer-only **tourist office** (May Mon 3–6pm, Tues–Fri 11am–1pm & 3–6pm; June & Sept Mon 3–5pm, Tues–Fri 11am–1pm & 3–6pm, Sun 3–5pm; July & Aug Mon–Fri 10am–1pm & 3–7pm, Sun 3–7pm; ☏05.53.57.52.64, ⓦwww.dordogne-vezere.com), and offers an unexpected range of **accommodation**. Adjacent to the cloister, the monks' dormitories have been turned into an excellent and very friendly ⚤ HI **youth hostel** (☏05.53.73.28.78, Ⓔcadouin@fuaj.org; dorms €13.50; closed mid-Dec to end Jan) with a well-equipped kitchen, bikes on loan and fantastic double height private rooms with shower, desks and mezzanine floor sleeping area (❶); rates include breakfast. Then, on the opposite side of the church, the *Restaurant de l'Abbaye* (☏05.53.63.40.93, Ⓕ05.53.63.40.28; ❷; closed Mon) has five simple en-suite rooms. It also does very good-value meals (menus from €13; mid-Nov to March closed eves except Sat). Also good is *Le Prieuré chambre d'hote*, on rue du St-Suaire on the road that heads towards Le Buisson (☏05.53.24.18.37, ⓦwww.priorygetaway.com, ❹). Entered through ivy-covered iron gates into a lovely walled garden, the rooms have wood floors and are decorated in cool pastel shades. For a bite to **eat** head for the *Salon de Thé Myoso'Tea* on rue de la République (daily 10.30am–7pm), a breezy space filled with white cane chairs and old books complemented with a soundtrack of mellow jazz. Teas, crêpes salads, and cakes are on the menu as are home-made jams and condiments to take away. *Du Côté de chez Cathy et Paulo* opposite the church on the main square is a good choice for pizzas and salads.

Those looking for **campsites** are equally well provided for. Closest is *Les Jardins de l'Abbaye* (T05.53.61.89.30; Ejardins-abbaye@wanadoo.fr; mid-June to mid-Sept), just above the village on the Montferrand road. With your own transport, however, you can reach the extremely welcoming and well-equipped three-star *La Grande Veyière* (T05.53.63.25.84, Wwww.lagrandeveyiere.com; April–Oct) 3km southwest on the road to Molières.

Leaving Cadouin, most people drop straight down to the Dordogne at Le Buisson, from where the caves around Les Eyzies (see p.229) are within easy striking distance. But if time allows, take a short detour east through the woods to **URVAL**, where you'll find a mere handful of houses and a fortified Romanesque church which is really no more than a tower containing a diminutive nave.

Travel details

Trains

Bergerac to: Alles-sur-Dordogne (1–2 daily; 40min); Bordeaux (4–8 daily; 1hr–1hr 30min); Le Buisson (2–6 daily; 40–50min); Castillon-la-Bataille (4–10 daily; 40–50min); Couze (1–2 daily; 20min); Lalinde (2–6 daily; 15–20min); Lamothe-Montravel (2 daily; 35–40min); Libourne (6–8 daily; 1hr–1hr 10min); Montcaret (1–3 daily; 30–40min); St-Émilion (1–3 daily; 55min); Ste-Foy-La-Grande (5–9 daily; 20min); Sarlat (2–6 daily; 1hr–1hr 20min); Siorac-en-Périgord (1–3 daily; 1hr); Trémolat (2–5 daily; 30–40min).

Le Buisson to: Agen (2–5 daily; 1hr 30min); Bergerac (4–6 daily; 40–50min); Le Bugue (2–6 daily; 8min); Couze (Mon–Fri & Sun 1–2 daily; 25min); Les Eyzies (2–6 daily; Lalinde (4–6 daily; 20min); 15min); Périgueux (3–6 daily; 45–50min); Sarlat (3–7 daily; 30min); Trémolat (4–6 daily; 10min).

Castillon-la-Bataille to: Bergerac (5–10 daily; 40min); Bordeaux (4–8 daily; 30–40min); Lamothe-Montravel (2–4 daily; 5min); Montcaret (1–3 daily; 10min); St-Émilion (1–3 daily; 8min); Ste-Foy-La-Grande (5–10 daily; 15–20min).

Ste-Foy-La-Grande to: Bergerac (4–8 daily; 20min); Bordeaux (4–8 daily; 1hr); Castillon-la-Bataille (5–10 daily; 15–20min); Lamothe-Montravel (2–4 daily; 15–20min); Montcaret (1–3 daily; 10min); St-Émilion (1–3 daily; 35min).

Buses

Bergerac to: Eymet (Mon–Fri 1–2 daily; 1hr–1hr 20min); Issigeac (Mon–Fri 1–2 daily; 30–40min); Lalinde (school term Mon–Sat 1–3 daily, school holidays Tues–Thurs & Sat 1 daily; 40min); Marmande (Mon–Fri 1 daily; 2hr); Périgueux (Mon–Fri 3–4 daily; 1hr); Port de Couze (as for Lalinde; 25min); Port de Lanquais (as for Lalinde; 20min); Villeneuve-sur-Lot (Mon–Fri 1–2 daily; 1hr 15min).

Cadouin to: Lalinde (by reservation only, Les Cars Boullet T05.53.61.00.46; 15min).

Eymet to: Allemans-du-Dropt (Mon–Fri 2 daily; 15min); Bergerac (Mon–Fri 1–2 daily; 1hr); Issigeac (Mon–Fri 1–2 daily; 20min); Marmande (Mon–Fri 3 daily; 45min–1hr).

Lalinde to: Bergerac (school term Mon–Sat 1–3 daily, school holidays Tues–Thurs & Sat 1 daily; 40min); Cadouin (by reservation only, Les Cars Boullet T05.53.61.00.46; 15min); Port de Couze (as for Bergerac; 5–7min); Port de Lanquais (as for Bergerac; 6–10min).

Sarlat and the Périgord Noir

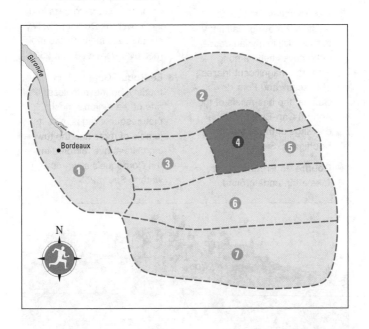

CHAPTER 4

Highlights

✳ **Sarlat** Wander the cobbled lanes of this beautifully preserved medieval town, which hosts one of the region's best markets. See p.218

✳ **Manoir d'Eyrignac** These formal gardens, with their manicured hornbeam hedges and trompe l'oeil parterre, are as much a work of art as of nature. See p.225

✳ **Vézère valley** Prehistoric artists left moving testimony of their skill in myriad decorated caves here, among them the magnificent friezes of Lascaux and Font-de-Gaume, the bas-reliefs of the Abri du Cap-Blanc and the drawings of the Grotte de Rouffignac. See p.227

✳ **Gouffre de Proumeyssac** Take a trip underground to marvel at the stunning limestone formations, from delicate needles to petrified waterfalls, in this "crystal cathedral". See p.239

✳ **La Roque-St-Christophe** Multi-storey living medieval-style in these dozens of rock-shelters cut into the limestone cliffs. See p.239

✳ **Château de Castelnaud** This archetypal feudal fortress lording it over the Dordogne valley contains a superb museum of medieval warfare. See p.250

✳ **La Roque-Gageac** Very touristy, but nevertheless one of the region's most picturesque villages, with its jumble of roofs and the towering cliffs above mirrored in the Dordogne's slow-moving waters. See p.253

△ Beynac-et-Cazenac

Sarlat and the Périgord Noir

The central part of the Dordogne valley and its tributary, the valley of the Vézère, form the heart of the **Périgord Noir**. This is distinctive Dordogne country: deep-cut valleys enclosed within limestone cliffs, with fields of maize in the alluvial bottoms and dense, dark oak woods on the heights. Orchards of walnut trees (cultivated for their oil), flocks of ducks and low-slung grey geese, and primitive-looking stone huts called *bories* are other hallmarks of the region. You'll also find mottled-grey roofs made of limestone slabs (*lauzes*), although the cost of maintaining these – the stones weigh on average 500kg per square metre – means that they are gradually being replaced with terracotta tiles. A floor made out of *lauzes* is called *pisé*, and is commonly found in châteaux and chapels, the stones inserted upright into a bed of clay and lime. None of these features is unique to the Périgord Noir, of course, but their prevalence here adds a defining stamp to the region – no more so than in the well-preserved medieval town of **Sarlat-la-Canéda**, the capital of the Périgord Noir. Though it boasts no great monuments, the warren of old lanes, hidden courtyards and fine architecture, the background for many a period drama, not to mention its excellent weekly market, are not to be missed. And there's no shortage of sights in the country around, of which the **Manoir d'Eyrignac** stands out for its evergreen gardens. Sarlat is also within spitting distance of the highlight of the Périgord Noir, the **Vézère valley**, which cuts diagonally across the region from the northeast. The valley's slightly overhanging cliffs have been worn away by frost action over the millennia to create natural rock-shelters where humans have sought refuge for thousands of years, leaving an incredible wealth of archeological and artistic evidence from the late Paleolithic era. There are enough **prehistoric caves**, shelters and related sites around **Les Eyzies**, the Vézère's main town, to keep enthusiasts happy for days. For most visitors, however, a selection will suffice, starting with the most beautiful of the caves still open to the public, the **Grotte de Font-de-Gaume**, where the quality of the paintings is quite outstanding; also nearby is the **Abri du Cap Blanc**, famous for its frieze of horses exquisitely depicted in bas-relief, while in the **Grotte des Combarelles**, prehistoric artists went to town with hundreds of animal engravings.

Nature has also gone to work in the limestone caves along the Vézère, with dazzling displays of multicoloured stalactites and stalagmites, columns,

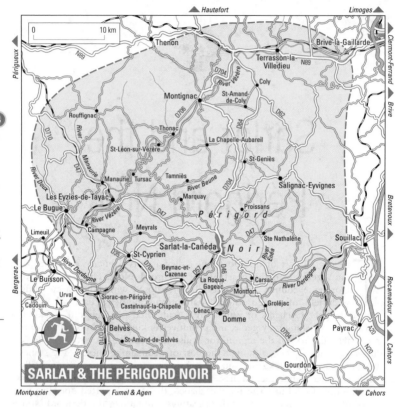

Map labels:

Hautefort ▲   Limoges ▲

Périgueux ◀   Clermont-Ferrand ▶

0   10 km

Thenon

Brive-la-Gaillarde

N89

Terrasson-la-Villedieu

N89

Brive ▶

Coly

Montignac   St-Amand-de-Coly

Rouffignac

Thonac

La Chapelle-Aubareil

St-Léon-sur-Vézère

St-Geniès

Bretenoux ▶

Manaurie Tursac   Tamniès

River Beune

Salignac-Eyvignes

Les Eyzies-de-Tayac   Marquay

Le Bugue   Proissans

P é r i g o r d

Limeuil   Meyrals

Campagne   Ste Nathalène

Souillac

Sarlat-la-Canéda   *N o i r*

St-Cyprien

Beynac-et-Cazenac   Carsac

Le Buisson   La Roque-Gageac   River Dordogne

Rocamadour ▶   Cahors ▶

Urval   Montfort

Cadouin   Siorac-en-Périgord   Grolejac

Castelnaud-la-Chapelle   Cénac

Domme

Belvès   Payrac

St-Amand-de-Belvès

Gourdon

SARLAT & THE PÉRIGORD NOIR

Montpazier ▼   Fumel & Agen ▼   Cahors ▼

fistules, draperies, eccentrics, triangles and pearls – the weird and wonderful shapes of crystallized calcite. The big daddy of crystal caves around here, despite all its commercialization, is the **Gouffre de Proumeyssac** near the southerly town of **Le Bugue**. Following the Vézère upstream, the valley's most eye-catching sight is the kilometre-long cliff of **La Roque St-Christophe**, where people lived for at least 50,000 years, first in simple shelters and then building increasingly sophisticated dwellings against the rock face until, in medieval times, it constituted a self-sufficient town. But the prime reason everyone treks up here is **Lascaux**, or rather Lascaux II, the brilliantly executed copy of the **cave paintings** of oxen, horses and other animals closed to the public in 1963, which number among the most significant discoveries in the history of art.

Having sated on prehistory, it's now the turn of châteaux and sublime river views as you head back to the Dordogne and track it eastwards. **Beynac** and **Castelnaud**, two semi-ruined fortresses on either side of the river, are without doubt the most spectacular – both as supreme examples of medieval military architecture and for the magnificent panoramas from their dizzying eyries. Closer to river-level, **La Roque-Gageac** presents a more homely scene. From a distance, save for its red-tile roofs, the village is barely distinguishable from the vertical cliff into which it nestles. This is also a good place to hop on a **canoe** and take a leisurely trip downstream for a different view of the river. At **Domme**,

Where we haven't given a specific information number contact the relevant tourist office.

Late May or early June Sarlat: La Ringueta (℡05.53.31.53.31). At Pentecôte (Whit Sunday) in even-numbered years, place de la Grande-Rigaudie is the venue for traditional games and sports of the Périgord.

Mid-July to early August Sarlat: Festival des Jeux du Théâtre (℡05.53.31.10.83). One of France's most important theatre fests, ranging from children's theatre and mime to classical pieces by Maupassant and Molière. It's staged over three weeks, including many open-air performances (tickets required) and theatre workshops.

Mid- to late July Montignac: Festival de Montignac (℡05.53.50.14.00, ⓦwww .alm.assoo.org). Major arts festival featuring local and international folk groups from as far afield as South America and China. As well as ticket-only events, there are street performances, food stalls, exhibitions and crafts demonstrations during the week.

Second fortnight in July Belvès: Festival Bach. Dedicated to the composer and comprising two or three concerts in Belvès church (tickets available from the tourist office).

August St-Léon-sur-Vézère and around: Festival du Périgord Noir (℡05.53.51.61.61). Baroque and classical music concerts in the churches of St-Léon, St-Amand-de-Coly and others throughout the region.

Early August Les Eyzies and around: Festival Musique en Périgord (℡05.53.30.36.09). Interesting mix of medieval and classical works alongside traditional music from around the world. Concerts take place over ten days in the Romanesque churches of Les Eyzies, Campagne and Audrix, among other venues.

Early November Sarlat: Festival du Film (℡05.53.29.18.13). One-week festival previewing films from around the world, including special screenings of student productions. Various discount tickets available.

Markets

The main **markets** in this region are at Belvès (Sat); Le Bugue (Tues & Sat); Domme (Thurs); Montignac (Wed & Sat); St-Cyprien (Sun); St-Geniès (Sun); Sarlat (Wed & Sat); Terrasson (Thurs).

an engaging *bastide* town upstream again, it's back to bird's-eye views from its 160m-high belvedere.

With so many first-class sights in such a compact area, it's not surprising that this is one of the most heavily visited inland areas of France, and as a result has all the concomitant problems of crowds, high prices and tack. It is really worth coming out of season, but if you can't, seek accommodation away from the main centres, try to visit places first thing in the morning and always drive along the back roads – the smaller the better – even when there is a more direct route available.

Though you'll need your own transport for exploring much of the Périgord Noir, two **train** lines cut through the area. Sarlat is the terminus of a line from Bordeaux via Bergerac, while trains between Agen and Périgueux stop at Le Bugue and Les Eyzies; you can change between the two lines at Siorac-en-Périgord and Le Buisson (see p.208). In addition, the northern Vézère valley can be accessed from Terrasson, on the Brive–Bordeaux main line. There is also a smattering of **bus** routes, though as usual services are not always very frequent nor at particularly convenient times.

Sarlat-la-Canéda and around

Very picturesque and very touristy, **SARLAT-LA-CANÉDA** (usually known just as Sarlat) is held in a green hollow between hills 10km or so north of the River Dordogne. You hardly notice the modern suburbs, as it is the mainly fifteenth- and sixteenth-century houses of the old town in mellow, pale ochre-coloured stone that draw the attention. Sarlat has one of the best-preserved centres you could wish for, an excellent example of organic, medieval growth where cobbled lanes open onto delightful little squares and where you'll find steep roofs stacked with characteristic *lauze* tiles. Of the many fine bourgeois houses scattered about the district, the most notable are the **Maison de La Boétie** and **Hôtel Plamon**. None is open to the public, however, so unless you are in Sarlat for the Saturday market, it won't take more than half a day to explore. Sarlat's range of **accommodation** options, both in and just outside the town, also makes it the most natural base for exploring the Périgord Noir.

The hills above Sarlat contain a good range of sights, from the **Moulin de la Tour**, a water mill making walnut oil by traditional methods, to the topiary gardens of the **Manoir d'Eyrignac**, with perhaps a detour to the picturesque village of **St-Geniès**. Heading westwards, the still-occupied **Château de Puymartin** tends to be overshadowed by the more famous castles along the Dordogne, but contains some unusual interior decorations, while the nearby **Cabanes de Breuil**, a harmonious group of what were probably shepherds' huts, represent a completely different architectural tradition.

Some history

Though it started life as a Gallo-Roman settlement, Sarlat really came to prominence in the late eighth century when Benedictine monks established an **abbey** here, later dedicated to a former bishop of Limoges, St Sacerdos. In 1147 **Bernard of Clairvaux** also left his mark when he preached to the Second Crusade – according to legend he miraculously cured the sick by offering them bread he had blessed. In spite of this, the townspeople were keen to gain independence from church rule, and in 1298 were eventually granted the right to elect their own consuls by Louis VIII. In return, they remained loyal to the French Crown during the Hundred Years' War and staunchly Catholic in the Wars of Religion, when the town suffered considerably at the hands of the Protestants. Prosperity returned, however, in the mid-fifteenth century, which led to a building boom whose legacy is the **Renaissance** facades you see to this day. That they are so well preserved is largely due to the fact that Sarlat went into slow decline after the late 1700s and thus for the most part escaped the ravages of modernization. Indeed, by the early twentieth century the centre was in a pretty poor state, but was saved from further decay by the **Malraux Act** of 1962, which helped fund a huge restoration project and brought life back to the town. As a result, it's now one of the most popular tourist destinations in the whole Dordogne valley, packed to the gunwales in summer, though still relatively undisturbed during the winter months.

Arrival and information

Sarlat's **gare SNCF** is just over 1km south of the old town on the road to Souillac. **Buses** from Brive, Périgueux and Souillac pull in to place Pasteur, immediately south of the centre at the south end of Sarlat's main street, rue de la République. If you're driving you can **park** for free around the ring road (except boulevard Eugène-Le-Roy on the west side); otherwise, the most

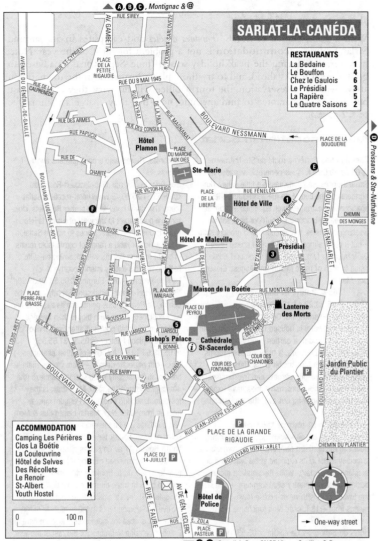

SARLAT-LA-CANÉDA

RESTAURANTS

La Bedaine	1
Le Bouffon	4
Chez le Gaulois	6
Le Présidial	3
La Rapière	5
Le Quatre Saisons	2

4

SARLAT AND THE PÉRIGORD NOIR | Sarlat-la-Canéda and around

▶ **Ⓓ**, Proissans & Ste-Nathalène

Hôtel Plamon

PLACE DU MARCHÉ AUX OIES

Ste-Marie

Hôtel de Ville

Hôtel de Maleville

Présidial

Maison de la Boétie

Lanterne des Morts

Bishop's Palace

Cathédrale St-Sacerdos

Jardin Public du Plantier

ACCOMMODATION

Camping Les Périères	D
Clos La Boétie	C
La Couleuvrine	E
Hôtel de Selves	B
Des Récollets	F
Le Renoir	G
St-Albert	H
Youth Hostel	A

0   100 m

N

→ One-way street

Hôtel de Police

▼ **Ⓖ, Ⓗ**, Gorodká, Gare SNCF, Vitrac, Souillac & Beynac

convenient pay-parking is on place de la Grande-Rigaudie, from where pedestrianized rue Tourny takes you north into the old centre and to the **tourist office** on place de Peyrou (April–Oct Mon–Sat 9am–7pm, Sun 10am–noon & 2–6pm; Nov–March Mon–Sat 9am–noon & 2–7pm; ☎05.53.31.45.45, ⓦwww.ot-sarlat-perigord.fr). Amongst all sorts of useful leaflets, they produce a free English-language walking guide to the medieval city, while from April to September you can join one of their **guided tours** (2–3 daily; 1hr 30min; €4). They also sell maps of hiking and bike trails around the Périgord Noir (€1.50 per map; €13 for all 29 maps).

Accommodation

With a good choice of hotels, *chambres d'hôtes* and campsites in and around Sarlat, finding **accommodation** is not a problem for most of the year. Note, however, that during the peak holiday season (June–Sept) you'd be advised to book several weeks ahead, and to try those places further from the town. If you arrive without a reservation, the tourist office will do what they can to assist, but they can't guarantee to find anything; note that they charge a nominal fee of €2 to €3.

Accommodation in Sarlat

Camping Les Périères route de Ste-Nathalène ☎ 05.53.59.05.84, @ les-perieres@wanadoo.fr. Sarlat's closest campsite lies in a little valley 1km northeast of the centre up rue Jean-Jaurès. It's spacious and extremely well equipped – facilities include heated indoor pool, outdoor pool, sauna, washing machines, tennis courts and grocery shop – but it costs almost as much as a cheap hotel. Daily rates for two people start at around €20, rising to €25 or more in July and August. Closed Oct–March.

Clos la Boétie av Gambetta ☎ 05.53.29.44.18, ⓦ www .closlaboetie-sarlat.com. Central Sarlat's newest and plushest hotel is housed in a lovely old building entered through a garden courtyard filled with plants and flowers. It boasts eleven rooms decked out with four-poster beds, flatscreen televisions, deep-pile carpets and hydromassage showers. The more expensive ones have expansive balconies looking out over the lush green gardens ❽

La Couleuvrine 1 place de la Bouquerie ☎ 05.53.59.27.80, ⓦ www.la-couleuvrine.com. Built into the northern ramparts, *La Couleuvrine* has a medieval feel in its exposed stone walls and big fireplaces downstairs, while the smallish rooms are decked out with country-style furniture – best is the tower room with views across town. Restaurant menus from €18 (closed Mon lunchtime & three weeks in Jan). ❸

Hôtel de Selves av Gambetta ☎ 05.53.31.50.00, ⓦ www.selves-sarlat.com. The sister hotel to the *Clos la Boétie* is a clean, modern place. Communal areas are adorned with bold pieces of art and the large rooms have a/c and large curved glass

balconies. There's also a pool, gardens and Wi-fi access. ❸

Des Récollets 4 rue Jean-Jacques-Rousseau ☎ 05.53.31.36.00, ⓦ www.hotel-recollets-sarlat .com. This small hotel, in the former Récollets' cloister on a quiet street to the west of rue de la République, is one of the nicest places to stay in Sarlat; a warm welcome, and a range of comfortable rooms in bright modern colours with gleaming en-suite bathrooms, plus a leafy interior courtyard. ❸

Le Renoir 2 rue Abbé-Surgier ☎ 05.53.59.35.98, ⓦ www.hotel-renoir-sarlat.com. Slightly out of the centre, *Le Renoir*'s plus points are its spacious and well-equipped rooms with bigger than average bathrooms, a small pool and attentive service. ❻

St-Albert place Pasteur ☎ 05.53.59.11.55, ⓕ 05.53.59.19.99. A choice of rather characterless – but perfectly decent – rooms in the main hotel or in the slightly more spacious annexe (the *Montaigne*) across the road. Main draw is the restaurant, serving traditional Périgord cuisine (menus from €19; Nov–March closed Sun & Mon). The buildings are on the main road immediately south of town, so ask for a room at the back. ❸

Youth Hostel 77 av de Selves ☎ 05.53.59.47.59. Relaxed, old-fashioned municipal hostel five minutes' walk north from the old centre, with just sixteen beds in three dorms; reservations are obligatory. There's a small kitchen area and space for five two-person tents in the garden. In theory the hostel is open for individuals only from April to October, catering to groups for the rest of the year, but it's always worth ringing in the off-season to see if there are places to spare. HI membership not required. Closed Jan. €12 for the first night; €10 thereafter.

Accommodation around Sarlat

L'Arche Les Chanets, Proissans ☎ 05.53.29.08.48, ⓦ www.arche.fr.fm. Well-priced *chambre d'hôte* in a lovely Périgord farmhouse beside a country lane to the southwest of Proissans village, about 5km northeast of Sarlat. The immaculate en-suite rooms

are pretty in a frilly sort of way, with lots of knick-knacks. Closed mid-Nov to Feb. ❷

Aux Trois Sources Pech-Lafaille ☎ 05.53.59.08.19, ⓦ www.hebergement-sarlat .com. Another *chambre d'hôte* in a handsome seventeenth-century manor house, in this case 3km east of Sarlat on the road to Ste-Nathalène. The rooms, rather squeezed into a converted barn, are well equipped with free Internet access and en-suite bathrooms, but for attractiveness they don't quite live up to the surrounding park, with its chestnut trees and pond. ❷

Camping La Palombière Ste-Nathalène ☎05.53.59.42.34, ⓦwww.lapalombiere .fr. A four-star job, this is one of the region's best campsites, roughly 10km east of Sarlat on the D47. It's in a lovely, peaceful location in eight hectares of woodland, is very well equipped – including restaurant, bar, grocery store, pool and tennis courts – and puts on all sorts of kids' events in summer. Closed Oct–April.

Camping Les Terrasses du Périgord Pech d'Orance ☎05.53.59.02.25, ⓦwww.terrasses-du-perigord.com. Another welcoming, well-tended campsite, this time in a superb hilltop position 2.5km north of Sarlat on the Proissans road. Plenty of flowers and spacious plots make this one of the nicest sites around. Closed Oct–April.

La Hoirie rue Marcel-Cerdan, La Girange ☎05.53.59.05.62, ⓦwww.lahoirie.com. This vine-covered thirteenth-century hunting lodge with a pool and small park lies 2km south of Sarlat, signed off the Souillac road. Though a touch on the expensive side, the rooms are a decent size and decor ranges from rustic beams to huge fireplaces and period furniture. There's also a good restaurant (dinner only; closed Tues) with menus from €20. Closed mid-Nov to mid-March. ❹

Le Relais de Moussidière Moussidière-Basse ☎05.53.28.28.74, ⓦwww.hotel-moussidiere. com. Turn left off the busy D57 Bergerac road beside the Citroën garage to find this luxury hotel nestled among trees in a seven-hectare park. It occupies a modern wing attached to a very attractive Périgordin manor house and incorporates open-plan communal areas full of palms and comfortable nooks and crannies. Most of the 35 rooms have their own balcony or terrace and brightly coloured hessian wall-coverings, tiles and chunky wooden furniture. Closed Nov–March. ❼

La Treille Vitrac ☎05.53.28.33.19, ⓦwww .la-treille-perigord.com. On the banks of the Dordogne some 7km south of Sarlat, this friendly, family-run hotel has just eight pretty rooms and an excellent restaurant (menus €17–33; closed Mon, also mid-Oct to mid-June closed Sun eve). ❸

The Town

The ramparts surrounding old Sarlat were torn down in the late 1800s, at about the same time that the north–south **rue de la République** was cut through the centre to create its main thoroughfare. The streets to the west remain relatively quiet; the east side is where you'll find the majority of sights. Note that from June to September (daily 11am–midnight), Sarlat's medieval core is closed to traffic, while rue de la République is pedestrianized in July and August.

Sarlat's labyrinthine lanes fan out from **place de la Liberté**, the central square where the big Saturday **market** spreads its stands of geese, flowers, foie gras, truffles, walnuts and mushrooms according to the season; it's mostly foodstuffs in the morning and general goods

△ Maison de la Boétie, Sarlat

after lunch. There's also a smaller fresh-foods market on Wednesday mornings and a covered market most days in the former church of Ste-Marie, which dominates the north side of place de la Liberté. The square's finest building is the **Hôtel de Maleville**, tucked into its southwest corner. The facade facing onto the square consists of a tall, narrow building in French Renaissance style with ornate window surrounds; turn down the lane beside it to see its more classical Italianate frontage, with a balustraded terrace and two medallions above the door representing Henry IV and, according to popular belief, his mistress Gabrielle d'Estrée. The lane continues through a series of passages and geranium-filled courtyards to emerge beneath Sarlat's most famous house, the **Maison de La Boétie**. Though its prominent gables and tiers of mullion windows, each within a sculpted frame, are certainly eye-catching, much of the building's fame derives from the fact that the poet and humanist Étienne de La Boétie, a close friend of Michel de Montaigne (see p.202), was born here in 1530. He went on to study law in Orléans, where he wrote his most famous work, *Discourse on Voluntary Servitude*, though it wasn't published until after his premature death at the age of 33. A treatise on the tyranny of power, and thus a very early expression of anarchism, the *Discourse* later struck a cord with Rousseau and other radical thinkers in the run-up to the Revolution.

Opposite the Maison de La Boétie, the former bishop's palace also sports a Renaissance gallery and windows, while the large and unexciting **Cathédrale St-Sacerdos** to which it is attached mostly dates from a seventeenth-century renovation. More interesting are the two pretty courtyards to the south of the cathedral – **cour des Fontaines**, filled with the sound of playing water, and **cour des Chanoines**, surrounded by a pleasing assembly of buildings – and the passage around the chevet where Sarlat's nobles were laid to rest in arched niches, *enfeux*, let into the wall. Less illustrious mortals were buried in the cemetery above, presided over by a curious bullet-shaped tower, the **Lanterne des Morts**, built in the twelfth century. Its exact purpose is unknown. Although it's called a "Lantern of the Dead" – after similar such monuments found further north in the Limousin – in this case there's no access to the upper chamber where the fire would normally be lit. Local tradition maintains that it commemorates St Bernard's visit in 1147 (see p.218).

Further north along the same slope you come to the **Présidial**, the former seat of royal justice, now a restaurant (see opposite). It's distinguished by its great stone staircase and interior court lit by a lantern under a peculiar, bell-shaped roof several sizes too large. From here, drop back down to place de la Liberté and pass behind the back of the badly mutilated church of Ste-Marie to find the place du Marché-aux-Oies – a delightful corner decorated by three bronze geese – and the **rue des Consuls**. Of several handsome houses along here; the most remarkable is the **Hôtel Plamon**: built by wealthy drapers in the fourteenth century, it was then added to over the next three hundred years, starting with a lovely row of flamboyant Gothic windows on the first floor.

It's worth crossing over rue de la République to wander the western sector, particularly rue Jean-Jacques-Rousseau. There's nothing in particular to see, beyond more cobbled lanes and ornate doorways or the odd defensive tower, but this side of Sarlat is less touristy and quieter by far.

Just outside Sarlat, 4km south off the D704 in the direction of Gourdon, **Gorodka** (15 June to 15 Sep daily 10am–12am, 16 Sep to 14 June 2pm–9pm by appointment; €7.50; ☎05.53.31.02.00, Ⓦwww.gorodka.com), the home and gallery of conceptual artist Pierre Shasmoukine, is well worth a visit. This is a rambling place with four different galleries crammed full of inventive pieces of art. The extensive grounds serve as an offbeat gallery of the weird and wonderful including a giant dragonfly made from the body of a helicopter, and bizarre, sinister-faced plastic totems that glow in the dark. It is also possible to stay in simple *chambre d'hote* accommodation, contacts as above (**①**).

Eating and drinking

During the main tourist season Sarlat is chock-a-block with **restaurants**. Many are of dubious quality and overpriced, yet such is the demand you'll need to reserve or eat early to be sure of a seat. In winter the pickings are thinner, but those that do stay open tend to be the better quality places patronized by locals. Though they all offer foie gras, duck and walnuts in various guises, you'll find good fish dishes and even vegetarian fare. Look out, too, for *pommes sarladaises*, potatoes crispy-fried in duck fat with lashings of garlic, parsley and, sometimes, mushrooms. For a coffee, drink or light snack, head for the **cafés** and **brasseries** around place de la Liberté; though by no means the cheapest in town, you can't beat them for location.

Restaurants

La Bedaine 4 rue du Présidial ☎05.53.59.44.07. A good bet, this place has a dining room with stone walls and bright pieces of modern art as well as a terrace opposite the entrance. Delicacies include quail stuffed with foie gras and cêpes cream and gizzard salad with raspberry vinaigrette. Menus from €14.

Le Bouffon 11 rue Albéric-Cahuet ☎05.53.31.03.36. Reliable regional restaurant behind the *Hôtel de Maleville*, with a pretty courtyard and exposed-stone interiors serving reliable favourites such as coq au vin and duck confit. Menus start at €13.

Chez Le Gaulois 1 rue Tourny ☎05.53.59.50.64. Charcuterie addicts will love this cosy restaurant festooned with cured Savoy, Corsican and Spanish hams and sausages. They're served, along with Savoy cheeses, in salads and open sandwiches (around €10–12) or you can buy to take away. Sept–May closed Sun & Mon, also closed school holidays in Oct & at Christmas.

Le Présidial 6 rue Landry ☎05.53.28.92.47. Consistently reliable and classy restaurant to the east of the centre in the former tribunal with a walled garden and airy, elegant rooms. The cuisine is a cut above other local restaurants, offering delicacies such as kidneys and sweetbreads with lentils and soya. Menus start at €26. Closed Sun, Mon lunchtime & mid-Nov to March.

La Rapière place du Peyrou ☎05.53.59.03.13. Popular restaurant opposite the cathedral, known for its good choice of fresh fish dishes in addition to standard Périgord fare. Menus from €14. Reservations recommended at any time of year. Closed Jan.

Les Quatre Saisons 2 Côte de Toulouse ☎05.53.29.48.59. Small restaurant to the east of rue de la République that's best in fine weather, when you can eat on their flowery terrace. Portions aren't huge, but the food is imaginative and beautifully presented. A starter and main dish will cost around €20, three courses €28 or so. Closed Wed & for lunch on Thurs.

Listings

Bike rental Bikes are available from: Cycles Sarladais, 36 av Thiers ☎05.53.28.51.87, ⓦwww.sscc24.com; Christian Chapoulie, 4 av de Selves ☎05.53.59.06.11. The latter also rents scooters.

Books and newspapers For foreign-language newspapers and magazines, try the Maison de la Presse, 34 rue de la République; or Librairie Majuscule, 43 rue de la République.

Bus departures Regional buses for Brive (CFTA; ☎05.55.86.07.07), Périgueux (CFTA;

☎05.53.59.01.48) and Souillac (SNCF; ☎05.53.59.00.21) depart from place Pasteur on the south side of town; Souillac-bound buses also call at the train station.

Canoe rental In summer you can rent canoes from Canoës-Loisirs (☎05.53.28.23.43, ⓦwww .perigord-insolite.net) beside the bridge at Vitrac, 7km south of Sarlat.

Car rental Europcar (☎05.53.30.30.40) is on place de Lattre-de-Tassigny near the train station.

Hospital The Centre Hospitalier is on rue

Jean-Leclaire (☎05.53.31.75.75) to the northeast of the centre.

Internet access You can log on to the Internet at Easy Planet, 16 av Gambetta (Mon–Thurs 10am–7pm, Fri & Sat 10am–midnight, Sun 6pm–midnight).

Police Commissariat de Police, 1 bd Henri-Arlet ☎05.53.59.05.17.

Post office The main post office is at place du 14-Juillet, 24200 Sarlat.

Shopping While the markets are the best place to buy foie gras, walnuts, walnut oil, prunes and other local foods straight from the farmer, place de la Liberté, rue de la Liberté and rue des Consuls are full of speciality shops. On the former, the Distillerie du Périgord (🅦 www.distillerie-perigord.com) makes delectable liqueurs from walnut and plum, amongst other things, and fruits in alcohol – try their Guinettes, containing local morello cherries.

Taxis Allo Philippe Taxi ☎05.53.59.39.65; Brajot ☎05.53.59.41.13.

Around Sarlat

While the **Dordogne valley's** major sights are its castles and towns (see pp.245–256), there are a number of worthwhile destinations in the hilly country above Sarlat. Heading eastwards, you can see what happens to at least some of the local walnut crop at the **Moulin de la Tour**, where creaking antique mills and presses, all driven by water power, produce various nut oils. Five kilometres further up into the hills, an abundance of water also helped create the surprisingly lush and very beautiful **Jardins du Manoir d'Eyrignac**, famous for their topiary. From there you can head further north again to admire the classic Périgord village of **St-Geniès**, or drop down to the west of Sarlat to the **Château de Puymartin**. Its fairy-tale towers, machicolations and crenellations make a stirring sight, while inside you'll find an interesting collection of tapestries and murals. The **Cabanes de Breuil**, northeast of Puymartin, consist of a more lowly clutch of traditional stone-built huts which are nonetheless preserved as a historic monument. With the exception of St-Geniès, which lies on the Sarlat–Périgueux bus route, you'll need your own **transport** to reach any of these places.

East and north of Sarlat

On the banks of the River Enéa, 9km east of Sarlat and 2km north of **STE-NATHALÈNE** on the Proissans road, a sixteenth-century water mill still grinds out walnut oil in time-honoured fashion. The pressing room of the **Moulin de la Tour** (30min guided tours: April & May Wed & Fri 9am–noon & 2–7pm; June & Sept also open Sat 2–7pm; July & Aug Mon, Wed, Fri 9am–noon & 2–7pm, Sat 2–7pm; Oct–March Fri 9am–noon & 2–7pm; €4; 🅦 www .moulindelatour.com), where creaking cog-wheels drive a cylindrical grinding stone set at right angles to the flat base, is dark, cosy and full of the most delicious aromas. Here the nuts – ready-shelled by local pensioners – are ground to a paste, heated gently over a wood fire and then pressed to extract the oil; an average pressing gives roughly fifteen litres of oil from thirty kilos of nuts.

Autorail Espérance

In July and August a **tourist train**, the *Autorail Espérance*, runs along the Dordogne valley from Sarlat to Bergerac, via Lalinde and Le Buisson; various local products are served en route, including a glass of wine. The train departs from Sarlat mid-morning for the hour and a half-long journey (Mon–Sat), after which you return on a regular SNCF service. Tickets cost €13 return (there are no one-way fares) and reservations are required: phone ☎05.53.59.55.39 to make a booking, or the Association l'Autorail Espérance on ☎05.53.31.53.46 for further information.

It's best to time your visit for a grinding day (as detailed in the hours above); at other times, only the shop (Mon–Sat 9am–noon & 2–7pm) is open, selling the mill's own walnut, hazelnut and almond oils.

The River Enéa rises among oak woods on a plateau to the north of Ste-Nathalène. Though the hills appear scrubby and dry, one of the Enéa's tributaries is fed by seven springs, the same springs that prompted a seventeenth-century noble, Antoine de Costes de la Calprenède, to build a manor house here, the **Manoir d'Eyrignac**, and which now sustain his descendants' glorious **gardens**, signed to the northeast along back roads from Ste-Nathalène (1hr guided tours daily: Jan–March 10.30am–12.30pm & 2.30pm–dusk; April 10am–12.30pm & 2–7pm; May–Sept 9.30am–7pm; Oct–Dec 10.30am–12.30pm & 2.30pm–dusk; €8; house not open to the public; ⓦwww.eyrignac .com). The gardens aren't huge, but, consisting of lush evergreens – mainly hornbeam, box, cypress and yew – clipped and arranged in formal patterns of alleys and borders, achieve remarkable effects with almost no colour, the regimented lines softened by the occasional pavilion or fountain and by informal stands of trees framing the countryside around. The original formal garden was laid out by an eighteenth-century Italian landscaper, and later converted to an English romantic garden according to the fashion of the times. What you see today is the work of the last forty years, the creation of the present owner's father in a combination of Italian and French styles. The most striking features are the **hornbeam avenue**, a hundred-metre-long alley lined with cylindrical yews between spiralling hornbeam ramps, and the parterre in front of the manor house, with its trompe l'oeil effect. To retain their immaculate lines, the hedges are cut – by hand – four times a year; it takes ten gardeners a full seven days to cut the hornbeam avenue alone.

The complex also contains a small **exhibition hall** next to the ticket office, where you can watch a video about the garden and its history, and a snack bar offering drinks, sandwiches and simple meals. You can also bring your own food and take advantage of their picnic tables.

With time to spare, cut across country northwestwards to the cluster of buildings some 14km north of Sarlat known as **ST-GENIÈS**. It's a typical Périgord Noir village, with its partly ruined château and fortress-like church all constructed from the same warm-yellow stone under heavy *lauze* roofs. Unless it's market day (Sunday morning), it won't take long to explore. Once you've done a quick circuit of the village, the only sight is the **Chapelle de Cheylard**, standing on its own on a small knoll to the east. The fourteenth-century frescoes inside have suffered over the years – at one time the chapel served as a dance hall – but a number remain visible: St Michael weighing souls in a balance, the martyrdom of St Catherine, St George slaying his dragon and, over the door, a particularly manic bunch pelting St Stephen with stones.

West of Sarlat

Eight kilometres northwest of Sarlat on the D47, the **Château de Puymartin** (45min guided tours: July 10am–noon & 2–6.30pm; Aug 10am–6.30pm; April–June & Sept 10am–noon & 2–6pm; Oct to mid-Nov 2–5.30pm) stands guard over the headwaters of the Petite Beune river which flows down to join the Vézère at Les Eyzies (see p.229). The castle, which underwent extensive remodelling in the seventeenth and nineteenth centuries, has been in the same family since 1450 and is remarkably well preserved. Among a large collection of family heirlooms, most noteworthy are the **tapestries**, particularly those in the grand hall, depicting the Siege of Troy. The Classical theme continues in the seventeenth-century *trompe-l'oeil*

Périgord walnuts

According to archeological evidence, **walnuts** have formed part of the Périgordin diet for more than 17,000 years. In medieval times, walnut oil was so valuable that it was sometimes used as a form of currency, and in the seventeenth century it was exported by river (via Bordeaux) to Britain, Holland and Germany. Walnuts are still central to the local economy today: rich in polyunsaturated fats, potassium, magnesium and vitamin E, both nuts and oil are marketed for their health-giving properties – they're said to help reduce cholesterol, stimulate the memory and protect against the effects of ageing. The nuts are also incorporated into bread, cakes, tarts and ice cream, or served whole with salads and the local *Cabécou* cheese. Green walnuts are often pickled in vinegar, but can also be made into jam or used to flavour wines and liqueurs. Not even the leaves are wasted: picked young, they give a distinctive tang to walnut apéritif.

In recognition of the walnut's importance to the economy – and indeed culture – of the region, four varieties (Grandjean, Marbot, Corne and Franquette) were granted an **Appellation d'Origine Contrôlée** (AOC) in 2002, to guarantee that you're buying only premium quality, locally grown produce. Walnuts are grown in the Lot, Corrèze and Charente *départements*, but the heart of the industry is the Dordogne, with more than 4000 hectares (40 square kilometres) of orchards. To capitalize on the AOC label, the local authorities have put together a **Route de la Noix**, along the Dordogne valley from Argentat to Beynac and north to Hautefort. Free leaflets outlining the four suggested itineraries are available from tourist offices, indicating producers and traditional oil mills open for visits as well as specialist patisseries and restaurants serving dishes with a nutty theme.

paintings on the chimneypiece here and in the guest bedroom, where Zeus visits Danaë in a shower of gold – presumably he would have been surprised to find her clothed and holding a cross, a liberty taken in the more puritanical 1800s. The same sensibilities demanded that a number of naked figures in the **mythological room** also be dressed. This is an extraordinary room, not large, but completely covered in monochrome scenes from mythology: snake-haired Medusa, Argus with his hundred eyes and Althaea murdering her son Maleagra by means of a burning brand. The general consensus is that the room was a place of meditation, though surprisingly it also served as a children's nursery for some time. Like all good castles, Puymartin also has its ghost, in this case La Dame Blanche, who supposedly haunts the north tower. In real life she was Thérèse de St-Clar, the lady of the household during the sixteenth century, who, on being surprised in the arms of a lover, was walled up in the tower until she died fifteen years later. More prosaically, it's worth climbing up into the roof here to admire the elaborate timber framework supporting the *lauzes*. If tales of ghosts don't put you off, the château also offers very comfortable **chambre d'hôte** accommodation (☎05.53.59.29.97, ✉ch.puymartin@voila.fr; closed Nov–March; ➐).

At the opposite end of the architectural scale are the **Cabanes du Breuil** (daily: March–May, Oct & Nov 10am–noon & 2–7pm; June–Sept 10am–7pm; €5; ⊛www.cabanes-du-breuil.com), a couple of kilometres up in the hills to the northwest of Puymartin. You'll find these dry-stone circular huts under conical *lauze* roofs scattered throughout the region, but none so picturesque as this group belonging to a small, working farm. Known locally as *bories*, the huts were originally used for human habitation, then for animals or storage. These particular examples are so in keeping with their location that they appear to grow out of the ground – especially the row of three under one undulating roof. In season (June–Sept) there's a video presentation explaining how the huts are made, but really these beautiful structures speak for themselves.

The Vézère valley and around

Billed as the "Vallée de l'Homme", the **Vézère valley** is home to the greatest concentration of **prehistoric sites** in Europe. They are by no means the oldest, but the sheer wealth and variety are quite stunning. It was here also that many important discoveries were made in the nineteenth and early twentieth centuries, which not only helped prove that early man did indeed possess artistic capabilities but also added greatly to our knowledge of our ancestors' way of life.

The valley, now listed by UNESCO as a World Heritage site, draws more than 300,000 visitors a year. The epicentre of all this activity is **Les Eyzies-de-Tayac**, where the National Museum of Prehistory contains many important finds and gives a good overview of what's on offer. The choice of sites is bewildering, but at the very least you should visit the **Grotte de Font-de-Gaume** and the **Abri du Cap Blanc**, both in the Beune valley to the east of Les Eyzies and harbouring the best cave paintings and bas-relief sculptures still open to the public. With a bit of extra time, the nearby **Grotte des Combarelles** also stands out for its wealth of engravings, while the **Grotte du Grand Roc**

The Cro-Magnon and their caves

The first signs of human habitation (in the form of flint tools) in the Vézère valley area date from around 450,000 years ago, but things don't really start to get interesting until the appearance of **Cro-Magnon** people – named after a rock-shelter in the middle Vézère valley where the first skeleton was found in 1868, but more broadly known as *Homo sapiens sapiens*, in other words, us – who swept across Europe a mere 30,000 to 40,000 years ago. The Cro-Magnon were nomadic people, tracking herds of reindeer across what was then steppe, only occasionally settling in riverside rock-shelters. Following on from their Neanderthal cousins, who were dying out around this time, they developed increasingly sophisticated tools using bone, ivory and antlers as well as stone, and then used fire to mould and strengthen them. They crafted ornaments such as necklaces and also started to decorate their tools and stone blocks with crude engravings and to sculpt small figurines.

By around 20,000 years ago the Cro-Magnon were depicting supremely realistic animals on their rock-shelter walls, by means of engraving and sculpting with flints or painting with dyes made from charcoal, manganese dioxide and red ochre. But the real explosion of prehistoric **cave art** was heralded by the widespread use of the tallow lamp, using reindeer fat, about 3000 years later at the start of the **Magdalenian** era (17,000–10,000 years ago); the era was named after the rock-shelter at La Madeleine (see p.238), but its apogee is to be found in Lascaux's painted caves (see p.243). The lamps allowed Magdalenian artists to penetrate deep into the limestone caves, where they covered the walls with drawings, paintings and engravings, the vast majority being animals, but also occasional human figures and various abstract signs – dots, rectangles and parallel lines being the most common – whose meanings are the subject of endless debate: they were perhaps forms of communication or ritualistic symbols. There is also much speculation as to why such inaccessible spots were chosen, but it seems likely that the caves were sanctuaries and, if not actually places of worship, they at least had spiritual significance. However, we will never know for certain, which in many respects adds to the attraction.

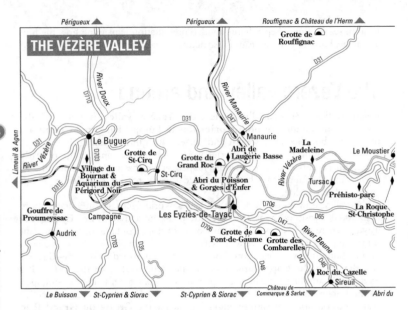

combines a classic rock-shelter with a limestone cave decorated with spectacular displays of stalactites and stalagmites. Further afield, directly to the north of
Les Eyzies, the **Grotte de Rouffignac** is one of the area's largest caves, where
the superb drawings of more than two hundred mammoths, horses and bison,
amongst others, seem so fresh they could have been done yesterday.

Towards the south end of the Vézère valley, near **Le Bugue**, there are more
colourful concretions in the **Gouffre de Proumeyssac**, with its very touristy
but nonetheless dramatic *son et lumière*.

Then north of Les Eyzies the sights begin to get more diversified. The semi-
troglodytic settlements at **La Madeleine** and **La Roque St-Christophe**
– where a whole town was built into a cliff-face – continue from where prehistoric man left off, and one of the most appealing châteaux along the Vézère,
the **Château de Losse**, stands further upstream near the picturesque village of
St-Léon. There are now several prehistoric parks in the area, of which **Le Thot**,
also north of St-Léon, is of most general interest for its collection of live animals
frequently depicted in cave art, and as an introduction to cave art, particularly
the legendary paintings of **Lascaux**. Located near **Montignac**, towards the
northern end of the Vézère valley, Lascaux cave itself is no longer open to the
public, but the paintings and engravings – with all their exceptional detail,
colour and realism – have been faithfully reproduced in **Lascaux II**.

Most of the Vézère sites can be visited only on **guided tours**. Some are
offered in English, while others provide a translated text, but they are tiring
– and the talks get repetitive – so it's best to select just a few of those covered
below. At several caves, notably Font-de-Gaume, Combarelles and Lascaux II,
visitor numbers are limited so you need to buy **tickets** in advance. And note
that in high season it pays to visit the more famous places in the early morning or at lunchtime, when they are quieter, or to concentrate on the less well-
known ones, some of which are every bit as enjoyable.

Finally, it's difficult, but not impossible, to explore the valley by a mixture
of public **transport**, taxis and walking – good planning is required to cover

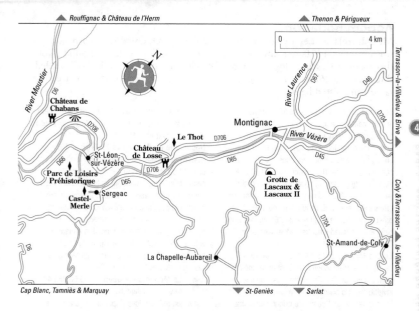

0   4 km

River Moustier

D6

Château de Chabans

D706

River Laurence

D67

D46

Montignac

River Vézère

Le Thot   D706

D45

Château de Losse

St-Léon-sur-Vézère

D66

D706

D65

Parc de Loisirs Préhistorique

D65

Sergeac

Grotte de Lascaux & Lascaux II

Castel-Merle

D704

D6

St-Amand-de-Coly

La Chapelle-Aubareil

4

SARLAT AND THE PÉRIGORD NOIR | The Vézère valley and around

more than one site per day. Les Eyzies, Le Bugue and Terrasson, the northern gateway to the valley, are all on major train lines, while with a few early starts, Montignac, Le Bugue and Rouffignac can all be reached by bus.

Les Eyzies-de-Tayac

The principal base for visiting the Vézère valley is **LES EYZIES-DE-TAYAC**, 20km northwest of Sarlat. Despite a promising position between the river and a towering cliff, it's a small, unattractive one-street town which nevertheless merits a visit for its museum, boasting the largest collection of Paleolithic art in France. While out of season it offers a good choice of hotels and restaurants, Les Eyzies gets completely overrun in summer.

Arrival and information

A stop on the Périgueux–Agen train line, Les Eyzies' **gare SNCF** lies about half a kilometre northwest of the centre along the main road, on which you'll also find the **tourist office** right in the town centre (April–June & Sept Mon–Sat 9am–noon & 2–7pm, Sun 10am–noon & 2–5pm; July & Aug Mon–Sat 9am–7pm, Sun 10am–noon & 2–6pm; Oct–March Mon–Sat 9am–noon & 2–6pm; ℡05.53.06.97.05, Ⓦwww.leseyzies.com). In addition to plentiful information on local sights, *chambres d'hôtes* and hiking trails, they also **exchange** cash and traveller's cheques (or there's a 24-hour ATM outside) and have one terminal for **Internet** access. You can also rent **bikes** and **cars** here (the latter through Avis), while **canoes** are available from Canoës Vallée Vézère (℡05.53.05.10.11, Ⓦwww.canoesvalleevezere.com; mid-April to Sept) and Les 3 Drapeaux (℡05.53.06.91.89, Ⓦwww.les3drapeaux.com; Easter–Sept), both located beside the bridge upstream from Les Eyzies on the Périgueux road, or from Loisirs Évasion (℡05.53.06.92.64, Ⓦcanoe-loisirsevasion-vezere-dordogne.com; May–Sept) out on the road to Le Bugue. If you need a **taxi**, call Taxi Tardieu (℡05.53.06.93.06).

Accommodation

Most **hotels** in Les Eyzies are pricey and may require *demi-pension* in high season, when it's better anyway to stay in one of the villages around. Note that many places also close in winter. The closest **campsite** is the well-tended, three-star *La Rivière* (April–Oct), 1km out of town, part of the hotel of the same name listed below.

Le Centenaire ☎05.53.06.68.68, ⓦwww.hotelducentenaire.fr. Les Eyzies' most luxurious hotel sits on a busy junction at the southeast end of town, though you soon forget the traffic once you're inside. While not huge the rooms are certainly plush and the service excellent. There's also a pretty garden and pool with views of the surrounding cliffs, and a top-class restaurant which offers best value with its lunch menu at €38; at other times the starting price is €68 up to a whopping €108 (closed lunchtime Mon–Wed & Fri). Closed Nov–April. ❽

Le Cro-Magnon ☎05.53.06.97.06, ⓦwww.hostellerie-cro-magnon.com. Just down the road from the station, the *Cro-Magnon* is a sunny, inviting-looking building with yellow shutters and ivy-covered walls. Rooms are bright with all the necessary comforts and there's a small library, a lounge with pool table and a good restaurant with menus from €23, dishing up hearty fare such as lamb stew or roast cod. ❹

Hotel des Falaises ☎05.53.06.97.35, ⒠hotel-des-falaises@wanadoo.fr. The cheapest hotel in Les Eyzies, and one of the few open all year, it has fourteen simple rooms above a café opposite the Musée de Abri Pataud. It's worth paying a little extra for the balcony rooms with proper en-suite bathrooms; cheaper rooms contain just a cubicle shower and partitioned-off toilet. ❷

Hotel de France 4 rue des Moulins ☎05.53.06.97.23, ⓦwww.hoteldefrance-perigord.com. Next door to the prehistory museum, this old-fashioned hotel has comfortable rooms decorated in shades of pastel blue and yellow. It's also home to the restaurant, the *Auberge du Museé* with good value menus from €10. ❹

Hostellerie du Passeur ☎05.53.06.97.13, ⓦwww.hostellerie-du-passeur.com. The ivy-covered *du Passeur* is in a prime spot right in the centre beside the tourist office, but set back from the road with a riverside terrace. The rooms are warm and cosy and there's a decent restaurant serving dishes such as roast pigeon with wild mushrooms and *dorade* flambéed in armagnac, with a lighter bistro menu available at lunchtime (menus €18.50–22; closed for lunch Mon & Tues). Closed early Nov to mid-Feb. ❹

Le Moulin de la Beune ☎05.53.06.94.33, ⓦwww.moulindelabeune.com. This converted mill in a lovely spot across the road from the *Centenaire* is undoubtedly the finest place to stay in Les Eyzies. The rooms offer extremely good value, not opulent but fresh with white walls and big windows all overlooking the millrace gardens. The restaurant, *Le Vieux Moulin*, is also excellent, both for the setting and its well-priced regional menus (€29–55; closed for lunch Tues, Wed & Sat). Closed Nov–March. ❹

La Rivière ☎05.53.06.97.14, ⒠la-riviere@wanadoo.fr. A good, inexpensive choice about 1km from Les Eyzies on the Périgueux road. There are just six unfussy rooms, all en suite, in a typical Périgord farmhouse with access to the same facilities as the campsite: pool, bike and canoe rental, river beach, and a restaurant with simple meals from €11. Closed Nov to early April. ❷

The Town

Les Eyzies' single, unnamed street runs parallel to the jutting limestone cliff which dominates the town. Beneath its overhang, Paul Dardé's 1930 statue of Neanderthal man, portrayed as an ape-like hunk, stands staring out over the Vézère, while beside him, the **Musée National de la Préhistoire** (July & Aug daily 9.30am–6.30pm; June & Sept Wed–Mon 9.30am–6pm; Oct–May Wed–Mon 9.30am–12.30pm & 2–5.30pm; €5; ⓦwww.musee-prehistoire-eyzies.fr) occupies the remains of a castle built into the rock as well as a smart new building built around it. The museum contains a vast array of increasingly sophisticated stone tools of the Paleolithic era (two million to 10,000 years ago) which enabled man to create the engravings and sculptures from the era on display. Some are copies, but many are originals: look out for the large limestone block with two aurochs (primitive wild cattle) beautifully superimposed to provide perspective, and some impressive reconstructions of prehistoric beasts.

There is plenty of information in English as well as a series of television points where you can sit and watch informative short films on a number of related topics, for example, a demonstration of how stone tools were made.

In the late nineteenth century local farmer Martial Pataud discovered prehistoric remains when he was cutting a new road beside what is now the National Museum. The rock-shelter (*abri*), which had been occupied for over 15,000 years before the roof collapsed around 20,000 years ago, yielded a rich hoard of finds, a selection of which are now on display in the next-door **Musée de l'Abri Pataud** (1hr guided visit: Feb–March & mid-Nov to Dec Tues–Thurs 10am–12.30pm & 2–5.30pm; April–June & Sept to mid-Nov Tues–Thurs & Sun 10am–12.30pm & 2–6pm; July & Aug daily 10am–7pm; €5.50; €13 for a combined ticket including Le Thot and Lascaux II), occupying what was previously the Patauds' wine cellar. Much of the excavation was carried out in the late 1950s and early 1960s, one of the first "modern" digs which enabled unusually precise analysis of the successive human occupations – unless you're an archeology buff this may not seem hugely exciting, but the guide's explanations help sort out all the different eras mentioned at other sites. The most famous find is the female figurine known as the **Vénus à la Corne** ("Venus with a Horn"). The exaggerated bas-relief, with her pendulous breasts and stout hips, now resides in Bordeaux's Musée d'Aquitaine (see p.89). Archeologists also found eleven skeletons, including a young mother with her newborn baby wearing a necklace; she is now closer at hand in the National Museum, though there's a copy here alongside a bronze statue modelled from her bone structure. Look out, too, for the enchanting little ibex (*bouquetin*) carved on the museum's rock ceiling.

Eating

When it comes to **eating**, there are some excellent choices among the hotel restaurants mentioned above. Otherwise, *Le Chateaubriant* (☎05.53.35.06.11; closed Wed & for dinner on Sun, also closed Jan), north along the main street from the tourist office, is your best bet. They're strong on grills and fresh fish, with good-value menus starting at €11; reservations are recommended in season, especially for the terrace. Or, for something cheaper, *La Grignotière*, east of the tourist office, has a pleasant outdoor courtyard and serves simple brasserie-style food: fish, steaks, omelettes and salads, as well as full menus from €10.80. *Du Côte de Chez Clos*, opposite the museum has a roof terrace café and salon de thé serving ice cream, crêpes and salads.

East of Les Eyzies

Les Eyzies sits on the confluence of the River Vézère and the Beune flowing in from the east. Like the Vézère, the Beune valley hides a wealth of prehistoric rock-shelters and caves, but here it is the great variety of **cave art** on offer that makes it so attractive. Closest to Les Eyzies, and arguably the best single sight in the whole area, the **Grotte de Font-de-Gaume** is one of the few places where you can still see original cave paintings on such a scale. Numbers are restricted so **advance booking** is highly recommended. The same applies to the **Grotte des Combarelles**, further east, the walls of which are covered with engravings. They're not always easy to make out, but the sense of mystery as you proceed deep into the dimly lit tunnel is compelling. To put it all in context the mock-up scenes at nearby **Roc du Cazelle** give an enjoyable view of what prehistoric life might have been like. You're back to the real thing, though, at the **Abri du Cap Blanc**, where early man sculpted an unusually large frieze of horses way up in the hills.

Grotte de Font-de-Gaume

Since they were first discovered in 1901, over two hundred Magdalenian-era (18,000–10,000 years old) polychrome paintings and engravings have been found in the narrow tunnel of the **Grotte de Font-de-Gaume** (45min guided tours daily except Sat: May 15–Sept 15 9.30am–5.30pm; Sept 16–May 14 9.30am–12.30pm & 2–5.30pm; €6.10; ℡05.53.06.86.00, ⑩www.leseyzies .com/grottes-ornees), just over a kilometre from Les Eyzies along the D47 to Sarlat. In order to preserve them, only 180 people are allowed to enter the cave each day, in groups of twelve. It is essential to book at least a week ahead, longer in July and August, though you may strike lucky and get a ticket on spec first thing in the morning, particularly on a Sunday when all tickets go on sale on the day. Sundays apart, phone reservations are accepted.

The cave mouth is no more than a fissure concealed by rocks and trees above a small lush valley. Inside is a narrow twisting passage of irregular height over 100m long, where you quickly lose your bearings in the dark. The majority of the **paintings** depict bison, but also horses, mammoths, reindeer and wild cats, and many unexplained signs such as the so-called "**tectiforms**", comprising a very gently inclined, upside down "V" with vertical lines beneath. The first you come to is a frieze of bison at about eye level: reddish-brown in colour, massive, full of movement and an almost palpable force. Further on a horse stands with one hoof slightly raised, resting, and another appears to be galloping or jumping. But the most miraculous of all is a frieze of five bison discovered in 1966. The colour, remarkably sharp and vivid, is preserved by a protective layer of calcite. Shading under the belly and down the thighs is used to add volume with a sophistication that seems utterly modern. Another panel consists of **superimposed drawings**, a fairly common phenomenon in cave-painting, sometimes the result of work by successive generations, but here an obviously deliberate technique: a reindeer in the foreground shares legs with a large bison to indicate perspective.

Grotte des Combarelles and Roc du Cazelle

The myriad engravings of the **Grotte des Combarelles** (1hr guided tours same hours as Font-de-Gaume; €6.10), a short distance further along the D47, were discovered a few days before Font-de-Gaume in 1901. Only five decorated caves had been discovered prior to this, and with the jury still out on primitive man's artistic abilities, they were an incredibly significant find. As with Font-de-Gaume, visitor numbers are restricted (there's a maximum of six people per tour) and pre-booking is recommended, especially in peak season; apply to the Font-de-Gaume booking office (see above).

Again, you make your way down a long, claustrophobic tunnel, stopping every now and then while the guide picks out a tiny selection of the six-hundred-plus **engravings** identified so far. It is a veritable Magdalenian menagerie: mostly horses, but also bison, reindeer, mammoths, rhinos, bears, ibex, aurochs and wild cats; stylized human figures and geometric symbols also feature. A good deal of imagination is required to recognize some of the fainter outlines, often superimposed one upon another, while others are astounding in their simplicity and realistic treatment – among the finest are the heads of a horse and a lioness, where the dips and projections in the rock provide eyes, nostrils and even bone structure.

Continue along the D47 for another couple of kilometres and you'll be greeted by mammoths roaring and the sound of people chipping flints at **Roc du Cazelle** (daily: March, April, Oct & Nov 10am–6pm; May, June & Sept 10am–7pm; July & Aug 10am–8pm; Dec–Feb 11am–5pm; €5.60; ⑩www .rocdecazelle.com), a theme park which reconstructs life 12,000 years ago. It's really best for children, but the imaginative design helps bring the surrounding caves to life. Various scenes – from hunting and gathering to painting and sculpting – are scattered around a wooded valley once occupied by prehistoric man, culminating in a real troglodyte fortress and a troglodyte farm that was inhabited up to the 1960s.

Abri du Cap Blanc and beyond

Not a cave but a natural rock-shelter, the **Abri du Cap Blanc** (1hr guided tours daily: April–June, Sept & Oct 10am–noon & 2–6pm; July & Aug 10am–7pm; closed Nov–March; €5.60) lies on a steep wooded hillside above the River Beune about 7km east of Les Eyzies; it's signed left off the D47 shortly after the Grotte des Combarelles. The shelter contains a superb **sculpted frieze** of horses and bison dating from the middle Magdalenian period (16,000–13,000 years ago), discovered in 1909 behind thick layers of sediment. Unfortunately, the excavation was carried out in such a hurry that the frieze had been badly damaged before anyone realized it was there. Even so, it is quite remarkable, mainly for its scale – the middle horse, which closely resembles the wild Przewalski horse of Central Asia, is virtually life-size – but also the depth of some of the sculptures. The bodies were obviously polished to set them off against the rough background, while traces of ochre and manganese pigments indicate that they were also painted at one time.

Continuing up the Beune valley from Cap Blanc you come to the elegant sixteenth-century Château de Laussel (closed to the public) and, on the opposite side, the romantic ruins of the **Château de Commarque** (daily: March & April 10am–6pm; May, June & Sept 10am–7pm; July & Aug 10am–8pm; €5.60; ⓦwww.commarque.com). Dating from the twelfth century, Commarque was a **castrum** – a fortified village made up of six separate fortresses, each belonging to a different noble family, of which the best preserved is that built by the powerful Beynac clan in the fourteenth century. The site was abandoned some two hundred years later, then left to moulder until the late 1960s when the present owner, Henri de Commarque, came to the rescue. The ruins have now been made structurally sound and it's possible once again to climb the Beynac's thirty-metre-high tower for views over the surrounding countryside. The easiest way to reach the château is by a footpath starting below Cap Blanc. Cars have to approach it from the south, following signs from the D47 Sarlat road; note that it's about 600 metres' walk from the car park to the entrance.

Accommodation and restaurants

The hills around Commarque hide a number of good **accommodation** and **eating** options which provide an alternative to Les Eyzies. There's a welcoming **ferme-auberge** (☎05.53.29.66.07, ⓦwww.grange-du-mas.com; menus €16–32; closed Tues lunchtime & Oct–Easter; ❸) at the Grange du Mas, just outside the village of **SIREUIL**. Heading eastwards, after about 4km you come to the little hilltop hamlet of **MARQUAY**, where the *Hôtel des Bories* (☎05.53.29.67.02, ⓦwww.members.lycos.fr/hoteldesbories; ❷; closed Nov–March) makes a pleasant alternative to staying in Les Eyzies. It's in a lovely spot, with marvellous views, a swimming pool and nicely rustic rooms; you need to book several months in advance for July and August. They also run the excellent *L'Estérel* restaurant, just round the corner, with a strong showing of fish and seafood – a welcome change from duck (menus from €13; April to mid-June & mid-Sept to Oct closed for lunch Mon–Sat; also closed Nov–March).

There's another good, slightly more upmarket hotel north of the Beune valley at **TAMNIÈS**, perched even higher, some 13km northeast of Les Eyzies. The geranium-decked *Hôtel Laborderie* (☎05.53.29.68.59, Ⓦwww.hotel-laborderie .com; ❸; closed Nov–Easter) occupies four separate buildings, with a big choice of rooms – the best are those in the newer blocks overlooking the extensive garden and pool – and a good restaurant with regional menus from €18 (closed Wed lunchtime). Again, early booking is advisable in summer.

❹

Northwest of Les Eyzies

As well as prehistoric cave art, you can see some truly spectacular stalactites and stalagmites around the Vézère valley. The closest of these to Les Eyzies is the **Grotte du Grand Roc**, just a few kilometres upstream. It can be combined with **Abri de Laugerie Basse** – another treasure-trove of Magdalenian art and artefacts – located under the same dramatic overhang. The Laugerie Basse finds are now scattered around various museums, including Les Eyzies' National Museum of Prehistory (see p.230), but one splendid piece of art in the area is still *in situ*. Up a little side valley known as the Gorges d'Enfer is the **Abri du Poisson**, named after the life-size salmon carved in the roof and well worth a visit. Then, way up in the hills to the north, the **Grotte de Rouffignac** is one of the largest decorated caves in Europe, so large that you enter by electric train to find caverns splattered with beautifully observed mammoths, horses, bison and other beasts deep in the bowels of the earth. If time allows, continue north to the **Château de l'Herm**, whose overgrown ruins provide an antidote to all these caves.

Grotte du Grand Roc and around

Two kilometres north of Les Eyzies on the D47 to Périgueux, the entrance to the **Grotte du Grand Roc** (30min guided tours daily: Feb–June, Sept to mid-Nov & Christmas school hols 10am–6pm; July & Aug 9.30am–7pm; €6.50; Ⓦwww.grandroc.com) lies under the cliffs that line much of the Vézère valley. There's a great view from the mouth of the cave and, inside, along some 80m of tunnel, a fantastic array of **rock formations**. Most unusual are the still-unexplained *excentriques* growing in all directions and triangles formed by calcite crystallizing in still, shallow pools.

The cave was discovered in 1924 in the continuing search for prehistoric art; sixty years earlier Edouard Lartet and Henry Christy had discovered a rock-shelter further along the same cliff. The **Abri de Laugerie Basse** (same hours as Grotte du Grand Roc; €5) was inhabited almost constantly over the last 15,000 years – most recently in the form of farmhouses built against the rock – and yielded hundreds of **engravings** and **sculptures**, not on the rock face but on pieces of bone or fashioned out of individual stones. The majority date from the late Magdalenian period (13,000–10,000 years ago) when prehistoric art reached its peak. They include a mysterious engraving of a very pregnant woman lying under a reindeer, and a sculpted female torso, the first so-called "Venus figure" – obviously symbols of fertility, though it's not known whether they relate to fertility rites – discovered in France. These and other important finds are presented in a slide-show before visiting the shelter; there's little to see otherwise, though during the visit you learn a lot about the history of the excavations and what conditions were like during the Magdalenian era.

More interesting, though, is the **Abri du Poisson** (1hr guided tours daily by appointment only, ☎05.53.06.86.00, Ⓦwww.leseyzies.com/grottes-ornees; €2.50), which lies on the road from Les Eyzies just before the Grotte du

Grand Roc. The rock-shelter – one of many along a side valley – contains one of the very few sculpted fish in prehistoric art. It's a real beauty too, a metre-long male salmon, complete with gills and beak, probably carved about 25,000 years ago. The deep-cut rectangular outline is not a prehistoric picture-frame, however, but the remains of an abortive attempt by a Berlin museum to acquire the salmon soon after it was discovered in 1912. Since then the shelter has been kept sealed up and can now be visited by a maximum of forty people per day.

You can, however, take a gentle stroll up the **Gorges d'Enfer** (daily: April–June, Sept & Oct 10am–6pm; July & Aug 9.30am–7.30pm; €4). Despite its name (the "Gorges of Hell"), the valley is small and very pastoral, with picnic tables and a few domestic animals roaming around for the children, but the main interest is the **footpath** winding past rock-shelters half-hidden among the woods. Although there's not a great deal to see – the excavations were completed many years ago – the shelters have been left in their natural state, with no mock mammoths or Cro-Magnon in sight.

Rouffignac and the Château de l'Herm

Soon after Grand Roc, the D47 turns northwest to follow the Manaurie valley. Seven kilometres beyond the village of **MANAURIE**, you'll pass a right turn signed to the **Grotte de Rouffignac** (1hr guided tours daily: July & Aug 9–11.30am & 2–6pm; April–June, Sept & Oct 10–11.30am & 2–5pm; €5.90; @www.grottederouffignac.fr), another 7km uphill among dense woods; unfortunately the tour is in French only and there's no English-language leaflet. It starts with a one-kilometre ride on a little electric train along the bed of an underground river which dried up about three million years ago. On the way the guide points out where hibernating bears scratched their nests and human visitors left their mark in the form of graffiti – including a priest, Abbé de la Tour, in 1808. In fact records show that the cave was known about in the sixteenth century, but it took until 1956 before the 13,000-year-old monochromatic drawings and engravings were recognized. Around 270 animal figures have been identified so far, the vast majority of which are mammoths, including a superb patriarch in the final chamber, his great tusks arcing under a piercing eye. The ceiling here is covered with mammoths, woolly rhino, horses, bison and ibex depicted with an astonishing economy of line.

The cave is located about 5km south of **ROUFFIGNAC** town, which was destroyed by German troops in 1944 and subsequently rebuilt. They drove everyone out before torching it; the only buildings to survive were the church, with its carved portal and unusual, twisted columns inside, and the adjacent house. Four kilometres further north, the **Château de l'Herm** (April to mid-Nov daily 10am–7pm; mid-Nov to March by appointment only; €5.50; ☎05.53.05.46.61, @www.chateaudelherm.com) also has an unhappy history, in this case a complicated tale of murders, forced marriages and disputed inherit-ance rights. In the end the castle was abandoned and has been crumbling away for more than three centuries to leave an atmospheric ruin engulfed by trees. Two big round towers and some decorative touches from the fifteenth and sixteenth centuries remain: a late Gothic doorway opens onto a spiral stone staircase, at the top of which is a beautifully worked palm-tree vault, while three sculpted fireplaces cling one above the other to the wall of an otherwise empty shell. Much is made of the fact that the château featured in local novelist Eugène le Roy's famous work *Jacquou le Croquant*, based on a sixteenth-century peasant revolt.

Le Bugue and around

LE BUGUE lies on the north bank of a meander in the Vézère 11km downstream from Les Eyzies, and is a good alternative base. It's not only marginally less crowded in season but is also a more attractive town, with a riverfront setting and scattering of old houses along the River Doux, which flows into the Vézère from the north, and the lane generously called Grande Rue, which runs east of and parallel to the Doux. Between the two, rue de Paris is Le Bugue's main shopping street, while the **place de Mairie**, on the river bank at the south end of rue de Paris, is what passes for the town centre; it also serves as the **market** square, with the main market on Tuesday mornings and a smaller one on Saturdays. From place de Mairie, avenue de la Libération heads south over the Vézère, and the main D703 to Les Eyzies, here called rue de la République, scoots southeast. On its way it takes you past Le Bugue's two rather second-tier sights, located side by side roughly 1km from the centre.

The more interesting, particularly for younger kids, is the **Village du Bournat** (daily: mid-Feb to April & Oct to mid-Nov 10am–5pm; May–Sept 10am–7pm; last entry 45min before closing; July & Aug €12.90, rest of year €8.90; ☎05.53.08.41.99 ⓦwww.lebournat.fr), a fair re-creation of a Périgord village in the early 1900s complete with *lauze*-roofed cottages, chapel, schoolhouse, baker, café and so forth – but no live animals. The entry price seems expensive, but there's a lot to see, including demonstrations of local crafts, such as clog- and barrel-making, potting and basketry, and you can come and go as you please within a day. Next door, the **Aquarium du Périgord Noir** (daily: April 10am–5pm; May & Sept 10am–6pm; June 10am–7pm; July & Aug 9am–7pm; €8.20; ⓦwww.parc-aquarium.com) will also appeal mostly to children. The aquarium concentrates on European freshwater fish – though they have more colourful tropical species as well – kept for the most part in open tanks, some of which you can walk under.

Practicalities

Trains on the Périgueux–Agen line pull into Le Bugue's **gare SNCF**, roughly 2km southeast on the D703; call Archambeau (☎05.53.07.10.70) if you need a taxi. You can also reach Le Bugue from Périgueux by bus (operated by Voyages Rey; ☎05.53.07.27.22); buses depart from near the *gendarmerie* at the north end of rue de Paris. The **tourist office** (April–June & Sept Mon–Sat 9.30am–12.30pm & 2.30–6.30pm, Sun 10am–1pm; July & Aug daily 9am–1pm & 3–7pm; Nov–March Mon–Sat 9.30am–12.30pm & 2.30–6pm; ☎05.53.07.20.48, ⓦwww.perigord.com/bugue) is on the river bank a short walk west of place de Mairie. In addition to the normal services, they offer Internet access and double as an SNCF ticket office; note that you can't buy tickets at the station. **Canoe rental** is available from Canoëric (☎05.53.03.51.99, ⓔcanoeric@wanadoo.fr), beside the Village du Bournat, and Canoës Courrèges (☎05.53.08.75.37, ⓕ05.53.03.98.02) on the Le Buisson road.

The cheapest place to **stay** is the welcoming, old-fashioned *Hôtel de Paris*, a short walk north of the central square at 14 rue de Paris (☎05.53.07.28.16, ⓕ05.53.04.20.89; ❶). *Le Cygne*, 2 rue du Cingle (☎05.53.07.17.77, ⓦwww.logis-de-france.fr; ❸; closed Jan & two weeks in Oct), is a smarter place just west of the tourist office. It offers well-priced rooms – overlooking the road at the cheaper end – and a popular traditional **restaurant** with menus from €13.50 (closed Sun eve & Mon out of season). If you'd rather be more in the country, try the friendly *Auberge des Fontenilles* (☎05.53.07.24.97, ⓕ05.53.07.24.70; ❷; closed Dec to mid-Jan), set back from the D703 a few kilometres southeast of

Le Bugue, with simple rooms, a pool and a decent restaurant (menus €13–28). A little further along the same road, the *Hôtel du Château* (☎05.53.07.23.50, ✉hotduchateau@aol.com; ❸; closed mid-Oct to Easter) is a traditional sort of place with big, bright rooms and a good regional restaurant (menus €18–45). It's located in **Campagne**, a pretty village gathered round a château and diminutive church, well-positioned between Le Bugue and Les Eyzies. *La Maison Oléa* (☎05.53.08.48.93, ⓦwww.olea-dordogne.com; May–Oct; ❸), two kilometres out of town in the direction of Sarlat, has five pretty rooms with good views of the surrounding countryside.

Le Bugue's closest **campsite** is the two-star riverside *Camping du Port* (☎05.53.07.24.60; May–Oct), immediately south of the river. However, with your own transport you'd do better to head 6km north up into the hills along the D31 to Manaurie and Rouffignac. Almost midway between Le Bugue and Les Eyzies, the *Camping Brin d'Amour* (☎05.53.07.23.73, ⓦwww .campings-dordogne.com/brindamour; April–Oct) is another two-star establishment, small, friendly, well-run and lacking the regimented feel of so many sites.

For somewhere simple to **eat**, there's the grill and pizza joint, *La Pergola*, 16 avenue de la Libération, just across the Vézère, which also offers salads, pasta, fondues and three regional menus from €15. At the other end of the scale, *L'Oustalou*, located in the *Royal Vézère* hotel on place de la Mairie, is well known for its original and varied cuisine (menus from €21; closed Nov–March).

Around Le Bugue

High-tech has hit the Vézère in a big way at the **Gouffre de Proumeyssac** (45min guided tours daily: Feb, Nov & Dec 2–5pm; March, April, Sept & Oct 9.30am–noon & 2–5.30pm; May & June 9.30am–6.30pm; July & Aug 9am–7pm; €7.90), a vast and spectacular limestone cavern 5km south of Le Bugue on the D31E. Its forty-metre-high vault dripping with multicoloured stalactites, ranging from fine needles to massive petrified waterfalls, is dubbed the "crystal cathedral". To heighten the sense of atmosphere you enter in the dark, then the music builds as lights pick out various formations before revealing the whole chamber in a grand finale. It's cleverly done, though some will find it too commercialized, even down to stacks of calcite-coated pottery souvenirs, and a far cry from when the cave was discovered in 1907. At that time the only way in was via a basket lowered through a hole in the roof under flickering torchlight – you can still make the descent by two-person basket for €15 per person including the entry fee.

Northeast along the Vézère: La Madeleine to Le Thot

The D706 tracks the Vézère as it meanders northeastwards from Les Eyzies. Here again the valley sides are peppered with cliff-dwellings, from prehistoric rock-shelters to the remnants of a full-blown town. One of the first you come to is the relatively recently abandoned village of **La Madeleine**, where a little chapel still survives, straddling the path, alongside the shells of several houses built into the rock cavity. Further on, the life-size replicas of prehistoric animals and people at **Préhisto-parc** will amuse the kids, while **La Roque St-Christophe** provides the most dramatic sight along this stretch of the valley. Until the sixteenth century this great wall of cliff provided accommodation for hundreds of people on five levels – a forerunner of the multistorey – accessed by ladders and just one heavily defended ledge-path. Beyond lies the exquisite riverside village of **St-Léon-sur-Vézère**, near which there's another imaginative theme park, the **Parc de Loisirs Préhistorique**, a cluster of **rock-shelters** and the **Château de Losse**. A handsome sight with its towers and turrets reflected in the Vézère, the château contains a particularly good collection of furniture and tapestries. Afterwards, head up over the lip of the valley to learn about cave art at **Le Thot**.

La Madeleine and the Préhisto-parc

First stop along the Vézère is a semi-troglodytic medieval settlement near the village of **TURSAC**, 5km upstream from Les Eyzies. **La Madeleine** (daily: July & Aug 9.30am–7pm; Sept–June 10am–6pm; €5; Ⓦ www.village-la-madeleine .com) lies on the river's north bank near the neck of a huge meander, where the Vézère takes a 3km loop to cover less than 100m as the crow flies. The cliffs here have been inhabited on and off for the last 15,000 years. Indeed, the prehistoric rock-shelter down by the water's edge yielded such a wealth of late-Paleolithic tools and engravings that archeologists named the era Magdalenian; one of the more intriguing finds was a carving of a man with a bestial head, believed to be a mask, now on display at Les Eyzies' museum (see p.230). Further up the cliff subsequent settlers constructed a whole village complete with fortress, drawbridge, village square and chapel, all dating back to the tenth century. Le Madeleine was inhabited until 1920 and the Resistance (see p.394) used it as a hideout, but now the chapel is the only building completely intact. Nevertheless, enough remains to give a good sense of what such cliff-dwellings were like.

Plastic Neanderthals hunting mock mammoths to an accompanying sound-track won't be everyone's cup of tea, but the **Préhisto-parc** (daily: March–June & Oct to mid-Nov 10am–6pm; July–Sept 9.30am–7pm; €5.50; Ⓦ www .prehistoparc.fr), a little further along the D706, is another attempt to re-create the daily life of prehistoric man. If you've already visited the more varied Roc du Cazelle (see p.232), you can give this a miss, but otherwise it's fun to take in, especially if you've got children in tow. Again, a woodland walk takes you past

△ Préhisto-parc

tableaux of encampments, people making flints, painting, sculpting and generally being busy in a prehistoric sort of way.

Tursac's central square is home to a simple village **restaurant**. *La Source* (T05.53.06.98.00, Wwww.restaurant-la-source.com; closed Sat & mid-Nov to mid-March) not only has a pleasant garden, but also caters for vegetarians, with an imaginative and well-priced menu at €13.50, other menus from €12. On the edge of the village, the ☀*Auberge du Pêche-Lune* (T05.53.06.85.85, Wwww .peche-lune.com; ⑤) is a rambling, eccentric **hotel** whose eclectic decor ranges from Mexican to Asian to North African. The rooms are cheerful and spacious, have women's names instead of numbers and are decorated with original pieces of art. There's also a restaurant (menus from €15) serving varied international as well as local cuisine, and a bar with regular entertainment including a belly dancer at times. The main lobby has a small display of pre-Columbian statues, masks and urns. There are also two good **campsites** in the area: first is the more basic but spectacularly located *La Ferme du Pelou* (T05.53.06.98.17, Wwww .leseyzies.com/le-pelou; mid-March to mid-Nov), a two-star site perched on the hilltop overlooking La Madeleine and its meander from the east; it's signed off the D706 to the south of Tursac. North of the village, *Le Vézère Périgord* (T05.53.06.96.31, Wwww.levezereperigord.com; Easter–Oct) is a well-run, spacious and friendly three-star site set back from the main road among trees.

La Roque St-Christophe

The enormous natural refuge of **La Roque St-Christophe** (45min guided tours daily: Feb–March & Oct–Nov 10am–6.30pm; July & Aug 10am–8pm; Nov–Jan 2–5pm; €6; Wwww.roque-st-christophe.com), 3km upriver from Tursac, is made up of about one hundred **rock-shelters** on five levels hollowed out of the limestone cliffs. The whole complex is nearly a kilometre long and up to 80m above ground-level, where the River Vézère once flowed. The earliest traces of occupation go back over 50,000 years, although permanent settlement dates from around the ninth century when the site's natural defences really came into their own. At its peak during the Middle Ages it had grown into a veritable town clinging to the rock face – with its own marketplace, church, prison, abattoir, baker and artisans' workshops – and was able to shelter over one thousand people in times of trouble. And there was no shortage of those, culminating in the Wars of Religion when Protestant sympathizers took refuge here. After they were kicked out in 1588, Henri III ordered the town and fortress demolished – which means you need a good imagination to re-create the scene from the various nooks and crannies hacked into the rock. The **guides** are instructive but during the summer peak the tour gets rather tedious – better if possible to come at lunchtime (noon–2pm) when you can wander at your own pace with the aid of their well-written English-language leaflet.

St-Léon-sur-Vézère and around

ST-LÉON-SUR-VÉZÈRE, 6km above Tursac, is by far the most attractive village along the whole Vézère valley. It sits in a quiet bend of the river guarded by two châteaux – one topped by a fairy-tale array of turrets – and boasts one of the region's most harmonious Romanesque churches. In summer the church serves as one of the principal venues, along with St-Amand-de-Coly (see p.244), for classical music concerts during the **Festival du Périgord Noir** (see box on p.217). For the best views of the whole ensemble, walk over the iron-girder bridge and turn left along a footpath on the opposite bank.

The path continues to a series of rock-shelters and the remains of a semi-troglodytic settlement known as Le Conquil, now part of the **Parc de Loisirs**

Préhistorique (daily: April & Sept 10am–6pm; May–Aug to 7pm; €7.80). The advertising is a bit twee, but the activities – fashioning flint tools and needles from bones, making fire and throwing spears, among others – are well organized and should appeal to all ages. On the whole the caves themselves aren't particularly interesting, with the exception of one pitted with square niches in rows along the back and side walls (one theory attributes them to a Neolithic burial site), but it's fun scrambling among the cliff dwellings, particularly the little fort right at the top, before you walk back through the woods.

Five kilometres west of St-Léon, the **Château de Chabans** (45min guided tours: May, June & Sept Mon–Fri & Sun 2–7pm; July & Aug daily 2–8pm; €6.80; ⓦwww.chabans.neuf.fr) stands on a ridge of hills known as the Côte de Jor. Chabans was built in the mid-fifteenth century, added to in the seventeenth and then abandoned after 1800, suffering more than two-hundred years of neglect before the present owner took it over in 1987. Since then she has poured money into its preservation, employing the best local artisans and using only traditional methods. The end result, which has received a number of architectural awards, is not so much a replica Renaissance château – the interiors are too pure, almost Romanesque – as a showcase for the owner's collection of period furniture, stained glass, chinoiserie and tapestries. Afterwards, you can take tea on the terrace and then wander round the vast estate, some of it planted with truffle oaks.

St-Léon's *Auberge du Pont* (closed Tues eve, Wed & Nov–Feb) is a lovely wisteria-covered **restaurant** beside the bridge, which offers various lunchtime *formules* (from €11.50) as well as more substantial menus (from €16) and a wicked array of home-made ice creams. Tucked down beside the church you'll also find the 🌿 *Déjeuner sur l'Herbe* (closed Mon & Jan). This tiny **shop** sells top-notch local produce and also does takeaways: a platter of cheese or charcuterie, for example, with a hunk of country bread, costs €12, while a sandwich comes in at €4.50. You can then decamp to the picnic tables along the riverbank. The closest **hotel** is *Le Relais de la Côte de Jor* (☎05.53.50.74.47, Ⓕ05.53.51.16.22; ❷–❸; closed Dec–March), in the pine-forested hills 2.5km north of St-Léon on the road to Château de Chabans, with views down the valley to La Roque St-Christophe. As for **campsites**, there's a choice between St-Léon's small municipal site beside the bridge (☎05.53.50.73.16, Ⓕ05.53.50.20.32; May–Sept), and the luxurious *Le Paradis* (☎05.53.50.72.64, ⓦwww.le-paradis.com; closed Nov–March) complete with heated pools, 3km down the road to Les Eyzies. You can rent **canoes** at *Le Paradis* and also through *Adventure Plein Air* (☎05.53.50.67.71, ⓦwww.canoevezere.com), who set up by the bridge in St-Léon from May through September depending on the weather.

South across the Vézère from St-Léon, the rock-shelters of **Castel-Merle** (April–June & Sept Mon–Fri 10am–noon & 2–6pm; July & Aug Mon–Sat 10am–7pm; €5; ⓦwww.castelmerle.com) are of fairly specialist interest, but the site is rarely crowded and you can borrow an unusually thorough English-language booklet outlining the history and importance of the four shelters. Only one still contains any **cave art**, including three rather poorly preserved bison sculptures from the same era as Cap Blanc (see p.233). However, the site has yielded a terrific number of **flints**, **bones** and **beads**. A good number of these are on show in a small private **museum** (no fixed hours; if the owner's not there, call ☎05.53.50.77.54; free) in the village of **SERGEAC**, 500m below Castel-Merle. The owner takes great delight in explaining the objects, many of them unearthed by his archeologist father, of which the highlight is a collection of six necklaces strung together about 30,000 years ago. One is made up of shells from the Atlantic, presumably obtained by trade, and another of various animal teeth including wolf's.

The same family also own a **hotel**, the *Auberge de Castel-Merle* (☎05.53.50.70.08, Ⓦwww.castelmerle.com; ❸; closed Oct–March) on the hill above the prehistoric shelters. It's a handsome Périgord building and the rooms are cheerful, but its main attribute is its clifftop terrace where on fine days you can **eat** lunch overlooking the Vézère (menus from €14; closed Mon & for lunch on Tues).

Château de Losse and Le Thot

Of several castles along the Vézère valley, the Renaissance **Château de Losse** (45min guided tours daily: April, May & Sept 11am–6pm; June–Aug 10am–7pm; €7; ☎05.53.07.24.60, Ⓦwww.chateaudelosse.com) stands out as the most striking. It occupies a rocky bluff 4km upstream from St-Léon on the main D706, though the best views are from the opposite bank, where the D65 provides a quiet and picturesque back road from St-Léon to Montignac (see below). The present castle was constructed in the 1570s by Jean II de Losse, royal tutor and the governor of Guyenne, on medieval foundations. It has changed little since then, a well-proportioned L-shaped building surrounded by dry moats and watchtowers. Inside, the château's present owners have established an impressive collection of sixteenth- and seventeenth-century **furniture** and **tapestries**. Among the latter, the Florentine *Return of the Courtesan* is particularly successful in its use of perspective, while the colours of this and the Flemish rendition of knights preparing for a tournament remain exceptionally vibrant. There's also a rare, tulip-decorated tapestry dating from around the time of the Dutch Tulipomania in 1634, when tulips cost more than gold. On your way out, note the inscription over the unusually imposing gatehouse which quotes one of Jean II's favourite maxims: "When I thought the end was in sight, I was only beginning." His perhaps jaundiced view is forgivable – of his five sons, four were killed in war and the fifth had no heirs to inherit the family estates.

It's back to prehistory at the next stop, **Le Thot** (Feb, March & mid-Nov to Dec Tues–Sun 10am–12.30pm & 2–5.30pm; April–June & Sept daily 10am–6pm; July & Aug daily 10am–7pm; Oct to mid-Nov daily 10am–12.30pm & 2–6pm; €5.50, or €13 combined ticket with Lascaux II and L'Abri Pataud; Ⓦwww.semitour.com), 1km into the hills west of the château. Somewhat whimsically described as an "Espace Cro-Magnon" (loosely translated as "space of the Cro-Magnon"), the combined museum and animal park focuses on prehistoric art, not only the technical aspects but also some of the **wildlife** that provided inspiration: reindeer, Przewalski horses with their erect manes, ibex, deer and European bison are all resident here. You'll also see **aurochs**, though these primitive wild cattle really died out in the 1600s – the beasts here are a close approximation achieved through selective breeding in the early twentieth century. The **museum** explains the different techniques and styles of cave art, but the most interesting part is a video showing the painstaking re-creation of the Lascaux caves (see p.243). For once, it's subtitled in English and the majority of displays here have English-language explanations.

Montignac and around

Some 26km upstream from Les Eyzies, **MONTIGNAC** is a more attractive town, with several wooden-balconied houses leaning appealingly over the river, and a vibrant annual **arts festival** in July, featuring international folk groups (see box on p.217). While there's nothing particular to do in Montignac itself,

Dhagpo Kagyu-Ling

South of Montignac and just above the village of **Le Moustier** is the Tibetan Buddhist centre, **Dhagpo Kagyu-Ling** (℡05.53.50.70.75, ⊛www.dhagpo-kagyu-ling.org). The centre was opened in 1977, under the auspices of the sixteenth Gyalwa Karmapa - the spiritual leader of the Kagyupa School, one of Tibet's four main spiritual schools - with the aim of spreading the teachings of the Buddha to those interested in France. Today, the centre welcomes people from all over Europe to its year-round workshops and retreats. **Courses** include meditation, Buddhist philosophy, sacred sculpture and Tibetan medicine and last anywhere from one day to one week. To follow a course you must take out a year's membership to the centre (€55) after which most courses cost €10 per day. Accommodation for those taking courses is also available in dorms, singles, twins or doubles, and all meals and accommodation are charged according to your monthly income. There are plans to expand the building and also to create a library, which will be open to the general public.

To reach the centre, follow the D706 from Montignac or Les Eyzies to Le Moustier. If coming under your own steam, take a train to Les Ezyies from where you can call a taxi on ℡05.53.50.68.62. All bookings should be made in advance.

apart from visiting the lively **market** – which spills out of central place Carnot on Wednesday mornings, with a smaller one on Saturdays – and wandering the riverbanks, it serves as the main base for exploring the Vézère valley's northern sights, foremost of which is **Lascaux**'s painted cave, though the Romanesque abbey church of **St-Amand-de-Coly** is also worth a visit.

Practicalities

Montignac straddles the Vézère, with its church and central square, place Carnot, on the west bank and the majority of tourist facilities across the river along rue de 4-Septembre. **Buses** from Périgueux, Brive and Sarlat stop on place Carnot and on place Tourny, the latter being at the east end of rue de 4-Septembre. Also on this road, the **tourist office** occupies the second floor of a sixteenth-century hospital on central place Bertran-de-Born (April–June, Sept & Oct Mon–Sat 9am–noon & 2–6pm; July & Aug daily 9am–7pm; Nov–March Mon–Sat 10am–noon & 2–5pm; ℡05.53.51.82.60, ⊛www.bienvenue-montignac.com). Below it you'll find the summer **ticket office for Lascaux II** (see opposite; April–Oct daily 9am–6pm). **Bikes** are available to rent from La Paléothèque at 59 rue de 4-Septembre (℡05.53.50.04.24), and there are two **canoe rental** outlets: Les 7 Rives (℡05.53.50.19.26; Easter–Sept) beside the more northerly Pont de la Paix; and Kanoak (℡06.75.48.60.47; mid-June to mid-Sept) below the old bridge.

As is usual in these parts, **accommodation** can be a problem in high season. The *Hôtel de la Grotte*, 63 rue du 4-Septembre (℡05.53.51.80.48, ⓔhoteldelagrotte@wanadoo.fr; ❶–❸), is the cheapest in town, with basic rooms (the cheapest with shared facilities), a small streamside garden and a restaurant (menus from €17). Next up is the more modern but less characterful *Le P'tit Monde Hotel* , further out along the Sarlat road at 54 rue du 4-Septembre (℡ & ℻05.53.51.32.76; ❷); with cheap, simple rooms with bath or shower rooms. From there it's a big leap up to the very comfortable *Relais du Soleil d'Or*, 16 rue du 4-Septembre (℡05.53.51.80.22, ⊛www.le-soleil-dor.com; ❹; closed mid-Jan to mid-Feb), whose menus start at €12.50 in the bistro and €24 in the more formal restaurant. They've also got a lovely big garden, with pool, but for not much more you can stay in the more homely ivy- and wisteria-clad *Hostellerie de la Roseraie*, across the river in quiet place d'Armes (℡05.53.50.53.92, ⓦwww.laroseraie-hotel.com; ❺; closed Nov to Easter; menus from €21; restaurant closed for lunch Mon–Fri). The rooms are prettily decorated with period furniture, and they boast an even bigger garden, landscaped pool and a riverside terrace. Finally, there's a well-tended, three-star camping and caravan site, *Le Moulin du Bleufond* (℡05.53.51.83.95, ⓦwww.bleufond.com; closed mid-Oct to March), on the riverbank 500m downstream.

Grotte de Lascaux and Lascaux II

The **Grotte de Lascaux** was discovered in 1940 by four teenagers in search of their dog, which had fallen into a deep cavern near Montignac. The cave was found to be decorated with marvellously preserved animal paintings, executed by Cro-Magnon people some 17,000 years ago, which are among the finest examples of prehistoric art in existence. Lascaux was opened to the public in 1948 and over the next fifteen years the humidity created by more than a million visitors caused algae and then an opaque layer of calcite to form over the paintings. The algae can be cured by disinfection, but the "white disease" is a more serious problem, and in 1963 the authorities decided to close the cave and build a replica.

Opened in 1983, some 200m from the original cave, **Lascaux II**, signed 2km south from central Montignac (40min guided tours: April–June & Sept daily 9.30am–6.30pm; July & Aug daily 9am–8pm; Oct to mid-Nov daily 10am–12.30pm & 2–6pm; mid-Nov to Dec & Feb–March Tues–Sun 10am–12.30pm & 2–5.30pm; €8; combined ticket with Le Thot and l'Abri Pataud €13; ⓦwww.culture.fr/culture/arcnat/lascaux/en), was the result of ten years' painstaking work by twenty artists and sculptors using the same methods and materials as the original cave painters. The almost perfect facsimile comprises ninety percent of the Lascaux paintings concentrated in the Hall of Bulls and the Axial (or Painted) Gallery, a distance of less than 100m. While it can't offer the excitement of the real thing, the reproduction is still breathtaking. In the **Hall of Bulls** five huge aurochs – one 5.5 metres long with an astonishingly expressive head and face – dominate the ceiling, while the **Axial (Painted) Gallery** is covered with more cattle surrounded by deer, bison and horses rendered in distinctive Lascaux style with pot-bellies and narrow heads. Some are shaded or spotted with different coloured pigments, while others, like the bulls, are drawn in black outline. You don't have to be an expert to appreciate the incredible skill employed by the prehistoric artists, who would have painted these animals from memory by the light of flickering oil lamps, nor to appreciate their sense of perspective and movement, and the sheer energy they manage to convey.

Even so, if you want to appreciate the paintings at their best, it's important to avoid July and August, when groups of forty are herded through conveyor-belt style. Two thousand **tickets** are on sale each day, but these go fast during the peak holiday periods, when it's best to buy in advance either by going to the ticket office in person or making a credit-card booking over the phone (July & Aug ℡05.53.51.96.23; Sept–June ℡05.53.05.65.65); bookings can be made up to seven days in advance. Note also that in winter (Nov–March) tickets are on sale at the site, while in season (April–Oct) they are available only from an office beneath Montignac tourist office – the system varies from year to year, however, so check in Montignac first before heading up to the cave. Tours are conducted in either French or English.

Nine kilometres east of Montignac, the village of **ST-AMAND-DE-COLY** boasts a superb fortified Romanesque **church**. Despite its size and bristling military architecture, the twelfth-century abbey church manages to combine great delicacy and spirituality. It is supposedly built over the burial place of the sixth-century St Amand, who gave up soldiering to become a hermit. Despite a promising start, however, the abbey never really prospered and had largely been abandoned by the late 1400s. In 1575 a Protestant garrison withstood a heavy siege here for six days, after which the building continued to crumble until 1868, when it was classified as a historic monument; since then it has been entirely restored. With its purity of line and simple decoration, the church is at its most evocative in the low sun of late afternoon or early evening. Its **defences**, added in the fourteenth century, left nothing to chance: the church is encircled by ramparts, its walls are 4m thick, and a passage once skirted the eaves, with numerous positions for archers to rain down arrows and blind stairways to mislead attackers. If you're lucky enough to be here in July or August you might catch a classical music concert in the church during the **Festival du Périgord Noir** (late July to late Aug).

Near the church, clean and simple **accommodation** offered by the small *Hôtel Gardette* (☎05.53.51.68.50, ⓦhotelgardette.free.fr; ❷; menus from €15; closed Oct–March) makes it possible to stay overnight in this tiny, idyllic place. There's also a very grand – but not sniffy – creeper-clad manor house, the *Manoir d'Hautegente* (☎05.53.51.68.03, ⓦwww.manoir-hautegente.com; ❻; closed Nov–March), some 3km north, beyond the village of Coly. Set in its own grounds well back from the road, the hotel has a pool, sumptuous rooms overlooking the grounds to the river and one of the region's best **restaurants** (menus from €46; closed lunchtimes Mon–Thurs).

Terrasson-la-Villedieu

Beyond Montignac the prehistoric sites die out and the Vézère valley becomes busier and more industrialized as it opens out towards Brive (see p.173) and **TERRASSON-LA-VILLEDIEU**, 15km upstream. The old part of Terrasson, a knot of lanes on the river's south bank leading up from the arched stone bridge to the church, merits a quick wander, but the main reason for coming here is to visit its resolutely contemporary garden, **Les Jardins de l'Imaginaire** (1hr 15min guided tours only: April–June & Sept to mid-Oct Mon & Wed–Sun 9.50–11.20am & 1.50–5.20pm; July & Aug daily 9.50am–6.10pm; €5.50) on a terraced hillside to the west of the church. Opened in 1996, the **gardens** were designed by American landscaper Kathryn Gustafson. In them she explores common themes found in gardens throughout history and among different cultures, from the Romans' sacred groves and the Hanging Gardens of Babylon to moss, water and rose gardens, the last a magnificent display of nearly two thousand varieties. In this respect it is much more than "just" a garden, which is why they insist you go with a guide to explain the complicated symbolism; English-language texts are available. Afterwards, however, you can wander at leisure to enjoy the garden on its own terms. It's full of imaginative touches: a forest of wind chimes, a stark line of weather-vanes and, above all, the use of water to splendid effect.

If you're travelling by public transport, you might find yourself passing through Terrasson since it lies on the Brive–Bordeaux train line and has bus links to Montignac and Brive. The **gare SNCF** lies on the north side of town at the far end of avenue Jean-Jaurès. **Buses** stop at the station and place de la

Libération, on the main west–east Brive road, near the old bridge. Place de la Libération is also where you'll find the **tourist office** (July & Aug Mon–Sat 9.30am–1pm & 2.30–7pm, Sun 10am–1pm & 3–6pm; Sept–June Mon–Sat 9.30am–12.30pm & 2–5pm; ℡05.53.50.37.56, ⓦwww.ville-terrasson.com). If you're looking for somewhere to **eat** near the gardens, *Les Saveurs des Jardins* (closed Mon eve & Tues, and Nov–March), just outside the entrance, does a range of soups, salads and sandwiches, followed by home-made ice creams garnished with edible flowers and flower-based syrups; in fine weather you can eat on their terrace – flower-decked of course. There's also a good and rather classy **restaurant**, *L'Imaginaire*, nearby on place du Foirail (℡05.53.51.37.27, ⓦwww.l-imaginaire.com; closed Sun eve & Mon lunchtime, & three weeks in Nov), in two elegant stone-vaulted rooms. Three-course lunch menus start at €19, while in the evening they're €35 and €49, though they also do slightly cheaper *formules*. It has recently expanded to become a **hotel** (ⓞ) and has seven large rooms with Wi-fi, flat screen televisions, wooden floors and minimalist bathrooms with roomy showers and baths.

The middle Dordogne: St-Cyprien towards Souillac

The stretch of river to the south of Sarlat sees the Dordogne at its most appealing, forming great loops between rich fields, wooded hills and craggy outcrops. This is also castle country, where great medieval fortresses eyeball each other across the valley. Most date from the Hundred Years' War, when the river marked a frontier of sorts between French-held land to the north and English territory to the south.

For the visitor today, things start slowly in the west with the service town of **St-Cyprien** and nearby **Belvès**, now a sleepy little place where people once lived in troglodyte houses beneath its streets, but châteaux come thick and fast thereafter. The first you reach on the river's north bank is **Beynac**. Clamped to the rock out of which it appears to grow, the château and its village of russet-hued, stone-roofed cottages cascading to the river, presents one of the valley's most dramatic sights – and, from the castle keep, one of its best panoramas. A short distance further upstream, the **Château de Marquey-ssac** provides respite among its Italian-style terraced gardens and woodland promenades, with views of both Beynac and its arch rival over on the south bank, the **Château de Castelnaud**. Castelnaud is all that a medieval castle should be: barbicans, curtain walls, inner courtyards, fluttering pennants and watchtowers surrounding a seemingly indomitable keep. It also contains an excellent museum of medieval warfare and, as at Beynac, the views are superb. Then a brief diversion westwards brings you to the far-from-militaristic castle of **Les Milandes**, once owned by the cabaret artist Josephine Baker and now set up as a museum in her honour.

Heading back upstream, the next stop is **La Roque-Gageac**. This lovely village caught between the river and the rock-face is up there with Beynac and Castelnaud as one of the Dordogne's most photographed – and visited – sights. Across on the south bank, **Domme**, a fortified *bastide* town perched on the cliff edge, is no pushover on either the tourist stakes or as regards its views. From up here you can take in a ten-kilometre sweep of the river, giving you a foretaste of the **Cingle de Montfort**, a particularly picturesque meander set off by

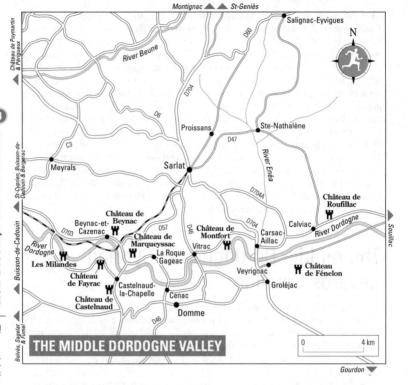

Montignac ▲▲ St-Geniès

Salignac-Eyvigues

River Beune

Château de Puymartin & Périgueux

Proissans

Ste-Nathalène

River Enéa

Meyrals

Sarlat

St-Cyprien, Buisson-de-Cadouin & Bergerac

Château de Roufillac

Château de Beynac

Beynac-et-Cazenac

Château de Marqueyssac

Château de Montfort

Carsac-Aillac

Calviac

River Dordogne

Souillac

La Roque Gageac

Vitrac

River Dordogne

Les Milandes

Château de Fayrac

Château de Fénelon

Veyrignac

Castelnaud-la-Chapelle

Cénac

Groléjac

Buisson-de-Cadouin

Château de Castelnaud

Domme

Belvès, Sagelat & Fumel

THE MIDDLE DORDOGNE VALLEY

0   4 km

Gourdon ▼

yet another glorious château to the east. Before you cross from the Dordogne *département* into the Lot, there's just one more castle to go, the **Château de Fénelon**, an attractive blend of medieval and Renaissance architecture with good collections of furniture and weaponry.

As far as public transport is concerned, although **trains** run along the valley from Le Buisson (see p.208) to Sarlat, the only intermediary station still functioning is Siorac-en-Périgord, between St-Cyprien and Belvès. Like Le Buisson, Siorac sits on the junction of the Sarlat–Bordeaux and Agen–Périgueux lines, with connections for Les Eyzies and the Vézère valley (see p.227). The only place accessible by **bus** is Carsac, a village with a pretty church just east of Montfort which is a stop on the Sarlat–Souillac bus route.

St-Cyprien and around

Despite its location, just 20km west of Sarlat and 10km south from Les Eyzies, **ST-CYPRIEN** remains a refreshingly workaday place set back from the busy D703. Admittedly, it hasn't got much in the way of sights, but the whole place really comes to life on Sunday mornings for one of the area's best **markets**. The hillside setting is also attractive and, with a number of decent hotels around, St-Cyprien makes an agreeable base. The old centre's narrow lanes of medieval houses and labourers' cottages, a good number still unprettified, hold the greatest interest. They zigzag up from the modern, lower town towards the austere **abbey church** founded by twelfth-century Augustinian monks. You certainly can't accuse the church of being pretty either, though there's a certain robust grandeur about its Romanesque tower and the echoing nave.

The helpful **tourist office**, on place Charles-de-Gaulle in the centre of the lower town (Mon–Sat 9.30am–12.30pm & 3–6pm, Sun 10am–12.30pm; ℡05.53.30.36.09, ⊛www.stcyprien-perigord.com), produces a good walking map of St-Cyprien.

Accommodation and eating

In town, the nicest is the *Hôtel de L'Abbaye* (℡05.53.29.20.48, ⓔschaller .abbaye@wanadoo.fr; ➎; closed mid-Oct to mid-April), on rue de l'Abbaye leading up to the church from the east. There are good views from the terraced gardens and pool and a beautiful courtyard, while antique furniture, comfy sofas and inglenooks give the place a country-house feel. Further down the same road, *La Terrasse* (℡05.53.29.21.69, ⊛www.logis-de-france.fr; ➋; Sept–June closed Sun eve & Mon, also closed mid-Dec to Feb) offers functional rooms – those in the newer block behind are bigger and better equipped – and good traditional **meals** (menus from €14.50).

There are a couple more good places to stay and eat in the hills 5km to the north of St-Cyprien near the typical Périgord village of **MEYRALS**. You'll need to book up early to get one of the twelve stylish **rooms** at ⚜ *La Ferme Lamy* (℡05.53.29.62.46, ⊛www.ferme-lamy.com; ➐) on the C3 north of the village. The whole place is immaculate, from the en-suite bathrooms to the big, landscaped pool and flower-filled garden, not to mention the breakfast-spread of home-made jams and breads. They don't offer main **meals**, but you only have to pop up the road to the *Ferme-Auberge de la Rhonie* (℡05.53.29.29.07, ⊛www.coustaty.com; ➌; closed Sun & Dec–Feb), where the Coustaty family serves up excellent country cooking (menus €22 & €33). For those that want to stay in this idyllic spot, they also offer good-value *chambre d'hôte* accommodation and a **campsite** (June–Sept) with space for just eight tents.

The other option is to head 8km downstream to **SIORAC-EN-PÉRIG-ORD** – a junction on the Sarlat–Bordeaux and Agen–Périgueux train lines – where there's a cheerful, British-run hotel, the *Auberge du Trèfle à Quatre Feuilles* (℡05.53.31.60.26, ⊛www.letrefle4feuilles.com; ➋; closed three weeks end Oct to mid-Nov), in the centre of the village; the **restaurant** is popular for its varied cuisine, from vegetarian dishes and curries to the likes of *crevettes* flambéed in pastis (menus from €16.50; closed lunchtimes except Sun, also closed Wed off season). On the north side of the river from Siorac, the *Petit Chaperon Rouge* (℡05.53.29.37.79, ⓔle-petit-chaperon-rouge@ wanadoo.fr; ➊–➋; closed Nov, and Tues off season) is an old-style country inn, all floral fabrics and a warm welcome, not to mention a good-value restaurant (menus from €11); cheaper rooms lack en-suite facilities. Campers are provided for by the friendly *La Faval* (℡05.53.31.60.44, ⊛www .lafaval.com; April–Sept), a three-star **campsite** immediately below the hotel with a restaurant, small pool and bike rental.

Belvès

Before setting off up the Dordogne from St-Cyprien, it's worth taking a detour south about 12km to **BELVÈS**. There's no mistaking the town's strategic importance, encircled by ramparts on a promontory above the Nauze valley and bristling with seven towers – even the central square is called place d'Armes. These days, however, the only battles likely to take place here involve haggling over prices at the Saturday-morning **market** under the old *halle*, or a hotly disputed game of boules.

In 1907 the wheel of a cart crossing place d'Armes broke through the roof of a warren of **troglodyte houses** (35min guided tours: mid-June to mid-Sept daily 10.30am–noon & 3–6pm; mid-Sept to mid-June Mon–Sat 11am, 3.30pm & 5.30pm; €3.50); note that it's best to confirm opening hours with the tourist office, which is where tickets are sold in any case. Hollowed into the rampart wall, these damp, dark and insalubrious dwellings were inhabited from the twelfth century up to the mid-1700s, after which they were blocked up and forgotten. So far eight "houses" have been opened, consisting of single rooms averaging a mere twenty square metres apiece for a family plus animals. It's hard to imagine what they must have been like to live in, even if the more sophisticated dwellings boast chimneys, raised sleeping areas and shelves cut into the soft rock. Afterwards, walk down rue Jacques-Manchotte, leading west from the market square and, if it's open, pop into the **Organistrum** at no. 14 (no fixed hours; free; ℡05.53.29.10.93), a combined museum and workshop producing medieval instruments. Music-lovers might also be interested in Belvès' principal annual event, the **Festival Bach**, dedicated to the composer, with a couple of concerts in the church largely during the second fortnight of July (see box on p.217).

Practicalities

Like Siorac, Belvès lies on the main Agen–Périgueux train line, with the **gare SNCF** down on the main road below the town. Its **tourist office**, 1 rue des Filhols (June 15–Sept 15 daily 10am–1pm & 3–7pm; Sept 16–June 14 Mon–Sat 10am–12.30pm & 3–6.30pm; ℡05.53.29.10.20, ⓦwww.perigord.com/belves), occupies the ground floor of the fifteenth-century Maison des Consuls, just off the market square, while the town's two **hotels** stand next to each other on place de la Croix-des-Frères, at the far west end of rue Jacques-Manchotte. First choice should be *Le Home* (℡05.53.29.01.65, ℉05.53.59.46.99; ❶; Oct–May closed Sun, & closed two weeks at Christmas), for its excellent-value rooms, friendly service and hearty country cooking (menus from €10). The *Belvédère* (℡05.53.31.51.41, ⓦwww.belvedere-perigord.com; ❸; closed Jan, & Oct–May closed Mon) is a smarter option, offering modern rooms complete with Wi-fi access as well as a decent restaurant. At Sagelat, a village 1km north-east of Belvès, comfortable **chambre d'hôte** accommodation is available in the handsome Périgord farmhouse of *Le Branchat* (℡05.53.28.98.80, ⓦwww.lebranchat.com; ❸). Finally, Belvès' nearest **campsite** is the three-star *Les Nauves* (℡05.53.29.07.87, ⓔcampinglesnauves@hotmail.com; mid-May to mid-Sept), in a quiet spot 4km southwest off the D53 Monpazier road.

Beynac-et-Cazenac and around

The stretch of river east of St-Cyprien sees the Dordogne at its most dramatic. The river still takes its time, but here the valley sides begin to close in as you approach the two great fortresses of **Beynac** and **Castelnaud**. They glare across at each other from their eyries, instantly recognizable from countless promotional posters, postcards and films. The area's second-tier sights inevitably pale by comparison. Close to Beynac the ridge-top gardens of the **Château de Marqueyssac** offer pleasant walks and expansive views, while **Les Milandes**, a Renaissance pile west of Castlenaud, serves as a sort of shrine to cabaret star Josephine Baker – much loved in France – who once owned it.

Beynac-et-Cazenac

Clearly visible on an impregnable cliff edge on the Dordogne's north bank, the eye-catching village and castle of **BEYNAC-ET-CAZENAC** was built in the days when the river was the only route open to traders and invaders. Now the busy main road squeezes between the cliffs and the water, creating a horrible bottleneck from July to mid-September. At this time you're best advised to arrive first thing in the morning to escape the worst of the crowds.

It's three kilometres by road from the waterfront to the **Château de Beynac** (1hr guided tours daily: March–May 10am–6pm; June–Sept 10am–6.30pm; Oct & Nov 10am–dusk; Dec–Feb 11am–dusk; €7) or, alternatively, it takes fifteen minutes to walk up the steep lane among the *lauze*-roofed cottages. The lichenous-grey castle is protected on the landward side by double walls and ditches; elsewhere the sheer drop of almost 150m does the job. The redoubtable Richard the Lionheart nevertheless took and held Beynac for a decade, until a gangrenous wound ended his term of blood-letting in 1189; apparently the heart-shaped keys and keyholes were fashioned in his memory. Though the English regained the castle briefly – thanks to the Treaty of Brétigny rather than any military prowess – in essence Beynac remained loyal to the French Crown during the Hundred Years' War.

The buildings are in surprisingly good condition thanks to a mammoth restoration project over the last forty years which is scheduled to continue until at least 2030. You enter into a **guardroom** lit by flickering oil lamps, one of the castle's more atmospheric rooms along with the **great hall**, where the nobles of Beynac, Biron, Mareuil and Bourdeilles – the four baronies of Périgord (see p.386) – met; note the unusual ox-skull motif over the fireplace, previously found at the Château de Lanquais (see p.205). Also good are the twelfth-century **kitchens**, complete with a cobbled ramp allowing horses access to the central courtyard, and kitted out with no-nonsense tables, vats, meat-hooks and great pulleys. If it looks familiar, that's because it featured in Luc Besson's epic, *Jeanne d'Arc*. For most people, however, it's the **views** that steal the show, notably from the top of the keep, where you get a stupendous – and vertiginous – sweep over the surrounding châteaux: Marqueyssac, Fayrac and Castelnaud (see below).

To get a very different perspective of all these castles, it's worth taking a **river trip** with Gabarres de Beynac (April–Oct 10am–noon & 2–6pm; €6.50; ☎05.53.28.51.15, Ⓦwww.gabarre-beynac.com) on one of the replica *gabarres*, the traditional wooden river-craft. Boats leave from a jetty beside the **tourist office** booth (June–Sept daily 10am–noon & 2–5.30pm; Oct–April Mon–Sat 9.30am–noon & 2–5pm; ☎05.53.29.43.08). You'll also find a small **car park** here and more along the road to the château opposite, but the only free parking is up at the château itself. This is classic **canoeing** country and there are a number of rental outfits: both Copeyre Canoë (☎05.53.28.95.01, Ⓦwww.canoe-copeyre.com) and Randonnée Dordogne (☎05.53.28.22.01, Ⓔrandodordogne@wanadoo.fr) have summer-only outlets near the tourist office, while Couleurs Périgord (☎05.53.30.37.61, Ⓦperso .wanadoo.fr/couleurs.perigord; open all year) is based about a kilometre east of Beynac where the railway crosses the river.

Accommodation and eating

Beynac's best all-round **hotel** is the *Hôtel du Château* (☎05.53.29.19.20, Ⓦwww.hotelduchateau-dordogne.com; ❷–❸; closed Dec 15–Jan 15), on a bit of a busy corner opposite the tourist office; ask for rooms on the back. Apart from simple rooms, it offers a tiny pool, a bar, Internet access and a good restaurant with a riverside terrace (menus €15–23, plus lighter meals from the brasserie menu; Oct–May closed Sun eve & Mon). Next choice would be the *Hostellerie Maleville* (☎05.53.29.50.06, Ⓦwww.hostellerie-maleville.com; ❸; closed Jan; menus from €15), which has the benefit of rooms in its annexe, the *Hôtel Pontet*, off the main drag on the road up to the castle. The most atmospheric option, however, is the old-fashioned *Hôtel Bonnet* (℡05.53.29.50.01; ❸; closed mid-Nov to March), right under the castle as you come into Beynac from the east, with a decent restaurant serving menus from €15; all rooms on the road are double-glazed. On the way to the *Bonnet*, you pass the English-run *Café de la Rivière* (℡05.53.28.35.49, ⊜cafe-de-la-riviere@wanadoo.fr; ❷–❸), with three attractive en-suite rooms and a restaurant (menu at €16; closed mid-Oct to mid-Nov), or you can simply enjoy a drink on its terrace – the view takes in no fewer than four châteaux. The riverside *Le Capeyrou* **campsite** (℡05.53.29.54.95, ⓦwww.campinglecapeyrou.com; mid-May to mid-Sept) lies immediately east of town.

The **restaurants** mentioned above offer plenty of choice, but for something a little different you could try the *La Petite Tonnelle* (menus €12–25; closed Nov–March except for Christmas hols), on the road to the castle. Alongside local fare, they rustle up exotica such as chicken saté and spring rolls with a spicy sauce; great chips, too.

Château de Marqueyssac

Three kilometres east of Beynac, the Dordogne loops south round a long and narrow wooded promontory, at the tip of which the **Château de Marqueyssac** (daily: Feb, March & Oct to mid-Nov 10am–6pm; April–June & Sept 10am–7pm; July & Aug 9am–8pm; mid-Nov to Jan 10am–5pm; €6.80, or €12.40 with Château de Castelnaud; ⓦwww.marqueyssac.com) presides over its terraced gardens. The château itself, a typically mellow Périgord mansion of the late eighteenth century, is rarely open to the public, but the **view**, encompassing the châteaux of Beynac, Fayrac and Castelnaud, is magnificent. The **gardens** were first laid out in the 1600s by the then owner, Bertrand Vernet de Marqueyssac, under the inspiration of Le Nôtre, the landscaper responsible for Versailles. However, most of the features you see today were added two centuries later when the half-kilometre long Grand Allée was established, thousands of box trees clipped into plump cushions, and six kilometres of woodland walks opened up along the ridge to the east. All paths lead to a 130m-high **belvedere** from where you can see La Roque-Gageac nestling under its cliff (see p.253). Between Easter and mid-November, the **salon de thé** serves light refreshments, and on Thursday evenings in July and August fairy lights give the gardens a magical touch.

Castelnaud-la-Chapelle

Rivals for centuries, the feudal fortresses of Beynac and **CASTELNAUD-LA-CHAPELLE**, on the Dordogne's south bank, now vie over visitor numbers. There's no question that Beynac has the edge with its more dramatic location and arguably the better views, but the **Château de Castelnaud** (Feb–Mar & Oct to mid-Nov daily 10am–6pm; April–June & Sept daily 10am–7pm; July & Aug daily 9am–8pm; mid-Nov to Jan Sun–Fri 2–5pm; Christmas hols daily 10am–5pm; €7.20, or €12.40 with Château de Marqueyssac; ⓦwww.castelnaud.com) provides the more entertaining visit – and more informative, thanks to the excellent English-language guidebook you can borrow; allow at least a couple of hours.

Like Beynac, Castelnaud was founded in the twelfth century and bitterly fought over on many occasions, starting with the bellicose Simon de Montfort, who seized it as early as 1214 during his Cathar Crusades (see p.387). Then during the Hundred Years' War the lords of Castelnaud sided with the English, slugging it out for nearly four decades with the French at Beynac until Charles

VII besieged Castelnaud in 1442. After holding out for three weeks, a treacherous English captain handed over the keys in return for his life and the princely sum of 400 crowns.

Heavily restored in the last decades, the château now houses a highly informative **museum of medieval warfare**. Its core is an extensive collection of original weaponry, including all sorts of bizarre contraptions, such as an "organ" which sprayed lead balls from its multiple barrels, and a fine assortment of armour. The displays are interspersed with interesting video presentations (in French only) on the history of warfare. In summer (July & Aug), staff give demonstrations of the various siege engines dotted around the ramparts, and evening visits led by guides in period costume are also on offer (Mon–Fri at 8.30pm; €8; in French only).

△ Castelnaud-la-Chapelle

On the road down from the village, where it joins the D57, it's worth stopping off briefly at the **Eco-musée de la Noix du Périgord** (April–Nov daily 10am–7pm; €4), for everything you ever wanted to know about nuts – **walnuts**, specifically. As well as detailing oil pressing, the exhibition reveals historical gems such as the fact that Louis XI's beard was trimmed using heated walnut shells, and that walnuts are used in the insulation of American spaceships. It also points out the nuts' many health benefits, before you're shepherded through to the well-stocked shop. If you're lucky the mill itself will be working, but otherwise there's a self-explanatory video featuring Ste-Nathalène's more authentic Moulin de la Tour (see p.224). The adjacent orchard, spattered with giant cement walnuts and picnic tables, is particularly good for young children.

While there are no hotels in Castelnaud, there's a quiet and well-managed three-star **campsite**, *Lou Castel* (☎05.53.29.89.24, ⓦwww.loucastel.com; May–Oct), among oak woods on the plateau a couple of kilometres to the south.

Les Milandes

From Castelnaud it's a scenic drive 5km west along the river past **Château de Fayrac** (not open to the public) with its slated pepper-pot towers – an English forward position in the Hundred Years' War, built to watch over Beynac – to **Les Milandes** (daily: April & Oct 10am–6.15pm; July & Aug 9.30am–7.30pm; May, June & Sept 10am–6.30pm; €7.80; ⓦwww.milandes.com). Built in the

Josephine Baker and the Rainbow Tribe

Born on June 3, 1906, in the black ghetto of East St Louis, Illinois, **Josephine Baker** was one of the most remarkable women of the twentieth century. Her mother washed clothes for a living and her father was a drummer who soon deserted his family, yet by the late 1920s Baker was the most celebrated cabaret star in France, primarily due to her role in the legendary **Folies Bergère** show in Paris. On her first night, de Gaulle, Hemingway, Piaf and Stravinsky were among the audience, and her notoriety was further enhanced by her long line of illustrious husbands and lovers, which included the crown prince of Sweden and the crime novelist Georges Simenon. She also mixed with the likes of Le Corbusier and Adolf Loos, and kept a pet cheetah, with whom she used to walk around Paris. During the war, she was active in the **Resistance**, for which she was awarded the Croix de Guerre. Later on, she became involved in the civil rights movement in North America, where she insisted on playing to non-segregated audiences, a stance which got her arrested in Canada and tailed by the FBI in the US.

By far her most bizarre and expensive project was the château of **Les Milandes**, which she rented from 1938 and then bought in 1947, including 300 hectares of land, after her marriage to the French orchestra leader Jo Bouillon. Having equipped the place with two hotels, three restaurants, a mini-golf course, tennis court and an autobiographical wax museum, Baker opened the château to the general public as a model multicultural community, popularly dubbed the "village du monde". Unable to have children of her own, in the course of the 1950s she adopted babies (mostly orphans) of different ethnic and religious backgrounds from around the world. By the end of the decade, she had brought twelve children to Les Milandes, including a black Catholic Colombian and a Buddhist Korean, along with her own mother, brother and sister from East St Louis.

Over 300,000 people a year visited the château in the 1950s, but her more conservative neighbours were never very happy about Les Milandes and the "Rainbow Tribe". In the 1960s, Baker's financial problems, divorce and two heart attacks spelled the end for the project, and despite a sit-in protest by Baker herself (by then in her sixties), the château and its contents were auctioned off in 1968. Still performing and as glamorous as ever, Josephine died of a stroke in 1975 and was given a grand state funeral at La Madeleine in Paris, mourned by thousands of her adopted countryfolk.

late 1400s, the ivy-clad château was the property of the Caumont family (the lords of Castelnaud) until the Revolution, but its most famous owner was the Folies Bergère star, **Josephine Baker** (see box above), who fell in love with it while visiting friends in the area in 1937.

It's easy to see why. The Renaissance château, sitting high above the Dordogne, has all the necessary romantic ingredients: towers, machicolations, balustrades, gargoyles, ornate dormer windows and terraced gardens shaded by great, glossy-leafed magnolias. After she bought Les Milandes in 1947, Josephine set about modernizing it, adding creature comforts such as the en-suite bathrooms, whose decor was inspired by her favourite perfumes – Arpège-style black tiles with gold taps and ceiling in one, Dioresque pink marble with silver-leaf in another. But it's really the stories surrounding Josephine and Les Milandes that are more intriguing than the château itself. Her roller-coaster life story is enough to fill a book, but you can trace the broad outlines from the collection of photos and posters. The few costumes which escaped the auctioneer's hammer in 1968 are also on display, though these are somewhat moth-eaten after mouldering in the cellar for 25 years.

From the terrace in front of the château, where they hold **falconry demon-strations** (April–Oct), you can look down on the J-shaped swimming pool belonging to one of the many fun-parks Josephine established in the area.

La Roque-Gageac

The village of **LA ROQUE-GAGEAC**, on the river's north bank 5km east of Beynac, is almost too perfect, its ochre-coloured houses sheltering under dramatically overhanging cliffs. Regular winner of France's prettiest village contest, it inevitably pulls in the tourist buses, and since here again the main road separates the village from the river, the noise and fumes of the traffic can become oppressive. The best way to escape is to slip away through the lanes and alleyways that wind up through the terraced houses. The other option is to rent a canoe and paddle over to the opposite bank, where you can picnic and enjoy a much better view of La Roque than from among the crowds milling around beneath the village, at its best in the burnt-orange glow of the evening sun.

Look carefully at the cliff above the village and you'll see guard-posts, ramparts and other remnants of a **troglodyte fort** (Easter–Oct daily 10am–6pm; €4). At one time belonging to the bishops of Sarlat, who built themselves a château within the ramparts, the fort provided the villagers with a virtually impregnable refuge from the Vikings' ninth-century invasions right up until the early 1800s when it was largely dismantled; only the Protestant armies were able to take it by force. The remaining defence-works are of only moderate interest, but it's worth tackling the vertigo-inducing ladder for the views.

A less athletic option, and highly recommended, is to take a **boat ride** down to Castelnaud. From April to October two companies offer these one-hour round-trips (with commentary in English) in a *gabarre*: Gabares Norbert (℡05.53.29.40.44, ⊛www.norbert.fr; €7.50), the main operator, and Gabarres Caminades (℡05.53.29.40.95; same price). If you'd rather go under your own steam, you can rent **canoes** from Canoë Dordogne (℡05.53.29.58.50, ⓔcontact@canoe-dordogne.fr) and Canoë Vacances (℡05.53.28.17.07), both east of La Roque towards Vitrac and Sarlat.

Practicalities

For more information about activities in the area, contact La Roque's **tourist office** (Easter–Oct daily 10am–1pm & 1.45–5.30pm; ℡05.53.29.17.01, ⊛www.la-roque-gageac.com), in a hut by the main car park on the Sarlat side of town. Since most people just come here for a day-trip, there's usually space if you want to **stay** the night outside the summer peak. The most pleasant and best-value option is *La Belle Étoile* (℡05.53.29.51.44, ⓔhotel.belle-etoile@wanadoo.fr; ❹; closed Nov–March), on the main road below the fort, whose restaurant serves good traditional cuisine at very reasonable prices (menus from €24; closed Mon & lunchtime Wed). Otherwise, set back from the D703 Sarlat road 1km out of La Roque, *La Ferme Fleurie* (℡05.53.28.33.39, ⊛www.perigord.com/la-ferme-fleurie; closed Nov–March) – which lives up to its name, with a flower-filled garden – would be another good choice, either for its *chambre d'hôte* rooms (❸) or a bed in the separate *gîte d'étape* (€19 per person including breakfast).

Of the many **campsites** in the vicinity, *Le Lauzier* (℡05.53.29.54.59, ⓕ05.53.29.51.66; mid-June to Sept) is one of the closest, while *Le Beau Rivage* (℡05.53.28.32.05, ⊛www.camping-beau-rivage.com; March–Sept) offers three-star luxury and lots of activities in season; they're both east of La Roque on the D703 Sarlat road.

Domme and around

High on the scarp on the south bank of the river, 5km southeast from La Roque-Gageac and 10km due south of Sarlat (see p.218), **DOMME** is an exceptionally well-preserved, terribly pretty *bastide*, now wholly given over to tourism. Its foremost attraction, however, is its position. From the chestnut-shaded **Esplanade du Belvédère** at the town's northern edge, you look out over a wide sweep of river country encompassing everything from Beynac to the Cingle de Montfort (see p.206). The drop here is so precipitous that fortifications were deemed unnecessary when the *bastide* was founded in 1281. They lived to regret it: in 1588 a small band of Protestants scaled the cliffs at dawn to take the town completely by surprise. The intruders stayed four years, during which time they destroyed the church amongst other buildings, before they were forced to abandon the town again to Catholic control.

Much of Domme's thirteenth-century walls and three of the gateways they skirted remain. Of the latter, the best-preserved and most interesting is easterly **Porte des Tours**, flanked by two round bastions. In 1307 a group of Templar knights was imprisoned here for eleven years; if you peer through the openings you can just make out the graffiti – Crucifixion scenes, the Virgin Mary, angels and various secret signs – they carved on the walls. Alternatively, you can visit by appointment with the tourist office, or there are photos of the carvings in the **Musée des Arts et Traditions Populaires** (daily: April–June & Sept 10.30am–12.30pm & 2.30–6pm; July & Aug 10.30am–7pm; €4) on central place de la Halle. Its displays of local life are nicely done, though not wildly interesting, whereas the **caves** (daily: Feb to mid-Nov; contact tourist office for hours & tickets; €6.50 including museum), which extend hundreds of metres under the village from beneath the timbered market hall, can definitely be given a miss. The concretions are badly discoloured with algae and can't compare with any of the area's other limestone caverns; the only good point is the exit onto the cliff-face with a panoramic lift up to the top and a pleasant stroll back along the promenade de la Falaise.

On the way to – or from – Domme, it's worth making a brief stop in **CÉNAC**, down by the river, to admire its Romanesque **church**, located a short distance along the D50 to St-Cybranet. Apart from a lovely *lauze* roof, its main draw is the remarkably distinct carving on the capitals, featuring various animals and demons, including Daniel taming the lions.

Practicalities

Domme's **tourist office** (Feb–June & Sept to mid-Nov daily 10am–noon & 2–6pm; July & Aug daily 10am–7pm; mid-Nov to Dec Mon–Fri 10am–noon & 2–6pm; ☎05.53.31.71.00, ⓦwww.ot-domme.com) is located on place de la Halle. On **market** days (Thursday mornings) stalls spill out of the square south down the main commercial street, the Grande-Rue, itself lined with souvenir shops. At the top of this road, *Le Nouvel Hôtel* (☎05.53.28.38.67, ⓦwww.dome-nouvel-hotel.com; ❸; closed Sun eve & Mon except in July & Aug, also closed Jan–March) offers several simple, reasonably priced **rooms** above a restaurant serving regional fare (menus from €15). For those on a more generous budget, the smartest place to stay is *L'Esplanade*, right on the cliff edge (☎05.53.28.31.41, ⓦwww.esplanade-perigord.com; ❼; closed mid-Nov to Feb); note that rooms with a view are premium-rated. *L'Esplanade* also has a recommended **restaurant** (closed for lunch Mon & Wed), with menus from €40.

The nearest **campsite** is Cénac's one-star municipal site (℡05.53.28.31.91, ℱ05.53.31.41.32; closed mid-Sept to mid-June) beside the bridge. In summer several **canoe rental** places set up here, including Randonnée Dordogne (℡05.53.28.22.01, ✉randodordogne@wanadoo.fr) and Cénac Périgord Loisirs (℡05.53.29.99.69, ✉cpl.infos@wanadoo.fr); the latter also has **bikes** for rent.

Upstream towards Souillac

Taking the prettier north bank of the Dordogne from Domme, a white-walled castle bristling with turrets soon hoves into view atop its well-defended promontory. So coveted was the superb strategic position that the **Château de Montfort**'s history is a long tale of destruction and reconstruction, most recently in the nineteenth century – hence the Disneyesque skyline (the château is not open to the public). To complete the picture it overlooks the almost perfect curve of the **Cingle de Montfort**, not the biggest but certainly the tightest of the Dordogne's many meanders, almost encircling a tongue of land covered in walnut orchards.

Two kilometres further on another inviting little Romanesque **church** below the village of **CARSAC** makes a good place to pause. Though the meadow setting is delightful, the church's **carvings** are the main point of interest: in this case Arabic-influenced capitals around the choir and some later keystones. Note, too, the Stations of the Cross made by Russian abstract artist Léon Zack, who was a refugee here during World War II. Carsac also has a couple of good **hotels**, which could be used as a base for Sarlat, only 10km to the northwest and accessible by bus. In the village itself, the family-run *Hôtel Delpeyrat* (℡05.53.28.10.43, ⓦwww.logis-de-france.fr; ❶–❷ closed Oct & Nov) is a charmingly old-fashioned place offering well-priced rooms, most of them set back from the road overlooking a small garden, and equally homely cooking (menus from €12.20; restaurant closed Sun eve & Sat midday). The more upmarket option is *Le Relais du Touron* (℡05.53.28.16.70, ⓦwww .lerelaisdutouron.com; ❹; closed mid-Nov to March; menus €14.50–32), set in extensive grounds a short distance along the Sarlat road. Its twelve bright and cheery rooms occupy a modern block, with a pool, behind the owners' lovely old manor house.

From Carsac you need to cross back over the Dordogne and continue along its south bank for some 5km to find the **Château de Fénelon** (Feb & Nov weekends 2–5pm; March & Oct Wed-Sun 2–5pm; May, June & Sept 10.30am–12.30pm & 2–6pm daily ; July & Aug 10am–7pm daily; €7), clamped to its own rocky outcrop. With its triple walls and great round towers topped with *lauzes*, the castle exudes all the might of the original medieval fortress. As you get closer, however, the Renaissance-era additions and other, later embellishments become more apparent – the large mullion windows and the gallery closing the interior courtyard, for example. The then lords of Fénelon swore allegiance to the English in 1360, but after it was taken by the French fifteen years later the castle came into the hands of the Salignac de la Mothe-Fénelon family, very big cheeses in the Périgord, who owned it for the next four centuries. Their most illustrious member was **François de Salignac de la Mothe-Fénelon**, who was born here in 1651. Private tutor to the heir to the throne and later archbishop of Cambrai, he fell from grace when King Louis XIV interpreted his work *Télémaque* – which recounts the adventures of Ulysses' son – as a thinly veiled attack on the Crown. His intention had been to teach the young prince the finer points of kinghood, but for his pains Fénelon was banished to Cambrai where he died in 1715. He is remembered with much pride at Fénelon today.

There's a mock-up of his study and numerous portraits, but the present owners have also amassed a worthwhile collection of period furniture, tapestries and medieval weaponry. The ornate walnut chimneypieces are also eye-catching.

From the Château de Fénelon the route continues east along the Dordogne, past one of its main rivals, the Château de Rouffillac (not open to the public), on the opposite bank, before finally reaching Souillac (see p.26) 17km later.

Travel details

Trains

Belvès to: Agen (2–5 daily; 1hr–1hr 15min); Le Bugue (4–5 daily; 20–35min); Le Buisson (4–5 daily; 15–30min); Les Eyzies (4–5 daily; 30–40min); Périgueux (4–5 daily; 1hr–1hr 15min); Siorac-en-Périgord (3–4 daily; 6min).

Le Bugue to: Agen (2–5 daily; 1hr 30min); Belvès (2–5 daily; 20–35min); Le Buisson (2–6 daily; 15min); Les Eyzies (4–5 daily; 7min); Limoges (1 daily; 2hr); Périgueux (4–5 daily; 35–40min); Siorac-en-Périgord (2–5 daily; 20min).

Les Eyzies to: Agen (2–5 daily; 1hr 40min); Belvès (2–5 daily; 30min); Le Bugue (2–5 daily; 7min); Le Buisson (2–5 daily; 15–20min); Limoges (1 daily; 1hr 50min); Périgueux (4–5 daily; 30–35min); Siorac-en-Périgord (2–5 daily; 30min).

Sarlat to: Alles-sur-Dordogne (1–2 daily; 35–50min); Bergerac (4–6 daily; 1hr–1hr 30min); Bordeaux (4–5 daily; 2hr 20min–2hr 45min); Le Buisson (4–6 daily; 30–45min); Castillon-la-Bataille (4–5 daily; 1hr 40min–2hr); Lalinde (4–6 daily; 40min–1hr); Ste-Foy-la-Grande (4–5 daily; 1hr 30min–1hr 50min); Siorac-en-Périgord (1–3 daily; 20min); Trémolat (4–6 daily; 35–50min).

Siorac-en-Périgord to: Agen (2–5 daily; 1hr 10min–1hr 20min); Belvès (2–5 daily; 6min); Bergerac (1–3 daily; 1hr–1hr 15min); Bordeaux (1–2 daily; 2hr 20min); Le Buisson (4–8 daily; 8–20min); Le Bugue (3–4 daily; 15–30min); Les Eyzies (3–4 daily; 25–40min); Périgueux (3–4 daily; 50min–1hr 10min); Sarlat (1–2 daily; 20–25min).

Terrasson-la-Villedieu to: Brive (4–7 daily; 15min); Périgueux (3–5 daily; 35–45min); Bordeaux (2–3 daily; 2hr–2hr 20min).

Buses

Le Bugue to: Périgueux (school term Mon–Fri 1–2 daily, school hols Wed only; 1hr).

Carsac to: Sarlat (4–5 daily; 20min); Souillac (4–5 daily; 30min).

Montignac to: Brive (Mon–Sat 1 daily; 1hr 15min); Périgueux (school term Mon–Fri 2–3 daily, school hols Wed 1–2 daily; 1hr); St-Geniès (as for Périgueux; 15min); Sarlat (as for Périgueux; 30min); Terrasson (Mon–Sat 1 daily; 25min).

Sarlat to: Brive-la-Gaillarde (school term Mon–Fri 1 daily, rest of year Tues, Thurs & Sat 1 daily; 1hr 40min); Carsac (4–5 daily; 20min); Montignac (July & Aug & school hols Wed 1–2 daily, rest of year Mon–Fri 2–3 daily; 30min); Périgueux (as for Montignac; 1hr 40min); St-Geniès (as for Montignac; 20min); Souillac (4–6 daily; 50min).

The Upper Dordogne valley and Rocamadour

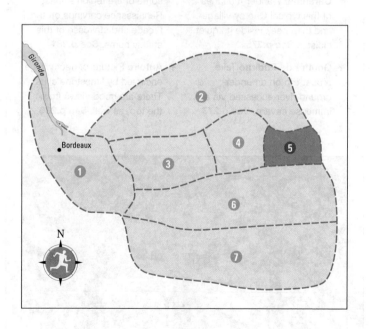

CHAPTER 5

Highlights

* **Souillac** In the abbey church of Ste-Marie the image of the prophet Isaiah is a masterpiece of Romanesque art. See p.261

* **Rocamadour** One of France's top pilgrimage sites defies gravity in its spectacular cliff-edge location. See p.265

* **Carennac** Wander the lanes of this typical Quercy village and then peek inside its quiet cloister. See p.275

* **Gouffre de Padirac** Take a boat trip on an underground river accessed via an immense cavern. See p.277

* **Château de Castelnau** Fans of military architecture shouldn't miss this brooding fortress. See p.278

* **Beaulieu-sur-Dordogne** Laid-back market town on the banks of the Dordogne which sees fewer tourists than it deserves. See p.280

* **Château de Montal** Admire some of the region's finest Renaissance carvings on the facade and staircase of this stately home. See p.281

* **Autoire** Picture-perfect village encircled by limestone cliffs. There are good views from the top, as well. See p.286

△ Èglise St-Pierre, Carennac

5

The Upper Dordogne valley and Rocamadour

I n its upper reaches the River Dordogne cuts a green swathe through the rocky limestone plateau of **Haut-Quercy**, as the northern sector of the Lot *département* is traditionally known. Though the cliffs rise to considerable heights in places, the valley here lacks the drama of the perched castles and towns immediately downstream. Instead, away from the main towns, it offers quieter lanes, more modest castles and a succession of unspoilt riverside villages where it's pleasant to relax for a couple of days.

The main gateway to the Upper Dordogne valley is **Souillac**, a busy little town whose major attraction is its domed abbey church, containing the finest of several examples of Romanesque carving scattered along the valley. A short distance upstream from Souillac, an attractive back road strikes off along the River Ouysse, a minor tributary of the Dordogne, heading southeast to the spectacular pilgrimage town of **Rocamadour**, whose seven religious sanctuaries are built almost vertically into a rocky backdrop. The town has been an important pilgrimage centre since the ninth century, though nowadays pilgrims are outnumbered by tourists, to the tune of one and a half million a year, who come here simply to wonder at the sheer audacity of its location.

Due north of Rocamadour, but on the other side of the Dordogne, the market town of **Martel** sees surprisingly few tourists, given its medieval centre full of turreted mansions, while further east **Carennac** merits a stop for its picturesque lanes and the twelfth-century carved portal adorning its church. Carennac also lies within striking distance of the **Gouffre de Padirac**, several kilometres to the south, where a collapsed cavern has left a gaping hole in the limestone plateau. Down below, a river leads deep underground through passages festooned with giant stalactites. East of Carennac the Dordogne valley begins to open out to form a broad plain around its confluence with the Cère. **Bretenoux**, the main town guarding the Cère valley, isn't in itself a particularly engaging place, but it's more than compensated for by the nearby **Château de Castelnau**, an impregnable fortress standing on

5

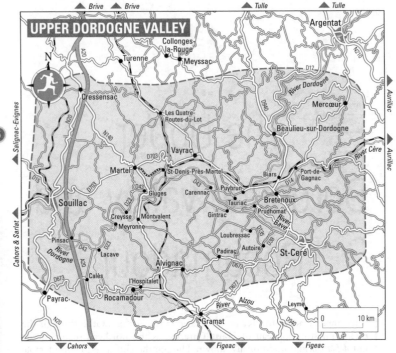

the frontier between the old provinces of Quercy and the Limousin, which still dominates the country for miles around. To the north of Bretenoux, **Beaulieu-sur-Dordogne** is a more pleasing town, featuring an abbey church with another magnificent tympanum carved in the same style as those at Souillac and Carennac.

To the south of Bretenoux, **St-Céré**, like Beaulieu, provides another good base for exploring the region, and beneath the brooding towers of its ruined château, a scattering of stone and half-timbered town houses attest to the town's fifteenth- and sixteenth-century heyday. There's more Renaissance architecture on show on the facade and in the superb stone staircase of the **Château de Montal**, a few kilometres to the west. The nearby villages of **Autoire** and **Loubressac**, meanwhile, are rooted firmly in the Quercy soil, their houses sporting little pigeon-lofts and the red-tile roofs splayed gently above the eaves which are typical of the region. From beside Loubressac's encircling walls or, better still, from the *cirque* above Autoire, there are sweeping views across the Dordogne valley and eastwards towards the river's source among the green foothills of the Massif Central.

Public transport in this region is patchy. You can reach Souillac, Rocamadour, St-Denis-Près-Martel (for Martel) and Bretenoux by train and, except for Rocamadour, by bus too. There are also buses to Martel, Carennac, Beaulieu and St-Céré, but services are fairly infrequent and the connections between the smaller towns are not particularly good. If you plan to do a lot of bus journeys, it would be worth getting hold of the comprehensive timetable, *Les Bus du Lot*; tourist offices in larger towns such as Souillac and Bretenoux should hold copies.

Festivals, events and markets

Second Sunday in May Beaulieu-sur-Dordogne: Fête de la Fraise. France's strawberry capital gets down to some serious baking with an 800-kilo strawberry tart. There's a strawberry market, too, and all sorts of fun and frolics.

Late May or early June Rocamadour: Fête des Fromages Fermiers. At Pentecôte (Whit Sunday) artisan cheese producers from throughout southern France gather above the town at L'Hospitalet to show off their wares. In addition to the cheeses, there are folk concerts and other events.

Mid-July Rocamadour: Les Éclectiques de Rocamadour (☏06.08.53.45.46; ☵www.leseclectiques.org). Living up to its name, this week-long music festival ranges from classical ballet to Eastern European folk groups. Ticket-only concerts take place in the Basilique St-Sauveur and the château.

Mid-July to mid-August St-Céré and around: Festival de St-Céré et du Haut-Quercy (☏05.65.38.28.08, ☵www.festival-saint-cere.com). Three weeks of opera, recitals, orchestral works and chamber music in St-Céré (including the châteaux of Montal and Castelnau), Beaulieu, Martel, Cahors and Souillac. Tickets required.

July and August Rocamadour: Les Mercredis de Rocamadour. Every Wednesday, a varied programme of street theatre, concerts and open-air cinema takes place in the old town or the valley below. Tickets required for some events.

Third weekend in July Souillac: Souillac en Jazz (☏05.65.37.81.56; ☵www.souillacenjazz.net). International jazz acts let rip in the streets of Souillac for six days of concerts, films, exhibitions and a feast on the final night. The big-name, ticket-only events take place outdoors next to the abbey church.

July 23 Martel: Foire à la Laine. A wool fair, in which the best fleeces are judged under the market hall.

Second weekend in August Souillac: Festival du Mime Automate (☏05.65.37.07.07). About fifteen groups of mime artists give performances (mostly free) in the streets of Souillac on the Friday and Saturday.

Early September Rocamadour: Semaine Mariale. The week dedicated to the Virgin Mary is celebrated with pilgrimages, prayers and Masses, including torchlight processions to the Chapelle Notre-Dame.

Last weekend in September Rocamadour: Rassemblement Européen de Montgolfières. Hot-air balloons take off from the valley below Rocamadour; for the best views, take up position early on the Belvédère in L'Hospitalet.

Markets

The main **markets** in this region are at: Beaulieu-sur-Dordogne (Wed & Sat); Bretenoux (Tues & Sat); Martel (Wed & Sat); St-Céré (Sat & first and third Wed of month); and Souillac (Fri). In addition to the weekly market, an annual truffle market takes place in Martel between mid-December and the end of January.

Souillac and southeast towards Rocamadour

Traffic-ridden **Souillac** suffers from being the major gateway to both Sarlat and the Périgord Noir to the west (see Chapter four) and to the upper reaches of the Dordogne valley to the east, and though the completion of the A20 *autoroute* has brought some relief, it will never be a particularly pretty place. The town's main attraction is the **Église Ste-Marie**, with its exquisite carvings, but it also has a small enclave of old streets, which are worth a quick wander, and an engaging museum containing a large collection of automated dolls.

Immediately upstream from Souillac, the valley is dominated by the new A20 road-bridge, but a few meanders of the river later and you're back among quiet lanes and unspoilt scenery. One place to head for is **Lacave**, a village on the south bank with some passably interesting limestone caves. From Lacave you can take an attractive detour south along a tributary river, the Ouysse, as it cuts its way through a mini-gorge in the limestone plateau, to visit a 600-year-old working flour mill. Continue on this route and you will eventually find yourself in Rocamadour (see p.265).

Arrival and information

Getting to Souillac by public transport is not a problem since it lies on the main Paris–Toulouse **train** line. The gare SNCF lies just over a kilometre northwest of town; take avenue Jean-Jaurès and then avenue Martin-Malvy, which will bring you out at the west end of avenue Gambetta, the old quarter's main east–west artery. **Buses** from Sarlat, Brive, Gourdon and St-Denis-Près-Martel (on the Brive–Figeac train line) mostly stop at the train station or the Sarlat road, while Eurolines buses (tickets from Voyages Belmon, avenue de Sarlat; ⊤05.65.37.81.15, ⓦwww.eurolines.fr), en route between Toulouse and London, Brussels, Hanover and Amsterdam, stop in central Souillac on the place du Foirail, a large square to the east of the main N20 (here called boulevard Louis-Jean-Malvy). This square also provides the most convenient **car parking** for the centre.

You can **rent cars** from the Renault garage on the road to Martel (Ets Sanfourche; ⊤05.65.37.73.03, ⓕ05.65.32.77.15) and bicycles from Carrefour du Cycle, 23 avenue de Gaulle (⊤05.65.37.07.52), the northern extension of boulevard Louis-Jean-Malvy. Bikes and canoes are also available from Copeyre Canoë (⊤05.65.37.72.61, ⓦwww.copeyre.com), next to the campsite (see opposite).

The **tourist office** (July & Aug Mon–Sat 9.30am–12.30pm & 2–7pm, Sun 10am–noon & 3–5pm; rest of year Mon–Sat 10am–noon & 2–6pm; ⊤05.65.37.81.56, ⓦwww.tourisme-souillac.com) is located in the town centre on boulevard Louis-Jean-Malvy, just across the road from place du Foirail. **Internet** access is available at Virtual Dragon on Place des Tailles (Mon–Wed 9am–8pm; Fri & Sat 9am–9pm; Sun 2–7pm). Souillac's main **market** takes place on Friday mornings: stalls selling fresh foods set up around the abbey church, while clothes and so forth can be found on place du Foirail.

Accommodation

Among Souillac's **hotels**, the best-value budget option is the homely *Auberge du Puits*, 5 place du Puits (⊤05.65.37.80.32, ⓦwww.auberge-du-puits.fr; ①; closed Sun evening, Mon & Dec–Jan), on a pretty square opening onto avenue Gambetta, which also serves copious country cooking with menus starting at €14. Moving up a notch, there's *Le Pavillion Saint-Martin*, at 5 Place Saint-Martin (⊤05.62.32.63.45, ⓦwww.hotel-saint-martin-souillac.com; ③), housed in a sixteenth-century mansion, and furnished with a variety of bright, comfortable rooms, ranging from old-fashioned floral to eye-assaulting reds and oranges. Souillac's most upmarket hotel is *La Vieille Auberge*, 1 rue de la Recège (⊤05.65.32.79.43, ⓦwww.la-vieille-auberge.com; ③; closed Nov to mid-Dec), across the old quarter at the west end of avenue Gambetta. The rooms in the main building are well equipped but disappointingly functional, while the annexe rooms, near the Musée de l'Automate, are larger, brighter and nicely furnished. Facilities include a pool, sauna and jacuzzi and a fine restaurant with menus from €22 (Jan–March closed Sun eve, Mon & midday Tues). Arriving by train, you could try the welcoming *Puy d'Alon*, a couple of minutes' walk south of the station down avenue Jean-Jaurès at 1 rue de Présignac (℡05.65.37.89.79, ⓦwww.hotel-dupuydalon.com; ❸), offering reasonable rooms, a pool and a small garden.

There's no shortage of hotels in the surrounding hills, either. You could do worse than check into the *Hôtel Chastrusse*, 10km southwest of Souillac in Nadaillac-de-Rouge (℡05.65.37.60.08, ⒺFrancis.chastrusse@wanadoo.fr; ❷; closed Mon & Nov). It's a delightfully unpretentious place with rooms either in the old block – the nicer option – or modern bungalows around the pool, with an excellent restaurant serving regional fare including home-made *confit*, foie gras and other meat preserves – they expect you to have a hearty appetite (menus from €11).

Souillac's nearest **campsite** is *Les Ondines* (℡05.65.37.86.44; closed Oct–April), a large, three-star municipal site down by the river to the south of town. Alternatively, with your own transport, you could head for the more luxurious four-star *Domaine de la Paille Basse* (℡05.65.37.85.48, ⓦwww.lapaillebasse .com), in a lovely, high spot 9km northwest of Souillac, signed off the D15 to Salvignac.

The Town

Souillac's two major sights are located in the compact old quarter to the west of boulevard Louis-Jean-Malvy. A handy landmark to aim for is the semi-ruined **belfry** of St-Martin church, partially destroyed in the Wars of Religion, on the southeast corner of the old centre.

Walk one block west of the belfry and you come to a wide open space dominated by the beautiful Romanesque **abbey church of Ste-Marie**. Its Byzantine domes are reminiscent of the cathedrals of Périgueux and Cahors, though on a smaller scale, while its largely unadorned interior conveys a far greater sense of antiquity. The first church on this site belonged to a priory founded in the tenth century which became an abbey five hundred years later. Badly damaged during both the Hundred Years' War and Wars of Religion, the church was restored in the seventeenth century before being abandoned during the Revolution. Sadly, only fragments of the **Romanesque sculptures** that once graced the main, west portal have survived, but those that do remain – now reassembled inside the west door – are superb. Those on the tympanum tell the story of a local monk, Théophile, who was dismissed from the treasury for corruption. Desperate to regain his position, he is said to have made a pact with the Devil, but then fell seriously ill and, full of remorse, beseeched the Virgin Mary for forgiveness. His luck was in – the final scene depicts Théophile's dream of the Virgin accompanied by St Michael driving the Devil away. Other carvings portray sin as an entangled couple, chaos as a seething mass of beasts devouring each other, and redemption as God staying Abraham's hand as he prepares to sacrifice his son Isaac. The greatest piece of craftsmanship, however, is the bas-relief of the prophet Isaiah to the right of the door. Fluid and supple, it appears that the elongated, bearded figure clutching his parchment and with one leg extended is dancing for joy as he proclaims news of the coming of the Messiah.

Behind the church to the west, the **Musée de l'Automate** (Jan–March, Nov & Dec Wed–Sun 2.30–5.30pm; April, May & Oct Tues–Sun 10am–noon &

3–6pm; June & Sept daily 10am–noon & 3–6pm; July & Aug daily 10am–7pm; €5) contains an impressive collection of nineteenth- and twentieth-century mechanical dolls and animals which dance, juggle and perform magical tricks. Most come from the once-famous Roullet-Decamps workshops in Paris and include such pieces as a life-sized 1920s jazz band, Charlie Chaplin and a woman doing the twist. Look out, too, for the irresistible laughing man.

Eating

The hotel **restaurants** mentioned above are all worth trying, but the best place to eat in Souillac – despite its inconvenient location about 1km south of the centre along boulevard Louis-Jean-Malvy – is *Le Redouillé*, 28 avenue de Toulouse (℡05.65.37.87.25; closed Sun eve & Mon, also Jan to mid-Feb; menus from €17), which makes innovative use of local produce to create such mouthwatering dishes as smoked duck breast and a *pastilla* of duck *confit* and *cèpes*). For simpler meals and snacks, try *Le Beffroi*, 6 place St-Martin (closed Sun eve & Mon; *plats du jour* at €6.50, menus €10–25), beneath the old bell tower, particularly if it's warm enough to eat out on the terrace under the wisteria. Alternatively, if you fancy a more novel eating experience, head for the *Lycée d'Hôtellerie*, avenue Roger-Couderc (reservations required, ℡05.65.27.03.00; closed weekends and during school hols; lunch menu at around €15, at least €20 in the evening), on a hill to the west of the old quarter, where you act as guinea-pigs for trainee chefs and waiting staff. Don't be put off, though – the food is generally excellent and you'll need to book up several days in advance.

Lacave and south towards Rocamadour

Following the Dordogne upstream along the D43 you soon leave the *autoroute* behind as you crest the hill and drop down to **LACAVE**, on the river's south bank 14km southeast of Souillac. A cavernous hole in the limestone cliffs overshadowing the village marks the entrance to a series of underground lakes, together making up the **Grottes de Lacave**, which can be visited on 1hr 30min guided **tours** (daily: March 10am–noon & 2–5pm; April–June 9.30am–noon & 2–6pm; July 9.30am–12.30pm & 1.30–6pm; Aug 1–25 9.30am–6pm; Aug 25 to Sept 30 9.30am–noon & 2–5.30pm; closed Oct–March; €7.70; ⓦwww .grottes-de-lacave.com). You travel the first few hundred metres by electric train, after which there's a lift up to the kilometre-long gallery resplendent with all manner of stalactites and stalagmites, from petrified "waterfalls" to great organ pipes. But the highlight here are the magical reflections in the lakes' mirrored surfaces – at one point they also use ultraviolet light to reveal the glittering fluorescence of the "living" water-filled formations while the older, dry deposits remain lost in the darkness.

There's a **hotel-restaurant** right opposite the cave entrance, but it's over-priced and very basic. If you can afford it, treat yourself instead to a meal at the Michelin-starred *Le Pont de l'Ouysse* (℡05.65.37.87.04; ⓦwww .lepontdelouysse.fr; ❶; closed mid-Nov to Feb), which also has fourteen immaculate rooms. It's in an idyllic spot beside the tumbling River Ouysse about a kilometre west of Lacave on the Souillac road, and you can enjoy a four-course feast here for a very moderate €32 (restaurant closed for lunch on Mon & Tues; menus from €32–120). Heading 2km out of Lacave in the oppo-site direction, on the D23 northeast to Meyronne, more rustic fare is available at the friendly *Ferme-Auberge Calvel* (℡05.65.37.87.20; reservations required; July to mid-Sept daily except Thurs; rest of year weekends only; menus at €13.50, €15 including wine), which also offers basic *camping à la ferme* with space for a handful of tents (closed mid-Sept to March).

From where the River Ouysse empties into the Dordogne just west of Lacave, a minor road heads south along the Ouysse, winding its way up the valley side with grand views as you climb up to the plateau near the village of **CALÈS,** 5km later. The village is a neat and tidy place with little more than a couple of decent **hotels** in its centre. The more appealing of the two is *Le Petit Relais* (☎05.65.37.96.09, ⑭www.le-petit-relais.fr; ❸; closed Christmas & New Year school hols; restaurant closed Sat lunch; good regional menus from €16), with a rustic atmosphere, spick-and-span rooms and a pretty, flowery terrace.

At Calès the road from Lacave joins the D673 and turns east before dropping back down to the Ouysse, which has here carved out a mini-gorge. For an interesting diversion, turn left just after crossing the river and about a kilometre later you'll reach the **Moulin de Cougnaguet**, a fourteenth-century fortified mill, which ceased working commercially only in 1959. During thirty-minute guided tours (daily: April to mid-Oct 10am–noon & 2–6pm; €3.50; ⑭www .cougnaguet.com), the enthusiastic owner points out its many defensive features – including arrow slits and sluice gates which, when opened from inside the mill, unleashed a torrent of water to sweep away anyone attempting to ford the millrace – and also puts the mill through its paces. Standing close to 1.5 tonnes of stone spinning at eighty revolutions per minute you get a real feel for the pent-up power of the water waiting calmly upstream.

From the mill it's only another 12km to Rocamadour. The D673 takes you back up onto the plateau and into Rocamadour from the north, but for a more dramatic approach follow the footpath (the GR6) along the valley. It runs alongside the River Ouysse past another mill – this was once big wheat country and even in high summer the Ouysse, part of which flows underground, never dries up – before turning eastwards along the River Alzou. Gradually the valley closes in until you round a bend and see the pilgrimage town of Rocamadour clinging to the cliff like a lost city.

Rocamadour

Halfway up the northern cliff-face of the deep and abrupt canyon of the River Alzou, the spectacular setting of **ROCAMADOUR** is hard to beat, with the turrets and spires of the **Cité Religieuse** at its heart, sandwiched between the jumbled roofs of the medieval town and the château's crenellated walls above. However, as you draw closer the spell is broken by the constant stream of pilgrims and more secular-minded visitors, particularly in summer, who fill lanes lined with shops peddling incongruous souvenirs. The main reason for Rocamadour's popularity – going back centuries – is the supposed miraculous properties of the statue of the **Black Madonna**, enshrined in the Cité's smoke-blackened **Chapelle Notre-Dame**. Modern tourists are also courted with a number of secondary attractions, including two wildlife parks, scattered on the plateau to the north and east of town. Even if those don't appeal, it's worth venturing up to the hamlet of **L'Hospitalet**, on the cliff to the east of Rocamadour, for the finest views of the town.

The first mention of Rocamadour's Chapelle Notre-Dame dates from 1105, although evidence suggests pilgrims started coming here as early as the ninth century. However, things really got going when a perfectly preserved body was discovered in a rock-hewn tomb beside the chapel in 1166. It was promptly declared to be that of Zacchaeus, later **St Amadour**; according to one legend, Zacchaeus – a tax-collector in Jericho at the time of Christ – was advised by the Virgin Mary to come to France and lived out his years in Rocamadour as a hermit. As tales of the saint and associated miracles spread, the faithful began to arrive in droves from all over Europe. St Bernard, numerous kings – including Henry II of England and Louis IX of France (St Louis) – and thousands of ordinary mortals crawled up the **Grand Escalier** (the pilgrims' staircase) on their knees to pay their respects and to seek forgiveness or cures. Others came simply to plunder the shrine – among them the Young King Henry (see box on p.274) – but they were easily outclassed by the Huguenots, who, in 1562, tried in vain to burn St Amadour's corpse and finally resigned themselves to hacking it to bits instead. In the meantime, centuries of warfare and plague led to a decline in the number of pilgrims. The buildings gradually fell into ruin until the bishops of Cahors, hoping to revive the flagging pilgrimage, financed a massive reconstruction in the early nineteenth century and so gave us the Rocamadour we see today.

Arrival and information

Getting to Rocamadour by public transport is awkward. There are no buses, and Rocamadour-Padirac **gare SNCF**, on the Brive–Figeac line, lies 4km away to the northeast. If you don't want to walk into town (it can be rather precarious as you're essentially walking along the side of a main road!), you can call a taxi (Taxi Floch ☎05.65.33.63.10). Note that the station is rarely staffed,

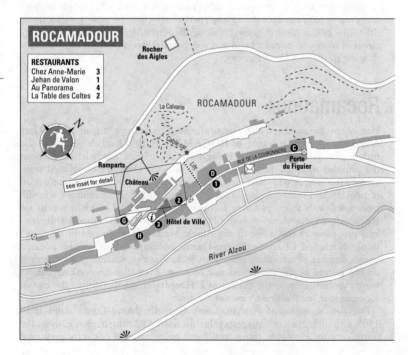

and there's no ticket machine so check the times of return trains carefully on arrival and buy a return ticket beforehand. Since Rocamadour is pedestrianized, if you arrive **by car** you'll have to park in L'Hospitalet or else in the valley several hundred metres below the town. A **lift** (daily Feb–April & Oct 8.30am–6pm; May, June & Sept 8.30am–7pm; July & Aug 8.30am–8pm; Nov 1–15 & Christmas school hols 9am–7pm; closed Nov 15 to Jan 31, except the school hols; every 3min; €2 one-way, €3 return) links the town's main street, rue de la Couronnerie, with the Cité Religieuse above, while **cable cars** (daily April & Oct 9am–6pm; May, June & Sept 8am–8pm; July & Aug 8am–10pm; Nov–March 10am–noon & 2–5pm; every 3min; €2.50 one way, €4 return) depart from just east of the Cité to emerge on the cliff-top near the château.

Rocamadour boasts two **tourist offices**: the main one is located on the western outskirts of L'Hospitalet (April daily 10am–noon & 2–6pm, closed Sat am; May to mid-July & mid-Aug to mid-Sept daily 10am–12.30pm & 2–6.30pm; mid-July to mid-Aug daily 9.30am–7.30pm; mid-Sept to mid-Nov Mon–Fri 10am–noon & 2–6pm, Sat & Sun 2–5.30pm; mid-Nov to March Mon–Fri 10am–noon & 2–5.30pm; ☎05.65.33.22.00, ⊕www.rocamadour.com), and you'll find a second on rue de la Couronnerie next to the Hôtel de Ville (daily April to mid-July & mid-Aug to mid-Sept 10am–12.30pm & 1.30–6pm; mid-July to mid-Aug 10am–7.30pm; mid-Sept to mid-Nov 10am–noon & 2–5.30pm; mid-Nov to March 2–5pm; same telephone number as above). Both sell a number of useful publications, including a town map (€1) and various walking and cycling guides, and can also help book accommodation and change money (3.5 percent commission or minimum of €2.50 for traveller's cheques

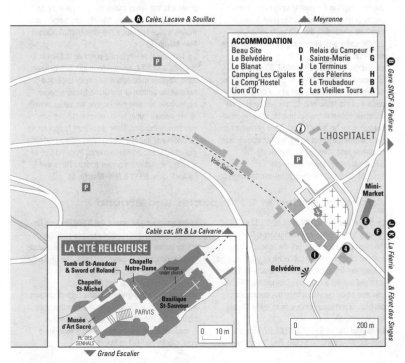

or cash), or there's a 24-hour ATM outside the L'Hospitalet office. This office also has **bikes** for rent (€10 per day).

The **mini-market** in L'Hospitalet sells basic provisions (see p.270), but otherwise the nearest food shops are in Alvignac, 7km northeast, which is also where you'll find the closest **pharmacy**.

Accommodation

One of the benefits of staying over in Rocamadour is that you can enjoy the town at its quietest in the early morning and late evening, and the **hotels** here are not too expensive. The downside is that everywhere is completely booked up in summer for miles around, and most places close during the winter months. Outside these periods, there are some good options, with a choice between central Rocamadour, the modern places in L'Hospitalet or somewhere in the surrounding countryside.

The two closest **campsites** are in L'Hospitalet: the two-star *Relais du Campeur* (☎05.65.33.63.28, ⓦwww.relais-du-campeur.com; closed Oct–March), situated next to the *Comp'Hostel* (see below), and under the same management; and the three-star *Camping Les Cigales* (☎05.65.33.64.44, ⓦwww.camping-cigales .com; closed Sept to late June), a little further east.

Hotels in the old town

Grand Hôtel Beau Site rue de la Couronnerie ☎05.65.33.63.08, ⓦwww.bw-beausite.com. Rocamadour's top hotel occupies a lovely old mansion – its entrance all flagstone floors and oak beams – right in the centre, with more modern rooms in an annexe across the road. It has an excellent restaurant, the *Jehan de Valon* (see p.272), and a pool 2km away. Closed mid-Nov to early Feb. ④

Lion d'Or Porte Figuier ☎05.65.33.62.04, ⓦwww.liondor-rocamadour.com. Just inside the old city gate at the east end of rue de la Couronnerie, this old-fashioned, family-run hotel is the cheapest option in the old quarter, offering small but adequate en-suite rooms. Their restaurant is right across the street with good but equally no-nonsense food. Closed Nov–March. ②

Sainte-Marie place des Senhals ☎05.65.33.63.07 ⓦwww.hotel-sainte-marie.fr.

If the *Lion d'Or* is closed, try this friendly place halfway up the Grand Escalier. The rooms are simple and some quite small, but the location and restaurant with tasty food and superb views down into the valley make up for it (*plat du jour* at €10.50 and menus €14–28). The terrace also makes a nice spot for a pre-dinner drink. Closed Nov–March. ③

Le Terminus des Pèlerins place de la Carreta ☎05.65.33.62.14, ⓦwww.terminus-des-pelerins .com. Another good option on rue de la Couronnerie at the bottom of the Grand Escalier. Some rooms have terraces overlooking the valley, while all are decked out in fresh, modern colours with spacious bathrooms. Their restaurant is popular for its traditional and regional cuisine, with a *plat du jour* at €10 and brasserie menus from €14.50 or €17 in the restaurant proper (closed Thurs eve & Fri April–June & Oct & Nov–March). ③

Accommodation in L'Hospitalet and around

Le Belvédère L'Hospitalitet ☎05.65.33.63.25, ⓦwww.lebelvedere-rocamadour.com. This is not the most beautiful hotel, but the rooms are decent and the location, on the cliff edge as you come into L'Hospitalet from Rocamadour – is superb. Make sure you ask for a room overlooking the Cité. You can also enjoy the views from the restaurant's big picture windows (menus from €15). Closed Nov–March. ③

Le Blanat Blanat ☎05.65.33.68.27, ⓦwww .gite-blanat-rocamadour.com. Four kilometres east

of Rocamadour, just across the N140 and in a tiny hamlet, *Le Blanat* offers three simple *chambre d'hôte* rooms in the main building plus *gîte d'étape* accommodation in a converted barn. The GR6 runs close by. ②

Le Comp'Hostel place de l'Europe ☎05.65.33.73.50, ⓦwww.hotel-comp-hostel.com. No views from this modern hotel a hundred metres north of the *Belvédère*, but acceptable rooms – some with a small terrace – and a swimming pool. Closed mid-Oct to March. ③

Le Troubadour Belveyre ☎ 05.65.33.70.27, ✆ troubadour@rocamadour.com. A small, spruce hotel, 1km north of L'Hospitalet on the D673, with flowery, en-suite rooms, where you can truly get away from the crowds. There's a pool and bikes, and a residents-only restaurant, open for dinner only (menus from €23; closed July, Aug). Closed mid-Nov to mid-Feb. ④–⑤

Les Vieilles Tours Lafage ☎ 05.65.33.68.01, ⓦ www.viellestours-rocamadour.com. A surprisingly affordable country-house hotel offering a spot of luxury 3km west of L'Hospitalet just off the D673. Set in large grounds, the buildings have been beautifully restored – one room incorporates a mini-tower – and there are splendid views all around, as well as a pool and an excellent restaurant (menus from €25; Mon–Sat closed midday). Half-board obligatory July & Aug. Closed mid-Nov to March. ④

The Town

Rocamadour is divided into two parts: the medieval town containing the **Cité Religieuse**, where you'll find all the most important sights, and the cliff-top hamlet of **L'Hospitalet**, one and a half kilometres by road to the east. The old town is easy enough to find your way around since there's just one street, pedestrianized rue de la Couronnerie, which runs west from Porte du Figuier – one of Rocamadour's four medieval gateways – to the wide stone staircase leading up to the sanctuaries roughly 300m later. Follow the main road east from Porte du Figuier, on the other hand, and it will take you winding up the valley side to L'Hospitalet; pedestrians can use the quieter Voie Sainte, a narrow lane which branches off left after a couple of hundred metres.

La Cité Religieuse

The steep hillside above rue de la Couronnerie supports no fewer than seven chapels, known collectively as "Les Sanctuaires", or the **Cité Religieuse**. There's a lift dug into the rock-face (see p.267), but it's far better to climb the 216 worn and pitted steps of the **Grand Escalier**, up which the devout once dragged themselves on their knees to the doors of the Cité. Inside lies a small square, the parvis, completely hemmed in by the various chapels. The largest of these, lying straight ahead of you, is the **Basilique St-Sauveur** (daily:

△ Rocamadour

5

THE UPPER DORDOGNE VALLEY AND ROCAMADOUR | Rocamadour

July & Aug 8am–9pm; rest of year 8.30am–6.30pm, though these times can vary), which up until 1900 provided lodgings for pilgrims who couldn't afford anything better. There's nothing much to see inside, however, so turn left for the little **Chapelle Notre-Dame** (same hours), nestled against the rock and the basilica wall, where the miracle-working twelfth-century Black Madonna resides. The crudely carved statue, less than 70cm tall, still wears a faint smile despite her mutilated state, though the adult-featured Jesus balanced on her knee looks decidedly out of sorts. The rest of the chapel is unremarkable, but note the empty recess in the rock outside, where St Amadour's body was found, and a rusty sword protruding from the cliff above. According to local tradition this is Durandal, the trusty blade of the legendary Roland whose heroic exploits are recorded in the twelfth-century *Chanson de Roland* (*The Song of Roland*), though it's not revealed exactly how it got here from northern Spain, where Roland supposedly died in battle against the Moors in 778. Beside the chapel's ornately carved door there are also some faded fifteenth-century frescoes depicting a macabre fight between the Living and the Dead.

Opposite the Chapelle Notre-Dame two incredibly well-preserved twelfth-century polychrome paintings of the Annunciation and the Visitation adorn the **Chapelle St-Michel**, which, along with the other four chapels, is only accessible on guided tours of the Cité (1hr: July & Aug Mon–Sat 8.30am–5pm, Sun 2–5pm; other school holidays Mon–Fri 8.30am–noon & 2–5pm; rest of the year for groups by appointment only; note that these times can vary and that tours leave according to demand; ☎05.65.33.23.23, ✆relais.des.remparts@wanadoo. fr; €5.50, or €10 including museum and ramparts); tickets are available from the guide on the parvis. However, don't worry if you miss it, since most of the chapels' remaining carvings, reliquaries and other treasures have been removed for safe-keeping to the **Musée d'Art Sacré** (daily: July & Aug 9am–7pm; Sept–June 9.30am–noon & 2–6pm; note that these times may vary; €4.70), located immediately inside the Cité gate on the left as you enter. The museum is dedicated to the French composer *Francis Poulenc* (1899–1963), who wrote his *Litanies à la Vierge Noire* after visiting the shrine in 1936, and contains a wide-ranging and well-presented collection of religious art from the twelfth to the twentieth century. Best are the earlier exhibits from Rocamadour's golden age (the twelfth and thirteenth centuries), such as the pilgrims' insignia, *sportelles*, which were made nearby on the place des Senhals, a fragment of stained glass from St-Sauveur and reliquaries covered in beautiful Limoges enamel.

East of the Cité there's a sandy esplanade and the cable car (see p.269) which will take you to the top of the cliff. Alternatively, you can walk up the shady zig-zag path, *La Calvarie*, past tableaux depicting the Stations of the Cross, or take a more direct and steeper path to come out near the château, a full 150m above the river below. While the château itself, a mostly nineteenth-century reconstruction, is private, you can walk round the **ramparts** (daily 8am–8pm; €2.60) for vertiginous views.

East to L'Hospitalet

The road leading west from the château brings you almost immediately to the first of Rocamadour's two wildlife parks, the **Rocher des Aigles** (☎05.65.33.65.45, ⊛www.rocherdesaigles.com; April–June & Sept Mon–Fri 1–5pm, Sun & school hols 1–6pm; July & Aug daily noon–6pm; Oct & Nov Mon–Fri 2–4pm, Sun & school hols 2–5pm; closed Dec–March; €6.50), a breeding centre for birds of prey. The cages seem uncomfortably small, but with a production rate of nearly a hundred chicks a year the birds can't be overly stressed about it. There's a film explaining the breeding programme, which aims to reintroduce a number of rare species to the wild, and you can also see the hatching room where scrawny chicks warm themselves under sun lamps. Best, though, are the thirty-minute flying demonstrations (April–June & Sept Mon–Fri 2pm, 3pm & 4pm, Sun & school hols also at 5pm; July & Aug 12.30–5.30pm roughly every hour; Oct & Nov Mon–Fri 3pm, Sun & school hols 3pm & 4pm), in which a dozen or so condors, fish eagles and other such majestic birds are allowed to soar free over the valley.

Continuing east about 700m along the cliff edge you join the main road, the D673 from Calès (see p.205), and then after another 150m reach the modern, plate-glass **tourist office** (see p.267), which marks the western extent of L'Hospitalet. The name refers to a pilgrims' hospital founded on the cliff-top here in the thirteenth century, of which only a few ruined walls and a chapel containing a copy of the Black Madonna remain. A crossroads lying immediately to the northeast of the chapel represents the centre of modern L'Hospitalet, which consists of a scattering of hotels, cafés and shops.

A hundred metres east of this crossroads, along the D36 to Gramat and Figeac, is **La Féerie autour du Rail**, essentially a landscaped model railway, albeit an amazingly detailed one, which took more than fifteen years to build. Forty-five-minute mini-*son et lumière* shows (daily April to mid-June & Sept four shows 11.15am–4.30pm; mid-June to mid-July five shows 11.15am–5pm; mid-July to Aug eight shows 10.45am–5.50pm; Oct 2.45pm & 4.15pm; closed Nov–March; €6.50; Ⓦwww.la-feerie.com) highlight different scenes: not only do trains scuttle about, but there are also automated cars, boats, fairs and fire engines, and even skiers and hot-air balloonists. It may not be everyone's cup of tea, but the whole thing is extremely well done and full of imaginative touches, and it's a must for kids.

Another couple of hundred metres east along this same road is the second of the wildlife parks, the **Forêt des Singes** (April & 1–15 Sept daily 10am–noon & 1–5.30pm; May & June daily 10am–noon & 1–6pm; July & Aug daily 9.30am–6.30pm; 16–30 Sep daily 1–5.30pm; Oct daily 1–5pm; Nov Sat & Sun 10am–noon & 1–5pm; €7; Ⓦwww.la-foret-des-singes.com); it's one of the better such parks, with some 130 Barbary apes roaming twenty hectares of oak and scrubland in relative freedom. Again, the aim is conservation – so far around six-hundred young monkeys have been reintroduced to North Africa. The monkeys continue feeding, grooming and playing regardless of human intruders, but the best time to visit is during the cool of the early morning or evening and in early summer when the youngsters are frisking about.

Even if none of the above sights appeals, it's still worth coming up to L'Hospitalet for the tremendous views of the medieval Cité from the cliff-edge *belvédère*, beside the eponymous hotel, just south of the central crossroads. It's stunning at any time, but particularly magical at night when the buildings are illuminated (March–Nov & Christmas hols). To return to Rocamadour from here, take the Voie Sainte, the old pilgrims' route running down beside the *belvédère* hotel to arrive beside the Porte du Figuier around eight minutes later.

Eating

Eating in Rocamadour is a mixed bag and there are a good few greasy fast-food joints and tourist traps. In general, the best of Rocamadour's **restaurants** are those attached to the hotels (see p.268), notably the superb *Jehan de Valon*, listed on p.272, along with a few more everyday recommendations; note that most places are closed in winter. The local speciality, which you'll find on most menus, is *Rocamadour*, a round disc of goat's cheese, often served on toast or with a walnut salad, or occasionally flambéed in brandy or drizzled with honey. Elsewhere in the region it is known as *Cabécou*, but cheeses produced around Rocamadour warrant their own special *appellation* – and even their own festival (see box on p.217). You can buy it at shops selling the inevitable foie gras and other regional produce, but for other **picnic fare** the only proper food shop hereabouts is the mini-market (April to mid-Oct) beside the *Comp'Hostel* in L'Hospitalet.

Chez Anne-Marie rue de la Couronnerie ☎05.65.33.65.81. A jolly little place just west of the *Hôtel Beau Site* that's popular for its cheap-and-cheerful mix of grills, omelettes and salads in addition to regional dishes. They also serve a vegetarian menu (€14.50). *Plat du jour* at €9 and menus from €11.50 with lots of choice.

Jehan de Valon rue de la Couronnerie ☎05.65.33.63.08. You need to book ahead for a table in this elegant restaurant, with panoramic views over the Alzou valley. Their seasonal menus include a good variety of fresh fish as well as local specialities, with prices starting at €21; count on at least €40 for the *à la carte* menu. Simpler fare is on offer in their adjoining brasserie

where a *plat du jour* will set you back around €9 and a three-course menu €14. Closed mid-Nov to early Feb.

Au Panorama L'Hospitalet. If you're looking for somewhere to eat in L'Hospitalet, try this unpretentious café-restaurant across from the *Belvédère* hotel. They serve an eclectic mix of regional dishes, salads and snacks. Salads cost €7–14, while full-blown menus start at €17. Closed mid-Nov to March.

La Table des Celtes rue de la Couronnerie. A few doors west from *Chez Anne-Marie* along the main street, this little crêperie isn't bad for a light lunch. Crêpes come in at around €7, salads €9 and a full menu €12.

Upstream from Lacave to Beaulieu-sur-Dordogne

Upstream from Lacave (see p.264), the Dordogne meanders in a northeasterly direction through walnut orchards and dozing villages. Its valley sides occasionally rise up to form rocky crags, the most dramatic of which are those around **Gluges** where the river has carved the **Cirque de Montvalent** out of the plateau. On the dry uplands to the north of Gluges, the market town of **Martel** somehow escapes the worst of the crowds, despite the attractions of its well-preserved medieval centre, while further east the river glides past the typical Quercy village of **Carennac**. The çarved portal on its abbey church is, like Souillac's, a superb example of Romanesque craftsmanship, and its cloister harbours a beautifully expressive entombment scene from the Renaissance era. With a couple of good hotels, Carennac also makes a good base for exploring this stretch of river, or for a foray south to the enormous limestone sinkhole known as the **Gouffre de Padirac**. From the bottom of the cavity you follow an underground river by boat and on foot through equally oversized caverns hung with gigantic stalactites.

At **Bretenoux**, some 10km to the east of Carennac, the River Dordogne turns northwards. Though the town has little to recommend it beyond a pretty medieval square and reasonable transport connections, the nearby **Château de Castelnau** makes a worthwhile excursion, if only to admire the fortress's impregnable defences or to take in the views from its ramparts. A short hop north of Bretenoux, **Beaulieu-sur-Dordogne** is a more attractive spot with its riverside walks and lanes of ancient houses, and is also home to another finely carved Romanesque portal ornamenting its abbey church.

Public transport along this stretch of the river is relatively good. St-Denis-Près-Martel, 7km from Martel, lies on both the Brive–Figeac and Brive–Aurillac train lines, while services on this latter line also call at Bretenoux-Biars, the nearest station for both Bretenoux and Beaulieu. Bus services are more comprehensive, covering Martel, St-Denis, Carennac, Bretenoux, Beaulieu and St-Céré, though they can involve a bit of backtracking.

From Lacave to Creysse and Gluges

From Lacave, the D23 takes a leisurely route northeastwards as it tracks the twists and turns of the Dordogne. Seven kilometres upstream you come to the sleepy hilltop village of **MEYRONNE**, where the road crosses from the south bank to the north. In the eleventh century the bishops of Tulle, northeast of Brive, built a château here to defend what was then an important bridging point. Their residence is now a splendid **hotel**, *La Terrasse* (℡05.65.32.21.60, ⓦwww.hotel-la-terrasse.com; ❹; closed Nov to early March), complete with spiral stairs, old chimneys and an excellent restaurant (menus from €20).

On the north side of the bridge turn right onto the tiny D114, which hugs the river for the next 4km east to **CREYSSE**. This idyllic hamlet, with its dinky market hall and fast-running stream, sits in the lee of a knuckle of rock where a fortified gate and scraps of wall are all that remain of a château once owned by the viscounts of Turenne (see p.180). Their twelfth-century **chapel**, standing immediately above the village (Mon, Thurs & Fri 3–5pm, Sun 10.30am–noon), has fared rather better, and is worth a look for its *pisé* floor and unique arrangement of two absidial chapels. There's a simple but very appealing **hotel**, the *Auberge de L'Île* (℡05.65.32.22.01, ⓦwww.logis-de-france.com; ❸; closed Nov to mid-March), straddling the stream in the village centre, whose plane-tree-shaded terrace is hard to resist; they offer a brasserie menu of salads, omelettes, sandwiches and so on in addition to full meals (menus from €19). Campers, meanwhile, should head for the excellent two-star **campsite**, the *Camping du Port* (℡05.65.32.27.59, ⓦwww.campingduport.com; closed Oct–April), down beside the Dordogne a hundred metres east of the village – **bikes** and **canoes** are available for rent on site from Port Loisirs (℡05.65.32.20.82, ⓦwww.portloisirs.com).

The cliffs lining the Dordogne valley get more dramatic upstream from Creysse. For the most impressive scenery, follow the D23 northeast for a good two kilometres and then branch off right along the D43. The road quickly narrows down to a single track – with passing spaces – cut into the rock. You emerge two kilometres later at another huddle of houses, **GLUGES**, whose prime attraction is its location under the cliffs and its views south to the **Cirque de Montvalent**, where the meandering river has carved a great semicircle out of the cliffs; for a sweeping panorama, climb up to the hilltop Belvédère de Copeyre, signed off the main road one kilometre above Gluges to the east. Otherwise, apart from a quick wander around Gluges' medieval lanes, the only thing to do is relax on the terrace of the welcoming **hotel** *Les Falaises* (T05.65.27.18.44, Wwww.les-falaises.com; ❸; closed Nov–Easter; restaurant for hotel guests from €25, evenings only) at the western entrance to the village. There's a three-star riverside **campsite** opposite, also called *Les Falaises* (T05.65.37.37.78, F05.65.32.20.40; closed Oct–April), though it's not under the same management. You can also rent canoes and bikes from Copeyre Canoë (T05.65.37.33.51, Wwww.copeyre.com) down by the water.

Martel

Five kilometres north of Gluges, and fifteen east of Souillac, **MARTEL**'s medieval centre is built in a pale, almost white, stone, offset by warm reddish-brown roofs. Another Turenne-administered town (see p.180), its heyday came during the thirteenth and fourteenth centuries when the viscounts granted certain freedoms, including the right to mint money, and established a royal court of appeal here. Martel was occupied briefly by English forces during the Hundred Years' War and suffered again at the hands of the Huguenots in the sixteenth century, but on the whole the compact old centre has survived remarkably intact.

The exception to this is the ramparts, which have been dismantled to make way for the wide boulevard which now rings Martel's pedestrianized centre. Take any of the lanes leading inwards and you will soon find yourself in the cobbled main square, **place des Consuls**. It is mostly taken up by the eighteenth-century *halle*, scene of a busy market on Wednesday and Saturday mornings, but on every side there are reminders of the town's illustrious past, most notably the grand Gothic **Palais de la Raymondie** on the square's east side, now occupied by the *mairie*. Begun in 1280, it served as both the Turenne law courts and fortress, hence the large square tower – one of seven which gave the town its epithet, *la ville aux sept tours*. On the square's south side is another of the towers – a circular five-storey turret belonging to the **Maison Fabri**. According to tradition, this striking building is where Young King Henry, son of Henry II, died in 1183 (see box below).

The tale of Young King Henry

At the end of the twelfth century, Martel provided the stage for one of the tragic events in the internecine conflicts of the Plantagenet family. When Henry Plantagenet (King Henry II of England) imprisoned his estranged wife Eleanor of Aquitaine, his sons took up arms against their father. The eldest son, also **Henry** (nicknamed the Young King since he was crowned while his father was still on the throne), even went so far as to plunder the viscountcy of Turenne and Quercy. Furious, Henry II immediately stopped his allowance and handed over his lands to the third son, Richard the Lionheart. Financially insecure, and with a considerable army to maintain, Young King Henry began looting the treasures of every abbey and shrine in the region. Finally, he decided to sack the shrine at Rocamadour (see p.265), making off with various artefacts, including Roland's famous sword, Durandal. This last act was to mark his downfall, for shortly afterwards he fled to Martel and fell ill with a fever. Guilt-ridden and fearing for his life, he confessed his crimes and asked his father for forgiveness. Henry II was busy besieging Limoges, but sent a messenger to convey his pardon. On the messenger's arrival in Martel, Young Henry died, leaving Richard the Lionheart heir to the English throne.

One block south of here, rue Droite leads east to the town's main church, **St-Maur**, built in a fiercely defensive, mostly Gothic style, with a finely carved Romanesque tympanum depicting the Last Judgement above the west door.

Practicalities

Without your own transport, the best way to get to Martel is via one of two **bus services**, both of which stop on the ring road to the southwest of the centre. One route comes from Brive and the second from Souillac, passing through Martel on its way to the **gare SNCF** at **ST-DENIS-PRÈS-MARTEL**, 7km to the east, on the Brive–Figeac and Brive–Aurillac train lines; if there's no convenient bus heading back from St-Denis to Martel, call Mme Daubet (℡05.65.37.34.87) for a taxi. In season, a **tourist train** runs along a splendid stretch of decommissioned line from Martel towards St-Denis and back – but not as far as St-Denis station – along cliffs 80m above the Dordogne (departures by diesel train: April–June & Sept Tues & Thurs 2.30pm; July & Aug Mon, Tues, Thurs & Fri 11am, 2.30pm & 4pm, Sat 2.30pm; €7 return; departures by steam train: April–Sept Sun & hols 11am, 2.30pm & 4pm, also mid-July to end-Aug Mon–Thurs same times; €9.50 return; ℡05.65.37.35.81). It departs from the otherwise disused station two hundred metres south of town; reservations are recommended.

The small **tourist office** in the Palais de la Raymondie on place des Consuls (April–June, Sept & Oct Mon–Sat 9am–noon & 2–6pm; July & Aug daily 9am–7pm; Nov–March Mon–Fri 9am–noon & 2–5pm; ℡05.65.37.43.44, ⓦwww .martel.fr) can provide further information about the train and about Martel's **festivals**, including the annual wool fair (see box on p.217 for more).

For an overnight **stay**, try *Auberge des 7 Tours* (℡05.65.37.30.16, ⓦwww .auberge7tours.com; ❷; closed Feb school hols; menus from €12.10; restaurant closed Sat lunch, Sun eve, & Mon) on Martel's northern outskirts on the road to Les Quatres-Routes, or, if you have money to spare, the expensive but absolutely gorgeous 🛏 *Relais Ste-Anne* (℡05.65.37.40.56, ⓦwww.relais-sainte-anne.com; ❺–❻; closed mid-Nov to mid-March), south across the ring road from the old centre down rue du Pourtanel. It occupies a former girls' boarding school set in gardens with its own chapel, pool and beautifully appointed rooms. For campers, there's a decidedly spartan municipal **campsite**, *La Callopie* (℡05.65.37.30.03, ℻05.65.37.37.27; closed Oct–April), with two stars, just north of town, opposite the *Auberge des 7 Tours*.

The best place to look for somewhere to **eat** is place des Consuls, where *Plein Sud* serves a decent pizza (€7–11) amongst other things (menus from €12). Just off the square's southeast corner, on rue Senlis, *La Mère Michèle* (℡05.65.37.35.66; closed Sun eve & Wed) is an attractive place and popular for its well-presented dishes at prices that won't break the bank (*plat du jour* €7.50; menus from €11). Another good choice, where you should always ring ahead, is the *Fermes Auberge Moulin à Huile de Noix* (℡05.65.37.40.69; closed Nov–March), attached to a working walnut-oil mill 3km east off the D703 to St-Denis and Bretenoux. Don't be put off by the modern concrete exterior; the dining rooms upstairs have a bit of character and the food – all regional dishes with a strong preference for duck and walnuts – is both excellent and plentiful (menus from €15).

Carennac and around

CARENNAC is without doubt one of the most beautiful villages along this part of the Dordogne valley. It sits on a terrace above the river's south bank

16km or so east of Martel; backtrack to Gluges and then head upstream on the D43 for the prettiest route. It is best known for its typical Quercy architecture and the richly carved tympanum of its Romanesque priory church. Founded in the eleventh century by Benedictine monks, the priory grew rich from pilgrims en route to Santiago de Compostela. Sacked during the Hundred Years' War (see p.388), it then enjoyed a second renaissance in the late fifteenth and sixteenth centuries, when the church was restored and a château built alongside. But by the 1700s the rot had set in as the monks became lazy and corrupt, and the priory was finally closed after the Revolution.

You get one of the best views of the village's towers and higgledy-piggledy russet-tiled roofs as you approach from the west. The houses cluster so tightly round the priory buildings that it's hard to tell them apart, but if you follow the road along the river bank, you'll soon find a gateway leading to a cobbled courtyard and the **Église St-Pierre**. Straight ahead of you the church's twelfth-century tympanum – in the style of Moissac and Cahors – dominates its recessed west door. The carvings are in exceptionally good condition: Christ sits in majesty with the Book of Judgement in his left hand, surrounded by the four symbols of the Evangelists and animated portraits of the Apostles (the twelfth is missing), ranged on either side. There's not a lot to see inside, but the church makes an atmospheric venue for the occasional concert.

South of the church, still inside the courtyard, you gain access to the **cloister and chapter house** (same hours as the tourist office, opposite; €2). The cloister's Romanesque and flamboyant Gothic galleries were somewhat mutilated during the Revolution, but they are in any case overshadowed by the late-fifteenth-century, life-size *Mise au Tombeau* (*Entombment of Christ*) on display in the chapterhouse. So supremely detailed is the sculpture that you can even see the veins in Christ's hands and legs. Joseph of Arimathea and Nicodemus, holding either end of the shroud, are richly attired as a fifteenth-century nobleman and pilgrim respectively, while behind them Mary Magdalene, her hair a mass of ringlets, ostentatiously wipes away a tear. The sculpture was overseen by the master-craftsman Jean Dubreuilh, who later worked on the cloisters of Cadouin and Cahors (see p.210 and p.300 respectively). Five statues by his apprentices are displayed nearby, alongside a sixteenth-century bas-relief telling the story of the life and passion of Christ in eight scenes (to be read from bottom left to top right) – beautifully crafted but lacking the simplicity and power of the Entombment.

In the sixteenth century the *doyens* (deans) in charge of the priory and its dependant churches built themselves a grand residence, referred to nowadays as the **château**, abutting the church's north wall. Its most famous occupant was François de Salignac de La Mothe-Fénelon (see p.255) who served as *doyen* of Carennac for fifteen years from 1681; according to local tradition he penned his infamous book *Télémaque* here. A few stone chimneypieces and the great hall's painted ceiling remain from this era, but little else, since the building has been partially modernized to serve as an **Espace Patrimoine** (Easter–June & Oct Tues–Fri 10am–noon & 2–6pm; July–Sept Tues–Sun same hours; closed Nov–Easter; free). Displays cover the geography, history, architecture and economy of the Dordogne valley from Bretenoux downstream to Souillac; it's not hugely exciting but provides a good overview of what the region has to offer. Staff here also organize a broad range of guided visits (to Carennac, Martel and Souillac, for example, some in English) and workshops based on the art and history of the Dordogne valley; contact the Service Animation du Patrimoine (☎05.65.33.81.36, ✉patrimoine-vallee-dordogne@wanadoo.fr) for further information.

Practicalities

Carennac's nearest **gare SNCF** is at Vayrac, 8km northwest on the other side of the river, on the Brive–Aurillac line; call ☎05.65.32.40.32 if you need a **taxi**. However, services are more frequent to St-Denis-Près-Martel, 10km to the west (see p.275), on the Brive–Figeac line. **Buses** from Gramat, St-Céré and Vayrac (with connections to Brive, St-Denis and Biars-Bretenoux) will drop you beside the *mairie* on the south side of town. Carennac's helpful **tourist office** is located in the priory courtyard (Jan–March & Oct Mon–Sat 10am–noon & 2–5pm; April–June & Sept Mon–Sat 10am–noon & 2–6pm; July & Aug daily 10am–12.30pm & 2–7pm; Nov–Dec Mon–Fri 10am–noon & 2–5pm, Sat 2–5pm; ☎05.65.10.97.01, ⓦwww.tourisme-carennac.com). They also have **Internet** access, for which you'll need a prepaid telephone card.

The village boasts two comfortable and reasonably priced **hotels**, both with pools and good restaurants specializing in traditional regional cuisine. Smarter of the two is the *Auberge du Vieux Quercy*, on the D20 immediately south of the village (☎05.65.10.96.59, ⓦwww.vieuxquercy.com; ❹; closed mid-Nov to March), whose restaurant offers well-priced menus from €20 (closed for lunch Mon–Fri). The alternative is the more rustic *Hôtel Fénelon* on the main street to the east of the château (☎05.65.10.96.46, ⓦwww.hotel-fenelon.com; ❸; closed Jan to mid-March, also Fri & Sat lunch except in July & Aug; restaurant from €20.50). There's also a good municipal **campsite**, *L'Eau Vive*, beside the river 1km east of Carennac (☎05.65.10.97.39, ⓕ05.55.28.12.12; closed mid-Oct to April), where you can also rent canoes in season from Saga Team (☎05.55.28.84.84, ⓦwww.dordogne-soleil.com).

In addition to the above hotels, you can also **eat** well, if more simply, immediately west of the château at *Le Prieuré*. It's primarily a crêperie, but they also do good big salads, omelettes and so on (*plat du jour* €10; menu at €17). There are also a few restaurants worth seeking out in the countryside around Carennac. For something special, try the *Côté Jardin* (☎05.36.38.49.51; reservations required; weekday menu at €17, or €24.50 at weekends), just north of Tauriac, a pretty village roughly 3km east of Carennac on the other side of the river. The well-prepared dishes using ultra-fresh ingredients taste their best on summer evenings under the fairy lights. The *Relais de Gintrac* (☎05.65.38.49.41; Oct–April closed evenings, also closed two to three weeks in Sept; menus from around €12), in the hamlet of Gintrac, about 3km from Carennac southeast along the D30, is a popular if isolated place, at the opposite end of the spectrum, offering wholesome country cooking washed down with well-priced wines.

The Gouffre de Padirac

Not surprisingly, local legend holds the Devil responsible for opening the gaping mouth of the **Gouffre de Padirac** (1hr 30min guided tours daily: April–July 6 & Sept 9am–noon & 2–6pm; July 7–31 9am–6pm; Aug 8.30am–6.30pm; Oct 9am–noon & 2–5pm, Nov school hols 10am–noon & 2–5pm; ⓦwww.gouffre-de-padirac.com; €8) in the middle of the limestone plateau 10km south of Carennac. The hole is over 30m wide and 75m deep, its sides festooned with dripping ferns and creepers, though the sense of mystery is somewhat diminished these days by the presence of a lift-cage built against the side. Rather than the Devil, the chasm was probably formed by a cave roof collapsing centuries ago; locals took refuge here during the Hundred Years' War and probably long before. The cave system was not properly explored, however, until 1889 when spectacular stalactites – the biggest a staggering 75m tall – and lakes were discovered.

The visit starts with a half-kilometre-long **boat trip** along an underground river, after which you walk on past barrages and massive cascades formed by calcite deposits over the millennia. The lakes are pretty, but the most notable feature here is the sheer scale of the formations and the height of the passages carved out of the rock, reaching nearly one hundred metres at their highest. Be warned, though: it is very, very touristy and best avoided at weekends and other peak periods, when you'll wait an age for tickets. And in wet weather you'll need a waterproof jacket.

The nearest **gare SNCF** is Rocamadour-Padirac, more than 10km to the west, from where you could take a **taxi** (☎05.65.33.63.10). There's a **tourist office** (Mon–Fri 9am–noon & 2–6pm; ☎05.65.33.47.17, ⓦperso.orange .fr/paysdepadirac) in Padirac village, a couple of kilometres south of the *gouffre*, while the best **accommodation** hereabouts is the ivy-covered *Auberge de Mathieu* (☎05.65.33.64.68, ⓦwww.aubergedemathieu.com; ❷; closed mid-Nov to mid-March; menus from €15), 300m south of the *gouffre* on the D90, with plain rooms but a nice terrace and garden. Alternatively, *Les Chênes* (☎05.65.33.65.54, ⓦwww.campingleschenes.com; closed mid-Sept to April) is a very well-organized four-star **campsite** just south of the *Auberge*, with a bar, restaurant and pool.

Bretenoux and around

Some 10km east of Carennac, the *bastide* town of **BRETENOUX**, founded in 1277 by the barons of Castelnau, sits on the south bank of the River Cère just upstream from where it joins the Dordogne. It was obviously a pretty little place at one time – the cobbled and arcaded **place des Consuls** behind the tourist office is a delight, especially on **market** days (Tues & Sat am) – but these days the town suffers from a busy main road and too much modern development. With its transport connections, however, Bretenoux is a useful staging post for the nearby towns of St-Céré and Beaulieu-sur-Dordogne (see p.281 & p.280).

It also lies within striking distance of the **Château de Castelnau** (30min guided tours daily: April 10am–12.30pm & 2–5.30pm; May & June daily 9.30am–12.30pm & 2–6.30pm; July & Aug daily 9.30am–7pm; Sept–March 10am–12.30pm & 2–5.30pm; €6.10), 2.5km to the southwest, which is one of this region's most outstanding examples of medieval military architecture. The great fortress dominates an abrupt knoll to the east of the village, its sturdy towers and machicolated red-brown walls visible for miles around. It dates from the mid-tenth century, but took on its present form – a triangular fort with a massive square keep and three round towers, the whole lot surrounded by ramparts and dry moats – during the Hundred Years' War under the ownership of the powerful barons of Castelnau. By the early eighteenth century, however, the Castelnau family had died out. Their abandoned château was sacked during the Revolution, sustained even greater damage in a fire in 1851 and was left to rot until it was salvaged, somewhat bizarrely, in 1896 by a celebrated tenor of the Parisian Comic Opera, Jean Mouliérat. He threw his fortune into its restoration and into amassing the valuable but rather dry collection of religious art and furniture from the fifteenth to eighteenth century which populates the handful of rooms you see on the guided tour. The views from the ramparts, though, are extremely impressive; on a clear day you can just make out the towers of Turenne, nearly thirty kilometres to the north (see p.180).

As you exit the castle's inner enclosure, turn left along the walls to take a quick look in the **Collégiale St-Louis**. Built of the same red stone and with powerful buttresses, this little Gothic church contains a fine fifteenth-century polychrome statue of the Baptism of Christ – note the startled expression of the angel holding his clothes – and a macabre treasure in the form of a bone from the arm of St Louis (alias King Louis IX of France). In 1970 the relic was taken to St Louis in America to commemorate the founding of the city.

Practicalities

Bretenoux's **gare SNCF**, on the Brive–Aurillac line, is officially known as Bretenoux-Biars since it is located some 2km north of the River Cère in the town of Biars; if you're heading east from here, the journey to Aurillac takes you through a very picturesque and otherwise inaccessible valley, a favourite for walkers and cyclists. **Taxis** wait outside the station (or call ☎05.65.10.90.90) and there are **buses** (operated by Chauvac; ☎05.65.38.08.28) from here to Bretenoux and St-Céré, but only on Wednesday, Thursday and Saturday; in Bretenoux the bus stop is on the main road, rue de la Libération, near the post office a couple of hundred metres south of the river.

On the way you'll pass the well-organized **tourist office** (July & Aug Mon–Sat 9am–noon & 2–6pm, Sun 9.30am–12.30pm; rest of year Mon–Sat 9am–noon & 2–6pm; ☎05.65.38.59.53, ⓦwww.ot-bretenoux.com) on rue de la Libération just south of the bridge. Carry on a bit further south along this road and you'll find Cycles Bladier (☎05.65.38.41.56), where you can rent **bikes** for a trip out to the Château de Castelnau.

Bretenoux has nothing to recommend in the way of **hotels**, but there are a couple of excellent small, family-run places 6km northeast on the D14 in the village of **PORT-DE-GAGNAC**, on the north bank of the Cère. The slightly more homely of the two is the *Auberge du Vieux Port* (☎05.65.38.50.05, ⓦwww.logis-de-france.fr; ❸; closed Dec 20–Jan 31), serving very good-value regional cuisine (menus from €12; Nov–Feb closed Sun eve). Just beyond it, the *Hostellerie Belle Rive* (☎05.65.38.50.04, Ⓕic05.65.38.47.72; ❸; closed two weeks at Christmas; restaurant closed Nov–March Sat & Sun, also closed April–June, Sept & Oct Fri eve, Sat lunch & Sun eve; menus €14–39) is a touch more upmarket – both the rooms and the restaurant. The other possibility is to stay in St-Céré, 9km to the south, or Beaulieu-sur-Dordogne, 8km to the north (see p.281 and p.280 respectively), or at one of the local **campsites**. The three-star *La Bourgnatelle* (☎05.65.38.44.07, Ⓔcontact@dordogne-vacances.fr; closed Oct–March), located on an island just across the bridge from Bretenoux, is not only the best option but also the most convenient. Otherwise, there's a quiet *camping à la ferme* (☎05.65.38.52.31; closed Oct–May) on the river bank a couple of kilometres west along the D14 towards Prudhomat. **Canoe** rental is available in July and August at the *Bourgnatelle* campsite (☎05.65.38.44.07, Ⓔbourgnatel@aol.com).

Again, Bretenoux has nothing much to offer in the way of **places to eat**, beyond a few cafés along the main road. The hotels in Port-de-Gagnac represent your best option, or you could head south to St-Céré (see p.281).

Beaulieu-sur-Dordogne and beyond

At Bretenoux the River Dordogne turns northwards as it leaves the Lot *département* for neighbouring Corrèze. The valley here is wide and industrial – with factories such as Andros churning out enough jam to make this the "jam capital" of Europe – but things get better as you recross the river 8km north of Bretenoux to find **BEAULIEU-SUR-DORDOGNE** beautifully situated on a wide bend in the river. It's a perfectly proportioned town, with an abbey church that boasts another of the great masterpieces of Romanesque sculpture, and yet is refreshingly untouristy. It even appears to be in gentle decline.

Arriving from Bretenoux, the main road skirts south of Beaulieu's compact and semi-pedestrianized core of old streets. On its way it passes through a large square, **place Marbot**, which represents the town's modern centre, off which rue de la République leads north to **place du Marché**. Here, you'll find some nicely jaded stone and half-timbered buildings, along with the twelfth-century **abbey church of St-Pierre**, a surprisingly large building, whose architecture reflects its position on the border between Limousin and Languedoc. The pairs of rounded arches piercing the belfry, for example, are typical Limousin styling, while the subject matter and style of carving on the magnificent **south portal** belongs firmly to the south. This doorway is unusually deep set but even a quick glance reveals similarities between the sculptures here and those at Souillac, Carennac and Moissac, both in the design and the wonderfully fluid lines; it is likely that they were all fashioned by craftsmen from Toulouse. In this case, the tympanum is presided over by an Oriental-looking Christ with one arm extended to welcome the chosen on the Judgement Day. Around him a mass of angels and Apostles, even the dead rising from their graves below, seem bursting with vitality.

It won't take long to cover the rest of Beaulieu, but it's worth devoting half an hour or so to wandering its maze of lanes. In particular, there are a number of half-timbered houses along **rue Ste-Catherine**, running east from place du Marché, while if you head northwest along **rue de la République** and **rue de la Chapelle** you'll pass some handsome sculpted facades before emerging beside the **Chapelle des Pénitents** in an attractive spot on the river bank. This twelfth-century chapel now makes a splendid venue for the occasional art exhibition or concert; if it's open, it's worth popping in to see the collection of religious art. In July and August traditional wooden **gabarres** depart from the river bank here for a one-hour jaunt upstream (℡05.55.27.68.05).

Upstream from Beaulieu, the Dordogne valley becomes wilder as you enter the first forest-covered foothills of the Massif Central. It makes for a lovely drive along the D12 as far as **ARGENTAT**, the last town of any size on the river, where it's easy to while away an hour or so sitting at one of the waterside cafés. Beyond Argentat, however, the Dordogne changes character entirely, due to a series of hydroelectric dams that turn the river into a succession of huge reservoirs.

Practicalities

It's just over 6km from Beaulieu to the Bretenoux-Biars **gare SNCF** (see p.279). Unfortunately there are no connecting **buses**, although you can get to Beaulieu by bus from Brive (℡05.55.86.07.07); services stop on place du Champs-de-Mars, a large shady square just west of place Marbot. If you need a **taxi** in Beaulieu, call ℡05.55.91.02.83. The **tourist office** is located on the south side of place Marbot (April, June & Sept daily 10am–12.30pm &

2.30–7pm; July & Aug daily 9am–7pm; Oct–March Mon–Sat 10am–12.30pm & 2.30–5pm; ☏05.55.91.09.94, ⓦwww.beaulieu-sur-dordogne.fr). It's well organized and offers **Internet access**.

The town has a decent range of **hotels**. Most appealing is the riverside ⚘ *Les Charmilles*, 20 bd St-Rodolphe-de-Turenne (☏05.55.91.29.29, ⓦwww .auberge-charmilles.com; ❹), on the northeast side of town, a bright, clean, cheerful place with just eight rooms and a flowery terrace – you'll eat well here, too; menus start at €18 (restaurant closed Tues & Wed except June–Sept). A good alternative is the *Hôtel Le Turenne*, in a former abbey on place Marbot (☏05.55.91.10.16, ⓔhotelleturenne@wanadoo.fr; ❸), with spacious rooms and a fine restaurant (closed Mon lunchtime & Jan; menus from €20). Cheaper rooms (not all en suite) are available further north in the old-fashioned *Étape Fleuri*, on place du Champ-de-Mars (☏05.55.91.11.04; ❶–❷; closed Fri eve, Sat & Sun from mid-Nov to mid-March; lunch menus from €10, eves from €17), and there's a welcoming ⚘ **HI hostel** (☏05.55.91.13.82, ⓔbeaulieu@fuaj .org; dorm bed €12; closed Oct–March) at the far end of rue de la Chapelle in a magnificent half-timbered and turreted building; it has comfortable modern dorms, a well-equipped kitchen, and breakfast is available as are meals on request for groups of four or more.

Beaulieu's two **campsites** are located on an island either side of the main road-bridge. The three-star *Camping des Isles* (☏05.55.91.02.65, ⓦwww .camping-des-iles.net; closed mid-Oct to mid-April), to the north of the bridge, is the better value and more attractive of the pair. The two-star municipal site, *Camping du Pont* (☏05.55.91.11.31, ⓕ05.55.91.24.73; closed mid-Sept to mid-June), lies immediately to the south. The latter offers **canoe** rental in July & August (☏05.55.28.84.84), while Adventures Dordogne Nature (ADN; ☏05.55.28.86.45, ⓦwww.adndordogne.org), which also has **bikes**, is over at the *base nautique* on the other side of the river; you can drive round or get there via a footbridge to the north of the town centre.

Once again, the hotel **restaurants** are the best places to eat, but there's also a nice little crêperie, *Au Beau-Lieu Breton*, on rue du Presbytère, behind the church, where you can get crêpes and salads for around €6–10 (closed Mon eve, Tue & Dec).

St-Céré and around

About 9km south of Bretenoux on the River Bave, a minor tributary of the Dordogne, you come to the medieval town of **St-Céré**, dominated by the brooding ruins of the *Château de St-Laurent-les-Tours*. The château is now home to an engaging museum dedicated to tapestry designer Jean Lurçat, who revitalized contemporary French tapestry, but the town's prime attraction is its old centre peppered with picturesque half-timbered houses.

St-Céré also makes a useful base for exploring the surrounding area. The town lies on the border between the empty but glorious wooded hills of the Ségala to the east and south, and the dry limestone *causse* to the west. However, the region's most impressive sight, and one not to be missed, is the Renaissance **Château de Montal**, 2km west of St-Céré, with its sculpted facade and grand staircase. From there you can loop south via the **Grottes de Presque** – a limestone cave with a tremendous variety of unusually colourful concretions – to arrive at the lip of the Cirque d'Autoire for dramatic views over the russet-red roofs of **Autoire** village, which provide a splash of colour in the valley far below.

On the way back to St-Céré the route passes through another captivating little village, **Loubressac**, which can hardly have changed for centuries.

It's possible to reach St-Céré by bus from Bretenoux, Cahors and Figeac, but you'll need your own **transport** to explore the rest of the area. If you've got the energy to tackle some of these hills, you can always rent a bike in St-Céré (see opposite).

The Town

Arriving in St-Céré from the north, the first things you see are the two powerful keeps of the Château de St-Laurent-les-Tours, once part of a fortress belonging to the viscounts of Turenne (see p.180). The town itself sits in the valley to the southwest where the old houses cluster round place du Mercadial and place de l'Église. These two squares lie north and south respectively of rue de la République, the main shopping street cutting through the old centre which, at its southeast end, comes out into **place de la République**. This big, open square is where you'll find car parks, cafés and the town's main tourist facilities.

St-Céré owes its existence to the martyrdom of **Ste Spérie** in 780. Born the daughter of the then lord of St-Laurent, Sérenus, Spérie pledged her life to God at an early age, and when later she refused to marry a local nobleman, she was beheaded by her brother and buried on the river bank. Later a chapel was erected on the spot around which the town began to develop in the tenth century. It lay initially under the jurisdiction of the counts of Auvergne, but was transferred to the Turenne viscounts in 1178. They beefed up the fortress and, as usual, granted the town a certain degree of autonomy. Its heyday didn't arrive, however, until after the fifteenth century when St-Céré's wealthy merchants began investing in the noble houses which can still be seen today.

The best of these lie in the streets to the north of rue de la République, notably around **place du Mercadial**, which, with its fountain and cobbles, is particularly appealing; to find it, walk one block north from rue de la République and turn left along rue du Mazel. You come out opposite the town's most eye-catching building, the **Maison des Consuls**, where the administrative council used to meet – it now hosts various free art exhibitions in summer. Beneath a steeply pitched tile roof, the building's most striking feature is the slightly overhanging upper storey of neatly layered brick in a timber frame. The same design is echoed in the **Maison Arnoud**, on the north side of the square, whose ground floor is a mere three metres wide. Rue St-Cyr, the lane to the right of this house, takes you east and then south past several elegant Renaissance buildings and into a recently renovated area of courtyards and alleys. Where rue St-Cyr eventually joins rue du Mazel, look out on the right for a particularly fine fifteenth-century residence with two round towers and a pair of escutcheons above the doorway.

There's less of interest on the south side of rue de la République, though the **church of Ste-Spérie**, largely rebuilt after the Wars of Religion, is worth a quick peek for its eighteenth-century altarpiece with a statue of Ste Spérie standing on the left. It was carved by a local monk who received 240 *livres* and, for some reason, four handkerchiefs for his pains.

St-Céré is rather prouder of another, more recent local artist, **Jean Lurçat** (1892–1966), who first came to the Lot to join the Resistance in 1941, then decided to settle in Château St-Laurent after the war. His wide-ranging talents took in sketching, painting, engraving and pottery, but he is best known for his big, bold tapestries, of which the most famous is the eighty-metre-long *Chant du Monde* (*Song of the World*), which portrays the vagaries of human existence and our inherent power for both good and evil. The tapestry is now on display in Angers, but you can get an idea of Lurçat's distinctive style – typically incorporating animals and birds, both real and fantastic, against dark blue or black backgrounds – by visiting the **Galerie d'Art Le Casino**, avenue Jean-Mouliérat (July–Sept daily 9am–noon & 2–6.30pm; rest of year daily except Tues same hours; free), 100m northeast of the old town; from place de la République walk north on boulevard Lurçat a short distance before turning right down avenue Jean-Mouliérat. Built as a casino in 1938 but never used, the gallery keeps at least thirteen Lurçat tapestries on permanent display.

You can see more of his work in his former studio in the **Château de St-Laurent-les-Tours** a kilometre or so above St-Céré – take avenue du Docteur-Roux heading northeast past the hospital and then follow the signs winding uphill. Of the Turenne fortress only the ramparts and two square towers remain, the smaller one dating from the late twelfth century and the taller, eastern tower from the 1300s. The rest of the castle was destroyed during the Wars of Religion, but around 1895 the then owner built himself a neo-Gothic mansion between the two towers. It is this building in which Jean Lurçat set up his studio in 1945 and which is now the **Atelier-Musée Jean Lurçat** (mid-July to Sept daily 9.30am–noon & 2.30–6.30pm; also two weeks at Easter same hours; ☎05.65.38.28.21; €2.50). Alongside his sketches and illustrations, a slide show of the *Chant du Monde* and a short biographical film, the museum's most interesting feature is the artist's unmistakable paintings covering the ceilings and doors.

Practicalities

The nearest *gare* **SNCF** to St-Céré is Bretenoux-Biars (see p.279), a good 10km to the north, from where there are **buses** on two days a week (Wed & Sat at around 12.30pm and 3pm; Chauvac; ☎05.65.38.08.28) on to St-Céré. You can also reach St-Céré by bus from Cahors via Gramat (also operated by Chauvac), and from Figeac (Cars Delbos; ☎05.65.38.24.19; ⓦwww.cars-delbos.com. All these services drop you on place de la République, on the north side of which you'll find the **tourist office** (July & Aug Mon–Sat 9am–noon & 2–7pm, Sun 10am–12.30pm; rest of year Mon–Sat 10am–noon & 2–6pm; ☎05.65.38.11.85, ⓦwww.tourisme-saint-cere.com). The office stocks English-language leaflets outlining a walking tour of the old centre and details of events in the area, of which the most important is the summer music festival (see p.261). For exploring the countryside around St-Céré, you can rent **bikes** from Peugeot Cycles, 45 rue Faidherbe (☎05.65.38.03.23), to the west of place de la République.

There are a couple of decent **hotels**, as well. You'll get a warm welcome at the Irish-French-run ⚇ *Hôtel Victor-Hugo*, 7 av des Maquis (☎05.65.38.16.15, ⓦwww.hotel-victor-hugo.fr; ❸; closed two weeks in March & three weeks in Oct), beside the old bridge in the southeast corner of place de la République. All the rooms, including the three family rooms with balconies, are en suite and have been decorated with flair by the chef, who also puts his artistic talents to good use in the restaurant (closed Mon & Oct–March also Sun eve; menus around €14–35). They also organize highly successful creative-writing weeks, golfing holidays and suchlike. The other option is the modern, more upmarket *Hôtel de France*, 139 av François-de-Maynard (☎05.65.38.02.16, Ⓔlefrance-hotel@wanadoo.fr; ❸; closed late-Dec to Jan), east off place de la République, with well-priced en-suite rooms, a pool and a flowery garden where you can eat out under a huge chestnut tree (Mon–Sat eves only, Sun & hols open for lunch & dinner; menu at €21). For campers, there's the three-star *Le Soulhol* **campsite** (☎05.65.38.12.37, ℱ05.65.10.61.75; closed Oct–April) beside the river, a short walk east of the *Hôtel Victor-Hugo*.

The *Victor-Hugo* is by far the best place to **eat** in St-Céré. Otherwise, there are cafés and brasseries around place de la République and place du Mercadial, where *Pizzeria du Mercadial* (pizzas €6–12.50; closed Sun & Mon, also two weeks in both Oct-Nov & March & the first week in June) is a popular spot. Just off the square on rue du Mazel, *Le Tama des Îles* (lunch menus from €12, eves from €14; closed Sun midday & Mon) is a convivial place which serves such exotic fare as spring rolls, samosas and rum punch. Or you could treat yourself to a meal at the Michelin-starred *Les Trois Soleils*, near the Château de Montal (see below). For picnic fodder, there's a small **market** on Saturday mornings on place du Mercadial and a much larger affair spreading throughout the old town on the first and third Wednesdays of the month.

Château de Montal

Two kilometres west of St-Céré, the **Château de Montal** (1hr guided tours: April–Sept daily except Sat 9.30am–noon & 2–6pm; €5) is a superb example of French Renaissance architecture. Its interesting history started in 1523 when Jeanne Balzac d'Entraygues, the widow of Amaury of Montal, started transforming the medieval fortress into a Renaissance palace, as was currently all the rage. But then came news that her eldest son, Robert, had been killed in Italy and poor Jeanne lost the heart to continue. Nevertheless the de Montal family continued to own the château up to the Revolution, after which it was bought by a certain Monsieur Macaire who gradually sold off the chimneypieces, sculptures and even the carved window surrounds. Rescue was at hand, however, in the form of Maurice Fenaille, a rich industrialist and patron of the arts, who bought the château in 1908 and began to restore it to its former glory. In just five years he managed to track down nearly everything that had been sold, including some of the original wall-coverings, and also filled the rooms with a fine collection of Renaissance and Louis XIII furnishings, before giving the whole caboodle to the state in 1913. Later, during World War II, Montal was chosen as a hiding place for thousands of paintings from the Louvre, including the *Mona Lisa*, which were moved from Paris for safekeeping.

As you approach, the rear of the château still exudes a thoroughly medieval air with its small windows, steep *lauze* roof and pepper-pot towers, but turn the corner into the **inner courtyard** and you're immediately transported to sunny Italy. The lovely pale stone of the two facades is worked into delicate carvings, including a frieze of mermaid-like sibyls and, above, busts representing three generations of the de Montal family: Jeanne is flanked by her husband and son Robert on the west wing, while her parents take pride of place over the front door.

The craftsmen went to work inside, too, on a magnificent **staircase** made from the same local limestone. As you climb up, notice the carving on the panels above, each bearing a different design, which gets finer and more elaborate towards the top. The rest of the interior can't quite compare, but there are some massive old oak tables, a good, homely kitchen and an excellent collection of tapestries, including a rare example featuring a pastoral scene with descriptive boxes of text, like an early cartoon.

As long as you make sure to book, you can combine a visit to Montal with a meal at 🍴 *Les Trois Soleils* (☎05.65.10.16.16, 🌐perso.orange.fr/trios.soleils; closed Nov to mid-Dec & Jan; Oct–March closed Sun eve to Tues midday

△ Autoire waterfall

inclusive), a one-star Michelin **restaurant** immediately west of the château surrounded by immaculate gardens. Their €30 menu is a bargain for such a perfect setting, and for dishes which see the best of the region's cuisine given a creative twist (other menus €35–70). Alternatively, you can eat in their grill, *Les Près de Montal* (same phone number), where menus start at €20 (closed mid-Oct to mid-March).

Grottes de Presque

About 3km southwest along the D673 from the Château de Montal the road cuts through a hillside as it climbs up onto the *causse*. When they were digging this road in 1825, engineers discovered the entrance to the **Grottes de Presque** (40min guided tours daily: mid-Feb to June & Sept 9.30am–noon & 2–6pm; July & Aug 9.30am–6.30pm; Oct to mid-Nov 10am–noon & 2–5pm; Ⓦ www.grottesdepresque.com; €6). The cave system is not only unusually accessible, with few stairs, but it also contains a marvellous variety of stalactites and stalagmites, some up to 10m high, as well as columns, semi-translucent curtains and glistening crystalline cascades. The other notable feature is the amount of colour, from pure white to grey, yellow and deep orange. This is the result of rainwater picking up iron, manganese and other minerals as it percolates through the 90m of rock above, minerals which are then deposited along with the calcite, drip by drip, inside the cave.

Autoire and Loubressac

Further west along the same line of hills, the River Autoire has carved an impressive canyon, the **Cirque d'Autoire**, into the limestone plateau; to get here from the Grottes de Presque, follow the D673 southwest for another 4km and then turn right on the D38. This brings you in above the *cirque* – for the best views, walk west from the car park for about five minutes, following the footpath across a bridge and up onto the opposite hillside. In the valley bottom, some 2km below you, lies the hugely pretty little village of **AUTOIRE** where the ochre-hued houses, including several rather grand piles built by nobles from St-Céré in the fifteenth and sixteenth centuries, snuggle round a very plain, solid Romanesque church.

The village also boasts a good **hotel** and pit stop in the form of the *Auberge de la Fontaine* (℡05.65.10.85.40, Ⓦ www.logis-de-france.fr; ❷; closed two weeks in Oct & Jan to mid-Feb, also Sun eve & Mon except in July & Aug) on the main street opposite the church, a simple country inn offering basic but well-kept rooms and family cooking washed down with local Coteaux de Glanes wines (menus from €10). In season there's also *La Cascade* across the road, serving crêpes, salads and regional dishes in a cheerful stone-walled room or on a terrace with views up to the *cirque* (closed Oct–March, also Mon eve & Tues except in July & Aug; menus from around €14).

It's only 8km back to St-Céré from Autoire, but it's worth taking a short diversion 6km northwest along the D135, little more than a country lane, to **LOUBRESSAC**. The narrow lanes of this fortified hilltop village are full of flowers and typical Quercy houses. You can't visit the château standing on the cliff edge, but there are grand views to be had from the lookout point immediately to the east of the village, taking in the whole sweep of the Dordogne, Bave and Cère valleys across to St-Céré and the châteaux of Castelnau and Montal.

In season a helpful **tourist office** (April, May & Sept Tues–Sat 2–6pm; June–Aug daily 10am–noon & 2–6pm; ☎05.65.10.82.18, ⓦwww.tourisme-saint-cere.com) opens up just outside Loubressac's southern gateway. There are also a couple of decent **hotels**. The simpler of the two is the *Lou Cantou* (☎05.65.38.20.58, ⓦwww.logis-de-france.fr; ❸; closed late Oct for three weeks, also Mon & Sun eve mid-Nov to March) on the southwest side of the village, with good views from its front rooms and the picture windows of its restaurant (menus from €12). Moving up a few notches, the modern *Relais de Castelnau* (☎05.65.10.80.90, ⓦwww.relaisdecastelnau.com; ❺; closed Nov–Easter, also Sun eve & Mon Oct & April) sits just outside the village on the main road west to Padirac. Apart from more splendid views, it also boasts a pool and a highly rated restaurant (menus from €17) but it has rather bland rooms and lacks atmosphere. There's also a very pleasant little three-star **campsite**, *La Garrigue* (☎05.65.38.34.88, ⓦwww.camping-lagarrigue.com; closed Oct–March), with a pool and restaurant among fields a couple of hundred metres south of the village.

Travel details

Trains

Bretenoux-Biars to: Aurillac (3–4 daily; 45min–1hr); Brive (3–4 daily; 35–40min); St-Denis-Près-Martel (3–4 daily; 15min); Vayrac (1–2 daily; 10min).
St-Denis-Près-Martel to: Brive (4–5 daily; 25min); Figeac (5–6 daily; 1hr); Gramat (5–6 daily; 20–30min); Rocamadour-Padirac (4–5 daily; 15–20min); Vayrac (2 daily; 5min).
Souillac to: Brive (6–9 daily; 25min); Cahors (6–9 daily; 40min–1hr); Gourdon (6–9 daily; 15min); Montauban (6–8 daily; 1hr 30min); Paris (5–6 daily; 4hr 30min); Toulouse (6–8 daily; 1hr 55min).

Buses

Carennac to: Gramat (school term Wed 1 daily; 20min); St-Céré (school term Mon–Fri 1–2 daily, rest of year Wed 1 daily; 20min); Vayrac (school term Mon–Fri 1–2 daily, rest of year Wed 1 daily; 10min).
Beaulieu-sur-Dordogne to: Argentat (July & Aug Mon–Sat 3 daily; 40min); Brive (school term Mon–Sat 1–3 daily, July & Aug Mon–Sat 1–2 daily, rest of year Tues, Thurs & Sat 1 daily; 1hr).
Bretenoux-Biars to: Bretenoux (Wed, Thurs & Sat 1–3 daily; 5min); St-Céré (Wed & Sat 2 daily; 15min).
Martel to: Brive (school hols Tues & Sat 1 daily; rest of year Tues 1 daily; 1hr); St-Denis-Près-Martel (Mon–Sat 1–2 daily; 10–15min); Souillac (Mon–Sat 2 daily; 35min).
St-Céré to: Bretenoux (Wed & Sat 2 daily; 5min); Bretenoux-Biars (Wed & Sat 2 daily; 10min); Cahors (Mon & Wed–Sat 1 daily; 1hr 45min); Carennac (school term Mon–Fri 1 daily, rest of year Wed 1 daily; 20min); Figeac (3–4 weekly; 1hr); Gramat (school term Mon–Sat 1–2 daily, rest of year Mon & Wed–Sat 1 daily; 30–40min).
Souillac to: Brive (school term Mon–Sat 1–2 daily, rest of year Tues–Thurs & Sat 1–2 daily; 1hr–1hr 15min); Martel (Mon–Sat 1 daily; 20–30min); St-Denis-Près-Martel (Mon–Sat 1 daily; 35–45min); Sarlat (3–5 daily; 50min).

6

The Lot valley and around

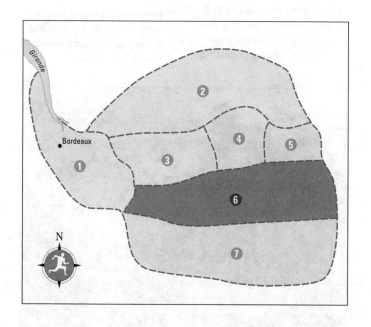

CHAPTER 6

Highlights

* **Pont Valentré** Cahors' signature sight is the fortified medieval bridge guarding the town's western approaches. See p.302

* **St-Cirq Lapopie** Perched high above the River Lot, this former feudal stronghold is now the preserve of craft shops and artisans. See p.306

* **Grotte de Pech-Merle** The combination of dazzling limestone formations and more than five hundred prehistoric drawings make this cave unmissable. See p.312

* **Figeac** Figeac's laid-back air belies its many attributes: medieval mansions, striking religious art and an engaging museum of writing. See p.314

* **Château de Bonaguil** One of the last medieval fortresses built in France, and now a magnificent ruin. See p.330

* **Bastides** Monpazier provides an almost perfect example of the region's myriad fortified towns. See p.335

△ Puy-l'Évêque

6

The Lot Valley and around

L
ike the Dordogne, the **River Lot** rises in the foothills of the Massif Central and is dammed in its upper reaches to form huge reservoirs. It begins to get more interesting, however, where it enters the Lot *département*, the boundaries of which roughly coincide with the old province of **Quercy**. Here the river has carved a wide gorge as it meanders back and forth in great lazy loops. In the east the land on either side is high and dry, part of the limestone plateau that extends north to the Dordogne and south almost to the Aveyron. Following the river westwards, the surrounding country suddenly becomes wooded and then gradually opens out into rolling farmland before the hills die out altogether where the Lot draws near to the Garonne.

The largest town in the Lot valley, and the capital of the *département*, is **Cahors**. It may lack the higgledy-piggledy charm of Sarlat or Bergerac, but compensates for this with a pleasingly workaday atmosphere and a wonderful location in the middle of a meander. It also boasts the best example of a fortified medieval bridge left in France, the **Pont Valentré**, while the country round about produces an extremely distinctive dark, almost peppery red **wine**.

The Lot valley is at its most picturesque upstream from Cahors. The scenery may not be as dramatic as the middle reaches of the Dordogne, but the cliffs here rise to considerable heights and host their fair share of perched fortresses and feudal villages. Foremost among these is **St-Cirq Lapopie**, one of the most spectacular sights along the valley, while the nearby **Grotte de Pech-Merle**, with its glittering rock formations and prehistoric cave art, draws almost as many visitors. Pech-Merle lies in the hills above the wild and pretty **Célé valley**, which leads northeast to **Figeac**, the Lot's second largest town. Figeac is a captivating place, just big enough to swallow the tourists who come to admire its web of medieval lanes, but not so large as to lose its intimacy.

North and west of Figeac stretches the **Causse de Gramat**, the biggest and wildest of the region's limestone *causses*. With its huge vistas, it makes a welcome change from the confining valleys and a great place for walking or cycling, though it has few notable sights beyond the village of **Assier**, in the far southeast, with its extraordinary church. On its western edge the Causse de Gramat suddenly gives way to a lovely area of gentle wooded hills known as the **Bouriane**. Again, there are no must-see sights, though its capital, **Gourdon**, a once-prosperous town built of butter-coloured stone, makes an engaging place to stay,

Late March to early April Figeac: Le Chaînon Manquant (☎05.34.51.48.88, ⊛www .reseau-chainon.com). Five days of contemporary performance art introducing up-and-coming talent from France and around the world. Mix of street performances and ticket events.

Late May or early June Puy-l'Évêque: Fêtes Médiévales. Over the weekend of Pentecôte (Whit Sunday), Puy-l'Évêque lets its hair down with all sorts of merry medi-eval japes: music, dance, games and a full-on medieval banquet (tickets required) on the Sunday night. Most events take place on place de la Truffière, by the tourist office.

Late May or early June Gramat: Festival Planète Animale (☎05.65.38.85.64, ⊛perso.wanadoo.fr/planete.animale). Workshops, theatrical events, films and walks with an environmental theme – for children and adults alike – over the Pentecôte (Whit Sunday) weekend.

Late June or early July Cazals: Encontre Chorégraphique (☎05.65.22.86.41). Well-regarded festival of contemporary dance held over three days (dates can vary, so if you do want to attend, it's best to call the number above to check). Mix of free and ticket-only events.

July and August Monpazier. Throughout the summer season, Monpazier stages a huge variety of events, including outdoor theatre and cinema, books and antiques fairs, concerts and crafts demonstrations.

Mid-July Cahors: Blues Festival (☎05.65.35.99.99, ⊛www.cahorsbluesfestival .com). Over five days, French and international artists bare their souls in the streets, Les Docks and the Théâtre de Verdure, rue Wilson (mostly free, though tickets required for some events).

Mid-July Assier: Assier dans tous ses États (☎05.65.40.42.42, ⊛www.festivalassier .com). Jazz and theatre festival with events taking place in local gardens, the village square, the church and the château courtyard. Some free events.

Mid-July to mid-August Cahors: Festival de St-Céré et du Haut-Quercy (☎05.65.38.28.08, ⊛www.festival-saint-cere.com). Three-week festival of opera,

---

and the nearby **Grottes de Cougnac**, with a smattering of prehistoric cave paintings and some exceptionally delicate limestone concretions, repay a visit.

Returning to the Lot valley, the river south of Cahors wriggles its way west-wards through vineyards and past ancient towns and villages. By far the most striking of these is **Puy-l'Évêque**. An outpost of the bishops of Cahors, the town's medieval and Renaissance houses jostle for space on a steep incline, reaching upwards like trees for light, though none is equal to the bishop's thir-teenth-century keep towering above. An even more dramatic sight lies in store in the country northwest of Puy-l'Évêque where the **Château de Bonaguil** is an outstanding example of late-fifteenth-century military architecture, its great bulk silhouetted against the wooded hillside.

Further downstream things begin to quieten down again as the valley flat-tens out towards **Villeneuve-sur-Lot**. Despite unattractive modern suburbs, Villeneuve holds a certain allure, with the river sliding through an old centre built of stone and warm red brick, and a decent supply of hotels and restaurants. Villeneuve – as its name indicates – was also one of the many "new towns", or *bastides*, founded in this area in the thirteenth and fourteenth centuries. The best examples of *bastide* architecture are to be found in the hills to the north, where the villages of **Monflanquin** and **Monpazier** seem hardly to have changed since the Middle Ages. The same can't be said for the much-altered **Château de Biron**, lying between the two, but its superb hilltop location makes it hard to resist.

orchestral works and chamber music, with ticketed concerts in Cahors' cathedral and Musée Henri-Martin.

Late July Cajarc: Africajarc (ⓦafricajarc.free.fr). Cajarc moves to an African beat during three days of concerts, exhibitions, crafts displays, markets and food stalls. Tickets required for the main concerts.

First weekend in August Gourdon: Grande Fête Médiévale. Gourdon lets rip with two days of junketing complete with jugglers, fire-eaters, musicians and the works. Entry €3.50.

Early August Puy-l'Évêque: Fête Votive. One of the area's most important local fêtes, lasting five days with a free dance every night, a funfair and a fireworks spectacular with music on the Sunday.

Early to mid-August Château de Bonaguil: Festival du Théâtre (ⓉⒸ05.53.71.17.17). The inner court and moats make a spectacular venue for this festival of French theatre held over eight or nine days. There's a play or other musical event every night (tickets required), as well as workshops, street theatre and lectures.

Mid-August Monflanquin: Journées Médiévales. Two days of mead, minstrels and merry japes as Monflanquin goes medieval. Jousting, banquets, siege engines – you name it. You can even rent costumes.

First Saturday in September Peyrusse-le-Roc: Spectacle Pyrosymphonique. The ruined towers of Peyrusse make a spectacular setting for a *son-et-lumière* cum fireworks display.

Markets

The region's main **markets** take place at Cahors (Wed & Sat); Cajarc (Sat); Figeac (Sat); Duravel (Sat); Fumel (Sun); Gourdon (Tues & Sat); Gramat (Tues & Fri); Luzech (Wed); Monflanquin (Thurs); Monpazier (Thurs); Monsempron-Libos (Thurs); Puy L'Évêque (Tues & Sat); and Villeneuve-sur-Lot (Tues, Wed & Sat).

Travelling by **public transport** is made relatively easy by two **bus services** running along the Lot valley from Cahors east to Figeac and west to Fumel, from where there's a connecting service downstream to Villeneuve. Other buses head north from Cahors and Figeac to Gramat, though Gramat is also served by trains on the Figeac–Brive main line. If you're planning to use the buses a lot, you'll need the departmental timetables for the Lot and Lot-et-Garonne available at larger tourist offices; otherwise contact the transport information desk of the relevant Conseil Général (Lot ⓉⒸ05.65.53.27.50; Lot-et-Garonne ⓉⒸ05.53.69.42.03).

You'll need your own transport, however, for exploring the Célé valley, the Bouriane and other places off the beaten track. Look out for the free **walking** map, *Carte de la Randonnée*, and the booklet *Promenades et Randonnées* (€8) available from local tourist offices or from the departmental office (see p.63). Another more leisurely possibility is to rent a **houseboat** and pootle along the Lot (see p.35).

Cahors

A sunny southern backwater built in a tight meander of the River Lot, **CAHORS** was the chief town of the old province of Quercy and is now the modern capital

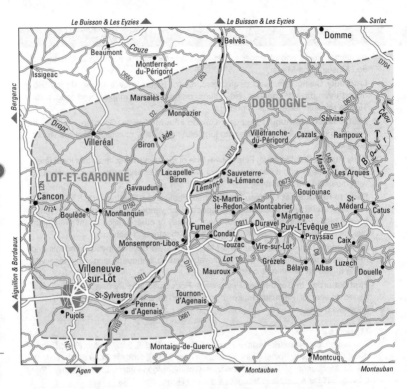

of the Lot *département*. Its somewhat troubled history has left a warren of dark medieval lanes, a rather knocked about cathedral and impressive fortifications, among them Cahors' famous landmark, the turreted **Pont Valentré**. Another reason to come here is to sample the local **wines**, heady and black but dry to the taste, which have undergone a revival in recent years (see box on p.296).

Some history

Both the names Quercy and Cahors derive from the area's first-known inhabitants, the local Gaulish tribe known as the **Cadurci**. During the first century BC they founded a settlement near a sacred spring, immediately across the river to the southwest of modern Cahors, which the Romans later called **Divona Cadurcorum**. Following successive Vandal and Frankish invasions after the fifth century, only a few fragments of Roman stonework remain, as well as the spring, which continues to supply Cahors' drinking water. It wasn't until the seventh century that the then Bishop (later Saint) Didier finally erected a wall to protect the nascent town and his rapidly growing cathedral.

The **bishops of Cahors** gradually spread their net until they not only ruled over a vast area extending down the Lot as far as Puy-l'Évêque but also controlled the all-important river trade. By the early thirteenth century Cahors was entering its **golden age**, as powerful local merchants known as Caorsins, together with Lombard bankers fleeing the Cathar Crusades, turned the town into Europe's chief banking centre. The more enthusiastic of these moneylenders earned such a reputation for usury that in his *Divine Comedy* (1321), Dante compared the town to Gomorrah when describing the structure of Hell.

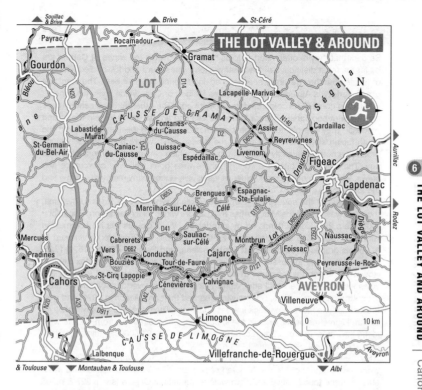

THE LOT VALLEY & AROUND

Nevertheless, the merchants helped finance any number of noble town houses, two new bridges, various embellishments to the cathedral and further fortifications enclosing the peninsula to the north. When the local Bishop Jacques Duèze was named **Pope John XXII** in 1316, Cahors had reached its apogee. His greatest legacy was a university, which remained one of the most important in France for the next four centuries.

By now, however, the English and French armies were at loggerheads. Cahors was never attacked during the Hundred Years' War, but the end result was the same: under the Treaty of Brétigny (1360) it succumbed reluctantly to **English occupation**. When French rule was eventually restored around 1440, the Cadurciens set about rebuilding their ravaged town, adding a few Italianate flourishes and developing a distinctive decorative style comprising carved or moulded rose blossoms, flaming suns and the so-called "*bâtons écotés*" ("pruned branches"), which is still in evidence today.

Unlike several of its neighbours, Cahors remained staunchly Catholic during the **Wars of Religion**. As a consequence it was sacked by the Protestant Henry of Navarre, the future King Henri IV of France, when he seized it after a brief battle in 1580. Later the same year, however, one of many peace treaties saw the town returned to the Catholic fold. By way of recompense, Henry later donated 6000 *livres*, half of which went towards restoring the cathedral.

Over the years Cahors gradually expanded to fill the entire peninsula, though it was not until the nineteenth century that Bishop Didier's ramparts were finally razed. They were replaced by a tree-lined boulevard which was later named after Cahors' most famous son, the politician **Léon Gambetta** (see box on p.300).

The wines and vineyards of Cahors

So dark that they're often referred to as "black wines", the red **wines of Cahors** are by far the most distinctive of the southwestern wines, hard and full-bodied with lots of tannin, and they generally need long ageing to bring out their best. The dominant **grape variety** is Auxerrois (also known as Malbec or Cot), which gives the wine its rich tannin content, its colour and its ability to age. The other thirty percent is made up of Merlot and Tanat – Merlot for roundness and aroma, Tanat to help the ageing process. They are planted on the clay-limestone terraces beside the Lot, on the south-facing slopes and even up on the *causse* itself, where the harsh conditions produce a correspondingly hard wine, but one which can improve dramatically with age. The distinctive bite of a young Cahors wine goes well with *charcuterie* and stews, while the more aromatic older wines usually accompany red meats, game and the local goat's cheese, *Cabécou*.

As in most of the southwest, it was the Romans who brought vines to the area, though it wasn't until the Middle Ages that Cahors wines really caught on. Pope John XXII (see p.295) kicked things off by introducing "Vieux Cahors" as his communion wine and table wine of choice. Then François I (1494–1547) ordered a vineyard of Auxerrois grapes to be planted at Fontainebleau, and Peter the Great (1672–1725) imported the wine to Russia, where it was adopted by the Greek Orthodox Church. However, the good times came to an abrupt end when **phylloxera** hit in 1877. The vines weren't replanted until after World War II, and then over a much smaller area. After struggling for a while, Cahors wines earned their *appellation* in 1971, and over the last decade have come back into fashion again. There are now approximately 43 square kilometres under vines in the *appellation*, which stretches from Cahors west along the Lot for 30km to Soturac, producing on average 240,000 hectolitres (roughly 32 million bottles) per annum.

Before **visiting the vineyards**, pick up a copy of the free *Livret du Vin de Cahors*, which gives details of the two hundred or so producers in the *appellation*; it's available from the tourist office and from wine merchants in Cahors (see p.297 & p.305 respectively), or from the Maison du Vin de Cahors, 430 av Jean-Jaurès (Mon–Fri; ☏05.65.23.22.24), opposite the station; note that the Maison du Vin does not otherwise cater to individuals. (For general tips on vineyard visits, see p.42.)

As an introduction to what's on offer, head for the imposing **Château Lagrézette** (daily 10am–7pm; ☏05.65.20.07.42, ⍟www.chateau-lagrezette.tm.fr), 10km north-west of Cahors on the D12 midway between Douelle and Mercués. In addition to sampling their award-winning wines you get a tour of the magnificent, state-of-the-art *chais* dug into the hillside. Also worth a visit for its reliably good wines – if not for its ambience – is the **Côtes d'Olt** co-operative (July & Aug Mon–Sat 8.30am–12.30pm & 1.30–6.30pm, Sun 10am–12.30pm & 2–6pm; rest of year same hours but closed Sun; ☏05.65.30.71.86, ⍟www.somillesimes.com/fr/public/cotes-d-olt.php), on the river's south bank about 17km west of Cahors on the D8 in the commune of Parnac.

In general you can expect to pay between €8 and €15 for a very decent Cahors, although some of the region's prestige wines fetch €70 or more.

Adorned with municipal buildings – the town hall, library, law courts and theatre – in Neoclassical style, it remains modern Cahors' principal thoroughfare.

Arrival and information

The heart of present-day Cahors is place François-Mitterrand, a wide, open square towards the middle of the main boulevard Gambetta. East of here medieval houses cluster round the cathedral, while the post-seventeenth-century

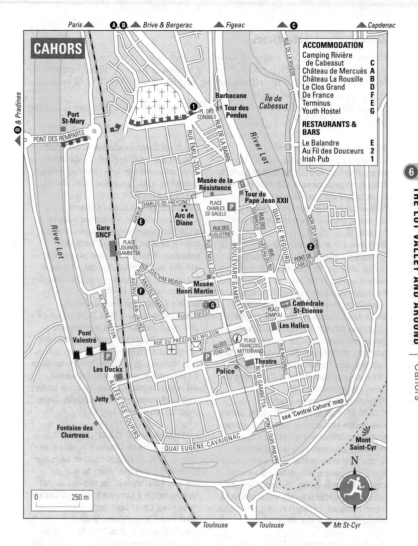

ACCOMMODATION

Camping Rivière de Cabessut	C
Château de Mercuès	A
Château La Rousille	B
Le Clos Grand	D
De France	F
Terminus	E
Youth Hostel	G

RESTAURANTS & BARS

Le Balandre	E
Au Fil des Douceurs	2
Irish Pub	1

town spreads west towards the **gare SNCF**, 500m away along rue Joachim-Murat. The station is also the terminus for some regional **buses**, while others stop on place de Charles-de-Gaulle at the north end of the main boulevard.

Cahors' **tourist office** (July & Aug Mon–Sat 9am–12.30pm & 1.30–6pm, Sun 10am–noon; rest of year same hours but closed Sun; ☎05.65.53.20.65, Ⓦwww.mairie-cahors.fr) occupies a handsome building on the north side of place François-Mitterrand. It provides detailed walking maps of the town, with an English-language insert, and also organizes **guided tours** in season (June & Sept Tues & Fri; July & Aug Mon–Sat; €5.50), covering either the cathedral or the medieval streets. The tours are occasionally conducted by a bilingual guide.

Accommodation

Cahors boasts a broad range of **hotels**, though the choice, particularly in the middle price categories, is not particularly inspiring. Instead, there's better value for money to be had in the **surrounding region**, though you'll need your own transport to take advantage of it.

Note that unless otherwise stated, the accommodation listed below is marked on the main Cahors map (p.297).

Hotels in Cahors

L'Escargot 5 bd Gambetta (see central Cahors map, p.299) ℡05.65.35.07.66, ℻05.65.53.92.38. This small hotel at the north end of the main drag is comfortable and good value; make sure you book well ahead in season. The rooms are cosy and well maintained. Closed occasionally mid-Oct to Easter. ❸

De France 252 av Jean-Jaurès ℡05.65.35.16.76, ⓦwww.hoteldefrance-cahors.fr. Large hotel in a modern block near the train station offering en-suite facilities, satellite TV and phone as standard, though the cheaper rooms are boxy and the furnishings bland. Closed Christmas and New Year hols. ❸

De La Paix 30 place Saint-Maurice (see central Cahors map, p.299) ℡05.65.35.03.40, ⓦwww.hoteldelapaix-cahors.com. This recently renovated hotel is the best mid-range choice in town. It has very calm, airy rooms decorated in blues and creams (one even has a great big Jacuzzi), staff speak English and there's a 24-hour reception. ❸

Terminus 5 av Charles-de-Freycinet ℡05.65.53.32.00, ⓦwww.balandre.com. Cahors' most opulent hotel occupies a nineteenth-century bourgeois residence near the station. Though extensively renovated, a few original features remain, such as big, tiled bathrooms with luxurious tubs in some rooms, while all boast the modern comforts of double-glazing, air-conditioning and satellite TV. The hotel is equally well known for its superb restaurant, *Le Balandre* (see p.303). Closed second two weeks in Nov. ❺

Hotels around Cahors

Château de Mercuès Mercuès ℡05.65.20.00.01, ⓦwww.chateaudemercues.com. High on its promontory 6km to the northwest of Cahors, for centuries this was the humble residence of the bishops of Cahors. It is now a luxury hotel with pool, tennis courts, excellent wine cellars (tastings available July & Aug; free) and a 1-star Michelin restaurant (closed Mon & for lunch Tues–Thurs; menus from €65). Closed Nov–Easter. ❾

Château La Roussille chemin du Moulin, Labéraudie, ℡05.65.22.84.74, ⓦwww .chateauroussille.com. A welcoming *chambre d'hôte* five minutes drive from Cahors centre; take the D8 in the direction of Moulin de Labéraudie. It has one room and two suites, all with their own individual character, a lounge, a billiard room, and is set in a large park complete with swimming pool. ❺–❻

Le Clos Grand 12 rue des Claux Grands, Labéraudie, Pradines ℡05.65.35.04.39, ⓦwww .clos-grand.com. In Pradines, a suburb 5km northwest of Cahors, this welcoming hotel looks out over fields and has a pleasant, shady garden. Most rooms occupy a purpose-built annexe beside the pool, each with a little terrace or balcony and en-suite bathroom. Locals come here for the good-value cooking (menus €16.90–38). Closed Christmas and New Year hols. ❸

Hostel and campsite

Camping Rivière de Cabessut rue de la Rivière ℡05.65.30.06.30, ℻05.65.23.99.46. Three-star campsite in a quiet spot beside the river just over 1km from Cahors across Pont de Cabessut. Facilities include a shop, snack bar, small pool and canoe rental. Closed Oct–March.

Youth Hostel 20 rue Frédéric-Suisse ℡05.65.35.64.71, ℻05.65.35.95.92. One of the more centrally placed youth hostels, occupying part of a former convent. It's not the friendliest of places, however, and the dormitories are squashed and rather spartan. Breakfast (€4) and other meals available (from €7 for three courses), as well as a laundry and TV room. No curfew. €12 per person per night.

The Town

Compact and easily walkable, Cahors is surrounded on three sides by the River Lot and protected to the north by a series of fourteenth-century fortifications. Most of interest lies within the cramped confines of the medieval streets on the peninsula's eastern edge, focused around the twin domes of the **Cathédrale**

St-Étienne. From here, **rue Nationale** leads south past the former homes of wealthy merchants to the flood-prone artisans' quarter, while north of the cathedral the land continues to slope gently upwards along **rue du Château-du-Roi**, where bankers and aristocrats once lived, towards the old town gate with its guardhouse and tower. Of medieval Cahors' three fortified bridges, only westerly **Pont Valentré** remains – one of the finest surviving bridges of its time. More recent history is commemorated in a couple of passably interesting **museums** and, on a fine day, there are good views to be had from the summit of **Mont St-Cyr**, which overlooks the town from the southeast.

The cathedral and around

The oldest and simplest in plan of the Périgord-style Romanesque churches, the **Cathédrale St-Étienne** dates largely from the early twelfth century, when Bishop Didier's original cathedral was rebuilt in part to house the relic of the Holy Coif. According to local legend, this cloth, said to have covered Christ's head in the tomb, was brought back from the Holy Land around this time by Bishop Géraud de Cardaillac; it's still on display in St-Gausbert's Chapel (see p.300). The cathedral underwent various modifications from the thirteenth century onwards. First the choir was rebuilt in Gothic style, and the massive west facade added to form the church's main entrance in place of the original north door. The cloister was then reconstructed in the late 1400s, after which there was a pause until the nineteenth century when extensive restoration work on the whole edifice was carried out, by Paul Abadie among others (see p.152).

Because of all these accretions, the St-Étienne's exterior is not exciting, with the notable exception of the elaborately decorated portal above the **north door**. Carved around 1140, it depicts Christ's Ascension. He dominates the

CENTRAL CAHORS

St-Barthélemy
PLACE BESSIÈRES
Musée de la Résistance
Tour du Pape Jean XXII Ⓐ
PLACE CHARLES-DE-GAULLE
Musée Henri Martin & Gare SNCF
RUE FEYDEL
@ 3.w.com
BOULEVARD GAMBETTA
RUE DU PORTAIL ALBAN
Château du Roi
Collège Péllegry
River Lot
RUE DU CHÂTEAU DU ROI
RUE DU FOUR-STE-CATHERINE
PLACE DE LA LIBÉRATION
PONT DE CABESSUT
QUAI DE REGOUD
Parc Olivier de Magny
RUE DAURADE
Maison du Borreau
QUAI CHAMPOLLION
RUE FOCH
Pont Valentré
Hôtel de Ville
RUE JOFFRE
PLACE JEAN-JACQUES CHAPOU
Cathédrale St-Etienne ❶
RUE WILSON
RUE SAINT-JAMES
Les Halles ❷
ⓘ
ALLÉES FÉNELON
PLACE FRANÇOIS-MITTERRAND
PLACE DE LA HALLE
RUE CLEMENCEAU
St-Urcisse ❸
RUE ST-URCISSE
❹ ❺
❼
RUE BERGOUGNIOUX
RUE LASTIE
PLACE ST-URCISSE ❻
Theatre
BOULEVARD GAMBETTA
RUE BRIVES
PLACE ROUSSEAU
RUE NATIONALE

RESTAURANTS & BARS
Auberge des Gabares 1
Le Bergougnioux 7
Curry Brian 2
Le Dousil 5
Le Lamparo 4
Marie Colline 3
Le St-Urcisse 6

ACCOMMODATION
L' Escargot A
De la Paix B

▼ Mt St-Cyr

299

tympanum, surrounded by the Apostles and angels falling back in ecstasy, while cherubim fly out of the clouds to relieve him of his halo. Side panels show scenes from the life of St Stephen (St Étienne), the first Christian martyr who was stoned to death around 35 AD, while the outer arch portrays people being stabbed and hacked with axes.

Inside, the cathedral is much like Périgueux's St-Étienne (see p.152), with a nave lacking aisles and transepts, roofed with two monumental domes. The extensive murals round the apse – depicting, for example, St Stephen's martyrdom and the Adoration of the Magi – suffered from rather heavy-handed nineteenth-century restoration work. The fourteenth-century frescoes high in the west dome are, however, original – they again depict the stoning of St Stephen, encircled by eight giant prophets. In 1988 further paintings from the same era were discovered behind layers of plaster just inside and above the west door. They consist of faded but beautiful Creation scenes, including Adam and Eve in the Garden of Eden and many finely observed birds and animals.

To the right of the choir, the aptly named **Deep Chapel** bears earlier scars from the Wars of Religion, when Protestant armies hacked away at its carvings. They also caused irreparable damage to the **cloister**, accessed by a door next to the Deep Chapel, though the flamboyant Gothic colonnades still retain some intricate craftsmanship. The best example occupies a niche on the northwest corner pillar, where the Virgin is portrayed as a graceful girl with broad brow and ringlets to her waist. The door surrounds are also beautifully carved, if rather battered; that on the northeast wall leads into **St-Gausbert's Chapel** (May–Sept Mon–Sat 10am–12.30pm & 3–6pm; rest of year contact the tourist office; €2.50), which holds the **Holy Coif** – a decidedly unimpressive, rather grubby looking piece of padded cloth – among chalices, gilded statues and other treasures. The unusually complicated vaulted ceiling and the mural adorning the chapel's west wall are of far greater interest. The latter portrays the Last Judgement, with the dead rising from their tombs as a dashing St Michael weighs their souls – despite the best efforts of a little devil trying to tip the balance in his favour.

The square on which the cathedral stands, **place Jean-Jacques-Chapou**, commemorates a local Resistance leader killed in a German ambush in July 1944. On its west side, look for a sign above what is now a bank announcing *Bazar Génois: Gambetta Jeune et Cie*. This is where **Léon Gambetta** (see box below), the son of an Italian grocer, spent his childhood. At its southern end the

---

Léon Gambetta

Heralded as the "father of the Republic", **Léon Gambetta** was born in Cahors in 1838. After graduating as a lawyer, he specialized in defending republican sympathizers accused of political crimes against Emperor Napoléon III. A charismatic man and great orator, the republicans soon rallied around Gambetta and, when Napoléon was forced to surrender to an invading Prussian army in 1870, he was among those who quickly proclaimed the **Third Republic**, the regime which continued to govern France until 1940. It had a rocky start, however. With the Prussians besieging Paris, Gambetta fled the capital by balloon to organize the war effort in the provinces. While he opposed the armistice signed in 1871, Gambetta and his band of moderate republicans, or "Opportunists", were able to keep the Republic afloat despite constant attacks from both the monarchist majority and the radical Left. He served as president of the National Assembly from 1879 to 1882, but later that year his career was cut short when he accidentally shot himself with a revolver, and died soon after.

square extends into place Galdemar, popularly known as place de la Halle. The covered **market hall** at its centre, built as a corn exchange in 1865, provides the focus for Cahors' lively markets. There's a fresh food **market** in the *halle* here (daily except Sun pm & Mon), and a more extensive market on Wednesday and Saturday mornings spreading north into the cathedral square; in winter (Nov to mid-March), the *halle* plays host to a Saturday morning *marché au gras*, selling all manner of duck and goose products. Nearby place François-Mitterrand also hosts an antiques fair-cum-flea market on the first and third Saturdays of the month.

The medieval streets

A warren of narrow lanes and alleys fills the area between boulevard Gambetta and the eastern riverbank, where the majority of houses, turreted and built of flat, thin southern brick, have been handsomely restored during recent decades. From the market square, **rue Nationale** cuts almost due south through the heart of medieval Cahors to where the old Roman bridge once stood – the foundations are still just visible when the water level is low. On the way it passes a number of eye-catching merchants' houses and some pleasing half-timbered frontages on place Rousseau. Other roads worth exploring in the area are canyon-like rue Bergougnioux and its easterly extension rue Lastié, which comes out among a pretty group of brick and timber buildings around place St-Urcisse.

One of Cahors' most attractive corners lies just north of the cathedral along **rue Daurade**, where a lovely row of buildings overlooks a little park named after the sixteenth-century poet Olivier de Magny, who lived at no. 12. His house is overshadowed, though, by the thirteenth-century **Maison du Bourreau**, the "executioner's house", with its big arched openings and line of double windows above. The name dates from the Revolution, when the public executioner lived here; naturally, the building is said to be haunted.

Continuing north along rue Daurade you reach the southern end of **rue Château-du-Roi** and its extension, **rue des Soubirous**. This is the "upper town", where the houses become distinctly grander. One of the most imposing is the fourteenth-century **Château du Roi** itself, built by cousins of Pope John XXII but later taken over by the king's emissary when the bishops lost their stranglehold on Cahors in the fifteenth century. Its massive, featureless walls now contain the local prison.

Wealthy Cadurciens were very fond of adding turrets to their homes and there are a number of examples scattered through the Soubirous quarter. To see them properly it's best to head down to the river – rue du Four-Ste-Catherine provides the most interesting route – to a vantage point across Pont de Cabessut. Cahors' skyline stretches in front of you from the cathedral domes in the south via Collège Pélegry, with its crenellated hexagonal turret, and the square, solid tower of the Château du Roi. In the far distance the **Tour du Pape Jean XXII** and the **Tour des Pendus** pinpoint Cahors' northern ramparts, which still stretch partway across the peninsula.

The museums

Back in the centre, Cahors' two museums deserve a brief stop. The first, in a small building on the north side of place Charles-de-Gaulle, is the **Musée de la Résistance** (daily 2–6pm; free), which documents very thoroughly the history of the local Resistance movement against the broader context of German occupation, deportations and finally, Liberation in 1945. The most interesting section, on the ground floor, deals with local history, where you can read about

Jean-Jacques Chapou, after whom the cathedral square is named (see p.300), and about the *Mona Lisa*'s sojourn in the area (see p.284).

Continuing south down rue Émile-Zola, you come to the **Musée Henri Martin** at no. 792 (Mon & Wed–Sat 11am–6pm, Sun 2–6pm; closed when changing temporary exhibitions; ☎05.65.20.88.66; €3), in the seventeenth-century former episcopal palace. Exhibits range from Gallo-Roman pots to works by nineteenth- and twentieth-century artists such as Dufy, Vlaminck and Utrillo. However, pride of place goes to seventeen oil paintings by local artist **Henri Martin** (1860–1943), whose mix of Impressionism and Pointillism perfectly evokes the lazy sun-filled landscapes of this part of France, and an important collection dedicated to **Léon Gambetta**. With over two thousand documents, photographs, sculptures and paintings, only a fraction is on show at any one time. The displays are predictably worthy, although the caricatures help liven things up a bit.

Pont Valentré

The reason most people venture to Cahors is to see the dramatic **Pont Valentré**, which guards the western river crossing. Its three powerful towers, originally closed by portcullises and gates, made it an independent fortress, which was so imposing, in fact, that the bridge was never attacked. Building it was a problem, however. Work started in 1308, but the bridge was not completed for another seventy years. According to legend, the Devil was to blame – at least in part. The story goes that the architect, exasperated at the slow progress, sold his soul in exchange for the Devil's assistance. As the bridge was nearing completion, he tried to wriggle out of the deal by giving the Devil a sieve with which to carry water for the masons. The Devil took revenge by creeping up the central tower every night to remove the last stone, thus ensuring that the bridge would never be finished. If you look carefully at the top of the tower's east face, you'll see a little devil which was added when Pont Valentré was renovated in 1879.

From April to October, Safaraid (☎05.65.35.98.88, ⓔbateaux .safaraid@club-internet.fr) operates **boat tours** round the Cahors meander from the jetty below Pont Valentré (1hr 30min; €8.50). Another company, Les Croisières Fénelon (☎05.65.30.16.55, ⓔbateaufenelon@wanadoo.fr), also put on a varied programme of excursions including daytrips upriver to St-Cirq Lapopie (€47); prices include a meal onboard. There are ticket booths for both companies beside the Pont Valentré jetty.

Mont St-Cyr

All around Cahors rise the dry, scrubby uplands of the *causse*.

△ Pont Valentré

These valley sides were carpeted with vines from Roman times until the nineteenth century when phylloxera set in, after which the land was used for grazing sheep; now, however, only the lines of tumbled-down stone walls and abandoned farmhouses remain. One of the few landmarks around is the red-and-white TV mast on the summit of **Mont St-Cyr**, overlooking Cahors to the southeast. At 264m, this is the place to head for bird's-eye views of the town: the division between medieval and seventeenth-century Cahors becomes very apparent from the summit, particularly in summer when tree-lined boulevard Gambetta picks out the former course of the ramparts. Pont Valentré is just visible in the distance, while on clear days you can see the Château de Mercuès way to the north.

It's a stiff but easy climb to the summit of Mont St-Cyr. From the southern end of boulevard Gambetta, cross Pont Louis-Philippe, then take the steps to the right of the Virgin's statue and keep going up for about twenty to thirty minutes. Though you can drive, it takes almost as long, as the road winds for about 5km among stunted oaks and pines across the plateau. Apart from the views, there are picnic tables at the top and a very welcome café-bar (closed Mon & Tues).

Eating and drinking

Cahors has no shortage of good **places to eat**, from the classy *Balandre* – the place to go for a splurge – to very much more modest establishments. Most are concentrated in the streets of the medieval town, though you'll also find brasseries, pizzerias and cafés along boulevard Gambetta.

Unless otherwise stated, the places listed below are marked on the central Cahors map (p.299).

Restaurants

Auberge des Gabares 24 place Champollion ℡05.65.53.91.47. This sort of traditional, single-menu restaurant is usually found in the depths of the country rather than in the middle of a town, albeit on a wisteria-covered terrace overlooking the Lot. The food, like the decor, is simple and unfussy, and it's good value, too, with five courses for a mere €13 including wine. There's more choice on Saturday evenings, when they stretch to two menus (€20 and €33). Reservations recommended for dinner. Closed Sun and for dinner on Mon except in July & Aug.

Le Balandre *Hôtel Terminus*, 5 av Charles-de-Freycinet (see main Cahors map, p.297) ℡05.65.53.32.00. Cahors' top restaurant serves refined takes on Quercy cuisine, with plenty of local lamb, duck, truffles and foie gras, in a dining room to match: all chandeliers, plasterwork and pretty Art Nouveau stained glass. They also offer a very impressive wine list, including over seventy Cahors wines. There are three menus at €40–70, or you can eat for around €40–45 from the *carte*. July to mid-Sept closed for lunch Sun & Mon; rest of year closed all day Sun & Mon.

Le Bergougnioux rue Bergougnioux. Hidden away from the main tourist drag this little gem has a

cosy dining room that spills out onto a tiny courtyard and serves simple, regional dishes such as duck breast in Noilly Prat. Closed Sun eve.

Curry Brian 44 rue St-James ℡05.65.23.24.88. This British-owned Indian restaurant is good if you fancy a change from the local cuisine and serves English-style curries including chicken tikka masala and tandoori. *Plats du jour* €9.50 or menus for €18.50. Closed Sun lunch.

Le Dousil 124 rue Nationale. This wine bar is a great place to sample local reds before setting off on the wine trail. They dish up good food, too, from cheese or charcuterie platters (€8–16) to open sandwiches (around €3) and more substantial fare such as beef bourguignon or *cassoulet* (around €12). Wine by the glass from €1.80. Closed Sun & Mon, also closed Oct in school hols.

Au Fil des Douceurs 90 quai de la Verrerie (see main Cahors map, p.297) ℡05.65.22.13.04. A floating restaurant moored on the far side of Pont de Cabessut, with splendid views of the Cahors skyline. The food is refined – crêpes with morsels of duck, lamb *brochette* and plenty of fish – but not outrageously expensive. Three-course menus start at €13 for a weekday lunch and otherwise at €18.20. Reservations recommended Sat eve. Closed Sun & Mon.

Le Lamparo place de la Halle. Large, bustling restaurant that spills out onto the square in summer. Decked out in sunny blues and yellows and with lots of greenery, it's justifiably popular for its generous portions and very reasonable prices. Though the speciality is pizza (from €7), there's something for everyone, including salads and local dishes plus enticing desserts to follow. *Plat du jour* €7.70, menus from €15. Closed Sun.

Marie Colline 173 rue Georges-Clemenceau ☎05.65.35.59.96. You need to reserve or wait till around 1pm to find space at this bright, airy vegetarian restaurant run by two sisters. The choice is limited – two entrées and two main dishes which change daily – but it's all freshly made, using locally produced vegetables. Save room for one of their scrumptious desserts. *Plat du jour* €8, or three courses for €14. Open lunchtime only Tues–Fri. Closed Aug.

Le St-Urcisse place St-Urcisse. ☎05.65.35.06.06. Stylish restaurant with a lovely big garden for al fresco eating. On the menu are salad, grilled meats with a bewildering variety of sauces and an excellent selection of seafood. Menus from €12.90. Closed Sun.

Nightlife and entertainment

There's little in the way of **nightlife**, especially out of season, but one of the livelier spots is the *Irish Pub* (daily 9pm–1am), to the northwest of place des Consuls, which hosts live bands on Saturdays. For other **events**, ask at the tourist office, which publishes lists of the many festivals (see box on pp.280–281 for more), exhibitions, concerts and plays taking place in Cahors. For plays, the principal venue is the Neoclassical – and very plush – **Municipal Theatre** on place François-Mitterrand (☎05.65.20.88.60, ⓦwww.mairie-cahors.fr/theatre /index.html), which puts on a varied programme of theatre, dance, concerts and opera. Classical concerts are also held in the cathedral, while live bands play Les Docks, 430 allées des Soupirs (☎05.65.22.36.38, ⓦwww.mairie-cahors.fr), a youth centre beside Pont Valentré.

Listings

Bike rental The nearest outlet is Antinéa Loisirs in Douelle, about 10km west of Cahors ☎05.65.30.95.79.

Boat rental If you fancy a quick potter on the Lot, Alliance Nautique, at Port Bullier beside the Pont de Cabessut (☎06.80.14.96.77), rents out five-person electric boats for periods up to 90 minutes. For more on boat trips, see p.35.

Books and newspapers The Maison de la Presse, 73 bd Gambetta, stocks the main English-language papers and magazines as well as local guides, while Librairie Calligramme, 75 rue du Maréchal-Joffre, is a more serious bookshop carrying a few English-language titles.

Bus information The tourist office stocks bus timetables, or phone the Conseil Général's central information desk (☎05.65.53.27.50). Tickets for Eurolines buses are available from Voyages Belmon, 2 bd Gambetta (☎05.65.35.59.30), at the north end of bd Gambetta.

Car parks Free parking is available towards the west end of allées Fénelon, along allées des Soupirs near the Pont Valentré and on place Charles-de-Gaulle.

Car rental Outside the train station, on place Jouinot-Gambetta, try: Avis ☎05.65.30.13.10; or Hertz ☎05.65.35.34.69.

Cinema Of Cahors' two cinemas, the three-screen ABC, 24 rue des Augustins (☎05.65.35.03.11), is the more likely to show English-language films, usually in the original version (*VO*). The other cinema is Le Quercy, 871 rue Émile-Zola (☎05.65.22.20.05), near the Musée Henri-Martin.

Hospital Centre Hospitalier Jean Rougier, 449–335 rue du Président-Wilson ☎05.65.20.50.50.

Internet access The cheapest place to log on is the Bureau Information Jeunesse du Lot, 20 rue Frédéric-Suisse, in the same building as the youth hostel (Mon, Tues & Thurs 1–6pm; Wed 9am–noon & 1–6pm; Fri 1–5pm). Another option is 3W.com, 37 bd Gambetta (Mon-Fri 10am–noon & 2.30–6.30pm).

Police Commissariat de Police, 1 rue de l'Ancienne-Gendarmerie ☎05.65.23.17.17.

Post office The main post office is at 257 rue du Président-Wilson, 46000 Cahors.

Taxis There are taxi stands outside the train station and on bd Gambetta, or call Allo Taxi on ☎05.65.22.19.42.

A taste of Périgord

This region – generally referred to as the Périgord when it comes to food – boasts one of France's great culinary traditions. Here you'll taste country cooking at its best, robust fare in which the flavours and textures speak for themselves. The staple ingredients are duck and goose, both of which are served in all sorts of delectable guises, while walnuts, game and wild mushrooms also feature prominently on regional menus. And to wash it all down, there's no shortage of excellent wines to choose from.

▲ Salade de gésiers

Duck and goose

Almost every bit of the **duck** and **goose** is used in Périgordin cuisine, kicking off with the justly famous foie gras, the fattened livers. The meat is preserved in its own salted fat to make succulent *confit*, which is either served on its own or goes into other dishes, such as soups and *cassoulet*, a no-nonsense concoction of *confit*, Toulouse sausage and haricot beans. Duck gizzards preserved in the same way are sliced and served warm on lettuce in a popular starter, *salade de gésiers*, while another delicacy is *cou farci*, goose neck stuffed with sausage meat, foie gras and truffles – both far more tasty than they sound. The thick juicy steaks of grilled duck breast known as *magret* are more instantly appealing and appear on practically every restaurant menu, in fancier places accompanied by a sauce laced with truffle, pepper or a seasonal fruit. Both duck and goose meat go into a coarse local pâté called *rillettes*, and their fat is used in the cooking of everything from omelettes to *pommes sarladaise*, a dish originating in Sarlat in which sliced potatoes are fried with lashings of garlic and parsley. The fat is also used to brown the garlic in *tourin* (or *tourain*), the region's traditional soup, served with an egg over thick country bread. Not even the carcasses (*demoiselles*) go to waste: they are roasted over a wood fire, after which you pick off the remaining morsels of meat.

Other meats and side dishes

It's not all duck and goose, however. You'll also find *poulet confit* and other **chicken** dishes, while **pork** features strongly too. In more traditional restaurants, look out for *enchaud périgordin*, sliced slow-roasted pork loin stuffed with garlic and, in fancier versions, with truffles as well; it's usually eaten cold. **Lamb** raised on the *causses* of Quercy or the Médoc's salt marshes is most frequently served roasted as *gigot* (leg), while towards the north and east, the excellent Limousin **beef** begins to feature more strongly. In summer, **snails** make their appearance on market stalls and at village fêtes, often cooked in a garlic or spicy tomato sauce. Later in the year, more upmarket restaurants offer *pigeonneau*, young pigeon, and hare (*lièvre*) among other types of **game**. Then there are the plump brown mushrooms, **cèpes**, which grow

Cheese and desserts

While you'll find good farm **cheeses** in the markets, the only local speciality cheese is *Cabécou*, a little flat medallion of goat's cheese from around Rocamadour. It's often served soft and fresh as a cheese course, or grilled as a starter on a bed of lettuce with walnut oil. **Walnuts** (*noix*) provide another mainstay of Périgordin cuisine. In addition to the oil, you'll come across walnuts in breads, cakes and desserts or simply as a garnish.

The best-known local **desserts** are *pastis*, a thin apple tart topped with almost transparent crinkled pastry and a hint of alcohol, and *clafoutis*, a pudding-cake made with cherries, pears or any other fruit. Walnut cakes and puddings are popular nowadays, as are strawberries from around Bretenoux and to the south of Périgueux. Agen, further south again, is famous for its prunes and all sorts of derived goodies.

throughout the region but are particularly prolific around Monpazier and Villefranche-du-Périgord. *Cèpes* come fried, grilled, stuffed and in omelettes.

Fish and seafood

Around Bordeaux and along the banks of the Garonne, **fish** and **seafood** hold sway. Salmon, eel, whelks, prawns, smelt, oysters and even farmed sturgeon can all be sampled in local restaurants according to the season. Young fried elvers (*pibales*) are expensive but popular along the estuary in January and February, while further inland shad (*alose*) is traditionally grilled over vine clippings. The least savoury of the local delicacies is lamprey (*lamproie*), an ugly, eel-like creature poached in Sauternes wine, leeks, onions and its own blood.

▲ Geese breeder, Vilatte Plassard Pompougnac

Fatty livers and black diamonds

One of this region's most celebrated foods is foie gras (see p.167), the fattened liver of duck or goose whose rich and buttery taste is an experience not to be missed. Though best eaten on its own in succulent slabs, foie gras is equally irresistible pan-fried with a seasonal fruit compôte, and makes a gloriously over-the-top garnish for various meat dishes. It's often combined with the region's other culinary star, truffles (*truffes*), aptly known as the "black diamonds of Périgord" (see p.171). These hugely expensive black fungi crop up in all sorts of dishes, from rich Périgordin sauces to the humble omelette. All too often, however, there's so little truffle or the other ingredients are so strong that it's impossible to detect its delicate flavour. Far better to splash out and order a simple, unadorned truffle you can really enjoy.

Wine Try the huge Atrium showroom (🖥 www
.g-vigouroux.fr), on the N20 as you come into
town from the south, which sells wines from
the châteaux de Mercuès, de Haute-Serre, Caïx
and Leret Monpezat at close to château prices,
offers tastings and advises on vineyard visits. In

town, head for the smaller Le Cèdre Valentré,
32 av André-Breton, at the east end of Pont
Valentré (closed mid-Jan to mid-Feb; 🖥 www
.quercy.net/com/cedre). Château Lagrézette
(see p.296) also has a boutique right beside the
bridge.

East along the Lot

Upstream from Cahors the Lot valley becomes narrower and the cliffs higher. The river is confined to ever tighter meanders and castles sprout from all the most inaccessible knuckles of rock, often with red-tiled villages clinging to their flanks. One such provides the most dramatic sight in the whole valley: **St-Cirq Lapopie**, 30km or so east of Cahors, perched precariously on the edge of a 100m drop. Its castle is now a ruin, but the village itself is a delightful – if very touristy – place where noble mansions stand testimony to a more illustrious past. Further along the river's south bank on the D8, the Renaissance **Château de Cénevières** also boasts an interesting history, as well as some unusual frescoes and a good collection of period furniture. The only major settlement along this stretch of river is **Cajarc**, an important market town and a stop on the pilgrims' road to Santiago de Compostela. Cajarc's only sight is an incongruous modern art gallery, featuring some world-class names, but it has sufficient accommodation and other facilities to provide a useful base. Upstream, the scenery takes over once again as the Lot winds its way past more medieval villages and castles, and beneath a 300-metre high belvedere, the **Saut de la Mounine**, on the valley's southern lip. There's nothing particular to stop for along the last stretch of river heading northeast to **Capdenac**, near Figeac (see p.314). Instead, you could take a diversion south across the *causse* to where the **Grotte de Foissac** harbours some prehistoric remains alongside a varied and colourful array of stalactites and stalagmites, and then continue on across country to the atmospheric ruins of **Peyrerusse-le-Roc**.

The Lot valley is unusually well served by **public transport**, with an SNCF **bus** running along the river's north bank from Cahors via Figeac to Capdenac. It stops at almost every village en route, though you'll have to walk across to those south of the river, and will need your own transport to explore the high country on either side.

Vers and Bouziès

Immediately east of Cahors, the Lot valley is taken up with a busy main road, train tracks and scattered modern developments, above which soars the bridge for the new A20 *autoroute*. However, things improve dramatically after the village of **VERS**, some 15km upstream, where the main D653 to Figeac strikes off northeastwards. Vers itself doesn't merit a stop, unless you are in search of overnight **accommodation**. The most attractive option – as long as you get a room in the main hotel rather than the old and noisy annexe across the road – is *La Truite Dorée* (☎05.65.31.41.51, 🖥 www.latruitedoree.fr; ❷; closed mid-Dec to Feb, also Sun eve & Mon Oct–May), at the entrance to the village overlooking the River Vers where it flows into the Lot from the north; it has a good-value **restaurant** with menus from €13 (also closed Fri eve in Oct & April). You can rent **bikes** at La Roue Libre, place du Communal

(☎ 05.65.31.45.57, ✉ larouelibre@aol.com), in the centre of the village near the church, which is also where you'll find the **bus stop**.

East of Vers, the D662 hugs the north bank of the Lot as it meanders back and forth beneath cliffs that loom ever higher as you near **BOUZIÈS**, located on the south bank across a narrow suspension bridge. The main reason for coming here is to walk along the **chemin de halage**, a towpath cut into the cliff just above water level on the river's south bank. In pre-railway days it was used by men hauling produce-laden *gabarres* boats upstream. It now forms part of the GR36 long-distance footpath, indicated by red and white markers, which you can join at the car park on the east side of Bouziès. The rock-hewn section starts after about 500m and extends for some 300m; if you're feeling energetic, you can then continue on to St-Cirq Lapopie (see below).

Another way of exploring the river bank is to take to the water. Bouziès is a **boating** and **canoeing** centre, with several companies setting up shop on the south side of the bridge in the summer. You can rent canoes from the hotel (see below), while in July and August Bateaux Safaraid (☎ 05.65.35.98.88, ✉ bateaux.safaraid@club-internet.fr) has "**picnic boats**" for rental by the hour (six-person boats at €25) and by the day (twelve-person boats €150); reservations are recommended at least one week in advance. Safaraid also runs one-and-a-half-hour **excursions** to St-Cirq Lapopie and back (April–Oct 3–4 trips daily; €8.50), with the option of an evening voyage on Fridays (mid-June to mid-Sept 10pm) to admire the floodlit cliffs. Finally, you can rent **houseboats** here through Nicols (see p.35 for more).

SNCF **buses** stop on the main road near the bridge. There's no tourist office, but Bouziès' welcoming **hotel**, *Les Falaises* (☎ 05.65.31.26.83; ❹; closed Nov–March; menus from €18), in the village centre, is a mine of information. Note that the rooms in the main building overlooking the pool and gardens are preferable to those in the older block behind.

St-Cirq Lapopie

Next stop up the valley is the cliff-edge village of **ST-CIRQ LAPOPIE**, 5km east of Bouziès, perched high above the south bank of the Lot. With its cobbled lanes, half-timbered houses and gardens virtually unspoilt by modern intrusions, the village is an irresistible draw for the tour buses, but it's still worth the trouble, especially if you visit early or late in the day.

There has been a **fortress** on this rocky protuberance, known as La Popie, since Gallo-Roman times if not before. So strategically important was the site that in the Middle Ages it was shared by the viscount of St-Cirq with the other three viscounts of Quercy (Gourdon, Cardaillac and Castelnau) and a feudal town grew up within the protection of its walls. It wasn't a particularly safe haven, though: St-Cirq took a battering from the English during the Hundred Years' War, then in the Wars of Religion it was seized by the Protestant Henry of Navarre, who ordered the castle destroyed in 1580 to keep it from the Catholics. Undaunted however, local craftsmen built up a reputation for their skill in **wood turning**, specifically of boxwood, which they fashioned into goblets, furniture and taps for casks. They continued to ply their craft into the nineteenth century, but following industrialization St-Cirq went into steep decline until it was rediscovered in the early twentieth century by the artistic fraternity, most famously **Henri Martin** (see p.302), **Man Ray** and the surrealist poet **André Breton**, who came to live here in the 1950s.

St-Cirq today consists of one main street running steeply downhill for 500m from Porte de la Payrolerie in the west to easterly Porte de Pélissaria; in between which it's variously known as rue de la Payrolerie, **rue Droite** – between the central market square, place du Sombral, and the church – and rue de la Pélissaria. All along are stone and half-timbered houses, under steeply pitched and gabled Quercy roofs. Starting from Porte de la Payrolerie, the first place to head for is the ruined **château** to the north of place du Sombral. Precious little remains of the castle, but the site is fantastic, plunging down to the river 100m below. Further east along the cliff edge, the fortified **church of St-Cirq** is now the village's dominant building. It's in a pretty sorry state itself, though you can still make out faint traces of thirteenth-century murals where the original Romanesque chapel was incorporated into a larger church three hundred years later.

Below the church to the east, the **Musée Rignault** (mid-April to Oct daily except Tues 10am–12.30pm & 2.30–6pm; July & Aug open until 7pm; €1.50) occupies a lovely fortified mansion with a romantic little rock garden and various other embellishments added by an art dealer who came to live here in 1922. A few pieces of his wide-ranging art collection are on display, while the rest of the space is given over to temporary exhibitions. On the way back up the hill, St-Cirq's local history museum, the **Musée de la Mémoire** (mid-March to mid-Nov & school hols daily 10am–noon & 2–6.30pm; €2), in a Renaissance mansion one block south of rue Droite, is worth a peek for its small exhibition on wood turning. **Maison Daura** (daily 3–7pm; ☏05.65.40.78.19), near the entrance to the village, was once the home of Catalan painter **Pierre Daura** and now serves as a residence for international artists and puts on regular modern art exhibits.

Practicalities

Buses on the Cahors–Figeac run drop you across the river in the hamlet of Tour-de-Faure; from there you can call a **taxi** (Lonjou; ☏05.65.31.26.15) or leg it up the steep hill for the last 2km. If you're driving, the most convenient **car park** is that outside Porte de la Payrolerie at the top of the village (Easter to mid-Nov €2 per day, including one free entry to both museums; rest of the year free). The **tourist office**, on place du Sombral (April–June, Sept & Oct daily 10.30am–1pm & 2–6pm; July & Aug daily 10am–1pm & 2–6pm; Nov–March Wed–Sat 10am–1pm & 2–5pm, Sun 1–5pm; ☏05.65.31.29.06, ⓦwww.saint-cirqlapopie.com), can furnish you with a handy English-language walking guide to the village.

There are various **accommodation** options, all of which get booked up weeks ahead in summer. Of the two hotels, ✣ *La Pélissaria* (☏05.65.31.25.14, ⓔhoteldepelissaria@wanadoo.fr; ❺–❻; closed Nov–April), in a sixteenth-century house perched on the cliff just inside St-Cirq's eastern gateway, provides the most atmospheric surroundings – all polished wood floors and exposed stonework, and a pretty terraced garden. The alternative is the *Auberge du Sombral* (☏05.65.31.26.08, ⓕ05.65.30.26.37; ❹; closed mid-Nov to March) on place du Sombral, which offers plain but perfectly adequate rooms. Cheaper accommodation is available in a very comfortable and well-equipped **gîte d'étape** in the same building as the Musée de la Mémoire (☏ & ⓕ05.65.31.21.51; €10 per person; closed Nov 11–Mar 14), and at two well-run three-star **campsites**: *Camping de la Plage* (☏05.65.30.29.51, ⓦwww.campingplage.com; open all year), down by the bridge, and the spacious *La Truffière* (☏05.65.30.20.22, ⓦwww.camping-truffiere.com; closed Oct–March), on the plateau 3km south-east of St-Cirq via the D42. *Camping de la Plage* offers **canoe** and **bike rental** as well as all sorts of other activities (including guided walks, rock climbing and pot-holing), through the Bureau des Sports Nature (☏05.65.24.21.01, ⓦperso.orange.fr/bureau-sports-nature).

As for **restaurants**, you can eat very well at St-Cirq's *L'Oustal* (☎05.65.31.20.17; closed mid-Nov to mid-March & Mon except in July & Aug; midday menus from €9.50), a tiny little place tucked into a corner at the top end of rue de la Pélissaria just south of the church. *Le Gourmet Quercynoise* (☎05.65.31.21.20; closed Mon eve except in July & Aug)on rue de la Peyrolerie at the top of the village, has a shady terrace and menus from €13.80; dishes include pork with honey and herbs and duck with truffles. Halfway up the hill on the main road to the village, the restaurant *Atelier* (☎05.65.31.22.34), offers stunning views over St-Cirq and the valley below and a simple menu of omelettes, salads and grills with menus from around €12. Great views are also to be had at the terrace of ⚜ *Lou Bolat* (closed mid-Nov to Feb, also Mon eve & Tues except in July & Aug), at the top of the village just inside Porte de la Payrolerie, which serves a varied menu of crêpes, salads and regional dishes, with menus starting at €17. In July and August there's a small **market** in place du Sombral on Wednesday mornings, but note that the nearest **food shop** is a small grocer down in Tour-de-Faure.

The Château de Cénevières and around

Travelling on eastwards from St-Cirq, rather than carry on along the main D662 it's preferable to take the smaller and quieter D8 along the river's south bank. Seven kilometres out of St-Cirq, you reach the **Château de Cénevières** (1hr guided tours daily Easter–Oct 10am–noon & 2–6pm; €4.50), perched on another rocky spur just beyond Cénevières village; the nearest **bus stop** is in St-Martin-Labouval, a good kilometre downstream and across on the north bank. The château, which largely dates from the sixteenth century in its present form, belonged to the **de Gourdon** family for nine hundred years until the line petered out in 1616. The last in line, Antoine de Gourdon, was a fervent supporter of the Reformation, so much so that the Protestant leader Henry of Navarre stayed here before attacking Cahors in 1580. Antoine brought back a rich haul which included the cathedral's principal altar – the boat carrying it, however, capsized and the altar is now somewhere at the bottom of the Lot. The château was saved from being torched during the Revolution by a quick-thinking overseer who opened the wine cellars to the mob, though he couldn't save the library, nor the coat of arms and other carvings on the facade. Cénevières was sold only once during its long history, to the ancestors of the present owners in 1793. Over the years they have uncovered several unusual Renaissance-era **frescoes**: notably, a frieze of the Istanbul skyline in the grand salon, and scenes from Greek mythology alongside what is believed to be a representation of an alchemist's fire and the philosopher's stone adorning a little vaulted chamber.

The valley's next rocky eyrie is occupied by the village of **CALVIGNAC**, 5km east from Cénevières on the D8, where a handful of ancient houses cluster round the remnants of another medieval stronghold. In fine weather you can soak up the views at the **restaurant** *La Terrasse Romantique* (☎05.65.30.24.37; closed mid-Sept to April; menus from €10.50), under the tower on the village's east side: the food is nothing special, the tiny terrace nestled into the rock face is a delight.

Cajarc

CAJARC, which lies on the river's north bank 9km upstream from Calvignac, is the biggest town on the Lot between Cahors and Capdenac. It consists of a small core of old lanes encircled by the boulevard du Tour-du-Ville, where you'll find facilities such as banks, food shops and a post office as well as cafés and brasseries.

The town's only sight as such is the **Maison des Arts Georges-Pompidou** (hours vary for each exhibition; ℡05.65.40.63.97; €3 for the mid-June to Aug exhibition, otherwise free) on the northeastern outskirts on the D19 Figeac road. The gallery is named in honour of the former French prime minister, who bought a holiday home near here in 1963, and hosts four major contemporary art exhibitions a year, including artists such as Jean-Pierre Bertrand and Vicente Pimentel; phone ahead to see if there's anything of interest.

SNCF **buses** stop on the north side of town on place du Foirail, a big open square where you'll also find the **tourist office** (June 11–30 & Sept 1–23 Mon–Sat 3.30–6.30pm, Sun 10am–12.30pm; July & Aug daily 10am–1pm & 3.30–7.30pm; ℡05.65.40.72.89, ℻05.65.40.39.05). A **market** takes place on Saturday afternoons on place du Foirail, with larger *foires* (country fairs) on the 10th and 25th of each month. **Bike rental** is available at Garage Couybes, also on place du Foirail (℡05.65.40.66.48).

Cajarc has two **hotels**, the smarter of which is *La Ségalière* (℡05.65.40.65.35, ⓦwww.lasegaliere.com; ❺; closed Nov–April), around 400m east on the D662 to Capdenac. It's a modern, concrete building – not beautiful, but airy and with nicely decorated rooms, some with a small balcony overlooking the pool and spacious gardens. There's also a good restaurant with menus from €14 (closed lunchtime Mon–Fri except in July & Aug). Cajarc's other hotel is *La Promenade*, place du Foirail (℡05.65.40.61.21, ℻05.65.40.79.12; ❷; closed Mon & late Dec to mid-Jan), with a handful of simple rooms above an equally unfussy but convivial restaurant (menus €13–28). There's also a two-star municipal **campsite**, *Le Terriol* (℡05.65.40.72.74, ℻05.65.40.39.05; closed Oct–April), beside the river roughly 200m southwest of the centre.

In addition to the above hotel **restaurants**, it's worth trying *Cajarc Gourmand* (℡05.65.40.69.50; June–Aug closed Wed midday, Sept–May closed Mon–Fri), on a quiet square beside the church. They serve inventive and well-presented cuisine such as duck carpaccio with basil and salmon with saffron sauce, and have various *formules* and menus ranging from €13 up to €25.

On to Capdenac

Upstream from Cajarc, the Lot twists through one more giant meander and then straightens out until you reach the next big loop at Capdenac. Buses follow the northerly route past a succession of picturesque villages and castles, but if you've got your own transport, the less-travelled roads along the river's south bank provide the more interesting route. They take you through walnut orchards and past weathered farm buildings snuggled into the landscape's folds, then up on to the *causse* where the scene changes to flat, empty country with little sign of habitation, past or present, save for the occasional dolmen or *cabane*, the traditional, stone-built shepherds' huts.

Where the D127 first climbs up from the river, 7km from Cajarc, it skirts along the edge of a 300-metre high cliff formed by the meander. The spot is known as the **Saut de la Mounine** ("Monkey's Leap"), after a legend concerning a local lord who ordered his daughter thrown off the cliff when she fell in love with a boy he disapproved of. A hermit took pity on the girl and secretly dressed a monkey in her clothes instead. When the poor beast was chucked over the edge, the lord repented, of course, and was only too relieved to discover he'd been outwitted. He apparently forgave his daughter, but history doesn't relate whom she married. Whatever the outcome, it's a marvellous view from up here, taking in the meander filled with patchwork fields and the ruined Château de Montbrun on the far hillside – where the lord and his daughter once lived.

A few kilometres further on you drop back down to the river along tiny lanes that wend their way northeastwards for about 15km before hitting the main D922. Turn left here and you'll be in Figeac (see p.314) in about ten minutes. Alternatively, if you cross over and follow the D86 along the river, another 7km will bring you to **CAPDENAC**, a major railway town on the south bank of the River Lot. There's a majestic view from the high ridge above the town and river to the north, but otherwise Capdenac is of little interest.

The Grotte de Foissac and Peyrerusse-le-Roc

On reaching the D922, instead of heading immediately north to Figeac or carrying on to Capdenac, it's worth taking a detour south towards Ville-franche to visit one of the less-frequented caves, the **Grotte de Foissac** (℡05.65.64.77.04, ⓦwww.grotte-de-foissac.com; 1hr guided tours: April, May & Oct daily except Sat 2–6pm; June & Sept daily 10–11.30am & 2–6pm; July & Aug daily 10am–6pm; €7.20); it's signposted about 6km down the D922 and lies another 3km west across the *causse* through Foissac village. The cave was discovered in 1959 by a local pot-holing club, who found not only a huge cavern of colourful and varied concretions, including delicate needles, some bulging out into onion shapes, but also evidence of human activity going back at least four thousand years. From the number of **skeletons** and their positions, it seems that, unusually, the cave was used as a cemetery. It was also a source of clay – you can still see where people dug it out with their hands, and they also left large and beautifully fashioned pots, probably for storing grain. But the most moving evidence is the lone footprint left by a child deep inside the cave.

Twenty kilometres to the east of Foissac, via beautiful back lanes through Naussac and along the Roselle, the ruined towers of **PEYRERUSSE-LE-ROC** are also well worth a look. The "modern" village, a tiny weatherworn huddle of half-timbered houses gathered round a seventeenth-century church, sits above a narrow valley. On the valley sides, hidden in the steep woods, lie the scattered remains of a fortified medieval town which once sheltered some 4500 people – a sizeable population in those days – who were seeking their fortunes in the local silver mines. But their luck ran out in the early sixteenth century, when silver from the recently discovered Americas began to flood the market, and the town was eventually abandoned around 1700. The site is gradually being tidied up and some of the buildings restored, but still remains a moving and atmospheric place.

A path leads from the northwest corner of the church square to a pinnacle of rock crowned by **twin towers**, all that's left of the medieval fortress which protected the town. If you've got a head for heights, you can scramble up the iron ladders for a vertiginous view of the gorge. From here a cobbled mule trail leads steeply down through the woods, where the stones of a Gothic church, synagogue and hospital stand roofless, to the river and a little thirteenth-century chapel, complete but not open to the public. To return to the modern village, follow the river downstream and pick up another path which takes you past the old market hall to the village gate. It's possible to do shorter circuits simply by following the signs, or you can buy a guidebook and map (€3.50) from the **tourist office** beside the church (May–Sept Tues–Sun 10am–12.30pm & 3–7pm; rest of year Mon–Fri 10am–noon & 1–5pm; ℡05.65.80.49.33, Ⓔpeyrusseinfo@wanadoo.fr).

The Célé valley

Instead of following the River Lot east from Cahors, you can take an alternative route to Figeac along the wilder and narrower **Célé valley**, which joins the Lot a kilometre or so upstream from Bouziès (see p.305). A single road winds through the luxuriant canyon-like valley, frequented mainly by canoeists and walkers on the GR651 footpath, which runs sometimes close to the river, sometimes on the edge of the *causse* on the north bank. The major settlement along here is **Cabrerets**, a village not far upstream from the Célé's confluence with the Lot, which serves as a base for the nearby **Grotte de Pech-Merle**. Well hidden on the scrubby hillsides to the west of the river, this enormous cave system combines superb examples of prehistoric art with an array of calcite deposits in all shapes and sizes. Continuing northeast, the valley is punctuated by a succession of villages and hamlets built against the cliff face. Of these, two in particular stand out: **Marcilhac-sur-Célé**, about halfway along the valley, for the atmospheric ruins of its abbey; and the tiny hamlet of **Espagnac-Ste-Eulalie** in the north, where another, more substantial church sports a delightfully whimsical belfry.

There's no **public transport** along the Célé, but you can rent bicycles at Conduché (on the bus route from Cahors to Figeac), where the Célé joins the Lot, at Bureau des Sports Nature (℡05.65.24.21.01, Ⓦperso.orange.fr /bureau-sports-nature). Another good option is to descend the Célé by canoe; rental outlets in St-Cirq, Figeac and near Cabrerets will organize the necessary transport.

Cabrerets

CABRERETS lies 4km up the Célé from its confluence with the Lot, the approach guarded by the sturdy **Château de Gontaut-Biron** (not open to the public), on a small flood plain where the River Sagne joins the Célé. It's a pretty enough spot, but the only real reason to linger here is to take advantage of its tourist amenities.

Firstly, there's a small **tourist office** in the village centre on the road to Pech-Merle (April–June & Sept Wed–Sun 10am–1pm & 2–6pm; July & Aug daily 10am–1pm & 2–7pm; ℡05.65.31.27.12, Ⓕ05.65.24.38.11), which sells handy guides detailing walks in the area. There's also a pair of two-star **hotel-restaurants**. In the village itself, overlooking the Célé, *Les Grottes* (℡05.65.31.27.02, Ⓦwww.hoteldesgrottes.com; ❷; closed Nov–Easter) is a welcoming place with functional rooms – the cheapest without an en-suite toilet – and a decent restaurant

△ The Célé valley

(menus from €14.50). The alternative is the slightly smarter and absolutely spotless *Auberge de la Sagne* (☎05.65.31.26.62, ⓦwww.hotel-auberge-cabrerets .com; ❸; closed mid-Sept to mid-May), 1km west of the village on the road to the caves; there's a pool, well-tended garden and a restaurant offering good-quality home cooking (evenings only; menus at €15 & €21; reservations recommended). In addition, there's simple **chambre d'hôte** accommodation available at *Chez Bessac* (☎05.65.31.27.04; ❷; closed Nov–Easter) near Cabrerets' tourist office; they also run a **gîte d'étape** (€8 per person) with its own kitchen and a modern dormitory. The last option is a small two-star **campsite**, *Le Cantal* (☎05.65.31.26.61, ⓕ05.65.31.20.47; closed Nov–March), immediately north of Cabrerets on the other side of the Célé.

Grotte de Pech-Merle

Up in the hills 3km west of Cabrerets by road, or 1km via the footpath from beside the *mairie*, the **Grotte de Pech-Merle** (1hr guided visits: April–Nov daily 9.30am–noon & 1.30–5pm; ☎05.65.31.27.05, ⓦwww.pechmerle.com; €7.50) takes some beating. Discovered in 1922 by two local boys, the galleries are not only full of the most spectacular limestone formations – structures tiered like wedding cakes, hanging like curtains, or shaped like discs or "cave pearls" – but also contain an equally dazzling display of more than five hundred **prehistoric drawings**. To protect the drawings tickets are restricted to seven hundred per day (it's advisable to book four or five days ahead in July and August and at least one day ahead at other times; Internet bookings must be made at least a week in advance), and the guides make sure you're processed through in the allotted time. If possible, it's worth allowing yourself time to visit the **museum**, located beside the ticket office (same hours; same ticket), before your scheduled tour. A twenty-minute film, subtitled in English, provides an excellent overview of Pech-Merle and its prehistoric art.

The drawings date mostly from the early Magdalenian era (around 16,000–17,000 years ago), contemporaneous with much of the cave art in the Vézère valley (see p.227), with which they share many similarities. The first drawings you come to are in the so-called **Chapelle des Mammouths**, executed on a white calcite panel that looks as if it's been specially prepared for the purpose; note how the artists used the contour and relief of the rock to do the work, producing utterly convincing mammoths with just two lines. In addition to the mammoths, there are horses, oxen and bison charging head down with tiny rumps and arched tails; the guide will point out where St-Cirq's André Breton (see p.306) added his own mammoth – he was fined but the damage was done. Next comes a vast chamber containing the glorious **horse frieze**, the oldest of the drawings (at around 25,000 years). Two large horses stand back to back, the head of one formed by a natural protuberance of rock, and their hindquarters superimposed to provide perspective. The surface is spattered with black dots of some unknown symbolic significance and silhouettes of hands, while the ceiling is covered with finger marks preserved in the soft clay. On the way you pass the skeletons of cave-hyena and bears that have been lying there for thousands of years, and, finally, the footprints of an adolescent preserved in a muddy pool some eight thousand years ago.

Upstream to Marcilhac-sur-Célé

Back on the D41 heading up the Célé from Cabrerets, you emerge from a tunnel after 3km to find old bikes, mannequins and even the shells of cars hanging from the rock face. They belong to the gloriously eccentric **Petit Musée** de l'Insolite, the "little museum of the extraordinary" (April–Sept 9am–1pm & 2–8pm; rest of year by appointment; ℡05.65.30.21.01; free), run by a wood sculptor with an engaging sense of humour. Both his garden and gallery are full of bizarre montages fashioned out of tree stumps, old machines and other bits of scrap. Along the river here you'll also find two **canoe rental** outlets: Les Amis du Célé (open all year; ℡05.65.31.26.73, ⓦwww.amisducele.com), and Nature et Loisirs (April–Oct; ℡05.65.30.25.69). Both organize descents of the Célé, while the latter also has **bikes** for rent and the former offers rock-climbing and pot-holing outings.

The next village of interest is **MARCILHAC**, 16km upstream from Cabrerets, whose partly ruined Benedictine **abbey** (same hours as tourist office – see below; €3; tickets from tourist office), with its gaping walls and broken columns, conjures a strongly romantic atmosphere. Founded some time prior to the ninth century, the abbey had the good fortune to be in charge of the modest sanctuary at Rocamadour (see p.265), in which St Amadour's body was discovered in 1186. The subsequent revenue from pilgrims and benefactors led to a brief golden age, which came to a grinding halt when English troops laid waste to the abbey in the Hundred Years' War. It never really recovered and was abandoned after the Reformation. Entering the abbey from the south, a rather primitive and badly damaged ninth-century Christ in majesty decorates the tympanum over the ruined door. In the damp interior of the church itself are late-fifteenth-century frescoes of the Apostles and another Christ in majesty, with the coats of arms of the local nobility below. The few religious treasures that survived – such as a seventeenth-century polychrome pietà and a nicely rendered statue of a pilgrim – are now on display in the small **Musée d'Art Sacré**, in a handsome half-timbered house immediately west of the abbey church which also doubles as a **tourist office** (April, May & Oct Tues–Sat 10am–noon & 2–5pm; June & Sept Tues–Sat 10am–noon & 2–6pm, Sun 2–5pm; July & Aug Mon 2.30–6.30pm, Tues–Sat 10am–12.30pm & 2.30–6.30pm, Sun 2.30–6.30pm; ℡05.65.40.68.44, ⓔmarcilhac@quercy.net).

It's worth timing your visit to **eat** at the attractive *Restaurant des Touristes* on the main street, to the northwest of the abbey (by reservation only, ℡05.65.40.65.61), where you'll feast on hearty home cooking for around €17. There's a **gîte d'étape** in the abbey (℡05.65.40.61.43; €6; closed Nov–Easter), as well as a two-star municipal **campsite**, *Le Pré de Monsieur* (℡05.65.40.77.88; closed Nov–March), just north of the village.

Espagnac-Ste-Eulalie

The tiny and beautiful hamlet of **ESPAGNAC-STE-EULALIE** lies about 12km upriver from Marcilhac and is reached across an old stone bridge. Immediately across the bridge, an eye-catching octagonal lantern crowns the belfry of the priory **church of Notre-Dame-du-Val-Paradis** (1hr guided tours: daily 10.30am, 4.30pm & 5.30pm by appointment, call Mme Bonzani on ℡05.65.40.06.17; €2 donation expected). The building itself is strangely ill-proportioned, a result of the nave being truncated in the Hundred Years' War, which somehow adds to its charm. Inside, apart from a typically over-the-top altarpiece of the Counter-Reformation, the most interesting features are the ornate tombs of the church's thirteenth-century benefactor, Aymeric d'Hébrard de St-Sulpice, a local man who became bishop of Coimbra in Portugal, and those of the duke of Cardaillac and his wife, who financed the rebuilding of the choir in the fourteenth century.

An ancient fortified gateway south of the church now houses a **gîte d'étape** (℡05.65.11.42.66; closed early Nov to Feb) with a choice between a dormitory (€7 per person), and rooms with three beds (€11 per person). Simple but good-quality **dinners** are available at *Les Jardins du Célé* (March, Sept & Oct Sat & Sun; July & Aug Mon–Sat; closed Nov–April; menu €15 including wine), in the row of houses next to the church; you must reserve in advance on ☎05.65.40.08.34. The only other accommodation around is at two good three-star **campsites** beside the river in **BRENGUES**, a hamlet 3km back downstream from Espagnac: the three-star *Le Moulin Vieux* (☎05.65.40.00.41, ℱ05.65.40.05.65; closed Oct–March), with a restaurant, pool and **canoe** rental, and the smaller municipal site (☎05.65.40.06.82, ℱ05.65.40.05.71; closed Oct–May).

❻ Figeac

Situated on the River Célé some 70km east of Cahors, **FIGEAC** is a most appealing town with an unspoilt medieval centre which is, surprisingly, not too encumbered by tourism. Its principal church, the **Église St-Sauveur**, contains a sumptuous rendition of the Passion of Christ in a side chapel, and there's an excellent **museum** devoted to famed locally born Egyptologist Jean-François Champollions. But best of all is simply to wander its narrow lanes, lined with a delightful array of houses, both stone and half-timbered, adorned with carvings, ornate colonnaded windows and elaborate ironwork.

Some history

Like many other provincial towns hereabouts, Figeac owes its beginnings to the foundation of an **abbey** in the early days of Christianity, one which quickly became wealthy thanks to its position on the pilgrim roads to both Rocamadour (see p.265) and Compostela (see p.385). In the Middle Ages the town flourished as a trading centre exporting wine and woollen fabrics throughout Europe, so much so that the wealthy merchants began to challenge the abbey's authority. In 1302 King Philip IV (the Fair) resolved the issue by sending his representative, the Viguier, to bring Figeac directly under royal control. At the same time he granted the town the all-important right to mint money. Figeac's fortunes declined during the Hundred Years' War, then revived at the time of the Renaissance, but it was the Wars of Religion that pushed it into eclipse. The town threw in its lot with the Protestants in 1576, providing them with an important safe-haven, until it was brought forcefully back into line in 1622. Figeac later became an important centre for tanning hides, and received a further boost with the arrival of the railway in 1862.

During **World War II** the Germans converted Figeac's Ratier metal workshop into a factory churning out propellers for Luftwaffe bombers. When the Resistance destroyed the plant in 1944, more than five hundred local men were carted off to labour and concentration camps, from which at least 120 failed to return at the end of the war. By the 1960s the town's old quarter had declined to such an extent that the majority of buildings were declared uninhabitable. It was designated a preservation zone in 1986, since when the authorities have put a tremendous effort into restoring the medieval and Renaissance buildings.

Arrival, information and accommodation

Figeac's **gare SNCF** – on the Toulouse–Clermont–Ferrand and Toulouse–Figeac–Brive lines – lies about 600m south of the town centre. SNCF **buses** from Cahors, Gramat and Villefranche-de-Rouergue stop at the train station, while most other services drop you at the *gare routière* on avenue du Maréchal-Joffre, a couple of minutes' walk west of the centre. If you're arriving **by**

car, note that the old quarter is largely pedestrianized. The most convenient parking is along the river bank or on place Vival, where you'll also find the **tourist office** (May, June & Sept Mon–Sat 10am–12.30pm & 2.30–6pm, Sun 10am–1pm; July & August daily 10am–7pm; Oct–April Mon–Sat 10am–noon & 2.30–6pm; ☎05.65.34.06.25, ⓦwww.quercy-tourisme.com/figeac), in the very striking Hôtel de la Monnaie building. They supply a useful do-it-yourself guide to Figeac, and sell booklets outlining walks in the surrounding area, while in summer you can sign up for one of their excellent **guided tours** (in French only), of which "*À la découverte de Figeac*" provides the best general introduction (April, May & Sept Sat 4.30pm; July & Aug daily 5pm; 1hr 30min; €5.50).

FIGEAC

0   200 m

Cardaillac & Brive

Célé Valley & Cahors

Brive

Capdenac & Rodez

Gare SNCF

Police

RUE DU GRIAL

AV. DU GENERAL-DE-GAULLE

AVENUE DES CARMES

AVENUE KASIMIR MARCENAC

PLACE DU FOIRAIL

BOULEVARD DU COLONEL-TEULIE

RUE DE LA FONTAINE AUX CHEVRES

AVENUE JULIEN-BAILLY

CHEMIN DU BATAILLE

RUE DES MAQUISARDS

RUE DE LA CROIX BLANCHE

RUE MALLEVILLE

RUE ST-THOMAS

RUE D'AUJOU

RUE SEGUIER

RUE JUSKIEWENSKY

AVENUE FERNAND-PEZET

BOULEVARD DOCTEUR G. JUSKIEWENSKY

RUE DE LA REPUBLIQUE

RUE GAMBETTA

RUE DU 11 NOVEMBRE

RUE CAVIALE

RUE DE LA GANTERIE

RUE STE-MARTHE

Gare Routière

RUE DES CORDELIERS

AVENUE DU MARECHAL-JOFFRE

Hôtel de la Monnaie ⓘ

PLACE VIVAL

RUE ORTABADIAL

RUE BALENE

RUE GAMBETTA

QUAI ALBERT-BESSIÈRES

Footbridge

River Célé

AVENUE JEAN-JAURÈS

AVENUE GEORGES-POMPIDOU

RUE R STJACQUES

RUE DE COLOMB

RUE DELCLOS

Notre-Dame du Puy

PLACE DU PAY

Espace Patrimoine

Maison du Griffon

Musée Champollion

IMP CHAMPOLLION

PL DES ECRITURES

PLACE CHAMPOLLION

RUE BOUTARIC

RUE DELCLOS

RUE TOMFORT

BOULEVARD DU COLONEL-TEULIE

RUE EMILE-ZOLA

RUE DU CONSULAT

RUE BADELE

RUE DE CLERMONT

PL AUX HERBES

R CAPOTE

PLACE E MICHELET

RUE BOODEFORT

RUE FERRER

PLACE DE L'ESTANG

Église St-Sauveur

RUE DU CHAPITRE

PLACE DE LA RAISON

AVENUE DU MARECHAL-FOCH

RUE DU 16 MAI

RUE DU 16 MAI

PLACE CARNOT

PONT GAMBETTA

RUE DU GRIFFOUL

ALLÉE VICTOR-HUGO

AVENUE DE LA GARE

AVENUE E. BOUYSSOU

RUE M. BARGEL

AVENUE GEORGES-CLEMENCEAU

N

① ② ③ ④ ⑤ ⑥ ⑦ ⑧ ⑨ Ⓐ Ⓑ Ⓒ Ⓓ Ⓔ Ⓕ Ⓖ @

RESTAURANTS & BARS
Le 5 Brasserie	3
La Cuisine du Marché	6
La Dînée du Viguier	2
La Flambée	4
Pizzeria del Portel	7
La Puce à l'Oreille	1
La Table de Marinette	8
Les Templiers	5

ACCOMMODATION
Des Bains	C
Camping Les Rives du Célé	E
Le Champolion	B
Château du Viguier du Roy	A
Hostellerie de l'Europe	F
Le Pont d'Or	D
Le Terminus St-Jacques	G

Figeac has a mixed bag of **accommodation**. There are three possibilities in the old quarter at completely opposite ends of the spectrum, and then a scattering over on the south bank of the river and towards the *gare SNCF*. The tourist office can supply lists of *chambres d'hôtes* in the area and there's a **gîte d'étape** at 26 chemin du Bataillé (ⓣ05.65.50.01.83; €11 per person; open all year) in the northeastern suburbs. The nearest **campsite** is the well-equipped three-star *Les Rives du Célé*, by the river 2km east of town in the Domaine du Surgié leisure complex (ⓣ05.65.34.59.00, ⓦwww.domainedesurgie.com; closed Oct–March). It contains a restaurant, grocery and several pools, and in July and August you can also rent **canoes** here through Figeac Eau Vive (ⓣ05.65.50.05.48), for trips down both the Lot and Célé.

Des Bains 1 rue du Griffoul ⓣ05.65.34.10.89, ⓦwww.hoteldesbains.fr. This recently renovated hotel just across from the old town is one of the nicest place to stay in Figeac. Rooms are spotless and well presented and the more expensive have a/c, balconies and Internet access. What makes the hotel special though, is the friendly and energetic hosts, who are a mine of information about the local area. ❸

Le Champollion 3 place Champollion ⓣ05.65.34.04.37, ⓕ05.65.34.61.69. This welcoming place offers ten surprisingly modern en-suite rooms above a popular café right in the centre. Try and get one of the two rooms overlooking the square. ❸

Château du Viguier du Roy rue Émile-Zola ⓣ05.65.50.05.05, ⓦwww.chateau-viguier-figeac.com. Figeac's one and only luxury hotel occupies a national monument, a magnificent medieval residence that was formerly the seat of the king's representative, the Viguier. Each room is individually designed in such styles as Renaissance or Venetian, and a pool, pretty cloister garden and a top-notch restaurant (see p.319), complete the picture. Closed late Oct to March. ❽

Hostellerie de l'Europe 51 allée Victor-Hugo ⓣ05.65.34.10.16, ⓦwww.hostelleriedeleurope.com. One block behind the *Hôtel des Bains*, on a busy main road, this recently renovated 1930s hotel is better than it looks from the outside. The rooms come with a/c and other two-star comforts, and there's a small pool. Closed Jan. ❸

Le Pont d'Or 2 av Jean-Jaurès ⓣ05.65.50.95.00, ⓦwww.hotelpontdor.com. Modern riverside hotel offering spick-and-span rooms with good-sized bathrooms; those on the riverfront have balconies. Other facilities include a brasserie-style restaurant (menus from €12.50; closed Sun eve except in July & Aug), a bar, rooftop pool and gym. They also serve a better-than-average breakfast buffet (€9). ❹–❺

Le Terminus St-Jacques 27 av Georges-Clémenceau ⓣ05.65.34.00.43, ⓦwww.hotel-terminus.fr. This small family-run hotel is handy for the train station and a favourite with walkers. Rooms are nothing special, but are comfortable enough, and there's a surprisingly smart restaurant (menus €25–50; closed Sun eve & for lunch on Mon & Sat). ❸

The Town

Figeac's old quarter sits on the north bank of the River Célé, its ramparts and ditches now replaced with a ring of boulevards. From the southern boulevard, the town's main artery and principal shopping street, pedestrianized **rue Gambetta**, leads north from the old stone bridge, **Pont Gambetta**, to place Carnot, with its market hall, and to neighbouring place Champollion.

The best place to start your explorations is on **place Vival** to the west of rue Gambetta, where the tourist office occupies the eye-catching **Hôtel de la Monnaie**. The building's origins go back to the thirteenth century when the city's mint was located in this district, and it's typical of Figeac's medieval merchants' houses, starting off with arcaded openings on the ground floor, while the colonnaded and sculpted windows above indicate the living quarters. These are now home to a none-too-exciting **museum** (same hours as the tourist office – see p.315; €2) of old coins and archeological bits and pieces found in the surrounding area, and an incongruous selection of presidential gifts

△ Place Champollion, Figeac

– Moroccan and Tunisian saddles, Indonesian ivory and the like – passed on by President Pompidou, who owned a holiday home near Cajarc (see p.308).

On the eastern side of rue Gambetta you'll find the much-altered **Église St-Sauveur** on a big, gravelled square overlooking the river. Its lofty yet restrained nave provides a striking contrast to the intimate **Notre-Dame-de-la-Pitié** chapel, to the south of the choir, decorated with heavily gilded but dramatically realistic seventeenth-century carved wood panels. The finest are those above the altar, where the Virgin Mary, her face full of sorrow, is flanked by scenes of the Descent from the Cross and the Entombment. Note also the unusual depiction of an infant Jesus asleep on the Cross surrounded by the instruments of the Passion – such as the cockerel and crown of thorns – to the bottom right.

Continuing north along rue Gambetta, cafés spread their tables under the nineteenth-century *halle* in the middle of **place Carnot**, surrounded by a delightful range of stone and half-timbered houses. Some sport open wooden galleries at the top; another typical feature of this region, these *solelhos* were used for drying and storing foodstuffs. The main weekly **food market** takes place here on Saturdays (dry goods are sold on place Vival). To the east, place Carnot opens into the grander but equally alluring **place Champollion**, named after **Jean-François Champollion**, who finally cracked Egyptian hieroglyphics by deciphering the Rosetta Stone (see box on p.318). The square's south side is dominated by a stunning, white-stone Gothic mansion with a row of handsome ornamental windows, filled with lacy trefoil stonework. Opposite, the **Maison du Griffon** on the corner with rue de Colomb is far less ostentatious, but this is Figeac's oldest house, built in the twelfth century and named after a barely visible griffin carved on the left-hand window arch (now blocked up) on the third floor.

Champollion was born nearby in a house at 4 impasse Champollion, to the northwest of the square, which now contains the fascinating **Musée Champollion**. The museum, which is currently being enlarged and is due to reopen mid-2007 (get an update from the tourist office or from Ⓦ www.ville-figeac.fr/musee), is dedicated not only to Champollion's life and work but also to the history of the languages and scripts of the lower Mediterranean basin. In addition to many beautiful examples of hieroglyphic script, it houses an excellent collection of funerary objects from the sixth and seventh centuries BC – sarcophagi, amulets and statues of the gods and goddesses, such as Bastet, a superb bronze cat, and an exquisitely crafted head of the god-king Osiris.

At the west end of this alley, a gigantic reproduction of the Rosetta Stone – the work of American artist Joseph Kossuth – forms the floor of the tiny **place des Écritures**, above which is a little garden with medicinal herbs and tufts of papyrus in pots. If it's open, you can cut through the **Espace Patrimoine** (April to early July & late Sept to early Oct Tues–Sun 2–6pm; early July to late Sept daily 10am–12.30pm & 3–7pm; free), a one-room exhibition illustrating Figeac's history and architecture, to rue de Colomb.

On the east side of place Champollion, it's worth walking along rue Émile-Zola past the front of the **Hôtel du Viguier**, now a luxury hotel (see p.316). As you go by, look out for three small sculptures on the facade: to the left a very fine portrait of the building's fifteenth-century owner; to the right an architect clutching his callipers; and in the middle the present owner, added during recent renovations. Round the corner on rue Delzhens, the large square tower looming over the street is the last vestige of the Viguier's fourteenth-century residence. You'll get a better view of it if you continue on up the hill to the **church of Notre-Dame du Puy**. Transformed into a veritable fortress by the Protestants in the late 1500s, then partially destroyed by Catholic

Champollion and the Rosetta Stone

Jean-François Champollion was born in Figeac in 1790, the son of a bookseller who opened a shop on place Carnot, in what is now *Le Sphynx* café. His interest in Egypt was first sparked by news coming back from Napoleon Bonaparte's 1798 Egyptian adventures, and when an acquaintance showed him the ancient Egyptians' so-far indecipherable script two years later, he became hooked. Declaring that he would solve the puzzle, Champollion set about studying ancient and Middle Eastern languages – he eventually mastered a mind-boggling total of twenty – and poring over hieroglyphs. One of the most important resources available was the **Rosetta Stone**. A slab of black basalt measuring around 120cm in height and 80cm wide, the stone was discovered in 1799 by French soldiers building fortifications around the town of Rosetta in the Nile delta; three years later it fell into British hands when they seized Egypt from the French, and it now resides in London's British Museum.

The crucial significance of the Rosetta Stone is that the same text – a decree issued in 196 BC recording the honours to be accorded to the young Pharaoh Ptolemy – is repeated in three different scripts: **hieroglyphics**, demotic (an abbreviated, cursive form of hieroglyphics used for everyday affairs) and Greek. By being able to translate the Greek, scholars then had fresh clues, but it took until 1822 before Champollion made the final breakthrough when he realized that hieroglyphs were, broadly, not pictograms but phonetic characters – within two years he had identified the majority of symbols. And all this without having set foot in Egypt. He made his one and only voyage to the country in 1828, but died of a stroke four years later at the age of 41.

reprisals, it now contains little of interest, but its cedar-shaded terrace is a peaceful spot from which to look down on the roofs of Figeac. When you've done, take cobbled rue St-Jacques twisting and turning down the hillside back to rue de Colomb and place Champollion.

Eating and drinking

Figeac's old centre is well provided with **restaurants**, offering everything from pizza to haute cuisine. When it comes to **cafés** or **bars**, your best bet is *Le Champollion* hotel (see p.316) on place Champollion, or, in winter, the cosy, British-style bar in the *Hôtel du Pont d'Or* (see p.316). For picnic food, there's a handy supermarket on the corner of rue Gambetta and rue de Clermont.

Le 5 Brasserie 51 place Champollion. Stylish new place with dark-brown leather furniture, vaulted ceilings, and huge picture windows. It serves up tasty French food with an Indian influence such as spicy frog's legs with sautéed rice and Goan *cassoulet*. Menus from €16.

La Dinée du Viguier 4 rue Boutaric ☏05.65.50.08.08. The restaurant of the *Château du Viguier du Roy* hotel (see p.316) isn't as expensive as one might expect for such rarefied cuisine: there's a good-value midday menu at €20 and three-course menus from €29, though you're looking at around €60 eating *à la carte*. There are only a handful of tables in its elegant stone-walled room, so reservations are essential. Closed Sat lunch & Mon, Sun eve Oct–May and three weeks in both early Jan & Nov.

La Flambeé 28 rue Caviale. Join the locals in this rustic little restaurant specializing in chargrilled meats and pastas. Main dishes cost €9 to €14, or you can opt for a three-course menu (including wine) for €14. Closed Sun & lunchtime Mon.

Pizzeria del Portel 9 rue Orthabadial. Another good-value and convivial place serving tasty pizzas, big salad platters and no fewer than seven varieties of *moules frites* including pesto and Roquefort. It also has the benefit of an outside terrace. Most dishes come in at under €12. Closed Sun lunch & Mon.

La Puce à l'Oreille 5 rue St-Thomas ☏05.65.34.33.08. Located north of place Carnot in a handsome fifteenth-century residence with an interior court for fine weather, and walls adorned with work by local artists, this place serves rich Quercy fare – make sure you leave room for one of their scrumptious desserts. Menus range from €14.80 to €38 and there's a fulsome regional wine list. Closed Sun eve & Mon except in July & Aug; also closed one week in June & three weeks in Oct.

La Table de Marinette 51 allée Victor-Hugo ☏05.65.50.06.07. It's worth venturing south across the river for the well-priced menus in this stylish Art Deco restaurant. Specialities include *cassoulet*, Quercy lamb and *pastis*, the local dessert of apple tart topped with a mountain of ultra-fine crinkly pastry. They offer a wide range of menus starting at €13 (€23 eves & weekends), while eating *à la carte* will set you back upwards of €35. Closed mid-Oct to May Sat & Sun eve.

Les Templiers 6 rue de la République ☏05.65.34.28.53. Attractive restaurant with a large first-floor terrace overlooking the rue de la République serving hearty regional cuisine such as pork braised in cider and onions and steak with port and mushrooms. Menus start at €12. Closed Mon.

Listings

Bike rental Office Intercommunal du Sport du Pays de Figeac/Cajard, 2 av du Général-de-Gaulle ☏05.65.34.52.54.

Books and newspapers For local guides and English newspapers, try Maison de la Presse, down by the river at 2 rue Gambetta.

Bus information For details of all bus routes, call the central information desk on ☏05.65.53.27.50.

Car rental ADA, on the road west to Cahors ☏05.65.11.62.92; Avis, on the south side of the river at 1 av Georges-Pompidou ☏05.65.34.10.28. Both offer station pick-ups on request.

Hospital Centre Hospitalier is to the west of the old quarter at 33 rue des Maquisards ☏05.65.50.65.50.

Internet You can log on at Dragoon-PL at 1 av E. Bouyssou; Tues-Fri 10am–noon & 2–7pm; Sat 10am–6pm.

Police Commissariat de Police, Cité Administrative, place des Carmes ☏05.65.50.73.73.

Post office The central post office is at 6 av Fernand-Pezet, 46100 Figeac.

Taxis Call Jean-Michel Luc on ☏05.65.50.00.20, or Didier Escribano on ☏05.65.50.01.73.

The Causse de Gramat

After the intimate beauty of the Lot and Célé valleys, the wide horizons of the **Causse de Gramat** to the north make a refreshing change. It's an empty land with few people and few villages, filled only with the sound of sheep bells and the cicadas' persistent clamour during the tinder-box-dry summers. Across the gently undulating landscape of scrubby pines and oaks, and close-cropped grass spattered with orchids and aromatic plants, you'll come across dolmens, shepherds' dry-stone huts and strange *lacs de St-Namphaise* – water holes hacked out of the rock – but little else to make you want to stop. The exceptions are mostly along the *causse's* southern boundary, starting off in the far southeast with **Assier**, a small village put on the map by a vainglorious military man who built a château and church here. From Assier the route tracks westward through a series of picturesque villages to the even more diminutive **Caniac-du-Causse**, last resting place of St Namphaise of *lacs* fame. At Caniac the route turns northwards into the wildest part of the *causse* towards the busy market town of **Gramat**, home to an above-average wildlife park.

The main towns in this area are well served by **public transport**. Assier and Gramat both lie on main **train** lines and are also accessible by **bus**. However, to do the *causse* justice you really do need your own means of getting about. With few roads and only a sprinkling of villages, this is a great area for **walking** or **mountain biking**; most tourist offices have maps of recommended routes.

Assier

If it weren't for the immoderate – and immodest – nature of Galiot de Genouillac, **ASSIER**, some 17km northwest of Figeac, would probably have remained an insignificant village. Chief of artillery under François I and an inspired tactician, de Genouillac really earned his stripes during the decisive French victory at Marignano in 1515 during the Italian Wars, after which he returned to his native village bathed in glory to erect a **château** befitting his status (April–June & Sept daily except Tues 10am–12.15pm & 2–6.15pm; July & Aug daily 10am–12.30pm & 2–6.45pm; Oct–March daily except Tues 10am–12.15pm & 2–5.15pm; €4.60). Built in the latest Renaissance style, it was said to rival the châteaux of the Loire, with its vast interior courtyard flanked by four round towers, its galleries, loggias and carved friezes – and liberal repetition of de Genouillac's motto: *J'aime fortune* ("In love with chance/success"). After 1768, however, the château and its contents were sold off lock, stock and barrel to raise money, leaving only part of the west wing – and even that is in a pretty poor state.

You can get a better idea of de Genouillac's decorative tastes from the **church** he also had built in the village square. It's an extraordinary edifice, not just because of its size and the feeling that it was built to the glory of de Genouillac rather than God, but mainly due to a frieze running round the exterior depicting Roman centurions, guns being hauled across the Alps, flame-spewing cannon and cities under siege – all beautifully realized but hardly normal church ornamentation. Less surprisingly, the most interesting feature inside is the great man's tomb in an intricately vaulted chapel near the west door. He appears twice: as a bearded man lying with his feet on powder sacks, and as a soldier leaning nonchalantly against a cannon.

Assier is a stop on the main Figeac–Brive train line, with a daily service direct to Paris. The **gare SNCF** lies nearly 1km west of the village. All **buses** running between Figeac and Gramat stop at the *gare*, and some also stop on the church square. There's a very helpful **tourist office** (mid-June to mid-Sept

Mon–Sat 10am–noon & 1–5pm; mid-Sept to mid-June Tues & Fri 3–5pm; ⓣ & ⓕ05.65.40.50.60) on the square's northeast corner and, opposite the church, an equally accommodating **restaurant**, *Chez Noelle* (closed Tues & Sun eves & three weeks in Sept), offering traditional family cuisine *(plat du jour* €7.50, menus from €10.50). A slightly smarter option is the *Auberge le Galiot*, just south of the main square on the road to Reyrevignes, which has a garden and pool and serves tasty Quercynois cuisine (ⓣ05.65.40.51.33; menus €12.50–25; closed Oct–Easter).

The southern causse

With your own transport, you can take a circuitous route from Assier through **the southern causse** before cutting northeast to Gramat. There are a few scattered sights to aim for, but on the whole it's the scenery that takes precedence in this high, open country with its grand vistas.

Five kilometres southwest of Assier on the D653, **LIVERNON** is the first of a string of attractive villages, in this case distinguished by a particularly appealing Romanesque belfry, with its rhythmically spaced arches. The route then meanders further south via **ESPÉDAILLAC** – a cluster of crumbling towers and pigeon-lofts – to **QUISSAC**, roughly 10km from Livernon. The main claim to fame of this tiny village is that the ninth-century soldier-turned-hermit **St Namphaise** lived in a nearby grotto. He's a terribly important person on the *causse*, since it was he who, according to legend, dug the shallow ponds in the rock which are characteristic of this region, thus providing water for the flocks of sheep; ironically, he is said to have been killed by an irate bull. There's a statue of Namphaise dressed as a soldier in Quissac church, and you can see one of his famous *lacs* about 1km south of the village beside the Coursac road.

The dying Namphaise supposedly threw away his hammer – with which he presumably created the ponds – and declared that he would be buried wherever it came to rest; it landed 8km away in what is now the village of **CANIAC-DU-CAUSSE**. It's a sleepy, flowery place undisturbed by the trickle of visitors come to view Namphaise's small, unadorned sarcophagus lying in a diminutive twelfth-century crypt beneath the village church.

From Caniac cut north across country on the D42, keeping a lookout on the right for signs down a dirt track to the Site de Planagrèze, a couple of kilometres later. At the end of the track various footpaths and biking trails strike out across the *causse*, while one of the more accessible dolmen stands a short walk south. On the way you pass a fenced-off area, in the middle of which is another typical feature of the *causse*, a limestone sinkhole, the **Igue de Planagrèze**; in this particular case pot-holers have so far explored 800m of tunnels.

From here the D42 continues north to Fontanes-du-Causse, where there's a choice of routes to Gramat: you can either stick to the back lanes, or cut west to the faster D677.

Gramat

The biggest town on the *causse*, and its capital, **GRAMAT** developed at the junction of two major Roman roads. Its fortunes increased further when pilgrims started passing through en route to Rocamadour (see p.265), and received another boost when the railway came here in 1863. Even today it's an important market town, with two weekly **markets** (Tues & Fri mornings) and bigger *foires* on the second and fourth Thursdays of each month. Though a few vestiges of the medieval town remain, Gramat is mostly of interest as somewhere to base yourself for a day or so; as well as being an ideal starting point for exploring the *causse*, it's within easy striking distance of Rocamadour, only 9km away to the northwest, and fairly convenient for sights in the upper Dordogne valley (see Chapter five).

Gramat would be more appealing if it weren't for the busy N140 and D677 funnelling through **place de la République**, a big square on the east side of town. If you walk west from here along the **Grande Rue**, though, you'll suddenly find yourself among the narrow lanes of the old quarter. There's not a lot to see, but both the place de l'Hôtel de Ville, at the top of the Grande Rue, and the market square, south of the Grande Rue down rue Notre-Dame, are attractive corners.

Heading south out of town, the newly planted **Jardins du Grand Couvent** (daily: May, June, Sept & Oct 2–6pm; July & Aug 10am–7pm; €4), behind the unmissable convent complex, will take some time to mature, but in the meantime you can see the lovely old wash house and bread ovens used by the nuns until fairly recently; they also run a small shop and tea room. Of more immediate interest, however, is the **Parc Animalier de Gramat** (daily: Easter–Sept 9.30am–7pm; Oct–Easter 2–6pm; €8, Ⓦ www.parcanimaliergramat.fr), a couple of kilometres further south on the D14. Encompassing half a square kilometre of the *causse*, the park is home to an unusually varied selection of animals: the 150 mostly European species include wolves, otters, bears, ibex – with their magnificent curved horns – and *mouflon*, a type of goat crowned with no less than four horns. If possible it's best to visit first thing in the morning, during feeding time, and to avoid the summer's midday heat when nothing stirs save the cicadas. Allow at least two hours if you want to cover the whole park.

Practicalities

Arriving in Gramat by train, you'll pitch up at the **gare SNCF** 1km south of the centre; if no **taxis** are waiting, call Adgié on Ⓣ05.65.38.75.07. Some **buses** call at the station but most drop you on place de la République, which is also where you'll find the **tourist office** (May, June & Sept Mon–Sat 9.30am–12.30pm & 2–7pm; July & Aug Mon–Sat 9.30am–12.30pm & 2–7pm, Sun 9.30am–12.30pm; Oct–April Mon–Sat 9.30am–12.30pm & 2–6pm; Ⓣ05.65.38.73.60, Ⓦ tourisme-gramat.com) on the east side of the square.

The most appealing place to **stay** in Gramat is the ⍫ *Relais des Gourmands* opposite the train station (Ⓣ05.65.38.83.92, Ⓦ www.relais-des-gourmands.fr; ❸; closed two weeks in Feb). It's a delightful, flowery spot, with airy rooms, a pool and an excellent restaurant serving all the classics as well as lighter versions of regional cuisine; on the menu are salad of sweetbreads with sweet and sour sauce and duck heart casserole with garlic and parsley (menus from €14.50; closed Sun eve & Mon lunch except in July & Aug). If it's full, try one of the two hotels on place de la République. The more refined *Lion d'Or* (Ⓣ05.65.38.73.18, Ⓦ www.liondorhotel.com; ❸–❹; closed mid-Dec to mid-Jan) occupies a handsome stone building on the north side of the square; its rooms are not particularly stylish, but comfortable enough, while the restaurant offers top-quality cooking (menus from €15). On the square's east side, you can't miss the electric-green shades of *Le Centre* (Ⓣ05.65.38.73.37, Ⓦ www .lecentre.fr; ❷; Oct–May closed Fri & Sat, also closed two weeks in Nov), which is equally cheerful inside, too, with good-value en-suite rooms and a restaurant (menus from €14).

If you'd rather be out in the countryside, you'll find a warm welcome at *Le Cloucau*, a very comfortable **chambre d'hôte** signed off the D677 roughly 4km west of Gramat (Ⓣ05.65.33.76.18, Ⓔ lecloucau@caramail .com); excellent evening meals are available on request from around €20.

Alternatively, there's a well-organized three-star **campsite**, *Les Ségalières* (℡05.65.38.76.92, ℱ05.65.33.16.48; closed mid-Sept to May), opposite the entrance to the Parc Animalier.

All the hotels mentioned above have recommended **restaurants**. In addition, *La Cuisine d'Alain*, in the old town at 2 rue de la Liberté (℡05.65.38.87.87; closed Sun & eves on Mon & Tues), makes a good pit stop. You'll need to get there early – or reserve – at lunchtime, when locals fill the two small rooms and pavement tables between scurrying serving staff. There's a bewildering choice of *formules* and menus with, for example, two courses at €9.50 and three at €13.

Gourdon and the Bouriane

Thirty-five kilometres west of Gramat, **GOURDON** is an attractive town, its medieval centre of butter-coloured stone houses attached like a swarm of bees to a prominent hilltop, neatly ringed by shady modern boulevards, known collectively as the **Tour-de-Ville**. While it has no outstanding sights, Gourdon makes a quiet, pleasant base, not only for the nearby **Grottes de Cougnac**, with their prehistoric paintings, but also for the **Bouriane** to the south, a hugely pretty area of luxuriant woods and valleys merging into neighbouring Périgord. The Bouriane is primarily a place to wander with no particular destination in mind, but anyone interested in twentieth-century art should visit **Les Arques**, in the south of the region, where a number of powerful, sometimes disturbing, sculptures by Russian exile, Ossip Zadkine are on display.

Gourdon lies on the main Toulouse–Brive **train** line and is also accessible by **bus** from Souillac. However, to explore the Bouriane you'll need your own means of getting about.

The Town

Where the ramparts once stood, Gourdon's medieval centre is now entirely surrounded by the **Tour-de-Ville**. The best-preserved gateway into the centre is southwesterly Porte du Majou, which stands guard over the old town's canyon-like main street, **rue du Majou**. The street is lined with mellow stone-built houses, some, like the **Maison d'Anglars**, at no. 17, with its ogive arches and mullion windows, dating back as far as the thirteenth century; look out on the right, as you go up, for the delightfully – and accurately – named rue Zig-Zag.

At its upper end, rue du Majou opens onto a lovely cobbled square beneath the twin towers of the massive fourteenth-century **church of St-Pierre**. Note the traces of fortifications, in the form of machicolations, over the west door, but you'll find nothing of particular interest inside, beyond some seventeenth-century gilded bas-reliefs by a local sculptor depicting the life of the Virgin Mary. The **Hôtel de Ville** – a handsome if unpretentious building whose arcaded ground floor once served as the market hall – stands on the west side of the square, while east of the church in place des Marronniers an ornately carved door marks the home of the Cavaignac family, who supplied the nation with numerous prominent public figures in the eighteenth and nineteenth centuries, including the notoriously brutal general who put down the Paris workers' attempts to defend the Second Republic in June 1848.

From the north side of the church, a path leads to the top of the hill where Gourdon's castle stood until it was razed in the early seventeenth century in the wake of the Wars of Religion. At 264m in height, it affords superb views over the wooded country stretching north to the Dordogne valley.

Practicalities

Gourdon's **gare SNCF** is located roughly 1km northeast of the old centre; from the station, walk south on avenue de la Gare, then turn right onto avenue Gambetta to come out on the south side of the Tour-de-Ville. **Taxis** come to meet the trains, or you could try calling one of the two local companies: Pasteur (☎05.65.41.08.63) or Gélis (☎05.65.41.36.31). Arriving by **bus**, services terminate on place de la Libération on the southwest side of the Tour-de-Ville. **Car rental** is available through Avis (☎05.65.41.03.95) at the train station, and Budget (☎05.65.41.02.19) on the Cahors road.

The **tourist office**, in the old centre at 24 rue du Majou (Feb–May & Oct Mon–Sat 10am–noon & 2–6pm; June & Sept Mon–Sat 10am–noon & 2–6pm, Sun 10am–noon; July & Aug Mon–Sat 10am–7pm, Sun 10am–noon; Nov–Jan Mon–Sat 10am–noon & 2–5pm; ☎05.65.27.52.50, ⊜gourdon@wanadoo.fr), dispenses town maps and details of Gourdon's festivities (see box on p.293). You can rent **bikes** from Nature Evasion, 73 av Cavignac (☎05.65.37.65.12), out on the west side of town. **Internet** access is available at *Informatique 46*, 18 rue du Majou and there's an excellent English **bookshop** *Books and Company* at 29 rue du Majour.

Accommodation and eating

For an overnight **stay**, head for the cheerful and very reasonably priced *Hôtel de la Promenade*, on the northwest side of the Tour-de-Ville at 48 bd Galiot-de-Genouillac (☎05.65.41.41.44, ⓦwww.lapromenadegourdon.fr; ❷–❸), with immaculate rooms and a decent restaurant (closed Sun lunch; menus from €12). On the opposite side of town, near the post office, is the *Bissonnier*, 51 bd des Martyrs (☎05.65.41.02.48, ⓦwww.hotelbissonnier.com; ❸; menu from €12.50) which has decent, if rather dingy rooms and a good restaurant. On Place des Cordeliers is the brand new *Hostellerie des Cordeliers* (☎05.65.27.05.10, ⓦwww.hostellerie-des-cordeliers.com; ❸). Housed in a thirteenth-century monastery, the hotel has a lovely courtyard garden and comfy wooden-floored rooms. Finally, you'll find a well-managed, three-star municipal **campsite**, *Écoute s'il Pleut* (☎05.65.41.06.19, ⓕ05.65.41.09.88; closed Oct–May), 1km north on the Sarlat road beside a leisure lake; the name, meaning "listen if it rains", comes from a mill which only functioned when there was sufficient rain to swell the river.

In addition to the hotels above, you'll find cafés and **restaurants** scattered around Tour-de-Ville. For picnic fare, there are fresh-food **markets** on Tuesdays beside the church in place St-Pierre, and on Saturdays beside the post office. In July and August an important farmers' market takes place on Thursday mornings in place St-Pierre, while the Tour-de-Ville is closed off on the first and third Tuesdays of the month for a traditional country fair.

The Grottes de Cougnac

Signed off the Sarlat road a couple of kilometres north of Gourdon, the **Grottes de Cougnac** (1hr guided tours daily: April–June & Sept 9.30–11am & 2–5pm; July & Aug 9.30am–6pm; Oct 10–11am & 2–4pm; €5.80) were discovered in 1949 by a local water-diviner. To begin with all the subsequent explorers found were rock formations – notably ceilings festooned with ice-white needles like some glitzy ballroom decoration – but three years later they hit gold when they came across **prehistoric paintings**. These date from between 25,000 and 19,000 years ago, when Cro-Magnon people ventured deep inside the caves to paint panels of ibex, reindeer and mammoths in elegant outline, using the rock's undulating surface to provide a sense of form and movement. They also left hundreds of mysterious signs – mostly dots and pairs of short lines – in addition to two human figures seemingly pierced by spears, a motif also found in Pech-Merle (see p.312).

Southwest through the Bouriane

The country southwest of Gourdon is a delight. Lanes tunnel through chestnut and pine woods, twisting up the valley sides past the occasional patch of vines and then popping out obligingly on high ground for the views. The **Céou valley** to the south of Gourdon provides one particularly beguiling route, although what sights there are in the Bouriane lie further west and are most easily accessed via the D673.

The first place of any size you come to along this road is the fortified village of **SALVIAC**, 14km from Gourdon, whose Gothic church was built in the late thirteenth century by Jean Duèze of Cahors, the future Pope John XXII (see p.295), and still contains fine stained-glass windows from that era. Seven kilometres further on, the *bastide* town of **CAZALS** has seen better days: its feudal château and ramparts were largely destroyed during the Hundred Years' War, though its big central square remains, and the whole place bursts into life in summer for a major contemporary dance festival (see box on p.292). From here, you can work your way 9km eastwards through enticing back lanes to **RAMPOUX**. This unusually scattered hamlet is home to a Romanesque priory church in which one of the original frescoes can still be seen – a very faded Christ in majesty in the apse. Better preserved are those from the fifteenth century in the south chapel, portraying the life of Jesus.

The next port of call, **LES ARQUES**, is equally buried in the countryside, 10km southwest of Rampoux and 6km south of Cazals. It's a nicely higgledy-piggledy village on a hillock above the River Masse, but its main draw is the Romanesque **church** and the neighbouring **Musée Zadkine** (daily: May–Sept 10am–1pm & 2–7pm; Oct–April 10am–1pm & 2–5pm; €2.50). A Russian émigré and well-known sculptor, **Ossip Zadkine** set up a studio in Les Arques in 1934 and worked on and off in the village until his death in 1967, producing big, powerful statues full of restless energy. Many are on a mythological or musical theme, such as those of Orpheus and Diana, the latter metamorphosing from tree to woman, and there's a strong Cubist influence, although his works grew more abstract towards the end of his life. Some of his most compelling pieces are displayed inside the church, whose cool stone interior provides the perfect foil for a passionate rendering of Christ on the Cross and, in the crypt, the *Pietà*. Mary sits without hope, her tortured face gazing off into the distance while the broken body of her son lies slumped across her knees, as if forgotten.

In season, it's worth timing your visit to have lunch in the old schoolhouse at the entrance to the village, now home to an attractive **restaurant**, 🥄 *La Récréation* (☎05.65.22.88.08; closed Jan & Feb; March & Oct–Dec closed Mon–Thurs; April–Sept closed Wed & Thurs). In July and August they serve a wholesome two-course lunch menu for €16, including coffee and wine, while at other times there's a single *menu carte* at €25 for five courses. Reservations are required at any time of year, but in summer you'll need to book at least two or three days in advance.

Another possibility for eating, or for an overnight stay, would be to continue southwest for 5km to **GOUJOUNAC**, whose **church** has rather worn Romanesque carvings of Christ in majesty and the four Evangelists over the south door. Opposite the church, the pretty *Hostellerie de Goujounac* (☎05.65.36.68.67,

@ www.hostellerie-de-goujounac.com; ❸; closed Dec 15–Jan 15, also Sun eve & Mon except in July & Aug) offers honest country cooking (menus from €12) in addition to five very simple **rooms**; if you want to stay here, you'll need to book well ahead in the summer season. Otherwise, there's a three-star **campsite**, *Camping La Pinède* (☎05.65.36.61.84; closed mid-Sept to mid-June), immediately west of Goujounac on the D660 Villefranche road.

West along the Lot from Cahors

The Bouriane's southern boundary is marked by the River Lot, which follows a particularly convoluted course downstream of Cahors as it doubles back on itself again and again between cliffs which gradually diminish towards the west. Standing guard over one of the larger meanders is **Luzech**, whose main claim to fame is the scant remains of a Roman encampment on the hill above the town. Continuing downstream, the route winds through a series of villages perched above the river, culminating in one of the most beautiful along the entire Lot valley, **Puy-l'Évêque**. A castle-town built on a terraced cliff, it dominates the last of the river's meanders, and its wandering lanes, tunnels, staircases and fountains together compensate for the lack of any first-rate sights. The area around **Duravel** and **Touzac**, further west again, with its fine selection of hotels and restaurants, provides a good base for visiting the impressive **Château de Bonaguil** in the hills to the north of the Lot. The last of the medieval castles to be constructed in France, and now partially in ruins, it still bristles with sophisticated defensive devices. Back on the Lot, **Fumel** is a major transport hub and service centre, though otherwise contains nothing to make you dally – better to hurry on downriver to where **Penne-d'Agenais**, with its striking basilica, lords it over the valley.

Public transport along this stretch of the river consists of an SNCF **bus** that threads along the valley from Cahors via Luzech, Puy-l'Évêque and Fumel to Monsempron-Libos, on the Agen–Périgueux train line. On the way it also passes through or close by most of the smaller villages cited below. From Fumel you can continue on by bus to Penne-d'Agenais and Villeneuve-sur-Lot (see p.332), but you'll need your own transport to reach the Château de Bonaguil and the villages north of the valley.

Luzech and around

Twenty kilometres downriver from Cahors, **LUZECH** is situated on the narrow neck of a particularly large meander and overlooked by a twelfth-century **keep**. There's a small area of picturesque alleys to the north of **place du Canal**, the central square spanning the isthmus, where you'll find, on rue de la Ville, the **Maison des Consuls**. Built in 1270, its most distinguished feature is the sturdy Gothic arch on the ground floor, offset by a pair of airy, double-arched windows worked in brick above. The building is now home to the tourist office and an interesting one-room **museum** of archeological finds from around Luzech (same hours as tourist office – see opposite; free). Though there are some delicate Gaulish safety-pins and needles, the exhibits demonstrate the huge leap in craftsmanship ushered in by the Romans in the first century BC: look out for the unusual folding spoon and the very fine red-clay pottery from the Tarn, not to mention the Roman coins chopped in half for small change.

The majority of items come from a fortress on a hill above the town, occupied since the early Iron Age and later reinforced by the Romans, who also erected a temple on the site. Little remains of their **Oppidum d'Impernal** beyond a few foundation stones, but it's worth trekking up for a splendid view over the Luzech meander. It's 1.5km by road, or you can walk up in about ten minutes: from the north end of rue de la Ville, follow signs for the GR36 footpath, past the castle keep and then just keep climbing. For a less strenuous jaunt, head south for about 2km to visit a tiny chapel, **Notre-Dame de l'Oesle**, surrounded by vines and walnut trees on the very tip of the meander.

Practicalities

Buses from Cahors pull in beside a roundabout at the east end of place du Canal, where you'll find the **tourist office** in the Maison des Consuls (May–Sept Mon–Fri 9.30am–12.30pm & 2.30–6.30pm, Sat 10am–noon & 2.30–3.30pm, Sun 10am–noon; Oct–April Tues–Fri 9.30am–12.30pm & 2.30–6pm, Sat 2.30–6pm; ☎05.65.20.17.27, ⍵www.ville-luzech.fr). For **accommodation** try the welcoming *Zotier chambre d'hôte* (☎05.65.30.54.22, ⍵www.zotier.com; ❸) on the western edge of the village with five very prettily decorated bedrooms, a shady garden and delicious evening menus on request (from €18). Alternatively, there's a two-star municipal **campsite**, *Camping de l'Alcade* (☎05.65.30.72.32, ✉maire.luzech@wanadoo.fr; closed Oct to mid-June), beside the river immediately west of town on the Albas road.

If you're looking for somewhere special to **eat** in the area, head north to St-Médard, where ⍲ *Le Gindreau* (☎05.65.36.22.27; July & Aug closed Mon and lunchtime Tues; Sept–June closed Mon & Tues) rates as one of the Lot's best restaurants serving up such delights as pig's trotters with panfried mustard greens or langoustine ravioli with ginger butter; the desserts in particular are real works of art and the chocolate fondant is divine. Menus start at an affordable €36, rising to a gastronomic €120. In summer tables are laid out under the chestnut trees.

Luzech marks the end of the navigable river descending from St-Cirq Lapopie. **Houseboats** are available through Nautic (see p.35), while pleasure **boats** can be rented by the day or half day from Navilot (☎05.65.20.18.19; mid-May to mid-Sept), both based a couple of kilometres north of Luzech near the village of **CAIX**. You can pitch your tent in Navilot's no-frills campsite, and also rent **canoes** both here and back in Luzech through Safaraid (☎05.65.30.47.47, ⍵www.canoe-kayak-dordogne.com).

Albas to Grézels

The prettiest route downstream from Luzech – and that followed by the bus – is the D8 along the river's south bank. It's especially beguiling in summer when the intense green of the vines and walnut trees in the valley bottom is offset against the dark grey cliffs. The river loops back and forth across the flood plain, with a village at the bottom of each meander. The first you come to, and the most attractive, is **ALBAS**, 5km from Luzech, instantly recognizable by its tall church spire. The church is nineteenth century and otherwise uninteresting, but the steep lanes below retain a few noble fourteenth- and fifteenth-century facades, a reminder of when the bishops of Cahors maintained a residence here.

There are a couple of good pit stops in Albas and its vicinity. In the town itself, the *Restaurant du Port* (☎05.65.20.15.95; closed Sun eve & Tues; mid-Sept to mid-June dinner by reservation only) occupies a small vaulted room on the road from the central square down to the river, and serves good old-fashioned menus from €10 (Sun & eves from €18). Two kilometres east, the *Auberge d'Imhotep* (☎05.65.30.70.91; closed Sun eve & Mon) is a friendly little **restaurant** named after the ancient Egyptian who supposedly discovered the art of *gavage* – the process of force-feeding ducks for foie gras – in 2600 BC. Naturally, duck features strongly on the menu, including innovative dishes such as duck kebabs with curry sauce, and they also offer an excellent Cahors wine list (menus at €13–39).

Two meanders and 18km west of Albas, **GRÉZELS** was another episcopal seat, though in this case its **château** – a very sober affair – has survived thanks to a seventeenth-century rebuild. But the prime attraction here, on the main road through the village, is another **restaurant**, the rustic *La Terrasse* (℡05.65.21.34.03; closed Sun & Mon eve, & first two weeks in Sept; Sept–June also closed eves), renowned for its jovial host and no-nonsense cuisine. There's only one menu which changes daily (€26 on Sun, €16 at other times). Make sure you've got a healthy appetite, and note that reservations are strongly recommended.

Puy-l'Évêque and around

Five kilometres from Grézels and 30km from Cahors by the main D911, **PUY-L'ÉVÊQUE** contends with St-Cirq Lapopie (see p.306) as the Lot valley's prettiest village. After 1227 it marked the western extremity of the Cahors bishops' domains and it's the remains of their thirteenth-century **château**, a big square keep like that at Luzech, which provides the town's focal point. Puy-l'Évêque changed hands any number of times during the Hundred Years' War, but then withstood a prolonged Protestant siege in 1580 during the Wars of Religion. Ardent anti-clerics tried to change the name to Puy-Libre during the Revolution, then Puy-sur-Lot, but the locals weren't convinced and it soon reverted to Puy-l'Évêque.

There are no great sights to speak of, just lanes of medieval and Renaissance houses built in honey-coloured stone. Beside the castle keep at the top of the town, the main **place de la Truffière** is the venue for the main weekly **market** (Tues morning); a small farmers' market also takes place on Saturdays in the lower town on place George-Henry, at the west end of rue des Platanes. From place de la Truffière, **rue du Fort** leads steeply down then flattens out beneath an imposing fourteenth-century building distinguished by its Gothic windows, which served as the bishops' audience chamber. As it curves round the hill, rue du Fort becomes rue Bovila and then peters out beside a staircase descending to rue des Capucins. This road heads back east along the hillside to **place Guillaume-de-Cardaillac** and then **place de la Halle**, the town's two most picturesque corners. Downhill from place de la Halle again, you come to rue de la Cale, with the dark alleys of the artisans' quarter off to the left, and the old **port**. For the best **view** of the whole ensemble walk out onto the modern bridge which crosses the Lot here. Alternatively, head for the belvedere in front of the **church of St-Sauveur** which guards Puy-l'Évêque's northeast quarter – literally, since it once formed an integral part of the fortifications; look carefully and you can still see where cannonballs found their target during the siege of 1580.

Practicalities

SNCF **buses** from Cahors stop in front of the church on place du Rampeau and down on rue des Platanes to the southeast of the old centre. The **tourist office** is behind the castle keep on place de la Truffière (July & Aug daily 9.30am–6.30pm; Sept–June Mon–Sat 9am–12.30pm & 2–5.30pm; ℡05.65.21.37.63, ⓦwww.puy-leveque.fr).

For an overnight **stay**, the refurbished *Hôtel Bellevue*, perched on the cliff edge on place de la Truffière (℡05.65.36.06.60, ⑤05.65.36.06.61; ❹; closed one month Jan–Feb), has very stylish rooms, all with highly contemporary decor and fine views, and with a restaurant to match; try the guinea fowl roasted with kiwis and foie gras (menus from €33, or €12.50 in the brasserie; closed Sun eve & Mon except in July & Aug). Opposite, *La Truffière* (℡05.65.21.34.54, @www.logis-de-france.fr; ❷; closed two weeks in both March and Oct) offers a more rustic atmosphere, with reasonably spacious en-suite rooms, while their restaurant draws the locals with its excellent-value menus (July & Aug closed Sun eve, rest of year closed Fri eve, Sat midday & Sun eve; from €12.50). Alternatively you could try the very reasonably priced, English-owned **chambre d'hôte** at *Maison Rouma*, 2 rue du Docteur-Rouma (℡05.65.36.59.39, @www.puyleveque.com; ❸), at the east end of the bridge. Its three rooms are immaculate and oozing with character, but the highlight is the glorious view of Puy-l'Évêque from the garden. There's also a Dutch-owned three-star **campsite**, *Camping Les Vignes* (℡05.65.30.81.72, @www.puy-leveque.fr/campingles%20vignes.htm; closed Oct–March), 3km south along the river on the D28.

As for **eating**, in wintertime *Le Fournil de l'Opéra Bouffe*, 24 Grande Rue (℡05.65.36.45.15; closed Tues except in July & Aug; menus from €15.10), on the main road leading from the lower to the upper town, is a nice cosy place offering grills cooked on a wood fire. In summer, on the other hand, the nicest option for a drink or a meal is the riverside *Le Pigeonnier* (℡05.65.21.37.77; closed Mon except July & Aug), on the far side of the bridge. Apart from splendid views, they also offer good-value salads, crêpes and grills as well as more substantial dishes in winter (a meal will set you back €10–15); reservations are recommended from June to September. You can also rent **canoes** here (June–Sept), while **bikes** are available from Loca-Lot (℡05.65.36.59.22, @www.loca-lot.fr.st), 5km downstream in **Vire-sur-Lot**.

Martignac

One of the best excursions in the vicinity is to the hamlet of **MARTIGNAC**, 2.5km north, where the much-altered Romanesque **church of St-Pierre-ès-Liens** contains some remarkable late-fifteenth- and early-sixteenth-century frescoes – hidden under plaster until 1938, they are reasonably well preserved. Characters on the north wall represent the Seven Deadly Sins being escorted to the mouth of Hell, each mounted on a different animal: Lust on a billy goat, Gluttony scoffing ham and wine and riding a pig, and scruffy Sloth on a donkey bringing up the tail. The Seven Virtues surround the apse, their grey robes tumbling about them, with Courage and Temperance being the easiest to recognize – the former holds a serpent, while Temperance carefully waters down her wine.

Duravel and around

Downstream of Puy-l'Évêque, the Lot valley begins to open out as the hills along the southern bank fade away. Those to the north continue a while longer, providing a green backdrop for the pretty eleventh-century **church** at **DURAVEL**, 6km from Puy-l'Évêque. Its crypt contains the remains of no less than three saints – Poémon, Agathon and Hilarion, their bodies having been brought back from the Holy Land in the eleventh century – but the village is unfortunately spoilt by the busy main road passing through its centre.

There are, however, a number of excellent **chambres d'hôtes** and **eating** options round about. First stop should be the welcoming *Aux Dodus d'Audhuy* (℡05.65.36.44.12, @auxdodus.free.fr; ❺; closed mid-Nov to Easter), signed just off the D911 3km northeast of Duravel. It has four bright rooms, a pool and garden, though is best known for its good, old-fashioned, home-cooked evening meals, available nightly in the summer (July–Sept), and on Fridays and Saturdays from Easter to May and October to mid-November (menus €24); the name, meaning "the roly-poly people of Audhuy", says it all. Reservations are strongly recommended. One kilometre to the south of Duravel, you'll also get a warm welcome and good food at *La Roseraie* (T05.65.24.63.82, Erigallaroseraie @wanadoo.fr), a busy working farm offering simple *chambre d'hôte* accommodation(❸; closed Nov–March), with meals on request (€18); they also run a farm shop selling their own wine and local produce ranging from duck to ostrich meat.

Five kilometres southwest across the Lot, you'll find an idyllic **hotel**, the *Hostellerie de la Source Bleue* (T05.65.36.52.01, Wwww.sourcebleue.com; ❺; closed Jan–March; menus from around €25, closed Wed), just south of the village of **Touzac**, in an ancient, spring-fed water mill swamped by luxuriant vegetation. Rooms are spacious and housed either in the the old mill or in the newer building next door. There's also a shady two-star **campsite**, *Le Clos Bouyssac* (T05.65.36.52.21, Wwww.leclosbouyssac.eu; closed Nov–March), a short distance south along the riverbank.

North to the Château de Bonaguil

With your own transport, you can cut northwest across country from Duravel to visit the magnificent ruined castle of Bonaguil. On the way it's worth taking a short detour to **MONTCABRIER**, just over 5km north of Duravel, if for no other reason than because this tiny *bastide* seems to have been forgotten by the renovators and tourist authorities. There's a clutch of once-noble residences around the chestnut-shaded main square, but the village is best known for a diminutive statue lodged in the north nave of its quietly crumbling **church of St-Louis**. It is one of the first stone representations of the saint, formerly King Louis IX, showing him as a bearded figure wearing a painted crown. It's also slightly macabre: when Louis died on a crusade in 1270, his body was immediately chopped into pieces and dispatched around Europe to meet the demand for relics. Apparently, one unspecified piece of the king now resides inside this little statue.

From Montcabrier take the D673 from below the village heading southwest, then turn west through the delightful hamlet of St-Martin-Le-Redon and start climbing. As the road crests the ridge you get a stunning view of the **Château de Bonaguil** (daily: Feb, March & Oct 11am–1pm & 2.30–5pm; April, May & Sept 10.30am–1pm & 2.30–5pm; June-Aug 10am–6pm; Nov school hols 11am–1pm & 2.30–5pm; Christmas school hols check hours on T05.53.71.13.70, Wwww.bonaguil.org; €6), 7km from Montcabrier, perched at the end of a wooded spur. The castle dates largely from the fifteenth and sixteenth centuries when Bérenger de Roquefeuil, from a powerful Languedoc family and by all accounts a nasty piece of work, inherited the partially ruined castle. Fearing revolts by his vassals, he decided to transform it into an impregnable fortress, just as his contemporaries were abandoning such elaborate fortifications. It took him around forty years to do so, constructing a double ring of walls, six huge towers, a highly unusual, narrow boat-shaped keep, and sophisticated loopholes with overlapping lines of fire. Perhaps because of such elaborate precautions, Bonaguil was never attacked, and although some demolition occurred during the Revolution, the castle still stands, bloodied but unbowed.

As a result, the site attracts up to two thousand tourists per day in July and August. It's best to arrive first thing in the morning to avoid the worst of the crush, and rather than joining the **guided tours** (1hr 30min; English tours available in July & Aug), which get tedious when it's very busy, it's preferable to buy a guidebook from the ticket gate and do it yourself. The château provides the backdrop for a **firework** extravaganza on the Friday following July 14 (€3.50), and then in early August makes a stunning venue for a **festival** of theatre (see p.293).

There are a couple of **eating** places below the castle, including the English-run *Auberge de Bonaguil* (closed mid-Nov to mid-March), which serves drinks and snacks all day as well as more substantial regional menus from €13. Another option is to head north 7km through the back lanes to **SAUVETERRE-LA-LÉMANCE**, where the friendly *Hôtel du Centre*, near the church (℡05.53.40.65.45, Ⓕ05.53.40.68.59; ❶; closed mid-Dec to Feb; menus from €12; restaurant closed Sat lunch from Oct to May), offers excellent-value regional cuisine in addition to a handful of basic rooms (no en-suite facilities).

Fumel and around

Eight kilometres southwest of Bonaguil and 12km west of Duravel, **FUMEL** – an important stronghold in medieval times – is now a busy industrial town which holds little of interest beyond its transport facilities and a decent hotel. It lies on the north bank of the Lot, spilling along the main road from its old centre – focused around **place du Postel** – in the east, past a huge factory making car parts, and then merges 4km later with the western suburb of **MONSEMPRON-LIBOS**.

It's in Monsempron-Libos that you'll find the **gare SNCF**, set back from the river near the new road-bridge at the end of avenue de la Gare. This is where SNCF **buses** from Cahors terminate, having first called in Fumel at place du Postel. Buses from Villeneuve-sur-Lot (operated by Cars Évasion; ℡05.53.40.88.20), on the other hand, drop you on place Voltaire, a short walk north of the old town.

You'll find Fumel's **tourist office** on place Georges-Escandes, immediately east of place du Postel (July & Aug Mon–Sat 9am–1pm & 2.30–6.30pm, Sun 9am–1pm; Sept–June Tues–Sat 10am–noon & 3–6pm; ℡05.53.71.13.70, Ⓦwww.fumel.fr). **Bike rental** is available from AJF Cycles, 8 place du Postel (℡05.53.71.14.57), and for a **taxi**, call Taxi Fumélois (℡05.53.71.39.50).

The best bet for an overnight **stay** is the modern and welcoming, Dutch-run *Hôtel Kyriad*, place de l'Église (℡05.53.40.93.93, Ⓦwww.kyriad.fumel.fr; ❸), perched on the cliff to the south of place du Postel. Most rooms have valley views, and there's also a pool and a decent **restaurant**, *La Soupière*, offering a choice of a self-service buffet at €9.50, menus from €10 and *à la carte* around €20. If you're looking for a **campsite**, head 3.5km east through the village of Condat to the two-star *Camping de Condat* (℡05.53.71.45.72, Ⓕ05.53.71.36.69; open all year), a relaxed but well-cared-for place beside the river; SNCF buses stop 1.5km up the road in Condat itself.

With your own transport, a better option is to head 9km southeast of Fumel, on the D5 Puy-l'Évêque road, to the *Hostellerie Le Vert* (℡05.65.36.51.36, Ⓦwww.hotellevert.com; ❺; closed mid-Nov to mid-Feb). It's a lovely old farm set in fields just east of **Mauroux**, with a heated pool and a handful of nicely refurbished rooms – the two more expensive ones in the annexe are the most characterful – and a good **restaurant** serving upmarket regional cuisine (closed Thurs eve, and lunchtimes except Sun; menu at €40 or around €32 *à la carte*).

Penne-d'Agenais

The last stop along the valley before Villeneuve-sur-Lot is the beautiful but touristy old fortress-town of **PENNE-D'AGENAIS**, 15km downstream from Fumel on the river's south bank, where a silver-domed **basilica** teeters on the cliff edge. **Notre-Dame-de-Peyragude** dates back to 1000, but had the misfortune to be built on a particularly strategic pinnacle of rock. After Richard the Lionheart erected a castle right next door in 1182, the chapel found itself in the crossfire on any number of occasions; in 1412 Penne changed hands no fewer than four times. The most recent construction was only completed in 1949; there's nothing particular to see inside, and the neighbouring castle was razed during the Wars of Religion, but the climb is rewarded with panoramic views.

From **place Gambetta**, the main square immediately south of the old town, **rue du 14-Juillet** ducks under a medieval gate. From there just follow your fancy uphill along narrow lanes lined with an alluring mix of brick and stone houses – all incredibly spick and span. A few twists and turns later you emerge beside the basilica.

Penne lies on the Agen–Paris main line, its **gare SNCF** a couple of kilometres southeast down the D103 to Agen. **Buses** between Fumel and Villeneuve-sur-Lot drop you 2km north across the river in St-Sylvestre. If you need a **taxi**, call Pallard on ☏05.53.41.22.66. The **tourist office**, just inside the medieval gate on rue du 14-Juillet (May–Sept Mon–Sat 9am–1pm & 2–7pm, Sun 2–7pm; Oct–April Mon–Sat 9am–12.30pm & 2–6pm, Sun 2–6pm; ☏05.53.41.37.80, ⓦwww.penne-tourism.com), can supply comprehensive lists of *chambres d'hôtes* and *gîtes* in the area. As for **campsites**, there's a choice between the small, two-star riverside *Camping Municipal de St-Sylvestre* (☏05.53.41.22.23; closed Oct to mid-May), beside the bridge over the Lot, and the three-star *Camping Municipal de Férrié* (☏05.53.41.30.97; open mid-June to Aug) beside a lake just north of Penne's gare SNCF. For something to **eat**, try *La Maison de la Place* (☏05.53.01.29.18; closed 2 weeks in Oct & 2 weeks in Dec–Jan), by the entrance to the village, for sophisticated country cooking in elegant surroundings, or *Le Bombecul* (☏05.53.71.11.76), on Place Paul Fromet, for more casual dining with a Moroccan twist.

Villeneuve-sur-Lot and around

Straddling the river 10km west of Penne-d'Agenais, **VILLENEUVE-SUR-LOT** is a pleasant, workaday sort of town. It has no terribly compelling sights, but the handful of attractive timbered houses in the old centre go some way to compensate, while the nearby hilltop village of **Pujols** makes for an enjoyable excursion. Founded in 1251 by Alphonse de Poitiers, Villeneuve was one of the region's earliest *bastide* towns (see p.336), and in no time it developed into an important commercial centre, which it remains to this day. As elsewhere, its ramparts have given way to encircling boulevards, but the distinctive chequerboard street plan survives, along with two medieval gates and the old, arched bridge.

Arrival, information and accommodation

While there is no longer a train station in Villeneuve itself, SNCF runs regular **bus services** from Agen, which is on the Bordeaux–Toulouse and

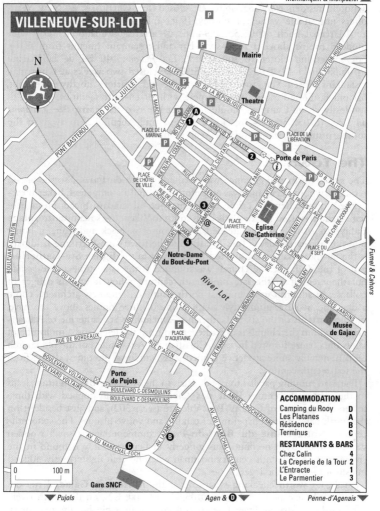

Agen–Périgueux lines. These buses call at Villeneuve's former *gare SNCF* (where there's an SNCF ticket office), a good five minutes' walk south of the centre, before terminating near the theatre on the opposite side of town. Other buses from Fumel, Bergerac, Marmande and Monflanquin stop by the theatre, at the old *gare* or near the post office, but the situation is not static: for further details call the central information desk (℡05.53.69.42.03) or ask at the **tourist office**, at 3 place de la Libération (July & Aug Mon–Sat 9.30am–12.30pm & 1.30-7pm, Sun 10am–1pm; Sept–June Mon–Sat 9am–noon & 2–6pm; ℡05.53.36.17.30, ⓦwww.tourisme-villeneuve-sur-lot.fr). **Internet** access is available at Cyber-phone.com at the corner of rue Parmentier and rue du Collège.

The best place to look for **accommodation** is around the former *gare SNCF*, where the friendly ⚓ *Résidence*, 17 av Lazare-Carnot (℡05.53.40.17.03,

@hotel.laresidence@wanadoo.fr; **❶**; closed for Christmas & New Year), offers unbeatable value for money. If it's full, try the nearby *Terminus*, 2 av Maréchal-Foch (☎05.53.70.94.36, @carrerea@wanadoo.fr; **❸**), with modern rooms above a retro-style bar and restaurant (menus from €10). For something closer to the centre, *Les Platanes*, 40 bd de la Marine (☎05.53.40.11.40, ☏05.53.70.71.95; **❶–❷**; closed two weeks at Christmas; restaurant closed Sun, from €13), on the old quarter's northwest corner, has old-fashioned rooms, the cheapest without en-suite facilities, but it's all spotlessly clean. Campers should head for the two-star **campsite**, *Camping du Rooy* (☎05.53.70.24.18; closed Oct to mid-April), 1.5km away in the southern suburbs, signed off the Agen road.

The Town

The *bastide*'s principal entrance was northerly **Porte de Paris**, also the prison – one of whose occupants was an unfortunate, and incompetent, baker incarcerated for the heinous crime of turning out substandard bread. From here semi-pedestrianized rue de Paris leads south to Villeneuve's main square, **place Lafayette**; surrounded by arcaded town houses in brick and stone, it bursts into life on market days (Tues & Sat). But the town's most striking landmark is the 55-metre-tall, octagonal red-brick tower of the **Église Ste-Catherine**, east of rue de Paris. The church was founded at the same time as the *bastide*, but then rebuilt in the late nineteenth century when it was in danger of collapse. In addition to an unusual north–south axis, the new architects chose a dramatic neo-Byzantine style, with a line of three domes above the nave, mosaic portraits of the six St Catherines – including St Catherine of Alexandria, to whom the church is dedicated, third from the left – and a multitude of saints on a frieze inspired by early Christian art. A few relics of the old church remain, notably some attractive stained-glass windows, the oldest dating from the fourteenth century.

The road running parallel to rue de Paris to the west, **rue des Cieutats**, leads to the thirteenth-century **Pont des Cieutats**, originally topped with three towers reminiscent of Cahors' Pont Valentré (see p.302), and, just beside it on the north bank, a tiny chapel full of candles and votive plaques. The sixteenth-century **Notre-Dame du Bout-du-Pont** commemorates a small wooden statue of the Virgin holding Jesus gingerly in her arms. It was found in the river here by a sixteenth-century boatman when his craft mysteriously stopped midstream – or so the legend goes.

Finally, it's worth checking what's on at the **Musée de Gajac**, 2 rue des Jardins (daily except Tues 2–6pm; ☎05.53.40.48.00; €2), on the north riverbank further upstream. Their fine art collection is missable, but the temporary exhibitions devoted to the history of the Lot, the river trade, its craft, boat-builders and so forth, are generally of interest.

Eating

Villeneuve has a good choice of **restaurants**. The prettiest is ❊ *Chez Câline*, 2 rue Notre-Dame (☎05.53.70.42.08; variable closing days; menus from €14), near the old bridge, serving fresh, inventive dishes in a tiny brick-vaulted room. The elegant *L'Entracte*, 30 bd de la Marine (☎05.53.49.25.50; closed Wed; menus from €12.50), caters for more traditional tastes, while *Le Parmentier*, at 13 rue Parmentier (☎05.53.70.35.01; closed Sun & Mon), has a range of options, from classic regional cuisine to club sandwiches; weekday lunch menus start at €18. *La Crêperie de la Tour*, on 5 rue Arnaud d'Aubasse (☎05.53.70.97.86) serves galettes, crêpes and salads with menus from €7.50. Alternatively, head south to Pujols (see below).

For picnic fare, the main **markets** take place on Tuesday and Saturday mornings on place Lafayette, with an organic market on Wednesday mornings on place d'Aquitaine, south of the river. Bigger fairs are held on the second and fourth Tuesdays of the month, while in July and August there are also farmers' night markets on Fridays on place Lafayette.

Pujols

Three kilometres south of Villeneuve, the two-street village of **PUJOLS** stands high above the plain behind its thirteenth-century ramparts. The town is a popular excursion destination, partly because it's a beguiling little place with its flowery nooks and crannies, and partly for views over the surrounding country – for locals, though, the main reason to come to Pujols is its restaurants.

Immediately inside Pujols' main north gate, it's hard to tell where the fortifications end and the tiny Gothic **church of St-Nicolas** begins. It contains nothing of particular note, whereas the **Église Ste-Foy** (open during temporary exhibitions; free), on the far side of the market square, is decorated with fifteenth- and sixteenth-century frescoes. Though faded, many are still visible, such as St George poised over the dragon and St Catherine with her wheel of torture, both around the apse. And look out, too, for a painting in the baptismal chapel (first on the left as you enter), depicting the old bridge at Villeneuve-sur-Lot sporting its three towers.

Top of the list for **restaurants** is the Michelin-starred *La Toque Blanche* (☎05.53.49.00.30, @www.la-toque-blanche.com; closed Sun eve, Mon & lunchtime Tues), just south of Pujols with views back to the village. Dishes include classics such as poached eggs in a Périgord sauce served with foie gras, and pears in millefeuille pastry served with creamed bitter almonds, but it's not outrageously expensive: weekday menus start €23, rising to €35 at weekends and holidays. The panorama is even better from the less formal *Lou Calel* (☎05.53.70.46.14; closed Tues eve, Wed & lunchtime Thurs), in Pujols itself overlooking the Lot valley; from around €20 you can enjoy beautifully cooked traditional but light menus.

The bastide country

Although *bastides*, or medieval new towns (see box on p.336), are by no means unique to this stretch of country to the north of the Lot, it's here that you'll find the two finest examples. The more southerly of the pair is **Monflanquin**, which makes a good place to start because of its museum outlining the history, architecture and daily life of the *bastides*. The route then heads northeast, skirting round the flanks of the imposing **Château de Biron**, seat of one of the four baronies of Périgord, before reaching **Monpazier**. This is the most typical of the *bastides*, with virtually no modern development around – where the rectangle of streets end the fields begin. There's a small museum here, too, but Monpazier's prime attraction is its atmosphere, "like a drowsy yellow cat, slumbering in the sun" as Freda White so aptly describes it in the *Three Rivers of France* (see p.401).

Nevertheless, some effort is required to reach it. Neither the Château de Biron nor Monpazier is accessible by **public transport**. The best on offer is the **bus** from Villeneuve to Monflanquin, but even that doesn't run every day.

Monflanquin

Some 17km north of Villeneuve-sur-Lot, pretty **MONFLANQUIN**, founded in 1252 by Alphonse de Poitiers, is nearly as perfectly preserved as Monpazier, but is less touristy and impressively positioned on top of a hill that rises sharply from the surrounding country and is visible for miles. Despite being constructed on a steep slope, it conforms to the regular pattern of right-angled streets leading from a central square to the four town gates. The ramparts themselves were demolished on Richelieu's orders in 1630, but otherwise Monflanquin has experienced few radical changes since the thirteenth century.

The main square, tree-shaded **place des Arcades** – where the **market** still takes place on Thursdays as decreed in the *bastide*'s founding charter – derives a special charm from being on a slope. Its grandest building is the Gothic **Maison du Prince Noir** in the northeast corner, where the Black Prince is said to have stayed. On this north side you'll also find the high-tech **Musée des Bastides**, above the tourist office (same hours – see below; €3), which is full of information about the life and history of *bastides*; most of the text is translated into English, but

Bastides

From the *Occitan bastida*, meaning a group of buildings, **bastides** were the new towns of the thirteenth and fourteenth centuries. Although they are found all over southwest France, from the Dordogne to the foothills of the Pyrenees, there is a particularly high concentration in the area between the Dordogne and Lot rivers, which at that time formed the disputed "frontier" region between English-held Aquitaine and Capetian France.

That said, the earliest *bastides* were founded largely for **economic and political** reasons. They were a means of bringing new land into production – this was a period of rapid population growth and technological innovation – and thus extending the power of the local lord. But as tensions between the French and English forces intensified during the late thirteenth century, so the motive became increasingly **military**. The *bastides* now provided a handy way of securing the land along the frontier, and it was generally at this point that they were fortified.

As an incentive, anyone who was prepared to build, inhabit and defend the *bastide* was granted various perks and concessions in a founding **charter**. All new residents were allocated a building plot, garden and cultivable land outside the town. The charter might also offer asylum to certain types of criminal or grant exemption from military service, and would allow the election of **consuls** charged with day-to-day administration – a measure of self-government remarkable in feudal times. Taxes and judicial affairs, meanwhile, remained the preserve of the representative of the king or local lord under whose ultimate authority the *bastide* lay.

The other defining feature of a *bastide* is its **layout**. They are nearly always square or rectangular in shape, depending on the nature of the terrain, and are divided by streets at right angles to each other to produce a chequerboard pattern. The focal point is the market square, often missing its covered *halle* nowadays, but generally still surrounded by arcades, while the church is relegated to one side, or may even form part of the town walls.

The busiest *bastide* founders were **Alphonse de Poitiers** (1249–71), on behalf of the French crown, after he became count of Toulouse in 1249, and **King Edward I of England**, Edward Plantagenet (1272–1307), who wished to consolidate his hold on the northern borders of his duchy of Aquitaine. The former chalked up a total of 57 *bastides*, including Villeneuve-sur-Lot (1251), Monflanquin (1252), Ste-Foy-la-Grande (1255) and Eymet (1270), while Edward was responsible for Beaumont (1272), Monpazier and Molières (both 1284) amongst others.

unfortunately not the audio-tapes. Then after a quick wander through Monflanquin's old centre, it's worth heading north past the **church**, which took on its
pseudo-medieval look in the early twentieth century, to end up on a terrace with
expansive views northeast to the next stop, Château de Biron (see below).

Practicalities

Buses from Villeneuve-sur-Lot stop on the main road below the *bastide* in
modern Monflanquin; simply walk uphill until you hit rue St-Pierre heading
north to place des Arcades, where you'll find the **tourist office** (April–June
& Sept–Oct Mon–Sat 10am–noon & 2–6pm, Sun 3–6pm; July & Aug
Mon–Sat 10am–7pm, Sun 10am–6pm; Nov–March Mon–Sat 10am–noon &
2–5pm, Sun 3–5pm; ☎05.53.36.40.19, ⓦwww.cc-monflanquinois.fr); they
can furnish you with details of the many **events** taking place here in summer
(see box on p.293).

As regards **hotels**, the *Monform* (☎05.53.49.85.85, ⓦwww.logis-de-france.fr;
❸; closed Feb school hols, & Sun from Oct to April), just west of centre on the
D124 Cancon road, is your best **hotel**. A modern and slightly soulless establishment overlooking a lake, it boasts a health centre (with heated pool, sauna and
gym) and a restaurant (menus €13–25). For atmosphere alone, however, it's
better to eat in one of the **cafés** and **restaurants** on place des Arcades. Pick
of the bunch is the welcoming *Le Bistrot du Prince Noir* (closed Jan–March, also
Tues & Wed from Oct to May) in the southwest corner of the square. It's both
a wine bar – with an excellent choice of local wines (from €2 for a glass) – and
restaurant, running the gamut from pan-fried foie gras or duck breast with a
spicy redcurrant sauce to a selection of Asian dishes; there's also a number of
vegetarian options and plenty of fresh fish (count on around €23–25 for three
courses from the *carte*). Another good option, in a flowery corner at the end
of a lane 5km north on the D676 to Villeréal, is the *Ferme-Auberge de Tabel*
(☎05.53.36.30.57; reservations required), where you'll feast on hearty regional
dishes; the farm is now English-owned, so provides an easy introduction to the
ferme-auberge concept. They offer a choice of six menus from €12 to €24, each
of no less than six courses revolving around farm produce such as pâtés, foie
gras and goose *confit*.

The best place for picnic fodder is the Thursday-morning **market** on place
des Arcades, though you can also buy provisions at the **supermarket** on the
main road immediately south of town. The neighbouring **wine co-operative**,
the Cave des 7 Monts (☎05.53.36.33.40; closed Sun), represents some two
hundred local vineyards producing some very palatable and reasonably priced
wines; tastings are available free of charge.

Château de Biron

Twenty-two kilometres northeast of Monflanquin, via a picturesque route along
the River Lède, the vast **Château de Biron** (Feb, March & mid-Nov to Dec
Tues–Thurs & Sun 10am–12.30pm & 2–5.30pm; April–June & Sept to mid-Nov
daily 10am–12.30pm & 2–6pm; July & Aug daily 10am–7pm; €5.50; ⓦwww
.semitour.com) dominates the countryside for miles around. It was begun in the
eleventh century and added to piecemeal over the years by the Gontaut-Biron
family, who occupied the castle right up to the early twentieth century. The
biggest alterations were made in the fifteenth and early sixteenth centuries, when
Pons de Gontaut-Biron started reconstructing the eastern wing. The result is an
architectural primer, from the medieval keep through flamboyant Gothic and
Renaissance to an eighteenth-century loggia in the style of Versailles.

△ Château de Biron

Rather than the guided tour (in French only; 45min–1hr), at busy times it's better to borrow the English-language text from the ticket desk and wander at will. The most striking building in the grassy **lower court** is the Renaissance chapel, where the sarcophagi of Pons and his brother Armand, bishop of Sarlat, lie. Though their statues were hacked about during the Revolution, the Italianate biblical scenes and three Virtues carved on the sides still show fine craftsmanship. On entering the cobbled and confined **inner courtyard** around its twelfth-century keep, the route takes you to a dungeon and through the lord's apartments, with their Renaissance chimney and wood-panelled hall, to a vast reception room and an equally capacious stone-vaulted refectory. If the rooms decked out as a tannery, torture chamber and weavers' workshop make you feel as though you're walking through a film set, you are – Biron is a favourite for period dramas, the most recent being *Le Pacte des Loups* in 2000.

If you're looking for somewhere to **eat**, you could try the *Auberge du Château*, beside the path up to the castle, which serves decent menus at €10–12 (☎05.53.63.13.33; closed Mon, evenings from Sept to Easter, from mid-Dec to mid-Feb and for two weeks in Sept). Or, better still, head back southeast 5km – by road or on the GR36 footpath – to **LACAPELLE-BIRON**, where *Le Palissy* (closed Wed & three weeks in Feb), on the main road, is a friendly, locals' place offering excellent-value menus from €10. The village also boasts one of the region's best **campsites**, *Sunêlia Le Moulinal* (☎05.53.40.84.60, ⓦwww.lemoulinal.com; closed mid-Sept to early April), beside a leisure lake and with four-star facilities including a shop, restaurant and bar and a cybercafé.

Monpazier

From the Château de Biron it's only another 8km north to **MONPAZIER**, the finest and most complete of the surviving *bastides*, built of a lovely warm-coloured stone on a hill above the River Dropt. It was founded in 1284 by King Edward I of England on land granted by Pierre de Gontaut-Biron, and picturesque and placid though it is today, Monpazier has a hard and bitter history, being twice – in 1594 and 1637 – the centre of **peasant rebellions** provoked by the misery that followed the Wars of Religion (see p.389). Both uprisings were brutally suppressed: the 1637 peasants' leader was broken on the wheel in the square and his head paraded around the countryside. In an earlier episode, Sully, the Protestant general, describes a rare moment of light relief in the terrible **Wars of Religion**, when the men of Catholic Villefranche-de-Périgord planned to capture Monpazier on the same night as the men of Monpazier were headed for Villefranche. By chance, both sides took different routes, met no resistance, looted to their hearts' content and returned home congratulating themselves on their luck and skill, only to find that things were rather different. The peace terms were that everything should be returned to its proper place.

It therefore comes as something of a surprise to find Monpazier has survived so well. Three of its six **medieval gates** are still intact and its central square, **place des Cornières**, couldn't be more perfect with its oak-pillared *halle* and time-worn, stone-built houses, no two the same. Deep, shady arcades pass beneath all the houses, which are separated from each other by a small gap to reduce fire risk; at the corners the buttresses are cut away to allow the passage of laden pack animals. On Thursday mornings the square comes to life for the weekly **market**, which expands on the third Thursday of each month into a fair. In mushroom season (roughly Aug & Sept depending on the weather) people also come here in the afternoons to sell their pickings.

Monpazier's main north–south axis is **rue Notre-Dame**, which brings you in to the northeast corner of place des Cornières, past the much-altered **church**. The thirteenth-century building opposite is a bit battered, but this is Monpazier's oldest house, where the tax collector received his share of the harvest. Of more interest is the local museum, the **Ateliers des Bastides** (April–Sept daily 10am–12.30pm & 3–6.30pm; free), west of the square along rue Jean-Galmot. It boasts a few prehistoric remains and other historical bits and pieces, but is largely devoted to local adventurer Jean Galmot, who was born here in 1879 and was assassinated in 1928 in French Guiana, then a penal colony, where he was aiding its fledgling independence movement.

During the summer months the museum also hosts a number of temporary **art exhibitions**, and the town puts on all sorts of other events to draw the tourists, from book fairs to medieval jamborees (see box on p.292). Outside these occasions, however, there's not much else to do in Monpazier beyond soak up the sun at a café on the market square.

Practicalities

Monpazier's very organized and helpful **tourist office** (April–June & Sept daily 10am–12.30pm & 2–6.30pm; July & Aug daily 10am–7pm; Oct–March Mon–Sat 10am–12.30pm & 2.30–6pm, Sun during school hols or during school term 2–6pm; ℡05.53.22.68.59, ⓦwww.pays-des-bastides.com) is located on the east side of place des Cornières. Amongst all sorts of useful information, they produce a free leaflet of six **walks** in the area, including a 17km round trip via the Château de Biron (see p.337). You can also rent **bikes** at Jean-Pierre Mouret, 17 rue St-Jacques (℡05.53.22.63.46), the road forming the west side of the market square.

Accommodation

One of the nicest places to **stay**, the *Hôtel de France*, 21 rue St-Jacques (℡05.53.22.60.06, ℔05.53.22.07.27; ❷; closed Nov–March, and Wed except in July & Aug), occupies a lovely medieval building on the southwest corner of place des Cornières. It has a fine regional restaurant (menus from €17;

closed Nov–March, and Tues eve & Wed except in July & Aug), while in summer it also offers lighter brasserie-style fare. Another good option is the *Hôtel de Londres*, Foirail Nord (☏05.53.22.60.64; ❷), just outside the north gate, also with a decent restaurant (menus from €10). There are two **campsites** in the vicinity: the very basic *Camping de Véronne* (☏05.53.22.62.22, ℱ05.53.22.65.23; closed mid-Sept to mid-June), beside a lake 3km northwest in Marsalès, and the luxurious, four-star *Le Moulin de David* (☏05.53.22.65.25, ⓦwww.moulin-de-david.com; closed early Sept to mid-May), in the Dropt valley roughly the same distance to the south. Make sure you reserve well in advance for the latter.

Eating

You'll eat very well in the two hotel **restaurants** cited above. Otherwise, browse around place des Cornières, or head north of the square along rue Notre-Dame, where *Le Privelège du Périgord* (☏05.53.22.43.98; closed Jan & Feb, and Tues year-round;) at no. 58 is a good bet, comprising a number of cosy rooms plus a few tables in the courtyard, and offering lunch *formules* at €10–14, or menus from €18. Two streets west, *La Bastide* at 52 rue St-Jacques (☏05.53.22.60.59; closed Feb, and Mon year-round; menus €13–40), packs a more traditional atmosphere – all pink linen and gleaming tableware – and has a well-deserved reputation for its beautifully presented dishes: try a plate of kidneys and sweetbreads with truffles, roast herbed lamb or zander with a red-wine sauce, but be sure to leave room for the luscious home-made ice cream or sorbet.

Travel details

Trains

Cahors to: Brive (8 daily; 1hr–1hr 10min); Gourdon (7-8 daily; 30min); Montauban (7–10 daily; 40–50min); Paris-Austerlitz (6 daily; 4–5hr); Souillac (7 daily; 45min); Toulouse (8–9 daily; 1hr–1hr 20min).

Figeac to: Assier (5–7 daily; 15–20min); Brive (5–6 daily; 1hr 20min–2hr); Cordes (5–8 daily; 1hr 10min–1hr 40min); Gramat (5–6 daily; 25–30min); Laguépie (5–7 daily; 1hr–1hr 20min); Najac (5–7 daily; 50min–1hr 10min); Paris-Austerlitz (2-3 daily; 5hr 30min–7hr); Rocamadour (5–6 daily; 30–40min); St-Denis-Près-Martel (5–6 daily; 50min–1hr 10min); Toulouse (5–7 daily; 2hr 15min–3hr); Villefranche-de-Rouergue (6–7 daily; 40min–1hr).

Gourdon to: Brive (7 daily; 40min); Cahors (5–8 daily; 30min); Montauban (4–7 daily; 1hr 10min); Paris-Austerlitz (4–5 daily; 4hr 45min); Souillac (7 daily; 15min); Toulouse (4–7 daily; 1hr 30min).

Gramat to: Assier (5–6 daily; 15min); Brive (5–6 daily; 45min–1hr); Figeac (5–6 daily; 30min); Najac (2–3 daily; 1hr 25min); Paris-Austerlitz (2 daily; 5hr 15min–6hr 15min); Rocamadour (5–6 daily; 8min);

St-Denis-Près-Martel (5–6 daily; 25min); Toulouse (1 daily; 3hr).

Monsempron-Libos to: Agen (5–6 daily; 40–55min); Le Bugue (4–5 daily; 50min–1hr); Les Eyzies (4–5 daily; 55min–1hr 10min); Penne-d'Agenais (5 daily; 15–20min); Périgueux (4–5 daily; 1hr 20min–1hr 40min).

Buses

Cahors to: Albas (4–8 daily; 30min); Bouziès (4–7 daily; 25–30min); Cajarc (4–6 daily; 1hr); Calvignac (4–6 daily; 45–50min); Figeac (4–8 daily; 1hr 45min); Fumel (4–6 daily; 50min–1hr 15min); Gramat (Mon & Wed–Sat 1–2 daily; 1hr–1hr 10min); Luzech (4–8 daily; 20min); Monsempron-Libos (4–6 daily; 1hr 15min); Puy-l'Évêque (4–8 daily; 45min); St-Céré (Mon & Wed–Sat 1–2 daily; 1hr 45min); St-Martin-Labouval (4–6 daily; 40min); Tour-de-Faure (4–7 daily; 35min); Vers (4–8 daily; 15–20min); Villefranche-de-Rouergue (school term Mon 1 daily; 1hr 30min).

Figeac to: Assier (Mon–Fri 1 daily; 25min); Cahors (4–6 daily; 1hr 40min–2hr); Cajarc (4–6 daily; 30–35min); Gramat (Mon–Fri 1 daily; 50min); St-Céré (school term Tues & Thurs–Sat 1 daily, school hols Tues, Thurs & Sat 1 daily; 50min–1hr 10min);

Tour-de-Faure (4–6 daily; 1hr); Villefranche-de-Rouergue (1–2 daily; 40min).

Fumel to: Cahors (4–6 daily; 1hr 10min); Condat (4–6 daily; 7min); Duravel (4–6 daily; 15min); Luzech (4–6 daily; 45min); Puy-l'Evêque (4–6 daily; 25min); St-Sylvestre (school term Mon–Sat 1 daily; 20min); Touzac (4–6 daily; 15min); Villeneuve-sur-Lot (school term Mon–Sat 1 daily; 40min).

Gourdon to: Souillac (school term Mon–Fri 1–2 daily, school hols Tues 1 daily; 1hr).

Gramat to: Assier (Mon–Sat 1 daily; 25min); Cahors (Mon & Wed–Sat 1 daily; 1hr–1hr 15min); Figeac (Mon–Sat 1 daily; 50min); St-Céré (school term Mon–Sat 1–3 daily, school hols Mon & Wed–Sat 1–2 daily; 35–40min).

Luzech to: Albas (4–8 daily; 10min); Cahors (4–8 daily; 25min); Monsempron-Libos (4–6 daily; 1hr); Puy-l'Évêque (4–8 daily; 30min).

Monsempron-Libos to: Cahors (4–7 daily; 1hr 15min); Condat (4–7 daily; 10–15min); Duravel (4–7 daily; 20min); Fumel (4–7 daily; 6–10min); Luzech (4–7 daily; 50min–1hr); Puy-l'Évêque (4–7 daily; 30min); Touzac (4–7 daily; 15min).

Puy-l'Évêque to: Albas (4–8 daily; 15min); Cahors (4–8 daily; 1hr); Condat (4–6 daily; 15–20min); Duravel (4–6 daily; 5–10min); Fumel (4–6 daily; 15–20min); Luzech (4–8 daily; 20–25min); Monsempron-Libos (4–6 daily; 20–25min); Touzac (4–6 daily; 10–15min).

Villeneuve-sur-Lot to: Agen (10 daily; 45min); Bergerac (Mon–Fri 1 daily; 1hr 15min); Fumel (school term Mon–Sat 1 daily; 45min); Marmande (Mon–Fri 1–3 daily; 1hr 15min–1hr 50min); Monflanquin (school term Mon–Fri 1 daily, school hols Thurs 1 daily; 40–45min).

7

South of the River Lot

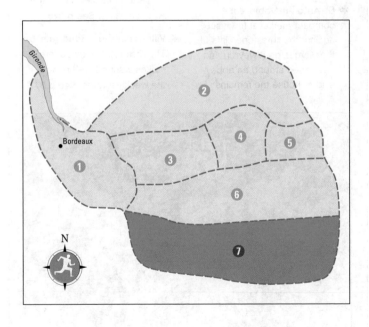

CHAPTER 7

Highlights

✳ **Moissac** The carvings decorating the south porch and cloister of Moissac's abbey church are masterpieces of Romanesque art. See p.357

✳ **Quercy Blanc** Take time to savour the bucolic countryside north of the Garonne, a soft, undulating landscape of vines, sunflowers and sleepy hilltop villages. See p.361

✳ **St-Antonin-Noble-Val** A compact medieval town set against the limestone cliffs of the Gorges de l'Aveyron and enveloped around an abbey said to house the remains of St Antonin, whose body, according to legend, was carried here in a boat led by two white eagles. See p.371

✳ **Cordes-sur-Ciel** Perched on its knuckle of rock, this fortified town is a favourite haunt of artists and artisans. See p.374

✳ **Najac** Climb the castle tower for vertiginous views over the Aveyron valley. See p.376

✳ **Villefranche-de-Rouergue** The arcaded central square makes a superb setting for the weekly market. See p.377

△ Moissac church carvings

South of the River Lot

The southern border of the Dordogne and Lot region is defined by the River Garonne in the west and by the Tarn and Aveyron in the east. On the whole this area to the south of the Lot offers more gentle and less dramatic scenery than further north, but by the same token it sees fewer tourists, and even in midsummer there are still quiet corners to be found. It is a fertile land, full of sunflowers and fruit orchards, particularly along the Garonne and spreading over the hills to the north: plums, pears, peaches, cherries, apples and nectarines all grow here, as well as melons, strawberries and the succulent chasselas grapes. In contrast with such agricultural bounty, the region has few outstanding sights, but, instead, endless opportunities to wander the country lanes between timeworn hilltop villages where life moves at a pace dictated by the slowly turning seasons, and where the local market is the high point of the week.

The first of the region's two gateways is **Agen**, the only major town on the Garonne between Bordeaux and Toulouse and more pleasant than it first appears, with an old centre built of pink-mottled brick and a fine local museum. Southwest of Agen, what's left of **Nérac**'s castle and its riverside pleasure gardens – where King Henri IV misspent his youth – still exudes a slightly decadent air. The river here is the Baïse, which flows north to join the Garonne near **Buzet-sur-Baïse** in the centre of a small wine region, from where it's worth continuing northwest again to see a tiny painting by Rembrandt in the church of **Le Mas-d'Agenais**.

Upstream from Agen, the one sight in this region not to be missed is the abbey church at **Moissac**. The carvings on its south porch and in its cloister are among the finest examples of Romanesque art to be found in France. The Garonne valley here is at its flattest and most featureless, but north of Moissac things improve as you climb up onto the low, rolling plateau of the **Quercy Blanc**, which stretches north almost to Cahors. It's a region of white-stone farmhouses, sun-drenched hilltop villages, windmills and *pigeonniers* – pigeon houses often raised on stilts – by the hundred. Of these, the prettiest is **Lauzerte**, but **Montpezat-de-Quercy** also merits a visit for its display of religious art, including a series of superb tapestries.

Near Montpezat the N20 and new A20 *autoroute* mark the eastern extent of Quercy Blanc and funnel traffic south to **Montauban**. This brick-red city,

Festivals, events and markets

Mid-May Montauban: Alors, Chante! ☎05.63.63.66.77, ⓦperso.orange.fr /alors-chante. Over Ascension weekend various well-known, and lesser-known, artists take part in this festival of French song (tickets required).

Late May or early June Moissac: Fêtes de Pentecôte ☎05.63.04.63.63. An important traditional fair on the banks of the Tarn over the Whitsun weekend, with fireworks on the Monday night.

July and August Moissac: Les Soirs de Moissac ☎05.63.04.06.81. Varied programme of concerts, choral works and recitals, including world music, held in the cloister or the church of St-Pierre, (tickets required). On the final Saturday evening there are free concerts in the church square and beside the Tarn.

Mid-July Villefranche-de-Rouergue: VISA Francophone ☎05.65.45.41.12. A one-week competition of French song held in the streets of Villefranche. Some ticket-only events.

Mid-July Cordes-sur-Ciel: Fête du Grand Fauconnier. This three-day medieval festival converts the town into a costumed extravaganza, complete with exhibitions on medieval crafts and falconry. Daily admission to the old town is €7.

Mid-July to mid-August Montauban and around: Jazz à Montauban ☎05.63.63.56.56, ⓦwww.jazzmontauban.com. International jazz and blues artists play in Montauban (mostly in the Jardin des Plantes) and various other towns around the *département* (tickets required for most events). There's also a "festival off" with free concerts in the cafés and streets of Montauban.

Late July Cordes-sur-Ciel: Musique sur Ciel ☎05.63.56.00.75, ⓦwww .festivalmusiquesurciel.com. Ten days of classical concerts, some by featured contemporary composers, in the church of St-Michel.

Late July to early Aug Aiguillon: Festival de Jazz ☎05.53.88.20.20. Open-air concerts featuring international and French groups take place over a weekend in

not far north of Toulouse and on the Paris main line, is the region's second gateway, and justifies a few hours' exploration thanks to its art museum and central square surrounded by elegant town houses. It sits on the banks of the Tarn in the midst of an alluvial plain which, in the east, gives way abruptly to hills. Running through them, the **Gorges de l'Aveyron** are punctuated with ancient villages perched high above the river, while **St-Antonin–Noble-Val**, with its core of medieval lanes, lies in the valley bottom caught between soaring limestone crags. Beyond St-Antonin, it's worth making a short detour south across the plateau to the aptly named **Cordes-sur-Ciel**, where noble facades line the steeply cobbled lanes, before rejoining the Aveyron beneath **Najac**'s much-contested fortress. The gorge opens out to the north of Najac, but it's worth continuing the last few kilometres to **Villefranche-de-Rouergue**, in the centre of which, in the monstrous shadow of its church tower, lies the most perfectly preserved arcaded market square.

Three major **train** lines fan out across this region from Toulouse: along the Garonne valley to Montauban, Moissac and Agen; north via Montpezat to Cahors; and northeast through Cordes, Najac and Villefranche en route to Figeac. Among the more useful **bus services** are those to Nérac, Lauzerte and along the Aveyron to St-Antonin and Laguépie. Another way to get about is by **boat** on the Canal latéral à la Garonne, which shadows the Garonne for nearly 200km from near Langon in the east (see p.117), passing through Buzet, Agen and Moissac, among other places, to Toulouse, where it joins the Canal du Midi.

front of the Château des Ducs (tickets required). A small "festival off" includes free concerts, workshops and masterclasses.

Late July to mid-August Lauzerte and around: Festival du Quercy Blanc ☏05.65.31.83.12. Concerts of classical and chamber music held mostly in churches around the region, including Lauzerte, Montcuq, Montpezat-de-Quercy and Castelnau-Montratier. Tickets available from local tourist offices.

Early August Villefranche-de-Rouergue and around: Festival en Bastides. Five days of contemporary theatre and performance art animate the streets of Villefranche and Najac, amongst other places. Some ticketed events.

August 15 Lauzerte: Foire brocante. Secondhand stalls fill the old village on the same day as the final concert of the Festival du Quercy Blanc, which takes place in the church (see above).

Third weekend in September Moissac: Fête du Chasselas and Fête des Fruits et des Légumes ☏05.63.04.63.63. Every even year the Fête du Chasselas celebrates the local grape, with tastings on offer and a competition to find the pick of the bunch; the event takes place in the market hall. In odd years the whole range of local fruits plus vegetables are on display and there are all manner of related events throughout the town.

Second weekend in October Auvillar: Marché Potier. Some forty exhibitors take part in this important pottery fair held on the place de la Halle.

Markets

The main **markets** in the region are at Agen (Wed, Sat & Sun); Aiguillon (Tues & Fri); Cordes (Sat); Laguépie (Wed & Sun); Lauzerte (Wed & Sat); Moissac (Sat & Sun); Montauban (Sat); Montcuq (Sun); Nérac (Sat); St-Antonin-Noble-Val (Sun); St-Nicolas-de-la-Grave (Mon); and Villefranche-de-Rouergue (Thurs).

Agen and around

AGEN, capital of the Lot-et-Garonne *département*, lies on the broad, powerful River Garonne halfway between Bordeaux and Toulouse. Close to the A62 *autoroute* and connected to both cities by fast and frequent train services, and to Paris by train and plane, it provides a useful gateway to the southern reaches of the Dordogne and Lot region. However, Agen is more than just a transport hub. Inside the ring of hypermarkets and industrial estates lies a core of old lanes lined with handsome brick houses, several churches worth a look and a surprisingly good fine arts museum. Add to that a number of excellent restaurants and a good choice of hotels, and Agen makes for a pleasant half-day's exploration, or a base from which to cover the surrounding country. The most interesting jaunts take you southwest to **Nérac**, where kings and queens disported themselves on the Baïse's wooded banks, and west to the wine town of **Buzet-sur-Baïse**. Further down the Garonne, **Aiguillon** provides more good hotel options as well as a clutch of picturesque medieval lanes, while **Le Mas-d'Agenais** hides a few surprises inside its church.

Of these places, only Nérac and Aiguillon are accessible by **public transport**: the former by bus from Agen, and the latter by train. However, since they all lie on navigable and interconnected waterways – the Baïse, Garonne and the Canal latéral – renting a **boat** would provide a leisurely way of exploring the area.

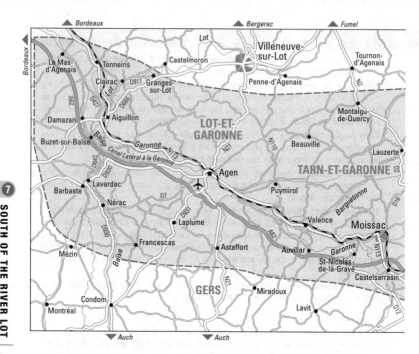

Arrival, information and accommodation

Flights from Paris arrive at Agen's La Garenne **airport**, around 3km southwest of town; a taxi into the centre costs roughly €14. The **gare SNCF** and **gare routière** are located next to each other on the north side of town. From in front of the station, boulevard du Président-Carnot leads south to place Goya, where it crosses the town's other main thoroughfare, the east–west boulevard de la République. For drivers, free car **parking** can be found along the riverbank and on cours Gambetta. You'll find the **tourist office** south of this crossroads at 107 bd Carnot (July & Aug Mon–Sat 9am–7pm, Sun 10am–noon; Sept–June Mon–Sat 9am–noon & 2–6.30pm; ☎05.53.47.36.09, ⓦwww.ot-agen.org).

Accommodation

Agen has some good **hotel** options scattered around its centre, especially at the budget end, though you'll also find four-star luxury at a reasonable price. There's a clutch of chain hotels (such as *Formule 1*, *B&B* and *Campanile*) at the exit from the *autoroute*; see "Basics", p.37 for more on these chains.

Alternatively, you can rent **houseboats** from Locaboat Plaisance on quai Dunkerque (☎05.53.66.00.74, ⓦwww.locaboat.com), and make your way northwest from Agen along the Canal latéral to Buzet, Aiguillon, and Le Mas-d'Agenais, from where you can enter the River Lot. Prices vary from €860–1500 per week for a three-to-five-person boat, depending on the season and level of comfort.

Des Ambans 59 rue des Ambans
☎05.53.66.28.60, ⓕ05.53.87.94.01. The best value of the budget hotels, at the very bottom of this price category, with nine small, tidy rooms; note that all but the most expensive lack an en-suite toilet. It's clean, friendly and central, which means you need to book well ahead for the summer season. Oct–March occasionally closed weekends. ❶

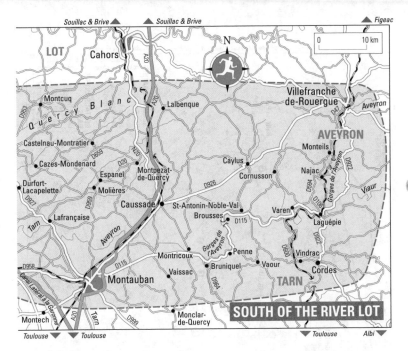

0   10 km

LOT   Cahors

Montcuq   B l a n c   Lalbenque   Villefranche-de-Rouergue   Aveyron

Q u e r c y

Castelnau-Montratier   **AVEYRON**

Monteils

Cazes-Mondenard   Espanel   Montpezat-de-Quercy   Caylus   Cornusson   Najac

Durfort-Lacapelette   Molières

Caussade   St-Antonin-Noble-Val   Varen

Lafrançaise   Brousses   Laguépie

Montricoux   Penne   Vindrac

Montauban   Vaissac   Bruniquel   Vaour   Cordes

TARN

Montech   Monclar-de-Quercy   **SOUTH OF THE RIVER LOT**

7

SOUTH OF THE RIVER LOT | Agen and around

Ibis 16 rue Camille-Desmoulins ☎05.53.47.43.43, ⓦwww.ibis.fr. A modern, mid-range hotel on a quiet side street near the tourist office. If the others are full then it's a decent enough choice but the rooms are rather boxy and lacking in character. ❸
Les Îles 25 rue Baudin ☎05.53.47.11.33, ⓕ05.53.66.19.25. One of Agen's more attractive hotels, in a lovely brick-built house full of plants and family furniture, about ten minutes' walk southwest of the station. Its rooms are simple but light and airy, while the cheapest share a toilet on the corridor. Again, with only nine rooms, it fills up quickly in peak periods. ❷
🏃 **Des Jacobins** 1 place des Jacobins ☎05.53.47.03.31, ⓦwww.chateau-des-jacobins.com. Agen's top hotel oozes character. It occupies an elegant nineteenth-century town house swathed in greenery beside the Jacobins church, and its rooms are decked out with antique furniture, gilt mirrors and plush fabrics. ❻–❼
Le Périgord 42 cours du Juillet XIV ☎05.53.77.55.77, ⓦwww.leperigord47.com. This large hotel is stuck in a bit of a traffic island, however, the rooms, decked out in country florals, are spacious and comfortable and reasonably priced. ❸
Régina 139 bd Carnot ☎05.53.47.07.97, ⓦwww.hotelreginagen.com. If the *Hôtel des Ambans* above is full, try this welcoming, rambling, old-fashioned hotel on the main road south of the station; it's best to ask for a quieter room at the back. Rooms are on the small side but with good-sized bathrooms and modern, pale-wood furnishings and the buffet breakfast is better than most. Note that there's an 11.30pm curfew. ❷

The Town

The old centre of Agen lies on the east bank of the Garonne. It is quartered by two nineteenth-century boulevards – **boulevard de la République**, running east–west, and north–south **boulevard du Président-Carnot** – which intersect at place Goya and make for easy navigation. To the northeast stands **Cathédrale St-Caprais**, somewhat misshapen but worth a look for its finely proportioned Romanesque apse and radiating chapels. However, Agen's foremost sight lies south-west on place Dr-Esquirol: beside the exuberant, Italianate municipal theatre, the **Musée des Beaux-Arts** (☎05.53.69.47.23; daily except Tues: 10am–6pm; closed

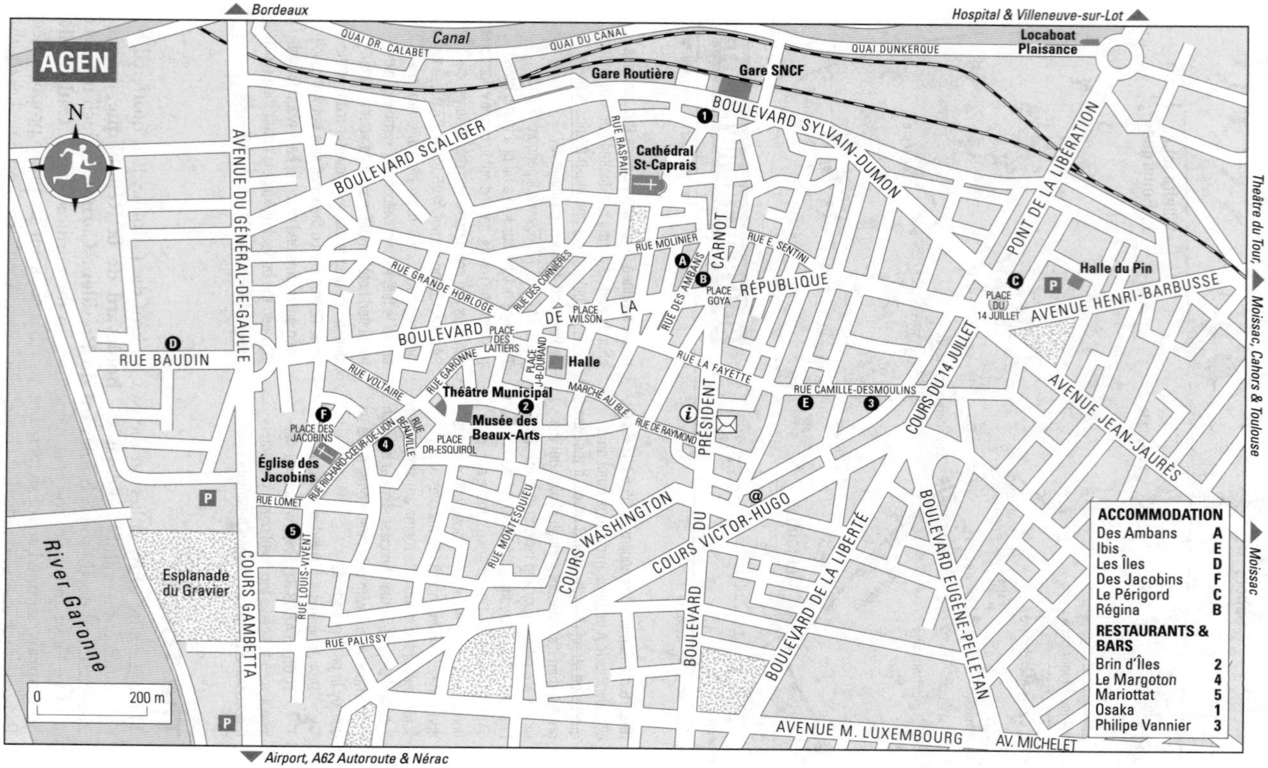
AGEN
N
Bordeaux
Hospital & Villeneuve-sur-Lot
Theâtre du Tour, Moissac, Cahors & Toulouse
Moissac
Airport, A62 Autoroute & Nérac
ACCOMMODATION
Des Ambans A
Ibis E
Les Îles D
Des Jacobins F
Le Périgord C
Régina B
RESTAURANTS & BARS
Brin d'Îles 2
Le Margoton 4
Mariottat 5
Osaka 1
Philipe Vannier 3
Canal
QUAI DR. CALABET
QUAI DU CANAL
QUAI DUNKERQUE
Locaboat Plaisance
Gare Routière
Gare SNCF
BOULEVARD SYLVAIN-DUMON
BOULEVARD SCALIGER
PONT DE LA LIBÉRATION
Cathédral St-Caprais
RUE RASPAIL
RUE MOLINIER
RUE E. SENTINI
CARNOT
RUE DES AMBANS
PLACE GOYA
BOULEVARD DE LA RÉPUBLIQUE
PLACE WILSON
PLACE DES LAITIERS
PLACE J-B-DURAND
Halle
Halle du Pin
PLACE DU 14 JUILLET
AVENUE HENRI-BARBUSSE
AVENUE JEAN-JAURÈS
COURS DU 14 JUILLET
RUE CAMILLE-DESMOULINS
RUE LA FAYETTE
MARCHÉ AU BLÉ
RUE DE RAYMOND
BOULEVARD DU PRÉSIDENT
RUE GRANDE HORLOGE
RUE DES CORNIÈRES
RUE GARONNE
RUE VOLTAIRE
Théâtre Municipal
Musée des Beaux-Arts
PLACE DR-ESQUIROL
RUE BEAUVILLE
PLACE DES JACOBINS
RUE RICHARD-CŒUR-DE-LION
Église des Jacobins
RUE LOMET
RUE LOUIS-VIVENT
RUE PALISSY
RUE MONTESQUIEU
COURS WASHINGTON
COURS VICTOR-HUGO
BOULEVARD DE LA LIBERTÉ
BOULEVARD EUGÈNE-PELLETAN
AVENUE M. LUXEMBOURG
AV. MICHELET
AVENUE DU GÉNÉRAL-DE-GAULLE
COURS GAMBETTA
RUE BAUDIN
Esplanade du Gravier
River Garonne
0 200 m

Agen grew rich at first on the trade of manufactured goods, such as cloth and leather, flowing through its river port, but the industrial revolution put paid to all that and since then the town's prosperity has been based on agriculture – in particular, its famous **prunes** and **plums**. Plums (*prunes* in French) were introduced to France by Crusaders returning from Syria in the eleventh century. It is believed that Benedictine monks at Clairac, near the confluence of the Lot and Garonne, were the first to cultivate the fruit, a variety known as *prune d'Ente*, which thrives on sun, high humidity and chalky soils and is also excellent for drying thanks to its size and high sugar content. Though plums now grow throughout the region, the dried fruit (*pruneaux*) were originally exported via the port at Agen – and are thus known as **pruneaux d'Agen**.

Nowadays **prunes** are one of the region's principal money-spinners and in late August the orchards are a hive of activity as the ripe fruit are shaken from the trees. They are dried slowly in hot-air ovens to retain the flavour – during which process they lose three-quarters of their weight. Even so, the biggest prunes weigh in at 20g.

You can learn more facts and figures about prune production in the specialist *confiseries* of Agen (see p.352) and also at an enjoyable **farm-museum**, Au Pruneau Gourmand (mid-March to mid-Sept Mon–Sat 9am–noon & 2–7pm, Sun 2–7pm; mid-Oct to mid-March Mon–Sat 9am–noon & 2–6.30pm, Sun 2–6.30pm; €3.30), near the village of Granges-sur-Lot, 10km northeast of Aiguillon (see p.356). And there's even a website devoted to this "strapping fruit": www.pruneau.fr.

1 January, 1 May, 1 November, 25 December; €3) is magnificently housed in four adjacent sixteenth- and seventeenth-century mansions adorned with stair turrets and Renaissance window details. Inside is a rich variety of archeological exhibits, furniture and paintings – among the latter, a number of Goyas and a Tintoretto rediscovered during an inventory in 1997. Best, though, are the basement's Roman finds which include intricate jewellery and a superb white-marble Venus.

To the west of place Dr-Esquirol, a clutch of brick and timber houses – the bricks forming neat zigzags within the timber frame – represent Agen's most attractive corner. From here a short and narrow alley, **rue Beauville**, cuts through to rue Richard-Coeur-de-Lion, with more eye-catching facades and the big, brick **Église des Jacobins** which often hosts temporary art exhibitions; ask at the tourist office for details. It was founded by Dominican monks in the thirteenth century, then served as the Protestants' headquarters before being used as a prison during the Revolution. If it's open, it's worth popping in to see the unusual Gothic frescoes of leaves and geometric patterns in *trompe l'oeil* on the walls and ceiling.

Continuing westwards you reach the river and the public gardens of **Esplanade du Gravier**, where a footbridge crosses the Garonne – from it you can see a 550-metre **canal bridge** dating from 1843 further downstream.

Eating, drinking and entertainment

In general, the best place to look for somewhere to **eat** in Agen is pedestrianized rue Émile-Sentini, cutting diagonally between boulevard Carnot and boulevard de la République. You'll also find a mixed bag of restaurants along rue La Fayette and its extension rue Camille-Desmoulins running east from boulevard Carnot near the tourist office, while there are a number of ethnic restaurants and fast-food outlets on rue Voltaire and rue Garonne further west. There are a couple of decent cafés on boulevard de la République and another group gathered at its western junction with avenue du Général-de-Gaulle.

With no fewer than three **theatres,** Agen has a reputation for its thespian activities. The main Théâtre Municipal, place Dr-Esquirol (℡05.53.66.26.60), puts on a varied programme of theatre, dance, concerts and opera by local and national artists, while the Théâtre du Jour, 21 rue Paulin-Régnier (℡05.53.47.82.08), stages more innovative works and doubles as a drama school. Last but not least, the Théâtre du Petit Jour, place Ste-Foy (℡05.53.47.82.09), offers a variety of children's entertainment.

Brin d'Îles rue des Cailles ℡ 05.53.87.79.65. This restaurant is popular for its smattering of Creole dishes and has a menu that changes weekly. It has particularly good desserts such as flambeé fruit kebabs and carpaccio of pineapple. Daily menu €19.50. Closed Sun, Mon & Sat lunch.

Le Margoton 52 rue Richard-Cœur-de-Lion ℡05.53.48.11.55. Stylish little place near the Jacobins church, serving a good range of seafood in addition to rich, gamey food such as guinea fowl, pigeon and venison. Menus range from €16 to €62, or around €30 from the *carte*. Closed lunchtime Sat & Mon, also late Dec to early Jan & the last two weeks in Aug.

Mariottat 25 rue Louis-Vivent ℡05.53.77.99.77. Agen's most elegant restaurant occupies a grand old villa with sumptuous interior to the south of the Jacobins church. They concentrate on mostly local produce, including duck in all its guises, with beautifully presented menus starting at a very reasonable €25 on weekdays, while eating *à la carte* will set you back about €55. Closed Sun eve, Mon & lunchtime Tues & Sat. Also closed Feb school hols.

Osaka 32 bd Sylvain Dumon ℡05.53.66.31.76. Japanese place opposite the station serving good sushi, *teppanyaki* and noodle soups. Menus start at just €8.90 at lunchtime. Closed Mon.

Philippe Vannier 66 rue Camille Desmoulins ℡05.53.66.63.70. ⒲www.philippe-vannier.com. A stylish restaurant with a cool, brick-walled dining room. There's a good-value lunchtime *formule* for €14.50 and the inventive menu includes salmon with coconut and melon, and a range of terrifically indulgent desserts. Closed Sun eve and for lunch on Mon & Sat.

Markets and shopping

A fresh produce **market** takes place daily (except Mon) in the covered market on place Jean-Baptiste-Durand. There are also two large farmers' markets held on Wednesday and Sunday mornings in the Halle du Pin, beside place du 14-Juillet, as well as a smaller one on Saturday mornings on the Esplanade du Gravier, and an organic market, also on Saturdays, on place des Laitiers, off boulevard de la République. The most interesting of several agricultural fairs are the *foire de la prune* (1st or 2nd Mon after Sept 15), devoted to plums and prunes, and the *foire aux oies et canards gras* (2nd Sun in Dec) for foie gras and all manner of products made from duck and goose. The fairs take place in varying locations around the town centre; contact the tourist office for further information.

The main **shopping** streets are boulevard de la République and boulevard du Président-Carnot, while pedestrianized rue Molinier, south of the cathedral, has a few smarter boutiques. *The* thing to buy in Agen is prunes. You'll find them in the markets and at a number of specialist shops, including Confiserie P. Boisson, (20 rue Grande-Horloge; closed Sun), southwest of the cathedral, which opened in 1835 and still uses traditional methods to produce chocolate prunes, truffle prunes, prunes in armagnac and stuffed prunes, amongst other delicacies. You can also ask to see a short explanatory film in English.

Listings

Airport Aerocondor (℡08.92.68.87.77, ⒲www .aerocondor.fr) operates daily flights to Paris from Agen's La Garenne airport, 3km southwest of centre; see website for further details.

Bike rental Bicycles are available from Méca Plus, 18–20 av du Général-de-Gaulle ℡05.53.47.76.76.

Bus information For up-to-date bus schedules ask at the tourist office or phone the transport desk of the Conseil Général on ℡05.53.69.42.03.

Car rental Avis, 12 bd Sylvain-Dumon (☎05.53.47.76.47), and Europcar, 120 bd du Président-Carnot (☎05.53.47.37.40), have outlets near the train station. Airport pick-ups are available on request.

Hospital Centre Hospitalier, rte de Villeneuve, located 1.5km northeast of central Agen on the N21 to Villeneuve-sur-Lot (☎05.53.69.70.71).

Internet Is available at Nauteus, 83 Cours Victor Hugo ☎05.53.87.96.55; Mon-Wed 10am-8pm, Thurs & Fri 10am-10pm, Sat 2-10pm, Sun 2-8pm.

Police Commissariat de Police, 10 rue Palissy, to the south of the old quarter (☎05.53.68.17.00).

Post office The central post office is at 72 bd du Président-Carnot.

Taxis There is a taxi stand at the station or call Alliance Taxi Azur on ☎05.53.47.88.88.

Nérac

Thirty kilometres across high, rolling hills to the southwest of Agen, you come to the castle town of **NÉRAC** on the banks of the River Baïse. It's hard to believe that this drowsy backwater, seat of the **d'Albret** family, once matched the Parisian court in its splendour and extravagance, and that here the bitter rivalries between Protestant and Catholic were played out. Nowadays, it's an attractive and prosperous little place, where you can happily spend a few hours wandering the riverbanks and what's left of the d'Albrets' castle.

The d'Albrets first came to Nérac around 1150 and over the next three centuries grew to become one of Aquitaine's most powerful dynasties – largely through a talent for marrying well. First they gained the Pyrenean kingdom of Navarre by marriage and then in 1527 Henri II d'Albret wed **Marguerite d'Angoulême**, sister to King François I of France. Intelligent and cultured, Marguerite surrounded her Nérac court with scholars and proponents of the new Protestant faith, including Jean Chauvin (John Calvin) who stayed here briefly in 1534. Neither Henri nor Marguerite converted, but their determined and ambitious daughter, **Jeanne d'Albret**, did so in 1560, thus making Nérac an important Protestant stronghold. Jeanne's son, also Henri, for his part married the young and beautiful **Marguerite de Valois**, sister of the king of France and Catherine de Médicis, in 1572 and so ushered in Nérac's golden era. Their court glittered with eminent writers, diplomats and nobles, poets and musicians, while Henri indulged in the innumerable amorous conquests that earned him the nickname, *Le Vert Galant*; Queen Margot, as she was called, was no retiring violet either, and the marriage was eventually annulled in 1599, by which time Henri had become **Henri IV** of France and removed his court to Paris.

All this time the d'Albrets had been adding to their **château** (June–Sept Tues–Sun 10am–noon & 2–7pm; Oct–May Tues–Sun 10am–noon & 2–6pm; €4) on the river's west bank – at the far end of the bridge coming into Nérac from Agen. By the sixteenth century they had made it into a comfortable palace, of which only the north wing with its Renaissance gallery still exists, the other three having been partially destroyed in 1621 and finished off during the Revolution. It now houses a local history museum, of which the most interesting displays relate to Henri, Queen Margot and their larger-than-life relatives.

To the north of the château stands the Neoclassical **Église St-Nicolas** which was built in the mid-eighteenth century and contains some good nineteenth-century stained-glass windows, depicting scenes from the Old and New Testaments. From the terrace here you get good views of the triple-arched **Pont-Vieux** and the ancient roofs of the area known as **Petit-Nérac** on the opposite side of the river. It's worth wandering over the bridge and turning right along rue Sederie, where the wooden balconies of old tanneries overhang the river, to come out beside Nérac "port", now bustling in summer with cruise boats, below the Pont-Neuf.

△ Boating at Nérac

Continuing south from the port across the main road, avenue Georges-Clemenceau, a shady woodland path, leads 1.5km along the riverbank. **La Garenne**, as the area is known, was laid out as a royal pleasure park in the sixteenth century. The aviaries of exotic birds, the arbours and minstrels have long gone, but it's still a pleasant place to stroll or picnic. Not far from the entrance, look out for the **Fontaine de Fleurette**, marked by a statue of a prostrate and scantily clad young woman. According to legend, Fleurette was a gardener's daughter who had the misfortune to be seduced by *Le Vert Galant* and, when his attentions drifted elsewhere, drowned herself in the river. The inscription reads: "She gave him all her life. He gave her but one day."

Practicalities

Buses from Agen (Citram; ☎05.56.43.68.68) stop on the central place de la Libération next to the château, while the **tourist office** is located opposite on avenue Mandenard (May, June & Sept Tues–Sat 9am–noon & 2–6pm, Sun 10am–noon & 3–5pm; July & Aug Mon–Sat 9am–7pm, Sun 10am–12.30pm & 3–5.30pm; Oct–April Tues–Sat 9am–noon & 2–6pm; ☎05.53.65.27.75, ⒺOffice-tourisme-nerac@wanadoo.fr). In summer you can rent pleasure **boats** at the port through Les Croisières de Prince Henry (☎05.53.65.66.66), for €80 for half a day or €120 for a whole day for 2–7 people or take a cruise with commentary on a traditional *gabarre* a short distance up the Baïse to the first lock and back (1hr; April–Oct; €7.50). There's also a **tourist train** the Train Touristique de l'Albret (☎06.85.62.77.47; ⓦwww.lafrancevuedurail.fr /ttalbret) that runs the thirteen kilometres southwest from the **gare SNCF** to the medieval village of Mézin. The journey takes an hour and a half and there's a guided commentary in French (July & Aug daily 10.30am, 2.30pm & 4.45pm; April–June & Sept–Oct times vary – call for details).

The most comfortable **accommodation** in Nérac is the centrally located *Hôtel du Château*, 7 av Mondenard (☎05.53.65.09.05, ⓦwww.logis-de-france. fr; ❷; closed Jan 1–15), on the main road west of the Pont-Neuf with quieter rooms at the back. It also has a swanky restaurant with menus from €28 (Oct–June closed Sat lunch and for dinner Fri & Sun). Alternatively, try the welcoming, family-run *Hôtel d'Albret*, 40 allée d'Albret (☎05.53.97.41.10,

@ www.logis-de-france.fr; ❷), on the wide boulevard a couple of minutes' walk southwest of the centre, with a wide choice of rooms and a cheerful restaurant serving well-priced regional menus from €16 (closed Sun eve). The *Auberge du Pont Vieux* (☎05.53.97.51.04; ❸) on the river's east bank at 19 rue Séderie, has comfortable, old-fashioned rooms with wooden shutters and flower-draped balconies overlooking the river, as well as a restaurant with good-value menus from €16.50.

Apart from the above hotel **restaurants**, you can get salads and crêpes (the sweet variety) in addition to the standard duck-based dishes at *L'Escadron Volant* (closed Sun eve & Mon from mid-Sept to mid-June) in a prime spot facing the château entrance. Around the corner on rue du Château is *Aux Délices du Roy* (☎05.53.65.81.12; closed Sun eve & Mon) an upmarket seafood place serving wonderfully simple, fresh fish dishes in an elegant blue dining room, with great daily specials and menus from €25. Across the river on rue Séderie ⅍ *Le Vert Galant* does a nice line in *tartines* – toasted bread with tomatoes in a white sauce –accompanied by regional produce (the speciality of the house is *tartine* with duck *confit*, pear and bacon). It also serves over sixty flavours of ice cream, including tomato and basil, Camembert and pumpkin. If you've still got room, you can pick up beautifully made goodies at *Chocolaterie Artisanale la Cigale* 2 rue Calvin, a couple of minutes' walk south of the *gare SNCF* (Tues–Fri 9.30am–12.30pm & 2–5.30pm; ☎05.53.65.15.73).

Probably the best place to eat in the area, however, is ⅍ *Le Relais de la Hire* (☎05.53.65.41.59; closed Sun eve & Mon), 10km southeast of Nérac in the village of Francescas, where you can feast on such dishes as artichoke and foie gras soufflé in an elegant eighteenth-century house or its flower-filled garden; menus are €23 and €31, or you can eat *à la carte* for around €45.

Downstream from Agen

East of Agen the Garonne is sandwiched between the *autoroute*, two busy main roads, and the Bordeaux train line, which doesn't make for a particularly scenic journey. If you're headed this way, however, there is a clutch of interesting places to stop en route. Near the confluence of the Baïse and the Garonne lies the wine town of **Buzet-sur-Baïse**, where the local wine co-operative merits a visit, while over on the Garonne's east bank, **Aiguillon**'s eighteenth-century château presides over the junction of the Garonne and Lot rivers. From Aguillon it's worth continuing downstream as far as **Le Mas-d'Agenais**. This village, which overlooks both the Canal latéral and the Garonne from the west, has an attractive old centre, but its prime draw is the wealth of carvings and a little oil painting inside its church.

Buzet-sur-Baïse

BUZET-SUR-BAÏSE lies roughly 30km west of Agen, in the shadow of the Château de Buzet (not open to the public), which stands high on the green hillside, now separated from its village by the *autoroute*. Buzet itself is rather dull but as the vines on this south bank of the Garonne indicate, you're back in wine country and you shouldn't miss the chance to visit the local **wine co-operative**, Les Vignerons de Buzet (July & Aug Mon–Sat 9am–12.30pm & 2–7, Sun 10am–noon & 2–6pm; Sept–June Mon–Sat 9am–noon & 2–6pm; ☎05.53.84.74.30, @ www.vignerons-buzet.fr), east of the village on the D642. Founded in 1953, this is France's largest wine co-operative, with around three hundred growers producing fourteen million bottles on average per year. The majority are strong red wines which benefit from ageing – Grande Réserve, Baron d'Ardeuil and

Château de Gueyze stand out among the many award-winning wines produced by the co-operative (free **tastings** available). It's also well worth arranging for one of their exceptionally informative **guided tours** of the vinification plant and *chais* (July & Aug two visits per day; Sept–June by appointment only; visits in English on request). The tour covers everything, from where the grapes are delivered and sorted, the in-house cooperage, the vast *chais* containing more than four thousand barrels, and the bottling plant, to the warehouse where you'll find yourself among some eight million glistening green bottles.

The other reason to visit Buzet is to rent a **boat** for a trip along the Canal latéral, the Baïse or the Lot. Aquitaine Navigation (℡05.53.84.72.50, Ⓦwww .aquitaine-navigation.com), based at the *halte nautique* on the canal below Buzet village, has both small pleasure boats for rent by the half day or day, as well as houseboats for longer excursions (prices vary seasonally).

Before setting off, you might want to refuel at one of Buzet's **restaurants**. The nicest option is *Le Vigneron*, on the broad main street (℡05.53.84.73.46; closed Sun eve & Mon), which offers well-priced menus, kicking off with a four-course *menu du jour* at €14 (€20 on Sun) including an hors-d'oeuvre buffet and a dessert trolley stacked with delectable home-made desserts – the house special is a confection of crêpes layered with cream, coated in meringue and baked.

Aiguillon

Six kilometres north of Buzet on the opposite bank, the hilltop town of **AIGUILLON** stands guard over the confluence of the Lot and Garonne rivers as it has done at least since Roman times. Nowadays Aiguillon's most imposing building is the eighteenth-century, Neoclassical **Château des Ducs** – now a school – which dominates the town centre. It was built by the duc d'Aiguillon who, having served as an army chief and governor of Brittany under Louis XV, returned to transform his medieval château into a mini-Versailles, though the grand balls and other festivities were soon cut short by the Revolution. The small area of medieval lanes with their half-timbered houses to the north of the château are worth a wander, but otherwise Aiguillon is more of interest for its hotels and transport connections.

Aiguillon's **gare SNCF**, on the Agen–Bordeaux train line, lies a couple of minutes' walk below the château to the southwest along avenue de la Gare. You'll find the **tourist office** beside the château on the central place du 14-Juillet (July & Aug Mon–Sat 9am–12.30pm & 3–6pm, Sun 10am–noon; Sept–June Mon–Fri 9am–12.30pm & 1.30–5pm; ℡05.53.79.62.58, Ⓦwww .tourisme.fr/tourist-office/aiguillon.htm). The most appealing **place to stay** is *La Terrasse de l'Étoile*, 8 cours Alsace-Lorraine (℡05.53.79.64.64, Ⓦwww .logis-de-france.fr; ❸), in a handsome stone and brick building at the east end of place du 14-Juillet; the rooms are full of character, and there's also a small pool and a good traditional restaurant (menus from €13). The only other hotel is *Le Jardin des Cygnes*, route de Villeneuve (℡05.53.79.60.02, Ⓦwww .jardin-des-cygnes.com; ❸; closed Dec 15–Jan 10 & last week in Aug), offering functional but perfectly comfortable rooms in an unmissable puce-coloured building – also with a garden, pool and decent restaurant (menus from €14) – on Aiguillon's northeastern outskirts.

Le Mas-d'Agenais

From Aiguillon, rather than taking the dreary N113, cross to the Garonne's west bank and follow the D427 northwest for 15km through orchards and poplar plantations to find another ancient village perched above the Garonne, **LE MAS-D'AGENAIS**. Traces of its ramparts still remain, but Le Mas' pride and joy is its cobbled central square with its old wooden *halle* and Romanesque **Église St-Vincent**. At first glance, the church's muddle of brick and stone, and its truncated tower don't look like much, but there's a surprising amount to see inside. Firstly, the exceptionally expressive carved capitals all around the choir and the triple-vaulted nave, depicting scenes such as Daniel in the lions' den, Abraham's sacrifice and David and Goliath. Then, in the southwest corner of the nave, there's a white-marble sarcophagus covered with geometric designs, which is said to have held the remains of St Vincent, the third-century evangelist, to whom the church is dedicated. But what most people come to see is a tiny painting in the north absidial chapel: the *Crucifixion* by **Rembrandt**. Dated 1631, the painting was donated to the church by a former parishioner in 1804; it belongs to a series of seven Stations of the Cross, the other six of which are in Munich. Christ is caught in a ray of light against an almost black background, his upturned face revealing the full agony of his question, "My God, why have you forsaken me?"

The Canal latéral runs immediately below Le Mas to the east, between the river cliffs and the Garonne. Here, beside the lock just north of the bridge over the Garonne, you'll find another **boating** centre, where Crown Blue Line (☎04.68.94.52.72, ⓦwww.crownblueline.com) has houseboats for rent. The canal itself makes a pretty route westwards, but otherwise there's little reason to stop beyond Le Mas until you reach La Réole, 30km downstream (see p.124).

Moissac and around

There is nothing very memorable about the modern town of **MOISSAC**, some 40km southeast of Agen, largely because of the terrible damage done by the flood of 1930, when the Tarn, swollen by a sudden thaw in the Massif Central, burst its banks, destroying 617 houses and killing more than a hundred people. Luckily, the one thing that makes Moissac a household name in the history of art survived, and that is the cloister and porch of the Benedictine **abbey church of St-Pierre**, a masterpiece of Romanesque sculpture and model for dozens of churches throughout the region. The flat plains to the south and west of Moissac are less exciting, not least because of the looming presence of a nuclear power plant, but there are, nevertheless, a couple of places worth visiting along the banks of the Garonne: **St-Nicolas-de-la-Grave**, for its little museum devoted to the founder of Detroit, after whom Cadillac cars were named, and **Auvillar** for its exquisite market square.

Moissac is well served by **public transport**, with train and bus connections to Toulouse, Montauban and Agen. For the rest of the region you'll be reliant on your own transport or taxis.

Arrival, information and accommodation

Moissac's **gare SNCF** lies about 500m west of the centre along avenue Pierre-Chabrié; from the station follow this road east and, where it curves northwards, you'll see steps leading down to the church square. **Buses** from Agen, Montauban and Toulouse, on the other hand, stop on the east side of town beside a roundabout known as the Tribunal on boulevard Camille-Delthil. The **tourist office**, 6 place Durand-de-Bredon (daily: April & May 9am–12.30pm & 2–6pm; June & Sept 9am–6pm; July & Aug 9am–7pm; Oct–March 10am–noon & 2–5pm; ☎05.63.04.01.85, ⓦwww.moissac.fr), at the west end of the church, has details of Moissac's festivals (see box on p.346 & p.247) and of concerts taking

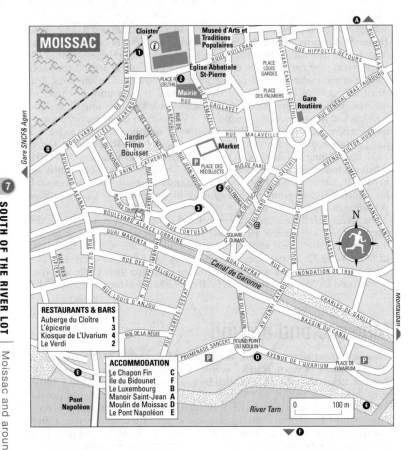

place in the church and cloister in the summer months. You can rent **bicycles** from Moissac Loisir, 29 rue Malaveille (℡05.63.04.03.48), on the north side of the market square. You can log on to the **Internet** at Video Pilote, 8 rue Camille-Delthi (Tues–Fri 3–8pm; Sat 10.30–noon & 3–8pm).

Accommodation

Le Chapon Fin 3 place des Récollets
℡ 05.63.04.04.22, ⓦ www.lechaponfin-moissac
.com. Situated on the south side of the market square, this comfortable hotel offers clean simple rooms and a decent restaurant (menus €15-35). Closed 3 weeks in Nov/Dec. ④
Île du Bidounet ℡05.63.32.52.52, ⓔ camping
.bidounet@wanadoo.fr. This is a good-value shady three-star campsite on a little island 2km from central Moissac across the Pont-Napoléon. Closed Oct–March.
Le Luxembourg 2 av Pierre-Chabrié,
℡05.63.04.00.27, ⓦ www.hotelluxembourg82.com.

A nicely old-fashioned place halfway along the road to the station, though it suffers slightly from road noise and the train tracks running behind, despite double-glazing. Even if you're not staying here, the restaurant is worth a visit for its good-value traditional meals (menus €12–26; closed Sun eve). ③
Manoir Saint Jean Saint-Paul d'Espis
℡05.63.05.02.34, ⓦ www.manoirsaintjean.com. Nine kilometres north of Moissac, the manor is set in its own pretty grounds and offers nine suites, all individually decorated with plush furnishings, paintings and chandeliers. There is also a first-rate restaurant (menus from €38) serving delicious

seasonal produce – organic wines, meat, and wild fish with fresh herbs from the garden. ❼

🏃 **Moulin de Moissac** Esplanade du Moulin ☎05.63.32.88.88, ⓦwww.lemoulindemoissac .com. Occupying a former water mill just east of the Pont-Napoléon, this is the most pleasant hotel in town. It's a large, not hugely attractive building, but inside has been beautifully refurbished and the rooms have large, very comfortable beds, swish bathrooms and mod-cons such as DVD players and Wi-Fi connections. ❸

Le Pont Napoléon 2 allées Montebello ☎05.63.04.01.55, ⓦwww.le-pont-napoleon .com. There are a few very classy rooms above this excellent restaurant (menus from €22, or around €48 à la carte; closed Wed), beside the bridge. The hotel overlooks a busy road, but inside, all is calm. ❷

The Town

Moissac sits with its back to the old river cliffs on the north bank of the Tarn just before its confluence with the Garonne. The town's compact centre is bordered to the south by the Canal latéral, to the east by boulevard Camille-Delthil and to the west by boulevard Lakanal, at the south end of which Pont-Napoléon carries road traffic over the Tarn. Moissac's main east-west thoroughfare, named rue Gambetta in the west, rue Ste-Catherine and then rue Malaveille, brings you into the central market square, **place des Récollets**, where you'll find the most convenient car park.

From this square, rue de la République leads north towards the red-brick belfry of the **Église Abbatiale St-Pierre**. Legend has it that Clovis first founded a church here in 506, though it seems more probable that its origins belong to the seventh century, which saw the foundation of so many monasteries throughout Aquitaine. The first Romanesque church on the site was consecrated in 1063 and enlarged the following century when Moissac became a stop on the Santiago de Compostela pilgrim route. Since then the church has survived countless wars, including siege and sack by Simon de Montfort in 1212, during the Crusade against the Cathars. Indeed, the fact that it is still standing at all is something of a miracle. During the Revolution the cloister was used as a gunpowder factory and billet for soldiers, who damaged many of the carvings, while in the 1850s it only escaped demolition to make way for the Bordeaux–Toulouse train line by a whisker.

Apart from the dumpy, red-brick belfry, the first thing you see approaching from the south is the great stone arc of the **south porch**, with its magnificent tympanum, completed in 1130. It depicts Christ in majesty, right hand raised in benediction, the Book resting on his knee, surrounded by the Evangelists and the 24 elders of the Apocalypse – every one different – as described by St John in the Book of Revelation. Below, the central pillar bears the figures of St Paul and St Jeremiah, the latter with the most beautifully doleful face imaginable, in the same elongated style as at Souillac (see p.261). In fact, the influence of this craftsmanship, assimilated with varying degrees of success, can be seen in the work of artists who decorated the porches of countless churches across southwest France.

There is more fine carving on the capitals inside the porch, and the **interior** of the church, which was remodelled in the fifteenth century, is painted with intricate patterns and filled with interesting wood and stone statuary. The most outstanding are those in the second chapel on the right as you enter: a lovely stone pietà in which Mary, enveloped in pastel blue, holds her son gently in her arms, and an equally compelling statue of Mary Magdalene with one arm outstretched and a thick tress of hair falling round her knees.

The adjoining **cloister** (same hours as tourist office – see p.357; €5) is accessed through the tourist office, behind the church to the west, where you can see a ten-minute video (in English on request) describing its main features. The cloister surrounds a garden shaded by a majestic cedar, and its pantile roof is supported by 76 alternating single and double marble columns. Each column supports a single inverted wedge-shaped block of stone, on which are carved, with extraordinary delicacy, all manner of animals and plant motifs, as well as 46 scenes from the Bible and the lives of the saints, among them Daniel in the lions' den, the Evangelists, fishermen on Lake Galilee, St Peter being crucified upside down and the decapitation of John the Baptist. Despite the damage done during the Revolution, they are in amazingly good shape. An inscription on the middle pillar on the west side explains that the cloister was constructed in the time of the Abbot Ansquitil in the Year of Our Lord 1100.

The same ticket gains you entry to the rather less interesting **Musée d'Arts et Traditions Populaires** (March–June, Sept & Oct Tues–Sat 10am–noon & 2–5pm, Sun 2–5pm; July & Aug Tues–Sat 10am–1pm & 3–7pm, Sun 3–7pm; closed Nov–Feb), housed in the former abbots' palace on rue de l'Abbaye immediately northeast of the church. Apart from a good collection of local ceramics, including *faïence* from Auvillar (see opposite), it contains a hotch-potch of furniture, ecclesiastical robes and religious treasures, portraits of old Moissac residents and a mock-up of a Quercy farmhouse interior.

Eating and drinking

In fine weather, the nicest place to **eat** in Moissac is the magnolia-shaded 🔺 *Auberge du Cloître*, on place Durand-de-Bredon beside the tourist office (closed Mon & eves on Wed & Sun), serving ultra-fresh local produce, some from the chef's own garden (weekday lunch menus from €12.50, others from €20). The cheap and cheerful *Le Verdi* (☎05.63.04.48.90), 8 place de la Mairie, is popular for its pizzas and *grandes assiettes* (large plates of salad, cheese and assorted meats or fish), while *L'Épicerie* on rue Jean-Moura (☎05.63.04.16.40) is a quaint little *salon de thé* selling teas from around the world, crockery, biscuits, and other gourmet goodies; it also has a couple of tables and a small menu of nibbles. The 🔺 *Kiosque de L'Uvarium*, on ave de L'Uvarium by the river, has a large terrace and serves grills, salads and pastas, all at around €10.50. The adjoining outdoor entertainment space hosts a variety of events on summer evenings, such as theatre, Latin dance displays and even hip-hop.

For picnic fodder, there's a small fresh produce **market** in the covered hall on place des Récollets daily except Monday, while on Saturday and Sunday morn-ings farmers' stalls fill the whole square, a marvel of colour and temptation.

St-Nicolas-de-la-Grave

Eight kilometres southwest of Moissac, the small *bastide* of **ST-NICOLAS-DE-LA-GRAVE** is dominated by a four-square château atop a low rise on the far side of the Garonne. Its oldest tower – the fatter of the four, on the northeast corner – is attributed to Richard the Lionheart, who passed through here on his return from the Third Crusade in the late 1100s. Nowa-days, however, it houses the *mairie*, and there's nothing to see inside.

St-Nicolas is prouder of its second claim to fame as the home town of **Antoine Laumet**, founder of Detroit in America, who was born here in 1658. His birthplace, just southwest of the central square, now contains the **Musée Lamothe-Cadillac** (July & Aug daily 10am–noon & 3–6pm; Sept–June apply to tourist office – see below; free), worth a quick look in passing as much for the story of Laumet's life as for any of the exhibits, which comprise mock-ups of a period bedroom and kitchen, and masses of documentation, some of it in English. Laumet was an adventurer who, on leaving for Canada in 1683, adopted the upper-crust name of de Lamothe-Cadillac. He later turned up in America in the service of King Louis XIV, where he founded a number of forts, among them a cavalry outpost called *le détroit* between lakes Erie and Huron in 1701. Two hundred years later, a Detroit car company was looking for a name at the same time as the city was celebrating its anniversary. They decided to honour Detroit's founding father, and thus were Cadillacs born.

You'll find the **tourist office** on place du Platane in front of the château (July & Aug daily 9am–noon & 2.30–6.30pm; Sept–June Mon 9am–noon & 2–5pm, Tues & Fri 2–5pm, Wed & Thurs 10am–noon & 2–5pm; ☏05.63.94.82.81, ⓦwww.stnicolasdelag.online.fr). St-Nicolas has no hotels, but the tourist office has details of *chambres d'hôtes* and there's a decent two-star **campsite** (☏05.63.95.50.00, Ⓕ05.63.95.50.01; closed mid-Sept to mid-June) 2km north of the village where the Garonne and Tarn rivers form a large lake; the campsite is part of a leisure complex with **canoe** and **bike rental** amongst other facilities. If you need somewhere to **eat**, try *Le Cadillac*, on the village's northwest corner; it's a simple place serving pizzas, grills, salads and a good hors-d'oeuvre buffet on the €11 *menu du jour* (closed Mon).

Auvillar

AUVILLAR, 14km west of St-Nicolas, is perched on a cliff on the Garonne's south bank. Its feudal château and ramparts were demolished in the eighteenth and nineteenth centuries, but thankfully the wonderful old village centre remains. From the main road skirting south of the village, you duck under the seventeenth-century **Tour de l'Horloge** to find yourself in the gently sloping triangular-shaped **place de la Halle** surrounded by a harmonious ensemble of brick and timber buildings with arcades running all around. At the square's cobbled centre stands a particularly pleasing circular stone-pillared market hall, built in the early nineteenth century. While you're here it's worth poking your nose into the **Musée du Vieil Auvillar** (Easter–Sept daily except Tues 2.30–6.30pm; Oct–Easter Sat & Sun 3–5.30pm; €3.50), on the square's north side, for its collection of local pottery. Auvillar was already known for its pottery production in the sixteenth century, but in the following century they began making *faïence* of sufficiently high quality to rival that imported from Holland and Italy. Local potters still have a good reputation, as witnessed by the big pottery fair held every October (see box on p.347 for details).

Auvillar's **tourist office** is on place de la Halle next to the museum (daily: April to mid-Oct 10am–12.30pm & 2–5.30pm; mid-Oct to March 2–5.30pm; ☏05.63.39.89.82, ⓦwww.auvillar.com). For somewhere to **stay** or **eat**, head for the *Hôtel de l'Horloge* (☏05.63.39.91.61, Ⓕ05.63.39.75.20; ❸; mid-Oct to mid-April closed Fri & lunch on Sat) beside the gate tower: in addition to a clutch of spacious en-suite rooms, they run a restaurant with menus from €27.

Quercy Blanc

As you head north from Moissac, the land rises gradually to gently undulating, green and woody country, cut obliquely by parallel valleys running down to meet the Garonne and planted with vines, sunflowers and maize, and apple and cherry orchards. It's a very soft landscape, the villages are small and widely scattered and the pace of life seems about equal with that of a turning sunflower. This is the **Quercy Blanc**, named after the area's grey-white soils and building stone, a region with few sights, but one which lives up to the image of deepest rural France. The single most interesting place to head for is **Lauzerte**, atop a river bluff 25km north of Moissac, though it won't take long to explore its well-kept central square and endearingly stocky little church, nor the clutch of once noble houses in the lanes around it. Further north again, **Montcuq** distinguishes itself with its solid square keep, the remnants of a twelfth-century fortress, standing guard over the medieval village, while way over to the southeast, **Montpezat-de-Quercy** is home to a Gothic church with a surprising collection of art treasures, including a beautiful and complete set of Flemish tapestries.

Public transport around Quercy Blanc consists of three separate bus services. You can reach Lauzerte from Moissac, and Montcuq from Cahors, while Montpezat is a stop on the route between Cahors and Montauban.

Lauzerte and Cazes-Mondenard

The first of the sleepy hilltop villages that you reach travelling north from Moissac is **LAUZERTE**. It stands on a promontory between two rivers, a press of white-walled houses contained within its medieval ramparts, with the "new" town spilling down the south and eastern slopes. The site's strategic importance was not lost on the counts of Toulouse, who took control of Lauzerte in the late twelfth century and granted it the status of a *bastide*, with all the rights and privileges that entailed, in 1241. The other notable event in its history took place fifty years later, when the townspeople threw out the English occupiers. In reward the French king, Philippe IV, elevated Lauzerte to capital of the Bas Quercy (Lower Quercy) region and seat of the royal Seneschal. However, its heyday came to an end in the late sixteenth century when Lauzerte was demoted to a mere district capital in the aftermath of the Wars of Religion.

Nevertheless, a few vestiges of its glory days remain in the old town, which lies clustered around the pretty, arcaded central square, **place des Cornières**, and the church of **St-Barthélémy**. The church's origins go back to the thirteenth century, but it was largely rebuilt after the Protestants wreaked their havoc, and its main point of interest nowadays is the gilded Baroque altarpiece, dedicated to the Virgin Mary and depicting scenes from her life, which fills the north chapel. Behind the church, there are good views to be had of the patchwork landscape all around from the **place du Château**, where the castle once stood on the promontory's northern tip. From here **rue de la Garrigue**, and its extension **rue de la Gendarmerie**, double back south of the church, running along the ridge past a number of thirteenth- and fourteenth-century merchants' houses with their big ground-floor arches and colonnaded windows above.

Once you've explored Lauzerte's compact centre, it's worth venturing southeast to visit a quirky museum near **CAZES-MONDENARD**, a village with a pretty Gothic church and a pleasant hotel (see opposite) 8km from Lauzerte. The core of the **Musée Yvan Quercy** (opening times vary, so phone to check ☏05.63.95.84.02; €5), at the end of a long lane signed off the D16 Molières road 2km east of the village, is its collection of hearses, which was started by chance when the owner – Monsieur Quercy – was given an old hearse thirty years ago. Since then he has amassed nearly a hundred different models, some horse-drawn, others pulled by hand, from the seventeenth century up to the first motorized model manufactured by

Peugeot in 1949. The collection also includes a large number of regular carriages, all in excellent condition, and some early caterpillar tractors. After the tour, you are offered tastings of wine, pâtés and other local produce, and in season they also run a restaurant (May–Sept daily; menus at €20 & €25; reservations required); the dining room is a bit dull but the food – nearly all regional dishes – more than compensates.

Practicalities

Lauzerte is served by twice-weekly **buses** from Moissac (Wed & Sat; ☎05.63.04.55.50), which drop you at the northern entrance to the lower village. It's then a steep walk along faubourg d'Auriac, or straight uphill via a series of steps and twisting paths, to reach the **tourist office** on place des Cornières (July & Aug daily 9am–1pm & 2–7pm; Sept–June Mon–Sat 9am–noon & 2–6pm, Sun 9am–noon & 2–7pm; ☎05.63.94.61.94, ⓦwww.quercy-blanc.net).

The **hotel** on faubourg d'Auriac, the *Hôtel du Quercy* (☎05.63.94.66.36; ❷; closed Sun evening & Mon), has a handful of old-fashioned but perfectly comfortable rooms, and a well-deserved reputation for its excellent **restaurant**. In addition to traditional local dishes, such as *cassoulet*, farm chicken cooked in Cahors wine and *confit de canard*, the latter also stuffed with foie gras, they serve a good range of fish and seafood dishes and game in season; menus start at €12 at lunch and €25 in the evening; reservations are recommended. The next closest hotel is *Le Luzerta*, north of the village beside the Cahors road (☎05.63.94.64.43, ⓦwww.hotel-quercy.com; ❷), which consists of several bungalows – functional but clean and en suite – around a pool. They also run a decent restaurant in a converted mill just up the road (closed Sun evening & Tues, also Nov–Feb; menus from €18).

In addition, there are two more good options in the countryside around Lauzerte. The smarter and more comfortable of the two is the Belgian-run *Aube Nouvelle* (☎05.63.04.50.33, ⓦwww.chez.com/aubenouvelle; ❸; good restaurant from €18), in a handsome brick-built manor house 9km south of Lauzerte on the D2, just before the village of Durfort-Lacapelette. Otherwise, try *l'Atre* (☎05.63.95.81.61, ⓦwww.logis-de-france.fr; ❷; closed Mon), a pleasant, country hotel, offering unfussy en-suite rooms and good home cooking (menus €13–35) in the centre of Cazes-Mondenard.

Montcuq and around

Thirteen kilometres northeast of Lauzerte along the Petite-Barguelonne valley, **MONTCUQ** – pronounce the "q" if you don't want to be saying "my arse" – is built around the flanks of a conical hill, on top of which stands a huge square keep. Like Lauzerte, Montcuq guarded the ancient road to Cahors and lies on the Santiago de Compostela pilgrims' route, but it seems to have had the knack of picking the wrong cause: it sided with the Cathars, was condemned for collaborating with the English and later became a Protestant stronghold. As a result, there's not much in the way of sights, though it's an attractive little place and less touristy than Lauzerte.

To get the lie of the land the best thing to do is climb up to the **tower** (July and Aug daily 3–7pm; €1.25); any of the lanes leading uphill from rue de la Promenade, the wide boulevard to the south of the old town, will take you up there. It was built at the turn of the eleventh century as part of a larger fortress, and although Louis IX ordered the ramparts destroyed, the ditches filled in and the tower's top knocked off in the aftermath of the Cathar Crusades, at 24m, it's still a fair climb. The effort is rewarded with all-round views; even when it's closed, the pinnacle of rock it stands on is high enough to give a good panorama. Wandering back down the slope through the maze of stone and half-timbered houses, the church of **St-Hilaire** stands out with its octagonal, brick tower, though there's nothing of particular interest inside.

Practicalities

Buses run to Montcuq from Cahors (Raynal Voyages; ☎05.65.23.28.28), stopping on rue de la Promenade near the **tourist office** (July & Aug Mon–Sat 9am–12.30pm & 3–7pm, Sun 10.30am–1pm; Sept–June Mon–Fri 9am–noon & 2–5pm, Sat 10am–noon; ☎05.65.22.94.04, ✉montcuq@wanadoo.fr). For a place to **stay**, try the welcoming *Hôtel du Parc* (☎05.65.31.81.82, ⓦwww .hotel-restaurant-du-parc.fr; ❸; closed mid-Oct to March), 500m west of Montcuq on the Belmont road, with old-fashioned but comfortable rooms, a big, quiet garden and a decent **restaurant** (open evenings only; menu at €20). Should you need a new supply of reading matter, on the other hand, Montcuq is also home to Chiméra, an English-owned **bookshop** selling mostly second-hand French and English titles; it's just off place de la République along rue du Faubourg-St-Privat – the road to Castelnau-Montratier.

Castelnau-Montratier and Montpezat-de-Quercy

The route southeast of Montcuq takes you on a roller-coaster ride across the valleys and intervening hills, on one of which stands **CASTELNAU-MONTRATIER**, 20km from Montcuq, with its incongruous neo-Byzantine church and spacious market square. Twelve kilometres further on through more country lanes you come to another, rather more interesting hilltop village, **MONTPEZAT-DE-QUERCY**. Traces of its medieval heyday remain in the arcaded central square and lanes of half-timbered houses, but the main reason to stop here is the **Collégiale St-Martin**, with its unusually rich hoard of treasures, standing at the southeast end of the promontory on which the village is built.

The church was founded in the early fourteenth century by Cardinal Pierre des Prés (1281–1361), a native of Montpezat, who grew wealthy in the service of the Avignon popes. With its high and severe single nave, the interior is unexciting, at least in comparison with the artworks of the fourteenth to sixteenth century arrayed in the side chapels. Best are the battered but still lovely *Vierge aux Colombes*, her face framed by golden ringlets, in the second chapel on the left, a polychrome pietà in the first on the right, and, next door, an English alabaster triptych depicting the Birth, Resurrection and Ascension of Christ – in the last only his feet are visible as he's whisked heavenwards. The church's finest treasures, though, are the five Flemish **tapestries** grouped around the choir. They were made specially for the church in the early sixteenth century, a gift from Jean IV des Prés, bishop of Montauban, and portray events from the life of St Martin de Tours, to whom the church is consecrated. The most famous scene is that in the first panel, where the future saint – at the time in the service of the Roman army – shares his cloak with a crippled beggar. The workmanship throughout is of superb quality, while the colours remain amazingly vibrant. Also in remarkably good condition is the white-marble sarcophagus and statue of Pierre des Prés, to the right of the choir, with his feet resting on a lion while his well-fed face is bathed in a contented grin.

Practicalities

SNCF **buses** between Montauban and Cahors (☎05.63.23.33.67) stop on the west side of the village on the boulevard des Fossés, near the helpful **tourist office** (April & Oct Tues–Fri 10.30am–12.30pm & 1.30–5.30pm; May Tues–Fri 10am–1pm & 2–7pm; June & Sept Tues–Thurs & Sun 10am–1pm & 2–7pm; July & Aug Mon 2–6pm, Tues–Sun 10am–1pm & 2–7pm; Nov–March Tues, Thurs & Sun 11am–5pm; ☎ & ⒻF05.63.02.05.55). The office doubles as a Maison des Vins where you can buy the local Coteaux du Quercy wines and pick up a brochure listing vineyards to visit, though they don't offer tastings.

While there are no hotels in Montpezat, there are two very comfortable **chambres d'hôtes**. Built into the southern ramparts, the German-English-owned *Le Barry*, faubourg St-Roch (☎05.63.02.05.50, Ⓦwww.lebarry.com; ❹; closed at Christmas), has a romantic garden, pool and views, and good-value meals available on request (eves only; €23). *Les Trois Terrasses*, rue de la Libération (☎05.63.02.66.21, Ⓦwww.trois-terrasses.com; ❻–❼; closed Jan & Feb), has terraced gardens overlooking the Collégiale. It's under French-English ownership and very stylish – the decor is an intriguing mix of the contemporary and the traditional, while one bathroom occupies a former chapel. Again, evening meals are available on request, costing €25 all-inclusive. You'll also **eat** well at the *Ferme Auberge de Coutié* (☎05.63.67.73.51; menus €16–31), on the D20, 9km southwest of Montpezat, signed to the east of Espanel hamlet, on a Quercy farm surrounded by ducks and orchards. There's a well-tended two-star municipal **campsite** (☎05.63.02.07.08, Ⓔmontpezat-accueil@wanadoo.fr; closed Nov–March) in a leisure park on Montpezat's northern outskirts.

Montauban

Lying 20km east of Moissac and 50km north of Toulouse, **MONTAUBAN** is a prosperous middle-sized provincial city, the capital of the largely agricultural *département* of Tarn-et-Garonne. Its beautiful old centre sits on the north bank of

△ Montauban

the River Tarn, a harmonious ensemble of warm, pink brick which looks its best at sunset, or at night when the steeples, massive old bridge and riverside facades are illuminated. The layout follows the typical *bastide* pattern: a regular grid of streets around an arcaded market square, the glorious **place Nationale**, but between the main streets lie enticing alleys, covered passages and interior courtyards. The greatest delight is simply to wander – the centre is only a ten-minute stroll from end to end – taking in the scattered sights as you go, of which the highlight is the **Musée Ingres**, dedicated to Montauban's most famous son.

Some history

The city's origins go back to 1144 when Alphonse Jourdain, count of Toulouse, decided to create a *bastide* here as a bulwark against English and French royal power. Indeed, it is generally regarded as the first *bastide*, the model for the medieval new towns found throughout this region (see p.336). Montauban has enjoyed various periods of great prosperity (as one can guess from the proliferation of fine houses), mainly based on trade in silk and other textiles. The first followed the suppression of the Cathar heresy and the final submission of the counts of Toulouse in 1229 and was greatly enhanced by the building of the Pont-Vieux in 1335, making it the best crossing point on the Tarn for miles. The Hundred Years' War did its share of damage, as did Montauban's opting for the Protestant cause in the Wars of Religion, but by the time of the Revolution it had become once more one of the richest cities in the southwest.

Arrival, information and accommodation

Montauban's **gare SNCF** lies roughly 1km west of centre across the Pont-Vieux at the far end of avenue Mayenne. Most regional **buses** terminate either at the station or nearby on place Lalaque, though buses from Laguépie drop you by the hideous market hall on place Prax-Paris on the northeast side of town. Eurolines buses stop at the top end of rue de Chateauvieux, about 600m north of the old centre. While central Montauban is eminently walkable, you might want to hop on a **city bus** from the train station to the centre (line #3; roughly every 15–20min), stopping on boulevard Midi-Pyrénées near place Prax-Paris; tickets, costing €1 for a single journey, can be bought on the bus.

The **tourist office** is located on the south side of place Prax-Paris (July & Aug Mon–Sat 9am–7pm, Sun 10am–noon & 3–6pm; Sept–June Mon–Sat 9.30am–12.30pm & 2–6.30pm; ☎05.63.63.60.60, ⓦwww.montauban-tourisme.com); you can pick up an English-language do-it-yourself walking map of the old centre here, and get information on local events (see box on p.346). There's a charge of €1.60 for booking accommodation, but this is money well spent in high summer when rooms are hard to come by.

This is partly because Montauban has a surprisingly limited range of **hotels**. The cheapest in the centre is the *Hôtel du Commerce*, 9 place Roosevelt (☎05.63.66.31.32, ⓦwww.hotel-commerce-montauban.com; ❸), beside the cathedral, which boasts en-suite facilities in all its rooms; they also lay on a good buffet breakfast (€6). There's a big jump up to the *Hôtel Mercure*, opposite at 12 rue Notre-Dame (☎05.63.63.17.23, ⓦwww.mercure.com; ❻; restaurant from €16), which is getting into the luxury bracket – and has modern, reasonably spacious rooms with excellent facilities. Otherwise, your best option is the *Hôtel d'Orsay*, 31 rue Roger-Salengro, outside the train station (☎05.63.66.06.66, ⓔcuisinedalain @wanadoo.fr; ❸; closed second & third week of Aug & Christmas hols); it doesn't look much, but the rooms are comfortable enough and it has an excellent restaurant (closed Sun & lunchtime Mon & Sat; from €23).

MONTAUBAN

ACCOMMODATION
Du Commerce   C
Mercure   A
D'orsay   B

RESTAURANTS & BARS
Agora   3
Bistrot Du Faubourg   6
Le Cosy   1
Le M....   4
Le Santa Maria   2
Le Ventadour   5

Gorges de l'Aveyron & Cahors

Moissac & Lauzerte

Cours Foucault

River Tarn

RUE INGRES

AVENUE GAMBETTA

RUE DU FORT

RUE LÉON-CLADEL

GRAND' RUE VILLENOUVELLE

R. JEAN MONET

PLACE PRAX-PARIS

Market Hall

Theatre

RUE DE LA MANDOUNE

RUE SAINTE-CLAIRE

R. LÉON-CLADEL

RUE DU DR.-ALIBERT

QUAI DE VERDUN

QUAI MONTMURAT

RUE ST.-JEAN

RUE DE LA COMÉDIE

RUE DE MALEVILLE

RUE VICTOR-HUGO

PLACE VICTOR-HUGO

R. PRINCESSE

PLACE BOURDELLE

Église St-Jacques

Musée Ingres

RUE DU COLLÈGE

RUE D'AURIOL

PLACE NATIONALE

BOULEVARD MIDI-PYRÉNÉES

RUE BESSIÈRES

RUE MICHELET

RUE SOUBIRONS

RUE DE LA RÉSISTANCE

PLACE DU MARÉCHAL-FOCH

R. N.-DAME

Cathédrale Notre-Dame

RUE DE LA RÉPUBLIQUE

RUE D'ORLACAZE

PLACE ROOSEVELT

ALLÉE DU CONSUL-DUPUY

Jardin des Plantes

GRAND'-RUE SAPAC

FAUBOURG LACAPELLE

RUE DE L'HÔTEL-DE-VILLE

RUE ALPHONSE-JOURDAIN

PONT VIEUX

PONT NEUF

PLACE ALFRED-MARTY

QUAI DE VILLEBOURBON

RUE DU GÉNÉRAL-SARRAIL

RUE ARISTIDE-BRIAND

PLACE M. LENOIR

PLACE LALAQUE

RUE JEAN-JAURÈS

AVENUE MAYENNE

AV. CHAMIER

AV. ROGER-SALENGRO

Gare SNCF

Castelsarrasin

Agen, Bordeaux & Cahors

Toulouse

Toulouse

N

0   200 m

The Town

Montauban couldn't be easier to find your way around. The most interesting part is the small kernel of streets based on the original *bastide*, enclosed within an inner ring of boulevards between **boulevard Midi-Pyrénées** to the east and the river on the west. The main shopping streets are pedestrianized **rue de la Résistance** and **rue de la République,** which intersect in the *bastide's* southern corner.

In the centre lies the city's finest point, **place Nationale**, the hub of the city's social life. Rebuilt after a fire in the seventeenth century, it is surrounded on all sides by a double row of arcades beneath two- and three-storeyed town houses, their uniformity tempered by the square's irregular shape. The distinctive octagonal belfry of the **Église St-Jacques,** a couple of minutes' walk away, shows above the southwestern rooftops. First built in the thirteenth century on the pilgrim route to Santiago de Compostela, the church bears the scars of Montauban's troubled history, not only in its mix of architectural styles, but in the holes gouged out of the belfry's fortified base by cannonballs during an unsuccessful siege by twenty thousand Catholic troops – held off by just six thousand locals – in 1621.

On the banks of the river south of the church stands a massive half-palace, half-fortress, begun by the counts of Toulouse, then continued by the Black Prince in 1363. He left it unfinished when the English lost control of the town, and so it remained until 1664 when the bishop of Montauban chose this very prominent spot for his residence. It is now the **Musée Ingres** (Tues–Sun 10am–noon & 2–6pm; €4), which houses paintings and more than four thousand drawings left to the city by locally born **Jean-Auguste-Dominique Ingres** (1780–1867). The collection includes several of the supremely realistic, luminous portraits of women which are the artist's trademark, though not to everyone's taste. It also contains a substantial collection of works by another native, **Émile-Antoine Bourdelle** (1861–1929), the ubiquitous monumental sculptor and a student of Rodin, alongside a hotch-potch of other exhibits, from Gallo-Roman mosaics to fifteenth- and sixteenth-century European fine art. In the early days of World War II, the museum hosted more illustrious visitors when the Louvre dispatched over three thousand works of art to Montauban for safe-keeping prior to the German invasion. When southern France was occupied in 1942, however, they were moved again to more remote locations, including the Château de Montal (see p.284).

Providing a stark exception to Montauban's red-brick homogeneity is a cold, sore-thumb of a building, the **Cathédrale Notre-Dame**, ten minutes' walk southeast up rue de l'Hôtel-de-Ville. It was erected on the city's highest spot at the turn of the seventeenth century as part of the triumphalist campaign to reassert the Catholic faith after the cruel defeat and repression of the Protestants. Inside the dazzling white Classical facade lies an echoing nave, whose main point of interest is another Ingres painting, *Le Voeu de Louis XIII*, hanging in the north aisle. Specially commissioned for the cathedral, the vast canvas depicts Louis offering France, symbolized by his crown and sword, to a Virgin and Child and is strongly influenced by Raphael's romantic style.

Eating, drinking and entertainment

The simplest way of finding a place to **eat** is to browse round the place Nationale, where you'll find the *Le Couvert des Drapiers* under the arcades at no. 27 (closed for dinner Sun–Wed), serving good-value lunchtime *plats du jour* at around €8, and the *Agora* at no. 9 (closed Sun evening & lunchtime Mon), with salads and *plats* at around €7.50 and menus from €12. For traditional cooking, however, you can't beat the *Bistrot du Faubourg*, east of the cathedral at 111 faubourg Lacapelle (℡05.63.63.49.89; closed Sat & Sun, also first two weeks in Aug & one week at Christmas), a popular locals' place offering excellent value for money: at lunch or dinner you can eat for €12 including wine. Last but not least, there's Montauban's top restaurant, ⚒ *Le Ventadour*, 23 quai Villebourbon (℡05.63.63.34.58; closed Sat lunchtime, Sun & Mon, also two weeks in both Jan & Aug; menus €22–42), magnificently sited in an old house on the west bank near the Pont-Vieux: *the* place for a splurge.

The best place for a **picnic**, on the other hand, is the Jardin des Plantes, a pleasant green space south of the cathedral along the banks of a small tributary of the Tarn. You can buy provisions at the sandwich shops, pâtisseries and delicatessens on rue de la République and rue de la Résistance. While you're at it, keep an eye open for the **local speciality**, *Montauriols*, a chocolate-coated cherry preserved in armagnac; you'll find them at pâtisseries all over town.

When it comes to a **drink**, you could try *Le Cosy*, on rue d'Auriol (open daily) which is rather more stylish than the other options, with a minimalist brown and white interior and a soundtrack of Latin and dance music as well as a small menu of meals and snacks. Another good option is *Le Santa Maria*, north of the Musée Ingres on quai Montmurat (closed Sun), with a terrace overlooking the Tarn; they also serve tapas and more substantial Tex-Mex meals. *Le M…* bar on rue de la République has a lively atmosphere, a good selection of cocktails and fruit smoothies and is open daily from lunchtime onwards.

Listings

Airport The nearest airport is Toulouse-Blagnac ℡05.61.42.44.00, ⊛www.toulouse.aeroport.fr.

Boat rental On summer afternoons you can rent electric-powered boats from the *embarcadère* below the Musée Ingres (July & Aug; from €8 for one person, up to €22 for five people).

Car parks The most convenient option is the pay parking on place Prax-Paris or place Roosevelt. Free parking is available along the riverbanks beneath the Pont-Vieux and north of the theatre on rue de la Mandoune.

Car rental Both Avis, 23 av Mayenne ℡05.63.20.45.73, and Europcar, 21 av Roger-Salengro ℡05.63.20.29.00, are located near the train station.

Hospital Centre Hospitalier, rue Léon-Cladel ℡05.63.92.82.82, to the north of the old quarter.

Internet access Within the city centre try Cyber World, rue de la Comédie.

Markets A few stalls sell fresh produce every day on place Nationale, but the main farmers' market takes place on Saturday mornings on place Prax-Paris. In winter (Nov–March) there's a small *marché au gras* on place Nationale on Wednesday morning.

Police Commissariat de Police, 50 bd Alsace-Lorraine ℡05.63.21.54.00, northeast of the centre, off av Gambetta.

Post office The central post office is on the bd Midi-Pyrénées, 82000 Montauban.

Taxis There are taxi stands at the station and the north end of bd Midi-Pyrénées, or call ℡05.62.88.70.70.

The Gorges de l'Aveyron and around

In its lower course the Aveyron glides across the dull flood plain surrounding Montauban, offering little reason to stop other than the village of **Montricoux**, with its museum dedicated to a forgotten artist. The scenery begins to get more interesting, however, about 30km east of Montauban where the river has sliced a narrow defile through the hills. The entrance of the **Gorges de l'Aveyron** is guarded by the fortress village of **Bruniquel**, its ancient houses smothered with summer roses, while further east **Penne** is perched beneath a crumbling castle. From here on the gorge gets increasingly dramatic as you work your way upriver to **St-Antonin-Noble-Val**, which, with its compact medieval centre and choice of hotels, makes an excellent base for exploring the gorge and surrounding sights. The most compelling of these is the partially ruined **Abbaye de Beaulieu-en-Rouergue**, located 14km northwest, where the Gothic church has been converted into a contemporary art gallery. Beyond St-Antonin, **Laguépie** is less interesting but provides another possible base, from where you can hop south to the beguiling – if very touristy – hilltop town of **Cordes-sur-Ciel**. At Laguépie the Aveyron valley turns abruptly north, and its sides close in again to form a second increasingly deep, thickly wooded gorge, dominated by the ruins of **Najac**'s mighty fortress. It stands guard over the frontier of the former province of Rouergue, now the Aveyron *département*, and the southern approach to the *bastide* of **Villefranche-de-Rouergue**. A refreshingly unprettified town lying on a bend in the river, Villefranche is centred around a perfectly preserved, arcaded market square above which soars a colossal fortified church tower.

Buses run along the Aveyron between Montauban and Laguépie (GAU Autocars; ☎05.63.30.44.45), with onward services from Laguépie to Villefranche (SNCF; ☎05.65.45.03.16) and from Najac to Villefranche (Gauchy; ☎05.65.81.12.92). Note that these buses cater mostly to schoolchildren, which means they don't necessarily run every day and tend to be at inconvenient times. An alternative – and preferable – way of travelling between Laguépie, Najac and Villefranche is the Toulouse–Brive **train** line, which tunnels and weaves along the valleyside; these trains also stop at Cordes on their way south.

Montricoux

Just before you leave the flat alluvial plains, 25km west of Montauban, **MONTRICOUX** would hardly be worth the stop if it weren't for its intriguing art museum, the **Musée Marcel-Lenoir** (April–Oct daily 10am-12.30pm & 2.30-7pm; €5), on the west side of the village. Like Ingres (see p.368), Marcel Lenoir was another prolific local artist, who was born in Montauban in 1872 and died in Montricoux in 1931. He was much fêted during his early years, when he was at the forefront of Pointillism and Cubism, and he even presaged Art Deco as he searched for new means of expression. But Lenoir was also an irascible character and managed to offend so many critics, dealers and galleries that he was eventually cast into oblivion. And there he stays, despite the best efforts of the owner of this collection of 140 works spanning Lenoir's whole career. One of the most revealing is the *Kiss of Judas*, in which you see Picasso profiled in blue and Van Gogh cutting off Gauguin's ear, while Judas is portrayed as a well-known art critic of the time.

Buses from Montauban stop on the main road across from the village on the river's south bank, where you'll also find an old-fashioned **hotel**, *Le Relais du Postillon* (☎05.63.67.23.58, ℱ05.63.67.27.68; ➊), offering basic rooms (none with its own toilet) but excellent regional cooking (menus from €15; closed Sun eve & for lunch Mon & Tues). There's also a very swish riverside **restaurant**, *Les Gorges de l'Aveyron* (☎05.63.24.50.50; closed two days a week except in July & Aug; menus from €25), along a lane beside the bridge. For more comfortable accommodation, head 8km southwest to *Chez Terrassier* (☎05.63.30.94.60, ⓦwww.logis-de-france.com; ➋–➌; closed Sun & Fri eve, also two weeks in Nov & one week in Jan; menus from €19), a pretty, modern place with a pool in the middle of **VAISSAC**.

Bruniquel

East of Montricoux the hills rise suddenly and 5km later the **Gorges de l'Aveyron** really get into their stride as you sight the first of several fortified villages along these rocky crags. Once a Protestant stronghold, **BRUNIQUEL** shelters in the lee of its **castle** (April, June & Sept Mon–Sat 2–6pm, Sun 10am–12.30pm & 2–6pm; May & Oct Sun only same hours; July & Aug daily 10am–7pm; closed Dec–March; €2.50, or €3.50 for guided tour), teetering on the edge of a hundred-metre cliff. In fact there are two adjacent castles, since the original twelfth-century fortress had to be divided between rival cousins in 1484, but both are much knocked about and not of tremendous interest, save for the views they afford along the valley. More engaging is the **Maison des Comtes de Payrol** (April–Sept daily 10am–6pm; March & Oct Sat & Sun 10am–6pm; Nov–Feb by appointment only, ☎05.63.67.26.42; €3) to the west of the castle entrance. The thirteenth-century home of a wealthy merchant family, its vaulted cellars and panelled and frescoed rooms now house an unusually good local history museum, including an interesting collection of oil lamps and candle holders.

Buses stop about 250m below Bruniquel to the south, beside a road leading up to the church and the **tourist office** (April–Sept daily 10.30am–noon & 2–6pm; rest of year same hours but variable closing days; ☎05.63.67.29.84, ✉tourisme-bruniquel@orange.fr) at the entrance to the village. For an overnight **stay**, Marc de Baudouin runs a very good *chambre d'hôte*, to the right of the church (☎05.63.67.26.16, ⓦwww.chambres-bruniquel.fr; ❸; closed Dec & Jan; evening meals on request); he's also a keen mountain biker and is happy to advise on local trails and footpaths. Right opposite, the **restaurant** *L'Étape du Château* (closed Sat & mid-Nov to Feb) serves traditional menus from €13. There's also a small, two-star **campsite**, *Le Payssel* (☎05.63.67.25.95; closed Oct–April), about 700m south on the D964 to Albi.

Penne and on towards St-Antonin

Six kilometres upriver from Bruniquel you come to the even more beautiful ridge-top village of **PENNE**, once a Cathar stronghold, with its ruined **castle** perched on an impregnable pinnacle. Everything is old and leaning and bulging, but holding together nonetheless, with a harmony that would be impossible to create purposely. There's just one cobbled street leading from an arch under the church belfry and through a second gate – where ancient grain measures are cut into the wall – to a footpath scrambling among the castle ruins. There's not much left, but it's an atmospheric spot, the piles of stones overrun with dog-roses, clematis and honeysuckle, with a panorama taking in the village roofs and the wooded country beyond. If that's worked up an appetite or a thirst, head for the **bar-restaurant** *La Terrasse* (May–Aug daily, Sept–April open for lunch daily except Wed & open Sat eve; menus from €16), at the north end of the village, from the back terrace of which you get a first-class view of the castle's airy crag.

Beyond Penne the gorge becomes deeper and more dramatic. To appreciate it at its best, turn off the main road just after Cazals, 6km from Penne, following signs for the **Corniche**, a lane which climbs steeply for a kilometre or so on to the cliff's edge. You'll be rewarded with tremendous views and, a little further on, a superbly sited **restaurant**, *La Corniche* (☎05.63.68.26.95; closed Oct–March, also April–June & Sept closed Sun eve & Wed, July & Aug closed lunchtime Wed; menus from €16; reservation recommended), offering generous country dishes, in the hamlet of **BROUSSES**. Six kilometres later, you drop down to the river again to the west of St-Antonin-Noble-Val.

St-Antonin-Noble-Val

The finest and most substantial town in this lower stretch of the Aveyron valley is **ST-ANTONIN-NOBLE-VAL**, 16km northeast of Penne. It sits on the river's north bank beneath the beetling white cliffs of the **Roc d'Anglars**, where it developed in the ninth century around an abbey said to house the remains of the evangelizing **St Antonin**. According to legend, his body was carried here in a boat guided by two white eagles from Pamiers, in the Ariège, where the saint met his death. Since then the town has endured all the vicissitudes of this region's history: it sided with the Cathars, then the Protestants and each time was walloped by the alien power of the kings from the north, until it eventually sank into oblivion after the seventeenth century. Yet, in spite of it all, a marvellous heritage of houses endowed by wealthy merchants remains from its medieval glory days, when St-Antonin was an important commercial centre, manufacturing linen and leather goods.

The easiest landmark to head for is the spire of the large but uninteresting neo-Gothic **church**, towards the town's southeast corner. Along the church's west wall rue du Pont-de-l'Aveyron leads south to the bridge, while rue Guilhelm-Peyre curves northeast to **place de la Halle**. This square is St-Antonin at its most picturesque, with its cafés and pint-sized *halle*, the focus of an important Sunday-morning market, and the town's finest building, the **Maison des Consuls**, whose origins go back to 1125. The facade is pierced with arcades, pairs of colonnaded openings and a contrastingly severe oblong window on the first floor, on one pillar of which Adam and Eve hide their modesty; the old man on the pillar to the left, holding some books and a staff, is Emperor Justinian (483–565), who codified Roman law. The building's most striking feature, however, is the tower with its top-heavy loggia and too-perfect machicolations added by the controversial nineteenth-century architect Viollet-le-Duc (see p.118) – though he did save the building from collapse. It now houses the **Musée du Vieux St-Antonin** (July & Aug daily except Tues 10am–1pm & 3–6pm; Sept–June by appointment only, ☎05.63.68.23.52; €2.50), with an uninspiring collection of objects to do with the former life of the place, including various prehistoric finds.

Practicalities

Buses on the Montauban–Laguépie route stop near the Crédit Agricole bank on avenue Paul-Benet, the boulevard to the north of the old centre. The **tourist office** is in the *mairie* next to the church (June & Sept daily 9.30am–12.30pm & 2–5.30pm; July & Aug daily 9.30am–12.30pm & 2–6.30pm; Oct–May Tues–Sat 2–5.30pm; ☎05.63.30.63.47, ⊛www.saint-antonin-noble-val.com). St-Antonin is also the starting point for canoeing down this lower stretch of the Aveyron: you can rent **canoes** from a number of outlets, including Variation (☎05.63.68.25.25), on the town's eastern outskirts, and Découverte, 15 boulevard des Thermes (☎05.63.68.22.46), to the west of the bridge. Découverte also rents out **bicycles**, while both companies organize **caving** and **rock-climbing** expeditions in the area.

St-Antonin has two very good places in which to **stay**. Beside the bridge on boulevard des Thermes there's the simple *Hôtel Les Thermes* (☎05.63.30.61.08, ℱ05.63.68.26.23; ❷; restaurant €15–32, closed Tues & Wed except in July & Aug) – so called because there was once a spa next door – with a terrace overlooking the water and cheerful, en-suite rooms. The smarter option is *La Résidence*, 37 rue Droite (☎05.63.67.37.56, ⊛www.laresidence-france.com; ❹–❺; evening meals on request), a welcoming, Dutch-German-run *chambre d'hôte* on the road leading northwest out of place de la Halle. The rooms are large and light, with tiles or wooden floorboards and high ceilings and one even has its own roof terrace. If you'd rather be out in the countryside, head 7km upstream to the quiet village of Feneyrols, where another former spa now houses the

Jardins des Thermes (☎05.63.30.65.49, ⓦwww.jardinsdesthermes.com; ❸; closed Nov-Feb) set in its own grounds with comfortable, modern rooms and a good restaurant (menus €18-45; July & Aug daily; Sept-June closed Wed & Thurs).

The two-star *Camping d'Anglars* is St-Antonin's closest **campsite**, located beside the river 1km upstream on the D115 (☎05.63.30.69.76, ⓕ05.63.30.67.61; closed mid-Oct to mid-April). With your own transport, however, it is possible to follow the signs 6km north up onto the *causse* to the spacious and well-organized *Les Trois Cantons* (☎05.63.31.98.57, ⓦwww.3cantons.fr; closed Oct to mid-April), with three-star facilities including a heated pool, shop and snackbar.

As for eating in St-Antonin, the **restaurant** at *Hôtel Les Thermes* (see opposite) is a good bet. Or, for simpler, very traditional fare, along the lines of *steak-frites*, salads and basic regional dishes, try *L'Auberge du Pont*, 6 bd Thermes (closed Thurs and December; menus from €18).

Abbaye de Beaulieu-en-Rouergue

Apart from exploring the gorge itself, the best excursion from St-Antonin takes you 14km northwest to the beautiful Cistercian **Abbaye de Beaulieu-en-Rouergue** (April–Oct daily: 10am–noon & 2-6pm; €6.50), which lies deep among wooded hills. The abbey was founded in 1144, though the present buildings date from the turn of the thirteenth century, and are remarkably unscathed considering it was sacked and burnt during the Wars of Religion, looted again during the Revolution and then used as a barn until the late 1950s; in 1844 Viollet-le-Duc even wanted to rebuild the whole caboodle in St-Antonin but had to give up through lack of funds. The present owners have now restored the church to create a superb exhibition space for their collection of **contemporary art**; displays change several times a year, in combination with temporary exhibitions. The high, light nave with its clean lines and lack of ornamentation, save for the delicate rose windows and a few sculpted capitals, provides the perfect foil for works by Jean Dubuffet, Simon Hantaï and Henri Michaux, amongst others. There's not much else to see – a low, vaulted chapterhouse with a few unidentified frescoes which predates the church, and a vast wine storehouse – but the peaceful setting will make you want to linger.

Upstream to Laguépie

Upstream from St-Antonin, the Aveyron valley widens out for a while and is spoilt by stone quarries. The only reason to stop is the village of **VAREN**, 16km from St-Antonin on the river's north bank. Its Romanesque **church** and tiny area of old streets repay a quick wander, but the prime attraction is another excellent-value though more upmarket **restaurant**, this time a converted mill on the riverbank just east of the village. The *Moulin de Varen* (☎05.63.65.45.10; closed mid-Nov to Jan, also closed Mon & Tues except in July & Aug) serves a *menu à choix*, from which you select the number of courses you want; the choice is good and the food beautifully presented. Prices start at €15 for a soup, main course, cheese (except in July & Aug) and dessert.

LAGUÉPIE 9km east of Varen, where the cliffs begin to close in again, guards the confluence of the Viaur with the Aveyron, which here turns north. The village has nothing in the way of sights, but is pretty enough and provides a useful base, served both by buses from Montauban and by trains on the Toulouse–Brive line. The **church** pinpoints the village centre lying in a spit of land between the two rivers. The **gare SNCF** lies 500m northwest on the north bank of the Aveyron; **buses** terminate either here or beside the church. There's a small **tourist office** (July & Aug Mon–Sat 10am–12.30pm & 3–6.30pm,

Sun 10am–12.30pm; Sept–June Wed & Sat 2–5pm, Thurs 10am–noon; ⓣ & ⓕ05.63.30.20.34) on place du Foirail, a big open space with a café and a grocery to the southwest of the church.

Laguépie's one and only **hotel** is the old-fashioned but welcoming and well-priced *Les Deux Rivières* (ⓣ05.63.31.41.41, ⓦwww.logis-de-france.fr; ❷; closed two weeks in Feb), on the north side of the bridge across the Aveyron. It is also a good place to **eat**, offering a choice between a brasserie and a formal restaurant with menus from €15 (closed Sat lunch & for dinner on Mon, Fri & Sun). You'll find a one-star municipal **campsite**, *Les Tilleuls* (ⓣ05.63.30.22.32; closed Nov–April), in a good shady spot beside the Viaur roughly 1km to the east of Laguépie.

⑦ Cordes-sur-Ciel

While you're in this part of the world it would be a shame to miss out on the spectacularly sited fortified town of **CORDES-SUR-CIEL**, 15km south of Laguépie on the D922 across high, rolling farmland, and also accessible by train. The origins of the suffix *sur-ciel* ("in the sky") become obvious as you approach the foot of the sudden hill on which the town is built, girded by several concentric walls and endowed with a score of medieval houses. It is something of an open-air museum and artisan centre, best avoided during July and August, but otherwise an atmospheric place to spend a few hours.

Founded in 1222 by Count Raymond VII of Toulouse, Cordes grew rich on **leatherworking** and in the following century the walls had to be enlarged no fewer than seven times to contain the expanding population. Things took a downturn, however, with the arrival of the plague in the fifteenth century, but Cordes later recovered, and developed a notable lace industry in the nineteenth century. However, its real renaissance came in the 1970s, when hippies, including the **craftsmen** and **artisans** whose studios now cram the upper town, arrived to put Cordes back on the map, attracted by its beauty and abandon.

The Town

The traveller, who from the terrace of Cordes regards the summer's night, knows that he has no need to go further, and that if he allows it, day after day, the beauty here will raise him out of any solitude.

Albert Camus

Camus' words give some idea of the town's allure, and hard though it may be to achieve such a placid state when the streets are packed during summer days, in the evening or out of season the romance of Cordes returns. To watch the sun rise from the ramparts is worth getting up for, and with every other building a medieval mansion, walking the town before the crowds arrive is a delight. Its layout is simple: the old citadel – the "**upper town**" – runs along and down the sides of the long and narrow ridge which juts up from the plain, while the modern "**lower town**" consists of a clump of streets at the foot of the old town's eastern tip. The best route to the upper town is the knee-cracking Grande Rue Basse ascending from the lower tourist office (see p.opposite), although at busy times, it is more pleasant to take one of the picturesque but less crowded side-streets. Alternatively, a **petit train** (July & Aug; €2.50) makes frequent trips from outside the tourist office. Along the way a series of medieval **gates** leads to the compact upper town.

Entering the last of the fortified entrances, you'll reach the **Musée Charles-Portal** (Easter–June & Sept–Oct Sun & hols 3–6pm; July & Aug daily 11am–1pm & 3–7pm; €2.30), housing a display on the medieval wells which riddle the town, and which were used in time of siege for water supply or to store grain. Further along on Grande Rue, the elegant and symmetrical arcaded face of the fourteenth-century **Maison du Grand Fauconnier** conceals the **Musée d'Art Moderne et Contemporain** (Feb–March & Nov–Dec 2–5pm; April–May & Oct 11.30am–12.30pm & 2–6.30pm; June–Sept 11am–12.30pm & 2–7pm; €4), features works by the figurative painter Yves Brayer, who lived in Cordes from 1940, a French-only audio presentation explaining the town's lace-making tradition and a motley collection of modern art, including minor pieces by Picasso, Miró and Klee – hardly worth the stop. Across the street squats the ancient covered market, where you can peer down one of the town's famously deep wells. Continuing along Grande Rue, you'll see the **Maison de Grand Veneur** ("House of the Great Hunter") – whose otherwise plain stone facade is festooned with amusingly sculpted and extremely well-preserved medieval caricatures of beasts and hunters. A few doors down is the similarly impressively carved frontage of Raymond of Toulouse's old palace, now home to the *Grand Ecuyer* hotel (named after the finely sculpted horse figure) while, just beyond, the contemporary **Porte des ormeaux** ("Gate of the Eims") takes you out of the old town.

There are more than forty **boutiques** in Cordes, including some which are thinly disguised as "museums". If you would like to shop for leatherwork, metal and handicraft items and price is not an issue, you could easily spend an afternoon or two (and a considerable sum) here. Many of the stores double as workshops, so even window-shopping is quite interesting. One of the better deals is *Le Petit Bois*, in the place de l'Église, which has ingenious toys and gifts.

Practicalities

Trains stop 5km to the west of Cordes at **Vindrac** (℡05.63.56.05.64), from where it's a pleasant hour-long walk. Alternatively, you can hop on the **navette** for €4.50. **Buses** arrive near the lower-town summer-only **tourist office** (May–June 14 & Sept 1–15 Sat 2–6pm, Sun 10.30am–12.30pm & 2–6pm; June 15–31 Aug Mon 2–6pm, Tues–Sun 10.30am–12.30pm & 2–6pm; closed Sept16–April), while the main tourist office (Jan Sat & Sun 2–6pm; Feb–March daily 2–6pm; April–June & Sept–Oct Mon 2–6pm, Tues–Fri 10.30am–12.30pm & 2–6pm, Sat & Sun 2–6pm; July & Aug daily 10am–1pm & 2–7pm; ℡05.63.56.00.52, ⌨www.cordes-sur-ciel.org) is in the heart of the *cit*é. If you're driving, **parking** can be a challenge – in the summer months the area a few metres east of the lower tourist office soon fills up and cars line the roads leading into town. Don't be tempted to drive into the old town.

Famed Tarnaise pastry chef and chocolatier Yves Thuriès is the enlightened despot of Cordes' **hotels**, presiding over the lavish 4-star *Grand Ecuyer* (℡05.63.53.79.50, ⌨www.thuries.fr; closed mid-Oct to Easter; ⑥), housed in Raymond's former palace, the atmospheric 3-star *Vieux Cordes* (℡05.63.53.79.20, ⌨www.thuries.fr; closed Jan; ③) and the 2-star, *Hôtel de la Cité*, (℡05.63.56.03.53, ⌨www.thuries.fr; closed Nov–April; ④). For those who'd prefer canvas, there's also a decent **campsite**, *Le Garissou* (℡05.63.56.27.14, ✉legarissou@wanadoo.fr; open mid-Apr to Oct), in Les Cabannes on the west end of town. The best **restaurants** are in the town's hotels, including that in the *Grand Ecuyer*, a one-star Michelin restaurant known for its foie gras and other regional dishes (menus €40–80). Aside from these, there's plenty of choice for more economical fare around the central place de la Halle and adjacent place de la Bride, while *Les Ormeaux*, at 3 rue Saint-Michel (menus from €25; closed part Jan), offers an appetizing middle ground.

Najac

Back at Laguépie, the Aveyron valley turns northwards and the river flows through a wooded defile. The most picturesque route along the valley bottom is either the train or the GR36 footpath, while road users should take the D106 and D594 along the western line of hills. Either way, you eventually arrive at a bridge – 15km by road and slightly less on foot – beneath the brooding towers of **NAJAC**'s semi-ruined **castle**.

The castle occupies an extraordinary site on the peak of a conical hill isolated in the river's wide meander – a site chosen in the mid-1200s by **Alphonse de Poitiers** who wanted to bring the area's Cathar sympathizers to heel. He enlarged the original fortress and laid out a new town to the east in an elongated version of a *bastide* with its arcades and central market square. For a short while Najac prospered as the region's capital, but the site proved too restricted and by the end of the thirteenth century it had lost out to Villefranche-de-Rouergue (see opposite), leaving the castle to be fought over endlessly in the conflicts that ensued. The Protestants pillaged it in 1572 and the revolutionaries had their turn in 1793, but, in spite of all this, Najac survived.

The Town

The heart of modern Najac consists of a big, open square lying to the east of the medieval village, where grey-tiled houses tail out westwards in a single street along the narrow spur connecting the valley side to the castle hill. Entering from the east you come first to the **faubourg**, the elongated market square bordered by houses raised on pillars. It slopes gently downhill towards a cobbled street, overlooked by more ancient houses, which leads past a fountain to the **château** (daily: April, May, Sept & Oct 10am–12.30pm & 3–5.30pm; June 10am–12.30pm & 3–6.30pm; July & Aug 10am–1pm & 3–7pm; closed Nov–March; €3.50). The castle is a model of medieval defensive architecture: its curtain walls reach to over 20m in places, within which five round towers supplement the square twelfth-century turret, and the castle is equipped with unusual multistorey loopholes for archers. However, the main reason to visit is for the magnificent all-round view from the top of the keep, a full 200m above the river.

Just below the castle, in what was the original medieval village, stands the huge, very solid-looking and austere church of **St-Jean** (April–Sept Mon–Sat 10am–noon & 2–6pm, Sun 11am–noon & 2–7pm; Oct Sun only; free), which the villagers were forced to build at their own expense in 1258 as a punishment for their conversion to Catharism. In addition to a collection of reliquaries and an extraordinary iron cage for holding candles, the church has one architectural oddity: its windows are solid panels of stone from which the lights have been cut out in trefoil form. Below the church, a surviving Roman road leads downhill to where a thirteenth-century bridge spans the Aveyron.

Practicalities

Najac's **gare SNCF** lies on the north side of the old bridge, 2km by road below the village; **taxis** can be called on ℡05.65.29.72.48. The daily **bus** from Villefranche terminates on the square to the east of the village, while the **tourist office** is on the south side of the *faubourg* (April–June & Sept Mon–Sat 9am–noon & 2–6pm; July & Aug daily 9am–noon & 2–6pm; Oct–March Mon–Fri 9am–noon & 2–5pm, Sat 9am–noon; ℡05.65.29.72.05, ⓦwww.najac.com).

There's a good choice of **accommodation** in and around Najac, of which the nicest and most central is the *chambre d'hôte Maison Authesserre* (℡05.65.29.73.47;

❸; closed occasionally in winter), a lovely, blue-shuttered town house owned by an artist, at the west end of the *faubourg*. The rooms are all en suite, spacious and packed with character; there's also a peaceful courtyard garden at the back. At the *faubourg's* east entrance you'll find a very comfortable hotel, *L'Oustal del Barry* (☏ 05.65.29.74.32, ⓦ www.oustaldelbarry.com; ❸; closed mid-Nov to late Dec & Jan–March, also Mon from April to mid-June & Oct to mid-Nov), whose restaurant is renowned for its subtle and inventive cuisine (closed Mon & lunchtime Tues out of season; menus €22.80–41.50). Najac's other hotel is the welcoming, old-fashioned *La Belle Rive* (☏ 05.65.29.73.90, ⓔ hotel.bellerive.najac@wanadoo .fr; ❸; closed Nov–March), in a lovely riverside position near the train station, from whose garden you get an ant's-eye view of the château towering above. They also run an excellent restaurant serving good-value regional cooking with weekday lunch menus from €12.50, or €16 at other times. Najac's four-star riverside **campsite**, *Le Païsserou* (☏ 05.65.29.73.96 or ☏ 04.73.34.75.53 off season, ⓔ sogeval@wanadoo.fr; closed Oct–April), to the southwest of the old bridge, is spacious and very well equipped. In addition there's a **gîte d'étape** at the adjacent leisure centre (same ☏ & ⓔ), where you can also rent **canoes** and **bikes**.

As well as Najac's two hotel **restaurants**, *La Salamandre*, at the bottom of the *faubourg*, is a good bet; they serve simple, well-priced meals, with a *plat du jour* at €8.20 and a menu at €17.50 (closed Tues & Wed except in July & Aug; also closed Dec & Jan). For picnics, look out for *fouace*, a speciality bread sold in local shops.

Villefranche-de-Rouergue

The second stretch of the Aveyron gorge peters out about 10km north of Najac, but it's worth continuing upstream the same distance again to the laid-back market town of **VILLEFRANCHE-DE-ROUERGUE**, which boasts one of the most atmospheric central squares in the whole region. As its regular form and the die-straight streets indicate, this is a *bastide*, founded in 1252 by

△ Place Notre-Dame, Vilefranche-de-Rovergue

the ubiquitous **Alphonse de Poitiers,** as part of the royal policy of extending control over the recalcitrant lands of the south. Villefranche became rich on trade and on copper from the surrounding mines. In 1369 it was also made the seat of the Seneschal, the king's representative, with the right to mint money. While its wealthy merchants built the ornate houses that grace the cobbled streets to this day, conditions in the surrounding countryside were so desperate that in 1643, more than ten thousand peasants, known as **Croquants** (see p.390), besieged the town for a week. As elsewhere, the rebellion was harshly put down and the leaders strung up in the market square.

The Town

Villefranche's medieval quarter lies on the north bank of the Aveyron, accessed by a modern road-bridge beside its decommissioned fourteenth-century counterpart. From the old bridge, the town's main commercial street, pedestrianized **rue de la République,** runs northwards up a gentle incline into the heart of the *bastide*. It is attractive enough, but no preparation for the central square you come out into, **place Notre-Dame**. The square, too, is built on a slope and is surrounded by unusually tall houses, arcaded at ground-floor level, some of which bear elaborate window surrounds. If possible, try and visit on a Thursday morning when local merchants and farmers spread out their produce at the weekly **market**, presided over by the colossal porch and bell tower – nearly 60m high and fortified – of the **Collégiale Notre-Dame**, which dominates the square's east side. The church was started in 1260 but wars and fires intervened and it was not finally completed until 1519. Behind the altar are two fine mid-fifteenth-century stained-glass windows: the one on the left depicts the Creation; that on the right portrays sixteen characters from the Old and New Testaments. Also worth noting are the oak choir stalls alive with a superb array of beasts and demons, as well as scenes from daily life – they took the craftsman, André Sulpice, fifteen years to complete in the late fifteenth century.

On boulevard Haute-Guyenne, which forms the northern limit of the old town, the seventeenth-century **Chapelle des Pénitents-Noirs** (July–Sept daily 10am–noon & 2–6pm; €3.50) boasts a splendidly Baroque painted ceiling and an enormous gilded retable – resplendent after its recent renovation. Another ecclesiastical building worth the slight detour is the **Chartreuse St-Sauveur** (same hours; €3.50), in the grounds of a hospital about 1km south of town on the main D922 to Najac and Laguépie. It was completed in the space of ten years from 1450, giving it a singular architectural harmony. The highlight is the second of the two cloisters, a minuscule quadrangle of white, sculpted stone, while the church itself contains more examples of André Sulpice's craftsmanship on the screen and choir stalls.

Practicalities

The **gare SNCF** and **gare routière** are located together a couple of minutes' walk south across the Aveyron from the old centre, while **car rental** is available from Avis, on riverside place St-Jean (℡05.65.45.08.16), in the town's southeast corner. The **tourist office** sits on the river's north bank, on promenade du Giraudet (May, June, Sept & Oct Mon–Fri 9am–noon & 2–7pm, Sat 9am–noon & 2–6pm; July & Aug also open Sun 10am–noon; Nov–April Mon–Fri 9am–noon & 2–6pm, Sat 9am–noon; ℡05.65.45.13.18, ⓦwww.villefranche.com), beside the new bridge. **Internet** is available at Escape, 3 rue Jacques Borelly (Mon–Fri 9am–noon & 2.30–5.30pm).

For an overnight stay, there are two pleasant **hotels**: *L'Univers*, 2 place de la République (℡05.65.45.15.63, ⓦwww.logis-de-france.fr; ❷–❸), immediately across the river from the tourist office with a good traditional restaurant (closed three weeks in Jan, also Fri eve & Sat except July to Sept; menus from €15); and the more modest but cheerful and friendly *Bellevue*, 3 av du Ségala (℡05.65.45.23.17, ℻05.65.45.11.19; ❷; closed school hols in Feb & Nov, also Sun & Mon lunch except in July & Aug), which also boasts a decent restaurant (menus €15–46), a little further out of town on the Rodez road. Even cheaper accommodation is on offer at the HI-affiliated 🏠 *Foyer de Jeunes Travailleurs* (℡05.65.45.09.68, ℻05.65.45.82.82; €12.50), in a wood-faced building next to the train station. It offers individual en-suite rooms – some of which are huge, with mezzanine floors and separate seating areas – kitchen facilities and canteen meals. There is also a big three-star municipal **campsite** the *Camping du Rouergue* (℡05.65.45.16.24, ⓦwww.villefranche.com/camping; closed Oct to mid-April), 1.5km to the south, signed off the D47 to Monteil.

As far as **restaurants** are concerned, you're assured of a warm welcome at the convivial *Restaurant de la Halle*, a workers' diner beside the covered market hall immediately east of the church, where you can eat substantial meals for €10 at communal tables. Another simple but good option is the *Globe*, a bustling, modern brasserie just across the old bridge (*plat du jour* €8, menus from €12), or you could try *La Gabelle*, 10 rue Belle-Isle (closed Sun lunch & Mon), one block south of the church where you can eat pizzas, home-made pastas and grills from around €10. Finally, for more upmarket regional cuisine, try *L'Assiette Gourmande*, one block north of the church on place André-Lescure (closed Sun, also Tues–Thurs eves except in July & Aug; ℡05.65.45.25.95; menus €14.50–33); meals are served in a pleasant stone-vaulted room or out on the square in fine weather.

Travel details

By plane

Agen to: Paris Orly (1–3 daily except Sat; 1hr 30min).

By train

Agen to: Aiguillon (6–8 daily; 15–20min); Bordeaux (15–20 daily; 1hr 10min–1hr 30min); Moissac (3 daily; 30min); Monsempron-Libos (6–8 daily; 30–40min); Montauban (12–16 daily; 40–50min); Périgueux (3–4 daily; 2hr–2hr 30min); La Réole (5–8 daily; 1hr); Toulouse (16 daily; 1hr–1hr 20min).
Cordes-sur-Ciel (Cordes-Vindrac) to: Brive (1–2 daily; 2hr 45min); Figeac (4–6 daily; 1hr 30min); Laguépie (4–5 daily; 20min); Najac (4–6 daily; 30min); Paris-Austerlitz (1 daily; 8hr 45min); Toulouse (5–6 daily; 1hr); Villefranche-de-Rouergue (4–6 daily; 45min).
Laguépie to: Cordes-sur-Ciel (6–7 daily; 20min); Figeac (4–5 daily; 1hr–1hr 20min); Najac (4–5 daily; 10min); Paris-Austerlitz (1 daily; 8hr 20min); Toulouse (5–6 daily; 1hr 25min); Villefranche-de-Rouergue (4–6 daily; 25min).
Moissac to: Agen (3–6 daily; 30min); Bordeaux (2 daily; 1hr 40min); Montauban (5–6 daily; 20min); Toulouse (4–6 daily; 45min–1hr).
Montauban to: Agen (12–16 daily; 40–50min); Brive (7–8 daily; 1hr 40min–2hr); Cahors (8–10 daily; 40–45min); Moissac (3–5 daily; 20min); Toulouse (20–30 daily; 30–40min).
Najac to: Cordes-sur-Ciel (6–7 daily; 30min); Laguépie (6–7 daily; 10min); Figeac (4–6 daily; 1hr–1hr 15min); Paris-Austerlitz (1 daily; 8hr 15min); Toulouse (5–6 daily; 1hr 30min); Villefranche-de-Rouergue (4–6 daily; 15min).
Villefranche-de-Rouergue to: Brive (1–2 daily; 2–3hr); Cordes-sur-Ciel (6–7 daily; 45min); Figeac (5–8 daily; 40min); Laguépie (6 daily; 25min); Najac (6 daily; 15min); Paris-Austerlitz (1 daily; 8hr); Toulouse (5–7 daily; 1hr 40min).

By bus

Agen to: Moissac (Mon–Fri 2 daily; 1hr 20min); Nérac (Mon–Sat 1–5 daily; 35–40min); Toulouse (Mon–Fri 1 daily; 3hr); Villeneuve-sur-Lot (10 daily; 45min).

Contexts

Contexts

History

W hile France has existed in name since the tenth century, for much of its history the country has consisted of fiercely independent duchies, baronies and counties that, while they might have paid homage to the French king, were often a law unto themselves. One of these was the duchy of Aquitaine and another the county of Toulouse. Their boundaries varied over the years as their fortunes ebbed and flowed, but between them they ruled over southwest France, including the areas now known as the *départements* of Dordogne and Lot.

The beginnings

Primitive flint tools found in the Dordogne indicate a human presence dating back at least 400,000 years. However, the region's archeological treasure trove really gets going with the **Neanderthal** people, who arrived on the scene some 100,000 years ago. Despite their brutish image, evidence now suggests that Neanderthals were surprisingly sophisticated. They developed not only an increasingly elaborate range of stone tools but also complex burial rituals. This didn't, however, equip them to compete with the next wave of immigrants sweeping across Europe between 30,000 and 40,000 years ago, and Neanderthals gradually died out.

Early archeologists named the newcomers **Cro-Magnon** after a rock-shelter near Les Eyzies where the first skeletons were identified. Now they are better known as *Homo sapiens sapiens* – in other words, our direct ancestors. While Cro-Magnons developed ever more sophisticated tools, they also began to scratch fertility symbols into the rock, made various pigments and then took the great leap into abstraction that led to drawing, painting and carving. The earliest evidence of **prehistoric art** dates from around 30,000 years ago, but reached its apogee during the **Magdalenian** era (10,000–17,000 years ago) – also named after a shelter in the Dordogne's Vézère valley. It was during this era that Cro-Magnon people covered the walls and ceilings of the region's caves with art of a quality that would not be seen again for several millennia (see colour insert for more on cave art).

Around 10,000 BC the all-important reindeer herds, the Cro-Magnons' one-stop source of meat, fat, skin, bone and sinew, began to move north as the climate grew warmer and wetter. Over the next three thousand years these nomadic hunter-gatherers were gradually replaced by settled **farming and pastoral communities** who left hundreds of **dolmen** (megalithic stone tombs) scattered over the region. This Neolithic era in its turn made way for the great metal-working cultures, culminating in the Iron Age, from around 700 BC. About the same time **Celtic** people began to spread into the region from north and central Europe, establishing trade routes and building towns and hilltop fortresses. They were skilled manufacturers and had their own coinage, but instead of a cohesive entity, comprised individual or loosely allied clans, continuously fighting amongst themselves. It was these disunited tribes that the Roman legions encountered when they arrived in what they called **Gaul** – roughly equivalent to modern France – in the second century BC.

The Roman occupation

At first the **Romans** contented themselves with a colony along the Mediterranean coast, but in 59 BC the threat of a Germanic invasion and various Celtic uprisings prompted **Julius Caesar** to subjugate the entire area. It took him just eight years. By 56 BC he had pacified southwest Gaul and the only real opposition came from a young Arvenian (modern-day Auvergne) chieftain called **Vercingetorix** who managed to rally a united Gaulish opposition in 52 BC. The Gauls had some initial victories, but in the end were no match for Caesar's disciplined armies. Vercingetorix was taken back to Rome in chains in 52 BC and the following year the Gauls staged their final stand at **Uxellodunum**, generally believed to be the Puy d'Issolud, to the east of Martel (see p.274).

The battle was one of the major turning points in the region's history. In 16 AD Emperor Augustus established the new Gallo-Roman province of **Aquitania**, stretching from Poitiers south to the Pyrenees. Its capital was Burdigala (Bordeaux), and regional administrative centres were set up in Vesunna (Périgueux) and Divona Cadurcorum (Cahors), each with its forum, amphitheatre, law courts and temples. During more than three centuries of peace – the **Pax Romana** – that followed, the Romans built roads, introduced new technologies, traded, planted vineyards and established an urbanized society administered by an educated, Latin-speaking elite. Gradually, too, Latin penetrated the rural areas, where it eventually fused with the local Celtic dialects to form two broad new language groups: the *langue d'Oïl* (where "yes" is *oïl* – later, *oui*), spoken north of the Loire, and the *langue d'Oc*, or *Occitan* (where "yes" is *oc*), to the south.

In the meantime, serious **disruptions** of the Pax Romana had begun in the third century AD. Oppressive aristocratic rule and an economic crisis turned the destitute peasantry into gangs of marauding brigands, who were particularly rampant in the southwest. But more devastating were the incursions across the Rhine by various restless **Germanic tribes**, starting with the Alemanni and Franks, who pushed down as far as Spain, ravaging farmland and looting towns along the way. In response, urban centres such as Périgueux were hurriedly fortified while the nobles hot-footed it to their country villas, which became increasingly self-sufficient – economically, administratively and militarily.

The crunch came, however, in the fifth century when first the Vandals and then the **Visigoths** stormed through the region. For nearly a hundred years the Visigoths ruled a huge empire extending across southern France and into Spain, with its capital at Toulouse. But they, too, were pushed out in their turn by more invaders from the north.

The Franks

By 500 AD the **Franks**, who gave their name to modern France, had become the dominant power. Their most celebrated and ruthless king, **Clovis**, consolidated his hold on northern France and drove the Visigoths out of the southwest in 507. But the **Merovingian** Dynasty (as Clovis and his successors were called) failed to re-establish the same over-arching authority as the Romans. Aquitaine in particular displayed the first inklings of its independent streak, as it became first a semi-autonomous duchy and then a kingdom from 781 to 877 (see below).

All this while **Christianity**, which had arrived from Rome in the early fourth century, was spreading slowly through France. Many of the early evangelizers of the southwest met a grisly end, though they were later commemorated in the abbeys and churches founded by the nascent Christian communities they left in their wake. Clovis himself embraced Christianity around 500 AD and devolved a great deal of everyday administration to increasingly powerful local bishops, such as those at Cahors.

The Merovingian Empire began to disintegrate in the late seventh century, leaving the way clear for their chancellors, the Pepin family, to take control. One of their most dynamic scions, **Charles Martel**, defeated the Spanish Moors when they swept up through the southwest as far as Poitiers in 732. His grandson, **Charlemagne**, continued the expansionist policy of the **Carolingian** dynasty – so called for their fondness for the name Charles, or "Carolus" – to create an empire which eventually stretched from the Baltic to the Pyrenees.

To secure the allegiance of the southwest, in 781 Charlemagne created the nominally independent **kingdom** of Aquitaine – an area extending from the Loire to the Cévennes and from the Rhône to the Pyrenees – in the name of his infant son, the future King Louis the Pious. Within the kingdom, the Carolingians continued to administer through royally appointed bishops, now joined by a growing number of counts, of Quercy and Périgord for example, who had been awarded territory in exchange for their loyalty.

While the Carolingian Empire dissolved into a long-drawn-out battle of succession following Charlemagne's death in 814, the next wave of invaders was on its way from Scandinavia. The Vikings (also known as Normans, or Norsemen) had been raiding coastal areas for decades, but in 844 they

The Way of St James

According to the Bible, **St James the Apostle** was decapitated in Jerusalem in 44 AD. There is nothing to suggest how his remains came to be buried in northwest Spain, but in 820 it was declared that they had been discovered there, and during the fervent religious revival of the Middle Ages millions of pilgrims began flocking to his supposed tomb in **Santiago de Compostela**. The route took on a life of its own: monasteries, churches and hospitals were founded and villages grew up along the way to cater for the pilgrims wearing their distinctive cockleshell badge.

The pilgrimage faded out during the sixteenth century, partly because of the wars sweeping France and partly because the cathedral canons rather carelessly lost the saint's remains; the relics were allegedly hidden to keep them out of the hands of Sir Francis Drake, who was then sniffing around Galicia, but later no one could remember where they'd put them. By another "miracle" they were rediscovered by archeologists in 1879, declared by the pope to be the genuine article, and the pilgrimage revived, though on a far more modest scale.

In 1998 the whole system of paths and associated buildings was inscribed on the UNESCO World Heritage list. As a result, to walk the **chemin de St-Jacques** (Way of St James) – or at least some of it – is becoming increasingly popular again, partly as a spiritual quest, but also simply as a walking holiday. Three of the four main routes – from Vézelay, Le Puy-en-Velay and Arles – have been waymarked as long-distance footpaths (*grandes randonnées*, or GRs). Of these the GR654 from Vézelay and the GR65 from Le Puy pass through the Dordogne and Lot region; booklets outlining the routes are available in the Topo-guide series (see p.401 for more).

385

penetrated deep inland along the Garonne, Dordogne, Isle and Lot rivers, plundering towns and churches. In the face of these destabilizing invasions the Carolingians were obliged to delegate ever more autonomy to the provincial governors until these eventually grew more powerful than the king. The last of the Carolingian kings was succeeded in 987 by Hugh Capet. In theory Capetian rule extended over the whole of France; in practice he had authority only over a small area near Paris. Nonetheless, Hugh Capet founded a dynasty that lasted until 1328.

The Middle Ages

Even as the Carolingian Empire crumbled, the local aristocracy in the south began to jostle for power. In the tenth century Périgord was carved up into four **Baronies** (Beynac, Mareuil, Bourdeilles and Biron), while Quercy was divided between five powerful families (Turenne, Gourdon, Cardaillac, Castelnau and St-Sulpice). At the same time, the counts of Poitou (based at Poitiers) and Toulouse were fighting for control of what was once again the **Duchy of Aquitaine**. The former emerged victorious, thus creating a vast territory which by the twelfth century reached from the Loire to the Pyrenees. The Poitou counts also ushered in a period of relative peace, rapid economic growth and renewed religious vigour, which saw a wave of church building. To them we owe the lovely Romanesque churches seen throughout the region to this day. At least some of this building activity was spurred and financed by the great procession of **pilgrims** passing along the route to Santiago de Compostela in Spain (see box on p.385).

Also wandering the southern highways and byways were the **troubadours**. Both poets and musicians, the troubadours flourished in the late twelfth century among the vibrant and cultured nobility of southern France. Their lyric poetry, written in Occitan, idealized courtly love and laid down codes of chivalry, the influence of which eventually spread throughout Europe. The person who set it all off is generally held to be Guillaume IX, Duke of Aquitaine (1071–1126), whose court at Poitiers was regarded as one of the most civilized and sophisticated of its day.

Another famous troubadour was **Bertran de Born**, Viscount of Hautefort (c.1140–1212), who, among many others, wrote countless songs in praise of Guillaume's granddaughter, **Eleanor of Aquitaine** (1122–1204; see box on p.387). Eleanor inherited her father's domains of Aquitaine and Poitou in 1137 at the tender age of 15. Fifteen years later, her marriage to **Henry of Anjou** created an empire comprising Anjou and Normandy in addition to Eleanor's possessions. This in itself was a disastrous blow to the Capetians, but it was compounded in 1154 when Henry succeeded to the English throne (as Henry II). As a result, almost half of France fell under English rule. Much of it would remain so for the next three hundred years.

With the major exception of **Richard the Lionheart** (Richard Coeur de Lion), Eleanor's third son, who plundered the region ruthlessly, the **English overlords** proved to be popular. For the most part they ruled indirectly and ensured the loyalty of their southern subjects by granting a large degree of independence to many of Aquitaine's rapidly growing towns. The economy flourished on the back of the Bordeaux wine trade and dozens of new towns, or *bastides*, were founded to accommodate the rapidly expanding population.

Eleanor of Aquitaine

The life of **Eleanor of Aquitaine** (1122–1204) is an incredible tale of romance and tragedy, of high farce and low intrigue that rivals any modern-day pot-boiler. As Duchess of Aquitaine and Countess of Poitou she was already a key figure in twelfth-century Europe. She then married two kings and gave birth to three more, effectively ruled England for a time and died at the grand old age of 82.

It all began when she was just 15. On the death of her father, the Duke of Aquitaine, in 1137, Eleanor inherited the domains of Aquitaine and Poitou. She not only owned most of the land from the Loire to the Pyrenees, but was also clever and exceptionally beautiful – the troubadours Bertran de Born and Bernard de Ventadour, among others, composed many songs in her honour. Not surprisingly, there was no shortage of suitors but King Louis VI of France nipped in and only three months after her father's death Eleanor married the king's son and heir in July 1137 in Bordeaux's St-André Cathedral. Exactly one week later Louis VI died, leaving the young couple king and **queen of France**.

Though **Louis VII** was no mean catch, the marriage bore no male heirs and soon vivacious, sophisticated Eleanor grew bored. She was accused of several affairs, notably with her uncle Raymond of Poitiers, Prince of Antioch, when she accompanied Louis on the Second Crusade. But the grounds for their **divorce** in March 1152, largely on Eleanor's instigation, was consanguinity through her grandfather.

The previous year Eleanor had met the handsome, charismatic and extremely ambitious **Henry of Anjou** when he came to pay homage to Louis. Though eleven years her junior, Henry was far closer in temperament. They were married with little ceremony in May 1152. The following year she bore him the all-important heir and, when Henry II succeeded to the English throne in 1154, Eleanor found herself queen of England.

Although Eleanor spent much of her time in France, she and Henry produced at least eight children. Of these Richard, Geoffrey and John all became kings of England, while only two, John and Eleanor, outlived her. In the meantime, since Henry proved reluctant to delegate power, his sons rebelled against him in 1173, supported by both Eleanor and her former husband, Louis VI; the latter hoped to put a more compliant neighbour on the English throne – and was possibly also out for a spot of revenge.

But the rebellion soon collapsed and Henry placed his wife under house arrest. She remained closely guarded until his death in 1189, but her problems had by no means ended. Richard I (the Lionheart), Eleanor's favourite son, was next in line. All went well until he was captured in 1192 while returning from the Third Crusade. The indomitable seventy-year-old waded in as unofficial regent, while also keeping her French possessions under control, for the next two years.

Eleanor withdrew from public life after Richard's release, and even more so after his death in 1199. She retired to the Abbey of Fontevraud, in the Loire valley, occasionally venturing out to tour her French domains. On the whole she was a popular, shrewd and effective ruler, well able to control her notoriously hot-blooded southern vassals. Nevertheless, Eleanor died almost unnoticed at Fontevraud in 1204 while her last remaining son, John, was busy losing Normandy, Anjou and Poitou for the English Crown.

The Cathar Crusades

Over to the east of Aquitaine, meanwhile, the powerful **counts of Toulouse** were getting into hot water. From the mid-twelfth century on, the so-called **Cathars** (also known as Albigensians) had won a great deal of support in the area, which extended as far as the Dordogne valley, by preaching that the

material world was created by the Devil and the spiritual world by a benevo-
lent God. They also believed in reincarnation and that the only way to escape
the mortal coil was to lead a life of saintly self-denial. All of which completely
undermined the role of the clergy. To put an end to such **heresy**, Pope Inno-
cent III unleashed a **crusade** against the Cathars in 1209, starting off with a
particularly murderous attack led by **Simon de Montfort** in which the entire
population of the Mediterranean town of Béziers, estimated at twenty thousand
people, was slaughtered; the papal legate in charge of the assault is famously
supposed to have proclaimed, "Kill them all. God will know his own."

A series of crusading armies, comprised largely of land-hungry northern
nobles, then proceeded to rampage through the region on and off for the next
twenty years. This was followed by an equally vicious **inquisition** designed to
mop up any remaining Cathars, which culminated in the siege of Montségur,
in the eastern foothills of the Pyrenees, in 1244, when two hundred people
were burnt alive.

As a result of the Cathar Crusades, the French Crown now held sway over
the whole of southeastern France, including Toulouse. The new count of Toulouse was **Alphonse de Poitiers**, brother of the future Louis IX, whose lands
stretched north through Quercy into Périgord, and west along the Garonne as
far as Agen. Like his English neighbours, Alphonse started establishing a rash of
bastides in order to impose his authority over his new domains.

The Hundred Years' War

Though the English had lost their possessions north of the Loire by the mid-
thirteenth century, they remained a perpetual thorn in the side of the French
kings thanks to their grip on Aquitaine. Skirmishes took place throughout the
century, followed by various peace treaties, one of which, in 1259, took Quercy
and Périgord back into the English domain. But the spark that ignited the
ruinous – and misnamed – **Hundred Years' War** (1337–1453) was a Capetian
succession crisis. When the last of the line, Charles IV, died without an heir in
1328, the English king, **Edward III**, leapt in to claim the throne of France for
himself. It went instead to Charles's cousin, **Philippe de Valois**. Edward acqui-
esced for a time, but when Philippe began whittling away at English possessions
in Aquitaine, Edward renewed his claim and embarked on a war.

It started off badly for the French. Edward won an outright victory at **Crécy**
in 1346 and seized the port of Calais as a permanent bridgehead. Ten years later,
his son, the **Black Prince**, took the French king, Jean le Bon, prisoner at the
Battle of Poitiers and established a capital at Bordeaux. To regain his liberty Jean
was forced to sign the **Treaty of Brétigny** (1360) in which he ceded more
than a quarter of his kingdom to the English. In exchange, Edward renounced
his claim to the French Crown.

The peace was short lived. Jean's successor, Charles V, waded in again and by
1377 the great military leader **Bertrand du Guesclin** had pushed the English
back until they were reduced to a toehold in Bordeaux and a smattering of
other Atlantic ports. There they stayed until 1415 when Henry V came back
with a vengeance to inflict another crushing defeat on the French army at
Agincourt. In the treaty that followed, Henry was named heir to the French
throne and it seemed that France was unravelling at the seams.

Just in the nick of time, however, **Jeanne d'Arc** (Joan of Arc) arrived on the
scene. In 1429 she rallied the demoralized French troops, broke the English

△ Château de Bonaguil

siege at Orléans and tipped the scales against the invaders. The English were slowly but surely driven back to their southwest heartland until even that was lost at the **Battle of Castillon** in 1453 (see p.203).

Apart from this last, no major battles of the Hundred Years' War were fought in southwest France, though most towns and castles were attacked at some point and many changed hands on numerous occasions, either by treaty or force. By the end of the war farms and villages lay abandoned and roving bands of **brigands** terrorized the countryside. The population had been reduced by roughly a half to under twelve million, partly by warfare, but largely through famine and disease; millions died as the bubonic **plague** repeatedly swept through France during the fourteenth and fifteenth centuries.

Gradually the nightmare ended. Though the south now had to kow-tow to the hated northerners, Louis XI proved to be an astute ruler who allowed some of the privileges granted by the English to remain. The Bordelais smarted for a while, but were eventually brought round with the establishment of their own parliament in 1462. Trade – particularly the wine trade – began to revive, towns were rebuilt and land brought back into production.

The Wars of Religion

In the early sixteenth century the ideas, art and architecture of the **Renaissance** began to penetrate France as a result of an inconclusive military campaign in Italy. As elsewhere in Europe, the Renaissance had a profound influence on every aspect of life, engendering a new optimism and spirit of enquiry which appealed in particular to the new class of wealthy merchants. At the same time increased trade and better communications, including the invention of the printing press, helped disseminate ideas throughout Europe. Among them came the new **Protestant** message espoused by Martin Luther and John Calvin that the individual was responsible to God alone and not to the Church.

Such ideas gained widespread adherence throughout France, but nowhere more so than in the southwest, where the Catholic clergy were closely linked to the oppressive feudal regime. The first Protestant (also known as **Huguenot**) enclaves to be established in the region were at Ste-Foy-la-Grande and Bergerac in the 1540s, followed soon after by Nérac, the fief of the **d'Albret** family (see p.353). As the Protestant faith took hold and Catholics felt increasingly threatened, the sporadic brutal attempts to stamp out Protestantism, such as a massacre in Cahors in 1560, erupted two years later into a series of bitter civil wars. Interspersed with ineffective truces and accords, the **Wars of Religion** lasted for the next thirty years.

The fighting was particularly vicious in the southwest, where whole towns opted for one side or the other – while the Protestants held Bergerac, Montauban and Figeac, for example, Sarlat and Périgueux remained staunchly Catholic – and Catholic and Protestant armies vied with each other in their savagery. By far the blackest event was the **St Bartholomew's Day Massacre** in 1572, when some three thousand Protestants, gathered in Paris for the wedding of Protestant **Henri d'Albret** to Marguerite de Valois, the sister of Henri III of France, were slaughtered. The bloodbath was repeated across France and led to yet more Protestant reprisals.

By a twist of fate, however, Henri d'Albret – king of Navarre and leader of the Protestant army – became heir to the French throne when Henri III's son died in 1584. Five years later, Henri III himself was dead, leaving a tricky problem, since a Protestant could not be king. After trying to seize the crown by force, Henri d'Albret eventually abjured his faith and became **Henri IV** of France. "Paris is worth a Mass," he is reputed to have said.

Once on the throne Henri IV set about reconstructing and reconciling his kingdom. Under the **Edict of Nantes** of 1598 the Protestants were accorded freedom of conscience, freedom of worship in specified places, the right to attend the same schools and hold the same offices as Catholics, their own courts and the possession of a number of fortresses, including Montauban, as a guarantee against renewed attack.

Not surprisingly, the ructions didn't end there. When Henri IV was assassinated by Catholic extremists in 1610, southern Protestants rebelled and several towns, such as Bergerac, were seized by the Catholics. Then in 1685 Louis XIII revoked the Edict of Nantes, forbade Protestant worship and set about trying to eliminate the faith completely. Orders were given for the destruction of Protestant churches and of the castles of its most fervent supporters. Thousands of Protestants fled the southwest for the safety of the Netherlands, Germany and England.

The stirrings of discontent

Once again, the countryside lay in ruins and the cost of the wars and rebuilding fell squarely on the peasants' shoulders. Ruinous taxes, a series of bad harvests, high prices and yet more outbreaks of the plague combined to push them over the edge in the late seventeenth century. There were **peasant rebellions** in Normandy and Brittany, but the worst of the "**Croquants**'" (yokels') uprisings broke out in the southwest in the late sixteenth century and rumbled on for two hundred years. The first major revolt occurred in the winter of 1594, when a number of towns and castles, including Monpazier, Excideuil and Puy-l'Évêque, were attacked. It was quickly and savagely put down by the allied forces of the local nobility, but the uprisings of May 1637 were altogether more serious. In the face of one tax demand too many, a **peasant army** ten thousand strong tried unsuccessfully to seize Périgueux. Instead, they took Bergerac and then marched on Bordeaux. They were stopped, however, at Ste-Foy-la-Grande and the final show-down took place soon after against 3400 royal troops at La Sauvetat-du-Dropt, south of Bergerac, leaving at least a thousand Croquants dead. The leaders were executed, one in Monpazier (see p.338), while the surviving rebels returned to the land.

By the 1640s things were getting even more complicated since the **aristocracy** themselves were starting to protest, partly at the increasing tax demands, but mainly at the loss of privileges threatened by an increasingly centralized state. The **Fronde** (meaning "a catapult" or, more generally, "a revolt"), as the series of uprisings between 1648 and 1652 were known, were at their worst around Paris and Bordeaux, though other southwestern towns, such as Sarlat and Périgueux, also rebelled against royal authority. In Bordeaux the protests spilled over into a more widespread republican revolt which was brought under control only when the royal army was sent in again in 1653.

Things gradually settled down after 1661 as **Louis XIV** instigated major administrative and financial reform. At the same time, France was beginning to establish a **colonial empire** in North America, Africa, India and the Caribbean, and, as trade from these places began to grow in the early eighteenth century, so Bordeaux and the other Atlantic ports prospered. Indeed, the late seventeenth and eighteenth centuries were something of a **golden age** for Bordeaux and its hinterland. On the back of colonial commerce and a booming **wine trade,** it grew to be the country's foremost port. The city centre was almost completely rebuilt and intellectual life flourished under the leadership of **Montesquieu** (see p.111) and other liberal visionaries.

Revolution

For the majority of people, however, little had changed. The gap between rich and poor grew ever wider as the clergy and aristocracy clung on to their privileges and the peasants were squeezed for higher taxes. Their general misery was exacerbated by a catastrophic harvest in 1788, followed by a particularly severe winter. Bread prices rocketed and on July 14, 1789, a mob stormed the **Bastille** in Paris, a hated symbol of the oppressive regime. As the **Revolution** spread, similar insurrections occurred throughout the country, accompanied by widespread peasant attacks on landowners' châteaux and the destruction of tax and rent records. In August the new National Assembly abolished the feudal rights and privileges of the nobility and then went on to nationalize Church lands.

In these early stages the general population of the southwest supported the Revolution, as did Bordeaux's elected deputies, known as the **Girondins**. However, as the Parisian revolutionaries grew increasingly radical and proposed ever more centralization of power, the Girondins found themselves in bitter opposition. Towards the end of 1792, as the **First Republic** was being declared, they finally lost out to the extremists and in October the following year **The Terror** was unleashed as mass executions took place throughout France; estimates run to 3000 in Paris and 14,000 in the regions. Amongst the victims were the Girondin deputies, the last of whom were tracked down and killed in St-Émilion in 1794.

Though revolutionary bands wrought a fair amount of havoc in the south-west, looting and burning castles and churches, hacking away at coats of arms and religious statuary, on the whole the region escaped fairly lightly; many aristocrats simply fled and their possessions were sold off at knock-down prices. Among many administrative changes following the Revolution, one of the most significant was the creation of **départements** in 1790 to replace the old provinces. Thus began a process of national unification which continued in the nineteenth century with moves to stamp out Occitan and other regional dialects. So, gradually, was the traditionally independent southwest drawn into mainstream France.

From Napoleon I to the Third Republic

By the end of 1794, more moderate forces were in charge in Paris. However, continuous infighting left the way open for **Napoleon Bonaparte**, who had made a name for himself as commander of the Revolutionary armies in Italy and Egypt, to seize power in a coup d'état in 1799. Napoleon quickly restored order and continued the process of centralization, replacing the power of local institutions by appointing a *préfet* to each *département* answerable only to the **Emperor**, as Napoleon declared himself in 1804. Nevertheless, the Dordogne and Lot *départements* supported the new regime by providing many military leaders – and more lowly troops – for Bonaparte's armies: the most notable examples were Périgueux's Baron Pierre Daumesnil (see p.154) and Joachim Murat (1767–1815), the son of a village innkeeper near Cahors, who was proclaimed king of Naples in reward for his numerous military successes. As elsewhere, however, it was the burden of the unceasing **Napoleonic wars** that cost the emperor his support. The economy of Bordeaux in particular and the southwest in general was hard hit when Napoleon banned commerce with Britain, to which Britain responded by blockading French ports in 1807.

Few tears were shed in the region when Napoleon was finally defeated in 1815. The subsequent restoration of the **monarchy**, on the other hand, saw opinions divided along predictable lines: the aristocracy and the emerging *bourgeoisie* (the middle classes) rallied to the king, while the working population supported the uprising in 1848 – a shorter and less virulent reprise of the 1789 Revolution – which ended in the declaration of the **Second Republic**. The new government started off well by setting up national workshops to relieve unemployment and extending the vote to all adult males – an unprecedented move for its time. But in elections held later in 1848 the largely conservative vote of the newly enfranchised peasants was sufficient to outweigh the urban, working-class radicals. To everyone's surprise, Louis-Napoleon, nephew of the former emperor, romped home. In spite of his liberal reputation, he restricted the vote again, censored the press and pandered to the Catholic Church. In 1852, following a coup and further street fighting, he had himself proclaimed **Emperor Napoleon III**.

Like his uncle, Napoleon III pursued an expansionist military policy, both in France's colonial empire and in Europe. And also like his uncle, this brought about his downfall. Napoleon III declared war on Prussia in 1870 and was quickly and roundly defeated by the far superior Prussian army. When Napoleon was taken prisoner the politicians in Paris – Cahors' Léon Gambetta among them (see p.300) – quickly proclaimed the **Third Republic**. Though it experienced a difficult birth, the Third Republic remained in power until 1940.

Into the twentieth century

Napoleon was more successful on the economic front, however. From the 1850s on, France experienced rapid **industrial growth**, while foreign trade trebled. The effect on the Dordogne and Lot region, however, was mixed.

Bordeaux and the towns along the region's great rivers benefited most from the economic recovery. Bordeaux in particular prospered once again thanks to its colonial trade. Although the region had no coal or mineral resources to stimulate large-scale industrialization (beyond metalworking around Fumel), industries were established along the navigable rivers – tanneries, paper mills, textile and glass industries. At the same time, agricultural areas within easy access of the rivers grew wealthy from exporting wheat, wine and tobacco. Many towns were given a facelift as their ramparts were torn down, wide avenues sliced through the cramped medieval quarters and a start was made on improving sanitation and water supply. Transportation was also modernized, although the **railways** came late to the Dordogne and Lot and were never very extensive. The region's first railway, the Bordeaux–Paris line, was completed in 1851, while the following year saw the opening of the **Canal latéral**, linking the Garonne with the Canal du Midi and thus the Mediterranean.

All this created pockets of economic growth, but the **rural areas** between became increasingly marginalized. Local industries dwindled in the face of competition from cheap manufactured goods and imports, while the railways simply provided the means for people to quit the country for the cities.

But by far the biggest single crisis to hit the area's rural economy in the late nineteenth century was **phylloxera**. The parasite, which attacks the roots of vines, wiped out almost one third of the region's vineyards in the 1870s and 1880s. For a while growers tried all sorts of remedies, from flooding the fields to chemical fumigation, before it was discovered that vines in America, where phylloxera originated, were immune and that by grafting French vines onto American root-stock it was possible to produce resistant plants. The vineyards were slowly re-established, but over a much smaller area. Many farmers turned to alternative crops, such as tobacco around Bergerac and sheep-rearing on the *causse* above Cahors.

The world wars

Such problems paled into insignificance, however, when German troops marched into northern France following the outbreak of **World War I** in 1914. The French government fled south to Bordeaux while thousands of southern men trekked north to lose their lives in the mud and horror of Verdun and the Somme battlefields. By the time the Germans were forced to surrender in 1918, the cost to France was 1.3 million dead, a quarter of whom were under 25 years of age, and three million wounded. Every town and village in the Dordogne and Lot, as elsewhere in France, has its sad war memorial recording the loss of this generation of young men.

In the aftermath of the war, agricultural and industrial production declined and the birth rate plummeted, although this was offset to some extent in the southwest by an influx of land-hungry refugees from Spain in the late nineteenth century and from Italy in the first decades of the twentieth. At the same time, however, Bordeaux's old-fashioned maritime industries were in terminal decline as the 1930s **Depression** hit home. The French government lurched from crisis to crisis while events across the border in Germany became increasingly menacing.

In April 1940, eight months after the outbreak of **World War II**, Hitler's western offensive began as he overran Belgium, Denmark and Holland. In June the French government retreated to Bordeaux again and millions of refugees poured south as Paris fell to the Germans. **Maréchal Pétain**, a conservative 84-year-old veteran of World War I, emerged from retirement to sign an armistice with Hitler and head the collaborationist **Vichy government**, based in the spa town of Vichy in the northern foothills of the Massif Central. France was now split in two. The Germans occupied the strategic regions north of the Loire and all along the Atlantic coast, including Bordeaux, while Vichy ostensibly governed the "Free Zone" comprising the majority of southern France. The frontier, with its customs points and guard posts, ran from the Pyrenees north through Langon and Castillon-la-Bataille to just south of Tours, and from there cut east to Geneva. Then, in 1942, German troops moved south to occupy the whole of France until they were driven out by Britain, America and their allies after 1944.

Resistance to the German occupation didn't really get going until 1943 when **General de Gaulle**, exiled leader of the "Free French", sent **Jean Moulin** to unify the disparate and often ideologically opposed Resistance groups. Moulin was soon captured by the Gestapo and tortured to death by Klaus Barbie – the infamous "Butcher of Lyon", who was convicted as recently as 1987 for his war crimes – but the network Moulin established became increasingly effective. Its members provided information to the Allies, blew up train tracks, bridges and factories, as well as undertaking daring raids into enemy-held towns; the high, empty uplands of Dordogne and Lot *départements* afforded safe bases for many Resistance fighters. But for every action, the Germans hit back with savage **reprisals**. In May 1944 the SS Das Reich division, based at Montauban, set out to break the local resistance by massacring civilians and torching houses in some twenty towns and villages, of which the worst atrocities took place in Terrasson-la-Villedieu, Montpezat-de-Quercy, Mussidan and Frayssinet-le-Gélat.

Soon afterwards the Germans were being driven out, but the fighting didn't stop there. In the weeks following **liberation** thousands of **collaborators** were executed or publicly humiliated – women accused of consorting with the enemy had their heads shaved and were sometimes paraded naked through the streets. Not surprisingly, the issue of collaboration left deep scars in rural communities throughout the region, a bitterness which occasionally surfaces to this day in local disputes.

Into the new millennium

The new millennium sees the same issues that have dominated the last fifty years in the region remaining paramount. One of the main themes, as in much of rural France, is one of **depopulation**. On average there are now 25 percent fewer people living on the land than at the end of the nineteenth century, rising to thirty percent or more in the worst hit areas, such as parts of Lot-et-Garonne. Once again this has been partly offset by immigration, in this case by *pieds noirs* (black feet) – French colonialists forced to flee Algeria after independence in 1962 – many of whom settled on farms in the southwest, and by north Europeans in search of the good life. Agricultural production is in slow decline as the younger generation leave the land, though this has partly been offset by a massive push towards mechanization and the amalgamation of small farms into larger, more efficient holdings – albeit often propped up by subsidies from the European Union.

Agriculture remains the backbone of the region's economy, notably wine production but also poultry, maize, fruit, tobacco, fishing and forestry. The Bordelais vineyards alone account for around four percent of Aquitaine's GDP and six percent of its employment; some sixty thousand people in the region depend directly and indirectly on viticulture. **Industry**, on the other hand, employs around fifteen percent of the active population. The biggest industrial city is Bordeaux, with its aeronautical, electronic, optical and pharmaceutical businesses. Agen is also known for pharmaceuticals, while other main towns such as Périgueux, Figeac, Montauban, Fumel and Villeneuve-sur-Lot boast modest industrial sectors.

The **unemployment** rate, which has fallen gradually over recent years, now hovers just below the national average of 9.5 percent. Even so, the region didn't escape the **riots** which erupted in French cities in October 2005 after two teenagers were accidentally electrocuted in a Paris suburb. Three weeks of rioting followed, mostly among the disaffected children of North African immigrants living in sink estates, including some relatively limited trouble in the suburbs of Bordeaux and Montauban. Rioters vented their anger over high youth unemployment, racial discrimination and lack of opportunities by torching some nine thousand vehicles and causing damage estimated at around €200 million. Things eventually calmed down amid much debate about how France has failed to integrate its immigrant minorities.

Just a few months later it was the turn of the **students** to take to the streets in protest against the Contrat Première Embauche (CPE, or "first employment contract"). Ironically, this was one of the initiatives introduced by Prime Minister Dominique de Villepin to tackle youth unemployment by encouraging firms to employ people under 26 years old – the incentive was a mix of financial measures and the ability to fire employees on a CPE within two years without having to provide a reason. While almost everyone agrees something needs to be done about France's restrictive labour laws, the CPE met with widespread opposition. Massive, and occasionally violent, demonstrations by students, trade unionists and workers marching through streets lined with riot police or manning the barricades brought back memories of the student-led revolt of 1968. The demonstrations in Bordeaux, with its high student population, were amongst the largest in France. As the protests spread – on April 4, 2006 as many as three million people demonstrated throughout France – and there were calls for a general strike, de Villepin finally caved in and withdrew the law. In theory, a new version is under discussion, but with presidential elections due in 2007 no one's holding their breath.

Besides agriculture and industry, **tourism** plays an increasingly important role in the regional economy. In recent years an enormous effort has gone into improving facilities and marketing the region, not just the honeypot attractions of Sarlat, Les Ezyies and the Dordogne valley châteaux, but also in the successful promotion of "green holidays", tempting people away from the Mediterranean and Atlantic coasts to discover all that the countryside has to offer. One of the largest such projects was the reopening of the River Lot and the Canal latéral to navigation, but at a local level almost every town and village now puts on a programme of summer events to lure visitors.

When you add to this the region's wealth of historic and natural attractions, it's hardly surprising that thousands of tourists flock here each year and that many decide to stay. Since the 1960s both nostalgic Parisians and north Europeans – predominantly British, but also increasing numbers of Dutch and other nationalities – have been snapping up property in the area. Initially, this meant holiday and retirement homes but nowadays there is a noticeable trend towards younger people coming to settle and work.

The French reaction to this invasion has been one of welcome, or at least tolerance, and not just because the newcomers restore the derelict farmhouses and pump money into the local economy. Even after all these centuries, there still exists a vague and undoubtedly romantic sentiment among the resolutely independent, anti-Parisian southwesterners that they were better off under English rule, when at least the economy boomed and their forbears enjoyed a high degree of autonomy. Down the intervening years the region's strong sense of identity has been tested on many occasions, but has survived to resurface these days as a deep-burning pride in the land, its produce and its traditions.

Books

T here are few English-language history books specifically devoted to the Dordogne and Lot region, and a surprising dearth of novels, whether in English or in translation. A few of those that do exist – and are worth recommending – are detailed below, along with a number of general history books and classic texts which provide the background to events that have occurred in the region. Books that are out of print are indicated by the abbreviation o/p.

History

Lesley and Roy Adkins *The Keys of Egypt* (HarperCollins). The surprisingly gripping story of how hieroglyphics were first deciphered, the hero of the tale being Jean-François Champollion, a native of Figeac.

Marc Bloch *Strange Defeat* (W W Norton). Moving personal study of the reasons for France's defeat in 1940 and subsequent caving-in to fascism. Found among the papers of this Sorbonne historian after his death at the hands of the Gestapo in 1942.

Christy Campbell *Phylloxera* (HarperCollins). A detailed but readable account of how phylloxera almost killed off the French wine industry and the desperate search for a remedy. In the end it was American rootstock that saved the day – though it seems the disease is making a comeback.

Richard Cobb and Colin Jones (eds) *The French Revolution* (Simon & Schuster; o/p). One of the best offerings on the 1789 Revolution, with lots of pictures, original texts and clear explanations by a host of historians.

Alfred Cobban *A History of Modern France* (3 vols: 1715–99, 1799–1871 and 1871–1962; Penguin). Complete and very readable account of the main political, social and economic strands in French history, from the

death of Louis XIV to mid-de Gaulle.

Robert Gildea *France Since 1945* (Oxford University Press). Pithy but serious contemporary history, with a particular interest in France's national self-image.

Mark Girouard *Life in the French Country House* (Weidenfeld & Nicholson, UK; Yale University Press, US). Girouard meticulously recreates the social and domestic life that went on within the walls of French châteaux from the first castles to modern-day marriage venues.

Christopher Hibbert *Days of the French Revolution* (HarperPerennial). Well-paced and entertaining narrative treatment by a master historian.

Johan Huizinga *Waning of the Middle Ages* (Dover Publications). Primarily a study of the culture of the Burgundian and French courts – but a masterpiece that goes far beyond this, building up meticulous detail to re-create the whole life and mentality of the fourteenth and fifteenth centuries.

Colin Jones *The Cambridge Illustrated History of France* (Cambridge University Press). A political and social history of France from prehistoric times to the mid-1990s, concentrating on issues of regionalism, gender, race and class. Good illustrations and an easy, unacademic writing style.

H. R. Kedward *In Search of the Maquis: Rural Resistance in South France 1942–44* (Clarendon Press, UK; Oxford University Press, US). Slightly dry style, but full of fascinating detail about the brave and often fatal struggle of the countless ordinary people across France who fought to drive the Germans from their country.

H. R. Kedward *La Vie en Bleu* (Penguin). This provacative and perceptive book looks at France from 1900 to the present day. Though not an easy read, Kedward's insights into contemporary France more than repay the effort.

Don and Petie Kladstrup *Wine & War* (Hodder & Stoughton, UK; Broadway, US). The role of wine in World War II and the often courageous and ingenious strategies used to prevent the best wines from being plundered by the German army; fascinating reading.

Max Hastings *Das Reich: The March of the 2nd SS Panzer Division Through France* (Pan). Max Hastings brings his journalistic skills to bear on the story of the infamous 2nd SS Panzer Division (Das Reich) as it marched north through the Dordogne and Limousin in the wake of the 1944 D-Day landings. Harassed by members of the French Resistance and Allied Special Forces, the German troops left a trail of savage reprisals.

Emmanuel Le Roy Ladurie *Montaillou* (Penguin, UK; Gardners Books, US). Village gossip and details of work and everyday life, extracted by the Inquisition from Cathar peasants in the fourteenth century, and stored away until recently in the Vatican archives. Though academic and heavy-going in places, most of this book reads like a novel.

Ian Littlewood *History of France* (Rough Guides). This pocket-sized guide offers a handy chronology plus background snippets on cultural movements and key historical figures.

Marion Meade *Eleanor of Aquitaine* (Weidenfield & Nicholson, UK; Penguin, US). Highly accessible biography of one of the key characters in twelfth-century Europe. The author fleshes out the documented events until they read more like a historical novel.

Nancy Mitford *Madame de Pompadour* (Penguin, UK; New York Review Books, US). Mitford's unashamedly biased admiration for Pompadour – Louis XV's mistress and France's greatest art patron – makes this a fascinating read.

Robin Neillands *The Hundred Years' War* (Routledge). This concise and eminently readable history of the war between the English and French that dragged on from 1337 to 1453 provides a good introduction to the subject.

Stephen O'Shea *The Perfect Heresy* (Walker & co). Lively if partisan non-academic account of the history of the Cathars and the Catholic campaign mounted to wipe them out.

Ian Ousby *Occupation: The Ordeal of France 1940–1944* (Cooper Square Press). Somewhat revisionist 1997 account looking at how widespread collaboration was and why it took so long for the Resistance to get organized.

Simon Schama *Citizens* (Penguin, UK; Vintage, US). Bestselling and highly tendentious revisionist history of the Revolution, which pretty well takes the line that the ideologues of the Revolution were a gang of fanatics who simply failed to see how good the *ancien régime* was. Nevertheless, it's well-written, racy and provocative.

J. M. Thompson *The French Revolution* (Sutton Publishing). A detailed and passionate account, first published in 1943, but still a classic.

🏃 **Barbara Tuchman** *A Distant Mirror* (Ballantine Books). The history of the fourteenth century – plagues, wars, peasant uprisings and crusades – told through the life of a sympathetic French nobleman whose career took him through England, Italy and Byzantium, and finally ended in a Turkish prison.

Paul Webster *Pétain's Crime: The Full Story of French Collaboration in the Holocaust* (Pan). The fascinating and alarming story of the Vichy regime's more-than-willing collaboration with the Holocaust and the bravery of those, especially the Communist resistance in occupied France, who attempted to prevent it.

Alison Weir *Eleanor of Aquitaine* (Pimlico, UK; Ballantine Books, US). A more scholarly account than Marion Meade's biography (see p.398), but still very readable. In telling

Eleanor's tale, the author also gives a broad overview of twelfth-century French and European history.

Ean Wood *The Josephine Baker Story* (Sanctuary Publishing). Wood traces the extraordinary life of this legendary entertainer with affection, from childhood to celebrated cabaret star, war heroine and then to her last, troubled years when she was forced to sell her Dordogne château, Les Milandes.

Alexander Worth *France 1940–55* (Beacon Press, US; o/p). Extremely good and emotionally engaging portrayal of the taboo Occupation period in French history, followed by the Cold War and years of colonial struggle in which the same political tensions and heart-searchings were at play.

🏃 **Theodore Zeldin** *The French* (Harvill, UK; Kodansha, US). Urbane and witty survey of the French world view – chapter titles include "How to be chic" and "How to appreciate a grandmother".

Travel, art and literature

Patricia Atkinson *The Ripening Sun* (Arrow). The ultimately uplifting tale of an English woman who struggles against all kinds of adversity to establish a well-respected vineyard near Bergerac.

🏃 **Michael Brown** *Down the Dordogne* (Sinclair-Stevenson, UK; Trafalgar Square, US). In the late 1980s, Michael Brown fulfilled a long-held ambition to follow the Dordogne from its source in the Massif Central to the Gironde estuary. The story of his journey – on foot, by canoe and bicycle – provides a lyrical introduction to the region.

🏃 **André Chastel** *French Art* (Flammarion). Authoritative,

three-volume study by one of France's leading art historians. Discusses individual works of art – from architecture to tapestry, as well as painting – in detail in an attempt to locate the Frenchness of French art. With glossy photographs and serious-minded but readable text.

Michael Crichton *Timeline* (Arrow, UK; Ballantine Books, US). A time-travelling history professor and his assistants get up to all sorts of scrapes in the Dordogne valley circa 1357, in the midst of the Hundred Years' War. An enjoyable romp by the author of *Jurassic Park.*

🏃 **Arthur Conan-Doyle** *The White Company* (Dover

Publications). A far cry from Sherlock Holmes, here Conan-Doyle turns his talents to historical fiction, depicting a Hundred Years' War where the English have hearts of gold and all the rest are jolly rotters.

Kenneth J. Conant *Carolingian and Romanesque Architecture, 800–1200* (Yale University Press). Good European study with a focus on Cluny and the Santiago de Compostela pilgrim route.

Betsy Draine and Michael Hinden *A Castle in the Backyard* (University of Wisconsin Press). Two American academics fall in love with the Dordogne and decide to buy a holiday home. This is the affectionate story of their search – which ends in Castlenaud – and subsequent summers spent exploring the region.

Louise Franklin Castanet *Bananas in Bordeaux* (Léonie Presse). Entertaining tale told in diary form by an English woman settling to married life – and new baby – in Bordeaux before French husband Eric relocates the family to embark on a new career and subsistence existence in the countryside.

Joanne Harris *Chocolat* (Black Swan). Set in the Garonne valley near Agen, this bittersweet bestseller gives little in the way of specific regional colour, but is worth reading for its beautifully rendered view of life in claustrophobic small-town rural France, albeit one wrapped inside a fairy-tale coating.

Jeremy Josephs *A Vineyard in the Dordogne* (Metro Books). If you're thinking of buying a vineyard in France, even with a few million in the bank, read this book first. Josephs charts the ups and downs of the English Ryman family (founders of Rymans stationery business) as they follow their dream to run a vineyard in France.

Mirabel Osler *The Elusive Truffle* (Black Swan). Part recipe book, part travelogue: Osler goes in search of the rapidly disappearing traditional cuisine of France, including Périgord.

Michael Sanders *From Here You Can't See Paris* (Bantam Books). American Michael Sanders spent a year living in Les Arques (p.325), watching the inner workings of the local restaurant as it brought new life to this tiny village. A compelling glimpse behind the scenes and a tribute to the determination of the chef and his family.

Christian Signol *La Rivière Espérance* (Robert Laffont, UK; Pocket Presses, US). Set in the 1830s, this French novel – which was made into a hugely successful TV film – follows the adventures of a young sailor working the *gabarres* which then plied the Dordogne. This nostalgic tale commemorates the end of an era as the railways relentlessly destroy the romanticized river life.

Ruth Silvestre *A House in the Sunflowers* and *A Harvest of Sunflowers* (Allison & Busby). These two books tell a gentle, engaging tale of restoring a tumbledown farmhouse in the Lot-et-Garonne. Singer-actress Ruth Silvestre and her family are swept up into local life – the grape harvest, plum harvest, village fêtes and gargantuan meals – thanks to their generous and exuberant neighbours. Together they witness modern life gradually intrude into this deeply traditional corner of rural France.

Marguerite Smith *A House Among Vines* (Robert Hale). In the 1970s Marguerite Smith found herself living alone with little money in a remote corner of southwest France. She describes her life and her neighbours – French and otherwise – with humour and compassion.

Freda White *Three Rivers of France* (Faber; o/p), *Ways of Aquitaine* (Faber; o/p). Freda White's classic books portray France in the 1950s before tourism came along to the backwater communities that were her interest. They are evocative books, slipping in history and culture painlessly, if not always too accurately, and still provide a valuable and vivid overview of the region.

Guides

Glynn Christian *Edible France* (Grub Street). A guide to food rather than restaurants: regional produce, local specialities, markets and the best shops for buying goodies to bring back home.

Cicerone Walking Guides (Cicerone, UK). Neat, durable guides, with detailed route descriptions. Titles include *The Way of Saint James; A Walker's Guide* and *The Way of Saint James; A Cyclist's Guide*, both of which follow the route from Le Puy to Santiago (GR65), and *Walking in the Dordogne*.

Brigitte Durgeon & Claude Feigné *La Gironde à Vélo* (Éditions Sud Ouest). Over 1000km of cycle trails divided into thirty circuits taking in the Médoc to the Entre-Deux-Mers.

Footpaths of Europe Series (Robertson McCarta). English-language versions of the Topo-guide route guides (see p.402) covering the system of GR footpaths, illustrated with 1:50,000 colour maps.

Peter Knowles *White Water: Massif Central* (River Publishing). Don't be put off by the series title, this guide covers rivers suitable for a spot of gentle family canoeing and canoe touring, including parts of the Dordogne, Lot, Tarn, Vézère, Célé and Aveyron. Packed with good, practical advice.

Joy Law *Dordogne* (Pallas Athene). Erudite and accessible thematic guide-cum-history text written by a long-time resident of the *département*, packed with interesting anecdotes and local colour.

Helen Martin *Le Lot* (Columbus Books; o/p). It's well worth trying to get hold of this book if you're going to be spending any length of time in the Lot. Though some of the practical details are out of date, the author's passion for the area provides plenty to inspire you in the general descriptions.

Hugh McKnight *Cruising French Waterways* (Adlard Coles Nautical). Essential reading for anyone going boating in France. It's not only a practical guide on navigating French rivers and canals, but also covers historical aspects and general tourist information.

Nouveaux Guides Franck *Dordogne, Périgord* (Éditions Glénat). A ring-binder comprising thirty walks of between two hours and two days around Périgueux, Lalinde, Sarland and Gourdon. It includes a plastic holder and an IGN map.

Victoria Pybus *Live and Work in France* (Vacation Work). An invaluable guide, packed with ideas and advice on everything from job-hunting, tax and bureaucracy to health care.

Alain Roussot (ed) *Discovering Périgord Prehistory* (Sud-Ouest, France). Translated into English, this guide provides a solid introduction to the prehistoric caves of the Périgord. It covers the most significant caves in chronological order, while the

C

CONTEXTS | Books

illustrations give a taste of what's on offer.

Les Sentiers d'Emilie (Rando Édi-tions). A series of guides, including a book on the Dordogne and the Gironde, each containing 25 easy walks of up to 2hr 30min for all the family.

Jeanne Strang *Goose Fat and Garlic* (Kyle Cathie). Com-prehensive cookbook covering the classics of southwestern cuisine, from *tourin* soup and scrambled eggs with truffles to *cassoulet* and *clafoutis*.

Paul Strang *Wines of Southwest France* (Kyle Cathie). A bit dated now, but still by far the best English-language guide to the region's wines. In addition to the history of viticulture and brief reviews of recommended producers in all the wine-producing areas from Figeac to Bergerac (excluding the Bordeaux

vineyards), the book gives a glimpse into local culture and traditions.

Topo-guides (Fédération Française de la Randonnée Pédestre, France). The best of the walking guides covering the long-distance paths, Topo-guides are widely available in France and not hard to follow with a working knowledge of French. The series includes guides to the GR65 St-Jacques pilgrimage routes, the *Tour des Gorges de l'Aveyron* (Topo-guide #323), the *Traversée du Périgord* (#321) and, for shorter walks, *Dordogne à Pied* (#D024) and *Lot à Pied* (#D046).

Paula Wolfert *The Cooking of South West France* (Grub Street). Rigorously researched cookbook containing a mix of traditional and modern dishes from the southwest. The recipes are sometimes lengthy and a bit complicated, but they work. For the serious cook.

Language

Language

Language

F rench can be a deceptively familiar language because of the number of
words and structures it shares with English. Despite this, it's far from easy,
though the bare essentials are not difficult to master and can make all
the difference. Even just saying "Bonjour Madame/Monsieur" and then
gesticulating will usually get you a smile and helpful service. People working in
tourist offices, hotels and so on, almost always speak English, though, and tend
to use it when you're struggling to speak French – be grateful, not insulted.

Phrasebooks and courses

Rough Guide French Phrasebook (Rough Guides). Mini dictionary-style
phrasebook with both English–French and French–English sections, along with
cultural tips for tricky situations and a menu reader.
Mini French Dictionary (Harrap/Prentice Hall). French–English and English–French Dictionary, plus a brief grammar and pronunciation guide.
Breakthrough French (Palgrave Macmillan). Excellent teach-yourself course
including audio-cassettes.
French and English Slang Dictionary (Harrap); **Dictionary of Modern
Colloquial French** (Routledge, UK). The key to French vernacular.
Á Vous La France; France Extra; Franc-Parler (BBC Consumer Publish-
ing/EMC Publishing). BBC courses, running from beginner's level to fairly
advanced; each consists of a book and two cassettes. In addition, Ⓦ www.bbc
.co.uk/education/languages/french has a range of online courses.

Pronunciation

One easy rule to remember is that **consonants** at the ends of words are usually
silent. *Pas plus tard* (not later) is thus pronounced "pa-plu-tarr". But when the following word begins with a vowel, you run the two together: *pas après* (not after)
becomes "pazaprey". **Vowels** are the hardest sounds to get right. Roughly:

a	as in hat	o	as in hot
e	as in get	o, au	as in over
é	between get and gate	ou	as in food
è	between get and gut	u	as in a pursed-lip version
eu	like the u in hurt		of use
i	as in machine		

More awkward are the **combinations** *in/im, en/em, an/am, on/om, un/um* at the
ends of words, or followed by consonants other than *n* or *m*. Again, roughly:

in/im	like the an in anxious	on/om	like the don in Doncaster
an/am	like the don in		said by someone with a
en/em	Doncaster when said with		heavy cold
	a nasal accent	un/um	like the u in understand

Consonants are much as in English, except that: *ch* is always "sh", *c* is "s", *h* is silent, *th* is the same as "t", *ll* is like the "y" in yes, *w* is "v", and *r* is growled (or rolled).

Basic words and phrases

French nouns are divided into masculine and feminine. This causes difficulties with adjectives, whose endings have to change to suit the gender of the nouns they qualify. If you know some grammar, you will know what to do. If not, stick to the masculine form, which is the simplest – it's what we have done in this glossary.

Basics

today	aujourd'hui	that one	celá
yesterday	hier	open	ouvert
tomorrow	demain	closed	fermé
in the morning	le matin	big	grand
in the afternoon	l'après-midi	small	petit
in the evening	le soir	more	plus
now	maintenant	less	moins
later	plus tard	a little	un peu
at one o'clock	à une heure	a lot	beaucoup
at three o'clock	à trois heures	cheap	bon marché
at ten-thirty	à dix heures et demie	expensive	cher
at midday	à midi	good	bon
man	un homme	bad	mauvais
woman	une femme	hot	chaud
here	ici	cold	froid
there	là	with	avec
this one	ceci	without	sans

Numbers

1	un	17	dix-sept
2	deux	18	dix-huit
3	trois	19	dix-neuf
4	quatre	20	vingt
5	cinq	21	vingt-et-un
6	six	22	vingt-deux
7	sept	30	trente
8	huit	40	quarante
9	neuf	50	cinquante
10	dix	60	soixante
11	onze	70	soixante-dix
12	douze	75	soixante-quinze
13	treize	80	quatre-vingts
14	quatorze	90	quatre-vingt-dix
15	quinze	95	quatre-vingt-quinze
16	seize	100	cent

101	cent-et-un	1000	mille
200	deux cents	2000	deux milles
300	trois cents	5000	cinq milles
500	cinq cents	1,000,000	un million

Days and dates

January	janvier	Sunday	dimanche
February	février	Monday	lundi
March	mars	Tuesday	mardi
April	avril	Wednesday	mercredi
May	mai	Thursday	jeudi
June	juin	Friday	vendredi
July	wjuillet	Saturday	samedi
August	août	August 1	le premier août
September	septembre	March 2	le deux mars
October	octobre	July 14	le quatorze juillet
November	novembre	November 23	le vingt-trois novembre
December	décembre	2006	deux mille six

Talking to people

When addressing people you should always use *Monsieur* for a man, *Madame* for a woman, *Mademoiselle* for a young woman or girl. Plain *bonjour* by itself is not enough. This isn't as formal as it seems, and it has its uses when you've forgotten someone's name or want to attract someone's attention.

Excuse me	Pardon	OK/agreed	d'accord
Do you speak English?	Parlez-vous anglais?	please	s'il vous plaît
		thank you	merci
How do you say it in French?	Comment ça se dit en français?	hello	bonjour
		goodbye	au revoir
What's your name?	Comment vous appelez-vous?	good morning /afternoon	bonjour
My name is . . .	Je m'appelle . . .		
I'm	Je suis	good evening	bonsoir
English	anglais[e]	good night	bonne nuit
Irish	irlandais[e]	How are you?	Comment allez-vous?/ Ça va?
Scottish	écossais[e]		
Welsh	gallois[e]	fine, thanks	Très bien, merci
American	américain[e]	I don't know	Je ne sais pas
Canadian	canadien[ne]	Let's go	allons-y
Australian	australien[ne]	See you tomorrow	Á demain
a New Zealander	néo-zélandais[e]	See you soon	Á bientôt
yes	oui	Sorry	Pardon/Je m'excuse
no	non	Leave me alone	Fichez-moi la paix! (aggressive)
I understand	Je comprends		
I don't understand	Je ne comprends pas	Please help me	Aidez-moi, s'il vous plaît
Can you speak more slowly?	S'il vous plaît, parlez moins vite		

Questions and requests

The simplest way of asking a question is to start with *s'il vous plaît* (please), then name the thing you want in an interrogative tone of voice. For example:

Where is there a bakery?	S'il vous plaît, la boulangerie?	Question words;	
Which way is it to the Eiffel Tower?	S'il vous plaît, la route pour la Tour Eiffel?	Where?	Où?
		How?	Comment?
Similarly with requests:		How many/how much?	Combien?
Can we have a room for two?	S'il vous plaît, une chambre pour deux?	When?	Quand?
		Why?	Pourquoi?
Can I have a kilo of oranges?	S'il vous plaît, un kilo d'oranges?	At what time?	À quelle heure?
		What is/Which is?	Quel est?

Getting around

bus	autobus/bus/car	Where are you going?	Vous allez où?
bus station	gare routière	I'm going to...	Je vais à...
bus stop	arrêt	I want to get off at the road to...	Je voudrais descendre à la route pour...
train/taxi/ferry	train/taxi/ferry	near	près/pas loin
boat	bâteau	far	loin
plane	avion	left	à gauche
train station	gare (SNCF)	right	à droite
platform	quai	straight on	tout droit
What time does it leave?	Il part à quelle heure?	on the other side of	à l'autre côté de
What time does it arrive?	Il arrive à quelle heure?	on the corner of	à l'angle de
a ticket to...	un billet pour...	next to	à côté de
single ticket	aller simple	behind	derrière
return ticket	aller retour	in front of	devant
validate your ticket	compostez votre billet	before	avant
valid for	valable pour	after	après
ticket office	vente de billets	under	sous
how many kilometres?	combien de kilomètres?	to cross	traverser
		bridge	pont
how many hours?	combien d'heures?	upper town	ville haute/haute ville
hitchhiking	autostop	lower town	ville basse/basse ville
on foot	à pied	old town	vieille ville

Accommodation

a room for one/ two people	une chambre pour une/ deux personne(s)	a room with a bath	une chambre avec salle de bains
a double bed	un lit double	for one/two/ three nights	pour une/deux/trois nuits
a room with a shower	une chambre avec douche	Can I see it?	Je peux la voir?

a room on the courtyard	une chambre sur la cour	cold water	eau froide
a room over the street	une chambre sur la rue	Is breakfast included?	Est-ce que le petit déjeuner est compris?
first floor	premier étage	I would like breakfast	Je voudrais prendre le petit déjeuner
second floor	deuxième étage		
with a view	avec vue	I don't want breakfast	Je ne veux pas de petit déjeuner
key	clef		
to iron	repasser	Can we camp here?	On peut camper ici?
do laundry	faire la lessive		
sheets	draps	campsite	un camping/terrain de camping
blankets	couvertures		
quiet	calme	tent	une tente
noisy	bruyant	tent space	un emplacement
hot water	eau chaude	youth hostel	auberge de jeunesse

Cars

car	voiture	put air in the tyres	gonfler les pneus
service station	garage		
service	service	battery	batterie
to park the car	garer la voiture	the battery is dead	la batterie est morte
car park	un parking		
no parking	défense de stationner/ stationnement interdit	plugs	bougies
		to break down	tomber en panne
		gas can	bidon
gas station	station service	insurance	assurance
petrol	essence	green card	carte verte
diesel	gazole/gasoil	traffic lights	feux
(to) fill it up	faire le plein	red light	feu rouge
oil	huile	green light	feu vert
air line	ligne à air		

Health matters

doctor	médecin	stomach ache	mal à l'estomac
I don't feel well	Je ne me sens pas bien	period	règles
medicines	médicaments	pain	douleur
prescription	ordonnance	it hurts	ça fait mal
I feel sick	Je suis malade	chemist	pharmacie
I have a headache	J'ai mal à la tête	hospital	hôpital

Other needs

bakery	boulangerie	to drink	boire
food shop	alimentation	camping gas	camping gaz
supermarket	supermarché	tobacconist	tabac
to eat	manger	stamps	timbres

bank	banque	telephone	téléphone
money	argent	cinema	cinéma
toilets	toilettes	theatre	théâtre
police	police	to reserve/book	réserver

Food glossary

Basic terms

l'addition	bill/check	moutarde	mustard
beurre	butter	oeuf	egg
bouteille	bottle	offert	free
chauffé	heated	pain	bread
couteau	knife	poivre	pepper
cru	raw	salé	salted/spicy
cuillère	spoon	sel	salt
cuit	cooked	sucre	sugar
à emporter	takeaway	sucré	sweet
fourchette	fork	table	table
fumé	smoked	verre	glass
huile	oil	vinaigre	vinegar
lait	milk		

Snacks and starters

un sandwich/	a sandwich	au plat	fried
une baguette		à la coque	boiled
au jambon	with ham	durs	hard-boiled
au fromage	with cheese	brouillés	scrambled
au saucisson	with sausage	pochés	poached
au poivre	with pepper	omelette	omelette
au pâté	with pâté	nature	plain
(de campagne)	(country style)	aux fines herbes	with herbs
croque-monsieur	grilled cheese and ham sandwich	au fromage	with cheese
		aux truffes	with truffles
croque-madame	grilled cheese and bacon, sausage, chicken or egg sandwich	charcuterie	pâté and cold meats
		crudités	raw vegetables with dressings
panini	toasted Italian sandwich	hors d'oeuvres	combination of charcuterie, crudités, smoked fish and other cold starters
tartine	buttered bread or open sandwich		
oeufs	eggs		

Pasta (pâtes), pancakes (crêpes) and flans (tartes)

nouilles	noodles	pissaladière	tart of fried onions with anchovies and black olives
pâtes fraîches	fresh pasta		
crêpe au sucre/ aux oeufs	pancake with sugar /eggs	tarte flambée	thin pizza-like pastry topped with onion, cream and bacon or other combinations
galette (de sarrasin)	buckwheat pancake		

Soups (soupes)

bisque	shellfish soup	potée	thick vegetable and meat soup
bouillabaisse	Mediterranean fish soup		
bouillon	broth or stock	soupe à l'oignon	onion soup with a chunk of toasted bread and melted cheese topping
consommé	clear soup		
garbure	potato, cabbage and meat soup		
miques	dumplings of maize or wheat flour served in a thick soup	tourain, tourin	garlic soup made with duck or goose fat served over bread topped with cheese
potage	thick soup, usually vegetable		

Fish (poisson), seafood (fruits de mer) and shellfish (crustaces or coquillages)

alose	shad	écrevisses	freshwater crayfish
anchois	anchovies	éperlan	smelt
anguilles	eels	escargots	snails
bigourneaux	periwinkles	esturgeon	sturgeon
brandade de morue	puréed, salted cod with oil, milk, garlic and mashed potato	flétan	halibut
		gambas	king prawns
		hareng	herring
brème	bream	homard	lobster
bulot	whelk	huîtres	oysters
cabillaud	cod	lamproie	lamprey
calmar	squid	langoustines	saltwater crayfish
carrelet	plaice	limande	lemon sole
colin	hake	lotte de mer	monkfish
coques	cockles	loup de mer	sea bass
coquilles St-Jacques	scallops	maquereau	mackerel
		merlan	whiting
crabe	crab	moules (marinière)	mussels (with shallots in white wine sauce)
crevettes grises	shrimp		
crevettes roses	prawns	raie	skate
daurade	sea bream	rascasse	scorpion fish

rouget	red mullet	thon	tuna
saumon	salmon	truite	trout
sole	sole	turbot	turbot

Fish dishes and terms

aïoli	garlic mayonnaise served with salt cod and other fish	grillé	grilled
		hollandaise	butter and vinegar sauce
		à la meunière	in a butter, lemon and parsley sauce
arête	fish bone		
beignet	fritter		
darne	fillet or steak	mousse/ mousseline	mousse
la douzaine	a dozen	pané	breaded
frit	fried	quenelles	light dumplings
friture	deep-fried small fish	thermidor	lobster grilled in its shell with cream sauce
fumé	smoked		

Meat (viande) and poultry (volaille)

agneau (de pré-salé)	lamb (grazed on salt marshes)	langue	tongue
		lapin, lapereau	rabbit, young rabbit
andouille/ andouillette	tripe sausage	lard, lardons	bacon, diced bacon
		lièvre	hare
bifteck	steak	merguez	spicy, red sausage
boeuf	beef	mouton	mutton
boudin blanc	sausage of white meats	oie	goose
boudin noir	black pudding	onglet	cut of beef
caille	quail	os	bone
canard	duck	poitrine	breast
caneton	duckling	porc	pork
contrefilet	sirloin roast	poulet	chicken
dinde, dindon	turkey	ris	sweetbreads
entrecôte	rib steak	rognons	kidneys (usually lamb's)
faux filet	sirloin steak	sanglier	wild boar
foie	liver	steak	steak
foie gras	(duck/goose) liver	tête de veau	calf's head (in jelly)
gibier	game	tournedos	thick slices of fillet
gigot (d'agneau)	leg (of lamb)	tripes	tripe
grenouilles (cuisses de)	frogs (legs)	tripoux	mutton tripe
		veau	veal
grillade	grilled meat	venaison	venison
hâchis	chopped meat or mince hamburger	volaille	poultry

Meat and poultry dishes and terms

aiguillettes	thin, tender pieces of duck	au four	baked
		blanquette, daube, estouffade, navarin, ragoût	types of stew
aile	wing		
au feu de bois	cooked over wood fire		

blanquette de veau	veal in cream and mushroom sauce	épaule	shoulder
		farci	stuffed
boeuf bourguignon	beef stew with Burgundy, onions and mushrooms	garni	with vegetables
		gésier	gizzard
		gigot (d'agneau)	leg (of lamb)
brochette	kebab	grillade	grilled meat
canard de périgourdin	roast duck with prunes, pâté foie gras and truffles	grillé	grilled
		magret de canard	duck breast
		marmite	casserole
carré	best end of neck, chop or cutlet	médaillon	round piece
		noisettes	small, round fillets
cassoulet	casserole of beans, duck and sausage	pavé	thick slice
		poêlé	pan-fried
choucroute	pickled cabbage with peppercorns, sausages, bacon and salami	poule au pot	chicken simmered with vegetables
		rôti	roast
		sauté	lightly cooked in butter
civet	game stew	steak au poivre (vert/rouge)	steak in a black (green/red) peppercorn sauce
confit	meat preserve		
coq au vin	chicken cooked until it falls off the bone with wine, onions and mushrooms	steak tartare	raw chopped beef, topped with a raw egg yolk
		tournedos rossini	beef fillet with foie gras and truffles
côte	chop, cutlet or rib		
cou	neck	viennoise	fried in egg and breadcrumbs
cuisse	thigh or leg		
en croûte	in pastry		

Terms for steaks

bleu	almost raw	bien cuit	well done
saignant	rare	très bien cuit	very well done
à point	medium		

Garnishes and sauces

américaine	white wine, cognac and tomato	chasseur	white wine, mushrooms and shallots
au porto	in port	diable	strong mustard seasoning
béarnaise	sauce of egg yolks, white wine, shallots and vinegar	forestière	with bacon and mushroom
		fricassée	rich, creamy sauce
beurre blanc	sauce of white wine and shallots, with butter	mornay	cheese sauce
		périgourdine/ périqueux	rich wine sauce, possibly with truffles
bonne femme	with mushroom, bacon, potato and onions	provençale	tomatoes, garlic, olive oil and herbs
bordelaise	in a red wine, shallot and bone-marrow sauce	savoyarde	with Gruyère cheese

Vegetables (légumes), herbs (herbes) and spices (épices)

ail	garlic	fèves	broad beans
artichaut	artichoke	flageolets	white beans
asperge	asparagus	haricots (verts, rouges, beurres)	beans (French/ string, kidney, butter)
avocat	avocado		
basilic	basil		
betterave	beetroot	lentilles	lentils
câpre	caper	mange-tout	snow peas
carotte	carrot	menthe	mint
céleri	celery	moutarde	mustard
champignon, cèpe, chanterelle, girolle, morille	types of mushrooms	oignon	onion
		persil	parsley
		piment	pimento
chou (rouge)	(red) cabbage	poireau	leek
choufleur	cauliflower	pois, petits pois	peas
ciboulette	chives	poivron (vert, rouge)	sweet pepper (green, red)
concombre	cucumber		
cornichon	gherkin	pommes de terre	potatoes
échalotes	shallots	radis	radish
endive	chicory	riz	rice
épinard	spinach	salade verte	green salad
estragon	tarragon	tomate	tomato
fenouil	fennel	truffes	truffles

Vegetable dishes and terms

à l'anglaise/ à l'eau	boiled	à la grecque	cooked in oil and lemon
beignet	fritter	jardinière	with mixed diced vegetables
biologique	organic		
duxelles	fried mushrooms and shallots with cream	mousseline	mashed potato with cream and eggs
		parmentier	with potatoes
farci	stuffed	pimenté	peppery hot
feuille	leaf	piquant	spicy
fines herbes	mixture of tarragon, parsley and chives	pistou	ground basil, olive oil, garlic and parmesan
garni	served with vegetables	râpée	grated or shredded
gratiné	browned with cheese or butter	sauté	lightly fried in butter
		à la vapeur	steamed

Fruit (fruits) and nuts (noix)

abricot	apricot	cacahouète	peanut
amande	almond	cassis	blackcurrant
ananas	pineapple	cérise	cherry
banane	banana	citron	lemon
brugnon, nectarine	nectarine	citron vert	lime

figue	fig	noisette	hazelnut
fraise (de bois)	strawberry (wild)	noix	nuts, walnuts
framboise	raspberry	orange	orange
fruit de la passion	passion fruit	pamplemousse	grapefruit
grenade	pomegranate	pastèque	watermelon
groseille rouge/ blanche	red/white currant	pêche	peach
		pistache	pistachio
kaki	persimmon	poire	pear
mangue	mango	pomme	apple
marron	chestnut	prune	plum
melon	melon	pruneau	prune
mirabelle	small yellow plum	raisin	grape
mûre	blackberry	reine-claude	greengage
myrtille	bluelberry		

Fruit dishes and terms

beignet	fritter	flambé	set aflame in alcohol
compôte	stewed fruit	frappé	iced
coulis	sauce of puréed fruit	macédoine	fruit salad
crème de marrons	chestnut purée		

Desserts (desserts or entremets), pastries (pâtisserie) and related terms

bavarois	refers to the mould, could be a mousse or custard	gênoise	rich sponge cake
		glace	ice cream
		île flottante/ oeufs à la neige	soft meringues floating on custard
bombe	moulded ice-cream dessert	macaron	macaroon
brioche	sweet, high-yeast breakfast roll	madeleine	small sponge cake
charlotte	custard and fruit in lining of almond fingers	mousse au chocolat	chocolate mousse
		omelette norvégienne	baked Alaska
clafoutis	cake-like fruit tart		
coupe/boule	a serving of ice cream	parfait	frozen mousse, sometimes ice cream
crème à l'anglaise	custard	pâte	pastry or dough
crème Chantilly	vanilla-flavoured and sweetened whipped cream	petit-suisse	a smooth mixture of cream and curds
crème fraîche	sour cream	poires belle hélène	pears and ice cream in chocolate sauce
crème pâtissière	thick, eggy pastry-filling		
crêpe	pancake	sablé	shortbread biscuit
crêpe suzette	thin pancake with orange juice and liqueur	savarin	a filled, ring-shaped cake
		tarte	tart
		tartelette	small tart
fromage blanc	cream cheese	tarte tatin	upside-down apple tart
gaufre	waffle	yaourt, yogourt	yogurt

Glossary

General vocabulary and terms

abbaye Abbey.

abri Prehistoric rock-shelter.

appellation (Appellation d'Origine Contrôlée; AOC) Wine classification indicating that the wine meets strict requirements regarding its provenance and methods of production.

auberge Country inn, frequently offering accommodation.

auberge de jeunesse Youth hostel.

autoroute Motorway.

bastide New town founded in the thirteenth and fourteenth centuries, built on a grid plan around an arcaded market square.

boules Popular French game played with steel balls (see p.48).

cabane, borie or gariotte Dry-stone hut, probably used by shepherds.

Capetian Capetian royal dynasty founded by Hugh Capet, which ruled France from 987 to 1328.

causse Limestone plateau extending from Dordogne *département* south through Lot and into Aveyron.

chai Barn or storehouse in which wines are aged.

chambre d'hôte Bed-and-breakfast accommodation in a private house.

chartreuse One-storey building typical of the Bordeaux wine region, slightly raised up and built on top of a half-buried *chai*; also a Carthusian monastery.

château Castle, mansion, stately home.

château fort Castle built for a specifically military purpose.

collégiale Church which shelters a community of priests.

colombage Traditional building style consisting of a timber frame filled with earth and straw or bricks.

commune The basic administrative region, each under a mayor (very occasionally, a mayoress).

confiserie Confectioner's (shop).

dégustation Tasting (wine or food).

département Mid-level administrative unit run by a local council – the equivalent of a county in Britain.

dolmen Neolithic stone structure, generally held to be a tomb, consisting of two or more upright slabs supporting a horizontal stone.

donjon Castle keep.

église Church.

falaise Cliff.

ferme auberge Farm licensed to provide meals in which the majority of the produce must come from the farm itself.

Festival off Fringe festival, set apart from the main programme, usually with free events.

foire Large market held once or twice monthly in some country towns.

formule Restaurant menu with two courses, usually comprising a choice of starter and main course or main and dessert.

fouille Archeological excavation.

gabare or gabarre Traditional wooden boat used to transport goods on the Dordogne and Lot rivers up until the late nineteenth century.

gavage Process of force-feeding ducks and geese to make foie gras.

gisement Deposit, stratified layers of an archeological excavation.

gîte Self-catering accommodation.

gîte d'étape Basic accommodation, usually restricted to walkers, pilgrims and cyclists.

gouffre Limestone chasm or sinkhole.

grotte Cave.

halle(s) Covered market (hall).

hôtel Hotel, but also an aristocratic town house or mansion.

lauze Small limestone slabs, a traditional roof covering in the Périgord.

navette Shuttle-bus, for example connecting a town with its airport.

Occitan Language (and associated culture) formerly spoken throughout most of south and southwest France.

pétanque Variation of the game boules (see p.48).

pigeonnier Dovecote, often built on stilts and used to collect droppings for fertilizer.

pisé Traditional Périgordin floor made out of small limestone slabs inserted upright into a bed of clay or lime.

porte Gateway.

retable Altarpiece.

seneschal Chief administrator and justice in medieval times, the representative of the king.

table d'hôte Meals served to residents of a chambre d'hôte.

tour Tower.

version originale (VO) film shown in its original language and subtitled in French.

Architectural terms

ambulatory Passage around the outer edge of the choir of a church.

apse Semicircular or polygonal termination at the east end of a church.

Baroque High Renaissance period of art and architecture, distinguished by extreme ornateness.

chevet East end of a church.

Classical Architectural style incorporating Greek and Roman elements: pillars, domes, colonnades, etc, at its height in France in the seventeenth century and revived in the nineteenth century as Neoclassical.

flamboyant Very ornate form of Gothic.

fresco Painting in watercolour on a wall or ceiling while the plaster is still wet.

Gallo-Roman Period of Roman occupation of Gaul (1st century BC to 4th century AD).

Gothic Architectural style prevalent from the twelfth to sixteenth century, characterized by pointed arches and ribbed vaulting.

machicolations Parapet on a castle, fortified church, gateway, etc, with openings for dropping stones and so forth on attackers.

Merovingian Dynasty (and art, etc), ruling France and parts of Germany from the sixth to mid-eighth century.

narthex Entrance hall of church.

nave Main body of a church.

Renaissance Architectural and artistic style developed in fifteenth-century Italy and imported to France in the sixteenth century by François I.

Romanesque Early medieval architecture distinguished by squat, rounded forms and naive sculpture, called *Roman* in French (not to be confused with *Romain* – Roman).

stucco Plaster used to embellish ceilings, etc.

transept Transverse arms of a church, perpendicular to the nave.

tympanum Sculpted semicircular panel above the door of a Romanesque church.

Regional names

Aquitaine Originally a Roman administrative region extending from Poitiers and Limoges south to the Pyrenees. It later became a duchy, which, at its apogee in the twelfth century, covered roughly the same area, though it fluctuated enormously. In the 1960s the name was resurrected with the creation of regional administrative units. Modern Aquitaine is based around Bordeaux and comprises the *départements* of Dordogne, Gironde and Lot-et-Garonne, amongst others.

Gascony The region to the west and south of the River Garonne, named after a Celtic tribe (the Vascons). In the early tenth century it became an independent duchy but

was soon subsumed into the duchy of Aquitaine, though still retained its own identity.

Guyenne A corruption of the name "Aquitaine" originating during the period of English rule. Prior to the Revolution, the province of Guyenne extended from Gironde to Aveyron. Nowadays, it is occasionally used to refer to an area roughly encompassing Entre-Deux-Mers and St-Émilion, although there is no strict demarcation.

Midi-Pyrénées The modern administrative region to the east of Aquitaine, based on Toulouse and incorporating the *départements* of Lot, Tarn-et-Garonne and Aveyron, amongst others.

Périgord The confines of Périgord have changed little since pre-Roman times, when it was the home of the Gaulish tribe, the **Petrocori**. In the eighth century Périgord became a county, and then a province of France until the name was officially changed to Dordogne when *départements* were created in 1790 (each *département* was named after its principal river). However, Périgord is still used frequently, especially in tourist literature. These days it is often subdivided into Périgord Vert (Green Périgord; the département's northern sector); Périgord Blanc (White; the central strip along the Isle valley including Périgueux); Périgord Pourpre (Purple; the southwest corner around Bergerac); Périgord Noir (Black; the southeast, including Sarlat and the Vézère valley).

Quercy Former province roughly equivalent to the modern *départements* of the Lot and the north part of the Tarn-et-Garonne. The latter is often referred to as Bas-Quercy, while Haut-Quercy comprises the Lot's northern region.

Small print and

Index

A Rough Guide to Rough Guides

Published in 1982, the first Rough Guide – to Greece – was a student scheme that became a publishing phenomenon. Mark Ellingham, a recent graduate in English from Bristol University, had been travelling in Greece the previous summer and couldn't find the right guidebook. With a small group of friends he wrote his own guide, combining a highly contemporary, journalistic style with a thoroughly practical approach to travellers' needs.

The immediate success of the book spawned a series that rapidly covered dozens of destinations. And, in addition to impecunious backpackers, Rough Guides soon acquired a much broader and older readership that relished the guides' wit and inquisitiveness as much as their enthusiastic, critical approach and value-for-money ethos.

These days, Rough Guides include recommendations from shoestring to luxury and cover more than 200 destinations around the globe, including almost every country in the Americas and Europe, more than half of Africa and most of Asia and Australasia. Our ever-growing team of authors and photographers is spread all over the world, particularly in Europe, the USA and Australia.

In the early 1990s, Rough Guides branched out of travel, with the publication of Rough Guides to World Music, Classical Music and the Internet. All three have become benchmark titles in their fields, spearheading the publication of a wide range of books under the Rough Guide name.

Including the travel series, Rough Guides now number more than 350 titles, covering: phrasebooks, waterproof maps, music guides from Opera to Heavy Metal, reference works as diverse as Conspiracy Theories and Shakespeare, and popular culture books from iPods to Poker. Rough Guides also produce a series of more than 120 World Music CDs in partnership with World Music Network.

Visit www.roughguides.com to see our latest publications.

Rough Guide travel images are available for commercial licensing at www.roughguidespictures.com

Rough Guide credits

Text editor: Lucy Ratcliffe
Layout: Anita Singh
Cartography: Rajesh Mishra
Picture editor: Nicole Newman
Production: Aimee Hampson
Proofreader: Anna Leggett
Cover design: Chloë Roberts
Photographer: Jean-Christophe Godet
Editorial: **London** Kate Berens, Claire
Saunders, Joanna Kirby, Ruth Blackmore,
Polly Thomas, Richard Lim, Alison Murchie,
Karoline Densley, Andy Turner, Keith Drew,
Edward Aves, Nikki Birrell, Alice Park, Sarah
Eno, Lucy White, David Paul, James Smart,
Sam Cook, Joe Staines, Duncan Clark, Peter
Buckley, Matthew Milton, Tracy Hopkins, Ruth
Tidball; **New York** Andrew Rosenberg, Steven
Horak, April Isaacs, AnneLise Sorensen, Amy
Hegarty, Ella Steim, Anna Owens, Joseph Petta,
Sean Mahoney
Design & Pictures: **London** Scott Stickland, Dan
May, Diana Jarvis, Mark Thomas, Jj Luck, Harriet
Mills; **Delhi** Madhavi Singh, Umesh Aggarwal,

Ajay Verma, Jessica Subramanian, Ankur Guha,
Pradeep Thapliyal, Sachin Tanwar
Production: Lauren Britton, Katherine Owers
Cartography: **London** Maxine Repath, Ed
Wright, Katie Lloyd-Jones; **Delhi** Jai Prakash
Mishra, Rajesh Chhibber, Ashutosh Bharti,
Animesh Pathak, Jasbir Sandhu, Karobi Gogoi,
Amod Singh, Alakananda Bhattacharya,
Athokpam Jotinkumar
Online: **New York** Jennifer Gold, Kristin
Mingrone; **Delhi** Manik Chauhan, Narender
Kumar, Rakesh Kumar, Amit Verma, Amit Kumar,
Rahul Kumar, Ganesh Sharma, Debojit Borah
Marketing & Publicity: **London** Niki Hanmer,
Louise Maher, Anna Paynton, Jess Carter, Libby
Jellie; **New York** Geoff Colquitt, Megan Kennedy,
Katy Ball; **Delhi** Reem Khokhar
Special projects editor: Philippa Hopkins
Manager India: Punita Singh
Series editor: Mark Ellingham
Reference Director: Andrew Lockett
Publishing Coordinator: Megan McIntyre
Publishing Director: Martin Dunford

ROUGH
GUIDES

SMALL PRINT

Publishing information

This third edition published April 2007 by **Rough
Guides Ltd**,
80 Strand, London WC2R 0RL
345 Hudson St, 4th Floor,
New York, NY 10014, USA
14 Local Shopping Centre, Panchsheel Park,
New Delhi 110017, India
Distributed by the Penguin Group
Penguin Books Ltd,
80 Strand, London WC2R 0RL
Penguin Putnam, Inc.
375 Hudson Street, NY 10014, USA
Penguin Group (Australia)
250 Camberwell Road, Camberwell,
Victoria 3124, Australia
Penguin Books Canada Ltd,
10 Alcorn Avenue, Toronto, Ontario,
Canada M4V 1E4
Penguin Group (NZ)
67 Apollo Drive, Mairangi Bay, Auckland 1310,
New Zealand
Cover concept by Peter Dyer.

Typeset in Bembo and Helvetica to an original
design by Henry Iles.

Printed and bound in China

© Jan Dodd, 2007

432pp includes index

A catalogue record for this book is available from
the British Library

ISBN 10: 1-84353-248-4

ISBN 13: 9-78184-353-802-8

1   3   5   7   9   8   6   4   2

Help us update

We've gone to a lot of effort to ensure that the third
edition of **The Rough Guide to Dordogne & the
Lot** is accurate and up-to-date. However, things
change – places get "discovered", opening hours
are notoriously fickle, restaurants and rooms raise
prices or lower standards. If you feel we've got it
wrong or left something out, we'd like to know, and
if you can remember the address, the price, the
time, the phone number, so much the better.
We'll credit all contributions, and send a copy of
the next edition (or any other Rough Guide if you

prefer) for the best letters. Everyone who writes
to us and isn't already a subscriber will receive
a copy of our full-colour thrice-yearly newsletter.
Please mark letters: "**Rough Guide Dordogne
Update**" and send to: Rough Guides, 80 Strand,
London WC2R 0RL, or Rough Guides, 4th Floor,
345 Hudson St, New York, NY 10014. Or send an
email to **mail@roughguides.com**
Have your questions answered and tell others
about your trip at
www.roughguides.atinfopop.com

Acknowledgements

Jan Dodd would like to extend a big thanks to Nana Luckham for her sterling work helping update this edition. Thanks are also due to Lance at the *Frog et Rosbif* in Bordeaux and, as ever, to the staff of numerous tourist offices for their patience in answering my questions. Also to everyone at Rough Guides, especially Lucy Ratcliffe for her work in editing the book, Anita Singh for typesetting, Nicole Newman for picture research and David Paul for indexing.

Nana Luckham would like to thank Jane and Richard in Moissac, Margot in Bergerac, Delphine in Agen, Shahrezad Razavi, Simon Macdonald, Linda Standen and Chyono Flynn for their help and advice. Thanks also to Lucy Ratcliffe for editing and to Jan Dodd for all her advice and support along the way.

Readers' letters

Thanks to all the readers who have taken the time to write in with comments and suggestions (and apologies if we've inadvertently omitted anyone's name):

Peter Austen, Gary Elflett, Brian Hassall, Margaret Kerr, Helen Martin, John Murphy, Harald Oldenziel, Ron Roskell, Chris Scott, Barry Weiss, David & Marion Williams.

SMALL PRINT

Photo credits

All images Jean-Christophe Godet © Rough Guides except the following:

Title page
Chateau de Hautefort © SIME/Mastrorillo
  Massimo/4

Full page
Bergerac and the River Dordogne © David
  Hughes/Robert Harding

Things not to miss
05 Basket of truffles ©Marto/Jupiter
08 Abbaye de Cadouin © Glenn Harper/Alamy
09 Monpazier's 13th century square © Patrick
  Ward/Alamy
12 Sarlat ©Rob Cousins/Robert Harding
14 Chateau at Najac © Charles Bowman/Robert
  Harding
16 Medieval festival at Eymet © Iteinerance
  medievale vallée du dropt/Public Relation
  Dordogne Tourist Board

18 Ancient festival © Hemis/Alamy
20 Chateau de Hautefort © Ian Dagnall/Alamy

Colour insert – Cave art
Lascaux II Montignac © Chris Howes/Wild Places
  Photography/Alamy
The prehistoric cave paintings at lascaux
  © images-of-france/Alamy

Black and whites
p.70 Chateau Pichon Longueville © Cephas
  Picture Library/Alamy
p.115 Chateau Y'Quem, Sauternes © Owen
  Franken/CORBIS
p.311 Cele Valley © guichaoua/Alamy
p.389 Bonaguil Chateau © Francesco Venturi/
  CORBIS

SMALL PRINT

Index

Map entries are in colour.

INDEX

INDEX

INDEX

Map symbols

maps are listed in the full index using coloured text

– – –	Chapter division boundary	—Ⓣ—	Tram stop
▬▬▬	Motorway	⛰	Mountains
▪ ▪ ▪	Motorway under construction	♜	Castle
═══	Main road	▮	Tower
───	Minor road	▪▪▪	Fortifications
⊪⊪⊪	Steps	∴	Ruin
- - - -	Footpath	⌂	Abbey
— —	Ferry route	⅄	Campsite
▬▬	Railway	🅿	Parking
∞∞∞	Tourist train	ⓘ	Tourist office
───	River	✉	Post office
◆	Point of interest	@	Internet access
⊠—⊠	Gate	⊞	Hospital
⌒	Cave	▮	Building
⅄	Viewpoint	┼	Church
✈	Airport	🝙	Cemetery
★	Transport stop	▦	Park/National park